Praise for *Jews, Judaism, and Success*

"With the same erudition and care that he has brought to his studies of medieval Jewish philosophy and the ethics of war and peace in Judaism, Robert Eisen here tackles the thorny question of how to account for the striking range and extent of Jewish accomplishments in modern societies. His answer – that long-nourished religious values of personal autonomy, freedom of thought, this-worldliness, and education uniquely prepared Jewish culture to thrive under the conditions of modernity – is developed in a clear and accessible fashion without sacrificing historical nuance. Given its many merits, *Jews, Judaism, and Success* deserves a wide readership, and given its subject, it will be sure to spark lively debate."

William A. Barbieri Jr., Ordinary Professor of Religious Ethics,
The Catholic University of America

"Robert Eisen makes a strong case for young Jews deeply exploring Rabbinic texts. Every Jewish day school educator and lay stakeholder – whether secular, Reform, Conservative, community, or Modern Orthodox – should read this book as a guide to creating an impactful curriculum; one that will strengthen our next generation of Jews. As Eisen correctly claims, Jews can sustain continued success if we strike the right balance between maintaining Jewish identity and being open to Western culture. That, in fact, is one of the mandates of any Jewish day school and is expressed articulately in this scholarly yet accessible work."

Sharon Freundel, Managing Director of the Jewish
Education Innovation Challenge

"In this provocative book, Robert Eisen demonstrates that traditional religious values cannot be simply washed out by the tidal waves of modernity. They run much deeper into the conscious as well as unconscious operations of the modern minds, and they exert powerful influences even on those who are staunchly committed to secularism. Eisen's story of Jewish success thus not only offers a new understanding of Rabbinic Judaism in the making of the Western world. More pertinently, it compels us to rethink the role of religion for all peoples who have undergone a sea of changes regarding reforms and revolutions in modern history."

Xiaofei Kang, Associate Professor of Chinese Religion,
Department of Religion, The George
Washington University

"Covering 2,000 years of intellectual and social history, *Jews, Judaism, and Success* could only have been written by a mature scholar like Eisen, who is well acquainted with the sweep of Jewish and Christian and secular intellectual history and knows the scholarly literature. In this well-written and organized book, Eisen has found a way to address both academics and the general audience interested in such issues."

Martin I. Lockshin, Professor Emeritus
of Humanities, York University

"Robert Eisen has asked a question that has intrigued Jews and non-Jews alike, and he offers answers that pierce the biases so often at play. His thesis is provocative, and his conclusions demand renewed engagement with the enduring legacy of Rabbinic Judaism. This is great news for rabbis and scholars of Judaism, each of whom, I believe, is obligated to consider the contributions of Eisen's book. But it is even better news for those who seek insight into how to expand the ability of society and all of its participants to thrive."

Rabbi Dr. (Hon.) Jack Moline, Rabbi Emeritus, Agudas
Achim Congregation, and President Emeritus,
Interfaith Alliance

"With thorough and up-to-date scholarship, this book argues that the political, economic, and cultural success of modern Jews is due to the continuing influence of Rabbinic Judaism and its values on modern Jews, even when most have long ceased to be governed by the authority of Rabbinic Judaism. *Jews, Judaism, and Success* definitely makes a significant contribution to its field."

David Novak, Professor and J. Richard and Dorothy Shiff
Chair of Jewish Studies, University of Toronto

"*Jews, Judaism, and Success* stands out for its deep engagement with Jewish history and tradition across the centuries. The breadth of scholarship, balanced analysis, and diversity of sources make for fascinating reading. Robert Eisen's impressive scholarship ranges over the full spectrum of Jewish history and thought throughout the rabbinic, medieval, and modern eras. The lucid writing and balanced analysis make the book a pleasure to read."

Jeffrey L. Rubenstein, Skirball Professor of Jewish Thought
and Literature, New York University

Jews, Judaism, and Success

How Religion Paved the Way to Modern Jewish Achievement

ROBERT EISEN

UNIVERSITY OF TORONTO PRESS
Toronto Buffalo London

ISBN 978-1-4875-4822-3 (cloth)   ISBN 978-1-4875-4824-7 (EPUB)
ISBN 978-1-4875-4823-0 (paper)   ISBN 978-1-4875-4825-4 (PDF)

Library and Archives Canada Cataloguing in Publication

Title: Jews, Judaism, and success : how religion paved the way to modern Jewish
   achievement / Robert Eisen.
Names: Eisen, Robert, 1960–, author.
Description: Includes bibliographical references and index.
Identifiers: Canadiana (print) 20230162134 | Canadiana (ebook) 20230162169 |
   ISBN 9781487548230 (paper) | ISBN 9781487548223 (cloth) |
   ISBN 9781487548254 (PDF) | ISBN 9781487548247 (EPUB)
Subjects: LCSH: Jewish ethics. | LCSH: Values – Religious aspects – Judaism. |
   LCSH: Success – Religious aspects – Judaism. | LCSH: Judaism. |
   LCSH: Talmud. | LCSH: Jews – Civilization.
Classification: LCC BJ1285.2 .E37 2023 | DDC 296.3/6 – dc23

We wish to acknowledge the land on which the University of Toronto Press
operates. This land is the traditional territory of the Wendat, the Anishnaabeg, the
Haudenosaunee, the Métis, and the Mississaugas of the Credit First Nation.

This book has been published with the help of a grant from the Federation for the
Humanities and Social Sciences, through the Awards to Scholarly Publications
Program, using funds provided by the Social Sciences and Humanities Research
Council of Canada.

University of Toronto Press acknowledges the financial support of the Government
of Canada, the Canada Council for the Arts, and the Ontario Arts Council, an agency
of the Government of Ontario, for its publishing activities.

Canada Council
for the Arts

Conseil des Arts
du Canada

ONTARIO ARTS COUNCIL
CONSEIL DES ARTS DE L'ONTARIO

an Ontario government agency
un organisme du gouvernement de l'Ontario

Funded by the   Financé par le
Government   gouvernement
of Canada   du Canada

Canada

MIX
Paper from
responsible sources
FSC   FSC® C016245
www.fsc.org

Dedicated to the memory of
Professor Sydney Eisen
(1928–2022)
whom I was blessed to have as my father and mentor

Contents

Part Three – Final Matters

Preface

There were good reasons *not* to write this book. Why that was the case may not be readily apparent from a description of it. The book addresses a mystery that, to my mind, has never been adequately solved despite numerous attempts to do so: how Jews in the modern Western world have achieved extraordinary success in a wide range of fields and disciplines. As for its audience, the book has been written for a wide range of readers. Needless to say, its subject-matter should be of interest to academics who specialize in Jewish Studies, as well as to Jews in general – two groups to which I myself belong. Yet, my book deals with an issue that has piqued the curiosity of many outside these groups, and it should therefore appeal to a broader readership. Moreover, in this book the approach I have taken to the issue of Jewish success has required me to explore fundamental issues regarding the success of the Western world as a whole, as well as the nature of success in general – topics that, I venture to guess, will be of interest to an even wider group of readers than those already mentioned. I have also invested considerable effort to make this book as accessible as possible to these various audiences by writing it in a conversational style, avoiding academic jargon, and providing explanations for all specialized terms and concepts. In short, my hope is that this book will be enjoyed by readers from any number of backgrounds, including academics and non-academics, Jews and non-Jews, Westerners and non-Westerners.

These goals may seem sufficiently worthy of the effort that normally goes into writing a book, but when I began working on it and spoke about it with friends, relatives, and colleagues, reactions were decidedly mixed. Some people were quite positive about the book, a few enthusiastically so. But a good number had reservations about it, some of them quite strong. A handful of people even recommended that I not write it.

Why the negativity? One objection expressed by some of my friends and relatives was that the book I planned to write might inflame antisemitism. Of those who voiced such concerns, some assumed that I was going to write a book that would attempt to demonstrate that Jews are inherently better than everyone else, a claim that was sure to arouse antisemitic sentiment. Others believed that my book would arouse antisemitism regardless of what it said. For them, the whole topic of Jews and success was toxic. These concerns were only heightened by the resurgence of antisemitism in the US in recent years. Those who were already negatively disposed to my project felt that in this situation, the book might only make things worse.

I did not dismiss these concerns. Antisemitism is an ongoing scourge in our world, and it has indeed enjoyed something of a renaissance in recent years, and yes, my book could play into the hands of those who indulge in that age-old hatred. But I wrote the book despite such concerns, and for good reasons.

First of all, let me clarify that I never had any intention of writing a book arguing that Jews are intrinsically better than everyone else. In fact, quite the contrary. One of my goals was to glean wisdom from the Jewish experience in the modern period that would be of value to others, a goal that presumed that all people had the same capabilities to achieve the success that Jews have had. Moreover, I intended to show that some of the wisdom provided by the modern Jewish experience was acquired by Jews because of unique historical circumstances that had nothing to do with the Jews themselves. Jews should certainly be given a good deal of the credit here. As I show in this book, they had visionary leaders who constructed a way of life that was remarkably enduring and that brought Jews great success when they were invited to become part of Western society. But that does not tell the whole story of why Jews have done so well in the modern period. So those who were worried that my book would fan the flames of antisemitism by engaging in ethnic chauvinism were completely mistaken.

Yet if the topic of this book itself was the problem, as some of my friends and relatives claimed, then it did not matter what its contents were; its very subject-matter would arouse antisemitism. I was not convinced that this concern was a valid one, but, to my mind, whether or not that was the case, was beside the point. I recoiled from the very idea of not writing the book just because there were hateful people in the world. The success that Jews have achieved in the modern West is a phenomenon that is both fascinating and highly instructive, and it is one that, as I mentioned above, has never been adequately explained despite a number of attempts to do so. An academic like myself lives for exploring a topic of this kind. I went into academia in part because, like most people who go into this line of work, I wanted to conduct research in an area of knowledge that I believed was of central significance to the human experience – in my case, religion, with a focus on Judaism – and that research can be particularly exciting when it involves a phenomenon precisely of the kind under discussion here, one that is highly intriguing but insufficiently understood. Many academics like myself regard such work as a calling that goes beyond personal interest; we see it as a sacred duty. We believe that uncovering truths about the human experience past and present is critical for the health of human civilization. I therefore found it unacceptable to avoid writing this book because there were people in the world who disliked Jews.

Reservations about this project of a very different kind emerged from conversations with my academic colleagues. Some of them were highly sceptical about my central thesis. The claim of my book is that Jews succeeded in the modern period because of values inculcated in them by traditional Rabbinic Judaism. That claim struck many of my colleagues as odd given that the modernization of Jews is usually understood as a process that involved the *rejection* of Rabbinic Judaism.

A response to this objection would be premature here, given that my entire book is devoted to supporting my claim. All I will say here is that while it is indeed true that the process of modernization among Jews involved the rejection of much of Rabbinic Judaism, I believe that this point underestimates the complexity of the relationship that modern Jews have had with Rabbinic Judaism. My contention is that some of the values of Rabbinic Judaism were retained by modern Jews unconsciously even as they consciously rejected it, and these values were critical for helping Jews achieve success in the modern period.

But there was another objection from my colleagues that I would like to address here in greater detail and that had to do with the way I planned to approach my subject. As I will argue in the coming pages, my belief is that one cannot understand the success of Jews in the modern West without seeing it in the context of the development of both Western culture and Jewish culture over the past two thousand years, and I will therefore be making far-reaching judgments about the evolution of the two cultures over a lengthy period of time. In other words, this book will deal with what academics in the humanities often call "big ideas," ambitious and sweeping claims that involve large chunks of history, or many cultures, or both.

The problem is that big ideas are less common in the humanities these days than they used to be because scholars in many of the fields in this sector of academia are increasingly sceptical that ideas of this kind have merit. Some academics even have contempt for them. As the scholarly literature in various disciplines in the humanities has grown in recent years, the academics producing this literature have become more and more specialized, and as a result, a good number of them have come to the conclusion that engaging with big ideas is no longer possible. The belief is that the knowledge required to formulate such ideas is now too extensive for any one person to master, except perhaps the rarest of individuals. Of even greater concern is the belief that big ideas cannot be true. Those who propose ideas of this kind have to make generalizations that cannot possibly be defended because our growing knowledge about all dimensions of the human experience past and present has brought with it an appreciation for the complexity of each and every one of those dimensions. Under such circumstances, making the kinds of generalizations that are needed to support big ideas is more likely to obscure the truth than enlighten us about it.

Thus, according to this way of thinking, scholars of European history, for instance, should not engage in research that cuts across more than one period. Each period now has a body of scholarly literature that is too large and complex for research of this kind to be done. Better to specialize, say, in just the Renaissance, where the amount of scholarship and its complexity are more manageable. And perhaps even the literature on *that* subject has become too unwieldy, and so yet a better choice would be to narrow oneself further and do research on a certain *aspect* of the Renaissance, one perhaps delimited by geographical location, time-period, or subject-matter.

A number of my colleagues confronted me with arguments along these lines. They intimated that it was simply not possible to write an academically respectable book that involved all of Western and Jewish intellectual history over the past two millennia. I was bound to run into problems trying to write authoritatively about two major cultures over such a vast expanse of time.

As a scholar who did highly specialized research for many years, I understood where these scholars were coming from. The growth in knowledge in the humanities and its increasing complexity have indeed made it more difficult to formulate and defend big ideas. However, I believe that scholars can still speak about such ideas; they just have to do so cautiously.

One thing that can be of immense help in this regard is simply consulting specialists in the various sub-fields upon which one's big ideas impinge. If, for instance, a scholar of European history wants to write about ideas that involve several major periods, that individual should seek guidance regarding the periods they are not versed in from those who are. That is, much of the problem about engaging big ideas can be solved by greater cooperation among scholars and a willingness to collaborate. Academics, for various reasons, are often reluctant to do that, and it is to their detriment.

In this project, I have done precisely what I am recommending here. I consulted academics in a wide range of fields about every aspect of the project, and I will be thanking them below. I could not have done the work without them. Has it saved me from all errors or from missing some things entirely? Almost certainly not, and I am sure I will be hearing criticism from one critic or another about what it is that I have got wrong. But I hope that consulting others has saved me from the most egregious transgressions of these kinds.

I also think that scholars not only *can* write about big ideas, they *should* write about them. We live in an era in which higher education is under increasing attack, and one of the major reasons for that is that universities are cultivating scholars who are so specialized, that they are less and less able to communicate with others about what they do. That includes undergraduate students, and yet, it is the parents of those students who are the ones supporting these scholars by paying high tuitions to the universities their children attend, and in the case of public universities, the taxpayers provide substantial support as well, whether or not they have children in the universities. One therefore has to wonder how long this situation can go on. At what point will the public no longer want to support institutions that pay scholars to do work that is less and less relevant to their lives and the education of their children?

One thing that academics can do to deal with this problem is to teach courses and write about issues that people outside the ivory tower care about, and one of the ways to do so is by engaging with big ideas, by grappling with fundamental questions that are of concern to large numbers of people. It is not that academics have to drop everything they are doing to become public intellectuals. They can still be specialists in their respective fields, and I, for one, have great respect for those engaging in that kind of work. It is just that scholars also have to find ways to communicate better with people about the work they do and why it is worthwhile, and again, that may mean entering the realm of big ideas.

Of course, many scholars are already taking this path. A number of my colleagues have written books for the popular market that deal with issues that are of major concern in the contemporary world, and they give public lectures about their work on a regular basis. However, these scholars still have to contend too often with colleagues who look down on this kind of work, who see it as tangential to the life of the true scholar, and that kind of response, to my mind, has to stop, given where we are with higher education.

Finally, if my book does contain errors or is incomplete because of its scope, I am still glad I wrote it, if for no other reason than for the fact that it was as exciting a project as any I have undertaken. I always tell my students that when it comes to class discussion, they should not hesitate to make comments that they think are incorrect because I like an interesting idea that is wrong as much as an uninteresting idea that is right. I can apply a similar ethos to this book. I may be proposing ideas in these pages that are flawed or even plain wrong because I took on a project that is exceedingly ambitious, but if those ideas are provocative and get good conversations started about important issues, then, as far as I am concerned, I will have accomplished as much as writing a book about ideas that are perfectly correct but are too narrow or dull to be of interest to anyone.

Acknowledgments

I mentioned that I have many people to thank for this book. First and foremost, Marc Saperstein was an invaluable resource for me at every stage of the development of this book. He helped me hash out the book's basic ideas when they were in preliminary form. He then meticulously reviewed an early draft of the book while making numerous suggestions for improving it and saving me from many errors. John Wood, my colleague at George Washington University, also read an earlier draft of the book and gave me a great deal of help with respect to the sections on Christianity. Daniel Schwartz, another colleague at GW, was also of great assistance at various points of this project. He too helped shape its direction and reviewed early drafts of a number of its chapters.

The following individuals also read through earlier drafts of the book and offered valuable feedback: Carmel Chiswick, Bernie Cooperman, Mohammed Faghfoory, Ephraim Kanarfogel, Xiaofei Kang, Jeff Kuperman, Yosef Lindell, Shaul Magid, Alan Mittleman, Derek Penslar, Jonathan Ray, Jeffrey Rubenstein, and Yudi Steiner. Needless to say, whatever errors remain in this book are entirely my own responsibility.

Helena Brantley, my publicist, deserves thanks for not only putting together a wonderful campaign to publicize the book, but for having encouraged me to write it in the first place. A casual conversation we had at an event in 2015 convinced me to take on the project. Several individuals took personal interest in this project and helped me find a publisher, and they include Jonathan Sarna, Jon Levenson, Neal Kozodoy, and Roger Freet. Roger also played a critical role in helping me shape the ideas of this book in its early stages. Special thanks go to David Novak, who suggested that I send the book to the University of Toronto Press, where it found a home. My experience with the press has been wonderful. Len Husband, the editor who guided the review process, was a pleasure to work with. He took a personal interest in the project that went beyond the call of duty. I should also mention that the experience of publishing with University of Toronto Press was enhanced by the fact that Toronto is the city where I grew up.

My mother, Doris Eisen, is the best proofreader I know, and she reviewed the manuscript for this book with utmost care as she has done with all my other books and caught many mistakes that eluded other readers. I have thanked my wife, Naomi, in every book that I have written, and there is no reason to break with that custom here. This book was made possible by the steady support she has always provided for my endeavours, and that support was especially appreciated during the many ups and downs that accompany a large project such as this one.

This book is dedicated to the memory of my father, an accomplished academic in his own right, who left this world a little over a month prior to the composition of these acknowledgments. Words cannot describe what a magnificent human being he was and how sorely he is missed by me, his family, and a large circle of friends and acquaintances.

Translations of Texts and Transliterations

All translations of passages in the Hebrew Bible will be from *Tanakh: The Holy Scriptures* (Philadelphia: Jewish Publication Society of America, 1985). I have sometimes altered the translation of a passage if I am discussing a rabbinic or medieval source that interprets the passage in a manner different from that of the Jewish Publication Society translation. All translations of other texts will be my own unless otherwise specified.

My transliterations from the Hebrew follow the *Encyclopedia Judaica*, except that "h" is used for ח, and "ts" is used for צ . Proper names are transliterated except when they have a form commonly used in English, in which case, that form is used.

Abbreviations

BT   Babylonian Talmud
JT   Jerusalem Talmud
M   Mishnah
T   Tosefta

JEWS, JUDAISM, AND SUCCESS

The Mystery of Jewish Success

The statistics are extraordinary. Since the beginning of the modern period roughly two centuries ago, the achievements of Jews have been wildly out of proportion to the size of their population. Nothing better illustrates the point than the statistics on how many Jews have won Nobel Prizes. From 1901, when these prizes were first established, to 2015, 22 per cent of all Nobel Prizes have gone to Jews, including 49 per cent in Economics, 26 per cent in Physiology or Medicine, 26 per cent in Physics, 21 per cent in Chemistry, 13 per cent in Literature, and 9 per cent in Peace.[1] And yet, while Jews were winning all these awards, they were only a tiny fraction of the world's population. At present, there are only 15 million Jews in the world, or just 0.2 per cent of that population.[2] That means that you could fit all the Jews in the world into the area of greater metropolitan New York and still have some room to spare. There were more Jews in the world before the Holocaust, but even then, Jews made up only 0.7 per cent of the global population – still a tiny fraction of the world's total. Thus, if one does the math, the world's Jewish population over the past century should have been five hundred to a thousand times larger than it has been for Jews to have received 22 per cent of all Nobel Prizes.

It is not just in the areas of interest to the Nobel committees that modern Jews have been remarkably successful. Their achievements are disproportionate to their numbers in just about every sphere of life that Westerners look to when gauging the success of individuals or groups, including economic status, intellectual accomplishments, and contributions to the arts. These three categories, in fact, provide a good framework for organizing the achievements of Jews in the modern period and appreciating their range, and so let us take a brief look at their achievements in each one.[3]

In the economic realm, the disproportionate success of Jews is quite striking. In general, Jews succeeded economically almost everywhere in the modern West where they were given a chance to – that is, when they were not subject to discrimination or persecution. Since the end of the Second World War, Jews in the Western world have been as free as they have ever been in any place or period, and they have consistently ranked at or near the top in surveys that measure affluence among ethnic and religious groups. In 2015, *Forbes* magazine reported that 11 per cent of the world's billionaires were Jews, as were 20 per cent of the top fifty billionaires.[4] American Jews, who constitute the largest Jewish community in the world outside Israel, have done particularly well in the economic sphere. Surveys of religious groups in the US over the past several decades have usually placed Jews first when it comes to annual income.[5] In 2009, the Forbes 400, which lists the 400 richest Americans, included 139 Jews, or 35 per cent of the list.[6] And all this from a group that makes up just 0.2 per cent of the global population and 2 per cent of the US population.

Mind you, not all Jews have done well from an economic standpoint. The phenomenon of Jewish poverty is often overlooked because of the economic success of most Jews. According to a survey conducted in 2013–14, between 16 and 20 per cent of American Jews had incomes of less than $30,000 a year. In another survey, conducted in 2017, 7 per cent of American Jews were living on $15,000 a year or less, and 7 per cent on incomes between $15,000 and $25,000.[7] Still, these figures do not negate the fact that on average, modern Jews have experienced remarkable success in the economic realm.

In the intellectual realm, the statistics on the number of Jews who have been awarded Nobel Prizes can be supplemented by other data that are no less impressive. Since the establishment of the Pulitzer Prizes in 1918, Jews have won 53 per cent of the awards in the non-fiction category and 14 per cent of the awards in the fiction category.[8] A survey in 2003 found that 21 per cent of students attending Ivy League universities were Jews,[9] and in 2009, the presidents of half these universities were also Jews.[10] It has also been widely noted that since the mid-nineteenth century, Jews have been overrepresented among the top scholars in the sciences and in mathematics.[11] Thus, here again, the disproportion of Jewish achievement is striking.

A similar disproportion is evident with respect to the accomplishments of Jews in the arts, both classical and popular. In the performing arts, the following statistics were current as of 2008:[12] Jews accounted for almost 30 per cent of the Kennedy Center Honors (established in 1978);[13] 14 per cent of the Grammy Lifetime Achievement Awards (established in 1962);[14] a remarkable 37 per cent of Academy Awards for Best Director (established in 1927);[15] and nearly 66 per cent of the longest-running musicals on Broadway were created by Jews.[16]

Even in sports, a field that does not usually come to mind when one thinks of Jewish achievement, Jews have experienced disproportionate success. In Olympic competition from 1901 to 2007, Jews won 401 medals, seven times more than would be expected given the size of their population.[17]

Many more statistics could be cited, but I think the point has been made. The question then is, "Why?" Why is it that Jews have done so incredibly well in the modern period?

This book is dedicated to that question. I am by no means the first one to broach it. A good number of scholars and popular writers have asked the same question and have offered theories attempting to answer it. But in my view, none of their theories have been entirely satisfactory, and so I have made it my goal in this book is to find one that is.

I should point out here for the sake of clarity that in tackling this question, I will not be concerned with moral issues. That is, when I speak about Jewish success, I will not be asking whether Jews have been successful from an ethical perspective. I will be speaking only about the types of success that are quantifiable. We can gauge how well Jews have done in Western culture in the economic, intellectual, and artistic realms because we have objective data on which to base such judgments. Morality, however, is a completely different matter. Whether an individual or group has succeeded in being moral is a question that does not easily lend itself to quantification. It is far more subjective, and so I will not take it up in these pages. Thus, readers should not expect me to engage in moral questions surrounding the State of Israel or the Israeli–Palestinian conflict. It is not that these issues are of no concern to me. It is just that they are not relevant to the matters that are the focus of this book.

Even so, the issues I will be addressing here are not entirely divorced from moral concerns. I will be dealing with the question of how Jews have succeeded in the economic, intellectual, and artistic spheres, and that question does have moral ramifications. An individual cannot get very far in life if they are not successful in one or more of these spheres, and much effort has been expended in the West on trying to figure out how to improve the lot of those who have had that problem. This point is particularly true for individuals who have not had success in the economic realm. Most people assume that making a decent living greatly increases the likelihood that a person will live a fulfilling and dignified life. So by attempting to understand how Jews have managed to succeed in the aspects of life I have chosen to focus on, I will in fact be tackling an issue that has moral ramifications.

Before I begin to search for an answer to the question about the success of modern Jews, I would like to say more about the question itself. The statistics I have cited in this introduction are reason enough to ask why Jews have done so well in the modern period, but the question becomes even more challenging in light of a number of other considerations.

The first is how suddenly the success of modern Jews came about. When academics and popular writers speak about the achievements of Jews since the beginning of the nineteenth century, they are referring primarily to Jews in the Western world, especially in Europe and the US. Yet as the nineteenth century began, it would have been hard to predict that Jews in either of these places would accomplish as much as they have in the past two centuries.

Let us begin with Europe. From the beginning of the sixth century up to the nineteenth – a time-span that encompasses the medieval and early modern periods – the Jews of Europe were a marginalized minority whose impact on European society was on the whole rather modest. The medieval Church determined that Jews were to be tolerated as the people whom God had initially chosen and who were the purveyors of his revealed truth in the Hebrew Bible, but they were also to be kept in a lowly condition because they had rejected the message of Jesus and were deemed responsible for his death. In the early medieval period, the Church's views had relatively little impact on the status of European Jews, but in later medieval times, especially after the eleventh century, these views resulted in the increasing exclusion of Jews from European life politically, socially, and economically, as well as spates of violence against them. The situation for them would not improve until the nineteenth century. There were, of course, notable exceptions. From the eleventh to the nineteenth centuries, Jews did quite well in some parts of Europe over substantial stretches of time. Still, life for them was precarious and insecure in the best of times, and in the worst of times, it was miserable. So it is not surprising that before the nineteenth century, the influence of Jews on the European world was not all that significant.

This is not to say that Jews had no impact at all in the medieval and early modern periods. In some parts of Europe, they did play a significant role in economic life. However, in the intellectual realm, their contributions were minimal. For instance, with regard to science, Jews were more conduits of knowledge than original contributors. In the late medieval period, they translated from Arabic into Latin large numbers of scientific treatises by Greek philosophers that Muslims had translated centuries earlier from Greek into Arabic. They also translated into Latin original works of science by Muslim thinkers. In this way, Jews played a critical role in advancing the study of science among medieval Christians. However, throughout the medieval and early modern periods, Jews produced few original scientific treatises and discoveries of their own. In the arts, the impact of Jews during these periods was practically non-existent.[18]

As for Jews in the US, their impact on the non-Jewish society around them also was not that significant before the nineteenth century. These Jews were granted citizenship and rights with the establishment of the US just prior to the beginning of that century. However, their numbers at this time were too small – between 1,000 and 2,500 – for them to have much influence on American society.[19]

But things would soon change. From the end of the eighteenth century onward, the situation for Europe's Jews went through a dramatic transformation. It began with the French Revolution that broke out in 1789. That revolution was inspired, in part, by the Enlightenment, an intellectual movement that declared that all human beings were created equal. Jews were beneficiaries of this new way of thinking. During the revolution, the Jews of France were granted citizenship and full rights in a European country for the first time, and over the next century or so, Jews in other parts of Europe gained the same privileges as Napoleon's armies brought the ideals of the Enlightenment to the territories they conquered.

It was in the wake of these momentous changes that Jews began to achieve success in Europe, and that success came with remarkable speed. As they started participating in European society, they rose quickly to prominent positions in a wide number of fields and disciplines, including politics, business, the professions, academia, and the arts.

American Jews also began to achieve success. As already noted, these Jews had been granted citizenship and rights when the American republic was founded in the eighteenth century, but their numbers were exceedingly small. However, the American Jewish community grew substantially in the middle of the nineteenth century with an influx of Jewish immigrants from central Europe. From 1830 to 1860, 200,000 Jews came to the US from that part of Europe. Most of them arrived impoverished, but they overcame their poverty in a relatively short period of time. Many started as peddlers but soon became middle-class store owners and businessmen. Some became very wealthy. Another wave of immigrant Jews came to the US in the late nineteenth and early twentieth centuries. This wave consisted of eastern European and Russian Jews and was far larger than the earlier one; 2.5 million Jews came to America's shores in those decades. Like their predecessors, most of these Jews came to the New World impoverished but managed to work their way up to a better life with impressive speed. Most of the newcomers initially resided in New York, where they had disembarked, and were employed in the garment industry, but they were determined to make a better life for their children, and most succeeded. By the Second World War, American Jews of all backgrounds were doing quite well and were having a significant impact on non-Jewish society.

Midway through the nineteenth century, non-Jews in Europe and America were beginning to take notice of the advances Jews were making. In 1846, Lord Ashley, a British parliamentarian, spoke admiringly of the "powerful intellect" of Jews, noting their accomplishments in music, poetry, medicine, and astronomy; in "every field," he concluded, they were "more than a match for their competitors."[20] At the end of the nineteenth century, the great American author, Mark Twain, would praise Jews even more enthusiastically:

> Properly the Jew ought hardly to be heard of, but he is heard of, has always been heard of. He is as prominent on the planet as any other people, and his commercial importance is extravagantly out of proportion to the small-ness of his bulk. His contributions to the world's list of great names in literature, science, art, music, finance, medicine, and abstruse learning are also away out of proportion to the weakness of his numbers. He has made a marvellous fight in this world, in all ages; and he has done it with his hands tied behind him.[21]

Twain made these comments before the twentieth century when Jewish achievements would reach even greater heights than they had in his own time.

Nothing better demonstrates the speed of Jewish success than their accomplishments in the sciences. As we have already noted, Jews had made few original contributions to the sciences before the nineteenth century. But by the second half of the nineteenth century, just a generation or so after their emancipation, Jews were making a significant mark on this domain of knowledge, and that trend would continue into the twentieth and twenty-first centuries.[22]

So the question is not only why Jews have done so well in the past two hundred years given their tiny population, but also how they have managed to do so well, so rapidly. Another consideration that makes it even more difficult to explain the success of Jews in the modern period is their unfortunate history. In my experience, most people – and that includes a good number of Jews – are unaware of the scope of Jewish suffering throughout the centuries. When people think of Jewish misfortune, they often focus on the Holocaust, but the troubles that Jews have experienced long predate that catastrophe.

I have already alluded to some of these difficulties: from the eleventh to the nineteenth centuries, European Jews were a marginalized minority. However, more detail is required to get a better picture of the challenges that Europeans Jews faced in these centuries. We can begin by noting the uncertainty that medieval Jews faced regarding their residence in any given locale. Jews resided where they did, at the pleasure of local rulers, and those rulers could expel them with little notice. This happened rather frequently, either for religious reasons – the rulers were loath to have Jews living in their territories – or for economic ones – Jews were competing with Christians for business. In fact, between 1290 and 1570, Jews were expelled from virtually every region of western and central Europe, with the exception of some parts of Germany and northern Italy, and had to find safe haven in other places, such as Poland, northern Africa, and the Ottoman Empire. And those expulsions were traumatic. Jews were forced to wander on treacherous routes to find another country that would take them in, with many not surviving the journey.[23]

Worst of all, hundreds of thousands of Jews died in anti-Jewish violence in these centuries. The first major instances of violence occurred during the First Crusade in 1096 when thousands of Jews in central Europe lost their lives to Crusader mobs. The Crusaders were on their way to the Holy Land to fight the Muslim infidels, but they found a much softer and more immediate target in the Jewish infidels whose communities they came across while marching through Europe. The fourteenth century was a particularly bad one for European Jews. Thousands of Jews in hundreds of communities were attacked in various regions in Europe for a number of reasons. For instance, Jews were deemed responsible for the Black Plague that decimated Europe in the middle of that century. They were accused of causing the disease by poisoning town wells or simply provoking God's wrath by their very presence. The early modern period witnessed violence against Jews that was just as bad, if not worse. Most notably, in the mid-seventeenth century, tens of thousands of Jews lost their lives in eastern Europe at hands of Cossacks and Tartars who had risen up against Polish rule and attacked Jews as part of their rebellion.

We might also note that while Jews living in Muslim lands in medieval and early modern times fared much better than they did in Christian Europe, they still experienced discrimination because of their religion. Moreover, violence erupted against them from time to time for the same reason it did in Christian Europe: Jews had rejected the true religion – but in this case, that religion was Islam.[24]

Salo W. Baron, the great twentieth-century Jewish historian, criticized Jewish historians of the nineteenth century for their tendency to read Jewish history as nothing more than a litany of disasters, a reading he called the "lachrymose" or tearful version of Jewish history. For Baron, Jewish history consisted of much more than a series of tragedies, and he dedicated his life's work to highlighting the vibrancy of Jewish life through the centuries.[25] Jewish historians since Baron's time have generally followed in his footsteps in giving a balanced portrait of Jewish history that does not dwell solely on its tragedies, and I will do the same in this study. But I also think that one should not overcorrect in the other direction and ignore the misery that Jews have experienced over the ages. One must take into account not just the actual violence against Jews in the medieval and early modern periods but also what life must have been like for Jews psychologically. Even in good times, Jews must have been plagued by uncertainty. Government policies towards Jews could change instantaneously, and even if such changes did not result in violence, there was always the fear of expulsion or economic deprivation. We must also appreciate the sense of humiliation that Jews must have felt throughout the centuries in Europe and in Islamic lands as a people who were often regarded as inferior to the majority population.[26]

For our purposes, the misfortunes that Jews have experienced are highly significant because when this aspect of Jewish history is taken into consideration, the record of Jewish achievement in the modern period becomes even more extraordinary. Their achievements came in the wake of centuries of adversity.

Most remarkably, even after the Holocaust, in which six million Jews died – more than one third of the Jewish people in the world at the time – Jews emerged from the catastrophe and continued to achieve success. Since the end of the Second World War, Jewish achievements in numerous areas of Western culture have been no less impressive than they were beforehand.[27] And whatever one's political views are on the State of Israel, the fact that the Jews were able to establish their own state right after the Holocaust was an amazing accomplishment.

Moreover, Israel, since its founding has epitomized the phenomenon of modern Jews achieving remarkable success in the face of adversity. Despite its short history, a tiny population that now numbers 9 million, and constant pressures from surrounding Muslim countries – all of which at some time or another have sought its destruction – Israel has achieved income levels that rival those of many First World nations, it has built top-rated universities, and in recent years, it has become a leader in technological innovation.[28]

Of course, there are other groups that have been highly successful in the modern world, and they have been the subject of much interest in recent years among authors attempting to understand why some groups have succeeded while others have not.[29] Yet the case of the Jews is unlike that of any other. No other ethnic group in modern times has quite the record of achievement that Jews have. None, for instance, has claimed nearly as many Nobel Prizes as Jews have. Nor have any of them had to overcome centuries of persecution in the way that Jews did in order to achieve success. The story of Jewish success is therefore a unique one.

Jews have often been compared to Asian Americans, who in recent years have also been noted for their achievements, and some have suggested that the success of the two groups is due to similarities in their cultures.[30] However, the phenomenon of Jewish success is much more difficult to explain than that of Asian Americans. As a recent study has shown, Asian Americans have succeeded in the US in part because they are a very select group. Changes in American law in 1965 favoured Asian immigrants who were highly skilled and highly educated, and so it is no surprise that their level of achievement in the US has been quite high. The level of achievement of Asian immigrants in other countries that have not had selective immigration laws is much lower. Most important, the level of achievement is even lower for the hundreds of millions of Asians who remain in their countries of origin and have not emigrated anywhere.[31]

Yet Jews who emigrated to the US from Europe in the nineteenth and early twentieth centuries were not selected for entry into the US because of their education or skills; many had neither when they arrived in America. Even so, they achieved immense success there. Moreover, the same can be said about the millions of Jews who remained in Europe and did not immigrate to the US. They too were extremely successful – particularly in western and central Europe – at least before the Second World War.[32]

How then did the Jews do it? How did they accomplish so much, so quickly, after having been persecuted for hundreds of years? And how have they sustained those accomplishments for two centuries?

Theories of Jewish Success

I mentioned earlier that various theories have been put forward to explain why Jews have done so well in the modern period. I will now discuss a number of them, as well as their shortcomings. As we will see, one particular theory will provide the basis for my own theory of Jewish success.

The Jews Are God's Chosen People

Some approach the matter through the lens of religious belief. Many Jews, as well as a substantial number of Christians, believe that the good fortune of the Jewish people over the past two centuries has been due to the fact they are God's chosen people. Their immense accomplishments are therefore a sign of divine blessing.[33]

In this book, I will not be pursuing that line of thinking. I am a committed Jew, but I am not a theologian, and I therefore do not feel qualified to speculate about God's intentions regarding the fortunes of the Jews and the world in general. I prefer to stay within the confines of academic scholarship.

The Jews Are Evil

A second type of explanation for Jewish success is, in some sense, the very opposite of the first. Some people believe that Jews have been successful because they are inherently evil and through their nefarious schemes have managed to dominate the world and its institutions, including governments, banks, businesses, and media.[34]

I have to say that there are times when I only wish this theory were true! I could certainly use a low-interest loan from the Jewish-owned banking industry to help pay my bills. But the truth is far different from what this theory proposes, and one does not have to speculate too deeply to understand its source. Human beings are prone to xenophobia and fear of the alien "other," and those traits often spawn conspiracy theories of the kind under discussion here. However, this type of theory plays into my hands in one important respect: it underscores just how accomplished Jews have been. Jews have done so well in the modern period that some have resorted to remarkably imaginative explanations to account for this phenomenon.

The Genetic Hypothesis

Another explanation for Jewish success is empirical in nature and is based on the science of genetics. This type of argument attributes Jewish success to a genetic predisposition to intelligence that evolved among Jews through a process of natural selection.[35] Explanations of this kind have been presented in numerous variations, only some of which I can summarize here.[36] According to one version, Jews have more "smart" genes than others because they were persecuted throughout their history, and therefore the more intelligent Jews tended to survive, while those with lesser intelligence did not. Over the centuries, the Jewish community was therefore composed of an increasing proportion of individuals of above-average intelligence, who then passed on their "smart" genes to subsequent generations.[37]

Yet another version of the genetic hypothesis claims that Jews themselves unwittingly engineered a smarter gene pool. In medieval Europe, the most intellectually gifted Jewish men were encouraged to become rabbis, and it was the custom for these rabbis to be married off to women from prestigious families that were quite wealthy. The rabbis could therefore afford to have more children than most Jews, and as a result, the proportion of intellectually gifted individuals in the Jewish community increased over time. By contrast, marriage practices in medieval Christian Europe had the opposite effect on its gene pool. The brightest men became monks, who were celibate, and therefore the smart genes of these individuals were lost. As a result, the gap between the average intelligence of European Jews and that of European non-Jews widened over time.[38]

Each of these genetic theories has elicited a number of criticisms, but a full summary of them would involve a much lengthier discussion than is needed here. I will just note several difficulties with this entire approach to Jewish success. First, the genetics of human intelligence are immensely complex, and our understanding of them is still quite primitive. There may be thousands of genes involved in intelligence, and we know relatively little about how they express themselves and interact with each other. Theories of Jewish success that rely on genetics are therefore based on arguments that can only be speculative.[39]

Second, it is unclear how intelligence should be measured. IQ tests are often the standard, and Jews have often been deemed more intelligent than other groups because their IQ scores are on average ten points above the rest of the population. But experts have increasingly questioned how much IQ scores can tell us about intelligence. Such tests measure a very narrow set of skills, and many of the accomplishments that Jews have achieved are in areas that have nothing to do with IQ, such as music and the writing of fiction. It has also been shown that IQ scores can be affected by environmental factors and can be improved through mental exercises, and these observations call into question how good a marker these scores really are for inherent intelligence. Some have also pointed out that the difference in average IQs between Jews and other groups is not large enough to account for Jewish accomplishments, such as the number of Nobel Prizes won by Jews.[40]

Third, even if it could be shown that Jews have more "smart" genes than others, there are questions about how much a role such genes even play in a person's success. We live in an era of mounting evidence that "nurture" is as important as "nature" in human development, if not more so, and therefore a genetic explanation of Jewish success is of limited use. No Jew, nor anyone else for that matter, has ever become accomplished only because they carried the right genes. One has to live in an environment that will allow those genes to be expressed and cultivated, and so environment is a key factor in a person's success.[41]

The Historical Hypothesis

Yet another type of explanation for the success of Jews in the modern period is what I will call the "historical hypothesis." Not surprisingly, this explanation has been favoured by scholars of modern Jewish history, particularly in recent years. It is a far more promising theory than the ones I have entertained so far, and I will discuss it in some detail.

According to this hypothesis, the extraordinary achievements of Jews over the past two centuries can be attributed mostly to historical circumstances and have little to do with any wilful action on the part of Jews themselves. As modern Western culture developed, Jews just happened to be in the right place at the right time and engaged in the right types of professions and activities to achieve success.

Scholars who take this approach usually make no effort to come up with an overarching theory of Jewish success. Rather, each of these scholars focuses on explaining how historical circumstances led to the success of Jews in one particular sphere – economic, intellectual, or artistic – or in one particular sub-sphere of these larger spheres, such as the sciences, which belong to the intellectual sphere. Sometimes the focus is even more narrow – for example, on the success of Jews in one of the three spheres in a specific country or geographic region.

Some examples will clarify how the historical hypothesis works. This hypothesis has had support among scholars of Jewish economic history, and it has become particularly popular in recent times among scholars who specialize in American Jewish history. Thus, Hasia Diner has argued that Jewish economic success in the US and a number of other Western countries in the twentieth century can be traced back to Jewish peddlers in the previous century, who numbered in the thousands in those countries and who made a living selling their wares door to door. Most of these peddlers earned a meagre living, but they eventually settled down and were able to establish businesses as shopkeepers, manufacturers, and financiers on the basis of the skills they had learned as peddlers and the networks they had established. These occupations, in turn, allowed Jews to do quite well economically, and some became quite rich as a result. Jews were then able to make headway in other parts of Western economies, especially in the US.[42]

Adam Mendelsohn has written a book in a similar vein in which he argues that economic prosperity among American Jews in the twentieth century can be explained by focusing on the involvement of Jews in the nascent garment industry in the previous century, an industry that eventually found its home in New York's Lower East Side. Jews were fortunate in entering the garment industry in its early stages of development because it ended up being quite lucrative. The success of Jews in that industry then paved the way for their entry into other sectors of the American economy in the twentieth century.[43]

The historical approach to Jewish success has also been taken up by those attempting to explain the accomplishments of Jews in the sciences. More than a century ago, Thorstein Veblen (1857–1929), the famous Norwegian-American sociologist, proposed a theory along these lines that was widely discussed at the time and is still the subject of debate. Veblen was a non-Jew fascinated by the fact that so many Jews were accomplished in the sciences, and he explained it by focusing on what he believed was the unique social position of Jews in Western society. He argued that when Jews became citizens of European countries in the nineteenth century, many of them left Jewish society but were not fully welcomed into European society, and they were therefore left in a kind of no man's land between the two cultures. That position turned out to have great advantages. Jews were free to think creatively about scientific questions in a way that non-Jewish Europeans were not, because Jews were not beholden to the burden of traditional patterns of thought in either society. The result was a flowering of innovative ideas among Jews in various scientific disciplines.[44]

More recently, Noah J. Efron has proposed another theory in accordance with the historical approach to explain why Jews have done so well in the sciences in the modern period. He argues that in the first half of the twentieth century, Jews in the US, Russia, and Palestine gravitated towards science because it gave them an opportunity to find a place in the modern world. Achievement in science was based on clear, objective criteria, and this allowed Jews to excel without having to fear discrimination based on old prejudices.[45]

All the scholars whose work I have just summarized are united in the belief that the success of Jews in the modern world has been primarily due to historical circumstances, though some, like Efron, concede that it was also in part the result of their own vision and initiative.[46] These scholars are also united in being highly focused in that they each examine how historical circumstances brought Jews success in one particular sphere. Some scholars focus even more sharply on one field in one particular country or geographical region.

The difficulty with this approach is that it fails to take into account the broader picture of Jewish achievement, and one has to see that larger picture in order to make sense of the more specific accomplishments of Jews. For instance, scholars who use the historical approach to explain Jewish success in the economic sphere do not grapple with the fact that Jews were also highly accomplished in a wide variety of other spheres that had nothing to do with the economic realm, such as the intellectual and artistic spheres. The same criticism can be made against scholars who use the historical approach to explain Jewish accomplishments in the sciences: they fail to recognize that Jews were successful in other fields and disciplines within the intellectual sphere, not to mention those in the economic and artistic spheres. Thus, scholars who adopt the historical hypothesis tend to be wearing blinkers: they forget that there is a much broader phenomenon of Jewish success in numerous disparate spheres and geographical regions and that no explanation of Jewish success in any one sphere or region is adequate without taking that wider context into account.

In the scholarship on Jewish economic history, one finds a similar problem within the field itself. Scholars like Diner and Mendelsohn have offered us important insights into the success of Jews in the US, but they do not grapple with the fact that Jews were also highly successful economically in other places in the modern period, in circumstances quite different from those in the US and in sectors of the economy quite different from those in which they excelled in the US.[47] If we go back to the early modern period, we see that Jews achieved remarkable success economically in a number of regions. Jonathan Israel has done pioneering work on the growth of Jewish trade networks in the seventeenth century that brought Jewish merchants considerable wealth. These networks connected Jewish spice and textile centres in the Ottoman Mediterranean and Balkans to merchants and bankers in northern Italy, Spain, the European Atlantic seaboard, and the Americas.[48] In the same period, Jews in Poland-Lithuania grew prosperous by managing the large estates of the Polish nobility as well as their commercial and industrial enterprises. These Jews tended to focus on the local production and sale of commodities from these estates, especially liquor, but they were also involved in marketing grain and timber to other European countries.[49] Jews in nineteenth-century Germany were another remarkable success story. In the eighteenth century, Jews in German lands – there was no Germany at the time – had high rates of poverty. But after their emancipation, Jews entered commerce, various service industries, and banking, and excelled in all three – particularly, banking. By the turn of the twentieth century, Jews constituted 4 per cent of Berlin's population but paid 30 per cent of its taxes. On the eve of the First World War, 32 per cent of the corporate elite in Germany were Jews.[50] A full explanation for Jewish economic success in the US would therefore have to account for the fact that this phenomenon was not solely an American one or restricted to particular industries. Over the past several centuries, Jews have managed to excel economically in a number of places and in a number of economic sectors. The same criticism can be made in reverse. Scholars who attempt to explain the economic success of Jews in regions in Europe in the early modern and modern periods generally do not take into account their success in the US.

This is not to say that all Jews were successful in the economic realm. There has certainly been plenty of poverty among Jews in the modern period, in both Europe and the US; I cited recent statistics on that earlier in this chapter. However, much of that poverty was the result of the antisemitic policies of governments (especially in Europe) that were determined to restrict the economic activities of Jews, and thus this poverty was not due to the failures of Jews themselves. And even if we concede that Jews were responsible for some of their own poverty, it is still remarkable in reading any survey of Jewish economic activity in the modern period to see how much success Jews experienced in this sphere in so many places when they were given the opportunity. Their consistent success in the US over the past century is the best evidence for this point.[51]

My criticism here of the historical hypothesis should not be construed as a rejection of the work of the scholars I have cited. Quite the contrary. Each of the scholars I have mentioned has made valuable contributions to our understanding of why Jews have been successful in the modern period. The problem with their explanations of Jewish success is that they are incomplete. If we take seriously all such explanations, the picture that emerges is implausible. We would be required to believe that all of the disproportionate success that modern Western Jews experienced in a wide range of spheres in a variety of geographic regions over two centuries were all because of different historical circumstances specific to each sphere and region, and that is an amount of good fortune that is too unlikely to be credible. What we need, then, is a more comprehensive approach to the success of Jews in the modern West, one that ties together all the achievements of Jews in many fields and in many geographic regions over two hundred years. There must be some common link, some underlying factor that connects these achievements.

Veblen's theory is the only one that has been discussed in this section that has the potential to provide such a link. In proposing that modern Jews were unusually successful because they inhabited a no man's land between the Jewish and non-Jewish worlds, Veblen suggests an explanation of Jewish success that cuts across the different geographic regions, time frames, and professions in which modern Jews achieved that success.

In some sense, that line of reasoning has been made explicit in a recent book by Norman Lebrecht, *Genius and Anxiety: How Jews Changed the World, 1847–1947*. Lebrecht's book consists mainly of a series of biographical sketches of significant modern Jewish figures, but as its title suggests, it also offers some reflection on why these Jews have been so successful. Lebrecht attributes this success to the fact that Jews have been perpetual outsiders in Western culture, a position that has brought with it several advantages. First, as Veblen argues, Jews were able to cultivate creativity more than their non-Jewish peers because they were not beholden to the norms of Western society. Second, Jews were forced to work harder than their non-Jewish peers in order to achieve recognition. Finally, the outsider status of Jews bred in them anxiety, and, according to Lebrecht, anxiety can prod individuals to great achievement.[52]

However, the approach taken by Veblen and Lebrecht to explaining the success of modern Jews is flawed in several ways. First, neither of them tests their theories in a larger global context. They do not explain why other minorities in the modern West, or in any other part of the world, have not been able to duplicate the success of Jews. These minorities have also found themselves in a no man's land between their ethnic communities and the majority society of which they have wanted to become a part, but these minorities have not racked up the record of accomplishment that Jews have. As for Lebrecht's notion of anxiety as a motivating force for creativity, Lebrecht never examines whether great figures in non-Jewish culture had their own anxieties. I suspect they did. Genius and anxiety are naturally paired because anyone attempting to revolutionize a field is likely to experience anxiety by virtue of that very ambition.[53] A second difficulty with the arguments of Veblen and Lebrecht is that they focus on elite intellectuals, musicians, and artists. Their theories do not tell us much about why ordinary Jews have done so well in Western culture relative to their non-Jewish peers.

Finally, neither Veblen nor Lebrecht takes into account that Jews have continued to experience remarkable success in Western culture since the Second World War – particularly in the US – even when they were no longer outsiders. Veblen lived well before this time period, and Lebrecht's book ends in 1947. Our search for a comprehensive explanation for the success of Jews in the modern period must therefore continue.

The Slezkine Hypothesis

Another scholar who has attempted to comprehensively explain Jewish success is Yuri Slezkine. His book, *The Jewish Century*, published in 2004, was devoted to this topic. Slezkine's book was highly original, widely read, and also quite controversial, and so it deserves its own separate discussion.[54]

Slezkine claims that Jewish success in the modern period can be attributed to the fact that Jews belong to a category of human communities that have existed throughout human history. He calls the people who make up these communities "Mercurians" after the Greek god Mercury. These communities are characterized by their nomadic and itinerant character. They are perpetual wanderers who move from place to place and cross borders between settled communities, and they are therefore never at home in any one location because of their unwillingness to settle down and because the settled communities tend to view them as foreigners. Mercurians make their living in ways that follow from their lifestyle: they specialize in the delivery of goods and services to the settled communities, and this labour does not require them to be rooted in a particular location. Their lifestyle also requires them to be highly adaptable to new circumstances, a quality that in turn encourages them to cultivate intelligence, cleverness, and wit.

According to Slezkine, there have been many Mercurian groups in the history of civilization in both the East and the West. In the West, Jews and Roma (formerly known as Gypsies) are perhaps the best-known examples, but Jews have been unusually successful at living the Mercurian lifestyle. In the medieval and early modern periods, Jews, like all Mercurians, were a mobile class that interacted productively with their host societies by specializing in the delivery of goods and services. They were merchants, traders, and moneylenders. As a result, Jews also excelled in the Mercurian quality of adaptability and developed the intellectual traits of intelligence, cleverness, and wit that usually go along with that quality.

Slezkine then contrasts "Mercurians" with "Apollonians," the other major category of human communities. Named after the Greek god

Apollo, Apollonians are the settled peoples to whom the Mercurians cater. They usually cultivate land to make their living, and they therefore place much greater value on manual labour than the Mercurians do. As a result, cerebral matters are not their interest. They also admire manly courage, and that is why they, not the Mercurians, field armies.

Slezkine claims that for the greater part of the past two millennia, Europeans have lived an Apollonian lifestyle, but that in the modern period, they have experienced revolutionary changes and have become Mercurians. The advent of capitalism has made the Mercurian way of life the preferred one, and therefore Europeans have been compelled to abandon their Apollonian lifestyle and adopt one more akin to that of the Mercurians. This explains why Jews have done so well in the West in the modern period: they are, after all, Mercurians *par excellence*.

And that is why Slezkine dubs the twentieth century "the Jewish century." The success of the modern West has been due to the fact that its inhabitants have adopted the Mercurian characteristics that Jews have been cultivating for so many centuries. It is not that Westerners have become more Jewish in any deliberate sense. Nor is it that Westerners have become Jewish in any religious sense. It is that Westerners have had to take on a Mercurian lifestyle and have therefore unwittingly become more Jewish in the process.

Slezkine's theory is highly original and is based on a remarkable range of learning, but it also has significant flaws. For our purposes, the most significant one is that he does not say nearly enough to explain why Jews have experienced success in the Western world so disproportionate to their numbers. If Westerners have become Mercurians like Jews, there should not have been a disparity between the two groups with regard to their respective achievements.

Slezkine addresses this issue briefly with two responses. First, Jews had an advantage over their European hosts because Jews entered European society already familiar with basic features of its culture, given that Jews shared a common religious heritage with Europeans. Second, Europe shifted to a Mercurian lifestyle in the modern period more so than any other Apollonian culture, and therefore Jews were far more at home there than in any other part of the world in this period.[55]

However, each of these arguments requires far more scrutiny than Slezkine provides. The first argument greatly underestimates the complexity of the relationship between Westerners and Jews with respect to religion both before and during the modern period. Jews shared much in common with the Western society of which they became part because of common religious roots, but the religious differences between Jews and European Christians have been substantial. Moreover, these differences were a source of great animosity for centuries before the modern period, and that animosity carried over into the new era. The second argument underestimates the complexity of both Western and Jewish society in the modern period. Even if the West did take on a more Mercurian character than other cultures did, it certainly did not leave the Apollonian way of life behind entirely. Conversely, when Jews joined Western society, many aspired to integrate into that society and succeeded so that their lifestyle was at least in part Apollonian.

It would also seem that neither of Slezkine's arguments really addresses the question of why Jewish success in the West was so disproportionate. His arguments merely tell us why Jews might have done as well as other Westerners did, not why they did so much better.

There are other difficulties with Slezkine's approach to Jewish success. His arguments about the Jews would be more convincing if he explained the discrepancy between the Jews and the other major Mercurian group in Europe, the Roma, who did not achieve the success Jews did. Moreover, there are other minority groups in Western culture that Slezkine does not discuss at all and whose experiences do not fit easily with his theory. For instance, how would he explain the success of Asian Americans in Western culture? Are they Mercurians as well? Nor does Slezkine explain why Mercurian communities in parts of the world outside the West have failed to achieve the kind of success that Jews have. Despite the originality of Slezkine's theory and his brilliant learning, I do not believe his approach to the remarkable success of Jews in the modern West is adequate.

The Cultural Hypothesis

I would now like to proceed to a theory for Jewish success that, I believe, supplies the critical ingredient for explaining this phenomenon. We might call it the "cultural hypothesis," for it presumes that what has been responsible for the achievements of Jews in the modern period is the religious culture that Jews lived by for centuries prior to that period. That is, the key to Jewish success has been, in a word, Judaism.

Some have adopted the cultural hypothesis to explain Jewish achievement in only one particular sphere. For instance, attempts have been made to account for Jewish success in the economic realm by looking to Jewish religious culture. This line of thinking goes back over a hundred years. The first major figure to take this approach was Werner Sombart (1863–1941), a German academic, who published a widely read and controversial book in which he argued that Jews not only were suited to capitalism but also had been instrumental in its creation, and that it was their religious culture that was responsible for their interest in it.[56] Sombart's work generated much discussion and debate, and despite its antisemitic overtones, some Jewish intellectuals were intrigued by it as well. A number of these intellectuals agreed with Sombart's premise that Jews were particularly well-suited to capitalism, though they disagreed with him about whether religious culture had anything to do with it, and if so, to what extent.[57] Much more recently, Jerry Z. Muller has argued that Jews have done well in capitalist economies in part because of their religious culture, but he has supported that position in a far more sophisticated way than Sombart did.[58] Attempts have also been made to explain the success of Jews in science by pointing to their religious culture, and these too have a long history. For instance, in the mid-twentieth century a number of Jewish intellectuals were inspired by the accomplishments of Albert Einstein, both during and after his lifetime, to argue for a connection between the accomplishments of Jews in science and their religious culture.[59]

While all these writers are to be commended for appreciating the influence of religious culture on the success of modern Jews, I believe they still do not go far enough because they are too narrowly focused in much the same way that supporters of the historical approach are. Again, what requires explanation is more than just the achievements of Jews in the economic, intellectual, or artistic realms, but their achievements in all three at once.

Some writers have attempted to answer this challenge by applying the cultural approach to all these spheres, and they usually identify the same attributes of Jewish religious culture as being responsible for the achievements of modern Jews in these areas: Judaism greatly values intellectual qualities, such as rationality, learning, and the ability to debate; it encourage virtues in the realm of behaviour, including moderation, discipline, and progress; and Jews have been able to cultivate these traits because Judaism has encouraged them to create stable societies in which great emphasis is placed on family life, communal networking, and education. Together, these characteristics explain why Jews have had such a spectacular record of achievement over the past two centuries.[60]

The cultural hypothesis when used in this comprehensive manner has the same advantage over the historical approach to Jewish success that the Slezkine hypothesis did. It identifies a factor common to all modern Jews that explains their success in a remarkable variety of fields and disciplines and in disparate geographical locations. Yet, while the Slezkine hypothesis looks to the socio-economic dimension of Jewish culture as the common factor, the cultural hypothesis looks to its religious dimension.

However, the cultural hypothesis also has its shortcomings. First, it has been supported mostly by popular writers whose arguments in favour of it have tended to be too superficial to be convincing. These writers have also been prone to inaccuracies, even when they are relatively knowledgeable.[61] For example, the feature of Jewish religious culture that is perhaps most talked about by popular writers as the source of Jewish success is education, on the assumption that Jews greatly valued learning when it came to their sacred texts and traditions and that they therefore invested a great deal in the education of their young. As I will show later in this book, that is not quite true. Throughout Jewish history, Jews valued learning but were not as committed to educating their young as many people believe.

The factual inaccuracies one finds in popular discussions of the cultural hypothesis for Jewish success often take the form of exaggerations – sometimes extreme ones. Some writers have been so enamoured of Jews and their accomplishments that they tend to place Jews on too high a pedestal, one from which they can only fall. For instance, Paul Johnson, author of the widely read *History of the Jews*, is no ignoramus on Jewish matters, yet he makes the following statement in his book: "The Israelites were the first people to bring their reason systematically to bear on religious questions. From Moses' day onwards, and throughout their history, rationalism was a central element in Jewish belief."[62]

That claim is hard to sustain. Israelite religion as it appears in the Bible was hardly rational or systematic. The rabbis who formed the Talmud in the first eight centuries CE used reason to adjudicate matters of Jewish law, but their discussions of law were equally based on biblical interpretation that was not rational at all. And when it came to formulating their religious beliefs, here too the rabbis depended mainly on biblical interpretation, not on reason. In fact, it was only in the tenth century CE, at least two thousand years after Moses's time, that Jews began analysing the theological premises of Judaism systematically and rationally, and their methods here were borrowed from ancient Greek and Islamic philosophy. It was, in fact, the Greeks who were the first to bring systematic reason to bear on religious questions in Western culture, and that was in the third and fourth centuries BCE, hundreds of years before the Hebrew Bible came into its final form. And even after Jews discovered rational methods for analysing their beliefs, many Jews in subsequent centuries were opposed to this approach to religion. In the medieval and early modern periods, the mystical schools of Kabbalah were far more popular among Jews than the rational philosophical schools of thinkers like Maimonides.

Let us look at another passage in Johnson's book:

To them we owe the idea of equality before the law, both divine and · human; of the sanctity of life and the dignity of the human person; of the individual conscience and so of personal redemption; of the collective conscience and so of social responsibility; of peace as an abstract ideal and love as the foundation of justice, and many other items which constitute the basic moral furniture of the human mind. Without the Jews it might have been a much emptier place.[63]

Here, Johnson praises the Jews for having invented a wide variety of ideas fundamental to modern Western culture, and as a Jew myself, I would like to believe that what Johnson is saying here is true. But I cannot. Judaism may have played a role in the development of the ideas mentioned by Johnson, but his assessment of that role goes too far. A full explanation of why that is the case would take us too far afield, but anyone with a familiarity with the history of Western culture will know that Christian and Greek thought were just as instrumental as Jewish thought was in the evolution of the ideas Johnson mentions, if not more so. In fact, we will be discussing the complex history of some of these ideas in the later chapters of this book, and when we do, it will be evident that Johnson's claims here are not accurate.

That is not to say that all popular treatments of the cultural hypothesis for Jewish success are without value. Special mention should be made of Steven L. Pease's work. Pease has written two books about the success of modern Jews, both of which support the cultural hypothesis, and one can only marvel at the amount of work he invested in the writing of these works. They are a valiant attempt to make a case for the cultural hypothesis.[64] Still, Pease's books suffer from some of the problems evident in the works of other popular writers who have written on the subject.

Yet the errors and exaggerations that have plagued popular treatments of the cultural hypothesis are not necessarily a fatal flaw in the hypothesis itself. It may still have merit if these problems are corrected. The difficulty is that there are other more serious challenges to the cultural hypothesis.

The difficulty that is most often noted by its critics is that some of the most successful Jews of the past two centuries have been secular, not religious, in orientation. Freud and Einstein certainly identified as Jews, but they were anything but Jewish from a religious standpoint. The same goes for the majority of Jews who have won Nobel Prizes, Pulitzer Prizes, Grammy Awards, and other prestigious international honours; these Jews have been mostly secular. The same observation can be extended to countless numbers of other Jews over the past two centuries who did not win international awards of any kind but nonetheless did very well in Western culture as professionals in such fields as medicine and law. It also has to be acknowledged that many of the Jews who have achieved success in the modern West were secular not just out of apathy; they consciously and openly *rebelled* against religion. Freud, for example, vilified religion as neurosis. How then can the claim be made that Jewish accomplishments in the past two centuries have been due to the influence of cultural values that are religious in origin?

A second difficulty with the cultural hypothesis that is also mentioned by some of its critics is that the achievements of Jews in the modern period have been heavily concentrated among Western Jews, not Mizrahi Jews, whose origins are in Islamic lands. Almost all the statistics about the success of Jews in the modern period that I listed at the beginning of this chapter are about Jews in the first category. Well, if Jewish religious culture was responsible for the success of Jews over the past two centuries, why did Jews from Islamic lands lag far behind their Western counterparts? While there were differences between the two groups when it came to religious practice, those differences were insignificant compared to what they shared. Thus, once again, there is reason to doubt the veracity of the cultural hypothesis for Jewish success.

There is a third difficulty with the cultural hypothesis that, to my knowledge, has not been noticed by anyone but is just as formidable as the other two. As I have just noted, the vast majority of modern Jewish achievements belong to Jews in the Western world, yet many of the features of Jewish religious culture that are deemed responsible for these achievements are features of modern Western culture as well. When Jews were invited to join European society in the nineteenth century, Europeans *also* valued education and family life; they *too* encouraged debate about intellectual matters and pushed for progress; and it was these features of European culture that were critical for its own success. In fact, Jews achieved their success in part because they were a minority in a majority culture that itself was immensely successful. What has been said here about Europe can be said about the US as well. American culture had many of the same positive qualities attributed to Jewish religious culture, and it too provided the environment for Jews to do well. If the cultural hypothesis is correct, how then did the characteristics of Jewish religious culture allow Jews to achieve such disproportionate success in the Western world if the culture of the West itself had many of the same characteristics? If Jews and Westerners had similar cultural values necessary for success, then Jews, on average, should have done about as well as Westerners did in the past two centuries, but that was not the case; Jews did better – *much* better, in fact – and the question is why. Without an answer to this question, the cultural hypothesis for Jewish success does not tell us very much.

In light of such difficulties, it is perhaps not surprising that the cultural approach to Jewish success has had very little support among scholars. In fact, to my knowledge, only two major academic studies in the past half-century have argued in favour of the cultural hypothesis for Jewish success. The first was Raphael Patai's *The Jewish Mind*, published in 1977.[65] Patai draws on a number of theories to explain the success of Jews in the modern period, but the cultural hypothesis receives the most attention from him, and he provides valuable insights into the manner in which religious culture helped modern Jews achieve as much as they did. However, his book reads like it is from another era. It has a polemical tone to it that harks back to a time when Jews were trying to prove their worth as citizens of the Western world. Patai's study is therefore of limited value.

The second study is much more recent: Maristella Botticini and Zvi Eckstein's *The Chosen Few: How Education Shaped Jewish History, 70–1492*, published in 2012. Botticini and Eckstein trace the economic success of Jews in the medieval period to the religious culture of Rabbinic Judaism that emphasized literacy and education.[66] However, this study does not deal with the modern period – though a second volume is projected that will carry the argument forward to the present day – and it deals with Jewish success only in the economic sphere. The book has also received highly critical reviews.[67]

The Cultural Hypothesis: My Contribution

The popular writers who have argued in favour of the cultural hypothesis have not been terribly successful in making their case, and academics do not find it convincing, apparently for good reasons. What, then, do I find so compelling about it? The rest of this book, in essence, will be devoted to responding to this question, and I would like to finish this introductory chapter by giving some idea of what form that response will take.

I believe that the key to presenting a convincing case for the cultural hypothesis is to provide a solution to the last of the three major difficulties with it that were just outlined: how can one claim that certain features of Jewish religious culture were responsible for the disproportionate success of Jews in the modern West if Western culture itself had many of the same features? As noted earlier, this problem has not been noticed by supporters of the cultural hypothesis, yet it may be the greatest challenge to their theory. The cultural hypothesis assumes that Jewish culture gave Jews an advantage when they became part of Western society, and the question being asked here casts doubt on that very assumption.

Addressing this problem will be the central task of this study, and it is a daunting one. It will require a lengthy and detailed investigation of how the traits seen as responsible for the success of both modern Jews and Westerners evolved over the better part of 2,000 years prior to the beginning of the modern era. Only with an investigation of this kind will we be able to discern why these traits helped Jews achieve success that was so out of proportion to their numbers when they became part of Western society two centuries ago.

In other words, we will be looking at the cultural hypothesis in a broad historical context, which others have not done. Most writers who support this hypothesis talk about the success of modern Jews without any reference whatsoever to historical context. Instead, they treat the cultural traits responsible for the success of modern Jews as timeless attributes that Jews have always possessed and that Jews were able to take advantage of as soon as they became part of the Western world. The reality, as we will see, was more far more complicated.

Mapping out the history of the cultural traits that allowed modern Jews and Westerners to achieve success will yield two major insights. The first is that Jews achieved the success they did in the modern period because the culture they fashioned during almost two millennia before modernity, in some respects, prepared them better than their non-Jewish neighbours for achieving success when the modern period arrived. For even though Jews and Westerners did indeed share many of the same cultural traits necessary for success in the modern period, a closer examination will reveal that those traits had a longer history and were more pronounced in Jewish culture than in Western culture. Westerners and Jews were both primed for success in the modern period, and for similar reasons – but Jews, more so, and it is that "more so" that will be our focus in the coming chapters.

The second major point that will emerge from our historical inquiry is that the pre-modern Jewish world view that prepared Jews so well for success in the modern West was rooted in a form of Judaism that academics refer to as "Rabbinic" Judaism, and that brand of Judaism can take much of the credit for the achievements of Jews over the past two centuries. This point will perhaps be the most important contribution this study will make to discussions about Jewish success, but I suspect that it will also be quite controversial since Rabbinic Judaism has generally been portrayed not as aiding the modernization of Jews but as hindering it. I am not denying that Rabbinic Judaism was, in many respects, an obstacle to the modernization of Jews, but I believe that the relationship that modern Jews have had with Rabbinic Judaism has been far more complex than has been appreciated up until now. I hope to show that while modern Jews have rejected the outward forms of Rabbinic Judaism, they have retained some of its patterns of thought and behaviour without necessarily being aware of it, and these have played a critical role in preparing Jews to achieve immense success in Western society.

For my readers who are not familiar with the term "Rabbinic Judaism," some explanation is in order. Simply put, Rabbinic Judaism is the Judaism of the rabbis, who emerged as a new class of leaders in the Jewish community after the first century CE.[68] Judaism had existed for hundreds of years by then, but up to that point, there were no rabbis – something that may be hard to imagine for those unfamiliar with Jewish history, given how central a role they play in contemporary Judaism.

The rabbis rose to prominence at a time when the Jewish community in the land of Israel was being ruled by the Roman Empire. In the first two centuries CE, Jews rebelled against the Romans twice, and both insurrections resulted in crushing defeat. Hundreds of thousands of Jews died, and the Temple in Jerusalem was destroyed. Because of this devastation, Judaism could have disappeared altogether, but the rabbis managed to confront the crisis in bold and innovative ways to prevent that from happening. They reconstructed and revolutionized Judaism so that Jews could deal with their new circumstances. The way of life they created went on to become the backbone of Judaism and allowed it to survive throughout the medieval and early modern periods, when Jews were scattered across vast distances in Christian and Muslim lands and were living among populations that were hostile to them. Judaism was now a religion based on the Bible as interpreted by the rabbis.

It was only in the eighteenth century that the authority of Rabbinic Judaism began to break down, and as the modern period evolved in the nineteenth and twentieth centuries, the majority of Jews would abandon it. However, my claim is that Jews still retained key elements of Rabbinic Judaism that prepared them particularly well for success in modern Western culture.

There should be no confusion between the rabbis I am referring to here and the rabbis in our contemporary world, who serve as clergy in the Jewish community. The rabbis of today are indeed connected historically to the rabbis of earlier times, but the office of rabbi in our day, which is defined primarily by pastoral duties, is largely a modern invention due to the centrality of the synagogue in contemporary Jewish life. When I speak of "the rabbis" in this study, I am referring to something different: I am referring to a group of religious leaders who rose to prominence in Judaism in the first centuries CE and continued to guide Jewish communities in the medieval and early modern periods. These figures also took on pastoral duties in the medieval period, but their main accomplishment was that they reshaped and revolutionized Judaism to cope with the destruction of the Temple and the exile of Jews from the land of Israel, and their Judaism became synonymous with Judaism in subsequent centuries.

There is one other potential point of confusion. When I speak about Rabbinic Judaism to my students or in public lectures, people tend to envision it as akin to today's ultra-Orthodox Judaism. That association is inaccurate. Ultra-Orthodox Judaism is a modern phenomenon. It arose in the nineteenth century as a reaction to the more liberal forms of Judaism that were gaining popularity in the Jewish community. Rabbinic Judaism, which defined Jewish life for hundreds of years before the modern period, was something quite different.

The role of Rabbinic Judaism has completely escaped the attention of writers interested in the success of modern Jews. To my knowledge, there are no scholars who have written about this issue and have properly appreciated the role of Rabbinic Judaism in this phenomenon. Popular writers, who have given the greatest support to the cultural hypothesis, have generally shown little or no acquaintance with Rabbinic Judaism. It is for this reason that the connection I will be drawing between Rabbinic Judaism and the success of modern Jews may be the most important contribution that this study will make to the literature on modern Jewish success.

These, then, are the main arguments I will be presenting in this book. But what about the other two difficulties with the cultural hypothesis that I described earlier? They too are serious challenges to any explanation for the success of modern Jews that depends on this hypothesis, including mine.

The one regarding Mizrahi Jews can be addressed immediately, and I will begin by noting that in the modern period, Western Jews have outnumbered Mizrahi Jews. In fact, by the mid-twentieth century, Western Jews *vastly* outnumbered them, and that was largely due to a population explosion among eastern European Jews in the late nineteenth and early twentieth centuries. Thus, on the eve of the Second World War, 90 per cent of world Jewry was of Western origin.[69] So if the statistics about Jewish accomplishments in the modern period belong mostly to Western Jews, it is in part because there were many more of them than Mizrahi Jews.

There are also questions about whether the success of Mizrahi Jews over the past two centuries can even be assessed in a manner that is meaningful for this study. To evaluate whether Mizrahi Jews were successful over the course of the past two hundred years, we would have to evaluate their success in that time frame relative to the larger societies in which they lived. However, before 1948, those societies were quite different from those of the West. That year marks the establishment of the State of Israel, and before that time, Mizrahi Jews lived mostly in Muslim countries that did not provide the kind of environment for Jews to succeed in the way that Western countries did. By the early nineteenth century, the Islamic world was steadily falling behind Europe with respect to standards of success as we have defined them.[70] So we should not be surprised if, according to these standards, Mizrahi Jews had fallen behind Western Jews by the mid-twentieth century. To put it succinctly, if Muslims themselves were not winning Nobel Prizes, one should not be troubled that Jews in Muslim countries were not winning them either. Therefore, "success" for Mizrahi Jews in Muslim lands before 1948 would have to be judged differently than for Jews in the West in the same period.

But there is another, more fundamental problem that makes even a relative determination of this sort difficult to make. Not enough scholarship has focused on Mizrahi communities in Islamic lands prior to 1948 for us to make accurate judgments about their levels of success in their respective Muslim societies. Moreover, if at some point scholars do enough research to make such judgments, these judgments will be more difficult to render than for Western Jews because we have a fair amount of statistical data about the latter group, at least from the late nineteenth century onward, whereas we have far less data about Mizrahi Jews in the same period.

We can more easily assess the success of Mizrahi Jews after 1948 because we certainly have data about Mizrahi Jews in the State of Israel since its creation. There are indications that while they started off poorly in Israel in the years after its founding, their situation has steadily improved in the past few decades. However, we lack sufficient data about how Mizrahi Jews have done who have emigrated to the West. For instance, surveys about income and education levels for Western Jews do not usually differentiate between Mizrahi Jews and Western Jews.

In light of all these observations, I think it best to set Mizrahi Jews aside for the purposes of this study. The state of our knowledge about these Jews is not sufficient to determine to what degree they have been successful in the past two centuries relative to the larger societies in which they have resided, and if they *have* been successful in this regard, it is hard to say whether the cultural hypothesis works for them as it does for Western Jews. Moreover, the vast majority of Jews over the past two centuries have been Western Jews, so we can still make meaningful judgments about Jewish success in general in the modern period by focusing just on them. I leave it to scholars who specialize in the history of Mizrahi Jewry to determine whether the insights of this study apply to that community as well.[71]

What about the matter of secular Jews? How can the claim be made that the success of modern Jews is attributable to Rabbinic Judaism if some of the most successful Jews were secular and have abandoned religion? I will be devoting an entire chapter to this issue, but here I would like to share some thoughts in anticipation of what is to come.

It is certainly true that these Jews left Rabbinic Judaism behind, but to say they must have then purged themselves of all vestiges of Rabbinic Judaism greatly underestimates the complex process by which cultures evolve, in general – as well as the complex process by which modern Jewish culture has evolved, in particular. Communities that go through major cultural shifts often carry over cultural traits from the previous era even when they are unaware of it and even when they are determined to leave the past behind, and I will argue later on in this book that this was likely the case for Jews entering the modern period as well. So it is quite plausible that while modern secular Jews rejected much of Rabbinic Judaism, they retained some of its key values, even if they were not cognizant of doing so, and that those values were critical in helping them achieve the success they did.

In this book, I will be expanding on everything I have discussed here. I will be delving more deeply into the cultural hypothesis and its historical context, the difficulties with this hypothesis, and how those difficulties can be solved. I hope that by the time all is said and done, I will have provided a convincing theory that finally solves the mystery of Jewish success in the modern period.

I should emphasize that the theory of Jewish success that I will be offering does not necessarily provide the entire explanation for this phenomenon. We are dealing with a complex issue here, and there were undoubtedly other factors involved. In fact, I have already acknowledged the value of the insights of scholars who suggest that historical circumstance played a role in the success of modern Jews. However, I believe that my theory provides a critical component, if not *the* critical component, of the explanation for this phenomenon.

The Plan for This Book

As I have just explained, the cultural hypothesis for Jewish success will be persuasive only if we examine how the cultural traits responsible for the success of modern Jewish and Western culture evolved in the two millennia before modernity. The greater part of this study will therefore be devoted to this task. I have also acknowledged that this task is a formidable one, given that we are talking about the evolution of basic features of two enormously rich cultures over a very lengthy stretch of time. The difficulty here will be compounded by the fact that there are numerous misconceptions about the development of these features in both Jewish and Western culture, and those misconceptions will have to be addressed. I will also have to contend with the challenge posed by secular Jews.

To deal with this series of tasks, I have structured this book in a somewhat unusual way. Rather than make a linear argument in which each chapter builds on the previous one, I will devote part 1 of this book (the next two chapters) to a basic overview of what I hope to prove in this study. Here I will be establishing the fundamental framework for a new and hopefully convincing version of the cultural hypothesis. In that way, my readers will get the big picture of what my version of the cultural hypothesis looks like without having to deal with its details. Once the framework is in place, part 2 will take up those details. It will demonstrate that, over two millennia, Western culture and Jewish culture both developed cultural traits that prepared them for success in the modern period, but that Jews developed those traits in more robust form. This discussion will span eight chapters. The two chapters in part 3 will summarize what has been learned from the previous chapters as well as the lessons emerging from my exploration that are relevant to Jews and non-Jews in our own time.

Methodology

It is important that I say something about my methodology. This book focuses mostly on intellectual history. That is, I will primarily explore the views of elite thinkers in the history of Christianity and Judaism in the West in order to make the case that cultural differences between Jews and Christians explain why Jews were better prepared than Christians for success in the modern period. That does not mean that I will be ignoring ordinary Christians and Jews. In fact, I cannot afford to do so, given that the success of modern Jews that I am attempting to explain involved large numbers of Jews who were not part of any elite, intellectual or otherwise. I will therefore do my best to draw into my discussion what we know about the views of ordinary Christians and Jews on the cultural values I am examining. That is, I will engage in social history, not just intellectual history.

However, my main focus will have to be on intellectual history because the intellectual elites in Christianity and Judaism left us copious writings on the cultural values I will be examining, whereas ordinary Christians and Jews did not. In many periods and places, our only insight into the views of Christians and Jews on such values will be those of the intellectuals. Still, I believe that my exploration of intellectual history will give some insight into the views of ordinary Christians and Jews as well. The views of the intellectuals in both communities were often quite influential on lay people, even if the latter were not educated or even able to read the views the intellectuals espoused, because it was often the intellectuals who led the way in shaping the fundamental religious ideas and practices of their respective societies. The teachings of the intellectuals often filtered down to the masses, albeit in simplified form, because the disciples of the intellectuals were the ones who often served as leaders and teachers in lay communities. An ordinary medieval Christian may not have been familiar with Thomas Aquinas's writings, and the same can be said about Jews in the same period with respect to the writings of Maimonides, but both Aquinas and Maimonides had a strong impact on medieval Christianity and Judaism respectively, and thus ordinary Christians and Jews were likely to have been taught or preached to by religious clerics who reflected the views of these masters.

I will assume, then, that while the views of intellectual elites do not necessarily reflect what ordinary individuals are thinking in any given era, one should not assume a complete disconnect between them either. Often the views of intellectual elites and lay people mirror each other. I believe that was particularly the case in premodern European Jewish communities with respect to the rabbinic values that, I will argue, prepared Jews for success in the modern period.[72]

Terminology

Some points of terminology should be clarified. The terms "Europe" and "the West" can be sources of confusion because in some contexts they can be used interchangeably, while in others they cannot. Moreover, "the West" itself is a loaded term that resists easy definition.

For the purposes of this study, "the West" will refer primarily to Europe and the US because it is in these places that most Western Jews have lived in the modern period. I will use the terms "Europe" and "the West" synonymously when speaking about the nineteenth century, because at that time, the centre of the West was clearly Europe. However, when I speak about the events in the twentieth or twenty-first centuries, I will tend to differentiate between Europe and the West, because in these centuries, the West encompassed both Europe and the US.

Another potential point of confusion concerns the terms "Christians" and "Europeans" as designations for the inhabitants of Europe. For most of the periods in European history that we will be dealing with in this book, the two are synonymous: the vast majority of Europeans were Christians. However, as we enter the early modern period, particularly the Enlightenment, it becomes more difficult to use the terms "Europeans" and "Christians" interchangeably since there were elements of European society by then that rebelled against Christianity. And in the modern period the two terms are not necessarily synonymous at all, given that significant sectors of modern European society do not identify as Christians. So from the Enlightenment onward, I will tend to speak of the inhabitants of Europe as "Europeans" and reserve the term "Christians" for those Europeans who continued to adhere to Christianity.

The terms "Christian" and "Christianity" themselves require some comment. When I use these terms in this book, the reader should assume that I am speaking about the Christianity that grew out of the Western Latin Church, including Protestant Christianity. There were certainly other branches of Christianity in various parts of the world, and there continue to be. However, these will not be our concern.

What about the term "Jews?" This word is actually rather problematic. There has been much discussion lately about whether the term refers to a unified group that has subsisted throughout history. The difficulty is that the Jews can be defined by a variety of factors: genealogy, religion, ethnicity, nationality, and culture – so one's definition of who is a Jew will depend on which of these factors, singly or in combination, makes one a Jew. Recent demographers have tried to simplify matters by settling on the definition that a Jew is someone who *says* they are a Jew, but the danger here is that it makes the definition very broad and entirely subjective.[73] Nonetheless, I believe this last definition will suit my purposes for this book; my interest will be in people, throughout the centuries, who have said they are Jews. It is these people who have survived centuries of persecution, have succeeded remarkably in the modern period, and are therefore the object of this study.[74]

A word is also in order here about periodization. I will be using a fairly standard scheme for time periods. When I refer to the medieval period, I am alluding to the years 500 to 1500. The years 500 to 1000 will be referred as the early Middle Ages, while the years 1000 to 1500 will be referred to as the late Middle Ages. Some scholars differentiate between the high Middle Ages (1000–1250) and the late Middle Ages (1250–1500), but I prefer to simplify matters by not using this distinction.

The early modern period will span the period 1500–1800, and the modern period covers the period from 1800 to the present. Periodization in Jewish history is not necessarily congruent with that of Western history, but throughout this study, unless I specify otherwise, I will be using the periodization scheme outlined here as my default even when discussing Jewish history. Here too, my goal is to simplify matters.[75]

My Intended Audience

I conclude this chapter by reiterating a point that I made in my preface, which is that this book is meant for several audiences. It has been written for academics and non-academics, for Jews and non-Jews, for Westerners and non-Westerners. I have therefore invested considerable effort in providing basic background for all the topics I have taken up. I have also explained all specialized terms and concepts while avoiding unnecessary academic jargon. As a result, this book is a good deal longer than it would have been had it been written for a more limited audience, and that may annoy some of my readers who have substantial background in the issues being discussed in the coming pages. Readers who encounter material that seems elementary to them always have the option to skim it, or skip it altogether.

My desire to reach a broad audience has also required me to simplify some matters in a manner that some of my more informed readers may find objectionable. Here again, I will beg the indulgence of such readers who, I hope, will understand why I have written the book as I have. Moreover, before readers pass judgment on me for not appreciating the complexities of a particular topic, they should check my footnotes, where I often address esoteric matters pertaining to the issues I address. These notes do not deal with all such matters, but they do discuss a good number of them.

PART ONE

The Cultural Hypothesis Revisited: An Overview

Chapter One

Western Culture, Jewish Culture, and Four Key Values

Part 1 of this book provides an overview of my theory for the success of Jews in the modern period. The theory I am proposing involves an enormous amount of material, and so I believe the reader will benefit by first getting acquainted with an outline of the theory before its details are laid out. This chapter will describe the basic features of my theory. The next one will confront the challenge to it posed by secular Jews.

The Success of the West: Four Critical Values

For the cultural hypothesis to be persuasive, we have to analyse the common cultural values developed by Westerners and Jews over the past two millennia that led both groups to achieve success in the modern period so that we can see how Jews were, in critical respects, better prepared for such success than Westerners were. Let us begin by identifying the common cultural values of which I speak here. I have in mind four:

1) human autonomy
2) freedom of thought and expression
3) the value of life in this world
4) education

These values are widely recognized by scholars as crucial to the West's modernization. They are discussed in practically every textbook that deals with the evolution of modern Western culture.[1] However, they are of interest to us for a somewhat different reason, which is their role in making the West successful. This point requires emphasis because the *modernization* of the West and the *success* of the West, while closely related, are not the same thing. The advent of modernity involved many changes in

Europe's intellectual, political, social, and economic life, not all of which were responsible for Europe's success. These changes included a belief in progress, the importance accorded to science, the shifting of power from monarchies and aristocracies to the middle class, the emergence of democratic forms of government, industrialization, the migration of populations from the countryside to urban centres, and the development of capitalist economies that replaced agrarian ones. The West's modernization is thus a much broader topic than that of the West's success, and we must keep that in mind as we discuss the four values that are at the centre of this study. Our interest in these values is due to their relevance to the latter topic, not the former one.

Before I go any further, it is appropriate for me to say a brief word about what I mean precisely by the term "success" when I speak about the success of Western culture. When I described the achievements of Jews in the modern West in the first chapter, I grouped them into three categories: economic, intellectual, and artistic. These same categories will be used for my discussion of the success of the West as well. In the economic realm, the modern West has led the world in the amassing of wealth. In the intellectual realm, it has led the world by building the its most prominent academic institutions and by outpacing others in scientific research and the development of technology. And in the arts, both classical and popular, the West has wielded enormous influence around the globe. This scheme is not the only one that could be used to examine the success of Western culture, but it sufficed for our treatment of Jewish success, and it can serve the same function for discussing Western success.

A point that I made in the previous chapter about my definition of Jewish success in the modern period also applies here. There I noted that while this definition did not necessarily include success in the moral realm, my discussion of the success of modern Jews still had moral import because others can glean positive lessons from this phenomenon to improve their lives. I take the same approach with respect to the West. From a moral perspective, the success of the West has, in fact, been a very mixed bag. The West has contributed a great deal to the world in the economic, intellectual, and artistic realms, but it has also been the source of great hardship and suffering because the success of the West in the economic and intellectual categories helped it achieve military might that it has often used to oppress non-Western nations. That was particularly the case in the colonial era, and an argument can be made that it continues to be the case to some extent in the present era. However, an understanding of how the West has succeeded in the three categories still has positive moral value as well, because it too has the potential to provide people with insight into how to better their lives, whether or not they are Westerners.

I will now briefly describe how the four values just enumerated played a role in the success of the West as I have defined it:

1) *Human autonomy.* I am referring here to autonomy in the meta-physical sense. Scholars, theologians, and philosophers often refer to this form of autonomy as "free will." For Europeans to achieve success in a variety of spheres in the modern period, they had to develop the notion that human beings were exalted, dignified, and powerful creatures with the freedom to conquer the world around them both literally and figuratively – that is, through physical and intellectual mastery. That meant Europe-ans had to get past the idea common in pre-modern Christianity that human beings were lowly and sinful creatures who were effectively enslaved to their natural impulses. Europeans also had to develop a new conception of God. They had to overcome the notion, also common in pre-modern Christianity, that God was an overpowering deity who left little or no room for human initiative. It is not that modern Europeans had to deny God's existence altogether to achieve success, nor did they have to give up on the idea that God was a powerful being. Rather, they had to believe that human beings were sufficiently empowered to become masters of the world around them, whatever God's role was in human affairs.

2) *Freedom of thought and expression.* This value is the political coun-terpart of the first value. In order to achieve success, Europeans had to have autonomy not just in relation to the cosmos but also in relation to each other. They had to pass laws guaranteeing freedom of thought and expression to ensure the cultivation of new and innovative ideas necessary for advancement in a wide range of disciplines from the sciences to the arts, and they had to do so no matter how threatening those ideas might have been to traditional religious beliefs and sentiments. Christianity prior to the modern period had tended to place restraints on what Europeans could believe and say, and this complicated efforts on their part to come up with pioneering ideas. Anything going against the fundamen-tal beliefs of Christianity could be branded as heresy. Only when Europeans began to erect strong protections for the expression of new ideas regardless of their religious implications were they able to pull ahead of the rest of the world in a number of fields and disciplines.

3) *Life in this world is inherently good.* Europeans not only had to have a robust belief in autonomy in the metaphysical and political realms in order to achieve success in the modern period, but they also had to believe that their autonomy in both senses should be directed towards this-worldly goals. For obvious reasons, modern Europeans could not have achieved what they did if they had not upheld this notion. Europeans had to come around to the idea that engaging in the world materially and intellectually was a valuable objective in its own right if they were going to be motivated to dominate in these spheres. And here too Europeans had to grapple with their pre-modern Christian world view. For centuries, Christianity had tended to devalue life in this world in favour of the afterlife and the messianic period.

4) *Education.* One more critical ingredient that was needed for Europeans to achieve success was that they had to actively cultivate the three values just described through education. There had to be recognition that all human beings, with proper instruction, could develop their metaphysical and political autonomy and engage in mastering the world around them. Moreover, Europeans had to build educational institutions for that purpose so that the best talent could be identified and nurtured in order to bring about progress. Pre-modern European society did not presume that all people needed to be educated, and so it did not set up educational institutions to that end. Thus, here as well, modern Europeans had to move beyond their pre-modern past.

These values did not appear out of nowhere when the modern period dawned. They had a long history prior to it. They were present in European culture in varying degrees as early as the beginning of the medieval period, but it took centuries for them to develop until they emerged in full bloom as modernity evolved. And their effects continue to the present day. Most Westerners nowadays in fact take them for granted.

Much has been written in recent years about the factors that helped Europe achieve what it did, and it is important that I explain how my approach to this issue fits in with that literature. Some scholars attribute the West's dominance in the modern period to material factors, including the West's aggressive pursuit of military technology and its investment in warfare,[2] or its fortunate circumstances with respect to geography and demography.[3] Other scholars attribute the dominance of the West in the modern period to non-material factors. They focus on its cultural traits in a variety of areas, including its intellectual life, politics, ethics, and religion.[4] The four values I will be examining are relevant to the second category of theories, but by focusing on these values, I am by no means rejecting the materialist theories.[5] I have chosen to focus on cultural factors only because they are the factors most relevant to the success of modern Jews. My argument is that it was in the realm of culture that modern Jews had advantages over their non-Jewish neighbours, and these advantages explain the explosion of Jewish achievement over the past two centuries. The materialist factors are not relevant to this argument because Western Jews and non-Jews benefited from them equally. Military technology and geography gave the two groups the same advantage since they were both defended by the same armies and lived on the same soil.

Yet even if I do not believe that the four values provide the entire explanation for the success of the West, I do believe that they provide a good part of that explanation. This point has to be highlighted because in recent decades a number of scholars have insisted that the dominance of the West came about only because of materialist factors and that culture had nothing to do with it. That is, the West's dominance has not had anything to do with its intrinsic virtues. These authors belong to a school of thought that arose in the 1960s in reaction to the long-standing favouritism towards the West that had characterized academic approaches to history up to this point, and this new approach has since become quite popular. It is tied in with the growth of multiculturalism, which has attempted to tear down the arrogance of the West, while bringing to light the accomplishments of other cultures. Part of this effort has also consisted of bringing to light the suffering and oppression that the West has brought on others.[6]

I am all for multiculturalism and I support those who have sought a more balanced understanding of world history. As a Jew, I should hope that there is appreciation for cultures other than that of the West. In fact, that is precisely what this book is about. I am also entirely in support of recognizing the horrific hardships that the West has inflicted on others. I just made note of those hardships myself. Moreover, Jews provide the best example of the West's brutality. Nothing better illustrates Western culture gone awry from a moral standpoint than the Holocaust.

However, if Western-centrism was a problem in academic treatments of history up to the 1960s, some of the correctives suggested by the multiculturalists have been no less of a problem. To say that the dominance of the West in the modern period has been only a matter of luck and circumstance and that it has had nothing to do with cultural values, or that Western culture has contributed nothing good to the world is as distorted as the Western-centrism that those supporting the multicultural approach hoped to replace. Thankfully, in recent years, some scholars have begun to react against the excesses of this approach.[7]

Most important for our purposes is that the four values I am focusing on have been a critical part of Western culture. These values were crucial in helping the West take a leading role in the world. They have also helped better the lives of people in other cultures. For instance, people throughout the world have enthusiastically embraced the notions of freedom of thought and expression and equal access to education as fundamental human rights.

The Four Values and the Success of the Jews

What does any of this have to do with the success of Western Jews over the past two centuries? A great deal, I will argue. When Jews were invited to become part of European society from the late eighteenth century onwards, they too lived according to the four values I have just described, as part of the process of acculturation to their new environment. Yet these values had their own rich history in Judaism. They had been latent in Jewish culture in the centuries before the modern era, just as they had been latent in pre-modern European culture, but in Jewish culture, they had a richer and more extensive history. When one compares the evolution of these values in the two cultures prior to the modern period, it becomes clear that each of these values arose in Jewish culture much earlier and took on a more mature form than in the culture of Europe. I am not saying that Jewish culture was already modern before modernity arrived. My argument is only that pre-modern Judaism was *closer* to being modern when compared to pre-modern European culture and that this was so only with regard to only *some* values – four to be precise – that would later become important for the success of Jews in the West.

If these observations are correct, we can explain why the characteristics of Jewish culture allowed Jews not just to achieve success in the modern Western world but to achieve it disproportionately, even though Western culture itself had similar features. The West certainly led the way here. Europeans built an impressive modern culture based on a series of traits that helped it become dominant in the world, and Jews were beneficiaries of Europe's achievements. Jews, in fact, could not have succeeded as they did without the European environment in which they resided. However, Jews also had their own culture, one in which similar traits had been cultivated over a longer period of time and had achieved a more mature form, and so when Jews were finally invited to become part of European culture after centuries of living lives apart from non-Jews, they were at an advantage. They were better attuned to the features of modernity that were important for achieving success, and as a result, they were in a strong position to make the best of the new world of which they would soon become part.

I do not want to give the impression that Jews had an easy time adjusting to modernity. It is not as if they settled into their new environment and happily succeeded without a hitch. That process was, in fact, quite difficult. It wreaked havoc on Jewish communities throughout Europe. Jews had been living in separate communities for centuries, and they were now part of a much larger European society that was foreign to them and that still harboured great antipathy towards them. Jews were also hit hard by the same intellectual currents that were challenging the validity of Christianity, and these forces caused many Jews to question whether Judaism as a religion had a future in Europe. Still, despite these challenges, Jews were in some respects rather well-prepared for modernity because basic features of Jewish culture meshed so well with the modern outlook, most notably the four values we have been discussing.

There are elements of my theory of Jewish success that may be familiar to some of my readers. Some may already know that Judaism is distinguished from Christianity by its emphasis on one or more of the four values I am focusing on in this study because Jewish intellectuals have spoken about these distinctions for some time. They began drawing attention to them early in the nineteenth century when Jews were just being admitted to European society. At this time, Jewish scholars and rabbis began probing the differences between Judaism and Christianity against the background of the momentous changes that were taking place in the modern period regarding the status of Jews and the revolutionary changes taking place in this period in general, and some of the differences they dwelled on were concerned precisely with one or another of the four values that are at the centre of this study.[8] In the twentieth century, Jews continued to explore these differences.[9] And in the twenty-first century, discussions of the distinctions between Judaism and Christianity have continued in popular discourse among Jews in various media.

However, my own exploration of these distinctions will be quite different from what others have presented. Much of the discourse over the past two centuries about the distinctiveness of Judaism vis-à-vis Christianity has had a polemical edge to it. Jews have often been eager to point out the differences between the two religions in order to argue for the moral superiority of Judaism. As a result, the treatments of these differences have usually lacked nuance and have been plagued by glib generalizations. The distinctions between Judaism and Christianity have frequently been put in black-and-white terms to the advantage of Judaism, including in discussions about the four values that are the focus of our concerns here.[10]

It is understandable that Jews have made these arguments. Even though Jews have become part of Western society over the past two centuries, the old prejudices against them and their religion have persisted, and Jews have therefore had to exert much effort to show that Judaism has a great deal to contribute to the Western world. The problem is that in their eagerness to make this case, Jews have overcorrected to the point of distortion. The argument has been that Judaism, far from being inferior to Christianity, is in fact superior to it, and this judgment is as problematic as the one it replaced.

I plan to avoid such distortions, as well as the polemics that lie behind them. In later chapters, I will subject the distinctions between Judaism and Christianity regarding the four values to an academic analysis. Such an analysis, to my knowledge, has never been attempted, and the result will be a much more thorough, nuanced, and accurate portrait of some of the most commonly discussed distinctions between Judaism and Christianity.

Most important, my purpose in drawing distinctions between Judaism and Christianity is not to weigh the moral value of the two religions. I am not interested in demonstrating that Judaism is better than Christianity. My aim is to explain a striking historical phenomenon: why Jews have done so well in Western culture in so many areas. It is only for that purpose that a comparison between Judaism and Christianity is being conducted here. Moreover, what I hope to show is that ultimately both religions deserve our admiration. My argument is that Judaism was responsible for Jews succeeding in the West but that Jews would never have had that success had Christianity not shaped Western culture in the way it did.

The Role of Rabbinic Judaism

I will now describe in greater depth the second major point that will be at the centre of my presentation of the cultural hypothesis, which is that much of the credit for Jewish success in the modern period goes to Rabbinic Judaism. As I explained in this book's introduction, when I speak about pre-modern Judaism containing the four values in unusually robust form, I am referring mainly to the Judaism that was created by the rabbis.

A Brief History of Early Rabbinic Judaism

The first thing I would like to do in this section is to provide more information about the history of Rabbinic Judaism for the sake of readers who may be unfamiliar with it. Readers who are already acquainted with this background may want to skip ahead to the next section.

In the first century CE, when the rabbis began to emerge as a distinctive group in the land of Israel, Judaism had been evolving for more than 1,000 years, and therefore the rabbis inherited a religion that already had a long history. Moreover, in the first century there were a number of different kinds of Judaism – much like today's denominations – with the rabbis representing only one of these. Nonetheless, a number of beliefs united most Jews in this period, including the rabbis, and they were as follows:

1) God had a special relationship with the Jewish people going back almost 2,000 years that began with their forefathers – Abraham, his son Isaac, and his grandson Jacob – as reported in the Bible. That relationship was concretized in a "covenant" (*berit*), a contract of sorts, in which both sides had to adhere to certain conditions: the forefathers and all their descendants had to obey God's will, and God would reward them by granting them the land of Israel and giving them material prosperity.

2) The covenant was further developed several generations later, by which time the descendants of the forefathers had grown into a large people, and their prophet and leader, Moses, had received the Torah from God on Mount Sinai. The Torah contained hundreds of commandments that the Israelites had to follow, commandments that consisted of two types: those that concerned proper behaviour towards God, and those that involved proper behaviour towards their fellow human beings. It is important to emphasize that there were many more commandments beyond the original Ten Commandments that had been given to Moses on Mount Sinai, because there is a common misconception among Christians, as well as a good number of Jews, that these commandments were the only ones that were given to the Israelites. That was not at all the case. According to the biblical narrative, many more commandments were imparted to the Israelites before they reached their homeland. In rabbinic tradition, 613 commandments were given by God to the Israelites – though how the rabbis arrived at that number would require a separate discussion.[11]

3) A significant number of the commandments were concerned with the worship of God through a variety of animal sacrifices. Under the reign of King Solomon in the tenth century BCE, a magnificent temple was built in Jerusalem that became the central location for performing the sacrifices.[12]

It is important to be aware that the 1,000 years of Israelite–Jewish history prior to the rabbis had been quite troubled. A series of empires had conquered and ruled over all or part of the land of Israel during most of that time. The Temple in Jerusalem had been destroyed by the Babylonians in 586 BCE but was then rebuilt in 515 BCE.

However, the most devastating catastrophes for the Jews occurred in the first two centuries CE. Jews were under the domination of the Roman Empire but were eager to regain their independence, and to that end they waged two rebellions against the Romans, one in the years 66–73, and another in the years 132–135, in the hope of achieving that aim. Both rebellions were brutally crushed, leaving large numbers of Jews dead and the land in ruins. Most significantly, during the first rebellion, the Romans destroyed the Temple in Jerusalem for the second and final time.

It is at this point in history that the rabbis began to emerge as an important class of leaders within the Jewish community. The challenges they faced were formidable. The Jews saw themselves as God's chosen people, and their history seemed to provide evidence of that. One empire after another had conquered them over the centuries, and some had attempted to destroy them, but none had succeeded. However, the suffering the Jews experienced at the hands of the Romans was different. The two rebellions had not only resulted in utter devastation to the land of Israel and its people, the Temple had been destroyed for a second time, and it eventually became clear that, unlike the first destruction, the Temple was not going to be rebuilt any time soon.[13]

Therefore, the question that must have been on the minds of most Jews at the time was whether Judaism could survive. The Temple had been the focal point of the relationship between God and the Jewish people for hundreds of years. It was there that Jews had worshipped God through the performance of sacrifices. It was there that they believed God's presence was concentrated and radiated blessings on the entire Jewish people. With the Temple now gone, how was Judaism going to continue? An even more serious question must have occurred to the Jews of the time: Was the covenant between God and the Jewish people now over? Was the destruction of the Temple perhaps punishment for sinful behaviour on the part of the Jews, behaviour that had so angered God that he no longer regarded them as his chosen people?

A number of groups now arose within the Jewish community that attempted to deal with the crisis caused by the Roman destruction, but it was the rabbis who provided a response that most Jews eventually accepted, and the rabbis were able to do so within the framework of the original covenant. The origins of these rabbis are something of a mystery, but most scholars believe that they evolved from, or were at least influenced by, a group of figures known as the Pharisees, who existed just prior to the destruction of the Second Temple. The Pharisees are well-known to Christians. In the New Testament, they are the notorious enemies of Jesus, and they have therefore been vilified in Christianity ever since. In Jewish tradition, their reputation is far more positive. They were the precursors to the rabbis, and rabbinic tradition therefore talks about them with great reverence.

The term "rabbi" originally had no religious connotation. It meant "my master" or "sir." But at the beginning of the second century, it began to refer to a new group of religious sages. The rabbis saw themselves as authoritative interpreters of the Bible. They studied the biblical text intensely in order to understand its every detail and to draw out of it as much wisdom and guidance as possible. The rabbis also made use of a large body of oral traditions to interpret the Bible, traditions they believed had been passed down for generations. They diligently collected, arranged, and systematized these oral traditions. They also formed study circles to explore them and understand their meaning.

In addition, the rabbis developed a theological framework to explain where these oral traditions originated. These traditions, according to the rabbis, were more than just the musings of prior sages on the meaning of the biblical text. They constituted an entire "Oral Torah" that had been given to Moses on Mount Sinai along with the written one. That is, God had not given one Torah on Mount Sinai, but two – one written and one oral – and the purpose of the Oral Torah was to supplement and explain the contents of the written one. The Oral Torah was also meant to remain oral, and it was therefore passed down from generation to generation in oral form. The rabbis saw themselves as merely the latest link in a chain of sages going all the way back to the time of Moses who were responsible for preserving the Oral Torah.[14]

The concept of the Oral Torah may have been the most important contribution that the rabbis made to Judaism. With this idea, a whole new dimension of Judaism was opened up. For the rabbis, Judaism was based not just on the Written Torah but also on a second Oral Torah, which greatly expanded the scope of Jewish ideas and practices.

How did all this help the rabbis cope with the destruction of the Jewish commonwealth and its Temple? We can answer this question by first looking at how the rabbis explained the destruction, beginning with the explanation the rabbis did *not* give for this event. None of the rabbis entertained the possibility that God had brought such suffering on the Jewish people because the covenant was over. According to the rabbis, the covenant was still very much in effect.

Why, then, had the destruction occurred? The most common response offered by the rabbis was that the Jews were being punished for their sins in accordance with the terms of the covenant itself. According to a number of passages in the Hebrew Bible, God's covenant with the Israelites included the provision that if they disobeyed his commandments, he would punish them, and the rabbis surmised that the suffering of the Jews at the hands of the Romans was a punishment of this kind.[15]

Yet the same Bible that explained *why* the Jewish people were suffering also explained that their suffering would eventually end, and the rabbis took the biblical text at its word here as well. The biblical text promised in a number of passages that God would eventually be reconciled with his people.[16] Some of these passages also spoke about a messianic era in which the Jews who were living in exile would return to the land of Israel, establish Jewish sovereignty there once again, and rebuild their Temple so that they could resume the sacrifices they were no longer able to perform.[17]

Yet there was still the practical question of how Jews could continue to serve God without the Temple. How would they be reconciled with God as the Bible promised if they could not perform the sacrifices that were so central to the body of commandments God had given?

The rabbis provided a number of responses to this dilemma. First, they maintained that there were still plenty of other commandments that Jews could observe in order to win back God's favour – enough, in fact, to occupy Jews practically every moment of the day. As noted earlier, the rabbis believed that the Torah contained 613 commandments, and even though a portion of those commandments concerned the sacrifices and other rituals that could be conducted only in the Temple, there were many others that had nothing to do with the Temple. The 613 commandments included prescriptions for numerous other rituals for worshipping God. They also included a myriad of imperatives governing ethical behaviour that did not require a Temple; in addition to worshipping God, Jews were required to build a just society. We also have to keep in mind that the 613 commandments were interpreted with the help of the traditions of the Oral Torah, which expanded upon and supplemented those of the Written Torah. So according to the rabbis,

Jews still had ample opportunity, even without the Temple, to devote themselves intensively to living in accordance with God's will so that they could repair their relationship with him.[18]

The rabbis also attempted to further the process of reconciliation with God by prescribing new rituals designed to maintain the memory of the rituals performed in the Temple. The presumed goal here was that God would see that the Jews felt remorse for their sins and longed to return to their old way of life. Thus, for instance, the rabbis instituted communal prayer three times a day as a substitute for the sacrifices. According to one rabbinic opinion, the prayer services were deliberately scheduled to take place at the same time of day that the sacrifices had been performed in the Temple.[19] It was as a result of these innovations that the synagogue soon became an important institution in Judaism. The synagogues, in effect, became mini-Temples to replace the one that had been destroyed.[20]

The rabbis envisioned that the daily affairs of Jews would be suffused with the observance of God's commandments so that, even without the Temple, every action would be an opportunity to bring his presence into their lives. The belief was that if Jews consistently dedicated themselves to God in this manner, they would surely be reconciled with him. He would send his messiah to redeem them. In the meantime, Jews had to observe God's commandments as interpreted by the rabbis and wait patiently until the messianic redemption arrived.[21]

The major work produced by the rabbis is the Talmud, a term that comes from the Hebrew word "to study." This is a massive, difficult work that extends to over twenty volumes in standard printed editions. It consists of two layers of material: an earlier layer known as the Mishnah that was edited in the third century, and a later layer known as the Gemara that came into its final form in the eighth century. In the Talmud, sections from these two layers alternate with each other.

The Talmud is mostly devoted to law. It explicates the commandments. However, it is not a law code. It contains rambling discussions and debates between the rabbis over hundreds of years about how to interpret the commandments.

Yet there are also substantial portions of the Talmud that are literary and philosophical in nature. In these sections, the rabbis tell stories about famous rabbis of the past, or they interpret and embellish the stories in the Bible. They also reflect on theological questions, such as why God has caused the Jewish people to suffer.

The rabbis also produced other works known as "Midrash." These works were anthologies of rabbinic interpretations of the biblical text, but the discussions here were arranged as line-by-line commentaries on

Scripture, not according to topic as in the Talmud. Over two dozen such works were produced by the rabbis.

The way of life the rabbis created had remarkable endurance. As we have already noted, it allowed Jews to maintain their identity as a people for centuries during which they were scattered across vast distances in Christian and Muslim lands and were residing among populations that were often hostile to them. Only in the eighteenth century did rabbinic authority begin to break down as Jews began to participate in modern European society.

Rabbinic Judaism and the Four Values

With this historical background in mind, we can now get back to our main concern, which is the connection between Rabbinic Judaism and the four values that are at the centre of this study. I contend that the rabbinic program of Jewish regeneration in the first centuries CE included these values in nascent form and that because Rabbinic Judaism became the dominant form of Judaism during these centuries, the four values became important for ordinary Jews in these centuries as well.

Moreover, it is important to keep in mind that the rabbis continued to be the leaders of Jewish communities everywhere in the Jewish world throughout the medieval period and well into the early modern period and, therefore, their form of Judaism remained the dominant type for Jews during these periods. The rabbis' authority broke down only in the nineteenth century, when most Jews adopted modern forms of Judaism, but even then, all modern forms of Judaism were beholden to rabbinic texts and ideas in varying degrees. What all this meant is that the four values that we will be focusing on remained embedded in Jewish religious culture well past the formative period of Rabbinic Judaism. They had an impact on Jews all the way up to the modern period.

It is not that the rabbis from early rabbinic to modern times focused on the four values consciously; rather, they were woven into the very fabric of rabbinic culture as fundamental, unstated premises. Nor, as I stated earlier, did the rabbis have any idea how important these values would become in the modern period. The rabbis were concerned with preserving Judaism in their own time. But the four values would turn out to be of critical importance in the modern period when Jews were allowed to become part of European society. In other words, the rabbinic program that allowed Jews to *survive* centuries of oppression and persecution in the Western world also allowed them to *thrive* in that world when Westerners dramatically changed their attitude towards

Jews in the nineteenth century and invited them to become part of their society.

I must reiterate that nothing I am saying here is meant to deny the fact that Rabbinic Judaism was a hindrance to the modernization of Jews. In many ways, Jews became modern by *rejecting* Rabbinic Judaism. My argument is only that Jews, while rejecting the outward manifestations of Rabbinic Judaism, retained elements of it without necessarily being cognizant of doing so, and these elements were key to their success in the new era. Moreover, as I will argue in the next chapter, there was nothing unusual about this. Cultural revolutions often overthrow the culture of the previous era while unwittingly retaining significant elements of that culture.

A difficulty with the assertions I am making here is that the rabbis rarely spoke with one voice when it came to any one value. Their texts are famously unsystematic. The editors of rabbinic texts tended to preserve many opinions on a given issue rather than settling on one in particular. It would therefore seem problematic to speak of the rabbis as a collective upholding the four values on which I plan to focus. However, as we will see, rabbinic texts, despite being multi-vocal, still reflect a coherent world view, and my claim will be that the four values we will be examining were well-represented in that world view. Moreover, the key issue here is how rabbinic views on the four values compared with those of Christians throughout the centuries, and I will demonstrate that even though the rabbis often entertained multiple positions on those values, their patterns of thinking regarding them were distinct from those of Christian thinkers.

I am not ruling out the possibility that other currents in Judaism played a role in Jews achieving so much in the modern period. The Jewish philosophical tradition in the medieval period, for instance, made important contributions in this regard as well, as David Biale has shown in a recent study, and I will be discussing this tradition, as well as other elements in medieval Judaism that made similar contributions.[22] But my belief is that the most important factor here was Rabbinic Judaism.

Views of Rabbinic Judaism

As already noted, the recognition of the importance of Rabbinic Judaism is a much needed corrective to the cultural hypothesis as presented by previous authors because these writers have generally failed to take this dimension of Judaism into account in their attempts to explain Jewish success. But the lack of appreciation for Rabbinic Judaism reflects a larger problem. I would venture to guess that most people in the

Western world have never heard of Rabbinic Judaism. They may know that Judaism has rabbis, but they usually have no awareness that Judaism existed for hundreds of years before it ever had rabbis and that much of the religion that has been called Judaism for the past two millennia was created by these figures in the first centuries CE. They are similarly unaware that the rabbis revolutionized Judaism by dramatically reshaping Israelite religion in the Hebrew Bible so that it could survive centuries of exile.

The reason for this gap in knowledge is that most people in the West equate Judaism with the Hebrew Bible on account of the fact that it is the only sacred text in Judaism they are familiar with. Christianity, which played a critical role in shaping Western civilization and continues to be its most popular religion, incorporated the Hebrew Bible into its own Scriptures, and it is therefore a text that Westerners have likely read or studied, if not as a book of religious value taught in a religious setting, then as a book of cultural value taught in an academic setting. The development of Rabbinic Judaism *after* the canonization of the Hebrew Bible, however, is entirely unknown to the vast majority of Westerners.

But the problem here is not just one of ignorance. Until relatively recently, Westerners who were familiar with Rabbinic Judaism had remarkably negative views of it, and that prejudice has a long history. The New Testament is filled with nasty remarks about the Pharisees who rejected Jesus, and Christian interpreters across subsequent centuries presumed that the Pharisees were rabbis.[23] They also presumed that Paul had the same group of people in mind when he famously spoke of Judaism as a religion concerned with the dead letter of God's law whereas Christianity was focused on its true spirit.[24]

For the better part of the modern period, Christian scholars and theologians adopted hostile views towards the rabbis because of these associations. In the nineteenth century, European scholars began studying Judaism in the early rabbinic period as part of their quest to understand the historical context in which the New Testament emerged, and they invariably portrayed the rabbis in unflattering terms. The rabbis were viewed as continuing the legacy of the Pharisees and as leading Jews away from the Christian truth. That perspective continued well into the twentieth century. Christian theologians also absorbed these prejudices during the better part of the past two centuries. They too had little good to say about Rabbinic Judaism.

What was wrong with Rabbinic Judaism, according to these scholars and theologians? Quite a bit, it would seem. The most common accusation was that the rabbis, like their Pharisaic predecessors, espoused a religion that was dry and legalistic. The rabbis required Jews to obey a myriad of religious laws based on the scores of commandments that God had given to the Israelites in the Torah.

Christian scholars and theologians developed this portrait of the rabbis in different ways. Some argued that the problem with Rabbinic Judaism was not just that it was dull and uninspiring; it was also rigid and severe. Rabbinic religion had so many commandments that one could never fulfil all of them. Failure was therefore guaranteed, along with the divine punishment that resulted from it. And there was no merciful deity here who was willing to overlook human weakness; the God of the rabbis was every bit as harsh as the rabbis themselves.

Other Christian scholars and theologians attributed to rabbinic religion the opposite problem. This form of religion made things all too easy. The rabbis believed that by simply observing God's many commandments, one would be rewarded, and therefore rabbinic religion was a mechanical enterprise. The rabbis were bean counters, so to speak, as was their God. That way of thinking also made the rabbis arrogant. It filled them with overweening pride because they believed that their obedience to God's laws would automatically result in winning his favour. Some scholars in this camp also argued that the arrogance of the rabbis made them manipulative. They engaged in endless arguments about the details of God's laws with the intent of bending them to their selfish interests. Terms like "casuistry" and "hair-splitting" were the common terms used to characterize rabbinic interpretation of the Bible for this purpose. Thus, according to this perspective, the rabbis, far from being too rigid, were in fact too flexible![25]

These were just a few of the problems with rabbinic religion, according to a good many Western Christian scholars and theologians. More problems could be cited. But the one thing they all had in common was that Rabbinic Judaism was a rather terrible religion and that Christianity had taken what was good in the Hebrew Bible and constructed a far better religion.

Furthermore, these biases against Rabbinic Judaism were not confined to professional Christian scholars and theologians. Christian priests, ministers, and popular writers expressed biases against Judaism in general, and these biases were often the same ones that Christian scholars and theologians expressed against Rabbinic Judaism in particular. Therefore, the prejudices of Christian scholars and theologians against Rabbinic Judaism that I have just described filtered into the Christian population at large and morphed into prejudices against Judaism as a whole.

Modern Jews have had some of the same difficulties with Rabbinic Judaism that one finds among Western scholars and theologians. The modern Jewish intellectuals I mentioned earlier who attempted to demonstrate the superiority of Judaism over Christianity rarely gave credit to Rabbinic Judaism for Judaism's ascendancy. Some even blamed Rabbinic Judaism for having held Jews back in pre-modern times. That argument was made during the Enlightenment by some Jewish intellectuals, who claimed that the poor condition of Jews at the time was due to their adherence to Rabbinic Judaism and that for Jews to become part of European society, they needed to get back to the Judaism of the Hebrew Bible. These views clearly had an apologetic motive. Jewish intellectuals had absorbed the criticisms of Rabbinic Judaism made by their non-Jewish peers, and they did their best to construe Judaism in a manner that would burnish the image of Judaism in the eyes of its opponents.[26]

Among lay Jews, prejudices against Rabbinic Judaism were accompanied by a growing ignorance of its contents. As the modern period progressed, many modern Jews turned their backs on Rabbinic Judaism in favour of more liberal brands of Judaism, or they abandoned religion altogether. In either case, the connection with Rabbinic Judaism was lost in subsequent generations.[27]

Thankfully, in the past half-century or so, scholars, Jewish and non-Jewish, have done a great deal of work to counter the negative portrayals of Rabbinic Judaism that were common even in educated circles. Scholars of early Christianity now paint a far more complex portrait of the Apostle Paul as an individual who maintained a stronger connection to Judaism than was previously assumed, and with that new interpretation has come a much more sympathetic depiction of Rabbinic Judaism than in prior scholarship.[28] Jewish scholars are now much less likely to engage in apologetics, with the result that criticisms of Rabbinic Judaism are less common among them as well.[29]

Yet negative views of Rabbinic Judaism persist in a good many places, and these are often combined with a profound lack of knowledge about it. In popular Christianity, prejudices against Rabbinic Judaism survive to this day in the form of prejudices against Judaism in general. Similar prejudices survive among contemporary Jews. I noted earlier that the bias that Jews have against Rabbinic Judaism is often expressed in their assumption that Rabbinic Judaism is identical to the severe form of Judaism practised by today's ultra-Orthodox Jews. That is, they perceive that medieval rabbis implemented a way of life for Jews that was oppressive and unenlightened, and only when the modern period came along were Jews finally freed from its shackles – except, of course, ultra-Orthodox Jews who have stubbornly maintained that medieval way of life.[30]

My intention in this book is to carry forward the project of reshaping the image of Rabbinic Judaism in a more positive vein. First, the coming pages will make abundantly clear to those who are not familiar with Rabbinic Judaism that Judaism for most of its history has *not* been synonymous with the Hebrew Bible. It is the Hebrew Bible as interpreted through the lens of Rabbinic Judaism. Even in the modern period, when Jews have rejected much of Rabbinic Judaism and no longer live according to its strictures, any understanding of Judaism still requires a familiarity with Judaism in its rabbinic form.

For readers who continue to uphold, wittingly or unwittingly, older prejudices against Rabbinic Judaism, the rest of this book will also demonstrate just how wrong-headed those prejudices are. The notion that Rabbinic Judaism was dry legalism and that it viewed God as unrelentingly wrathful is entirely inaccurate. Rabbinic Judaism could be severe, but so can almost any religion, including Christianity. In fact, as we will later see, Christians have often had even harsher views of God than the rabbis maintained. Furthermore, Rabbinic Judaism was quite a dynamic form of religion, and for many who still live by it, it remains that way. If it had not been, it is hard to understand why so many Jews adhered to it for so many centuries under such harsh conditions. Why would Jews have accepted a life of degradation and even risked death generation after generation for a religion that had nothing going for it? Surely there was more to Rabbinic Judaism than religious behaviourism and an angry, punitive God.

Similarly inaccurate is the view that the rabbis were manipulative and bent religious norms to their own interests. We will see that the rabbis did indeed infuse their religion with a lot of flexibility, but they did not do so out of arrogance or pride. They did so because their religious world view included bold and courageous perspectives regarding human beings and their capabilities. They believed that they could shape God's words in light of historical circumstances and pragmatic needs, and that was because God in fact wanted them to do so. And far from being a liability, this perspective should be commended in our day and age. Religion would be far less threatening to human welfare in today's world if religious leaders learned a lesson or two from the rabbis about how to balance religious imperatives with practical concerns.

As for the modern Jewish criticisms of Rabbinic Judaism, they too rest on inaccuracies. The medieval Judaism that was shaped by the rabbis was far more vibrant than many Jews assume, and, as pointed out in the introduction, ultra-Orthodoxy is in fact largely a modern phenomenon that arose in modernity to combat Jewish reform and the encroachment of modernity into the Jewish community as a whole. Ultra-Orthodox Judaism is, in many respects, as much a product of modernity as the liberal forms of Judaism it has opposed.

Most important for our purposes is that Rabbinic Judaism explains the achievements of Jews in the modern period. It inculcated in Jews a series of values over the centuries that made it possible for them to adapt unusually well to the new world they had entered when they became part of modern Western society some two hundred years ago.

Moreover, I would like to take the arguments in defence of Rabbinic Judaism a critical step further than its supporters have done up to now. My belief is that not only should Rabbinic Judaism be spared much of the criticism it has received, it should be appreciated as an extraordinary phenomenon. When properly understood, Rabbinic Judaism has to be regarded as one of the most successful forms of religion in history. The rabbis were a relatively insignificant group of religious figures in the context of world events when they began rising to prominence in the Jewish community in the first centuries CE, and the same can be said of the medieval and early modern rabbis who inherited their legacy. But they created a way of life that allowed an entire people to survive the destruction of their homeland and sacred shrine, tolerate eighteen centuries of exile among cultures that were not kindly disposed to them, and then emerge as the most successful subgroup in modern Western culture. The religion created by the rabbis has a record that is nothing short of astonishing, and one of the goals of this book is to bring that to light.

Jewish Women

It should be obvious from everything I have said thus far that my explanation for the success of Jews in the modern period is focused primarily on Jewish men, not Jewish women. This is unavoidable for two reasons. First, the rabbis, who, according to my theory, were responsible for preparing Jews for success in the modern era, were men. From the beginning of the rabbinic period up to the modern era, the title of rabbi was an exclusively male privilege. Rabbinic ordination also remained the province of men for the greater part of the modern period. The first ordination of a female rabbi took place in 1972 in Reform Judaism. Second, once the modern period began and Jews began to experience success, their most accomplished Jews were men. This is no surprise, given that over the past two centuries, Jewish men have had far more opportunity than Jewish women to cultivate their talents and make their mark in the public sphere.

However, several caveats to these observations are in order. First, it is not as if Jews were unique in manifesting the gender imbalance described here. The same imbalance was evident among non-Jewish Westerners. The groundwork for the West's success was laid in the medieval and early modern periods mostly by men because men had far greater opportunity to become leaders than women did. In the modern period, the dominance of the West in the economic, intellectual, and artistic realms was brought about primarily by men as well because again, it was men rather than women who had the opportunity to become leaders in these areas. The argument can also be made that the dominance of men in the modern period in both the Jewish and Western spheres was connected. The success of modern Jews was heavily dependent on the success of the Western world as a whole, and therefore, it would not have been possible for Jewish women to achieve success in the modern period any more than non-Jewish women could.

Even though my analysis of the success of modern Jews focuses mostly on men, it does not exclude women. While I will argue that male rabbis were the visionaries who shaped Judaism in a manner that brought Jews great success in the modern era, it will become clear that their success could not have been accomplished without women. One of my central claims is that the four rabbinic values that explain the success of modern Jews were so fundamental to Jewish culture from the beginning of the rabbinic period up to the modern era, that they were absorbed by *all* Jews – men and women alike. Women, then, may not have shaped Jewish culture in the medieval and early modern periods as much as men did, but they were nonetheless carriers of the four values whether they were conscious of it or not. One can also assume that because of their traditional role in the home, women were crucial inculcators of these values in children, male and female – and here too, the manner of transmission may not have been conscious. Put plainly, the eventual success of Jewish men in the modern period cannot be accounted for without acknowledging the role of women in bringing it about. Moreover over the course of the modern period, Jewish women increasingly rivalled men in their public accomplishments, just as non-Jewish Western women did. That was particularly the case after the 1960s, as the feminist movement began to take hold in Western society. Finally, I should emphasize that even though my account of the success of modern Jews is heavily weighted towards men, the lessons that can be learned from this account today, which I will spell out in my epilogue, can be applied to women as well.

Readers, however, should not expect a full account in this study of the contributions that Jewish women made to the success of Jews. It is too complex an issue to be dealt with adequately in this book. I will provide only a series of general impressions about the matter that I hope will spur further research.

Conclusions

The rest of this book will attempt to demonstrate the broad claims I have made in this chapter. That will entail an in-depth investigation of how the four values developed in both Western and Jewish culture before modernity, how rabbinic Judaism helped these values in more robust form, and how these values brought Jews disproportionate success in the modern period. I should reiterate what I said in the introduction; explanations for the success of modern Jews other than my own have merit. We are dealing with a complex phenomenon for which there is unlikely to be one single explanation. I believe, however, that my theory provides a critical component, if not *the* critical component, of the explanation for this phenomenon.

One of the ironies of the argument I am making is that its focus will not be primarily on the modern period, even though the success of Jews in the modern world is what it is attempting to explain. Instead, the focus will be on the eighteen or so centuries that preceded the modern period because my contention is that it was in these centuries that Rabbinic Judaism prepared the ground for Jews to amass the achievements they did when the modern period arrived.

For this reason, my readers should not be surprised when I do not provide lengthy discussions of the major modernizing movements in Judaism, such as the Haskalah (the Jewish Enlightenment), or the Reform movement. I do pay some attention to them, but they are ultimately tangential to the question this book is asking. The focus of this book is not on how Jews became modern. Nor is it even focused on how modern Jews became successful, but rather on how they became *disproportionately* successful, and I do not believe that modernizing movements such as the Haskalah and Reform Judaism explain why. Again, I contend that the best explanation can be found in Rabbinic Judaism and the way it shaped Jewish culture for the better part of two millennia prior to the advent of modernity.

Before I unpack the details of my argument, there is one more critical piece of its basic framework that has to be put in place: where modern secular Jews fit into it. That is the subject of the next chapter.

Chapter Two

Secular Jews (and Other Jews)

Anyone with even a cursory knowledge of modern Jewish history or a passing acquaintance with the modern Jewish community is likely to have doubts about the arguments laid out in the previous chapter because of a major difficulty I noted in my introduction: how can I possibly claim that Rabbinic Judaism was responsible for the success of modern Jews, if many of the Jews who were representative of that success were secular and had abandoned the rabbinic way of life? In fact, many modern Jews not only left that way of life but also did their best to distance themselves from it as much as they could. In this quest, they were inspired by some of the leading Jewish intellectual figures of the eighteenth and nineteenth centuries who guided the process of modernization among Jews. Many of these figures vilified Rabbinic Judaism as the major obstacle to enlightenment and progress in the Jewish community, and their views attracted a wider and wider following as the modern period evolved.

I became well aware of this problem early on in my research for this project. When I began discussing the project with fellow Jewish scholars, practically everyone I spoke to pointed to the problem posed by secular Jews as my biggest challenge. Some of my colleagues also noted another challenge that was, in some sense, the mirror image of the first: if Rabbinic Judaism was responsible for the success of modern Jews, why is it that Orthodox Jews, who have been so deeply committed to Rabbinic Judaism, have achieved so much less success than other Jews whose devotion to Rabbinic Judaism has been much weaker or non-existent?

This chapter is devoted to addressing these questions. Towards the end of this chapter, I will also discuss Jews who were neither secular nor Orthodox – that is, Reform and Conservative Jews – in order to give a full picture of how my theory about Jewish success relates to all Jews.

However, the bulk of my discussion will be focused on secular Jews, who represent the most significant stumbling block for my hypothesis.

It may seem premature to discuss this issue at such an early stage of my study, but it is important that I do so. My core arguments about the development of the four values in Western and Jewish culture will require a lengthy investigation spanning several chapters, and I would be asking a lot of my readers if I was to wade through such an investigation without the critical problem of secular Jews first being resolved. That is especially the case for readers who are familiar with modern Jewish history.

Jewish Secularism

Secular Jews have had a substantial presence in Jewish society in the West since the modern period began. It is widely acknowledged that today in the US, Jews are far more secular than any other ethnic or religious subgroup, and that has been true for some time.[1] Scholars have identified different varieties of Jewish secularism, but one feature that has consistently distinguished secular Jews from other Jews is their abandonment of the rabbinic beliefs and practices that defined Jewish life for centuries. In fact, one could argue that this feature has been the hallmark of secular Jewishness, and for our purposes it will suffice as the marker for this brand of Jewish identity.

However, one should not presume that secular Jews over the past two centuries rid themselves of all vestiges of Rabbinic Judaism just because they said they did. Such a presumption greatly underestimates the complex manner in which cultures evolve, in general, and modern Jewish culture has evolved, in particular.

Cultural Transformations: Change vs. Continuity

Unpacking this last assertion will require a good bit of explanation, and I will begin with some observations about the evolution of cultures, in general. When cultures transition from one era to the next, they always carry with them cultural values from the previous era; in such transformations, change is always accompanied by continuity. Often the older values are reshaped in the process of being absorbed into the culture of the new era. They do not necessarily appear in the new culture in the same precise form in which they did in the older one, but there is carryover from the previous era.

This is the case even when cultures undergo change that is revolutionary. Every major transformation in European culture over the past two millennia, for instance, can be characterized as a combination of change and continuity. The Renaissance, the Reformation, and the Enlightenment, to cite but three such transformations, all represented major shifts in Western culture, but they also built on cultural elements from the previous epochs. Scholars often debate the extent to which the dawn of a new cultural era represented something entirely new or continuity with the old, and those debates can be heated. Every era in Western history has been subject to disagreements of this kind. But no cultural revolution occurs in a vacuum; no new cultural era is simply created from scratch; there is always a residue from the culture of the era that preceded it, and the only question is how much.[2]

Sometimes this cultural carry-over is conscious, but often it is not. Representatives of the new era may even explicitly disavow the previous culture while still absorbing important elements from it in an unconscious manner. That is to be expected. Representatives of the new culture are often eager to establish the innovative nature of the transformation they are attempting to bring about, and so they tend to emphasize that the old ways have been entirely swept away when in reality they have not been. They often underestimate how beholden they are to the older values.

We can illustrate these observations by looking at an example central to our study: how the advent of modernity transformed Christianity. It is well-known that in many respects, modernity represented a rebellion against Christianity, but it is also recognized that modernity developed *out of* Christianity, and it could not have been otherwise. Christianity was so much part of the fabric of Western culture when modernity arrived, it so permeated every aspect of pre-modern European culture, that modern Westerners could not have possibly purged all vestiges of Christianity from their culture even if they had wanted to. And indeed, many Christian values survived in modern Western culture. This process was not necessarily conscious. Nor were the older values preserved in the same form they had taken in the previous era; those values were often secularized. But they survived nonetheless and became part of modernity, and they survive to this day. Moreover, ironically, some of those older Christian values may well have been instrumental in *undermining* Christianity in the modern era, and it would not have been the first time that a world view had elements in it that eventually resulted in its own demise.

Thus, for example, a modern Western atheist may disavow Christianity, but the minute the same person begins talking about the infinite value of each and every human individual, as secular Westerners often do, they are betraying the influence of Christianity on their world view. The extreme value that Westerners place on the individual *qua* individual is not necessarily found in other cultures, at least not in the robust form it takes in the West; rather, it is a value that is culturally specific, and it is traceable to Christianity.[3] It is rooted in the biblical notion that human beings are created in the image of God, and it was further shaped by the Protestant Reformation and the Enlightenment before it appeared in the secular form we are familiar with today. It can also be argued that the extreme value that Christianity placed on the individual ironically helped undermine Christianity. The modern notion that the individual is the ultimate arbiter in matters of religion and can even choose to reject religion altogether is often traced back to the Reformation, whose leading representatives spoke of justification through faith alone. That idea, for which Luther is usually given credit, morphed gradually into the idea of freedom of conscience in religious matters.[4]

Some academic readers may recognize that I have inserted myself into a long-running debate about the role Christianity has played in the shaping of modern culture and that I have, in effect, adopted an approach that lies between the two poles of that debate. This debate dates back to the 1960s when Hans Blumenberg (1920–96) took issue with Karl Löwith (1897–1973) on the influence that Christianity has had on modern secular culture. The debate was a complex one that cannot be easily summarized here, but one of the major points that divided the two thinkers was that Löwith argued that modern secular culture grew out of Christianity, while Blumenberg denied that this was the case. Central to their disagreement was the influence that the pre-modern notion of messianic redemption had on the modern idea of progress. Löwith claimed that this idea was a transmutation of the Christian notion of messianic redemption, while Blumenberg argued that there was no connection between the two.[5] More recent figures who have engaged in this debate include Charles Taylor (1931–) and Marcel Gauchet (1946–).[6]

I have often found that when it comes to debates over major questions of the kind being discussed here, the truth usually lies somewhere in the middle of the two positions. Questions involving large issues can rarely be settled unequivocally in one direction or the other, and that is precisely the position I take in this instance. The process by which Christianity was transformed in modernity is an excellent example. That process was remarkably complex, involving different levels of Western society widely spread out across a number of geographical regions. So we should avoid extremes on one side or the other. Christianity clearly was not absorbed into modern Western culture in the form that it had taken over the previous centuries. The advent of modernity was marked by revolutionary change, and one of those changes was the rejection of Christianity in its pre-modern form by large numbers of Westerners. However, Christianity had been part of every element of European life up to that point, and so it is unimaginable that it could have been got rid of altogether. We can therefore presume that elements of it survived in modern Western culture, even if they were preserved unwittingly and in secularized form. The example of the modern atheist cited earlier nicely illustrates the tensions between the two tendencies. Modern individuals who identify with secularism may openly reject the God of Christianity, but without being aware of it, they are also likely to uphold ideas rooted in Christianity that have been secularized, such as the value of the individual.

It is against this background that we can explain why the four values at the centre of this study helped Europe become dominant in the modern period. These values represented, in many respects, a rebellion against Christianity that was at the centre of European life for centuries prior to the modern period. However, in many ways, those values also grew *out of* Christianity. We who live in the modern period are often unaware that that was true, especially those who have no interest in Christianity or are openly hostile to it. Yet these values did indeed have roots in that religion, and part 2 of this book will discuss this issue in detail.

One can also argue that these four values were especially easy to co-opt into the modern world view because they could be preserved without a religious framework and could thus be accepted by secular Westerners no less than by religious Westerners. An individual can believe in a robust sense of human autonomy in relation to the cosmos, freedom of thought and expression, the value of life in this world, and the importance of education, without being religious. Moreover, the absorption of the four values in secularized form by Westerners who had rejected Christianity would have been encouraged by the benefit that Westerners derived from them. As already noted, the success of the West was due in part to the adoption of these values. We might also go one step further by speculating that the four values ironically *accelerated* the process of secularization despite their religious roots because the success these values brought to Westerners in their secular form only confirmed the merits of secularism.

The Modernization and Secularization of Jewish Culture

All these observations are highly relevant to our concerns here because Jewish culture, in becoming modernized, went through a process of transformation that was, in many respects, similar to that of modern

Western culture. The modernization of Jewish culture in the nineteenth and twentieth centuries can be characterized, like its Western counterpart, as one that involved revolutionary change alongside continuity with the pre-modern past.[7]

Efforts by Jews to deal with this tension resulted in a wide range of solutions that I can summarize only briefly here. Some Jews embraced change in a radical manner and rejected any continuity with the past. They welcomed modernity with open arms, severed all affiliations with the Jewish community, and did their best to assimilate into European society. Some of these Jews even converted to Christianity, thus fulfilling the worst fears that many Jews had about the effects of modernity.

However, this group was relatively small.[8] The vast majority of Jews maintained continuity with the past by retaining their Jewish identity, but what form that identity took depended on how much change they were willing to allow. Different viewpoints emerged in the Jewish community regarding this issue, and the result was the rise of a number of religious denominations. Reform, Conservative, and Modern Orthodox Judaism all emerged from this process, and each attempted to balance change with continuity in its own distinctive way, moulding its particular beliefs and practices accordingly. These various branches of Judaism flourished in western and central Europe, particularly Reform Judaism, which tended to emphasize change more than the other denominations did.

There was a third group of Jews who focused solely on continuity with the past and rejected change of any kind, taking a position that was, in effect, the diametric opposite of that held by the first group. These ultra-Orthodox Jews, as they were called, repudiated all modernizing influences in the Jewish community and did their best to keep themselves separate both from the non-Jewish world and from the rest of the Jewish community that had succumbed to its influences. These Jews were concentrated mainly in eastern Europe.[9]

Where then did secular Jews fit into this picture? Given that these Jews abandoned the religious beliefs and practices that had defined Jewish life for centuries, one may be tempted to assume that they belonged to the first group of Jews, who were interested solely in change and who rejected any continuity with the past. However, that was not the path most of them took. Scholars have recently begun to explore the history and world view of Jewish secularism, and there is general agreement among them that even though secular Jews abandoned pre-modern Judaism, their way of thinking was not defined solely by a desire for change.[10]

David Biale, who has provided us with the only book-length academic treatment of modern Jewish secularism, has demonstrated that secular Jews retained a sense of Jewish identity that was continuous with the Judaism of pre-modern times; it is just that they refused to embrace it in its traditional form. Instead, they selected elements of pre-modern Judaism and moulded them in order to construct a modern Jewish identity. That identity took a bewildering variety of forms, but most secular Jews based their new identity on Jewish culture, language, or ethnicity, or a combination of these. Many of these Jews also combined these forms of identity with political ideologies such as socialism, communism, nationalism, or Zionism.[11]

Some secular Jews tapped the resources of pre-modern Judaism to develop new forms of religiosity that they found more suitable to the modern era. Thus, when it came to matters of religious belief, secular Jews may have ceased adhering to the notion of a personal God as depicted in the Bible, but many of them came to believe in a God who was *im*personal – that is, a God who was an abstract spirit responsible for the laws of nature. In formulating this conception of God, secular Jews were inspired by Baruch Spinoza, the great early modern Jewish heretic whom many regard as the first modern Jew. But there is an argument to be made that they also drew inspiration from medieval Jewish philosophy and Kabbalah, which contained radical reflections on God's nature. We see a similar pattern with religious practice. Secular Jews may have rejected the divine commandments that had defined Jewish life for centuries in favour of universal ethical principles, but some held that these principles were rooted in the prophetic books of the Hebrew Bible.[12]

In short, recent scholarship has discovered that while secular Jews abandoned much of pre-modern Judaism, they also retained and reshaped elements of it. There were, of course, secular Jews who were determined to rid themselves of all traces of pre-modern Judaism. However, even these Jews could not have done so entirely as long as they wanted to retain some form of Jewish identity, which most of them did. Judaism functioned in pre-modern Jewish culture much like Christianity did in pre-modern Western culture. It had been intertwined with every aspect of Jewish life for centuries, and so when these Jews set about constructing a new Jewish identity, they could not have done so without co-opting into it in an unconscious manner at least some elements of their pre-modern religious past.

This phenomenon is evident in the major ideologies to which modern secular Jews were attracted. A salient example is Zionism. While the vast majority of Zionists were secular and were resolute about rejecting

Jewish religion and practice in favour of a secular Jewish nationalism, scholars have long speculated that their fundamental aspiration for a Jewish homeland in the land of Israel was a secular reworking of messianic hope that had its source in Jewish religion. Let us also not forget that the entire basis of Zionism – which called for the founding of a Jewish homeland in the land of ancient Israel – was inspired by the Bible, the foundational religious text of Judaism. Secular Zionists treated the Bible as a book of history, not as divine revelation, but the fact that it had been the most sacred text of Judaism for 2,000 years illustrates that secular Zionists were very much dependent on their religious heritage.[13]

There is nothing terribly surprising about any of this when viewed in light of our earlier discussion of cultural transitions. As already noted, when an ethnic group or nation moves from one cultural phase to the next, they always preserve cultural features from the earlier era, often without being aware of it, and that is true even when their intention is to rebel against that earlier way of life. Secular Jews are a wonderful example of all these tendencies.

Yet what I have said so far about secular Jews would seem applicable mostly to those who were part of the intellectual elite in the Jewish community or those who at least belonged to the lay sector of the Jewish community that was well-educated in Jewish matters. These were the Jews who were grappling with their Jewish identity in a serious manner and engaging with secular ideologies such as Zionism. But what about other secular Jews? Most Western Jews who have been secular over the last two centuries were neither part of the intellectual elite, nor were they well-educated in Jewish matters, and a good number of them were not terribly preoccupied with their Jewish identity and may have even been indifferent to it. Your average Jewish doctor, lawyer, or businessman in nineteenth- or twentieth-century Europe or America did not necessarily spend time thinking about the meaning of Jewish existence, and these people are central to the concerns of this study no less than the intellectual elite. After all, the phenomenon of Jewish success in the modern period includes these Jews as well.

Much less has been written about secular Jews of this kind, and that is understandable. Intellectuals often leave us with copious writings to analyse, whereas ordinary people do not, and so it is much easier to write about the former group than the latter one.[14] Still, I would maintain that even secular Jews who were not particularly engaged with questions about Jewish identity must have retained some elements of pre-modern Judaism. Again, religion had been intertwined with every aspect of Jewish life for centuries, and so it is highly unlikely that even secular Jews who were indifferent to their identity would have purged themselves of *all* vestiges of it. At the very least, they would have carried with them patterns of thought, speech, and behaviour from their pre-modern Jewish past even as they rejected its metaphysical aspects. And here as well, these Jews would not have necessarily retained these traits consciously or in their original religious form; they would have absorbed them subconsciously and secularized them in the process.

Of course, I am making some claims here that are not easy to prove. I am arguing that whether or not secular Jews were intellectually sophisticated, they must have preserved elements of pre-modern Judaism even if they did so subconsciously, and it is very difficult to make any firm determinations about what is in the subconscious mind of any individual, let alone an entire group. However, the principles of cultural transformation that I have invoked here are universal enough to make a case for what I am saying. Again, ethnic groups or nations that go through a major cultural change always retain cultural features of the previous era whether their adherents are aware of it or not, and that goes for the common folk no less than for intellectual elites. Also, the chances of cultural carry-over from the prior era are greatly increased for cultural features that were fundamental to the prior era. So even ordinary secular Jews had to have preserved some of the traits of pre-modern Judaism, given that it had been central to Jewish culture before the modern period.

My case here is strengthened when viewed in conjunction with another important consideration. Even after Jews were given citizenship and rights in Western countries, they remained socially isolated from their non-Jewish neighbours. Most Jews still lived in close proximity to other Jews, socialized with other Jews, and married other Jews. What is remarkable about this phenomenon is how widespread it was. Even though the process of modernization for Jews varied considerably from country to country, what I have just described here was true across the board.[15]

Part of the reason for Jewish self-segregation was that most Jews still felt a sense of ethnic and communal solidarity with other Jews despite the fact that the legal barriers between them and the non-Jewish world had come down. This self-segregation was also due to external pressures. Antisemitism persisted, and so when Jews were invited to become part of European society, the hatred against them that had festered for centuries did not go away; it remained ingrained in European culture. Antisemitism became particularly virulent at the end of the 1800s, with violence breaking out against Jewish communities in eastern Europe. So one of the reasons modern European Jews did not lose their identity was that they were not allowed to.

Most important for our concerns is that what we have said here applies to secular Jews not just Jews who were religious. Secular Jews also continued to live and socialize with other Jews and marry other Jews because of the same sense of ethnic and communal solidarity that other Jews felt, and that was the case even for secular Jews who did not think too deeply about their Jewish identity. Furthermore, secular Jews also experienced antisemitism, for even though the European hatred of Jews had originally been based on religion, that hatred now morphed into one that was more racial in character. So even Jews who had ceased being religious and who were indifferent to their Jewish identity were not spared the animosity of their non-Jewish neighbours.[16] Interestingly, even Jews who had converted to Christianity tended to live apart from non-Jews. They socialized with other Jews who had become Christians, intermarried, or had become Jews without religion, and they often married Jews who themselves had become Christians.[17]

These observations apply to American Jews as well. The vast majority of Jews who would make up the American Jewish community arrived during the great migration of 2.5 million Jews from eastern Europe between 1881 and 1924. These Jews for the most part retained their Jewish identity just as their European counterparts did. They tended to live alongside, socialize with, and marry other Jews. And here as well, this self-imposed segregation was found not just among religious Jews but also among secular Jews who represented a large portion of this immigrant group.[18]

These observations about the continued isolation of Jews are important because they bolster the case that secular Jews could not have left behind every aspect of pre-modern Judaism even if they had wanted to. We can presume that if these Jews lived among other Jews, socialized with them, and married them, then in their transition to modernity they would have also retained some of the patterns of thought, speech, and behaviour from pre-modern Jewish religious culture, even if they were not entirely aware of it.

To put matters another way, secular Jews would have preserved features of pre-modern Jewish culture because the transition they underwent was incomplete. Jews were invited to become part of modern European society, but most of them did not want to completely abandon the Jewish world they had come from, nor were they entirely welcome in the non-Jewish society that had opened its doors to them, and they therefore lived semi-segregated lives. As a consequence, it was inevitable that the average secular Jew preserved elements of pre-modern Jewish culture, even if they did so unwittingly.

Secular Jews and the Four Rabbinic Values

We can now address the question to which this chapter is devoted: how can we claim that Jews were successful in the modern period because of the influence of rabbinic values, if some of the most successful Jews were secular and had left the life of Rabbinic Judaism behind?

If secular Jews did indeed inherit some of the patterns of thought, speech, and behaviour of pre-modern Judaism, there is an awfully good chance that they also inherited the four rabbinic values that are at the core of this study – and here I am speaking about *all* secular Jews, whether they were among the intellectual elite or the common folk. We have to keep in mind that pre-modern Judaism was mostly Rabbinic Judaism. That form of Judaism was the common denominator that all pre-modern Jews shared, and the four values I am speaking of here were fundamental to it and undergirded it. Thus, if secular Jews retained any elements of pre-modern Judaism, it is highly likely that the four values were among them. And again, it is not that secular Jews had to be conscious of the rabbinic origins of these values. A secular Jew may very well have bid good riddance to Rabbinic Judaism while nonetheless preserving the four values unwittingly.

The plausibility of these conjectures is strengthened by observations made earlier about the role of the four values in the transformation of Western culture. In the West, the four values had their roots in pre-modern Christianity and were most likely retained in the modern period because they were easily secularized, and in their secular form they were of great benefit to Westerners. The same applies to Jews. The four values had developed in parallel fashion in Rabbinic Judaism and were most likely preserved by Jews in the modern period because here too, those values were easily secularized, and in their secular form, they were of great benefit to Jews. We also speculated that in Western culture the four values ironically accelerated the process of secularization, and we can do the same with respect to Jewish culture as well. These values, once secularized, may have further distanced modern secular Jews from their religious past by helping them succeed in the Western world that they had been invited to enter.

I recognize that in making these claims, I am going against the views of a number of highly reputable Jewish scholars who have spent their careers studying the transition of Jews to modernity. These scholars see no connection whatsoever between modern Jewish secularism and pre-modern Rabbinic Judaism. Quite the contrary. They take the architects of modern Jewish secularism at their word who said they were determined to abandon the Judaism of the rabbis.[19] However, my arguments here suggest that an alternative perspective is plausible – that there was some degree of continuity between modern Jewish secularism and the rabbinic past even as secular Jews rebelled against it. My arguments do not necessarily negate what has been said by the scholars to whom I have just alluded. Rather, it supplements their approach by suggesting that alongside the strident determination of secular Jews to abandon Rabbinic Judaism, more complex subliminal processes were at work. And I am not entirely alone here. Some Jewish scholars have made similar arguments regarding one or another of the features of modern Jewish secular culture.[20]

But there is another important question here: how could secular Jews have preserved the four values for so long? My theory is that modern Jews were highly successful because they carried with them four key values from Rabbinic Judaism for the past two centuries. How would that have been possible? Even if secular Jews initially absorbed the four values from Rabbinic Judaism in an unconscious manner early in the modern period, two centuries is a rather long stretch of time for subsequent generations of secular Jews to have maintained those values.

But, in fact, this scenario is not at all implausible, given that the segregation of Jews in Western society that I described earlier persisted well into the twentieth century. Jews did not fully begin to assimilate into Western society until the second half of that century. American Jews led the way here. After the decimation of the Jewish population in Europe during the Second World War, the Jewish community in the US became the largest one in the world, and it was also around this time that non-Jewish attitudes towards Jews changed for the better. With the rise of the civil rights movement in the US in the 1950s and 1960s, American society became far more tolerant and antisemitism diminished. As a result, intermarriage between Jews and non-Jews became common for the first time in the history of the West and Jews began to fully assimilate into non-Jewish society. However, up to this period, Western Jews were mostly segregated from non-Jews, which meant that even secular Jews had spent the better part of two centuries living a lifestyle that, in all likelihood, retained some of the features of Rabbinic Judaism, including the four values. These observations explain not only why secular Jews were successful when they first became part of Western society but also why they continued to be throughout the nineteenth century and the greater part of the twentieth.

Then there is the question of how, according to my argument, secular Jews could have continued to experience success since the 1960s when the remaining barriers between Jews and non-Jews in the West largely broke down. I do not believe that this development undermines my argument because the assimilation of a minority group into a majority culture does not happen overnight; it is a gradual process, and Jews are only in the second generation of that process. Even Jews who fully became part of non-Jewish culture in the 1960s – say, by marrying non-Jews and disavowing all Jewish commitments – did not necessarily stop being Jewish in all respects. It is likely that they still carried with them, consciously or unconsciously, vestiges of the Jewish culture they left behind, including the rabbinic values we have been speaking about. It is also plausible that these vestiges have been passed on to their offspring. Of course, if this process continues in subsequent generations, then rabbinic values that have been passed on without any reinforcement will eventually dissipate entirely, but we may not be at that point just yet.

What comes out of our discussion thus far is that the secularity of the most successful Jews in the modern West is no obstacle to the cultural hypothesis for Jewish success. The argument that Jews had an advantage over their non-Jewish neighbours because of the influence of the rabbinic tradition and the four values that underlay it can be applied to secular Jews no less than to Jews who were more committed to their religious heritage.

Orthodox Jews

Let us now address another issue that was raised at the beginning of this chapter. Up to now, we have been concerned with the question of how Rabbinic Judaism could be responsible for the success of modern Jews if the most successful modern Jews have been secular. We must now ask the inverse question: if Rabbinic Judaism was responsible for the success of modern Jews, why have so few Orthodox Jews been successful? After all, they are the sector of the Jewish community that is most beholden to Rabbinic Judaism. A good number of Orthodox Jews in the modern West have certainly done well in the economic realm as businessmen and professionals. Some Orthodox Jews have also won major international awards for intellectual achievement.[21] But on the whole, the achievements of these Jews lag far behind those of secular Jews. That is particularly evident in the arts, where Orthodox Jews have barely had an impact.[22] The gap is even greater for the ultra-Orthodox part of the Orthodox community. To my knowledge, not a single ultra-Orthodox Jew in the past two centuries has won a major international award for intellectual or artistic achievement, and when it comes to income levels, this part of the Jewish community has tended to be the poorest. My theory about the influence of Rabbinic Judaism on Jewish success would therefore have to account for the irony that those Jews in the modern period most committed to Rabbinic Judaism have been the least successful in the categories by which we are measuring success.

I believe that my theory *can* in fact account for this irony, and to explain why, let us start with ultra-Orthodox Jews. The reason why these Jews have not had a record of achievement like that of other Jews does not require much reflection. The hallmark of this form of Judaism has been its negative attitude towards the modern world, and as a result, ultra-Orthodox Jews have tended to live in close-knit communities that are both physically and culturally separate not just from the non-Jews but from other Jews as well. It is therefore not surprising that these Jews have not achieved success in the modern world the way other Jews have. They have not wanted to become part of that world in the first place. We have to keep in mind that modern Jews could not have achieved the success they did in the West had the West itself not been successful. The success of Jews was predicated on their ability to make the best of what the Western world offered them. Thus, ultra-Orthodox Jews who never became part of the West to begin with were not going to share in its success either.[23]

The low average income levels of ultra-Orthodox Jews have other causes as well. These Jews have high birth rates, and therefore resources have always been spread out thinly among them. Moreover, in the past century, a large portion of ultra-Orthodox men have been supported by their communities so that they can study Jewish texts full-time rather than seek employment, and that has made the economic situation of ultra-Orthodox Jews even more difficult.[24]

But not all Orthodox Jews have been ultra-Orthodox. In the nineteenth century we have the development of Neo-Orthodoxy, now termed "Modern Orthodoxy," particularly in Jewish communities in western and central Europe, but since the Holocaust, the centres of Modern Orthodox Judaism have moved to the US and Israel. Adherents to this form of Judaism live in accordance with the strictures of Rabbinic Judaism in much the same way that ultra-Orthodox Jews do, but they are different from the ultra-Orthodox in a number of ways. Most important, Modern Orthodox Jews are much more open to the modern world. That openness is in fact part of their credo and tells us why they refer to themselves as "modern." They believe it is incumbent on Jews to live in accordance with Rabbinic Judaism but that Jews should also interact with and learn from the non-Jewish world around them.

These Orthodox Jews have therefore followed a different trajectory from that of ultra-Orthodox Jews. When it comes to income and educational levels, they have tended to do as well as other Jews.[25] Where they lag behind is with respect to extraordinary achievements that involve

international recognition, such as Nobel Prizes. Yet there is a simple reason for that: their relatively small numbers. Over the past two centuries,
Modern Orthodox Jews have been only a minuscule percentage of the
world's Jewish population.[26]

Reform and Conservative Jews

I would like to round out my discussion here by making some observations about modern Jews who have been neither Orthodox nor secular
and have identified with Reform or Conservative Judaism. Any discussion of the success of modern Jews has to include these Jews as well
because they have been a major presence in the Jewish community in
the modern period. That has been true particularly in the US. Since the
mid-twentieth century, most American Jews have identified with one of
these two denominations.[27]

It is not difficult to see how my theory would apply to Reform and
Conservative Jews. Both Reform and Conservative Judaism were
beholden to the rabbinic tradition, and therefore Jews belonging to
these denominations would have had some contact with the rabbinic
values that I claim have been critical for the success of modern Jews.

The dependence of Conservative Judaism on the rabbinic tradition
was greater than it was in Reform Judaism. For most of its history, the
leading figures of Conservative Judaism depicted their form of Judaism as the most authentic expression of Rabbinic Judaism and thus
as the most authentic expression of Judaism in general. In their view,
Reform Judaism had strayed from authentic Judaism because in making concessions to modernity, it had abandoned too much of Rabbinic
Judaism. However, they also believed that Orthodoxy was problematic despite its commitment to Rabbinic Judaism because it interpreted
Rabbinic Judaism too rigidly and thereby distorted it. For Conservative Jewish thinkers, only their form of Judaism preserved the rabbinic
tradition in its genuine dynamic form, one that balanced tradition with
change. In fact, "tradition and change" became the motto of Conservative Judaism.

The relationship between Reform Judaism and Rabbinic Judaism
is often perceived as adversarial, but the truth is more complicated.
Reform Judaism has depended on Rabbinic Judaism as well, though
not to the same degree as Conservative or Orthodox Judaism. The
key shapers of Reform Judaism in the nineteenth century rejected the
authority of Rabbinic Judaism in their effort to create a form of Judaism more suitable to the modern period. They believed that a modernized Judaism should be based primarily on Jewish monotheism

and ethics, which, they held, had always been the core of Judaism, and they were intent on setting aside significant portions of Rabbinic Judaism in their attempt to construct a Judaism of this kind. But the leaders of nineteenth-century Reform Judaism did not reject Rabbinic Judaism altogether; they rejected only its authority as the supreme source of guidance for Jews and therefore took great liberties in choosing from it what appealed to them. Moreover, in the twentieth century, Reform Judaism, particularly in the US, which had by then become its centre, moved back towards traditional Judaism in some respects. This development was driven by lay Reform Jews who were more enamoured of the ritualistic and particularistic aspects of Judaism than their leaders were.[28]

It is not easy to determine the extent to which lay Reform and Conservative Jews throughout the history of their respective denominations have been cognizant of the rabbinic elements of the brands of Judaism they have adhered to. That said, it is likely that Rabbinic Judaism and its four values continued to influence Reform and Conservative Jews for all the same reasons they influenced secular Jews. As I have argued in this chapter, a modern Jew did not have to be committed to Judaism at all to have been influenced by Rabbinic Judaism and its major values, and so the same can certainly be said about religiously affiliated Jews in the Reform and Conservative movements.

In addition, there is reason to believe that many of the more informed Jews in these denominations would have had a sense of how Judaism differed from Christianity regarding one or more of the major rabbinic values. I base this assessment on observations noted in the last chapter. There I discussed the fact that leading rabbis and Jewish intellectuals throughout the modern period have spoken about the four values quite openly and with some degree of frequency. I also noted that at no point did these figures speak about the four values as a group, nor did they identify them as an explanation for Jewish success, as I have; instead, they discussed these values individually, with the intent of demonstrating how they made Judaism superior to Christianity.[29] But the fact that they discussed these values with some regularity throughout the modern period is significant, for it means that the notion that Judaism had such values and that they marked Judaism off from Christianity circulated among lay Jews. It is difficult to say to what extent these Jews were aware of such discussions. However, there is a good chance that a substantial portion of Jews in the Reform and Conservative movements were aware of them, especially those who were seriously engaged with their denominations and read the writings of the leading Jewish intellectuals of their day.

Conclusions

The picture that emerges from our discussion in this chapter is both complex and interesting. Many of the most successful Jews in the modern West were secular Jews who had moved away from the pre-modern rabbinic world but were not really part of the modern Western world either, and it would seem that it was in this space between the two worlds that these Jews were able to flourish.

What I am saying here sounds quite similar to the theory proposed by Thorstein Veblen, to which I referred in my introductory chapter. At the beginning of the twentieth century, Veblen suggested that European Jews had become unusually accomplished scientists because when they joined European society, they left their old Jewish way of life behind but did not entirely assimilate into the new world they had entered. Jews were therefore in a no man's land between the two cultures, a position that allowed them to be unencumbered by the intellectual restrictions of both worlds and thus gave them the freedom to engage in the sciences in highly creative ways. The result was a burst of remarkable accomplishments.[30]

I support a similar picture of secular Jews flourishing in the space between Jewish culture and non-Jewish culture. However, I differ with Veblen because my contention is that within this space, Jews flourished not because they were in some sort of void but because they were in a position to combine the best features of the two worlds and create a dynamic way of life. That is why secular Jews became so successful not just in the sciences but in a host of other fields as well. In other words, in being positioned between Jewish and non-Jewish culture, secular Jews were not in a *no* man's land; they were in an *every* man's land. These Jews had left the rabbinic way of life, but they had to have retained a number of its habits of thought, speech, and behaviour, and those habits likely included an adherence to the four values that are central to this book. At the same time, these Jews availed themselves of the wonderful opportunities presented by the Western world that was blossoming around them and in which they were invited to participate, a world ideally suited for those with precisely the type of values that Jews had absorbed from rabbinic culture.

The same argument explains why religiously affiliated Jews, with the exception of the ultra-Orthodox, were successful in the modern period as well. They too occupied a space similar to that of secular Jews in that they inherited the values of Rabbinic Judaism but were at the same time part of modern Western society. Religiously affiliated Jews were perhaps more conscious of their attachments to the rabbinic tradition than secular Jews were, but they were not so attached to it that they closed themselves off from modern Western culture. In fact, most of them embraced that culture with great enthusiasm. These Jews, then, were not all that much different from secular Jews in benefiting from the every man's land that stood between the two worlds.

Yet a serious difficulty emerges from my arguments in this chapter. My views on secular Jews are based on the assumption that many if not most of these Jews were beholden to specific values inherited from their rabbinic past in a subconscious manner, and I have admitted that it is awfully difficult to prove anything about the subconscious. My assumption has been bolstered by a number of considerations, but it still rests on a certain amount of conjecture about subconscious processes.

In truth, the same difficulty is evident in my theory as it applies to Jews who were religiously affiliated. These Jews were not much more aware than secular Jews were that rabbinic culture and its values were responsible for their success. Religiously affiliated Jews were openly devoted to the rabbinic tradition in varying degrees, but it is not as if they had a conscious plan to focus on its key values in order to succeed in Western society. My theory therefore presumes that the success of these Jews also came about because rabbinic values affected them subconsciously, and so here as well, I have not been able to entirely escape the conjectural nature of my arguments any more than I was in my discussion of secular Jews.

To put it succinctly, I am arguing, in effect, that *all* Jews, with the exception of ultra-Orthodox Jews, were inspired to achieve success in the modern period by subconscious forces that are very hard to probe and about which there can only be speculation and conjecture. So the best I can do is demonstrate that my theory about the success of modern Jews is plausible, not that it is, in fact, true, and this in turn casts doubt on the validity of my entire enterprise in this book.

I have a number of responses to this concern. First, while my approach is indeed speculative and conjectural because of its focus on subconscious forces, it can be strengthened by looking at evidence that is more concrete and empirical. For while the subconscious is certainly difficult territory to explore, one can sometimes make good judgments about its contents by looking at how it expresses itself in speech and behaviour. These often reveal indirectly what the subconscious is up to, and that is true as much for groups as it is for individuals. In fact, this premise is the basis of the social sciences. Disciplines such as psychology, sociology, and anthropology are predicated on the assumption that we can get information about subconscious forces that shape how we relate to the world around us by examining human speech and behaviours that betray the influence of such forces.

A handful of studies have been carried out by social scientists that provide valuable information of this sort regarding Jews and their connection to the rabbinic tradition – and here, we are speaking about Jews of all kinds, from religious to secular. In one study done in 2001, sociologists examined the style of public discourse used by Israeli Jews on TV talk shows, and what they discovered was that their discourse had the unmistakable features of Talmudic dialogue, even though the Israelis whose speech was being analysed were secular.[31] Another study done in 2002 arrived at a similar conclusion regarding the way in which members of the Israeli Parliament engaged in floor debate. Here too, the sociologists concluded that the verbal exchanges had the unmistakable marks of Talmudic dialogue, and that was the case for secular lawmakers no less than for religious lawmakers.[32] Yet another study suggests that the same may be true of American Jews. A study done by a sociologist in 1984 analysed the discourse of Jews in Philadelphia from religious and secular homes and concluded that these Jews also had a distinctive style of argumentation that might have roots in Talmudic discourse.[33]

These studies give support to my argument about the impact of the four values on Jews of all stripes. If religious and secular Jews have carried on habits of discourse that are rabbinic in origin without being aware of it, and have done so for generations since the beginning of the modern period, then it is quite possible that both groups of Jews have similarly carried on habits of thinking and behaviour informed by the four values embedded in Rabbinic Judaism.

The problem is that the studies I have cited here focus only on patterns of Jewish dialogue, and my theory of Jewish success deals with so much more. Moreover, these studies are not numerous enough for us to be certain of their conclusions even regarding the issue of dialogue.

Yet there is a better response to the concerns I have raised here. One must recognize that *any* explanation for the success of modern Jews that is truly comprehensive in the way that it should be is almost certain to involve subconscious forces and therefore *has* to be speculative. We are dealing with a phenomenon that is highly diffuse and elusive. It concerns the success of modern Jews over a period of two centuries, in a number of geographic regions, and in a wide array of disciplines, and again Jews certainly did not have a conscious and coordinated plan for achieving such success. So we have no choice but to explore the realm of subconscious forces that affected modern Jews and were responsible for this phenomenon, and in consequence, any theory of Jewish success in the modern period will have to involve some guesswork about the nature of these forces.

Yuri Slezkine's hypothesis is an excellent illustration of this point. As noted in my introductory chapter, he, more than any historian in recent years, has attempted to come up with a comprehensive explanation for modern Jewish success, and so he has had to indulge in speculations and conjectures regarding subliminal forces the way I am doing here. When Slezkine argues that Jews succeeded in the twentieth century because they were Mercurians, a class of people who were unsettled and who thrived by serving sedentary communities, he is relying on judgments about such forces. At no point did modern Jews consciously identify themselves as Mercurians or anything akin to them.

In fact, similar observations can be made about much of the work produced by scholars who study how cultures evolve. Often the evidence these scholars adduce to explain the development of the cultures they explore has to be speculative and conjectural because many of the processes involved in cultural evolution are subconscious or, at best, semi-conscious. That is particularly true when scholars examine the evolution of cultural values, as we are doing here, because cultural values are by their very nature abstract and thus harder to pin down.

What, then, are we to do in such a situation? How can we understand a historical phenomenon, such as the one we are concerned with, that by its very nature can be explained only by theories that have to be conjectural? The simple and straightforward answer is that we can still determine which theory is best because not all conjectures are the same; some are better than others. I hope to prove in the coming chapters that my theory of Jewish success, despite its speculative nature, is still the most convincing theory among those that have been offered.

We have already made a lot of headway in that direction. In my introductory chapter, I noted the critical weaknesses of other theories for the success of Jews in the modern period. The genetic approach is even more speculative than mine because of how little we know about the genetics of intelligence. The historical approach is the most empirical of all the approaches, but it deals with the issue of Jewish success in piecemeal fashion and therefore does not account for the highly varied and diffuse nature of this phenomenon. Slezkine's approach is comprehensive in focusing on broad subconscious forces that he believes were responsible for Jewish success, but to my mind, he focuses on the wrong forces. It is much more plausible that Rabbinic Judaism provided the subconscious impetus for the success of modern Jews than the Mercurian sensibilities that Slezkine speaks of. After all, we are certain that Rabbinic Judaism was at the centre of Jewish culture for centuries, while the same cannot be said about Slezkine's Mercurian sensibilities.

However, I will need the rest of this book to demonstrate just how plausible it is that Rabbinic Judaism was the critical factor that made modern Jews as successful as they have been. Hopefully by the time readers reach the end of this study, I will have made the case that my theory of the success of modern Jews is not only highly plausible but also the most persuasive one that can be offered.

PART TWO

The Cultural Hypothesis Revisited:
The Core Argument

My book at this point resembles a donut – or perhaps, for a book about Jews, I should say, a bagel. Everything is in place, but there is a big hole in the centre. I have established a framework for my theory of Jewish success in the modern period, but its core claims have yet to be proven. I have not yet demonstrated that both pre-modern Western Christian culture and Jewish culture developed four values that were critical for their success in the modern world and that Jews developed these values in more robust form than Christians did.

The next section of this book will be devoted to this task. Each chapter will look at one of the four values and will be divided in two. The first section will provide a history of the value being considered in pre-modern Western Christianity from the first century CE to the modern period; the second will provide a parallel history of that same value in pre-modern Judaism over the same span of time.

I could have just focused on the critical differences between Christian and Jewish culture with respect to these values, but I have chosen, for a number of reasons, to take the lengthier route of tracing their history in the two cultures over two millennia. First, it is only by seeing how each of the values gradually emerged in the two cultures that one can really get a sense of how the cultures differed in their approach to them. A presentation focusing only on the differences would not make nearly as convincing a case that those differences existed and were meaningful.

Second, it is my belief that the importance of a particular value in a culture is determined not just by how central it is in that culture but by how long it has been central. The longer a value has been part of a people's culture, the more it will be ingrained in their mindset and the more it will imprint itself on their habits of thought, speech, and behaviour. So it is critical to our enterprise to provide the full story of how the four values evolved in Western and Jewish culture because it will allow us to assess how deeply embedded they are in the two cultures.

A third reason for giving the full history of the four values in pre-modern Christian and Jewish culture is that basic misunderstandings are common regarding the four values and their development in the two cultures, and that is the case even for seasoned academic scholars. Scholars in each culture have had a tendency to claim that one or another of the four values evolved in these cultures much earlier than they actually did. Modern values such as human autonomy and freedom of expression are often projected anachronistically onto past eras. This tendency is understandable, given that scholars tend to be eager to show that the particular era they specialize in was one of dramatic breakthrough in anticipation of modernity and, thus, highly significant from a historical standpoint. Nonetheless, we must avoid this tendency because without an accurate account of how the four values evolved in Western and Jewish culture, the comparisons we will make between the two cultures to explain the success of modern Jews will have little merit. These observations thus provide another reason to offer a detailed history of how the four values evolved in both Christian and Jewish culture. It will allow us to weed out misconceptions about these values so that my explanation for the success of modern Jews rests on a reliable foundation.

Finally, a full history of the four values in Christian and Jewish culture is necessary because basic misunderstandings about them have often plagued the comparisons between Christian and Jewish views on the four values that have already been drawn by Jewish scholars. As I mentioned in an earlier chapter, I am by no means the first Jewish scholar to compare how the two cultures treated these values, but I also noted that such comparisons have almost always had a polemical edge to them, with Jewish scholars often attempting to use such comparisons to demonstrate the superiority of Judaism.[1] This provides yet another reason to offer a comprehensive history of the four values in Christian and Jewish culture. By doing so, I will be able to clear up common errors about the similarities and differences between the two cultures so that, once again, my theory for the success of modern Jews rests on a reliable foundation.

There is one more potential misunderstanding that I would like to pre-empt here. The goal of the following chapters is not to compare how Jews and Christians made the transition to modernity but rather to compare how they achieved success in the modern world. I made this point earlier.[2] There is a good deal of overlap between the two issues, but they are not the same. The transition to modernity for both groups is a far larger topic than I can tackle in the following pages, so readers will not find an adequate account of it here. My entire focus will be on the evolution of the four values that are at the centre of this study in Jewish and Christian cultures and how they explain the success of those cultures.

It is important that I also share some observations here about the sources that we will be analysing in this section of the book. We need to be aware that it is more difficult to determine Jewish views on theological issues than it is to determine Christian views on such matters. Christian thinkers tended to write on theological issues in a systematic way; that is, they analysed those issues in an organized and comprehensive manner. That was not always the case with Jewish thinkers, and, in fact, as I pointed out earlier, the most important Jewish theological literature after the Bible, which is found in the literature of early Rabbinic Judaism, is rather unsystematic in its approach to theology.[3] The rabbis who composed and edited this literature, which included the Talmud and various works of Midrash, did not provide comprehensive and organized treatments of theological concepts because they were more interested in systematizing laws than in systematizing beliefs. The rabbis certainly addressed theological issues, but the literature concerned with such matters took the form of brief and pithy statements, which were scattered throughout their works and sometimes were not consistent with each other.

Later schools in Judaism would attempt to systematize Jewish theology in a way that the early rabbis did not. Their efforts to do so defined the agendas of the schools of Jewish philosophy and Kabbalah that arose in the medieval period, and we will be looking at these schools as well. But the early writings of the rabbis will be the most important body of literature that we will be examining in the coming chapters because of their centrality in Judaism. Also, the schools of philosophy and Kabbalah constructed much of their systematic thinking from rabbinic teachings.

But despite the haphazard character of rabbinic sources that deal with theological matters, we can still make judgments about what the early rabbis thought about such issues. On any given theological topic, we may find a spectrum of opinions in rabbinic literature, but that spectrum usually is not unlimited in scope; it tends to have boundaries beyond which the rabbis were not willing to go. Moreover, one can often identify within the spectrum of rabbinic opinions on a given matter definable tendencies and patterns of thought that allow us to make at least some generalizations about the topic under discussion. We just have to be cautious in doing so.

Chapter Three

Human Autonomy I: Sin, Grace, and Salvation

We begin our foray into the four values by looking at the issue of human autonomy. Our concern here will be human autonomy in the metaphysical sense – or what philosophers and theologians often refer to as "free will." That is, we will be exploring human autonomy as it pertains to the relationship between human beings and God. The major question here will be how much freedom God grants human beings to act according to their own will.

As I pointed out in the previous section of this book, one of the reasons that modern Westerners achieved the success they did in the economic, intellectual, and artistic realms is that they developed a much stronger belief than their predecessors did in the freedom of human beings in relation to God. There was a new emphasis on the dignity and worth of human beings in God's scheme. For some Westerners, the belief in human freedom was so strong that they no longer felt they needed to believe in God at all; human beings could do just fine without a supreme deity. These sentiments naturally led to the view that human beings could take initiative and master the world around them. The same was the case for many modern Jews. They too developed a strong sense of human freedom and the notion that human beings could use that freedom to their advantage.[1] However, what I will show is that modern Jews were better prepared to adopt this conception of freedom than their non-Jewish neighbours were because of differences in their respective religious heritages.

Yet, the notion of metaphysical autonomy in the modern sense did not come easily either to Christians or to Jews. For centuries, both groups adhered to religions in which the preponderant view was that God was all-knowing and all-powerful, and therefore they had to question how much free will human beings had, if any at all. In a world created and governed by such a God, how was it possible for people to act on their own initiative? Was everything we did not predetermined by his knowledge and will? Our task is therefore to explore how Christian and Jewish thinkers prior to modernity grappled with these questions and how the solutions to them later paved the way for modern conceptions of autonomy. For that purpose, we will explore the following topics: (1) sin, grace, and salvation (2) religious authority, and (3) attitudes to the use of reason in exploring philosophical truths. A full chapter will be devoted to each topic.

The terms "sin," "grace," and "salvation," which will be dealt with in this chapter, are more Christian than Jewish in character, but they will still serve as a good focal point for our first attempt to compare the respective approaches of Christian and Jewish thinkers to human autonomy. The three terms are interrelated, and what unites them is the issue of divine judgment. This issue is highly relevant to the problem of free will because the question of how God judges human beings inevitably involves discussion about how much control human beings have over their actions so that they may earn divine reward. An examination of this issue is particularly valuable for our purposes because all Jews and Christians were concerned about it whether they were elite theologians or lay people.

I. Christian Perspectives

The Medieval Period

Let us start by looking at Christian perspectives on sin, grace, and salvation.[2] Any discussion of these matters has to begin with Augustine (354–430), the greatest theologian in early Christianity and perhaps of all time. His views on sin, grace, and salvation were more influential than those of any other Christian thinker.

Augustine's approach to sin was rather harsh. While his thinking on this issue evolved over time, he came to believe in his mature years that human beings were so depraved, so captive to their base instincts, that all they could do was sin. Even when human beings acted in obedience to God, there was always an element of ego emanating from their sinful disposition that crept into their motivations and blemished their actions.[3]

Augustine's assessment of human nature was rooted in his well-known views on Original Sin. Augustine was the first Christian thinker to give a clear and detailed exposition of this highly influential idea. According to him, the notion of Original Sin meant that human beings were born with a tendency to do evil because they had inherited it from Adam and Eve. When Adam and Eve rebelled against God by eating the forbidden fruit, their rational capabilities were permanently damaged, making them incapable of rendering clear moral judgments. Furthermore, the damage caused by their actions was passed on physically to all subsequent generations. The very act of sexual intercourse communicated the pollution of the first sin to one's offspring. The precise term that Augustine used to characterize the sinful tendencies inherited from Adam and Eve was "concupiscence," which was usually synonymous in his thinking with sexual lust. It was the sexual urge in people that was most responsible for their inability to be obedient to God because it tended to overwhelm their will more than any other human impulse; however, concupiscence could refer to any desire that was focused on selfish needs and that thereby clouded one's ability to obey God's will.[4]

The implication that Augustine drew out of these views was that human beings had no role to play whatsoever in their salvation, which, in Christian thinking, was equated with reward in the afterlife. Whether human beings made it to heaven was entirely in God's hands. One could be saved only if God granted salvation as a pure act of kindness on his part, a gift referred to as "grace."

Augustine took these considerations one step further with his doctrine of Predestination. According to this doctrine, only some human beings were recipients of grace, and the decision about who had been chosen for this privilege had already been made in the mind of God at the very beginning of time. Moreover, it was impossible for anyone to know whether they belonged to this group on the basis of the life they were living. A person who made every effort to overcome Original Sin and whose life was filled with piety and good deeds could still end up in hell, while a person who made no such effort and whose life was filled with wicked deeds could still end up in heaven. If that seemed unfair, Augustine argued that as sinful creatures, we were fortunate to have been given life by God and granted the opportunity to enjoy the pleasures of this world. Salvation was not a right we deserved.[5]

Did human beings then have *any* free will? It would seem that if human beings were utterly captive to their base instincts due to Original Sin, if their actions always contained an element of sin even when they tried to do good, then they had very limited freedom when it came to their moral behaviour. On top of that, human beings had no free will whatsoever with respect to the issue of greatest concern to Christians: their fate in the afterlife. God had already decided well in advance whether or not an individual would achieve salvation, and nothing they did could alter that decision.

Interestingly, Augustine still affirmed free will, and he presented a series of philosophical arguments to make his case. However, it is doubtful that these arguments were successful, and most scholars have therefore concluded that for Augustine, human beings did not have free will in any meaningful sense, despite his affirmations to the contrary.[6] Augustine seems to have recognized that his attempt to make room for free will was not adequate. In a book he wrote to Simplicianus, the Bishop of Milan, Augustine reflected on the tension in his thinking between God's power and human free will and concluded as follows: "In trying to solve this question, I made strenuous efforts on behalf of the preservation of free choice of the human will, but the grace of God defeated me."[7]

Augustine's views on these matters were disturbing to some of his contemporaries, and for understandable reasons. The most important critic was Pelagius (360–418), a British monk. Pelagius was deeply troubled by Augustine's understanding of sin, grace, and salvation – even though, when Pelagius first became familiar with Augustine's thinking on these matters, it was not as harsh as it would later become. According to Pelagius, what was the point of expending effort to be pious if one could not overcome the effects of Original Sin and if salvation was predetermined by God's mysterious will?

Pelagius therefore took positions on sin, grace, and salvation that were diametrically opposed to those of Augustine. He argued that human beings did *not* have damaged souls because of the actions of Adam and Eve; all of us were born good. If we sinned, it was solely because we had chosen to do so, not because sin was somehow ingrained in our very nature. As for God's grace, God certainly helped us achieve salvation, but he did so, not by giving it to us despite our sinfulness, but by instilling in human beings the ability to gain salvation on their own through choosing good over evil. God also provided us with guidance to achieve salvation through his prophets and his Scriptures. Pelagius thus insisted on an optimistic view of human beings and their capacity to achieve salvation on their own, an attitude that was in marked contrast to Augustine's thinking.

In the ensuing debate between those who supported Augustine's position and those who upheld the position of Pelagius, a third position emerged, the proponents of which tried to find a compromise between the two. The defenders of this position became known as "Semi-Pelagians," even though they could have just as easily been called "Semi-Augustinians." The Semi-Pelagians believed in Augustine's doctrine of Original Sin and that human beings needed God's grace in order to be saved, but they also argued that human beings had at least some role in their salvation. They had the freedom and capability at least to take the first step towards salvation by demonstrating a desire to achieve it. If they made this effort, God would then meet them halfway with the gift of grace and grant salvation. In this way, the Semi-Pelagians injected an element of free will into the process of salvation.[8]

By the beginning of the sixth century, the Church wanted the debate over these matters to be settled, and so in 529, at the Synod of Orange (in today's France), Western bishops convened to discuss the three positions. Their final decision was that Augustine's views on Original Sin and grace would become the official teachings of the Church, and Pelagius's views were declared to be heresy, as were the views of the Semi-Pelagians. Human beings were hopelessly tainted by sin just by virtue of being human. However, Augustine's victory was by no means complete. Significantly, the synod did not endorse Augustine's doctrine of Predestination. Perhaps the members were uneasy about the idea that our fate in the afterlife was entirely predetermined by God, for this raised serious questions of the type Pelagius had posed about whether there was any point in striving to be a good Christian.[9]

Nonetheless, debate over Predestination would persist among Christian thinkers up to the end of the medieval period, with some of them supporting Augustine's view, and others rejecting it. Gottschalk, a Saxon monk in the 800s, declared his support for Augustine's position on Predestination, and he was imprisoned for it. Yet several centuries later, Thomas Aquinas (1225–74), the greatest Christian theologian after Augustine, supported the latter's views on Predestination, and he did so with impunity. Another prominent theologian, William of Ockham (1287–1347), took what was effectively a Semi-Pelagian position in claiming that salvation depended in part on human will and effort, in part on divine grace. However, he was promptly condemned by Thomas Bradwardine (1300–49), a British theologian who staunchly supported Augustine's position on Predestination.

Adding to the confusion was that the type of Christianity the Church preached to the masses seemed to be tacitly in accordance with the Semi-Pelagian position, despite the Church's prior condemnation of it. The Church taught that if one sinned, one could repent in order to repair their relationship with God, and the Church instituted elaborate procedures of penance for that purpose. It seems then that in the Church's eyes, human beings had to have *some* control over their salvation; otherwise repentance would not have been possible.[10]

The medieval period therefore ended with little clarity on the Church's views regarding free will as it pertained to the process of salvation. The only thing that was certain was that the Church and all its major thinkers rejected the view of Pelagius that gave human beings complete free will to earn salvation. Beyond that, there were a variety of views on the matter. The Church and some of its thinkers either endorsed Augustine's views that effectively denied free will in the salvation process, or they endorsed views akin to those of the Semi-Pelagians that granted some degree of free will in that process, even though these views had been branded as heresy.[11]

The Renaissance

The last two centuries of the medieval period were also the first two centuries of the Renaissance, and many of the great thinkers of this period, particularly in Italy, developed a more exalted view of human beings than in previous centuries, according to which human beings were creatures with great dignity. However, these thinkers were not as secular in their orientation as scholars of the Renaissance once believed. As Charles Trinkaus has shown in his definitive study of religion in the Renaissance, these thinkers saw human beings as creatures infused with the divine who were placed by God on this earth in order to improve it; this conception was, in turn, based on the biblical idea that human beings were created in God's image.[12]

Most important for our concerns is that Renaissance thinkers were not fundamentally different from their predecessors on such issues as sin, grace, and salvation. They functioned within the same framework that their medieval predecessors had in acknowledging that human beings required God's grace through Jesus's death and resurrection in order to be the dignified creatures that they were meant to be. Petrarch and Lorenza Valla seem to have been particularly focused on this issue. Moreover, Valla appears to have acknowledged, much as Augustine did, that God's calculations regarding who should receive divine grace were a mystery. The exalted view of human beings that one finds in Renaissance thinking was thus tempered by the acceptance of traditional Catholic views on sin, grace, and salvation.[13]

It should also be pointed out that on such matters, ordinary Europeans in this period would not have necessarily been cognizant of the esoteric ruminations of the great thinkers of Renaissance Italy. These thinkers belonged to an elite whose reach beyond their intellectual circles was limited. Humanists were trained in schools that were open only to the upper classes.[14] The views of the common folk on sin, grace, and salvation would be far more affected by the Reformation, which overlapped with the final century of the Renaissance. It is to that movement that we will now turn.

The Reformation

The final century of the Renaissance was also the first century of the Protestant Reformation, and in this movement, there were important developments on the issue of sin, grace, and salvation. Augustine's harsh views on the matter received renewed emphasis. Martin Luther (1483–1546), the founder of Protestantism, was driven to rebel against the Catholic Church in large part by his desire to go back to Augustine's views on sin, grace, and salvation and discard the Semi-Pelagian elements that he believed had corrupted the Church's teachings and practices. Luther argued passionately, as Augustine did, that human beings were inherently sinful because they could not overcome the taint of Original Sin and that their fate in the afterlife was predestined by God's inscrutable will. Neither participation in the Church's sacraments nor the performance of good deeds could bring salvation. One could be saved only by God's grace, and one had no way of knowing whether one had merited that grace.

Did all this mean that human beings had no free will? Luther's views on this issue were as murky as those of Augustine, if not more so. However, it is quite clear that, like Augustine, Luther emphasized the overpowering nature of God's will when it came to our salvation, and he therefore denied that human freedom had a meaningful role to play in that aspect of life that was most important to human beings.[15]

Luther's views on sin, grace, and salvation had an enormous impact on Protestantism. They were adopted by John Calvin (1509–64), a central figure in the founding of the Reformed Church, which became the largest Church in Protestantism. The popularity of Calvin's writings and of the Reformed Church he helped spawn meant that the doctrines of Original Sin and Predestination became common features of the religious outlook of a substantial portion of Europe's Protestant population.[16]

After Calvin's death, developments in Protestantism ensured that the doctrines of Original Sin and Predestination would become even more prominent in this new brand of Christianity. In the second half of the sixteenth century, the three most powerful Protestant denominations – Lutheran, Reformed, and Anglican – began to systematize their respective beliefs, and for that purpose, these Churches provided lists of their most basic doctrines, lists known as "confessions." The confessions issued by the Lutheran and Reformed Churches identified the doctrines of Original Sin and Predestination as fundamental dogmas of Christianity.[17] The Anglican confessions were also influenced by Calvin's thinking on Original Sin and Predestination.[18]

That the Protestant Churches required lay people to assent to the doctrines of Original Sin and Predestination in their severe Augustinian formulation was unprecedented. As we have seen, in the medieval period the Christianity that the Church preached to ordinary Christians supported positions on sin, grace, and salvation that were effectively Semi-Pelagian in character. Yet in Protestant Christianity, Augustine's views on Original Sin and Predestination were not only supported by its leading theologians, they were explicitly taught to ordinary Christians.

It is important to point out here that the widespread inculcation of these teachings among Protestants did not result in apathy about life, for even though Protestants widely assented to doctrines implying that they had no control over their salvation, there is good evidence that they continued to go about their religious and mundane lives with great energy. In the religious realm, the most devout Lutherans and Calvinists focused intensively on making themselves better Christians. The Puritans in England and the American colonies were Calvinists, and they were particularly devoted to improving themselves in God's eyes through religious introspection. In the political realm, Calvinists were also highly active in several European countries and were known for their zealotry in spreading their teachings.[19] Moreover, Protestant countries that made Lutheranism and Calvinism their official Churches were as successful economically as other countries, if not more so. This prompted Max Weber, the renowned twentieth-century German sociologist, to propose a highly influential theory, according to which Protestantism was, in fact, the root cause for the development of capitalism. Whether Weber's theory was correct is another question, which I will be taking up in a later chapter. The important point is that the widespread diffusion of the doctrines of Original Sin and Predestination did not stop Protestants from being productive, even in the mundane realm.[20]

Still, the doctrines of Original Sin and Predestination certainly put a psychological burden on Protestants. Even if they continued to live their lives as if they had freedom, they were still preoccupied with the depth of human sin, and they still trembled at the thought of an all-powerful God who had predetermined their fate.[21]

As one might expect, the doctrines of Original Sin and Predestination eventually troubled some Protestant thinkers. Some of them had great difficulty with the severity of Luther's and Calvin's views on sin, grace, and salvation in the same way that Pelagius had difficulty with those of Augustine. These thinkers therefore parted company with Luther and Calvin on such issues. Human beings had to have enough free will to initiate the process of salvation, and God had to have enough mercy to take their efforts into account. These thinkers upheld the views of Luther and Calvin on Original Sin and the need for divine grace to achieve salvation, but they opposed the view that faith was given to us by God solely through grace. Instead, human beings had a choice to let God into their hearts, and if they did so, he would grant them salvation through grace despite the sins they had committed. In other words, these Protestants were Semi-Pelagians, even though they did not use that term.

This position was at first branded as heresy, and adherents to it often paid with their lives.[22] However, it eventually became accepted by a number of Protestant groups. Most significant here was John Wesley (1703–91), a British preacher who believed that God was primarily a God of love. He found it inconceivable that God would predestine human beings to heaven or hell without giving them a role in their own salvation. The movement that Wesley inspired eventually broke with the Church of England and became known as Methodism, and it would prove to be popular in England and even more so in the American colonies. By the mid-nineteenth century, Methodism was the largest denomination in the US, and it would play a critical role in shaping American evangelical Christianity that continues to be a significant force there.[23]

The Catholic Church also grappled with the issues of sin, grace, and salvation in light of the challenges posed by the Reformation. At the Council of Trent (1545–63), a gathering that provided the Church's formal response to the Reformation, the Catholic Church adopted what was, in effect, a Semi-Pelagian view on these matters. Original Sin made it impossible for human beings to achieve salvation on their own, but if they took initiative and opened themselves to God's grace, God would help them reach that goal. This move brought clarity to the Catholic Church's position on sin, grace, and salvation, which in the preceding centuries had been ambiguous.[24]

What emerges from our discussion thus far is that up until the eighteenth century, Christian views on human autonomy in relation to God swung between two poles. One pole was defined by Augustine and Luther, who maintained that human autonomy was highly restricted, and when it came to salvation, effectively non-existent. Human beings were too sinful to do good, and God chose some for salvation and others for damnation solely according to his mysterious will. The other pole was defined by the Semi-Pelagians, who argued that human beings had enough autonomy in this life to at least initiate the process of salvation but were dependent on God's grace to complete it.

The Enlightenment

Major developments regarding the issue of human autonomy took place in the next phase of European intellectual history, the Enlightenment, which extended from the second half of the seventeenth century through the eighteenth. Significant numbers of Christians had already denied the doctrine of Predestination and thus made room for free will in the salvation process, but European intellectuals now began sweeping aside all metaphysical constraints on free will by attacking the doctrine of Original Sin as well. This move was part of a larger agenda. Central to Enlightenment thought was a new and more positive view of human beings than had been bequeathed to them by Christianity in both its Protestant and Catholic forms, and this meant that the notion of Original Sin had to be discarded. According to the new perspective, human beings were born morally neutral and it was entirely up to the individual to decide what kind of moral life they would cultivate. The human will was inherently free. So widespread was the rejection of Original Sin during the Enlightenment that Ernst Cassirer, the great twentieth-century German philosopher, claimed that nothing united Enlightenment thinkers more than the opposition to this doctrine.[25]

These developments were encouraged by the first stirrings of academic scholarship on the Bible that began to emerge in this period. This new approach to the Bible cast doubt on the historicity of the Garden of Eden story upon which the entire notion of Original Sin rested. Also bolstering the positive view of human beings were major advances in the sciences that took place in the seventeenth and eighteenth centuries and helped convince many Enlightenment intellectuals that human beings had far more good in them than the doctrine of Original Sin presumed.[26]

Enlightened intellectuals thus rejected the doctrines of Original Sin and Predestination, not because they were leaving Christianity altogether but because they simply no longer viewed these concepts as rational. In their view, humans were noble and powerful creatures whom God had placed on earth to be stewards of his creation and they were capable of doing good or evil according to their own wishes. These thinkers still held the belief that God would reward and punish individuals in the afterlife for their deeds on earth, but significantly, they considered human beings to be entirely responsible for their actions while on earth. In other words, this new perspective revived the pure Pelagian viewpoint on sin, grace, and salvation, which had not received significant support among European thinkers since its founder, Pelagius, had lived fourteen centuries earlier.[27]

But just because a strong view of human autonomy became fashionable during the Enlightenment did not mean that the Augustinian or Semi-Pelagian perspectives disappeared. Large parts of Europe remained devoted to traditional Christianity in its Catholic and Protestant forms in the modern period, and therefore, the alternative perspectives on metaphysical autonomy lived on. Nonetheless, the new view on autonomy introduced by the Enlightenment would compete quite well with these perspectives. It would eventually give rise to a modern secular culture in which God was either relegated to a distant role in human affairs or dispensed with altogether. And most important for our purposes, this perspective would encourage Europeans to take control of the world around them as never before and would therefore play an important role in the success of Europe in the modern period.

II.   Jewish Perspectives

Let us now look at how Rabbinic Judaism approached sin, grace, and salvation. An obstacle here is that some of this terminology is foreign to Rabbinic Judaism. Concepts such as "grace" and "salvation" as we have understood them up to this point in our discussion are distinctively Christian and have no exact equivalent in Rabbinic Judaism. However, we do find ideas in the rabbinic world view that are sufficiently resonant with these concepts to make for a fruitful comparison between the two religions.

The main questions of concern to us here are as follows: what do the rabbinic ideas analogous to the Christian notions of sin, grace, and salvation tell us about the thinking of the rabbis on human autonomy in relation to God? And how do these ideas compare to those of premodern Christianity?

I am by no means the first to broach this question. Since the beginning of the modern period, Jewish intellectuals have commonly claimed that Judaism has no equivalent to the notion of Original Sin and that Judaism therefore has a far more robust notion of human autonomy than Christianity does. Popular Jewish writers have made the same argument and continue to do so.[28]

The difficulty with these pronouncements is that they have not been sufficiently scrutinized, and some scholars in recent years have begun to question whether they are, in fact, true. Some have found evidence that Judaism was not entirely devoid of the notion of Original Sin. We should also note that the claims of Jewish intellectuals and popular writers about Original Sin are suspect because they often have polemical overtones. Because the idea of human freedom in the metaphysical sense has become a pillar of modernity, modern Jews have had a vested interest in declaring that their religion supports this idea – more so, in fact, than Christianity does. Such declarations are often part of a broader attempt to demonstrate that Judaism plays a critical role in modern culture.

Our task in the remainder of this chapter is therefore to open up this whole issue again, to explore it in more depth than others have, and to do so without polemical intent. We must also expand our investigation beyond Original Sin, which has received a great deal of attention from modern Jewish intellectuals, and look at other concepts in our discussion that have received much less attention, such as Predestination and grace.

We will be focusing mostly on Rabbinic Judaism in its formative period – roughly the first eight centuries CE – because it was in this period that the rabbis formulated their views on the matters under discussion here, and those views would become central to Judaism for centuries to come. However, we will also give some attention to the views of the rabbis in the medieval and early modern periods.

Original Sin

We will begin by asking whether there were rabbis in early Rabbinic Judaism whose views had any resonance with the harshest views on sin, grace, and salvation in Christianity – those found in the Augustinian tradition. In particular, were there rabbis who upheld concepts akin to Augustine's notions of Original Sin and Predestination, concepts that made human freedom difficult if not impossible?[29]

Scholars have noted that elements of the doctrine of Original Sin do appear in some early rabbinic sources. For instance, a Talmudic statement informs us that the snake in the Garden of Eden injected Eve with a poison that affected subsequent generations and that when the Israelites received the Torah on Mount Sinai, the effects of the poison were neutralized.[30] Here, it would seem, the sin of the Garden of Eden was passed on physically by Eve to subsequent generations in a manner reminiscent of Augustine's doctrine of Original Sin. A number of passages in rabbinic literature also intimate that the punishment for Adam's sin was bequeathed to all subsequent generations because Adam was originally supposed to be an immortal being but became mortal when he disobeyed God's will, and that punishment has affected all human beings ever since.[31]

Yet while these rabbinic sources carry elements of the doctrine of Original Sin, they do not present us with that doctrine in its Augustinian form. The first passage informs us that the sin of Adam and Eve was no longer a problem for Jews once the Torah was given, and therefore the passage can be read as a statement *against* Original Sin, and not just the Augustinian version of it. We are told here that while the first sin was inherited from generation to generation, the Torah was its remedy and freed us from its negative influence.

As for the passages that speak about Adam's sin still being with us in that we are mortal beings, here too we have an approach that is quite different from Augustine's. For Augustine, it was the *impulse* to commit sin that was inherited from Adam, not just its *punishment*, while for the rabbis, it was only the latter that was inherited. In addition, for Augustine the impulse to sin inherited from Adam restricted human autonomy because it made it impossible for human beings to do anything out of purely good motives. For the rabbis, that was not the case because again it was only the punishment for Adam's sin that was inherited. Human beings were free to act as they pleased, though they had to understand that if they disobeyed God's will, they would be punished.

There is some similarity between Augustine's understanding of Original Sin and the way in which some rabbis approached the sin of the golden calf in a number of sources. In several passages in rabbinic literature, the claim is made that all the suffering that the Jewish people would experience throughout history would be due to that sin.[32] This idea, it would seem, resembles the Augustinian conception of Original Sin in that the sin of the golden calf affects generations of people who are not responsible for it and whose only connection to its perpetrators is genealogical. However, here again, the critical difference between Augustine and the rabbis is that for Augustine, it is the impulse to sin that is inherited, while for rabbis, it is the punishment, which means that the rabbis preserve human freedom in a way that Augustine does not.

It would seem, therefore, that the rabbis did not develop a concept of Original Sin according to its Augustinian understanding. But in order to fully appreciate the differences between Augustine and the rabbis on this issue, we have to go beyond individual passages in rabbinic literature and look at the larger rabbinic world view. The rabbis in general never developed the same fascination with the Garden of Eden story that Christians did. They were far more focused on the later stories of the Bible about the forefathers of the Jewish people and the Israelites who descended from them. More important, all of rabbinic religion was built on the premise that Jews were required and able to obey God's 613 commandments and that human beings therefore had to have enough good in them to obey God's commandments and thereby earn reward or punishment in this life and the next. So the rabbis generally believed that our sinful tendencies could be overcome.

We can better understand the distinction between Augustine and the rabbis on Original Sin by looking at how the rabbis explained sinful behaviour. The most frequent reason the rabbis offered to account for such behaviour was that human beings were born with two inclinations or forces in their souls, one good (*yetser ha-tov*) and one bad (*yetser ha-ra*), and these inclinations did battle with each other throughout a person's life to sway them towards good or bad behaviour.[33] Therefore, according to this theory, individuals have the capability to choose in any given situation whether to follow their good or evil inclination. And again, that was precisely what Augustine and his followers denied. For them, human beings could only choose to do evil because of the influence of Original Sin, and that was the case even when they were attempting to do good.

Predestination

What about Augustine's doctrine of Predestination? In order to determine whether there was anything similar to this doctrine in early rabbinic thought, let us first note that it presumes two ideas. First, God has decided the fate of each and every individual in the afterlife prior to the beginning of human history. Second, God's decisions here are entirely mysterious; there is no necessary correlation between our actions in this life and whether we achieve salvation in the next.

Let us look at whether there are any analogues to these ideas in early rabbinic thinking. The first idea does seem to have parallels in rabbinic literature. The rabbis generally presume that God is all-powerful and all-knowing, and therefore God has a plan for determining how major historical events will unfold. The rabbis without exception understood the grand prophecies in the Torah and the books of the Prophets about the future of the Israelites as accurate predictions of events that would occur later in Jewish history.[34] Clearly then, history was controlled by God's will. Some rabbis also presumed that God is in control of more minor events as well. Thus, we are told in one Talmudic source that "no person bruises their finger [in the world] below unless it was decreed in the world above."[35]

However, the rabbis appear to have accepted the paradox that human beings have free will despite God's power, and they therefore believed that everyone had the choice whether or not to obey God's commandments, and by implication they had control over whether they earned reward or suffered punishment.[36] The rabbis rarely spoke about this paradox, but its premises are presumed in their literature. There are also some passages that lay out the paradox quite explicitly. The best-known of these appears in the Mishnah in a passage that cites the following statement by R. Akiva: "Everything is foreseen, yet the power to choose is given."[37] That is, everything that happens in the world is foreseen by God, but we still have the power to choose how we act in our daily lives.

R. Akiva's dictum is painfully brief but still significant. It achieved authoritative status among Jewish thinkers in later centuries who discussed the relationship between divine will and human freedom, and there were a number of reasons for this. First, the dictum appeared in Tractate *Avot*, a portion of the Mishnah that became highly popular among Jewish thinkers of later centuries because it was the only portion of the Mishnah that dealt extensively with theological and ethical matters, as opposed to legal ones. Second, the author of the statement, R. Akiva, was one of the most revered personalities in early rabbinic literature.

But is the rabbinic attitude towards human freedom as encapsulated in R. Akiva's dictum really that different from the viewpoint of Christian thinkers who supported the doctrine of Predestination? Christian theologians who believed in Predestination recognized the same paradox. They too spoke of God's absolute control over history, but they also insisted that human beings had free will.

I believe that there is, in fact, a difference between the two viewpoints. Christian theologians like Augustine and Aquinas, who believed in Predestination, tended to focus more on God's power than on human freedom. In their discussions of Predestination, they expended most of their energy on explaining how God's determination of our fate prior to human history followed logically from God's omnipotence. The same theologians went on to affirm the existence of free will but with great difficulty. In other words, according to Christian theologians, divine power and human freedom coexisted, but the former took priority. Here we can be reminded of Augustine's statement to Bishop Simplicianus cited earlier. In grappling with the relationship between divine power and human freedom, Augustine wrote that he made every effort to preserve human free will but that the grace of God "defeated" him.[38] That is, for Augustine, divine omnipotence was easier to justify than human freedom.

When we look at the rabbinic side of this issue, the approach to the paradox between divine power and human freedom seems different. The rabbis appear to be less emphatic than Augustine and his followers about God's power. First of all, note that R. Akiva's statement is phrased in the passive voice: "everything is foreseen, yet the power to choose is given" – which has the effect of softening God's role in determining our actions. In fact, there is no explicit mention here of God at all. Moreover, R. Akiva speaks only of God's *foreknowledge* in determining our actions, not his *will*, as Christian proponents of Predestination had a tendency to do, and the difference here makes R. Akiva's statement less about God's power over us than about the consequences of God's nature as an all-knowing being.[39] Finally, the contrast between R. Akiva and Christian proponents of Predestination is evident when we look at the continuation of R. Akiva's statement. After informing us that divine power and human freedom can coexist, R. Akiva adds: "With goodness the world is judged, and everything is according to the majority of one's deeds." Here we are told that God is merciful, that we do not have to be perfect to win his favour, and that only the majority of our deeds have to be good for God to judge us favourably. What is striking here is that these observations are clearly in line with the idea that human beings have freedom of choice, not that God foresees everything. That is, even though R. Akiva accepts the contradiction between God's foreknowledge and our free will, he seems to underscore the side of the contradiction concerned with free will, not divine foreknowledge. Therefore, the emphasis here is the reverse of what is found in the discussions of Christian theologians supporting Predestination.[40]

Another rabbinic statement often cited by later Jewish thinkers when dealing with issues of human freedom seems to go even further in favouring free will over divine power. Several Talmudic passages assert that "everything is in the hands of heaven except the fear of heaven."[41] Here there is actually no paradox at all between divine power and human freedom: God controls everything in the world below; the one exception is our capacity to obey him. No Christian theologian supporting Predestination would have made such a statement. For these theologians, the relationship between divine power and free will was at best paradoxical. It could not be that there were any exclusions when it came to God's power over us.

In sum, the rabbis do not accept the first premise of Predestination, at least not in the same way that Christian theologians do. Both the Christian supporters of Predestination and the rabbis accept the paradox that human beings have free will despite the fact that God controls human events. However, the rabbis place more emphasis on the side of the paradox allowing for human freedom.

What about the second idea implied by Predestination, that God's decisions about our fate in the afterlife are entirely mysterious and that there is no necessary relationship between our actions in this world and whether we are rewarded or punished in the next?

There are certainly rabbinic sources suggesting that God's ways in meting out reward and punishment are mysterious to us.[42] However to my knowledge, all these sources pertain to reward and punishment in *this* world, not the next. When it comes to one's ultimate fate in the afterlife, the rabbis seemed to have been unanimous that here God's justice was manifest: the righteous received reward for being righteous and the wicked received punishment for being wicked. I know of no source in which the rabbis held the view that God's judgments in the afterlife were incomprehensible to us, or that the righteous could be punished and the wicked rewarded.

In fact, often according to the rabbis, the afterlife was where the moral logic of God's justice would become clear. For instance, a common explanation in rabbinic literature for the suffering of the righteous in this world is that God is punishing them in this life for the few sins they have committed so that he can reward them more fully in the afterlife. Conversely, the wicked may prosper in this world because God is rewarding them in this life for the few good deeds they have done so that he can punish them more fully in the afterlife. Thus, for the rabbis, the afterlife was in effect the place where the books were finally balanced when it came to divine justice.[43]

It is here that we see most clearly the gap between Christian theologians who believed in Predestination and the rabbis. For Christian advocates of Predestination, God's judgments about reward and punishment in the afterlife were inscrutable from our perspective. For the rabbis, there was no mystery here at all; everyone in the afterlife would get their just desserts. We can therefore conclude that while there is some degree of resonance in rabbinic thinking with elements of the doctrine of Predestination, that doctrine was mostly foreign to the world view of the rabbis.

The Early Rabbis: Semi-Pelagians or Pelagians?

If the rabbis did not subscribe to the Augustinian perspective that essentially deprived human beings of autonomy when it came to doing good in this life and earning salvation in the next, the next step is to ask whether the rabbis granted autonomy to human beings more in the manner of the Pelagians or that of the Semi-Pelagians. That is, did the rabbis hold, as Pelagius did, that human beings had *complete* freedom to choose between good and evil and thus gain divine reward on their own, or did they take the position of the Semi-Pelagians that human beings had only *partial* freedom to choose between good and evil and that God's assistance was needed to achieve reward?

PELAGIAN ELEMENTS IN EARLY RABBINIC JUDAISM

The common contemporary view among popular Jewish writers and intellectuals is that Judaism has always upheld a position akin to that of the Pelagians – though these writers and intellectuals do not state it in these terms.[44] According to this reading, Jews have always believed that human beings have full freedom to choose between good and evil and that their worthiness for divine reward or punishment is therefore entirely in their own hands. Human beings have two inclinations, one good and one evil, and so they are constantly being challenged to decide which inclination to follow. God plays no role here.

A good number of rabbinic sources do indeed endorse an attitude towards human freedom similar to that of the Pelagians. According to one Talmudic source, God "created the bad inclination," but he also "created the Torah as its antidote," and if one obeys the Torah, one "will not be delivered into its hand [i.e., the bad inclination]."[45] Here, the only factor involved in obeying God is one's willingness to do so.

A similar way of thinking seems to underlie a number of rabbinic sources that identify individuals who were perfectly righteous and had no taint of sin. The usual candidates for this distinction are the Patriarchs – Abraham, Isaac, and Jacob – and Elijah and Enoch, but other righteous individuals are sometimes included as well.[46] These sources clearly presume that human beings need no assistance from God to merit divine reward.

Relevant for our purposes are also a number of interesting rabbinic sources telling us that the evil inclination is not entirely evil. According to these sources, our goal is not to suppress the evil inclination altogether but to channel its energy for good purposes.[47] For instance, we are told in an often-cited midrash that "were it not for the bad inclination, no man would build a house, nor marry a woman, nor would he have children."[48] That is, the evil inclination is responsible for sexual desire, which can certainly lead to sin, but without it, no man would ever marry or have a family, the assumption here being that these are desirable and good things in God's eyes. So the message is that sexual desire has merit as long as it is directed towards proper goals. For our concerns, the passage also presumes a highly positive view of human nature in general. Human beings can be thoroughly good because even the evil inclination does not have to be evil.[49]

The rabbinic tendency to believe that human beings have control over their actions and are therefore fully capable of earning divine reward on their own comes through quite clearly in a number of rabbinic reflections on repentance. The most common view about repentance in rabbinic literature is that if one sins, the mistake is correctable; it does not remain as an indelible stain on the soul. One can make amends for sins by asking for forgiveness directly from God.[50] Moreover, the holidays of Rosh Hashanah and Yom Kippur were designated by the rabbis as special days to focus on repentance and repair one's relationship with God.

We thus see in many rabbinic sources a position that is absent in medieval and early modern Christian theology, which is the notion that human beings have full autonomy in their relationship with God when it comes to earning salvation. They have the freedom to choose between good and evil, and they are capable of being sufficiently good to earn reward in this life and the next without any help from God. The analogous perspective in the history of Christianity is Pelagianism, but Pelagianism was considered heresy in Europe throughout the medieval and early modern periods, and it was only in the era of the Enlightenment that this way of thinking became fashionable. In this way, the rabbis pre-empted the views of the Enlightenment about human nature by hundreds of years.

But there is more. Some rabbis went even further than Pelagius in asserting human autonomy. These rabbis believed that human beings were not only capable of making decisions about good and evil for themselves, but they were also capable of doing so for God. I am referring here to dozens of passages in rabbinic literature in which human beings – usually, biblical characters – argue with God in direct dialogue to protest against his actions when they seem unjust. And in some of these instances, God not only listens to the objections levelled against him, he accepts the arguments of his human opponent. Thus, in these passages, the tables are turned; it is human beings who judge God![51]

These sources are among the most radical and fascinating passages in rabbinic literature, and only by looking at examples does one get a sense of their flavour. In one passage in the Talmud, for instance, we are told that Moses confronts God after the sin of the golden calf and accuses him of causing the sin. Moses's argument is predicated on the fact that when the Israelites were taken out of Egypt, God, as we are informed in the biblical text, allowed them to collect valuables from the Egyptians[52] – a back-pay of sorts for several hundred years of slavery, one might say – and those valuables, Moses complains, included a large quantity of gold that was then used to build the calf. According to Moses, the making of the calf was therefore God's fault because God should have known what would happen when he provided the Israelites with gold. The Israelites were newly liberated slaves who had spent hundreds of years working for Egyptian idolaters, and so, was it any wonder that when they were provided with copious amounts of gold, they built an idol – especially after Moses, their leader, had disappeared on Mount Sinai for forty days to receive the Torah?[53]

The tradition of arguing with God would continue well into the Middle Ages. As Jews began to experience horrific violence in Christian Europe, particularly during the period of the Crusades, Jewish poets wrote deeply moving poems in which they demanded that God intervene and save them from their oppressors. A citation from one of these poems will show just how daring these writers were. Menachem ben Jacob of Worms (d. 1203) composed the following passage in response to the massacres of Jews during the Crusades:

> Who is like You among the mute, my God? You kept silent.
>   You were silent when they destroyed your Temple.
>   You remained silent when the wicked trod your children underfoot,
> and you sold your people without gain or profit.
>   We came through fire, water, and flame …
>   You are the zealous one and the avenger – where then is
> Your vengeance?[54]

God is being challenged here as directly as possible. The writer takes God to task for being silent in the face of the persecutions Jews are experiencing.

It is important to recognize that not all rabbis, early or medieval, protested against God or believed that one should do so. Some, in fact, were opposed to the idea, particularly in the first two centuries of Rabbinic Judaism.[55] However, the fact that rabbinic literature included dozens of sources that depicted human beings arguing with God and even winning on occasion indicates that at least a significant faction of rabbis believed this form of behaviour was acceptable and that their views were a legitimate part of rabbinic discourse. Moreover, for our purposes, these sources demonstrate that there were rabbis who went well beyond Pelagius in asserting that human beings had the autonomy to discern good from evil in their own behaviour. According to these rabbis, human beings could do so with respect to God as well.

Why did the rabbis differ from their Christian counterparts here? Why did they develop the notion that human beings could argue with God when no such idea was entertained by any major or minor premodern Christian thinker?[56]

The simplest answer, and the one most relevant to our concerns, is that the rabbis tended to have a more robust conception of metaphysical human autonomy than Christians did, and therefore, in rabbinic thinking, that autonomy could be turned against God himself. There are other reasons to explain why the protest motif appeared in Rabbinic Judaism but not in pre-modern Christianity. The different historical contexts in which these two religions evolved may have played a role. Rabbinic Judaism developed at a time when Jews had lost their Temple and homeland and were in a state of exile. One also has to keep in mind that by the time the rabbis appeared, Jews had already experienced centuries of subjugation to other nations. Between the eighth century BCE and the Roman period that began in the first century BCE, Jews were threatened or overrun by one empire after another. The Temple had been destroyed and the Jews exiled once before in the sixth century BCE. So against this background, it is perhaps no surprise that the rabbis would express anger at God and object to his actions. They certainly expressed great reverence for God throughout their literature, but their frustration with God's actions – or lack thereof – seems to have boiled over at times, and that is why we see passages in rabbinic literature in which they protest against him. In contrast, Christians began to achieve political success early on in their history. Once Christianity became the official religion of the Roman Empire in the fourth century, Christians would be the conquerors rather than those conquered, and since that time Christians have had considerable political power in one form or another. So there was much less reason for Christians to develop a literature of protest against God than there was for Jews.

Another important factor that helps account for the difference between Jews and Christians on the theme of protesting against God is the content of their respective Scriptures and how these were interpreted. Jews read only the Hebrew Bible, not the New Testament, and as already noted, in the Hebrew Bible, there are a number of instances in which biblical characters argue with God. In fact, two of the most important characters in the Hebrew Bible, Abraham and Moses, engage in such protests. When God decides to destroy the wicked cities of Sodom and Gomorrah, Abraham demands that God be merciful and not carry out his decree, and he manages to strike a bargain with God that the cities will be spared if they have ten righteous inhabitants. As it turns out, the cities fail to meet this condition, and so they are destroyed. Still, God was willing to listen and responded to Abraham's arguments without any irritation. The example of Moses is even more radical. He protests against God after the incident of the golden calf when God declares his intention to annihilate the Israelites on account of their sins, and God not only listens to Moses's arguments without getting annoyed, but actually changes his mind; the Israelites are spared. And there are a number of other examples of prophets challenging God in the Hebrew Bible.[57]

In light of these sources, the rabbinic stories that depict human beings arguing with God and even winning on occasion are not that revolutionary – at least not within the Jewish tradition. The rabbis were drawing on a long-standing biblical motif. Christians, of course, read the same Bible, but they focused far more on the New Testament than the Old, and therefore the stories in which such figures as Abraham and Moses protest against God perhaps did not make as much of an impression on them. We also have to keep in mind that the key figure in the New Testament – and in Christianity in general – experienced persecution and suffering but made a point of reacting with passivity. Jesus not only does not protest against God for his ill treatment at the hands of the Jews and Romans, he begs his disciples not to intervene even when he is arrested and slated for execution. Jesus makes it clear that his death is part of a divine plan.[58] So it makes sense that Christians would not take up the theme of protest against God from the Old Testament, even when they experienced persecution. The behaviour of Jesus, not that of Abraham or Moses, provided the role model for Christians to follow, and that required them to have faith and trust in God's plan, whatever fate he meted out to them.[59]

Still, none of these considerations nullifies our initial and most important observation regarding the protest motif. This theme in rabbinic literature underscores basic differences between Rabbinic Judaism and pre-modern Christianity regarding human autonomy in relation to God. It indicates that some rabbis were willing to entertain conceptions on this issue that were more radical than anything we find in pre-modern Christianity.

SEMI-PELAGIAN ELEMENTS IN EARLY RABBINIC JUDAISM

Yet, many early rabbinic sources go in a very different direction from those we have just looked at. These sources suggest that the distinction between rabbinic and Christian thinking on the role of human autonomy in earning salvation is not as sharp as modern Jewish interpreters would like to believe. Some rabbis took positions that were closer to the viewpoint of the Semi-Pelagians than to that of the Pelagians, a position that was therefore very much in line with mainstream elements of Christianity. For these rabbis, human beings had the capacity to choose between good and evil but were incapable of overcoming their evil instincts entirely on their own, and they were therefore unable to achieve divine reward without at least some divine assistance.[60]

For instance, a number of sources in rabbinic literature suggest that human beings are *not* perfectible; even the most righteous people sin at least once in a while.[61] Therefore, God, as a rule, has to exercise some degree of mercy in judging people. Otherwise, no one would ever be worthy of reward.[62] Some rabbis who take this viewpoint presume there is an unpredictable quality to God's mercy. God's wrath can alternate with his kindness, and it is not always certain which side of God one will experience.[63]

Some rabbis put the need for divine mercy in cosmic terms by surmising that God had to create the world with his attribute of mercy because had he done so with his attribute of strict justice, the world could not exist; it would be worthy of destruction. Here divine mercy is seen as a kind of metaphysical force that is woven into the very fabric of existence so that human beings, fallible creatures that they are, can survive in God's presence despite their sins.[64]

Therefore, some rabbis adopted views akin to the Semi-Pelagian notion of grace in presuming the need for human beings to have God's assistance in earning reward. The popular assertion that the rabbis consistently saw human beings as fully in control of their actions and the consequences they brought, is thus inaccurate. Some rabbis took this view, but others did not.

EARLY RABBINIC JUDAISM: CONCLUSIONS

To sum up what we have discovered so far, both early Rabbinic Judaism and pre-modern Christianity had a spectrum of views on how much freedom human beings have in earning divine reward, but the rabbis tended to be more willing than Christian theologians to accentuate that freedom. The spectrum of views in Christianity regarding this issue was defined by two poles. On one pole was a highly restrictive view of human freedom represented by Augustine and his followers. These thinkers effectively denied that human beings had autonomy in making the most important choices about their actions and in earning divine reward. The viewpoint that defined the other pole was that of the Semi-Pelagians, according to whom human beings had to have *some* degree of freedom in earning divine reward, even though they still needed God's grace to help them do so.

Opinions in early Rabbinic Judaism on this matter were also defined by two poles but on a spectrum that shifted more towards human freedom. On the restrictive end of the spectrum were rabbis who espoused views similar to those of the Semi-Pelagians: human beings had the freedom to earn divine reward but required some assistance from God. On the other end of the spectrum were rabbis who upheld views close to those of the Pelagians that existed in early Christianity but were absent in medieval and early modern Christianity and dictated that human beings had full autonomy to earn divine reward. We also saw that some rabbinic sources went even further by depicting scenarios in which human beings judged God for his faults and God actually listened. Here the tables were turned: instead of God taking human beings to task for wrongdoing, it was human beings who were doing so with God.

Thus, if we place the opinions of the early rabbis and pre-modern Christian theologians on a single spectrum ranging from those that restricted human autonomy in relation to God to those that allowed for full autonomy, the picture that emerges here is that there was much overlap between the opinions of the two groups in the middle of the spectrum. There were rabbis and Christian theologians who supported the position that human beings were able to initiate a relationship with God but were not sufficiently virtuous to merit salvation without his help. However, differences between the groups emerge when we consider the extreme ends of the spectrum. Christians were willing to entertain views on the end of the spectrum restricting autonomy that Jews were not, while, conversely, Jews were willing to take positions on the opposite end of the spectrum granting autonomy that Christians were not.

Sin, Grace, and Salvation in Medieval and Early Modern Judaism

As stated earlier in this chapter, I intended to focus the bulk of my discussion about sin, grace, and salvation on early Rabbinic Judaism because its texts and world view were the basis of Jewish life in the medieval and early modern periods and therefore its views on metaphysical human autonomy carried over to the Jewish community in these periods as well. However, there were new developments in Judaism regarding such matters in these later periods that are relevant to our discussion.

But first, some remarks about medieval Judaism in general are in order. By the year 1000, rabbinic literature had become the basis of Jewish life both in Christian Europe and in Islamic lands. Rabbinic discussions of the 613 commandments were becoming solidified as a system of law, and Jewish communities in the Christian and Muslim worlds were governed by it. Its regulations encompassed every aspect of Jewish life – ritual and ethical, communal and individual, religious and mundane.

Rabbinic literature in the medieval period focused largely on the legal dimension of Judaism because that was the anchor of Jewish life; however, medieval Jews also developed a literature concerned with the theological dimension of Judaism. Entire schools came into being in the medieval Jewish world devoted to this aspect of Judaism. Some of these schools were devoted to rational philosophy that applied reason and systematic arguments to determine Judaism's beliefs. Others were more mystical in orientation and fell under the rubric of Kabbalah, a term that means "tradition."

It is fair to say that for the most part, rabbinic views in the medieval and early modern periods on sin, grace, and salvation were continuous with those expressed by the rabbis of earlier centuries. However, some Jewish thinkers began espousing opinions on such matters that were more Christian in character than those of the early rabbis, and one suspects that some of these thinkers were influenced directly by Christianity.

One group of medieval Jewish figures who adopted views of this kind consisted of pietists who appeared in Jewish communities in Germany from the thirteenth to the fifteenth centuries (*Hasidei Ashkenaz*). These pietists were deeply concerned about the power of the evil inclination to dominate human thinking and behaviour, and they were thus highly focused on how to avoid falling prey to its influences. They also dwelled a great deal on repentance and how to make amends with God when the evil inclination got the upper hand, and they designed practices for this purpose that could be quite severe.[65]

It is possible that the strong focus of these pietists on sin and repentance was a natural outgrowth of Rabbinic Judaism. A fundamental principle of early Rabbinic Judaism was that Jews were in exile because of their sins, and one can imagine that as the centuries went by and the messiah had not come, some Jews focused on sin and repentance to the point of obsession. But the obvious question is whether the pietists were at all influenced by their Christian environment. As we have noted, medieval Catholic Christianity spent much energy contemplating the problem of sin and developing penance rituals to deal with it, some of which were exceedingly harsh. Monastic communities were also widespread in Europe, including Germany and France, and the monastics were especially concerned about these matters. So it is quite possible that the Jewish pietists in medieval Germany unwittingly absorbed elements of Christianity from their environment.[66]

However, for our purposes, there is no need for us to determine whether or not Christianity had an influence here. At the very least, we have an example of how some Jews in the medieval period took on positions regarding sin, grace, and salvation that were closer to those of Christianity than the earlier rabbis did.

Perhaps the best examples in medieval and early modern Judaism that point to Christian influence regarding sin, grace, and salvation involve the doctrine of Original Sin. Scholars have pointed out that this concept found its way into the writings of a number of Jewish thinkers and schools in the medieval and early modern periods. It crops up among Jewish thinkers who were broadly rabbinic in orientation.[67] It is also found in the schools of Jewish philosophy and Kabbalah that arose in these centuries.[68]

The Kabbalists seem to have taken particular interest in ideas that were resonant with the doctrine of Original Sin, and that was especially true of the school of R. Isaac Luria in sixteenth-century Palestine. According to this school, Adam's sin had allowed the evil inclination to dominate human beings in subsequent generations, and all of human history was to be understood as a series of attempts to overcome its influence. Only in the messianic era would the evil inclination be defeated. As a consequence, the issue of sin and repentance received a great deal of attention in Lurianic Kabbalah, much as it did in medieval German pietism. Here too, one wonders if this emphasis was due to Christian influences.[69]

Yet none of these medieval developments signalled a major change from the views of early Rabbinic Judaism with regard to human autonomy. The influence of German Pietism on medieval Jews was confined largely to defined circles of followers in a particular geographic region, and only for a couple of centuries. Moreover, its views on sin seem to have had no lasting impact on Judaism. Similar observations can be made about the rabbinic thinkers and medieval Jewish philosophers who supported ideas akin to the notion of Original Sin. These figures were isolated individuals. On top of that, those who engaged in philosophy took an approach to Judaism that was highly esoteric. The impact of these thinkers regarding sin was therefore negligible.

Matters were different with respect to Kabbalah. By the seventeenth century, Lurianic Kabbalah had spread far and wide in the Jewish world, it dominated Jewish theology, and it would continue to do so until the modern period. Moreover, by this point in history, Kabbalah was being studied by significant numbers of Jews. So Kabbalah's adoption of ideas that were resonant with the doctrine of Original Sin cannot be dismissed as inconsequential.

That said, Kabbalah was not at odds with early Rabbinic Judaism regarding the scope of metaphysical human autonomy. Even if Kabbalah incorporated ideas about Original Sin, it granted powers to human beings in their relationship with God that were far greater than in any other school of Judaism.

To explain how that was the case, a few remarks about Kabbalah are in order. The foundation of Kabbalah was the notion that God had ten attributes, called *sefirot*, that explained everything that human beings could know about God. There was a standard list of names for these attributes: crown, wisdom, understanding, lovingkindness, judgment, beauty, eternity, glory, foundation, and divine presence. These attributes were more than just character traits. They were semi-independent entities, and each was a world in its own right. For this reason, the Kabbalists spent much energy exploring the many facets of each attribute.

According to the Kabbalists, God's ten attributes were supposed to function in perfect harmony with each other. However, they did not: since the creation of the world, they had been out of sync with each other. God was still master of his universe, but he could not govern as well as he was supposed to because his attributes were not working together in perfect coordination.

This problem explained why the world was such a troubled place. All evil in the world could be traced to the fact that God's attributes were out of harmony with each other. If God lacked inner harmony, then the world had the very same problem.

Kabbalists gave a number of explanations for the disarray within God's being. A common theory was that the problem started with Adam and Eve in the Garden of Eden. Their rebellion threw God's attributes out of kilter, and they have remained that way ever since. As we have already noted, this notion became central to Lurianic Kabbalah, a school that developed in Palestine in the sixteenth century and soon dominated Kabbalah.

But the Kabbalists claimed to have a solution to the chaos that Adam's sin had caused. God's attributes could be brought back into line with each other if Jews observed the 613 commandments – or at least, as many of them as were still applicable after the destruction of the Second Temple. Each time a Jew fulfilled a commandment, they had a direct influence on God's attributes and created greater harmony among them. And if Jews were consistent enough in performing the commandments, the cumulative effect over time would result in God being in perfect harmony with himself once again. Once that state of affairs was achieved, the world would also experience messianic redemption. The well-being of the world depended on God's well-being, and so the world would be redeemed once God's attributes were functioning properly. Sin had precisely the opposite effect. If Jews violated the commandments, they would further damage God by reinforcing the lack of harmony among his attributes, and that would also delay the messianic redemption.

The Kabbalists thus understood the relationship that human beings had with God in a highly original manner. God was a deity who effectively had been "broken" by human beings but who could be "fixed" or "repaired" by them as well. In fact, the process of bringing God's attributes into harmony with each other through the performance of the commandments was known as *tikkun*, which literally means "repair."[70]

What becomes clear in Kabbalistic theology is that while human beings may have lost some of their autonomy because of Adam's sin, that loss was more than compensated for by the immense power they were given to correct that sin. By obeying God's commandments, human beings not only saved themselves from its effects, they also saved God from its effects as well. Thus, according to this scheme, not only did God save human beings, human beings also saved God!

In Kabbalah, then, we have the most radical conception of human autonomy that we have encountered in Judaism thus far. Moreover, Kabbalah widens the gap between Judaism and Christianity on the question of human autonomy perhaps more than any other dimension of Judaism before modernity. The idea that human beings had an obligation to repair God would have seemed ridiculous for mainstream Christians in the medieval and early modern periods. In Christianity, human beings were viewed as corrupt creatures who could not fix themselves, let alone God.

Of course in Christianity, God, in effect, had been "broken" when Jesus was crucified. However, there is no real analogy here with Kabbalah. Jesus's death on the cross was a one-time event, and after it, Jesus was resurrected. So even if God was "broken" here in some sense, that state of affairs was not an ongoing one, as it was in Kabbalah. Furthermore, Jesus's death was considered a victory for humanity because it atoned for all human sin, whereas in Kabbalah, God's brokenness was viewed negatively because it was the source of evil in the world. It was a problem that needed to be corrected.

Our understanding of the contrast between Christians and Jews here can perhaps be enriched by placing it once again in historical context. Jews throughout the medieval and early modern periods believed that they were God's chosen people, but their situation did not seem terribly consistent with that conviction. The Kabbalistic notion of *tikkun* should perhaps be understood against this background. That suggestion was made by Gershom Scholem, the greatest academic scholar of Kabbalah since the inception of the field. According to Scholem, what the doctrine of *tikkun* did for Jews was make them feel immensely powerful. If they did not have power in the political arena, then they had it in the metaphysical realm, which, from their perspective, was far more important. Jews, far from being weak and insignificant, were in fact gradually repairing God's being through their performance of the commandments and, indirectly, repairing the world as well. In other words, Jews were still God's chosen; it is just that their chosenness was not evident in the visible realm.[71] Christians, by contrast, did not have any incentive to think in such terms about human action. Christians were *already* powerful in the visible realm, and so they did not have to view themselves as having special powers to fix God in the metaphysical realm, nor did they have to think of God as needing to be fixed in the first place. He was already doing a splendid job running the world. The success of Christianity was evidence of that.

It would seem that our discussion of Kabbalah has taken us beyond Rabbinic Judaism, but that is not entirely true. The Kabbalistic notion of *tikkun* was likely inspired in part by Rabbinic Judaism. There are a handful of sources in rabbinic literature in which the rabbis depict God as being empowered or weakened by the actions of human beings. These sources inform us that when the Jews obey God's commandments, they give God strength, and when they sin, they take his strength away.[72] The Kabbalists, in formulating the concept of *tikkun*, were therefore beholden to some extent to their rabbinic predecessors.

In sum, Kabbalah was the only major school of thought in medieval and early modern Judaism that may have been significantly influenced by Christian thinking on Original Sin. However, as we have seen, not only did this idea fail to compromise human autonomy in Kabbalah, the Kabbalists granted human beings a degree of autonomy that was far greater than in any other school of Judaism and that Christians would have considered shocking.

Conclusions

The conclusions that were drawn earlier about Rabbinic Judaism in its formative period carry over into the medieval and early modern periods. Again, if one places the views of pre-modern Christian and Jewish thinkers regarding the freedom of human beings to earn divine reward on a single spectrum, there was a good deal of overlap in the middle of the spectrum where human beings had *some* autonomy in this regard but not *complete* autonomy. However, large sectors of the Christian tradition placed strict limits on human autonomy in earning divine reward that were unthinkable in Judaism, while large sectors of the Jewish tradition allowed a degree of human autonomy in earning divine reward that were unthinkable in Christianity.

A key factor that helps explain the different ranges of views that Christian and rabbinic thinkers were willing to entertain here is that it was difficult for Christians to grant the kind of full autonomy to human beings that Jews did because of the role that Jesus played in Christianity. It was a fundamental Christian belief that Jesus's death atoned for the sins of humanity, and this belief assumed that human beings could not atone for their sins on their own. Therefore, the most that Christian thinkers could offer regarding human autonomy in relation to God was partial autonomy of the kind the Semi-Pelagians espoused. Human beings could make the effort to achieve salvation but could not succeed without the assistance of Jesus. And some of the most important Christian theologians, as we have seen, were not willing to grant human beings even that much.[73] However, the rabbis did not believe in an intermediary between God and human beings for the purpose of atonement, and they could therefore give individuals greater autonomy in earning reward from God. Some rabbis preferred to give human beings only partial autonomy in the way the Semi-Pelagians did, but many of the rabbis saw human beings as fully autonomous in the sense that no help from God was needed for individuals to perfect themselves and win God's favour.

There is an irony in the conclusions that have come out of this chapter. A popular belief among contemporary Christians – particularly conservative Protestants – is that Judaism is a harsh and strict religion, whereas Christianity is a religion characterized by gentleness and love. According to this view, the Old Testament set a severe tone for Judaism in that God demanded obedience to his commandments and threatened punishment if any one of them was violated. Also, given how many commandments there were, human beings could only fail to be righteous and achieve salvation. In the New Testament, however, a new era began in which God no longer required the observance of so many commandments and forgave people for their sins, and anyone could achieve salvation merely by asking for God's grace. In the new era, God took on a more loving and merciful persona. This way of thinking about Judaism and Christianity is implied throughout the history of Christian thought from Paul onwards, but it became especially fashionable during the period of the Enlightenment, and since then has made its way into popular Christianity.[74]

But it turns out that from everything we have seen in this chapter, this characterization of the differences between Judaism and Christianity is inaccurate. We have observed that Christians were often willing to entertain conceptions of God that were far harsher than anything one finds in Rabbinic Judaism and that Rabbinic Judaism often conceived of God as more merciful and forgiving than many Christians did. Moreover, according to the strand in Rabbinic Judaism that supported the protest motif, the gulf between the all-powerful God and his human subjects was far narrower than anything we find in Christianity.

What does all this have to do with the success of Jews in the modern West? As we have noted, the West revived the Pelagian view regarding human autonomy in relation to God during the Enlightenment after centuries of it being dormant. That view increasingly dominated Western thinking after the Enlightenment, and it was a critical ingredient in encouraging Westerners to master the world around them by inspiring them to believe that human beings were dignified, powerful, and independent creatures. Yet what our discussion in this chapter has shown is that a viewpoint akin to that position was well-represented in Rabbinic Judaism many centuries before the Enlightenment. In fact, it was represented in the earliest texts of rabbinic literature. It was not the sole view in that literature. Analogues to the Semi-Pelagian position were espoused by some rabbis. Nonetheless, a position akin to Pelagianism was common in their writings.

Most significant is that Jews did not have to overcome anything resembling the Augustinian position in the way that Westerners did. That position, according to which human autonomy in relation to God was either severely restricted or non-existent, cast a shadow over all discussion in pre-modern Christianity about the relationship that human beings had with God. Judaism had thinkers who espoused elements of that position, but their influence on Jewish thinking was not nearly as great as that of the Augustinian tradition in pre-modern Christianity. So when Jews joined European society in the nineteenth century, they were in some respects better prepared for the new way of thinking about human autonomy than their non-Jewish neighbours were, and thus, to some extent, better prepared to achieve success as well.

Another way to look at it is that modern Jews could easily adapt to the modern approach to human autonomy because Westerners, in reviving Pelagianism, had unwittingly adopted a position regarding this issue that was in fact similar to one found in Rabbinic Judaism. Tatha Wiley, in her study of the idea of Original Sin in Western thought, points us in the direction of this insight. She argues, as others do, that Immanuel Kant, more than any other figure in the Enlightenment, was responsible for convincing Europe's intellectuals to adopt the Pelagian view that human beings had freedom in making moral choices. But Wiley also notes that Kant's views here were, in one significant respect, more resonant with Judaism than with Christianity. As she puts it, Kant had a theory of human nature that was "more akin to the ancient Jewish conception of two interrelated orientations co-existing in human persons – yetser ha-tov, the inclination to do good, and yetser ha-ra, the inclination to do evil – than that of Augustine and Luther."[75]

Of course, Kant himself would never have put matters in these terms. He was no fan of Judaism and criticized it on a number of grounds.[76] Nonetheless, Wiley's observation is valid. Kant, without realizing it, had more of an affinity with Rabbinic Judaism than with Christianity in his belief that human beings were not burdened by Original Sin and were therefore free to choose between right and wrong. Once we recognize this point, we can better understand why Jews were able to adapt so well to modern Western society and achieve in it as much they did. Rabbinic Judaism had long anticipated a feature of modern Western culture that was key to its success.

A difficulty with my analysis here is that the differences between Rabbinic Judaism and Christianity that I have explored here were differences between elite intellectuals in the medieval and early modern periods, not necessarily between ordinary individuals who made up the vast majority of the Jewish and Christian populations. We have few written records from these centuries that can tell us what views the lay sectors of the populations in the two communities held about metaphysical autonomy, but it is likely that the vast majority of their constituents would not have been familiar with the intricate and arcane discussions of the intellectuals on the matters that have been discussed in this chapter. The argument could thus be made that what has been explored here tells us little about the mindset of lay Jews in the medieval and early modern periods regarding metaphysical autonomy, and it thus tells us little about why most Jews became disproportionately successful when the modern period began.

However, I believe that the views of Jewish and Christian intellectuals that we have analysed must have had an impact of some kind on lay people in their respective communities, particularly from the late medieval period onwards. Ordinary Jews and Christians from this point in history forward may not have been familiar with the esoteric discussions of sin, grace, and salvation that intellectuals were conducting, but many of them must have been aware of the major lines of thinking about such matters. By the twelfth century, both Jewish and Christian societies in Europe had become quite religious. Jews had established communities in Europe that were guided by rabbis and Jewish law, Christians had become more interested in religious piety than in previous centuries, and both societies would be suffused with religion up to the modern period. Furthermore, the issue of divine reward and punishment was too fundamental in both religions for lay people in these centuries to have had no cognizance of the basic approaches that their respective religions took towards this issue. Ordinary Jews and Christians were engaged enough in the reciting of liturgy and the performance of rituals involving the expiation of sin to have had a sense of the nature of the relationship that they had with God as determined by the intellectuals in their respective religions. For Jews, the most significant holidays on the calendar, Rosh Hashanah and Yom Kippur, were centred on that theme. In Christianity the same theme was even more central, as exemplified by the Eucharist, and in Protestantism, in particular, the catechisms required lay people to recite doctrinal formulas that highlighted this theme. The awareness that lay Jews and Christians had about the nature of divine reward and punishment in their respective religions would have also been strengthened by the preaching of clerics in churches and synagogues, who frequently focused on this issue.

On the Jewish side, there is also reason to believe that the basic doctrines of Kabbalah were known to a good number of lay Jews from the seventeenth century onwards. At this time, Kabbalah was no longer confined to esoteric circles; its ideas were being widely disseminated in Jewish communities throughout the world.[77] That meant that the radical notion of human autonomy assumed in Kabbalah would have been widely known among Jews as well.

Ordinary Jews and Christians must have therefore absorbed the approaches of their respective religions towards sin, grace, and salvation, even if they could not have had an articulate discussion about them of the kind that the intellectuals had. So it is quite plausible that lay Jews and Christians came to the modern period imbued with the different approaches to metaphysical autonomy that have been described in this chapter.

Our discussion of this issue is not yet complete. In this chapter, we have covered only the first of three topics that concern the issue of metaphysical autonomy. In the next chapter, we will take up the second of these topics, which is concerned with religious authority.

Chapter Four

Human Autonomy II: Religious Authority

The topic we will now look at regarding the issue of human autonomy in the metaphysical sense is religious authority. I am referring here to the area of religion that deals with how religious communities make decisions about their beliefs and practices, and its main concerns are identifying who is qualified to make such decisions and determining the manner in which they make them. How Christian and Jewish thinkers prior to the modern period handled these questions had obvious implications for their views on metaphysical human autonomy because they involved how much freedom religious authorities possessed in interpreting God's word. Did these authorities approach Scripture with the presumption that their interpretations had to be in perfect agreement with God's will? Or did they presume that their interpretations allowed some room for human originality and creativity? What we will discover is that by the time the modern period began, Judaism had developed a much stronger tendency than Christianity to grant religious authorities autonomy in the interpretation of God's word.

I. Christian Perspectives

The Medieval Period

In medieval Christianity in Europe, religious authority was relatively well-organized. The Catholic Church established a hierarchy of clergy early on to guide its followers on all matters concerning religion. At the top of the hierarchy was the pope. Below him were the bishops, who had authority over specific regions in Europe, and below the bishops were the priests who had authority over the communities in which they resided.

The popes and the bishops were the ones who made the fundamental decisions about Christian belief and practice. These decisions were determined largely through the interpretation of Scripture and tradition. "Tradition" here referred to teachings not contained in Scripture that were believed to have been passed down from Jesus's Apostles and the Church Fathers to subsequent generations.

The priests mainly had ritual functions. They performed the sacraments, rituals that were central to the Christian religious life and were believed to attract God's grace. These included baptism, the Eucharist, and marriage.

The medieval Catholic Church justified the authority of their clergy with the concept of "apostolic succession," which was the notion that this authority could be traced back to Jesus's Apostle Peter. According to this concept, Jesus identified Peter as the founder and head of God's Church and the first bishop of Rome, and he then passed his authority on to subsequent bishops of Rome, thereby generating a line of successors.[1] The bishop of Rome soon became known as the pope, and he ordained other bishops to serve under him. These bishops in turn ordained priests, who led congregations throughout Europe. In this way, the popes, bishops, and priests all shared in the authority conferred by apostolic succession.[2]

What is clear from this bare-bones description of the medieval Church hierarchy is that even though the Church tended to have a negative view of human beings when speaking about sin, grace, and salvation, it viewed its religious authorities in a somewhat more positive light, and that is because it had to. The clergy throughout the Church hierarchy had to be seen as sufficiently empowered by God in order to lead the Christian faithful.

The Reformation

The Reformation brought with it enormous change on the question of religious authority. One of the major features of Luther's revolution was that it denied the validity of the entire system of authority on which the Catholic Church had been based. Luther argued that the popes, bishops, and priests in the Church hierarchy were no nearer to God than other Christians and therefore had no special advantage in determining Christian belief and practice, performing sacraments, or leading people to salvation. All human beings were born equally sinful, which meant that one was granted salvation by God only through having faith in his saving power. This idea was encapsulated in the phrase the "priesthood of all believers," which implied that all believers were their own priests. Luther concluded from this that the offices of the Church hierarchy were of no use and should be abolished. Congregations could have leaders, but these "ministers," as they were eventually called, were to be chosen by the congregations, not appointed by Rome, and they could only guide human beings to receive grace and achieve salvation; they could not bring these about by the performance of sacraments.[3]

This new orientation towards religious authority inspired the Protestant denominations to adopt models of Church governance that gave lay people a much greater say in how Christianity should be understood and practised. Calvin instituted a "presbyterian" model that became standard in the Reformed Church. A congregation elected presbyters, or elders, who in turn were given the authority to send representatives to assemblies that had authority over a number of congregations. In this scheme, authority flowed in two directions. The higher assemblies of presbyters had authority over the congregations on matters of belief and practice, but congregations selected their presbyters, and they could also send agenda items up the hierarchy of assemblies to be considered for adoption as official Church teaching.[4]

The "congregational" model in Protestantism went even further in empowering lay people. According to this scheme, which was adopted by the radical Reformers and the Baptists, individual congregations functioned independently of each other without any of them having to answer to higher assemblies. The belief was that each congregation was guided directly by the Holy Spirit. Congregations could therefore appoint ministers and elders for guidance, but the status of these figures was not intrinsically higher than that of the other members of the congregation.[5]

However, some Protestant denominations retained a hierarchical model similar to that of the Catholic Church. The "episcopal" model, as this form of governance was known, was adopted by the Anglican Church. Individual congregations had priests, above them were bishops, above the bishops was the Archbishop of Canterbury, and presiding over this whole structure was the British monarch.[6]

Exaggerations have often crept into discussions of the Reformation regarding these developments. On account of the innovations just described, the Reformation is frequently credited with giving birth to the modern notion of the individual and the belief in freedom of religious conscience. The argument is that it spawned these ideas by removing religious authority from the hierarchy of officials in the Catholic Church and granting it to each and every Christian who forged a direct and unmediated relationship with God through faith. The truth is more complicated and not quite as dramatic. First, Luther's notion of the individual was paradoxical. For even though Luther's idea of justification through faith implied the importance of the individual in their relationship with God, one has to keep in mind that he simultaneously held, as Augustine did, that the individual was helpless before God in achieving salvation and that it was achievable only through divine grace, a view that gave the individual little independence.[7]

More important for our purposes is that Protestant denominations still had formal authority figures who determined religious beliefs and practices; otherwise, the denominations would have descended into chaos. Most followed Luther's suggestion that authorities be appointed by lay people, and they did so according to a variety of schemes, but each of the denominations was guided by religious leaders who implemented beliefs and practices that all their constituents were expected to uphold. We are therefore still at some distance from the notion that human beings should be free to make their own choices regarding religion. Protestantism may have removed religious authority from the hierarchy of officials in the Catholic Church, but it did not grant it to each and every Christian.

The limitations placed by the Protestant denominations on individual freedom were also evident in the fact that they could be quite dogmatic and that they often persecuted, sometimes ruthlessly, those who did not agree with their respective viewpoints. The Protestant Churches were intolerant not just of Catholics but of each other as well.[8]

Nonetheless, Protestantism did take an important step towards strengthening human autonomy in religious matters by developing a somewhat more individualistic approach to religion than Catholic Christianity had. Calvinism, in particular, developed the notion of the priesthood of all believers and salvation through faith by placing great emphasis on the individual's private and personal relationship with God. That emphasis was accentuated in the Puritan branch of Calvinism that had so much influence in the US. It was also accentuated in Pietism, a movement that arose in Germany. In these strains of Protestantism, everyone was expected to explore their inner religious life through intense self-reflection and self-examination.[9] Moreover, Protestantism implicitly strengthened the notion of metaphysical human autonomy simply by breaking the monopoly of the Catholic Church on Christianity in Europe. With the rise of so many different versions of Christianity, Europeans began to slowly accept the possibility that there was no single Christian truth to which everyone should adhere.

The Enlightenment

When we come to the heart of the Enlightenment, two hundred years after the beginning of the Reformation, the ideas latent in the Reformation regarding religious authority began to take a more radical shape. Luther's idea of the "priesthood of all believers" developed into the notion that religion was indeed a matter of individual choice and the right to that choice had to be legally protected. Each person was to decide for themselves what kind of religious life they should live. Those adhering to this position initially spoke of tolerance only within Christianity. That is, Christians had a right to choose what kind of Christians they would be, but that did not mean that non-Christians were to be tolerated. Yet some also began to speak of granting non-Christians the same right; they too should be allowed to practise the religion of their choice, even if they were living in error. Luther would not have been happy to see that the notion of the priesthood of all believers had developed in this manner. He never intended it to be a principle for justifying tolerance. But this would not be the first time in history that an idea had unintended consequences.

Much of the impetus for these developments came from external events. Europe in the sixteenth and seventeenth centuries witnessed a series of devastating wars both between states and within states that were partly driven by divisions between Catholics and Protestants, and millions died in these wars. The most important of these wars were the civil wars in France (1562–98), the Thirty Years' War (1618–48) that involved most countries in Europe, and the Puritan revolution in England (1642–8). With the signing of the Treaty of Westphalia that put an end to the Thirty Years' War, Europeans began making a concerted attempt to neutralize the threat that religious divisions posed to the peace and welfare of the entire continent. The treaty was meant to defuse religious conflict by specifying that monarchs would choose the form of Christianity to be recognized in their respective states and that people whose religion differed from that of the state could seek asylum in another state that upheld their version of Christianity. The belief thus began to grow that the only way for Europeans to move forward was by tolerating different forms of Christianity.[10]

We will have much more to say about these important developments in a later chapter, but for now what is important to recognize is that by the time of the Enlightenment, Europeans had begun to conceive of human beings as having autonomy before God not only by rejecting the concepts of Original Sin and Predestination but by strengthening the notion of autonomy in a more positive way. They transformed the individualism implied in Protestant theology into the idea that God allowed each person to decide what kind of religious life they wanted to live.

The emphasis on the individual as the sole source of religious authority would become one of the hallmarks of modernity. As the modern period evolved, Westerners became increasingly committed to the idea that when it came to matters of religion, the only authority over the individual should be the individual themselves. It was up to each and every person to decide which religion they would adhere to, or whether they would adhere to any religion at all.

II.   Jewish Perspectives

Early Rabbinic Judaism

In turning now to rabbinic views on religious authority, we will begin by noting that the way this matter was treated by the early rabbis bears some resemblance to that of pre-modern Christianity in both its Catholic and Protestant forms. The rabbis grounded their authority, as both these forms of Christianity did, in the idea that God's will was expressed in Scripture, that it was supplemented by traditions that helped explain his will, and that both had to be interpreted by qualified individuals. As for the manner in which those qualified individuals were chosen, the rabbis were perhaps closer to Catholicism than to Protestantism in that the rabbis, like the Catholic clergy, formed a distinct class of individuals who passed their authority on directly to the next generation of successors. Here the chain of authority extended all the way back in time as apostolic succession did, but it originated with Moses, whom the rabbis viewed as the first rabbi. However, the rabbis conceived of their actual function in ways that in some respects were closer to Protestantism. The rabbis, like the Protestant clergy, did not see themselves as intermediaries between God and ordinary Jews, at least not as a rule, nor did they have the exclusive right to perform ritual functions.

Much more can be said about the similarities and differences between rabbinic and Christian views on these matters, but what is important for our purposes is to compare the views of Rabbinic Judaism and Christianity on how authority should be exercised. What were the limits of authority in both religions? How creative and original could authority figures in the two religions be in interpreting Scripture before running the risk of overstepping their bounds?

THE NATURE OF THE ORAL TORAH

In order to answer these questions, we first have to say more about the rabbinic concept of the Oral Torah. There was a good deal of ambiguity regarding this concept in the first few centuries of Rabbinic Judaism. At times, the rabbis appeared to view the Oral Torah as a body of traditions that had been given to Moses on Mount Sinai and was passed down orally from one generation to the next, and its purpose was to supplement and fill in details regarding the 613 commandments in the Written Torah. From this perspective, the rabbis saw themselves as nothing more than passive recipients of these oral traditions who were charged with guarding them and communicating them to their followers. Yet at other times, the rabbis seemed to view themselves as active *creators* of these traditions. The Oral Torah was a body of wisdom that the rabbis could expand upon by interpreting the Written Torah with their own creative and original insights. According to this second perspective, God was willing to share his authority with human beings, and the rabbis were the ones designated as his partners in this regard. There may also have been different schools of thought on this issue: some rabbis may have taken the first approach, while others took the second. The difficulty is that it is often hard to tell in any given rabbinic passage which paradigm of the Oral Torah its author had in mind – or if they had any paradigm in mind at all – because the rabbis did not usually explain the theory behind their particular interpretations; they simply presented them in succinct and straightforward fashion.[11]

It should be obvious why this ambiguity is critical for our concerns. The rabbis who saw themselves only as recipients of the Oral Torah did not regard themselves as exercising autonomy in the interpretation of God's word; they were merely acting as conduits for traditions that had been passed down to them. But the rabbis who saw themselves as *creating* the Oral Torah in some manner did regard themselves as having autonomy in interpreting God's word, and it was an autonomy of a rather impressive kind. These rabbis believed that they could determine God's truth.

An example will illustrate the ambiguity. The famous rule of "an eye for an eye" appears in a number of places in the Torah that deal with the punishment meted out to someone who has physically injured another individual.[12] According to the literal meaning of the rule, an individual who has committed such a crime is to be punished by having the same injury inflicted on them that they inflicted on their victim.

Yet the rabbis who edited the Talmud did something interesting with this rule. They rejected its literal meaning and came to the conclusion that what the Torah actually meant when it spoke of "an eye for an eye" was that if a person injures someone else, that person will pay only monetary damages to the victim. That, in fact, is how injuries are handled in our modern-day American court system.

The rabbis based their understanding of "an eye for an eye" on arguments drawn from a number of biblical sources. For instance, R. Ashi cites Deuteronomy 22:29, which informs us that a man who rapes an unmarried woman is to be punished by paying damages to the victim's father and agreeing to marry the woman. According to R. Ashi, this law provides proof that if an individual injures another, the punishment is to pay damages, and he bases his interpretation on the use of the preposition *tahat*, which in this instance means "for" and appears in both cases in the biblical text. That is, in the case of rape, the text says that the man must pay for damages and marry the woman "for" (*tahat*) having afflicted the woman, and in the case of bodily injury, the perpetrator is to be punished according to the principle of an eye "for" (*tahat*) an eye. The fact that the same preposition appears in both passages indicates that in the case of bodily injury, one pays damages just as one does in the case of rape. The notion that one can draw an analogy like this on the basis of the same word appearing in two seemingly unrelated passages is common in rabbinic legal discourse.[13]

Modern readers may, of course, be offended that the monetary compensation is paid to the father, not to the woman herself, and that the rapist is invited to marry his victim, but these are issues we cannot take up here, nor are they relevant to our concerns. The point is that, according to the rabbis who edited the Talmud, we have proof here that bodily injury – in this case, sexual assault – is to be punished by having the perpetrator pay monetary compensation, not by inflicting physical harm on him.

Yet this argument seems forced, for it is predicated on the use of a single word appearing in both the case of rape and bodily injury. Why then did the rabbinic editors of the Talmud read the Bible in such a convoluted way? Why not simply obey the Torah's commandment regarding "an eye for an eye" according to its obvious meaning?

The rabbis do not give us any further insight on these questions because again, they do not usually reflect on the theory behind their interpretations of the biblical text, so we can only speculate, and here we must return to the issue of the Oral Torah and its ambiguity. One possibility is that the rabbis were merely reporting an interpretation they had received from earlier rabbis and was believed to have been originally given to Moses on Mount Sinai as part of the Oral Torah. Therefore the rabbis regarded this interpretation as the true meaning of God's word, regardless of how convoluted it seemed. And if this possibility is correct, then the implication is that the rabbis, at least in this instance, saw themselves as mere recipients of the Oral Torah with no autonomy to shape its meaning.

A second possibility is that the rabbis interpreted "an eye for an eye" in the way they did because they deliberately chose to, and one could well imagine why they might have done so. They may have been repelled by the literal meaning of "an eye for an eye" because it suggested that an act of violence would be punished by another act of violence, and the rabbis may have found that notion morally problematic. (*We* certainly would, and that is why we do not do it in our own courts.) Therefore, the rabbis perhaps read the biblical text in a convoluted manner so that they could rule that the perpetrator would only pay damages. The implication of this possibility is that the rabbis in this instance saw themselves not as mere recipients of the Oral Torah, but as active creators of it. That is, they read their own personal views *into* the biblical text rather than *out of* it. And if that is true, the rabbis here saw themselves as having great autonomy in their role as religious authorities. They could impose their own meaning on God's word in order to align it with their own moral preferences.

There is yet another possibility, which is that the rabbis here were influenced by moral considerations as the second possibility suggests, but that these considerations were subconscious. That is, the rabbis were not fully aware that their moral sensibilities were affecting their understanding of the biblical text. If that was the case, then we are back to where we were with the first possibility with respect to the issue of human autonomy: the rabbis in this instance did not see themselves as creators of the Oral Torah, even if on a subliminal level, they actually were.

Which one of these possibilities is correct? It is impossible to say with certainty. Scholars tend to side with possibilities two or three, and for good reason. It does seem as if the rabbinic editors of the Talmud were affected by moral considerations in their interpretation of "an eye for an eye."[14] But the rabbis do not provide enough information for us to determine which of the two possibilities is correct, and for our concerns, there is a big difference between them. Possibility two suggests that the rabbis were interpreters with a strong sense of their own autonomy as religious authorities, while possibility three does not support this assessment. We also do not have absolute proof that the first of the three possibilities suggested above should be ruled out because, again, the rabbis do not give us sufficient information about how they arrived at their reading of God's word. We therefore have to remain open to the notion that the rabbis in this case saw themselves as doing nothing more than conveying well-established traditions of biblical interpretation.

Plenty of other passages in rabbinic literature could be analysed in a similar manner, though the focal points of concern are often different from the passage about "an eye for an eye." In that passage, the question was whether the rabbis interpreted the biblical text in light of moral considerations, while in other rabbinic passages, the same type of question arises but with respect to a host of other considerations, such as those involving political, social, or economic matters, or those having to do with historical circumstances. That is, there are many passages in rabbinic literature in which the rabbis appear to interpret the biblical text in light of a variety of outside considerations, not just moral ones, and once again, because the rabbis did not usually say enough about how they arrived at their interpretations, we cannot be sure in these passages that they took these considerations into account in a conscious and wilful manner. As a consequence, the role of human autonomy in these cases is no less ambiguous than it was in the case of an "eye for an eye."

We can illustrate this point by looking at fundamental elements of the rabbinic agenda. Much of Rabbinic Judaism was an attempt to reconstruct Judaism to cope with a dire historical situation. The loss of the Second Temple and Jewish political independence were devastating blows, and the rabbis responded to this crisis by insisting that the covenant between God and the Jewish people was alive and well and that Jews should continue observing the commandments that remained. They also set out to preserve the rituals of the Temple symbolically. The sacrifices, for instance, were replaced by communal prayer, with the understanding that the synagogue served as a substitute for the Temple.

These adaptations were all justified by highly creative, and sometimes eccentric, readings of the biblical text that characterize rabbinic literature as a whole, and we therefore have the same ambiguity here that we had with the case of "an eye for an eye." It is hard to tell in these instances whether the rabbis, in reading the biblical text the way they did, saw themselves as mere recipients of traditions from the Oral Torah or as creators of the Oral Torah, and, if the latter, whether they were creators of the Oral Torah in a conscious or subconscious manner.

The problem with the ambiguity I am describing here has to be emphasized, because popular writers, as well as a good number of academic experts, have been tempted to see the rabbis as figures who as a rule regarded themselves as having a remarkable amount of autonomy in shaping Judaism. That approach to the rabbis is understandable because it appeals to our modern sensibilities. These writers will there-fore read a rabbinic text, such as the one concerned with "an eye for an eye," as clear proof of a robust sense of autonomy on the part of the rab-bis. However, as we have shown here, one has to be cautious in making such judgments. Matters are not so simple.

RABBINIC LAW OUTSIDE DIVINE WILL

From what we have said thus far, the rabbis were not much different from religious authorities in pre-modern Christianity. Scholars of Chris-tianity will tell you that like the rabbis, these authorities based their beliefs and practices on the Bible; they came up with highly creative readings of the biblical text to accommodate moral, political, social, and economic concerns; they said little about whether their interpretations were shaped by those concerns; and therefore it is often unclear how conscious they were of their creativity.

Augustine provides an excellent example of these tendencies. He displayed great ingenuity in developing notions such as Original Sin and Predestination from his reading of Scripture. These ideas did not appear explicitly in the Bible, but he was able to draw them out of the biblical text with interpretations that were highly original. However, Augustine provided no acknowledgment that he was doing anything creative here; he simply presented his interpretations as the authentic reading of Scripture as he saw it, and so it is hard to know whether he was at all conscious of his own creativity.

I now turn to a series of rabbinic sources that reveal significant dis-tinctions between the rabbis and their Christian counterparts regard-ing biblical interpretation and the role that human autonomy played in that endeavour. Many passages in rabbinic literature reveal that the rabbis were not only innovative interpreters of Scripture but also clearly *conscious* of being innovative. Therefore, in these passages, there is no ambiguity. Such passages reflect a clear and robust sense of human autonomy that at best has been only implied in the rabbinic texts we have discussed so far. Most important, these passages have no analogue in pre-modern Christianity. At no point did Christian thinkers assert their autonomy in interpreting God's word in the way the rabbis did in these cases.

A well-known example of what I am referring to here concerns the biblical law in Deuteronomy 21:18–21 about the "rebellious son." The case involves parents who are unable to discipline an unruly son, presumably someone in his teenage years or older. Despite all their efforts, he remains "a glutton and drunkard." The Bible tells us that in such an instance, the parents may take their son to the "elders" of the community to attest to his bad behaviour, and if found guilty, the son will be put to death by stoning.

The notion of having one's child executed for bad behaviour would be revolting to most people, and it would seem that most of the rabbis felt the same way. In their discussion of this law in the Talmud, the majority of rabbis read the biblical text in a manner that allowed them to attach numerous conditions to the law, some of them patently ridiculous, and the result was that the law could not be implemented. By the time these rabbis were done interpreting the biblical passage containing the law, a rebellious son would be executed only under the following conditions: he had to be between the ages of thirteen years and one day, and thirteen years and three months (meaning that there was only a three-month window in the son's life when the law applied); he had to have stolen a specific quantity of meat and wine from his parents (other foods did not count, and the quantity of meat and wine had to be exact); the food had to be eaten outside the parents' premises (if eaten inside the home, the law did not apply); and it had to be eaten in the company of wastrels (if eaten alone or in more refined company, the law, again, did not apply).[15]

In the Talmud, R. Shimon asks the obvious question: "Because one eats a *tartemar* [i.e., a specific measurement] of meat and drinks a half a *log* [i.e., another specific measurement] of Italian wine, shall his mother and father have him stoned!?" R. Shimon answers his own question with the declaration that the case of the rebellious son is pure fiction: it "never happened and *will* never happen" (my emphasis). That is, R. Shimon, in essence, recognizes that the conditions the rabbis attached to the law render it effectively null and void. Clearly, for R. Shimon, a law that allows parents to execute a rebellious son is too immoral to implement.

R. Shimon then asks why the law appears in the Bible at all. His answer is that it was written "so that you may study it and receive reward."[16] That is, the biblical passage and its attendant rabbinic interpretations are only meant to be studied, not implemented, and one will be rewarded by God for the effort expended on doing so.[17]

In the same passage, R. Jonathan disagrees with R. Shimon and states that the case of the rebellious son was not fictional at all. R. Jonathan even claims to have sat next to the grave of one such individual who had been executed.[18] However, the thrust of the Talmudic discussion is clearly in line with R. Shimon's view. The ridiculous conditions that its editors placed on the execution of the rebellious son make that clear.

This case is similar to that of "an eye for an eye." In both instances, the rabbinic editors of the Talmud seem to have interpreted biblical law in light of their moral sensibilities. However, scholars generally agree that in the case of the rebellious son, it is much more obvious that moral concerns come into play because the rabbis seem intent on entirely disabling a law that is morally problematic by interpreting it in a patently ridiculous manner, and they do not do so with the case of "an eye for an eye." In the latter instance, the law is transformed but also preserved in some sense.

AMENDMENTS TO BIBLICAL LAW

There are instances in which it is even clearer that the rabbis saw themselves as having the authority to add to or modify God's laws. Sometimes they proposed legislation that supplemented biblical law when it was deemed to be inadequate. When the rabbis were confronted with unprecedented circumstances in the social, political, or economic realms, and the Bible provided no guidance, they were willing to propose new legislation to deal with the problem. The rabbis referred to the type of legislation used in these instances as a *takkanah*, a term that comes from the word "to repair" and is related to the word *tikkun* that we encountered in our discussion of Kabbalah. That is, the rabbis in instituting a *takkanah* saw themselves as "repairing" the Torah when it had to be fixed.[19]

One way to understand the notion of a *takkanah* is to see it as similar to an amendment to the US Constitution. An amendment adds to or modifies the Constitution when there is broad consensus among Americans that such a correction is warranted in light of new conditions. The rabbis did the same thing with the Torah. The *takkanah* mechanism was meant to add to or modify the laws of the Torah when there were pressing reasons to do so. However, the *takkanah* was more radical than an amendment to the Constitution because, with a *takkanah*, the words that were being amended were the words of God, not those of human beings.

A number of examples will give us a better understanding of how rabbinic amendments worked. We will begin with an instance in which the rabbis attempted to fill a gap in biblical law. We are told in the Talmud that the rabbis devised a marriage contract so that men could not rashly divorce their wives. According to some rabbinic sources, the rabbis inserted conditions into the marriage contract to accomplish that purpose. Other sources credit the rabbis with coming up with the whole idea of a marriage contract.[20] Whatever the case, the rabbis in this instance openly describe their legislation as an addition to biblical law, one motivated by moral concerns. Thus, we have an excellent example of the rabbis making a ruling on a fundamental issue in Jewish law that openly and explicitly added to God's commandments in Scripture and was inspired by the rabbis' moral concerns.[21]

In some instances, the rabbis seem to have made rulings that did not just supplement biblical law but modified it in some fashion. The most famous example of this kind of rabbinic legislation involves an economic matter, and it will require a bit of background information to explain. In the Bible, God commands the Israelites to let farmers take a year off work every seven years and let their fields lie fallow.[22] All farmers in ancient Israel were on the same seven-year cycle, and because the economy of ancient Israel was primarily agricultural, the seventh year was a year-long national holiday of sorts.[23] In addition to the commandment to desist from agriculture in the seventh year, there was another commandment in the Torah specifying that, in that same year, all debts across the nation were to be cancelled.[24] This law was probably instituted to ensure that individuals would not be impoverished because of their debts, or worse yet, become enslaved to their lenders in order to pay them off.

The law of debt cancellation was probably not terribly disruptive to the economy in ancient Israel because at the time, the Israelites did not have an economy that relied much on the lending of money and buying things on credit. Again, the Israelite economy was primarily agricultural. But by the first century, when the rabbis began to emerge as religious leaders, the economy in the land of Israel had become more dependent on money transactions, and so the law of debt cancellation had potential to bring about economic disaster. With such a law in place, individuals were unlikely to lend money, and money-based economies depend on loans.[25]

So the rabbis had to find a way to cope with this situation, and we are told in the Mishnah that Hillel, one of the great first-century rabbis, did just that. He made a ruling that allowed individuals to collect debts even after the seventh year. The effect of Hillel's ruling was that it negated a divine commandment because of new economic conditions that had made the commandment unworkable.[26]

Some commentators have noted that in the Gemara, the later layer of the Talmudic text, the rabbis attempt to soften the radicalism of Hillel's innovation. However, a full discussion of whether that is indeed the case should not preoccupy us here.[27] The important point is that in implementing rabbinic amendments, the rabbis clearly saw themselves as going beyond divine law in some fashion. The notion of amending the law implied that a solution to a given legal problem could not be found through the normal channels of interpretation of biblical law and that the rabbis either had to add to that law or modify it.[28] Thus, the very idea of a *takkanah* had a radical element.

Moreover, the rabbis seem to have been aware that making a *takkanah* was a radical move because they did not take this responsibility lightly. Such amendments were invoked sparingly. They were implemented only in situations in which there was a pressing moral, political, social, or economic problem that could not be solved within the normal parameters of God's laws.[29] Thus, the fact that the rabbis were willing to implement amendments to God's law at all is remarkable. These amendments reflected an extraordinary level of confidence in their own authority.

An even clearer example of the courage of the rabbis in modifying God's laws involves the composition of the Talmud itself. According to a passage in the Talmud, the rabbis believed that there was a biblical commandment that prohibited them from putting the Oral Torah, or any part of it, into writing. They based this commandment on their own idiosyncratic reading of the biblical text. When God revealed to Moses the second set of tablets of the Ten Commandments on Mount Sinai, God instructed Moses as follows: "Write down these commandments, for in accordance with these commandments I make a covenant with you and Israel."[30] God mentions the commandments twice in this verse, and a plain reading would suggest that they are the very same body of commandments. However, the rabbis often treat repetitions and redundancies in the Bible as signifying something significant. God, after all, could not just be wasting his words. Thus, in this instance, the rabbis claim that two references to the commandments must refer to different bodies of commandments; the first reference alludes to the commandments in the Written Torah, while the second alludes to the commandments in the Oral Torah. The rabbis also base this latter association on a pun in the verse that is difficult to translate.[31] What is most important for our purposes is that God does not instruct Moses to write down the commandments in the second half of verse that the rabbis believe are the commandments of the Oral Torah, and that is because these commandments are supposed to remain oral.

Yet the rabbis did, in fact, write down the Oral Torah – or at least, their discussions of it – and the same Talmudic source that reports the prohibition against doing so suggests that the decision to record the Oral Torah in written form was made not long after the destruction of the Jewish commonwealth by the Romans in the first and second centuries. The source intimates that in the wake of the devastation of this period and all the disruption in communal life that accompanied it, the rule about keeping the Oral Torah oral was no longer tenable; the Oral Torah had to be committed to written form because it was in danger of being forgotten.[32]

The writing down of the Oral Torah may seem like a trivial violation of God's will, but we have to understand that for the rabbis, it was a serious matter. According to them, the imperative that the Oral Torah remain oral was one of God's commandments, and so the ruling that the Oral Torah could now be recorded was an outright transgression of a divine imperative. Moreover, the writing down of the Oral Torah was central to the entire rabbinic enterprise. It resulted in the composition of the Talmud, which became the central work of Rabbinic Judaism. The rabbis did not explicitly refer to their ruling about writing down the Oral Torah as a rabbinic amendment, but it certainly had the earmarks of one, and later halakhic interpreters would use that term for this move. Most important, here it is clear that the rabbis saw themselves as overruling God's commandment when there was a need to do so because of pressing external circumstances – in this case, the dire situation of the Jewish people.

What is most interesting here is not just that the rabbis acted in so bold a manner, but how they justified their action. They cite a verse in the book of Psalms that reads: "It is time to act for the Lord, they have violated your Torah" (Psalms 119:126). The only sensible way to read this verse is that "it is time to act for the Lord [because] they have violated your Torah." The first clause is a consequence of the second; hence, my insertion of the word "because." You need to act on God's behalf when people have violated the Torah. However, the Talmudic source reads the verse as follows: "It is time to act for the Lord; [therefore,] they have violated your Torah." In this reading, the second clause is a *consequence* of the first; hence, my insertion of the word "therefore." So here the meaning of the verse is completely reversed. The way you act on God's behalf is to violate his Torah! The Talmudic passage has not technically rewritten the biblical verse here because there is an ambiguity in the Hebrew that allows for the alternative reading, but the meaning derived from the verse is the opposite of what it clearly intended. And with this highly creative interpretation, the rabbis are telling us explicitly that in some situations, they have to violate the Torah with new legislation in order to save it! It is for this reason that the prohibition against writing down the Oral Torah had to be ignored.

The boldness of this interpretation goes beyond the particular instance at hand. What the Talmudic source is saying is that there are times when the rabbis are justified in transgressing God's commandments. This passage thus confirms the same message we have gleaned from sources we have already looked at regarding the power of rabbinic authority, but it does so in a particularly dramatic manner.

ARGUING WITH GOD AGAIN

The notion that the rabbis had the power to overturn God's word is illustrated even more vividly by an extraordinary story that appears in the Talmud and is cited in practically every introductory textbook on Judaism. It opens with an argument taking place among a group of rabbis in the second century about an arcane issue in Jewish law: whether an oven with a particular construction is susceptible to impurity. The details of the issue being debated here are not important. What is significant is that the rabbis come to a unanimous opinion on the matter, except for one revered rabbi, R. Eliezer, who stubbornly refuses to go along with his colleagues. The story proceeds with R. Eliezer attempting to convince his colleagues that his view is correct; he even performs a series of miracles to demonstrate his authority. He uproots a tree and causes a river to reverse course by simple command. The rabbis, however, are unimpressed and stick with their ruling. But R. Eliezer will not give up, and he finally calls on God himself to support him, at which point a divine voice comes from heaven and announces to the rabbis that R. Eliezer is indeed right. But shockingly, the rabbis tell God that they will not change their minds. The Torah, they say, has been given to them, and it is they who will decide how to interpret it. God is told, in effect, to stay out of the argument, even though it is about a law in his own Torah! What is God's reaction to all this? We are informed that in heaven at that very moment, God laughed and said, "My children have defeated me, my children have defeated me." Not only was he not bothered by what happened, he was apparently rather amused.[33]

In this case, the rabbis have expressed their autonomy in a manner that is even more daring than if they had simply implemented a rabbinic amendment. While a rabbinic amendment can override God's written word, here the rabbis override his word in a direct conversation.[34]

Moreover, as we already know, this is not the only instance in rabbinic literature in which human beings argue with God and win. In the previous chapter, we noted that there are numerous passages in rabbinic literature in which individuals engage in direct debate with God, and in some of them, they too come out victorious. There are some differences between the sources cited in the last chapter and the story we have just recounted. The dispute with God over the oven concerns a matter of Jewish law, while in the passages discussed earlier, the debates with God were about moral issues, with God being accused of failing to live up to his own ethical standards. Also, in the passage about the oven, it is the rabbis who argue with God, while in the passages discussed earlier, the person arguing with God is often a biblical character. Still, the important point is that the story about the rabbis overruling God on a matter of law should not be considered unusual by rabbinic standards. It presents a scenario that appears in a number of variations in other passages in rabbinic literature.

CAVEATS

I do not want to overstate the case here. Modern Jewish thinkers have often used the sources cited in this section of our discussion to suggest that according to the rabbis, human interpreters had unlimited freedom to interpret God's word as they saw fit, and that is not at all the case. With regard to rabbinic amendments, we noted that the rabbis issued such amendments only on rare occasions. They knew that they could not just amend God's laws whenever they wanted to without undermining the entire system of Jewish law.

Furthermore, the rabbis viewed their authority for instituting an amendment as coming from God's own words. It was not something they did without warrant; God had granted them that authority. We have already seen that one Talmudic passage cited a biblical verse in Psalms that was read to mean that, in some instances, one must violate the Torah in order to save it. We can add that in another Talmudic passage, R. Aviya supports the authority for making amendments by citing a verse from the Torah that is quite explicit about the power of human authority in interpreting God's commandments. In the book of Deuteronomy, the Israelites are told by Moses that when they encounter a situation in which they are unsure about how to apply God's law, they should seek guidance from the proper authorities in their time:

> If a case is too baffling for you to decide, be it a controversy over homicide, civil law, or assault – matters of dispute in your courts ... [you shall] appear before the levitical priests, or the magistrate in charge at the time, and present your problem. When they have announced to you the verdict in the case, you shall carry out the verdict that is announced to you ... observing scrupulously all their instructions to you.[35]

According to R. Aviya, the authorities referred to here were none other than the rabbis, and the scope of powers granted to them by this passage included the right to issue rabbinic amendments.[36] Thus, if the rabbis were bold legislators, it was because they assumed that God himself had given them the right to be.

We also should not exaggerate the importance of the Talmudic passage about the debate over the oven. This passage, while very provocative, did not reflect the opinions of all rabbis in the Talmud. The rabbis never declared that in principle it was acceptable to go against the divine will in interpreting the biblical commandments. In fact, there were clearly some rabbis who took a more conservative approach, and R. Eliezer seems to have been one of them. That is why he stubbornly stuck to his viewpoint in the argument with his colleagues over the oven.[37]

Still, we should not overcorrect too much in the other direction and *under*estimate the radical elements of rabbinic literature that we are discussing. Certainly, rabbinic amendments were used sparingly. Yet, the fact that the rabbis used them at all reflects an impressive amount of courage on their part.

Nor does the fact that the rabbis cite verses in the Bible to justify rabbinic amendments entirely blunt the boldness of the practice, because the verses cited were themselves read in highly creative ways. As we have seen, the verse in Psalms that was adduced for this purpose was interpreted in a convoluted fashion to give the rabbis the authority to write down the Oral Torah. The verse in Deuteronomy that was used for the same purpose by R. Aviya was read in similar fashion; it speaks only about the need for Israelites to consult the authorities of their time to make judgments about the *application* of God's law, but R. Aviya uses it to justify the notion that the rabbis may come up with legislation *overriding* God's law. Thus, the rabbis did not have to read these biblical passages as warrants for them to do something as radical as implementing an amendment to the Torah; they *chose* to read them this way.[38] The rabbis therefore displayed their boldness as interpreters not just in issuing rabbinic amendments but also in the way they chose to read verses in the Bible giving them the authority to do so.

Similar observations can be made about the story regarding the oven in which the rabbis overrule God directly. Not all rabbis in Talmudic times would have dared to do such a thing, and the fact that some of them did on this occasion is remarkable. Moreover, the actions of the rabbis who behaved in this manner were not treated as anything unusual by the editors of the Talmud. The story appears in the flow of discussion in the Talmudic text without any special attention being drawn to it. Thus, the Talmudic editors seem to have accepted the fact that, according to at least one group of rabbis, one could challenge God when it came to adjudicating matters involving his commandments. In sum, while we should not exaggerate the radicalism of the sources we have cited in which the rabbis had strong views about their own authority, we should not minimize it either.

CONCLUSIONS: EARLY RABBINIC JUDAISM

What has been established here is that the early rabbis were often remarkably bold interpreters of God's word. They usually did not acknowledge that they were, and so it is hard in most cases for us to know how conscious they were of their originality. The case of "an eye for an eye" provided an excellent illustration of this point. But in some places, the rabbis openly depicted themselves as taking unusual liberties with the divine word. They disabled biblical laws that were morally problematic by attaching so many conditions to them, that they could not be practised; they added to or modified biblical laws by issuing amendments when there was a pressing moral, political, social, or economic reason to do so. In one such instance, the rabbis even spoke explicitly about the need to violate God's law. Perhaps most surprising of all was an instance in which the rabbis overruled God about a legal matter face-to-face when he attempted to enter into one of their disputes. Moreover, what the rabbis were doing in all these cases should be seen in relation to the strand in rabbinic tradition analysed in our previous chapter that depicted human beings as having the right to argue with God when his actions seemed unjust or immoral.

The most important question for our concerns is how rabbinic views on authority compared with those of Christianity. I will hold off making a judgment about this issue until we explore how rabbinic views on authority evolved in later centuries because it was only then that both Rabbinic Judaism and Christianity began to grapple more systematically with the question of religious authority.

The Late Medieval and Early Modern Periods

In the late medieval and early modern periods, the tendency of the rabbis to accentuate human autonomy in relation to God became even more pronounced. We can appreciate this development by first looking at the way in which they grappled with the concept of the Oral Torah. As we have seen, the views of the early rabbis on this central idea were ambiguous, and much of the difficulty had to do with the fact that the rabbis did not provide much discussion about it. However by the medieval period, a number of rabbis, including some of the most prominent, had begun to reflect extensively on the Oral Torah in order to get a firmer understanding of its contents and the role it played in Jewish law. These reflections were often part of larger discussions about the nature of Jewish law and its history, discussions that were, in turn, inspired by the challenges Jews faced in their environments. The vast majority of Jews resided either in Christian or Islamic countries, and they were usually looked down upon by their neighbours because of their stubborn refusal to accept the religion of the majority in these countries. Jews therefore felt the need to justify why their religion was still God's one and only truth. That need led Jews to explore the premises of their religion in greater depth than they ever had done before, and an important focus of those explorations was the nature and history of Jewish law because of its central role in their lives. The motivation of Jews to engage in such explorations was made more urgent by periodic attempts on the part of their non-Jewish neighbours to actively convince them to abandon their faith and adopt the religion of the majority culture, an endeavour that was sometimes accompanied by threats or outright violence. Also inspiring the rabbis to conduct such an exploration was the existence of communities of Karaites, Jews who had rejected Rabbinic Judaism in favour of a more biblically based Judaism. Karaism arose in the ninth century in Iraq, and it thrived among Jews in Islamic countries in some periods and places.

THE NATURE OF THE ORAL TORAH

Let us now focus on the aspects of these rabbinic discussions about the nature and history of Jewish law that are of greatest relevance to our concerns. What did these discussions have to say about the contents of the Oral Torah when it was given to Moses on Mount Sinai? What kind of evolution did it undergo, if any, in subsequent generations? And what implications did the answers to these questions have for human autonomy in the metaphysical sense?

Medieval rabbis developed several approaches to the Oral Torah, but we cannot look at all of them, and so I will focus on the approaches taken by the two most prestigious rabbis who dealt with this issue.[39]

The first view belongs to R. Moses ben Maimon (1138–1204), better known as Maimonides, the most famous of the medieval Jewish legal authorities. He held that the Oral Torah that Moses received on Mount Sinai was not fully fixed, nor was it comprehensive. It consisted of a limited number of laws to supplement the Written Torah, and these laws were the only ones about which there had been no disputes in subsequent generations. However, there was an inevitable need to greatly expand the laws of both the Written Torah and the Oral Torah because there were constant demands for legislation to deal with new situations. Thankfully, God had anticipated this problem and had given to Moses, as part of the Oral Torah, rules of legal interpretation for that purpose. Maimonides was referring here to a well-known list of thirteen rules of interpretation recorded in early rabbinic literature that were attributed to R. Ishmael.[40] With these rules, the rabbis could derive new laws from the Written and Oral Torah. The problem was that each rabbi had different intellectual capabilities, which meant they applied the rules of interpretation in different ways, resulting in multiple views on any given law. So there was a need to settle those disputes through debates, and it is these debates that were recorded in the Talmud and subsequent rabbinic literature.

Thus, according to this theory, what God gave to Moses on Mount Sinai was an Oral Torah that was mostly undefined. It was the task of the rabbis to use divinely-sanctioned methods of legal reasoning to build a comprehensive law-system as new situations arose requiring new applications of the laws.[41]

The second viewpoint on the nature of the Oral Torah was supported by a number of medieval rabbis who based their insights on those of R. Moses ben Nahman (1194–1270) – often referred to as Nahmanides and perhaps the greatest medieval rabbi after Maimonides. According to this approach, the Oral Torah consisted of disputes from the outset. That is, what God revealed to Moses on Mount Sinai was not a body of fixed laws at all – not even a small number as Maimonides proposed – but all the various possible opinions about those laws that could arise in any situation. Those opinions were then passed on to subsequent generations as oral tradition, and when a law had to be applied to a new situation, it was the task of the rabbis to determine through debate which of the various possible opinions about the law they supported. Whichever opinion had the endorsement of the majority of sages was the one deemed correct.[42] This viewpoint was in some sense the opposite of that of Maimonides. While Maimonides believed that disputes among the rabbis about the Oral Torah proliferated over time as the rabbis attempted to fill in its gaps, the followers of Nahmanides claimed that all the disputes were present from the beginning and were reduced in number over time as they became settled.

The important point here is that in both paradigms, human autonomy plays a significant role in determining the contents of the Oral Torah. According to the first model, the rabbis had a significant amount of autonomy with regard to the Oral Torah because when it was originally given on Mount Sinai, it was not complete, nor was it meant to be. It was up to the rabbis to fill in its details by applying divinely sanctioned techniques of interpreting the biblical text. The second model accorded even more autonomy to the rabbis by claiming that the original Oral Torah consisted of a series of open-ended possibilities about how the laws of the Written Torah could be interpreted, and that it was the responsibility of the rabbis to decide which possibility was correct in a given situation.

An argument can be made that the two positions on the Oral Torah we have just outlined are less radical than those found in earlier rabbinic sources because both positions remove the possibility that there could be any real conflict between God's will and that of the rabbis. As we have seen, in earlier rabbinic sources such conflict was indeed possible and the rabbis sometimes solved the problem by setting aside God's will in favour of their own. We even encountered a passage in which that occurred in a direct confrontation with God himself. But according to the later positions on the nature of the Oral Torah that we have just described, conflicts of this kind were not possible. The first theory of the Oral Torah held that its body of laws was largely incomplete from the outset and that God had given the rabbis the right to fill in what was missing. According to the second theory, the Oral Torah had no laws from the outset, only a series of opinions *about* the laws, and therefore the rabbis were charged by God with the obligation of determining what those laws should be.

However, the reason why there could be no conflict in either of the paradigms between God's will and the will of the rabbis is that each of the paradigms assumed that God had granted the rabbis a remarkable degree of autonomy in the first place. Therefore, the two theories were no less radical than earlier rabbinic sources; they were just radical in a different way. These theories managed to take away the problem that God's will could conflict with the will of the rabbis regarding his laws by presuming that God at the outset had granted the rabbis a great deal of freedom to interpret his laws.

COMMUNAL AMENDMENTS

Another way in which the rabbis in the medieval and early modern periods accentuated human autonomy in the metaphysical sense involved rabbinic amendments. Medieval and early modern rabbis were willing to invoke this mechanism to amend Jewish law when necessary just as the earlier rabbis were.[43] However, medieval rabbis also began extending the authority to issue rabbinic amendments to lay leaders in Jewish communities.

To understand this development, some background is needed. From the tenth century onwards, each Jewish community governed its own affairs both in Europe and in the Islamic world. Jewish communities were, of course, under the jurisdiction of the non-Jewish ruler in whose territory they resided, but these rulers were generally happy to let Jews govern their own communities as long as they were obedient to him and paid their taxes. So the Jews in each city set up their own governments for that purpose. These governments were fairly uniform in their structure across the Jewish world. They were semi-democratic in character. The Jewish community in each city elected a council. The councils then legislated on civil matters, such as those involving administration and taxation. It also legislated, in some instances, on criminal matters.

What was extraordinary was that rabbinic authorities approved of such legislation even when it conflicted with elements of Jewish law. It could not conflict with the essential principles of Jewish law; basic principles of justice and equity had to be maintained. Still, rabbinic authorities gave community leaders considerable latitude in shaping legislation to suit the needs of their subjects. The rabbis referred to this kind of legislation as a *takkanah*, the same term they used when they themselves produced legislation to amend God's laws – except that here it was lay people who did the amending. This right did not extend to matters involving more purely religious concerns, such as ritual practices or marriage; in the latter areas, only the rabbis could set the rules. Still, the fact that the rabbis permitted elected councils of lay individuals to legislate on civil affairs, even when it went against Jewish law, was remarkable. It demonstrates that medieval and early modern rabbis, even more than the earlier rabbis, believed that Jewish law had been placed in the hands of human beings to adjudicate.[44]

I do not want to paint too idyllic a picture here. The legislation of lay authorities did not always meet with the approval of the rabbis. The rabbis also had different views about how much power should be ceded to lay authorities in the first place, and as a result, there was often tension between the rabbis and the lay authorities regarding the latter's legislation. Moreover, in such conflicts, lay authorities often came out on top because the rabbis had been hired by them and were paid by them and thus could also be fired by them. The position of the rabbis grew even weaker in the early modern period when the rabbis were being challenged more and more by ordinary Jews, and cracks in the edifice of rabbinic authority began to show.[45] However, what is significant here is that in principle, the rabbis approved of lay authorities making decisions on matters normally governed by Jewish law.

Religious Authority: Christianity vs. Rabbinic Judaism

We are now finally ready to explore the main question, which is how, prior to modernity, Rabbinic Judaism compared with Christianity regarding the issues we have discussed. From everything that has been said in this chapter so far, it would appear that Rabbinic Judaism had far bolder views than Christianity on the autonomy of religious authorities in relation to God.

The medieval Catholic Church was certainly bold on this issue to the extent that human beings were empowered to express God's will and interpret his word in matters of both theology and law. By far the most important figure in this regard was the pope. He was considered to be the representative of Christ on earth, a notion that was fully consolidated by the twelfth century, and he therefore had supreme authority when it came to all aspects of Christian doctrine and practice. But the pope did not usually act alone. On the most important matters, he made decisions in consultation with councils made up of the most powerful clerics in the Church hierarchy. On minor matters, decisions could also be made by lower-level clergy. Furthermore, from the twelfth century onwards, the Catholic Church put an enormous amount of effort into the consolidation and organization of its laws on religious matters, and this body of "canon law," as it was called, required the expertise of lawyers to determine the contents of this law and to apply it in real-life situations. Thus, in the medieval Catholic Church, human beings with various levels of authority were empowered to make decisions about religious matters.

Yet Rabbinic Judaism clearly went much further than Catholicism did regarding the power that human beings had to interpret God's will. Once again, in early rabbinic literature, some of the rabbis deliberately disabled morally problematic laws; they explicitly implemented amendments to biblical law in light of moral, political, social, and economic pressures; they spoke of the need to violate God's Torah in order to save it; and in one instance, they overruled God's opinion regarding a particular law when he personally attempted to intervene in one of their disputes. In the medieval period, the rabbis, in some respects, went even further. The radical view of authority that had been represented only in some early rabbinic sources became the standard position with the backing of the greatest medieval rabbinic authority: Maimonides. The medieval rabbis also extended that power in some degree to ordinary Jews by allowing those who governed Jewish communities to amend divine legislation on civil matters.

We find no parallel to any of this in medieval Catholicism. The popes and their councils were considered conduits for God's will, and therefore there was no sense in which they could argue or negotiate with God on the meaning of his word, nor was there any notion that God had abdicated his authority to them. Their job was to implement God's word according to his intent as they understood it, not to challenge it in any way. Furthermore, once the pope and his councils made determinations regarding matters of doctrine or law, lower-level clerics could not question those determinations. They could perhaps interpret them, but again, only for the purpose of getting to the true intent of what the pope and his councils had legislated. And there was certainly no mechanism by which ordinary Christians could make amendments to divine law in the way that the rabbis permitted ordinary Jews to do. In short, underlying the Catholic approach to religious authority was the presumption that the divine will was immutable and could never change. Human beings therefore had to approach God's directives with that presumption in mind.[46]

The differences between Rabbinic Judaism and the medieval Catholic Church are wonderfully highlighted by the way in which Church authorities reacted to the Talmudic story involving the oven in which the rabbis overruled God. The story became known to Christian authorities in the later centuries of the medieval period when they first became familiar with the contents of the Talmud, and they were horrified by it. They expressed consternation at the idea that the rabbis would not only argue with God but make a ruling in contradiction to his will. They took it as evidence that Jews were hopelessly rebellious and blasphemous.[47]

This reaction speaks volumes about larger differences between medieval Jews and Christians regarding human autonomy in relation to God. Christian authorities simply could not relate to a story in which human beings would engage in a debate with God and reject his word. For Christians, the story highlighted the insolence of the Jews. But that is not at all how the rabbis understood the story. For them, the story underscored the exalted status of human beings as partners with God in the shaping of the Torah. It was a tribute to human freedom and dignity.

Protestantism increased the empowerment of human beings to determine the content of God's will by greatly widening the circle of those who were considered religious authorities. As we have noted, in the presbyterian model, religious authority devolved onto communities of elders, but their congregants were involved in choosing those elders and determining the issues the elders would take up once elected. In the congregational model, the members of the communities themselves were the religious authorities. However, on the issues of greatest importance to this discussion, Protestants were not much different from Catholics, for even though religious authority in Protestantism involved far more people and was more democratic than in Catholicism, Protestants were no more willing than Catholics to entertain the possibility that one could argue with God, overrule him, "repair" his law, or "violate" it. ·

Conclusions

Both the rabbis and their Christian counterparts in the Catholic and Protestant Churches had a certain degree of autonomy when it came to religious matters. Both groups of authorities were innovators because they had to be. No religion can survive for long without its leaders being granted the power to be creative. Religious communities are constantly being challenged to deal with new circumstances in the moral, political, social, and economic realms, and innovation is a must if a religion is going to have the dynamism to deal with these challenges. A religious community that lacks this capacity is one that will soon disappear.

However, the main question in this chapter is whether the authorities in Rabbinic Judaism and Christianity before the modern era were ever *conscious* of being innovators. Were they aware that the guidance they were providing their followers was, at times, at odds with what God had commanded in Scripture? We have seen that some rabbis in early Rabbinic Judaism *were* aware of this and that, in the medieval period, this strain of thinking was eventually accepted as normative by the rabbis. In Christian thinking, by contrast, there was no such phenomenon. Christian authorities consistently saw themselves as providing guidance that was in accordance with God's immutable will.

What explains the differences here between Rabbinic Judaism and Christianity? Part of the answer, I believe, is obvious. The rabbis had to assert a significant amount of power in the interpretation of God's laws for Judaism to survive, even if it was at God's expense. After the destruction of the Jewish commonwealth and its Temple in the first century, and with a large portion of the Jewish people now living in exile, Judaism might not have lasted long if it had consisted of a body of laws that were fixed and inflexible. These catastrophic events changed everything for the Jews, and a dynamic response was needed so that their way of life could continue. That is what the rabbis provided. They went about reshaping Judaism to deal with the new circumstances. On the one hand, the rabbis insisted that God's covenant with the Jewish people was still in force and that the laws laid down in the Bible that defined the covenant still had to be observed. On the other hand, the rabbis believed that they could shape those laws so that Jews could continue to live in accordance with them. The rabbis therefore fashioned a Temple-less Judaism in which sacrificial rituals were no longer the central means to worship God. They also took upon themselves the responsibility of interpreting God's laws that could still be observed in light of the new conditions under which Jews lived. The result was that Judaism continued as a vital religion while its adherents began to live in exile, subjugated to other nations. In short, historical circumstances played a large role in encouraging the rabbis to adopt an expansive approach to human autonomy in the metaphysical sense. The rabbis were pressed to adopt a highly pragmatic approach to their religion in which they had to constantly take into account not just what God's word meant but its implications over the long term, and those implications required them to take positions at odds with the original intent of that word.

Medieval and early modern Christians did not face the same challenges that Jews did. In these periods Christians wielded immense political power in one form or another. This meant that Christians did not have to adopt views on authority and autonomy that were as radical as those of the rabbis. They could afford to take a more conservative approach to interpreting God's word. That is not to say that Christianity lacked original thinking; in fact, its thinkers were brilliantly creative in interpreting religious doctrine and practice. It is just that Christian authorities were not pressed to see themselves as interpreters with the same freedom that the rabbis had to take upon themselves to ensure Judaism's survival.

But historical circumstances were not the only reason the rabbis adopted a more robust notion of human autonomy in relation to God than Christians. The rabbis themselves have to be given credit here as well. They were visionary leaders who understood that they had to take courageous steps in order for Judaism to continue, and that courage was evident in the role they took upon themselves in interpreting God's word. So we have to recognize the rabbis for the remarkable leaders they were.

They did not have to be so courageous. They could have taken a far more restrictive and conservative approach to interpreting God's will. Going in that direction, of course, could have brought about the end of Judaism. History is filled with examples of religions that have not survived, and the rabbis easily could have taken Judaism down that path. Alternatively, the rabbis could have fashioned a Judaism that largely retreated from the concerns of the world. In fact, it is not unusual for religions to do so in the face of suffering. But the rabbis did not adopt either of these options. They asserted themselves as authorities whose role it was to confront the challenges that Jews faced with creativity and flexibility, and the religion they fashioned remained fully engaged with the world in all its mundane detail. What is remarkable is that Rabbinic Judaism allowed Jews to survive not only the catastrophic events that befell them in the first centuries CE but also subsequent periods in which Jews would be living as a beleaguered minority among populations that were often hostile to them.

Our insights in this chapter should help correct common misconceptions about Rabbinic Judaism that we described in chapter 1.[48] One such misconception is that the rabbis were severe and rigid religious authorities who insisted that Jews adhere to a large body of impossibly harsh and demanding laws. Our discussion in this chapter demonstrates just how inaccurate and wrong-headed this perspective is. The early rabbis certainly saw themselves as charged with enforcing God's laws, and these laws were indeed demanding; yet plenty of early rabbinic sources indicate that at least some of the early rabbis also regarded themselves as having the authority to adapt and reshape God's laws in accordance with the needs of their followers, sometimes in radical ways, and this approach to divine law became normative in the medieval period. Moreover, Christian authorities were more rigid than the rabbis! Religious authorities in pre-modern Christianity were much less inclined than the rabbis were to take liberties with God's word.

Our discussion in this chapter should also lay to rest criticisms of the rabbis that come from the very opposite direction. As we also noted in chapter 1, the rabbis have often been accused of being manipulative and dishonest.[49] According to this viewpoint, they deliberately twisted God's words in order to suit their own needs. That is, the problem with the rabbis according to this criticism is not that they were too rigid, it is that they were too flexible. Our discussion demonstrates that this second perspective represents no less a misunderstanding of Rabbinic Judaism than the first. The early rabbis were certainly innovative, but there is no evidence that they were manipulative. The most innovative among them seemed to assume that God had empowered them to interpret his word to accommodate pragmatic concerns. By the medieval period, prominent rabbis stated this assumption explicitly. Bold interpretation of God's word was not only permitted, it was mandated, and it was mandated by God himself. Moreover, even the most creative rabbis recognized that there were limits to how creative they could be. None of the rabbis saw themselves as having the power to say anything they wanted to about God's laws. They were not going to permit idol worship or move the Sabbath to another day of the week, no matter how clever their interpretations were. Some readings of the biblical text were clearly off limits. In sum, the picture that has emerged here is that the rabbis constantly struggled to find the correct balance between obeying God's word as received, and engaging in innovative interpretation in order to deal pragmatically with a host of extraneous considerations and circumstances, and according to the rabbis, striking this balance was precisely what God wanted from them.

The rabbis never developed hard and fast rules about how to weigh the ideal and the practical, and therefore we find a considerable variety of approaches to Jewish law in the history of Rabbinic Judaism. Some rabbis could be quite conservative in their legal rulings; others could be rather liberal. But on the whole, the rabbis had to chart a path that took both elements into consideration.

What we have learned in this chapter helps us better understand how Jews weathered hundreds of years of subjugation and persecution after the first century. The balance that the rabbis struck between the ideal and the practical in adjudicating God's laws was critical in this regard. It provided Jews with a way of life that gave them a strong sense of religious identity but at the same time was nimble and adaptable enough to cope with their difficult and ever-changing circumstances.

More important, this chapter's insights allow us to take a step forward in understanding why, when the modern period arrived, Jews achieved disproportionate success. In the previous chapter, I argued that one explanation for this phenomenon is that before the modern period, Rabbinic Judaism ingrained in Jews a stronger sense of autonomy than Christianity ingrained in Christians, and I demonstrated how that was the case by focusing on concepts related to the question of divine judgment. In this chapter, I have made the same argument with respect to the issue of religious authority. Therefore, I have shown that in two major areas of Jewish religious life, the rabbis cultivated an unusually robust sense of autonomy in Jews, a trait that was key for success in the Western world.

A challenge that was posed in the last chapter can be posed here as well. Most of the material analysed in this chapter is unlikely to have been known by lay Jews and Christians in the medieval and early modern periods. Over those centuries, discussions about religious authority of the kind we have looked at were limited to esoteric circles in both Judaism and Christianity. One can therefore question how significant these discussions were for explaining the success of ordinary Jews in the modern period.

My response to this challenge will be similar to the one I provided in the previous chapter. While ordinary Jews and Christians in the medieval and early modern periods may not have been aware of the intricate and arcane discussions of their respective intellectual leaders about authority, they would have certainly had some sense of how that issue was treated by these figures even if they could not have articulated it. The issue of religious authority was too fundamental to Judaism and Christianity not to have had an impact on ordinary Jews and Christians in their daily lives.

That would have been the case particularly from the beginning of the late medieval period onwards when Jewish and Christian societies had become quite religious and were heavily influenced by the decisions on religious matters that were being made by their respective religious authorities. In Christian Europe, that influence increased with the consolidation of canon law and its application in daily life. Among Jews, a sense of how religious authority functioned would have been even greater. Jews tended to live in tightly knit communities in which religious law governed every aspect of their lives and was adjudicated primarily by rabbis. Thus, there is good reason to believe that by the time the modern period arrived, the different approaches to religious authority in Judaism and Christianity had been absorbed by lay individuals in their respective communities along with the differing approaches to metaphysical freedom that these approaches entailed.

But we are not yet finished with the issue of autonomy in the metaphysical sense. In the next chapter, we explore one last area in which Jews, prior to modernity, outdid their Christian neighbours in developing a sense of autonomy that would serve them so well once the modern period began.

Chapter Five

Human Autonomy III: Reason and Philosophy

The thinkers in Christianity and Judaism who addressed the question of free will most directly and thoroughly before the modern period were the philosophers. They specialized in examining questions of ultimate meaning through the use of systematic, rational argumentation, and the issue of free will was one such question. The philosophers often dedicated entire sections of their treatises to this topic.

We have already encountered the views of some of these philosophers on issues such as sin, grace, and salvation, but we have not looked at the discussions they devoted specifically to the issue of free will, and in fact, I do not plan to do so here or elsewhere in this book. This may come as a surprise to some of my academic colleagues, especially those familiar with the history of philosophy. It may be particularly surprising to those of my colleagues who are aware that I devoted the first fifteen years of my career to medieval Jewish philosophy. But I can explain my decision, and I believe it makes a good deal of sense. The problem with the discussions of pre-modern Christian and Jewish philosophers about free will is that they are exceedingly complex and abstract. They are also difficult to interpret, and thus they often elicit widely different readings from modern scholars. In addition, some of the philosophers affirmed free will but in ways that go against our conventional understanding of that concept.[1] Most important, in the medieval and early modern periods, the influence of such discussions on Christians and Jews outside philosophical circles was very limited, far more so than the topics we have taken up in the past two chapters. Few ordinary Christians and Jews would have had any cognizance of them. In light of all of this, it is not clear that we can learn much from these discussions for the purposes of this book.

Nonetheless, I do not want to ignore the medieval and early modern philosophers altogether, and so I have chosen to discuss in this chapter their treatment of another issue that is important for our concerns: the place of reason in probing questions of ultimate meaning. This issue was perhaps the most basic one that pre-modern philosophers took up; it grappled with the question of how far reason could go in its explorations of philosophical matters. Was reason the ultimate arbiter of truth? Or did it have limitations, and if so, what were they? The answers that the philosophers provided to such questions are important for our concerns because they offer critical insight into their views on human autonomy. The fundamental issue here is the extent to which human beings are able and permitted to explore all aspects of existence, both physical and metaphysical.

The advantage of examining the discussions of this issue over those dealing with free will directly is that the former discussions are far more accessible, and by the same token, they are more likely to have been known by Christians and Jews outside philosophical circles in the medieval and early modern periods. Few people outside these circles would have been able to follow the intricate discussions of Christian and Jewish philosophers on free will, but some of them were aware of how these philosophers viewed reason and its capacities. In these centuries, Christians who attended universities would have had some cognizance of this matter because philosophy was a basic subject in the university curriculum. Jews did not have universities, but many of them were educated enough in philosophical matters to have debated the place of philosophy and human reason in the exploration of religious truths. In fact, controversy over that very issue engulfed Jewish communities in the Jewish world in the twelfth and thirteenth centuries.

I.   Christian Perspectives

The Medieval Period

We will begin our discussion with medieval Christian philosophy, but we must first understand more precisely what the term "philosophy" meant in the medieval era for both Christians and Jews. As I have already noted, philosophy is a discipline in which questions of ultimate meaning are explored through systematic, rational argumentation. Medieval Christians and Jews defined philosophy in a similar manner, but their approach to philosophy was different from that of the modern period in a number of respects.

One such difference was that all medieval Christian and Jewish philosophers were religious thinkers since religion was the lens through which medieval Christians and Jews addressed questions of ultimate meaning. In modern times, philosophy has become a largely secular pursuit, with only one branch of it designated for religious questions, a branch usually referred to as "philosophy of religion." Conversely, when religious thinkers nowadays engage in rational explorations of religion, this activity is referred to as "theology." In short, medieval Christian and Jewish philosophy combined what are now thought of as two separate disciplines: philosophy and theology.

Another difference between medieval and modern philosophy is that in the medieval period, Christian and Jewish philosophy included the study of the hard sciences, because the philosophers in both religious traditions held that studying the physical world was absolutely necessary for examining the truths of religion, an enterprise that, as we have just stated, was included in medieval philosophy. The belief was that science offered insights into God's creation and that these insights in turn provided an understanding of God himself and his activities. The philosophers included science as part of their discipline also because they believed that science and religion used the very same rational methods for acquiring knowledge and that the knowledge generated in both realms was firm and certain. Nowadays we do not think this way. We tend to believe that religion and science are separate and that we can achieve certainty in science but not in religious matters. In the medieval period, there was no such distinction; both could be explored by rational methods. That is why in the medieval period there was no such thing as "science" as an independent discipline or series of disciplines. That term, as we understand it today, came into vogue only in the nineteenth century. In the medieval period, what we know as "science" was referred to as "natural philosophy" – that is, the sector of philosophy that dealt with nature. However, in this discussion, I will use the term "science" rather than "natural philosophy" because it is the one with which we moderns are most familiar.

Yet another distinction between medieval and modern philosophy is that medieval Christian and Jewish philosophers relied heavily on Greek philosophy in their rational deliberations, particularly that of Plato and Aristotle. These two men had lived hundreds of years before Christians and Jews began engaging in philosophy, but their thinking was so powerful and sophisticated that it continued to be influential long after their lifetimes. In modern philosophical discourse, Greek philosophy is still influential among philosophers but far less than it was in the medieval times.

In sum, philosophy for medieval Christians and Jews was a much broader discipline than it is now. It encompassed practically the entire body of knowledge with which Christians and Jews were familiar. The fields we now include in science – such as physics, astronomy, botany, and zoology – were all included in philosophy, as were topics that now belong to religion and theology, such as God's existence and the nature of prophecy. All these areas of knowledge were believed to be governed by a common rational method that led one to truth, a method adopted from the ancient Greek philosophers.

One more important point: among the various subjects included in medieval Christian and Jewish philosophy, religion was considered by far the most important. The ultimate goal of philosophy was to acquire a better understanding of the divine truths explored in theology, and for this reason, it was imperative that human beings engage in philosophy.[2]

I have spoken so far only about the medieval period, but much of what I have said also applies to the early modern period. It is certainly the case that philosophy underwent important developments in this latter period, and some of the observations I have made up to this point become less applicable as we approach the modern period, and new ways of thinking come into vogue. Nonetheless, these observations provide an adequate starting point for us, and we can now proceed to focus on medieval Christian philosophy.

The major question we will examine is how far medieval Christian philosophers were willing to go in the exercise of reason. Did reason merely confirm the truths of religion, or could it question them? For the most part, medieval Christian philosophers believed that there were limits on what reason could do, a point that is not always sufficiently emphasized when writers talk about the contribution of medieval philosophy to the development of Western culture.[3] Reason could not function entirely on its own in order to achieve truth because it had been damaged by Original Sin. Therefore, guidance was also needed from "revelation," which consisted of the wisdom God had revealed to human beings, either through prophecy or divine inspiration. That wisdom had been recorded in Scripture or preserved by tradition that had been passed down through the generations. Medieval philosophers consulted these sources of revelation in conjunction with their rational speculations in order to ensure that nothing they said contradicted God's word. Thus, while the discipline of philosophy encouraged Europeans to believe that they were autonomous creatures before God, it also presumed that this autonomy remained restricted.

Christian interest in philosophy goes back to the beginning of Christianity. The Church Fathers became familiar with philosophy because the study of Greek and Roman philosophy was already popular in intellectual circles in the Roman Empire when Christianity first appeared. However, the Church Fathers had divided opinions on its value. On the one hand, Greek philosophy seemed unconnected to Christianity, or even antithetical to it. The founders and expositors of philosophy were pagans who had neither knowledge of the Bible nor any apparent need for it. They explored philosophical questions through the use of reason, and reason alone. On the other hand, in some respects, the Greek philosophical tradition seemed to confirm some of the key truths espoused by Christians. Greek philosophers often spoke of the existence of God and the need for human beings to lead moral lives, and this very much resonated with Christianity. Moreover, the sophistication of Greek philosophy was hard to ignore.[4]

Augustine favoured using Greek philosophy to explore Christianity, and because of his stature, later generations of Christian thinkers were inclined to do the same. Augustine was particularly enamoured of Neoplatonism, a school of philosophy with religious overtones that had developed out of Plato's thought.[5] However, the use of Greek philosophy and the philosophical method it employed did not really take hold in Christianity until much later in the Middle Ages with the rise of "scholasticism" in the twelfth century. This was a school that arose and flourished in the universities, which were then relatively new institutions. Scholastic thinkers were devoted to exploring Christianity through rational philosophical methods, and they continued the legacy of Augustine and some of the Church Fathers by using Greek philosophy as their inspiration.[6]

A major factor in the growth of the scholastic schools in the twelfth century was the influence of the newly discovered works of Aristotle. Up to this time, Christians were more familiar with Plato's works than with those of Aristotle because Christians did not have most of Aristotle's works in their possession; they had been lost for centuries. In the twelfth century, these works were rediscovered and began coming to light.[7]

Aristotle's philosophy had a powerful impact on Christian philosophers. They were impressed that his methods were far more empirical and less abstract than those of Plato or Neoplatonism. Christians were also impressed by Aristotle's reflections on how reason should be used in studying philosophical questions. Aristotle's works included entire books devoted to logic, a discipline not discussed by Plato. Thus, by absorbing Aristotle, Christian philosophy took on a different character than before. It became a more rigorous, structured discipline that combined hands-on observations of the physical world with well-thought-out methods of rational deduction in order to explore philosophical truths in all their variety, from science to theology. The greatest representative of scholasticism was Thomas Aquinas, whom we have already encountered.[8]

But again, we must be aware of the limits that medieval Christian philosophers placed on the use of reason. Aquinas believed that while reason had great capabilities, the most important truths were beyond the reach of the rational faculty, such as those concerning the Trinity, Original Sin, and salvation. These truths were revealed only in Scripture and tradition, and they were the most important truths concerning the relationship that human beings had with God.

Medieval Christian philosophy was not entirely free of radical thinking. William of Ockham (1285–1347), a rather conservative philosopher, placed more restrictions on reason than Aquinas did, but he also took some positions that rankled the Church. His scepticism about what human beings could know prompted him to cast doubt on the notion that the Church's authority resided in the pope and its clergy. He held instead that it resided in the souls of all Christian believers, a position that implicitly challenged the authority of the entire Church hierarchy.[9]

The Church tended to clamp down on philosophical thinking that had radical implications. Ockham was excommunicated for his views. Also, in the period just prior to Ockham, the Church took measures on more than one occasion to suppress the views of Christian philosophers that it deemed to be too radical. An edict known as the Condemnation of 1277 is the best known of these.[10]

Thus, by the end of the medieval period, Christian philosophers had established a strong beachhead for human autonomy in medieval Europe. According to these thinkers, human beings were capable of exploring every dimension of knowledge, and they therefore possessed significant powers in their relationship with God and the cosmos. However, the same philosophers also believed there were limits to what reason could probe. Moreover, the Church was determined to protect what it believed to be the fundamental doctrines of Christianity, and so it placed restrictions on the philosophers when it felt that their thinking raised questions about those doctrines.

The Renaissance

In an earlier chapter, we noted that the Renaissance was no less an age of faith than the medieval period. Christianity still held sway in European society, and most of the Renaissance's great thinkers were devoutly religious.[11] Philosophers in the Renaissance followed the same basic rules governing the relationship between human reason and religion that the medieval philosophers had. One could use reason to probe the physical and metaphysical worlds so long as the fundamental truths of Christianity were not challenged. Moreover, the Church continued to apply repressive measures when it felt that philosophers had overstepped their bounds.

To be sure, Renaissance philosophy was innovative in some respects. The philosophers of this era bypassed the scholastics and preferred to engage the sources of ancient Greek philosophy directly. This was the age of humanism, a school of thought that looked back to the great minds of antiquity for inspiration and ignored medieval thinkers on the belief that they had corrupted the teachings of these great minds. The humanists worked tirelessly to recover the works of the ancient philosophers in their original languages. Still, philosophy remained a pursuit for the purpose of deepening faith. Reason continued to be viewed as a God-given faculty that was meant to confirm the truths of religion.[12]

As in the medieval period, there were certainly thinkers who tested the limits placed on reason. Pietro Pomponazzi (1487–1525), an Italian philosopher, entertained views that aroused the ire of Church authorities. In his writings, he denied the immortality of the soul, claimed that many miracles in the Bible could be explained naturally, and seemed to deny the validity of religion altogether by stating that its function was entirely political in ensuring that people acted morally and obeyed authority. However, for every heretical statement Pomponazzi made in his writings, he made another one that contradicted it by upholding traditional Christian teaching. It is not clear whether he did so out of a genuine uncertainty about his beliefs or because he was trying to protect himself from the Church.[13]

Giordano Bruno (1548–1600) was another Italian Renaissance philosopher who held views that were objectionable to the Church. He supported Copernicus's heliocentric view of the universe, argued that the universe was infinite, and claimed that it contained an infinite number of other worlds with intelligent beings – ideas that all contradicted the Church's teachings. Like Pomponazzi, Bruno also believed that the primary function of religion was political. In some passages, Bruno also directly criticized Christianity, and he did so in rather harsh terms.[14]

Mention should also be made here of Niccolò Machiavelli (1469–1527), the great Italian political philosopher, who in some his writings criticized Christianity because of its otherworldly focus. Christianity, in his view, sapped human vitality. Like Pomponazzi and Bruno, he also expressed the view that religion's main function was political. But he was also similar to Pomponazzi in being inconsistent in his statements on religion. In some passages, he struck a conciliatory tone towards Christianity by praising the Church and the pope, and as with Pomponazzi, we are left wondering whether he was merely inconsistent or was making an effort to protect himself from the Church.[15]

Most Renaissance philosophers, however, sought to confirm rather than question the truths of Christianity. All the while, the Church continued to quash any views it deemed unacceptable. Pomponazzi was charged with heresy by the Church but was not tried, though his books were banned after his death. Bruno was less fortunate; the Church executed him. Machiavelli was fortunate to have escaped punishment.

The Reformation

The Reformation, at least initially, viewed human reason in a far less positive light than the scholastics and Renaissance figures did. The tone was set by Luther, who emphasized the lowliness of human beings due to their sinful nature and who therefore despised scholasticism for even suggesting that the human mind could probe the realm of religion. Luther also opposed the use of Greek philosophy by the scholastics because it was pagan in origin and was not informed by divine revelation. Luther's feelings about scholasticism were encapsulated in his description of it as "that great whore." He also expressed dismay at scientific developments that went against the Bible, and for this reason, he strongly opposed Copernicus's heliocentric theory.[16]

For Luther, reason was not entirely bad. It was a gift from God that could be used for exploring the natural world, and since that world had been created by God, its exploration could help one better appreciate God's handiwork. John Calvin was even more enthusiastic than Luther about the capacities of reason to increase our appreciation of God's creation. However, both Luther and Calvin believed that when Adam and Eve sinned, the faculty of reason was permanently damaged as Augustine had argued, and therefore its capacities were limited. Neither believed, as the scholastics did, that reason was of any use for exploring the mysteries of the divine realm.[17]

The Scientific Revolution

In the seventeenth century, the confidence of Europeans in the powers of human reason made a comeback as science took enormous steps forward. This period is commonly referred to as the Scientific Revolution, but it was not a revolution in any conscious sense. Rather, it was deemed a revolution by later historians who argued that in this period, changes occurred in the study of science that were so momentous that they added up to what was, in effect, a revolution.

What was revolutionary here was, first of all, the new and innovative ways in which Europeans approached science. They began to employ methods for exploring the physical world that included mathematics, a discipline that thus far had not played a prominent role in scientific exploration. These methods also included the employment of experiments to test hypotheses, a procedure that ensured certainty in one's findings. As far as the actual content of science was concerned, the Scientific Revolution resulted in a number of important discoveries, most significantly in the field of astronomy. Isaac Newton (1643–1727) was the leading figure here. Newton combined the views of Copernicus and Kepler, which suggested that the earth rotated around the sun, with his theory of universal gravitation, and the result was an entirely new model of the universe and how it worked, a model that was comprehensive, convincing, and elegant.[18]

The new science spawned innovative philosophical thinking. Philosophers applied the scientific method to philosophical issues and took into account the discoveries of science. Some of these philosophers were "rationalists." They began with ideas they believed were fundamental in our minds, and they then used them to construct arguments about what human beings could know about the physical and metaphysical realms.[19] Other philosophers were "empiricists." These thinkers attempted to understand the physical and metaphysical realms by beginning with observations about the concrete world.[20]

We also begin to see in this period the emergence of thinkers who believed that reason was so powerful that it was superior to religion. Thomas Hobbes, the great political philosopher, cast doubt on the fundamental dogmas of Christianity in various passages in his writings. However, Hobbes, like his Renaissance predecessors, was not entirely consistent on matters of religion. In some passages in his works, he seemed to support Christianity, and here again it is not clear whether such statements were genuine or attempts to ward off punishment from the Church.[21]

Baruch Spinoza was the only major figure in this era who was unequivocal in placing reason above religion as a source of truth. Spinoza was a Dutch Jew who was excommunicated by the Jewish community because of his radical philosophical views but then went on to become a highly influential philosopher in the non-Jewish world. And his views were indeed radical. He constructed a philosophy in which God was identified with nature. Nature, in turn, was governed by laws that could not be violated. Miracles were therefore impossible. Spinoza also argued that the Bible was not of divine origin; it had been written by human beings, and to prove his point, he conducted an examination of the Hebrew Bible that was among the first attempts to use empirical and historical methods to explain its origin and contents. In this way, he openly challenged the basic premises of both Judaism and Christianity.[22]

However, it would be a mistake to assume that in this period, Europeans on the whole were prepared to leave religion behind. Most of the great scientists in this era were religious individuals who, much like the medieval philosophers, saw science as a means to confirm their Christian beliefs, not reject them. Science was still referred to as "natural philosophy" because it continued to be viewed as part of the philosophical enterprise, and it therefore remained subordinate to theology. Newton himself viewed science through this lens. His new model of the universe had the potential to undermine Christianity because it raised questions about whether God was really necessary for the universe to function, but Newton himself did not see it that way. He regarded the conception of the universe that emerged from his theory as confirming the existence of the Creator and the glory of his creation.[23]

So even during the Scientific Revolution, European views on the relationship between reason and religion were pretty much consistent with those that had dominated European thinking from the beginning of the medieval period. Most European thinkers still saw the wisdom revealed in religion as superior to that constructed by reason, and reason continued to be religion's handmaid.

To sum up our discussion thus far, prior to the Enlightenment, the intellectual tradition in Europe that cultivated philosophy and science also developed bold views on the powers of reason. According to the thinkers who were engaged in these disciplines, human beings had the capacity to probe and understand the workings of the physical and metaphysical realms. Some thinkers even used reason to question the basic tenets of religion – most notably, Spinoza. However, the boldness of the European intellectual tradition had its limits. The common belief was that reason required the help of God's revealed word to truly understand the mysteries of the physical and divine worlds and that reason could not contradict that word. Moreover, the Catholic and Protestant Churches were willing to prosecute those who thought otherwise.

The Enlightenment

In the eighteenth century, the confidence of European intellectuals in reason grew stronger. It was becoming increasingly clear that reason could function independently of religion and that the study of the natural world was its own discipline and had its own methods. Eventually, the enterprise of exploring the natural world was longer referred to as "natural philosophy." It was now "science," an area of study independent of both philosophy and theology. That term would not become fashionable until 1830, but when it did, its creation reflected changes in European thinking that had begun in the previous century.[24]

One reason why science was now seen as an independent discipline was that it was being used to solve practical human problems as never before. Science was inspiring the invention of new technologies with the aim of controlling nature in order to make life easier and more comfortable. There were significant improvements in agriculture, the raising of livestock, mining, forestry, and public health. The view now began to take hold that the goal of science was not just to gain insight into the world of nature but to benefit humankind, and in that role, science did not need to have a relationship with religion.[25]

The growing confidence in reason also affected the way Europeans approached human society. There was now a belief that human interactions could be studied in the same way that the interactions of all other objects in nature had been studied because human beings also behaved according to laws that could be discerned through reason. This way of thinking gave rise to a series of new disciplines that we now call the "social sciences."

There was also the growing belief that the science of human behaviour was meant not just for descriptive purposes but for prescriptive ones as well. If one could understand the laws governing human interactions, one could then construct an ideal society that would be just and peaceful and that would maximize the potential of its citizens. Intellectuals now spoke of constructing law systems in accordance with "natural law," a body of law governing human behaviour that was discerned through reason and against which all particular human law systems could be judged.[26]

In light of all these developments, perhaps it was inevitable that some Europeans began to think that reason and the science it produced were not just independent of religion but actually superior to it. This perspective was encouraged by the fact that some scientific discoveries, far from confirming the truths of religion, now seemed to undermine them.

Most influential in this regard was Newton's conception of the universe. As noted earlier, Newton believed that his discoveries confirmed the truths of Christianity; yet many Enlightenment thinkers drew the opposite conclusion. The universe, as Newton conceived it, seemed not to require a God who was constantly involved in its operations. It functioned according to a series of scientific laws that made it a graceful and harmonious mechanism, and therefore the need for God's intervention in the world's affairs seemed minimal at most. That way of thinking also undercut one of the most important premises of Christianity: that

God performs miracles. Miracles were fundamental to Christianity; the biblical narrative was filled with them. However, miracles violated the laws of nature, and in light of the new science, it was difficult to imagine that this was possible. Miracles would disrupt and irreparably damage the harmony of the universe. Thus, in some respects, reason and religion were now on a collision course, with reason gaining the upper hand in some circles.[27]

Another casualty of the advances in science was the doctrine of Original Sin. We noted in an earlier chapter that in the Enlightenment, the doctrine of Original Sin was rejected by most intellectuals in this period, and we can now understand better why that happened. One reason for the dismissal of this idea was that scientific advances had convinced Enlightenment thinkers that nature was inherently good; the universe that God had set in motion according to Newton's paradigm was harmonious and beautiful. And if nature was good, *human* nature had to be good as well; it could not be inherently evil. Thus, the world was not a fallen place, nor were the people who inhabited it. The belief began to grow that people were born in a neutral state from a moral standpoint and that it was up to them to choose whether to be good or evil throughout their lives.[28]

Other tenets of Christianity were undermined by the new science. Evidence was mounting that the world was far older than the Bible implied. Some Enlightenment thinkers began to challenge the status of the Bible itself as a revelation from God, as Spinoza had. This approach to the Bible was inspired in part by the discovery of stories in other civilizations that seemed awfully similar to those in the Bible, an indication that the Bible could be understood as just one example of ancient Near Eastern literature. Furthermore, new methods of textual analysis indicated that traditional claims about the authorship of the Bible were not necessarily true. For example, a close reading of the Torah made it difficult to believe that it had been written by Moses, or any one single author, as Christians and Jews had held.[29]

These developments would result in a new approach to human beings and their relationship to the cosmos. Some Europeans began to view human beings as masters of the world around them. God was pushed into the background as an impersonal being who was responsible only for sustaining nature's operation, or he was dispensed with altogether. Spinoza, who was mentioned earlier, was perhaps the first major thinker to adopt a world view of this kind, but European thinkers were now supporting it in significant numbers.

During the Enlightenment itself, the most radical thinkers were found in France and England. Voltaire (1694–1778), perhaps the leading proponent of the French Enlightenment, rejected Christianity, though he still believed in a God who was in charge of the world.[30] The antipathy towards Christianity that Voltaire and other French thinkers had cultivated came out in full force in the French Revolution that began in 1789. Many of the revolutionaries wanted to get rid of Christianity altogether, and for a short period they got their wish. During the revolution's most violent phase, the Reign of Terror (1793–4), the revolutionaries replaced Christianity as the official religion of France with a newly contrived religion called the "Cult of the Goddess of Reason," which celebrated human rationality and its capabilities. The traditional Christian calendar was replaced with a new one that eliminated Sundays and Christmas. The clergy were pressured to renounce their faith. These changes would soon be overturned, and France would bring back much of the older religious order, but France would continue to be a country marked by mixed feelings about institutional Christianity, and it would become a bastion of secular European culture in the modern period.[31] These events were significant not just because of the radical ideas being espoused here but also because the new way of thinking among Europe's intellectuals was beginning to have an impact on ordinary Europeans.

Yet it is important to recognize that not all Enlightenment intellectuals were as radical as those just described. In fact, most intellectuals across Europe during the Enlightenment remained attached to Christianity, but the kind of Christianity these intellectuals adhered to was a rational Christianity, a "religion of reason," as they called it. It was a form of Christianity that they believed greatly improved on the Christianity of past centuries.

The intellectuals who took this approach differed about what rational Christianity was, but we can identify common patterns in their thinking. They usually rejected the God who performed miracles, but they still believed in a God who governed the world through the laws of nature. They often denied Jesus's divinity, but they still saw him as an extraordinary human being who provided a role model for morality that everyone should emulate. They tended to reject the notions of heaven and hell in the afterlife, but they still believed in an afterlife of a more abstract kind that provided individuals with rewards for leading morally good lives. They tended to believe that Christianity was not necessarily the only religion that had rational elements in it, but they held that its rationality was far greater than that of other religions and that it was by far the most enlightened.[32]

However, the important point to recognize here is that both the radical intellectuals of the Enlightenment who largely rejected Christianity, and the more moderate intellectuals who reshaped it into a religion of reason, adopted the notion that human beings could penetrate the world's mysteries with their unaided reason. In this way of thinking, human beings were the primary arbiters of truth.

Matters were quite different for another sector of the European population at the time of the Enlightenment. Plenty of European intellectuals continued to adhere to Christianity in its pre-modern forms, as did most of Europe's lay people. This observation is one that scholars of the Enlightenment were reluctant to acknowledge until recently.

The eighteenth century also saw the rise of Christian movements that encouraged Europeans to *deepen* their religious commitments to traditional Christianity by adopting a form of religious devotion that cultivated the inward, spiritual, and emotional dimensions of religious experience. These movements were widespread and reached ordinary Europeans in a way that Enlightenment intellectuals did not. Germany had the Pietists, England the Methodists, and France the Jansenists, and the US experienced a religious revival known as the Great Awakening that was partly inspired by Methodism. Thus, as the nineteenth century began, Christianity, as it had been understood and practised before the Enlightenment, was still a powerful force in European society and the US.[33] The popularity of these older forms of Christianity during the Enlightenment meant that large numbers of Europeans would not have been as assertive about the powers of human reason as those who either rejected Christianity entirely or reinterpreted it as a religion of reason.

There was also opposition in this period from conservative Christian quarters to the notion that the human intellect was as powerful as many Enlightenment thinkers were claiming. Many in this segment of the European population were resistant to science in particular because they saw it as undermining Christian tenets, and they believed that it made human beings seem more powerful in God's world than they really were.

To sum up, by the nineteenth century, the notion had taken hold in Europe that human beings had rational capabilities that allowed them to understand and master the world. However, this new view of human beings took a long time to evolve – longer, in fact, than some scholars have been willing to acknowledge. It had roots in the medieval philosophical tradition, but it was not until the Enlightenment that it emerged in full force. We must also recognize that even during the Enlightenment, the new way of thinking was not to everyone's taste, particularly ordinary Europeans. Much of Europe remained religious in the traditional sense.[34] Still, the idea that human reason was the ultimate judge of truth became increasingly popular as the modern period began, and it would become highly influential in the Western world as a whole. Most important, this way of thinking had an impact on the West's relationship with the rest of the world. It no doubt helped the West to become dominant in the economic, intellectual, and artistic realms and to expand its power and influence around the globe.

II. Jewish Perspectives

The Medieval Period

As we noted earlier, medieval Jews developed schools of philosophy that were based on principles similar to those that informed the philosophical schools in medieval Christianity. Jewish philosophers, like their Christian peers, used reason to probe religious questions: this pursuit included the study of science, and it was aided by insights from ancient Greek philosophy.

By far the greatest of the medieval Jewish philosophers was Maimonides (1138–1204), a figure we have already encountered. His major philosophical work, *The Guide of the Perplexed*, had an immense impact on Judaism not just in the medieval period but in subsequent periods as well. It became one of the most important books in the history of Judaism.

Maimonides' philosophy is therefore a good starting point for our discussion. The problem is that it is notoriously difficult to interpret and will require a far lengthier exposition than was needed for any of the Christian philosophers. The source of the problem is that at the beginning of the *Guide*, Maimonides states that he will conceal his true positions throughout his treatise. He even tells us at one point that for this purpose he will deliberately contradict himself. His goal in writing in this manner is to hide philosophical truths that he believes will be harmful to the uneducated masses, who know little about philosophy. But he assures us that those educated in philosophy will be able to discern his true views.[35] Sure enough, the ensuing treatise is filled with ambiguities, provocative innuendos, and contradictions about all the topics it takes up, which cover the entire range of philosophical issues in which medieval Jewish thinkers were interested.

For centuries, interpreters have tried to discern what Maimonides' true philosophical views were, but opinion, on this matter, has not been settled. It can be divided into two major schools of thought that emerged at the end of Maimonides' lifetime and that have persisted to this day, and they give widely different accounts of his beliefs. According to one view, what Maimonides was trying to conceal was the fact that he was a radical philosopher, a thinker whose ideas were completely at odds with those of traditional Judaism. According to the second view, Maimonides was no radical at all. His philosophical positions supported the basic tenets of traditional Judaism, but he felt the need to conceal some of his philosophical thinking out of fear that it would be misunderstood by the masses, who were not versed in philosophy.[36]

These two portrayals of Maimonides have different implications with respect to the powers of human reason, and so I will discuss each one in turn, beginning with the radical interpretation. But in order to understand this interpretation, we need to say more about the philosophy of Aristotle, whose thinking had as big an impact on medieval Jewish philosophy as it did on medieval Christian philosophy, including the philosophy of Maimonides.

As noted earlier in this chapter, Aristotle's philosophy had a great deal to offer philosophers in both Judaism and Christianity because it seemed to provide rational proof for some of the most fundamental beliefs of the two religions. Most important, Aristotle demonstrated that there was a single God who was invisible, all-powerful, and all-knowing, and Jewish and Christian philosophers therefore celebrated the fact that a pagan philosopher had used sophisticated rational arguments to arrive at a conception of God that was much like that of the Bible. Aristotle showed that one did not have to read the Bible to know that such a God existed. It was an idea accessible to all human beings through reason.[37]

The problem was that the God of Aristotle and the God of the Bible resembled each other only up to a point. In critical respects, they were quite different. Aristotle's God was what scholars refer to as an "impersonal" God. He contained within himself all the ideal prototypes for things in the world and all the laws that allowed the universe to function, but he did not have "personhood" in the way that the biblical God did. Aristotle's God could not perform miracles, speak to humans, or even change his mind from one moment to the next. As a result, this God was incapable of creating the world, and so the world must have existed for all eternity.

Perhaps the best way for us moderns to picture the God of Aristotle is to think of God as a giant computer program that is responsible for running all of nature's processes. A computer program is composed of an enormous number of functions coded into it that allow it to perform a wide variety of tasks. However, the program is not "aware" of the things it is doing. It simply does them. The program also is not capable of changing itself; its functions are set. It was the same with Aristotle's God. He too was made up of a large number of functions – the ideal models of all species of objects in the world and the natural laws that governed them – and these were responsible for everything that existed in the world and all events that happened in it. However, he was unaware that he was making the world function, nor could he actively alter anything in it through a change of will.

Did this mean that, according to Aristotle, people could give in to their basest instincts and live a life of wanton pleasure without fear of divine punishment? They certainly could, given that God was incapable of rewarding and punishing human beings for their actions, but for Aristotle this way of life was not at all advisable. He believed that human beings should still refine their morals by indulging in the physical pleasures of life in moderation. That way they could develop their minds through the exercise of reason and the amassing of knowledge. The cultivation of the intellect was, for Aristotle, the ultimate goal towards which human beings should strive. It brought human beings the greatest possible amount of well-being and happiness. Thus, even if a life of wanton pleasure did not bring punishment from God, one would, in effect, end up punishing oneself by failing to experience the true pleasures that came from cultivating the life of the mind, and so the latter lifestyle was much preferred.

The life of the mind also had practical benefits, according to Aristotle. It made one more intelligent so that one could make choices in daily life to maximize good fortune and avoid physical harm as much as possible. Aristotle also believed that the cultivation of the intellect had ramifications for the afterlife. It prepared the soul to survive the death of the body. And here too, no wilful action on God's part was needed. The mind, as the highest part of the soul, was the only part of us that could achieve immortality, and therefore by developing the mind in this life, one was guaranteeing that it would live on in the next. The process was an entirely natural one.

Most medieval Jewish and Christian philosophers who were influenced by Aristotle found a compromise between Aristotle's philosophy and that of the Bible, and they proposed a number of ways for doing this that we cannot delve into here. But the general strategy was to draw insights from both Aristotle and the Bible to construct a philosophy that had some of the characteristics of both. In this way, the philosophers in the two religious traditions could make use of Aristotle's carefully reasoned arguments but without giving up their most cherished religious beliefs.

With all this background in mind, we can now understand the radical reading of Maimonides. According to this reading, Maimonides did not try to find a compromise between Aristotle's philosophy and the Bible;

instead, he adopted Aristotle's philosophy *in place of* the Bible. That is, he believed in the same impersonal God that Aristotle envisioned, a God who did not create the world, perform miracles, speak to human beings, or intervene in the world below in any way. In fact, this God was not really interested in human beings at all because he spent all his time contemplating his own essence. The world functioned only as a by-product of the energy God invested in that contemplation. As for human beings, here too Maimonides adopted Aristotle's views. Maimonides believed we should live lives of moderation and cultivate our intellects. Perfecting the intellect brought us pleasure, guided us to the best course of practical action in our daily lives, and guaranteed the survival of the soul after death.

But did that mean that, for Maimonides, the Bible and traditional Judaism had no value? And if so, why did Maimonides continue being an observant Jew to the end of his life? According to the radical reading of Maimonides, the Bible still had great value for him, as did traditional Judaism in general. First, religion provided people uneducated in philosophy with enough wisdom so that they would have some sense of the truth. Thus, for instance, these people would learn from religion that there was a supreme deity, even if their conception of this deity was not entirely accurate. This modicum of philosophical wisdom might even allow them to achieve immortality. Second, religion helped promote a stable society by convincing the uneducated masses that there was a God who was watching over them at all times and would punish them if they lived immoral lives. God, in fact, did no such thing, but if people *believed* he did, the world would be a more peaceful place. As we have seen, a number of radical Christian thinkers in the Renaissance adopted this view of religion as well.

As for Maimonides' own lifestyle, it made perfect sense that he lived as a traditional Jew despite his radical views. The masses had to believe in the truth of traditional religion for the reasons just stated; it had personal and political value for them. Therefore, Maimonides had to adopt the appearance of being a traditional Jew while concealing his true views.

All of this explains why Maimonides wrote the *Guide* in the manner that he did. The truths of philosophy had to be concealed from the uneducated masses, for if they were taught these truths, they might not cultivate their minds to achieve intellectual perfection but instead might live in accordance with their worst instincts, and society would descend into chaos. What held the masses in check was the fear of a God who would punish them for living this way. Therefore, in the *Guide*, Maimonides hid his radical beliefs through ambiguity, innuendo, and outright contradiction. Still, he left enough clues about his true views so that those versed in philosophy would be able to discern them.

The implications of this interpretation of Maimonides are startling. If it is true, then the most important Jewish philosopher of the medieval period, and perhaps of all time, was really a heretic in disguise! Maimonides' views would also have startling implications for our topic; they would assume that human reason had great power and was, in fact, superior to religion as a source of truth. Everything one had to know about the universe was reflected in the kind of philosophy that Aristotle espoused, a philosophy that did not depend at all on the Bible or on any other text produced by divine revelation.

Yet many students of Maimonides, both medieval and modern, have not gone along with this radical reading. They have found the notion that Maimonides was an Aristotelian heretic in disguise unconvincing, even preposterous. For them, Maimonides was a traditional, pious Jew, very much devoted to the Judaism of the Bible and the rabbis. Maimonides may have adopted some insights from Aristotle, but he in no way accepted Aristotle's entire way of thinking. And if Maimonides concealed some of his true views, that was because he did not want to be misunderstood by Jews who were unfamiliar with philosophy, who might draw incorrect conclusions from his ideas. In other words, Maimonides was not himself a heretic, but he was afraid his *readers* might become heretics if they did not understand him properly, and that is why his writing on philosophical matters was so elusive.

As far as human autonomy goes, this reading of Maimonides granted human beings considerable freedom as well, but not to the extent that the radical reading did. Reason was still a powerful faculty because of its capacity to explore the physical and metaphysical worlds, but it had definite limits. There were truths that it could not penetrate in the metaphysical realm and that could only be imparted through revelation.

My sense is that the majority of modern academic scholars have tended to side with the radical reading of Maimonides. However, opinions vary on how much of an Aristotelian he really was.[38] In some respects, I sympathize with the radical reading of Maimonides, though I am not always sure how deep Maimonides' radicalism was.[39] Yet while the debate about the real Maimonides is a fascinating one and has consumed the attention of Jewish scholars for hundreds of years, this is not the place to settle it; indeed, chances are that it will never be settled. What is important for our purposes is to understand each of these readings of Maimonides and the implications they have for the place of reason in probing religious matters.

The two readings of Maimonides are also critical for giving us insight into the views of the medieval Jewish philosophers who came after him. These philosophers can be divided roughly into two camps that parallel the two readings of Maimonides. In the radical camp were philosophers who composed works that attempted to unveil the radical secrets in Maimonides' philosophy, or who wrote treatises that presented their own radical philosophy, or who penned works of both types.[40] Included in this camp was R. Levi ben Gershom, known by modern scholars as Gersonides (1288–1344), who is considered to be the greatest medieval Jewish philosopher after Maimonides. In the second camp were more traditional Jewish philosophers, who composed works in a variety of formats similar to those of the radical philosophers.

Soon after Gersonides's lifetime, Jewish philosophy took a conservative turn. Hasdai Crescas (1340–1410/11), a Spanish philosopher, heralded the beginning of this phase of medieval Jewish philosophy. He was born shortly before Gersonides's death and produced a highly influential work that attempted to dismantle the Aristotelian philosophy upon which Maimonides and Gersonides had based their thinking. By the fifteenth century, there was no longer a rivalry between the radical and traditional Jewish philosophers. The latter group now dominated.

The Early Modern Period

As the early modern period got under way, several Jewish thinkers in Europe continued to study philosophy and incorporate it into their thinking, but they tended to be traditional in orientation and thus used philosophy to support Rabbinic Judaism. Also, philosophy was no longer the influential discipline among Jews that it once was.[41] It was now being overshadowed by Kabbalah, which became the dominant thought-system in Judaism until the modern period. We saw earlier that Kabbalah had some radical elements in it, but with regard to the role of reason in speculating about questions of ultimate meaning, Kabbalah was even more traditional than the most traditional of Jewish philosophers. It rejected philosophy on the premise that ultimate truth was beyond the reach of human reason and could be attained only through revelation, and the Kabbalists claimed that their theology had been received in this manner.[42] The popularity of Kabbalah in the early modern period was due, in part, to the fact that the largest community of Jews in Europe was in eastern Europe, and that community was highly traditional.

Philosophy eventually made a comeback. A new era in Jewish philosophy began at the tail end of the early modern period with Moses Mendelssohn (1729–86). Mendelssohn was a German Jew who broke new ground for Jews by becoming one of the leading figures in the German Enlightenment. His early works treated general philosophical questions that were not specifically Jewish, but he eventually began to write on Jewish themes. His major work, *Jerusalem*, is often regarded as the first great work of modern Jewish philosophy.[43]

Mendelssohn's philosophy of Judaism was relatively traditional. In the mid-nineteenth century, however, Jewish philosophy began taking a more radical turn, inspired in part by the Reform movement, which fundamentally rethought basic Jewish beliefs and ideas. Some Jewish intellectuals seeking to modernize Judaism in this manner looked to philosophy as the means to do so.[44]

Mention should be made here of Spinoza, an early modern figure whom we have already encountered in this chapter. Spinoza was, in effect, an heir to the radical strand in medieval Jewish philosophy discussed earlier by adopting views similar to theirs. As we have noted, Spinoza adopted an impersonal conception of God and denied the divinity of the Bible. He was also familiar with the philosophical works of the great medieval Jewish philosophers, most notably Maimonides and Gersonides, though it is hard to say whether his radicalism was inspired by these figures.[45] Nonetheless, Spinoza's thinking, whatever its source, was certainly radical, and it was very much in line with the type of radical thinking that some Jewish philosophers had entertained centuries earlier.

It took time, however, for Spinoza's approach to win adherents in the Jewish community. His views were too radical for the Jews of Amsterdam in his time, and he was excommunicated as a result. But in the nineteenth century, with the advent of the Reform movement in Judaism, and with radical Jewish philosophy finding a footing in the European Jewish community, Jewish thinkers revived the notion of an impersonal God. Perhaps the most important Jewish philosopher who went in this direction was Hermann Cohen (1842–1918), a German intellectual whose thinking had a great impact on subsequent Jewish philosophers as well as on the Reform movement in Judaism. Some modern Jewish thinkers would also embrace Spinoza.[46] From this point onwards, the type of thinking that was once branded as radical was no longer regarded as such, and it began to find a permanent place in Jewish discourse. For many Jews, reason was now the ultimate arbiter of truth in the same way that it had become so in large sectors of Christian Europe.

Jewish Philosophy vs. Christian Philosophy

Let us now take stock of what we have discussed so far in this chapter by comparing the views of medieval and early modern Christian and Jewish philosophers on the powers of reason. What comes out of our analysis is that in Europe, radical philosophy took root among Jewish thinkers much earlier than it did among Christian thinkers. According to this type of philosophy, reason had immense power in that it was superior to religion in determining truth. In Judaism, a school of philosophy espousing this way of thinking developed in the thirteenth century on the basis of Maimonides' thought. Gersonides, the greatest medieval Jewish philosopher after Maimonides, could be included in this camp, though his thinking was somewhat less radical than that of the most radical interpreters of Maimonides. It is also quite plausible that the radical interpreters of Maimonides were correct and that Maimonides himself was the radical philosopher they believed him to be, and if that is true, then the two greatest medieval Jewish philosophers were radicals.

There is also reason to believe that lay Jews were aware of this radical strain in philosophy over the centuries in which its proponents were active, particularly in southern France, Spain, and Italy. Jews in these countries did not have universities in which to study philosophy as Christians did, but there were private itinerant tutors in Jewish communities that Jews could hire to study this discipline, and the evidence would suggest that the number of Jews who availed themselves of such instruction was not negligible. Medieval rabbis in the countries just mentioned delivered sermons in synagogues and communal events, and many collections of those sermons, some of which include philosophical material, have been preserved. Clearly, then, lay audiences for these sermons must have had some knowledge of philosophy.[47]

But did lay Jews necessarily encounter philosophy in its radical form? And if so, did they understand its implications? There is evidence for an affirmative answer on both counts. Gersonides's biblical commentaries were quite popular among medieval Jews, as evidenced by the fact that some of them were among the first Hebrew books to be printed and that they were reprinted numerous times. These works contained all the major elements of Gersonides's philosophical teachings, which, as already noted, could be quite radical.[48]

But the strongest evidence that radical medieval Jewish philosophy had an impact on ordinary Jews is that it provoked widespread controversy in the Jewish community from the last years of Maimonides' life at the end of the twelfth century to the beginning of the fourteenth century. In this time frame, significant portions of the Jewish world in Christian and Islamic lands were engulfed in bitter disputes about the place of Maimonides' philosophy in Judaism, as well as the study of philosophy in general. In these disputes, Maimonides, and philosophy in general, had critics and defenders. The rabbis of communities in France and Spain took one or the other side and publicly issued decrees of excommunication against their opponents. And even after the worst of the disputes died down, opinions in the Jewish community remained sharply divided over the place of philosophy in Judaism.[49] So it is clear that the views of the radical Jewish philosophers seemed to have circulated enough in the Jewish community at large to have become a source of extensive strife. How deep this dispute penetrated into the lay sectors of Jewish communities is not easy to determine, nor is it easy to determine how much this sector of the Jewish public truly understood the thinking of the most radical of Jewish philosophers. Nonetheless, the Jewish public could not have been completely unaware of what the dispute was about.[50]

Jewish philosophy became more conservative in the early modern period, with the notable exception of Spinoza. Spinoza left the Jewish community after his excommunication and wrote his major works after that event. Yet he was part of the Jewish community into his adult life, and his thinking was shaped in part by medieval Jewish philosophy. So in some respects, he represented a continuation of the radical strand found in medieval Jewish philosophy that had existed several centuries earlier.

Among Christians in the medieval period, there were certainly philosophers who entertained radical ideas that irritated the Church; we have already mentioned William of Ockham and the philosophers who were the object of the Condemnation of 1277 as examples of such thinkers. But in neither case were the ideas that were censured nearly as radical as those held by the radical interpreters of Maimonides or by Gersonides. Historians once believed that the Condemnation of 1277 was directed against a group of radical philosophers who challenged fundamental Christian doctrines on the basis of Aristotelian principles. However, this hypothesis has largely been abandoned.[51] As for Ockham, the problem here was a very specific element in his thinking that undermined the authority of the Church hierarchy; it was not that he engaged in a wholesale rethinking of basic Christian beliefs. Ockham was, on the whole, a conservative philosopher.

In the fifteenth century, we see the emergence of radical views on religion among Christian philosophers in Renaissance Italy, and we have noted the examples of Pomponazzi, Bruno, and Machiavelli as evidence of this trend. But only Machiavelli had significant influence, and his interests lay primarily in political philosophy, not religion. Moreover, these thinkers did not spawn a widespread debate about philosophy in Christian communities the way the radical Jewish philosophers had in Jewish communities in the thirteenth and fourteenth centuries. Later on in seventeenth-century England, Hobbes expressed radical views on religion, but he too was interested mainly in political philosophy, and he did not initiate widespread controversy about religious ideas.

It was only in the eighteenth century that radical philosophy began to take hold in Europe on a significant scale. French philosophers, such as Voltaire, took the lead by openly and systematically challenging the fundamental tenets of Christianity, and the assault on the Church and on Christianity reached its high point in the French Revolution. In sum, radical philosophy took hold in Christian Europe at least four hundred years after it did among Jews.

What explains the difference here? Why did radical philosophical thinking establish itself among Jews so much earlier than it did among Christians?

One obvious reason is political. European Christianity in the medieval and early modern periods was governed by powerful Churches that could crush dissent and crush it violently. Thus, for instance, in the medieval period, the Catholic Church arranged for the slaughter of thousands of Cathars and Waldensians, who had challenged its sacrosanct doctrines and practices. The medieval Church never used violence against Christian philosophers on a scale of this kind, but it did outlaw their views when it felt that the philosophers had gone too far in their thinking, as was the case with the Condemnation of 1277. From the Reformation onwards, the Protestant Churches also silenced thinkers whose views were deemed radical. Thus, the power of the Churches in medieval and early modern Europe was undoubtedly a factor in ensuring that Christian philosophy did not become too radical.

The rabbis in Jewish communities during the same periods did not have the political power the Churches did, and so when they had to discipline dissenters, their options were more limited and less effective. The rabbis could excommunicate such individuals. In fact, in the century after Maimonides' death, some European rabbis excommunicated whole communities because of their support for the study of Maimonidean philosophy. But the rabbis had no armies at their disposal to quash dissent in the way that the Catholic Church did. Excommunication in Rabbinic Judaism meant only that individuals who received this punishment were socially ostracized – an unpleasant punishment to be sure, even devastating from a psychological standpoint, but not as serious as physical violence, imprisonment, torture, or execution.[52] Furthermore, there was no central rabbinic institution that wielded power over all Jews in the way that the Catholic Church did for all medieval European Christians, which meant that rabbinic excommunication was only as effective as the authority of the rabbis promulgating it. As a consequence, excommunication sometimes was not effective at all. The communities that were excommunicated in medieval Europe for studying Maimonidean philosophy had their own rabbis, who promptly excommunicated the rabbis who had excommunicated them. Thus, given the differences between Jews and Christians regarding the power that religious authorities wielded, radical thinking could survive in Jewish communities in a way that it could not among Christians.[53]

Another factor that may explain the difference between Jews and Christians regarding radical philosophy was the influence of historical circumstances. Jews in general may have tended to be more comfortable with this type of philosophy than Christians were because, as the centuries went by, the Jewish exile seemed to be persisting without end, the condition of the Jews was worsening in some places – especially in Christian Europe – and therefore Aristotle's impersonal God may have made more sense to some Jews than the traditional Jewish conception of God did. Hundreds of years of suffering may have made medieval Jews open to the idea that God was detached from history and did not intervene in world events.

The situation of Christians was quite different. For centuries, Christendom was quite powerful, and so Christians had less need than Jews to take issue with the traditional conception of a God who was involved in human affairs. According to their perspective, the job he was doing was fine. At times, Christians certainly felt threatened and suffered. Since the advent of Islam, there were constant fears in European Christendom about the growing power of the Islamic empire, and indeed those fears were justified. By the later centuries of the medieval period, Muslim armies were making inroads into Christian Europe; the Crusades were partly a response to those inroads. Still, Christians in Europe were far more secure than Jews were.

An important question for our purposes is what the nature of the connection was between Jewish philosophy, including its radical element, and Rabbinic Judaism. Modern scholars tend to downplay that connection, and for good reason: the medieval Jewish philosophers were attempting to reinterpret Judaism in light of Greek philosophy, and the concepts and methods of Greek philosophy were alien to Rabbinic Judaism. That was particularly true of the most radical medieval Jewish philosophers, who adopted views that were entirely at odds with those of Rabbinic Judaism.

However, an argument can be made that there was indeed a connection between medieval Jewish philosophy and Rabbinic Judaism and that this connection helps explain the radical philosophical thinking that developed in medieval Judaism. Most of the great medieval Jewish philosophers, including Maimonides and Gersonides, were also rabbis. Remember also that Rabbinic Judaism had its own radical ideas about God, and while none of the rabbis in the Talmud and its related literature adopted an impersonal conception of God of the kind that the radical medieval Jewish philosophers did, these rabbis sometimes depicted God as a deity who was less than omnipotent, or as a deity who was willing to relinquish his power and share it with humans. Thus, the ideas of the radical philosophers regarding God were not entirely at odds with those of the Talmudic rabbis. If, according to the rabbis, it was possible to overrule God on a matter of law or accuse him of moral failings, then the notion of an impersonal God of the kind that the radical medieval Jewish philosophers upheld merely took those ideas a critical step or two further.

Moreover, the rabbis of the Talmud certainly valued the use of reason when it came to matters of Jewish law. The type of reason employed by the rabbis here was different from that of Aristotle. Rabbinic reasoning focused mainly on legal matters and was based on the Written and Oral Torah, which had been given directly by God. It also had its own idiosyncratic logic. Aristotle's reasoning was concerned with philosophical issues and did not depend on divine revelation of any kind, and its logic was meant to be universal. However, the rabbis certainly valued the power of the human mind to explore divine matters, and this way of thinking also had something in common with what the medieval Jewish philosophers were trying to do, including the radical ones. Thus, while the radical dimension of medieval Jewish philosophy was in some ways a rejection of Rabbinic Judaism, it was not entirely inimical to it and may even have been beholden to it in some respects. In sum, a combination of external and internal factors help explain why Jews developed radical philosophical thinking so much earlier than Christians did.

Conclusions

In the past three chapters, we have examined how Rabbinic Judaism, medieval and early modern Jewish philosophy, and Kabbalah dealt with the issue of human autonomy in the metaphysical sense prior to the modern period and how these branches of Judaism compared with pre-modern Christianity in their treatment of that theme. We can now draw conclusions that tie together what we have explored.

What has emerged from our deliberations is that from the first century CE up to the modern period, many Jewish thinkers in various schools of Judaism entertained views on human autonomy in relation to God that gave human beings significantly more freedom than Christian thinkers did. In some instances, Jewish thinkers took positions on that issue that, by Christian standards, were quite radical, even heretical. There is also good reason to believe that the difference between Jewish and Christian thinkers on this matter could not have been confined to intellectuals. It is likely that the contrasting attitudes of the intellectuals in the two religions towards human autonomy filtered down to some extent to ordinary people in their respective communities, even if we have no written records to prove it.

Not all Jewish thinkers accentuated human autonomy in the radical ways we have just described. Many upheld far more moderate beliefs. Christians thinkers also entertained a diversity of opinions on human autonomy. So each religion had a variety of opinions on this matter, ranging from restrictive views to more libertarian ones. However, Jewish views skewed towards the more libertarian end of the spectrum, and Christian views skewed towards the more restrictive end.

It is possible that Jewish thinkers entertained more libertarian views on human autonomy due to historical circumstances. As the long centuries went by and no end of the exile appeared to be in sight, Jews were perhaps inspired to consider bold ideas about this kind of autonomy in a way that Christians were not. Because Jews were subjugated and persecuted, they had to think of themselves as powerful in the metaphysical realm in order to make up for their loss of dignity as God's chosen people in the physical realm. Political factors may have also played a role here. Rabbinic authorities did not have as much power as Christian authorities did to enforce what they regarded as proper beliefs among their followers, and therefore Jews had greater opportunity to develop radical thinking on the question of metaphysical human autonomy. That seems to have been a factor in explaining why medieval Jewish philosophy developed a radical branch.

However, the bold speculations of the rabbis, philosophers, and Kabbalists regarding the relationship between human beings and God should not be attributed entirely to their environment. We also have to give credit to these groups themselves for their innovative views. They were courageous thinkers.

From everything we have seen in the past three chapters, the argument can be made that when Jews were invited to join modern Western society in the nineteenth century, they were, in some respects, better prepared than their non-Jewish counterparts for the modern period. At that time, Western society was rapidly progressing in the economic, intellectual, and the artistic spheres, and that was in part because of a growing belief that human beings were autonomous, powerful, and dignified creatures in relation to God and the cosmos. However, Jews had developed this conception of human beings in radical form centuries earlier, and thus they were also better suited to adopt the mindset of the new world they were entering than their non-Jewish peers were.

European thinkers in the medieval and early modern periods certainly had advantages over Jews when it came to the actual exercise of human autonomy. Most notably, Europeans developed the sciences, particularly in the early modern period, and their scientific discoveries would play a critical role in convincing Europeans that human beings were powerful creatures who could function independently of God or that God did not exist at all. There were Jewish scientists as well in the medieval and early modern periods, but they were few in number, and their contributions to science paled in comparison to those of Europeans.[54] Yet when Jews were invited to become part of European culture in the nineteenth century, they quickly made up the lost ground. They imbibed scientific knowledge with great energy and enthusiasm, and by the second half of the century, they were already beginning to excel in the various scientific disciplines. By the mid-twentieth century, Jews were represented in the sciences disproportionately and they were winning international awards in the sciences in even greater disproportion.

One possible explanation for such success in the sciences is everything we have discussed in the past three chapters. Jews may not have entered modern European society with centuries of accomplishments in the sciences, but they came with something that was perhaps just as valuable, if not more so: centuries of philosophical and theological speculations granting human beings autonomy in relation to God and the cosmos that were more radical than those entertained by Christian Europeans. These ideas about human autonomy primed Jews to be receptive to the sciences when they were finally given the opportunity to study them. A people that for hundreds of years believed that God could be argued with, overruled, and even "repaired" by human beings was a people that could easily adapt to scientific exploration, a pursuit that also presumed an exalted view of human capabilities.

None of this is to say that Jewish speculations on human autonomy in the metaphysical sense were the only reason why Jews were well-prepared to engage with the modern sciences. We will see in the coming chapters that the other three values responsible for Jewish success also played a role here. My argument is only that centuries of Jewish speculations on human autonomy in the metaphysical sense were an important ingredient that helped groom Jews for the scientific disciplines.

What I have said here about Jewish success in the sciences also applies to the other two realms in which Jews were successful: the economic and the artistic realms. Jews entered the modern period behind Europeans in these realms as well – particularly in the arts – but here too, they made up for lost ground fairly quickly, and I believe that, again, this was in part because of an unusually strong sense of human autonomy that had been so central to their religious culture.

It is also important to keep in mind that everything that has been said here applies to modern secular Jews no less than to those who were religiously affiliated. As I argued earlier in my chapter on secular Jews, there is very good reason to believe that secular Jews were affected by rabbinic values, even though they had cut their ties with institutional Judaism, and that would have been especially true for a value such as human autonomy. Once secularized, this value was of utility to modern secular Jews as much as it was to those who remained in the religious fold.

In fact, the last three chapters may help us understand why secularism made such inroads among modern Western Jews in the first place. As also noted in my chapter on secular Jews, modern Jews have been known for their affinity to secularism – particularly in North America, where Jews, for some time now, have been identified as the most secular subgroup.[55] Why is that the case? A common premise for those who identify with secularism is that either God does not exist, or if he does, he is a distant or impersonal deity. In light of what has been discussed in the past three chapters, one can see why Jews, when they became modernized, may have been more open to this type of thinking than their Western neighbours were. For centuries, Jews had entertained more radical views on human autonomy in relation to God than Christian Westerners had, and so Jews may have had an easier time conceiving of a universe in which God either was absent or was minimally involved. I am not arguing that this is the entire reason for the popularity of secularism among modern Jews. My claim is only that it may have been a significant factor in bringing about this phenomenon.

We have explored only the first of the four values that are at the centre of this study. We will examine three more, beginning with freedom of thought and expression, which is the subject of the next chapter.

Chapter Six

Freedom of Thought and Expression

The previous three chapters analysed how Western and Jewish culture developed the notion that human beings had autonomy in the metaphysical sense – that is, in their relationship with God and the cosmos. We will now explore how the two cultures developed the idea that human beings had autonomy in relation to each other, with a specific focus on freedom of thought and expression. The question here is how these cultures came to believe that human beings should be permitted to think and say what they wanted without running into trouble with other members of their society, particularly those in positions of power in the political and religious spheres.

As I noted when I introduced the four values in chapter 1, the development of the principle of freedom of thought and expression was critical for the success of the West in the modern period. The West was able to achieve the dominance it did in part because Westerners believed in the freedom of individuals to engage in innovative thinking and to disseminate new ideas without fear of retaliation from political and religious authorities. Had the modern West not developed such freedom, it is unlikely that the West would have made the advances it did in a wide array of fields and disciplines that were necessary for it to become so powerful.

I also touched on this type of freedom in my discussion of how the West developed the idea of autonomy in the metaphysical sense because the two values are connected. During the Enlightenment, the Protestant notion of "the priesthood of all believers" morphed into the conviction that an individual's religious choices were an entirely private matter between the individual and God, and this conviction then paved the way for the idea that those choices should be made without interference from religious authorities. Nevertheless, the freedom that the West granted its citizens to openly express their convictions deserves its own separate discussion because the path of development this value took was different in a number of respects from that of autonomy in the metaphysical sense. Furthermore, I have not yet discussed this right in the political realm, and this is an issue that is important for the concerns of this study.

This chapter will also explore what Rabbinic Judaism had to say about freedom of thought and expression and how the development of its views on this matter compared with those of the West. The rabbis did not make explicit reference to this value, nor did they provide the kind of systematic theoretical treatment of it that one finds in the Western intellectual tradition. Nonetheless, one can construct a picture of how the rabbis felt about the issue from numerous statements scattered throughout their writings and from their overall patterns of thought, and here again, it can be shown that the rabbis, in critical respects, anticipated modernity more than their Western neighbours did. That, in turn, helps explain why Jews were so successful when they became part of the Western world. When they joined Western society, Jews were instinctively prepared for the kind of vibrant and bold exchanges of ideas that characterized the new environment they entered.

I.   Christian Perspectives

Preliminary Considerations

Throughout human history, the type of opinion that has landed people in trouble most often has been the criticism of political leaders. Over the centuries, countless individuals have been threatened or imprisoned, or even lost their lives, for voicing opposition to those with political power. That was very much the case throughout the history of pre-modern Europe. Political dissent usually was not tolerated by those in power, and when it threatened their rule, it was almost always met with repression or violence.

However, another factor that restricted the free expression of opinion in pre-modern Europe and that is more relevant to our concerns was the power wielded by institutional religion. In medieval Europe, the Catholic Church wielded a great deal of control over what people could think and say and it too was prepared to threaten people, imprison them, or even take their lives when it considered their ideas objectionable. In the early modern period, the major Protestant Churches acted no differently. These Churches also regulated what people thought and said, and they were no less ruthless than the Catholic Church in punishing dissenters.

For our purposes, the control Europe's Churches exerted over ideas and their expression is far more important than that exerted by its political leaders. While Europe's political leaders were mostly concerned about opinions that might challenge their power, Church authorities were concerned about opinions on a much wider range of issues. Christianity provided an all-encompassing world view that determined how people should understand and interact with the world around them in both the natural and human realms, and therefore Christian authorities placed limits on the development of new ideas in a number of areas of knowledge. The story of Europe's success in the modern period is therefore in part the story of how Europeans stripped the Churches of their political power so that Europeans could make advances in knowledge in the material, intellectual, and artistic realms.

The Churches were determined to regulate ideas and their expression for several reasons. First, Christianity was, from its beginnings, a missionizing religion. A fundamental tenet of Christianity was that all people should be Christians. This meant that the presence of dissenters from God's truth in society was believed to represent a failure on the community's part in God's eyes and could therefore lead to divine punishment for the community as a whole. For this reason, when Christianity became aligned with political power in the late Roman period, it was all but inevitable that the Church would use its power to ensure that the inhabitants of the empire upheld its teachings, and that is precisely what happened. When Christianity was adopted as the official religion of the Roman Empire towards the end of the fourth century, the Church persecuted dissident Christian groups that did not follow its prescriptions, as well as pagans who had not accepted any version of Christianity in the first place. In the medieval period, when there were no longer pagans to contend with, religious dissenters within Christianity continued to be targeted, as well as out-groups, such as Jews. In later centuries, Protestants would turn out to be no different from Catholics in this regard. After the Protestant Churches were founded, they too became aligned with political power and adopted similar repressive measures against individuals and groups perceived as deviant.

The control that the Churches exercised over Europeans concerned not just their beliefs but their practices as well. The Church set standards for moral behaviour that affected the way society was structured and how its members should conduct themselves in their daily activities. However, the regulation of ideas and their expression was of particular concern to Christian authorities because Christianity has always accorded great importance to this dimension of religious experience. The litmus test for being a Christian has usually involved assenting to a series of beliefs. The tricky part, of course, has been to define precisely what those beliefs are, and there has been much disagreement among Christians throughout the centuries about this issue, some of it violent. Still, whatever differences Christians have had on matters of belief, they have tended to be united in placing a high premium on this aspect of religion. In all the major branches of Christianity, the affirmation of correct beliefs has been the key factor to membership in their respective communities, and that is why for so many centuries Christian authorities in Europe were particularly determined to regulate what their followers thought and what opinions they expressed. Thus, it was the missionizing element in Christianity, combined with the importance it accorded to beliefs, that resulted in the intense regulation of ideas and their expression by the Churches in pre-modern Europe.

It would appear from what has been said thus far that the effect of the Churches on the development of ideas and their expression was entirely negative. However, there is another side here. While the Churches placed limits on what ideas could be entertained by Christians, they also supported and encouraged the development of knowledge that was deemed beneficial for Christianity, and this included the cultivation of knowledge in a wide range of subjects. Moreover, as already noted, ideas within Protestantism would eventually lead Europeans to the belief that freedom of thought and expression was a right that all human beings possessed. Thus, the irony is that while Christianity in pre-modern Europe was perhaps the major obstacle to the development of the principle of freedom of thought and expression, it also in some respects paved the way for it. It is this paradox we must make sense of in order to comprehend how the notion of free thought and expression became fundamental to Western culture.

The New Testament and Early Christianity

With these general observations in mind, let us now get a better understanding of how Christianity came to emphasize uniformity of belief among its adherents and how that emphasis eventually gave way to a commitment to the principle of freedom of thought and expression. The concern in Christianity for proper belief originated in the writings of Paul. One of Paul's central teachings was that the experience of "faith" (*pistis* in the Greek) was more important in God's eyes than obedience to "the law" – that is, the scores of commandments that God gave to the Israelites in the Hebrew Bible. It was faith that led one to salvation.[1]

But faith is a rather vague word, and so the next question is what Paul meant by it. He seems to have identified it with the belief that Jesus had been sent by God to fulfil a unique mission on earth by dying on the cross and being resurrected. However, Paul's notion of faith meant more than just an intellectual acceptance of these ideas. It also involved an ongoing trust in God's saving power, a trust that these ideas engendered. Faith was a commitment that permeated one's entire life. As noted in an earlier chapter, Martin Luther would adopt that view of faith centuries later.[2]

The impact of Paul's emphasis on faith on the development of Christianity was evident in later centuries as Christianity started to take shape. First, it meant that God's salvation was more easily accessible to non-Jews than it was in Judaism because one could achieve it by merely committing to a life of faith. In Judaism, matters were not so easy. Rabbinic Judaism had developed procedures for conversion to Judaism, and the convert had to take on the observance of God's 613 commandments, a rather formidable commitment. This was one reason why Christianity won a large numbers of converts and became a major world religion in a way that Judaism did not.

The emphasis on faith also had a strong impact on Christianity's internal development. In the three centuries after Paul, the primary goal of Christian theologians was to define precisely what Christians should believe if they were to be regarded as true Christians. The earliest attempt of this kind was the Apostles' Creed, which dates to the mid-second century. It consisted of a series of statements about God, Jesus, and the Holy Spirit that would later be identified with the three parts of the Trinity. It also touched on the role of the Church, divine judgment, and the resurrection at the end of history.[3]

However, the question of what Christians should believe was far from settled, and Christian theologians engaged in lengthy and complex discussions to bring clarity to the matter. Most important in this regard was the Arian Controversy, which erupted in the fourth century over fundamental aspects of Christian theology and which would preoccupy Christians for more than a century. This controversy focused mainly on the nature of the relationship between God and Jesus, which up to that point had not been precisely defined.

A brief description of these controversies will be helpful because it will convey just how important precise formulations of beliefs were for Christians. The Arian Controversy began when Arius (250[256?]–336), a priest and theologian from Alexandria, argued that Jesus had been created by God and therefore was neither God nor co-eternal with him. Athanasius (c. 296–373), the bishop of Alexandria, vehemently disagreed with Arius, arguing that Jesus was begotten by God as a father begets a son and was therefore of the same nature as God and thus co-eternal with him. Two camps emerged that supported these respective viewpoints, and the dispute became divisive enough that it got the attention of Constantine, the Roman emperor, who convened a council of the major Christian authorities throughout the empire for the purpose of settling the disagreement. The council met in 325 at Nicea, near modern-day Istanbul, and after much deliberation, Athanasius emerged as the victor. The Council of Nicea declared that God and Jesus were "of the same substance" and that Jesus was therefore co-eternal with God. That formulation became the basis of the Nicene Creed, the creation of which became a landmark event in the history of Christianity.

But matters were still not entirely resolved. More disputes soon arose regarding the relationship of God and Jesus, this time focused on what that relationship meant for Jesus's nature. If Jesus was of the same substance as God but was also incarnated as a human being, did Jesus also have a human element in his nature? And if so, to what extent? The resolution of this question required the convening of several more councils by subsequent Roman emperors in the fourth and fifth centuries. Finally, the Council of Chalcedon in 451 brought some clarification to the issue. The council declared that Jesus was simultaneously divine and human, but without these elements being united or mingled. Most Christian authorities adopted this formulation.[4]

As noted earlier, a critical factor that made the Christian focus on belief so significant for Europeans in the medieval and early modern periods was that the Churches had political power that allowed them to dictate what opinions could be expressed on matters of religious belief. The marriage between Christianity and politics began with the conversion of the Roman emperor Constantine to Christianity in 312. A year later, Constantine issued the Edict of Milan, which gave Christianity equal status with the various pagan cults in the Roman Empire. From that point in time until his death in 337, Constantine issued a number of other decrees that gave Christianity favoured status among the empire's religions. However, Constantine still allowed pagans to continue living in accordance with their religious customs. That changed when Theodosius I became emperor more than half a century later. In 380, he made Christianity the official religion of the Roman Empire and implemented intolerant policies towards paganism. Pagans were not forced to convert to Christianity, but their temples were closed and rededicated as churches and some of their practices were outlawed. Around the same time, discriminatory laws were passed against Jews.[5]

I do not want to give the impression that just because the Church was so concerned with correct beliefs, it had no interest whatsoever in correct deeds. While Paul certainly focused a great deal on faith, he also affirmed that Christians had to be righteous in their actions in order to gain God's favour. In several passages in his letters, he tells his audience that they have to behave towards their fellow human beings with love and that they are required to live moral and upright lives.[6] Moreover, passages in some of the non-Pauline books in the New Testament speak about the importance of deeds. The Letter of James is commonly cited in this connection. In the second chapter of James, we are told that "works" are just as important as "faith," perhaps more so (James 2:14–26). Moreover, as Christianity took shape at the end of the Roman era and the beginning of the Middle Ages, the ritual dimension in Christianity took on great importance. The Church implemented a series of sacraments, such as baptism and the Eucharist, that were believed to attract divine grace and aid in the process of salvation. Thus, here too, deeds mattered a great deal.

Yet despite these observations, it was still the case that in early Christianity, Christian identity was tied more to creed than to deed. The most intensive discussions and debates during this phase of Christianity were about issues involving belief.

The Medieval Period

The Church's political power continued into the medieval period but increased significantly after the year 1000. As life in Europe settled down politically and socially after centuries of instability, and the wealth of Europeans began to grow, the Church became better organized and more centralized. It was now in a stronger position to dictate to Europe's rulers how they should conduct their affairs and to its ordinary inhabitants how they should live their lives.

The growth of the Church's political power was accompanied by a growing determination on its part to regulate ideas and their expression regarding religious matters. Heretics were now persecuted in unprecedented ways. The twelfth and thirteenth centuries, in particular, saw a sharp rise in violence against those who were deemed religiously deviant – most notably, the Cathars and Waldensians, whom we mentioned in the previous chapter. These groups sprang up in the thirteenth century, and after several attempts by the Church to get them to renounce their beliefs, the Church convinced the political powers in the regions in which these groups resided to launch military campaigns against them. Both groups were slaughtered by the thousands.

From the twelfth century onwards, the Church also established Inquisitions in various parts of Europe to root out heresies. The Inquisitions were charged with bringing heretics back into the Catholic fold, first through persuasion and then, if necessary, through imprisonment and torture. If those measures failed, execution often followed. Several thousand Europeans lost their lives in this manner.[7]

In the same centuries, the Catholic Church also imposed limits on what its own intellectuals were allowed to believe and say. The targets were usually scholastic thinkers whose views the Church opposed. Thus, for instance, in the thirteenth and fourteenth centuries, Church authorities in France periodically compiled lists of ideas that the faculty at the University of Paris – home to many of the most prominent scholastic thinkers in this period – were prohibited from discussing. Sixteen lists of this kind were issued over the two centuries, the most famous of which was mentioned in the previous chapter. The "Condemnation of 1277," as it was called, prohibited 219 ideas, and it appears to have specifically taken aim at ideas drawn from Greek and Islamic philosophy that the scholastics were discussing.[8]

Christian theologians sometimes imposed limits on *themselves* regarding which ideas were acceptable. As we saw in the previous chapter, Thomas Aquinas, who belonged to the school of scholasticism, believed that reason could be used to probe truths in the physical and metaphysical realms but that it could not be used to examine the most central of Christian doctrines, such as the Trinity and Original Sin. Only God's revealed word in the Bible could provide insight into these issues.

Here too, I do not want to give the impression that Christianity was concerned only about correct beliefs. In the medieval period, the sacraments continued to play an important role in Christian life, and the Church expanded their number to include seven rituals. In this period, the Church also developed the notion that Christians should cultivate seven virtues while avoiding seven vices. The Church's concern for deeds was also evident in the development of medieval canon law, which regulated the actions of clergy and lay people. However, the concern for correct belief remained at the centre of the Christian experience, as was evident in the manner in which the Church enforced adherence to its dogmas and persecuted those who rejected them.

The Reformation and Early Modern Period

In early modern Europe, the Catholic Church's persecution of those who denied its doctrines continued, but it now had a much more formidable heresy to deal with than at any time in its history: Protestantism. The Catholic Church persecuted adherents to this new form of Christianity as ruthlessly as it had any other group of heretics. One of the most horrific examples was the Catholic treatment of the Huguenots in France. In the sixteenth and seventeenth centuries, French Catholics killed thousands of Huguenots in a number of violent outbursts. In the eighteenth century, these persecutions diminished. Even so, by the end of that century the Huguenots had nearly been wiped out.[9]

The Protestants were not much better than the Catholics in their treatment of dissenters. As mentioned earlier, the issue of proper belief was as much a concern for the Protestant Churches as it was for the Catholic Church, especially during the phase of the Reformation when Protestant Churches were solidifying and organizing their beliefs.[10] Therefore, in those areas of Europe where the Protestant Churches had power, they were just as determined as the Catholic Church to enforce adherence to their doctrines and punish those who were considered heretics. Thus, for instance, in various parts of Europe in the sixteenth century, thousands of Protestants in the radical denominations of the Reformation were killed by their fellow Protestants because of their religious beliefs and practices. Protestants were also prone to violence against Catholics, who were just as heretical from a Protestant perspective as Protestants were from a Catholic one. In France, for instance, the Protestant Huguenots displayed as much willingness as the Catholics did to engage in bloody conflict over religious differences.[11]

Yet at this time, there were significant developments within Protestantism that began to open the door to greater freedom regarding the expression of ideas than the Catholic Church had allowed. The notion of the "priesthood of all believers" suggested the possibility that it was up to the individual, and the individual alone, to determine what kind of relationship they would have with God, though it was only in the Enlightenment that the full implications of that idea were taken seriously. Meanwhile, other developments were occurring in Protestantism that also allowed for greater freedom on religious matters than the Catholics had permitted. As discussed in an earlier chapter, some Protestants groups introduced new political structures in their communities that were semi-democratic in character, such as presbyterianism and congregationalism, and these allowed for greater freedom of expression in the religious sphere.[12]

A critical question that deserves separate attention here is the extent to which the repression of ideas by the Catholic and Protestant Churches in the medieval and early modern periods affected the development of science. This question is important because scientific discoveries would be essential for allowing Europe to achieve dominance in the modern period.

Until the 1970s, most scholars assumed that institutional Christianity throughout the medieval and early modern periods was hostile to science. The persecution of Galileo (1564–1642) by the Catholic Church was held up as prime evidence for that assessment. Galileo followed in the footsteps of Copernicus and Kepler in placing the sun at the centre of the universe, and the Catholic Church forced him to recant this view in 1616.

However, scholars have now revised this approach and are now of the opinion that in the medieval and early modern periods, the attitude of institutional Christianity towards science was complex. At times it was negative, at other times quite positive, and on balance the latter tendency most often prevailed.[13]

This approach certainly has merits. It is true that in the medieval period, the Catholic Church largely encouraged the study of science. Philosophers, including Thomas Aquinas, viewed science – or "natural philosophy" as it was then called – as central to the scholastic enterprise because they believed it was critical for understanding God and his activities in the world. The openness of medieval Christian philosophers to scientific knowledge was particularly evident in their willingness to consult the scientific works of non-Christian philosophers, such as Aristotle and Averroes – an important twelfth-century Muslim philosopher who was an interpreter of Aristotle – in order to gain insight into workings of the natural world. During the Reformation, the same positive attitude towards science was evident among Protestants as well. Isaac Newton is a superb example of a Protestant figure whose engagement with science was an expression of Christian piety. As noted in our previous chapter, he regarded the new model of the universe that he had formulated as a testimony to the glory of God's creation. As for the Galileo affair, there is now a consensus among scholars that the actions of the Catholic Church were more against Galileo the person than against his science. Galileo had an arrogant and petulant personality, and he seemed to do his best to antagonize Church authorities, including the pope himself. Thus, when these authorities went after him for his scientific views, it was likely a cover for settling a series of personal scores. The Catholic Church's treatment of Galileo therefore does not prove much about how the Church, or Christians in general, viewed science prior to modernity.

Yet the attitude of institutional Christianity towards science in the medieval and early modern periods was not always warm, and that needs to be emphasized to counterbalance the tendency among some recent scholars to paint too rosy a picture of the relationship of the Churches to science.[14]

To fully understand the negative impact that the Churches sometimes had on science, we have to keep in mind a number of points that have already been made in earlier chapters. First, in the medieval and early modern periods the distinction between philosophy and science had not yet been clearly drawn. What we now call "science" was a branch of philosophy and it was therefore referred to as "natural philosophy." Second, natural philosophy was seen by medieval and early modern thinkers as a mere stepping stone for the most important branch of philosophy: theology, which was concerned with religious matters. And third, the marriage of science and theology was based on the belief that the two areas of inquiry made use of the same rational methods. What all this meant was that when the Church placed limits on the ideas philosophers could entertain regarding religion, as they often did, they were also placing limits on which ideas were acceptable in the study of science. Theology and science were intertwined too inextricably for it to be otherwise.

A case in point is the Condemnation of 1277. A number of the ideas banned by the Catholic Church in this instance concerned the philosophical question of how the world was created. This question may seem to have been a purely religious one, but it was not. For medieval Christian philosophers, the question of creation was also a scientific one because it was intimately bound up with the discipline of physics. So here, the Church, in restricting speculation about a topic in theology, was in effect also putting limits on the study of science.[15]

Therefore, the relationship that institutional Christianity had with science before modernity could be contentious. The Churches gave Christian philosophers wide latitude to explore the natural world, but when those explorations threatened sacrosanct religious doctrines, the Churches sometimes stepped in to set limits on them.

It is also likely that the restrictions placed by the Churches on ideas in the medieval and early modern periods convinced some scientists to not even broach some issues that might have interested them. This judgment, of course, is difficult to prove because it is based on what the scientists did *not* say rather than on what they *did* say. We obviously do not have records of all the scientific treatises that medieval European thinkers did not write out of fear. However, the Church had shown on multiple occasions that it meant business when it identified threats to its doctrines, and throughout history, the threats of powerful institutions have often been highly effective in silencing those under their jurisdictions. Scientists in medieval and early modern Europe would have been no exception.

The picture that emerges thus far is that in the medieval and early modern periods, the Catholic and Protestant Churches supported a certain degree of freedom of thought and expression. Most significantly, they endorsed the exploration of both religious and scientific questions with rational methods. However, the Churches also put significant restrictions on such explorations, restrictions that affected a range of disciplines. Those restrictions were mainly concerned with religious matters, but they also impinged on scientific ones as well. Thus, Europeans in the medieval and modern periods had a vibrant intellectual culture, particularly from the twelfth century onwards, but they did not yet have a sufficient degree of freedom to explore new ideas that would allow them to leap ahead of other cultures and become dominant in the world.

The Enlightenment

In the early modern period, major changes took place with respect to the issues of interest to us here. The Enlightenment brought a new orientation to Europe regarding freedom of thought and expression. That development was in part a reaction to the devastating wars that had plagued Europe in the sixteenth and seventeenth centuries. As noted in an earlier chapter, religion was a factor in these conflicts as the tensions between Protestants and Catholics played themselves out in the wake of the Reformation. The Treaty of Westphalia in 1648 that brought an end to the Thirty Years' War was the first step in a new approach towards the role of religion in European society that attempted to pre-empt a recurrence of such violence. It determined that the monarchs, not the Churches, would have the right to decide which brand of Christianity was to be recognized in their respective territories. Those who lived in a region in which their type of Christianity was not the same as that of the monarch would be encouraged to relocate to one where it was. This arrangement had first been suggested at least a century earlier, but it was now enforced, and the hope was that it would put an end to wars waged in the name of religion.[16]

What is significant here is that the new arrangement recognized the need for the different Christian denominations to tolerate each other. However, by the eighteenth century, some Enlightenment intellectuals began to argue that this arrangement was not sufficient to prevent conflict. They believed that each individual should be allowed to decide independently what kind of Christian they wanted to be, no matter where they resided. Some went even further and suggested that tolerance should be accorded to those who were not Christians.[17]

Other developments taking place in European intellectual life helped foster this new way of thinking. In the past three chapters, we examined several factors that inspired the notion among Europeans that the individual was a free and autonomous creature in relation to the cosmos. As this idea began to take hold, it encouraged Europeans to believe that they should be autonomous in relation to each other as well. Individuals had to be allowed to make their own decisions about their religious convictions without fear of persecution.

England was the first country where these new sentiments resulted in legislation. Like the rest of Europe, England throughout most of the seventeenth century was plagued by religious wars – in this case, a series of civil wars between Protestant factions. The strife ended in 1688, and a year later the British Parliament passed legislation designed to pre-empt religious wars in the future. The Toleration Act of 1689 gave freedom of religion to Protestant groups that dissented from the Church of England. It did not extend the same freedom to Catholics, but it still constituted a major step towards religious freedom that would have been hard to imagine a short time earlier.

Around the same time, John Locke, the great British philosopher, made a case for religious freedom that would have great influence not just in England but elsewhere as well. In his "Letter On Toleration" (1690), he presented the argument – which in retrospect seems so simple – that it was pointless to coerce religious beliefs, because beliefs that had been imposed on an individual were not genuine at all; one could not control what was in another person's heart when it came to religious convictions. Religious communities were therefore voluntary associations by their very nature. However, Locke's plea for toleration did not extend to atheists or Catholics. These groups, he believed, could not be trusted to uphold the interests of England.[18]

Alongside the development of the notion that people should be free to think and say what they wanted regarding religious matters was the growth of the idea that people should have the same freedom in the political realm. The two freedoms were not necessarily related in the minds of Europeans in the early modern period. Locke called for significant restrictions on free speech when it came to politics even as he made the case for freedom when it came to religion. But views on the two freedoms became increasingly intertwined. As the notion of freedom of religious thought and expression came into vogue, it was inevitable that the idea of granting people the same freedom in the political realm would become fashionable as well. Moreover, the presbyterian and congregational models of Protestantism had already introduced democratic elements into Church governance, and so it was natural for the members of these Churches to expect something similar in the political realm.

Here again, England led the way. In 1694, the British government's censorship of publications was abolished.[19] The twin freedoms to choose one's religion and to speak one's mind on political matters were also embraced elsewhere. In France, these rights were established at the start of the French Revolution with the Declaration of the Rights of Man and the Citizen. In the newly established United States, the First Congress passed the Bill of Rights in 1791, and its first article guaranteed the same rights.[20]

The granting of freedom in the religious and political realms was connected to yet another advance in the lives of Europe's citizens: the growth of democracy. Here again, England, France, and the US led the way. Democracy enhanced political freedom by giving ordinary individuals an actual say in how their government functioned.

By the end of the eighteenth century, England, France, and the US had made enormous advances on the issues of freedom of thought and expression in the realms of politics and religion; they had also taken significant steps towards establishing democratic government. However, much more still needed to happen for the three countries to provide the kind of comprehensive rights that their citizens nowadays take for granted. Despite the commitments to freedom of religion, there was still discrimination against minority religious groups.[21] Despite the commitments to freedom of opinion on political matters, individuals could still be punished for their political views.[22] And when it came to democracy, voting rights in the three countries were restricted mostly to men, and only to men who possessed a certain amount of wealth. Moreover, most other countries in Europe lagged behind England, France, and the US in establishing the principle of freedom of thought and expression in the religious and political realms, and the same was true for democracy. Still, what these three countries accomplished represented a significant turning point. As the modern period began, the rights to free thought and expression that they established in the religious and political spheres were gradually expanded, as were voting rights. As for other European countries, most eventually gave their citizens these rights as well.[23]

Most important, by the end of the nineteenth century, the right to freedom of thought and expression was firmly enough in place in Europe to allow Europeans to make remarkable advances in a wide range of areas. Most significant for our concerns were the advances that Europeans made in the sciences. A bewildering array of scientific discoveries paved the way for Europeans to come up with new technologies that would play a large role in making Europe wealthy and powerful. Those technologies included the heavy machinery that made it possible for industries to flourish, weapons that brought victory in war, and more efficient means of travel and communication that aided both these enterprises. Advances in some of the social sciences produced important benefits as well. The development of the discipline of economics, for instance, would allow for a more sophisticated understanding of how wealth was generated and was therefore important for Europe's advances in the material realm. The progress made in all these areas helped Europe become dominant as the modern period matured.

II.   Jewish Perspectives

The question of how much Judaism supported freedom of thought and expression is intimately connected, as it was in Christianity, with the question of how much emphasis Jews placed on adherence to a set of beliefs in defining religious identity. As we have seen, a major obstacle to establishing the principle of freedom of thought and expression in the West was that much of Christian identity was defined by a commitment to a series of beliefs, and religious authorities were therefore inclined to place strict limits on ideas and their expression out of fear that they would undermine those beliefs. The question then is whether Judaism was similar. Did its religious authorities also insist on a set of doctrines that all Jews had to uphold, thereby limiting free thought and expression in the way that Christian authorities did?

This question has received a great deal of attention from Jewish intellectuals throughout the modern period, beginning with Moses Mendelssohn (1729–86), the first major modern Jewish philosopher, whom we have already encountered. Mendelssohn famously declared that Judaism had no dogmas. To be a Jew, one did not have to be committed to any beliefs whatsoever. Instead, one had to observe a series of laws regulating deeds. According to Mendelssohn, one had to go no further than the Torah to verify this claim. When God revealed himself to Moses on Mount Sinai in order to instruct the Israelites about how to worship him, God did not demand that they uphold beliefs of any kind: the focus was entirely on norms of behaviour.[24]

Mendelssohn's position clearly had polemical intent. He wanted to show that Judaism was a greater proponent of free thought and expression than Christianity was, that Judaism was therefore more enlightened than Christianity was, and that Jews and Judaism should thus have a respected place in modern European society. But as is often the case with positions that are polemical in nature, Mendelssohn greatly simplified matters, and it was only a matter of time before Jewish thinkers disputed his claims. Saul Ascher (1767–1822), a German-Jewish book dealer and journalist, wrote a book that rejected Mendelssohn's views on Jewish dogma. He was the first to argue that Judaism had an "essence" – an idea that would become very important for subsequent Jewish thinkers. He also claimed that this essence was based on several characteristics, including ten abstract principles centred on revelation, redemption, and resurrection, in which Jews had to believe. The Reform movement in Judaism, which began to gather momentum in the mid-nineteenth century, issued platforms periodically that attempted to define its beliefs in a series of succinct principles. The first of these was the Pittsburgh Platform in 1885.

Solomon Schechter (1847–1915), a prominent Jewish intellectual, also challenged Mendelssohn's position that Judaism had no dogmas. Schechter showed that in fact there was a history of efforts by Jewish philosophers to come up with a set of dogmas for Judaism, though he made no attempt to determine which dogmas Jews should adhere to in the modern period.[25]

Mendelssohn also had his defenders. In the twentieth century, for instance, Leo Baeck (1873–1956), another prominent Jewish thinker, argued that Mendelssohn was correct regarding the question of dogma in Judaism to the extent that Judaism had no dogmas that were determinative of Jewish identity in the way that Christianity did.[26] Moreover, throughout the modern period, rabbis and popular writers have supported Mendelssohn's claim, though without necessarily citing Mendelssohn. The notion that Judaism has no sacrosanct beliefs has often been taken as a given. Moreover, these writers often make this claim for the same reason Mendelssohn did: it provides evidence that Judaism is superior to Christianity. Again, the implied argument is that because Judaism has no required beliefs, Judaism allows for freedom of thought and expression in a way that Christianity does not.[27]

In tracing the history of freedom of thought and expression in Judaism, we will therefore be going over some well-trodden ground. Nevertheless, it behooves us to do so. First, this study would be incomplete if it did not address the debate over free thought and expression in Judaism. Second, as I have just noted, there are many who still believe, as Mendelssohn did, that Judaism has no required beliefs, and we need to show that matters are more complicated than this claim suggests. Finally, by embedding a discussion of this issue in a study about the success of modern Jews, we will be looking at the entire matter from a new angle.

We will begin by examining freedom of thought and expression in pre-modern discussions of Jewish theology. We will then examine the same issue in pre-modern discussions of Jewish law.

Jewish Theology

THE HEBREW BIBLE AND EARLY RABBINIC JUDAISM

The Hebrew Bible contains a significant amount of material relevant to both deeds and beliefs, but it does not deal with either in detailed or systematic fashion. When it comes to deeds, the Torah has many passages which list the laws that God expects the Israelites to observe, but they are not organized in a coherent framework and are not described extensively enough to constitute a fully functioning system of law. The same is true with regard to beliefs. The Hebrew Bible intimates that the Israelites are expected to uphold certain convictions – most importantly, the notion that God is the supreme deity and that he will reward and punish them depending on their commitment to obey his commandments.[28] But these ideas are never laid out in a comprehensive manner. Some of the later books of the Bible certainly reflect on theological matters in some detail, such as Job and Ecclesiastes, and the ideas they entertain are at times quite provocative. Yet even in these books, there is no attempt to systematize such matters. Both books leave us with a series of loose ends regarding the theological questions they raise.

When the rabbis reconstructed Judaism in the wake of the destruction of the Second Temple, they showed much more interest in the biblical material pertaining to deeds than to that concerned with beliefs. The rabbis conducted lengthy and elaborate discussions about the Torah's laws and eventually built a comprehensive legal system out of them on the assumption that the way for Jews to repair their relationship with God after the destruction of the Temple was by meticulously observing his commandments. The rabbis conducted far fewer discussions regarding beliefs, and that is why medieval Judaism was a religion in which the practice of Jewish law took priority over the inward experiences of faith and adherence to dogma.

It did not have to be this way. Christianity is proof that the religion of the Hebrew Bible could be shaped into one in which the emphasis was on faith and dogma. The rabbinic focus on deeds was therefore a conscious choice.

The emphasis on deeds in Rabbinic Judaism is perhaps what led some, like Mendelssohn, to claim that Judaism has no dogmas whatsoever. That assertion, however, takes things a bit too far. While the rabbis were far less focused on beliefs than on deeds, they were not completely uninterested in beliefs because they could not afford to be; they had to assume the truth of a number of dogmas if their world view was to make any sense. The observance of Jewish law, which for the rabbis was the centre of Jewish life, required that Jews believe that God was the only true God, that they were his chosen people, that he gave them the Torah, and that he would reward and punish them depending on whether they observed his 613 commandments. To be more precise, the rabbinic world view depended on belief in the historical accuracy of the Hebrew Bible, and that meant accepting all the principles just listed.[29]

Moreover, while the rabbis did not dwell extensively on matters of belief, they did discuss such matters when it was necessary to draw a sharp distinction between themselves and other factions in the Jewish community that they regarded as heretical. A well-known passage in the Mishnah informs us that three groups of people will not receive a share in the world to come: those who declare that the resurrection of the dead in the messianic age is not stated in the Torah; those who claim that the Torah is not from heaven; and the *epikoros*.[30] Scholars have identified all three of these forbidden beliefs as convictions upheld by the Sadducees, a group of Jews who were rivals to the Pharisees, the precursors to the rabbis. The Sadducees denied the resurrection of the dead and the notion that the Torah was entirely from heaven. *Epikoros* is a Greek term and is not defined by the Mishnah, but it probably refers to the followers of the Roman philosopher Epicurus, who denied God's providence over the world, a position that appears to have been upheld by the Sadducees. In this source, then, the rabbis were speaking about matters of belief in order to differentiate themselves from a group of Jews whom they felt were not adhering to Judaism as they understood it.[31]

Still, the concern for proper practice was at the centre of the rabbinic world view in a way that the issue of proper belief was not. While the rabbis had to assume certain dogmas for their world view to make any sense, they spent the vast majority of their time discussing and systematizing laws of behaviour, not dogmas. And even though they sometimes went out of their way to differentiate themselves from rival groups that held beliefs inconsistent with their own, discussions of their differences with these groups were few and far between.

Most important for our purposes is that the deed-oriented nature of Rabbinic Judaism put it on a course that was quite different from that of Christianity. The rabbis, in focusing as much as they did on observing God's commandments, allowed their followers far more latitude than their Christian counterparts did on matters of belief. Rabbinic sources have a wide variety of views on all the theological issues that concerned them but without making any systematic attempt to determine which views were correct.

There is no better way to illustrate the distinction between Rabbinic Judaism and Christianity than by looking at what their respective authorities were doing in the fifth century. As we saw earlier in this chapter, Christianity in that century was at a critical stage of its development characterized by intense, lengthy, and detailed discussions about such theological matters as the relationship of Jesus to the two other parts of the Trinity and the relationship between Jesus's divine and human natures. At the same time that these discussions were taking place, Rabbinic Judaism was also at a critical stage of development, and its authorities were also steeped in debates that were just as intense, lengthy, and detailed as those of the Christians. However, the discussions here were of a very different kind. The focus for the rabbis was on legal issues, such as what damages were to be paid when someone's ox gored his neighbour's cow, or what quantity of wine had to be consumed when a blessing was made over it before the Sabbath meal. *These* were the issues that preoccupied the rabbis.

MEDIEVAL JUDAISM

During the Middle Ages, the rabbis began to show greater interest in the question of what Jews should believe. That development was inspired in part by the rise of the schools of Jewish philosophy and Kabbalah. These schools attempted to systematize Jewish theology, and they engaged in heated debates about theological issues. Those debates often consisted of philosophers on one side and Kabbalists on the other. But there were also plenty of debates in which philosophical thinkers squared off against each other, and the same can be said about the Kabbalists as well.

The most serious dispute between Jews in the medieval period regarding theological issues is one we have already discussed. After Maimonides' death in 1204, Jews throughout Europe and the Islamic world became engaged in a series of bitter disagreements over his legacy that would persist for a century and a half, and at stake were a number of fundamental issues regarding what Jews should believe. This controversy went through several phases and involved philosophers and Kabbalists, as well as rabbis who belonged to neither group.[32]

It is in the Middle Ages that we also see the first serious attempts by Jewish thinkers to compose lists of dogmas that all Jews were expected to uphold. This interest was partly due to outside pressures. The vast majority of Jews were now living in Christian Europe and Islamic lands, and both Christianity and Islam were more focused on dogma than Rabbinic Judaism was – Christianity, particularly so. It is therefore no surprise that the rabbis were motivated to examine this dimension of their own religion. The desire to better define Jewish belief was also strengthened by the fact that Jews were under pressure – in subtle or not so subtle ways – to convert to the religions of their non-Jewish over-lords. The rabbis therefore felt it was important to demarcate what it was precisely that Jews should believe.[33]

The interest medieval Jews took in spelling out the dogmas of Juda-ism was also inspired by a schism within the Jewish community. The Karaite movement, mentioned in an earlier chapter, arose within Iraq's Jewish community in the ninth century and was premised on the rejection of Rabbinic Judaism. The Karaites believed that only the Hebrew Bible represented God's will and that the Oral Torah was an invention of the rabbis. Therefore, for the Karaites, all of rabbinic liter-ature, including the Talmud, had no authority. The Karaite movement spread to other parts of the Jewish world in subsequent centuries, and in some places and times it posed a significant threat to Rabbinic Judaism, though it never became dominant. The Karaites were thus another factor that prodded the rabbis to examine the theological dimension of Judaism – in particular, the nature of revelation and its transmission.[34]

By far the best-known list of Jewish dogmas not just in the medieval period but in the early modern and modern periods as well was the one composed by Maimonides. He listed thirteen dogmas that he believed were fundamental to Judaism:

1. God exists.
2. God is one.
3. God is incorporeal.
4. God is prior to the cosmos.
5. God alone may be worshiped.
6. God communicates to human beings through prophecy.
7. Moses's prophecy is superior to that of all other prophets.
8. The Torah came from God.
9. The Torah will never change nor be exchanged with another one.
10. God knows individuals.
11. The righteous will be rewarded, and the wicked, punished.
12. The messiah will come.
13. The dead will be resurrected in the time of the messiah.[35]

Most striking about Maimonides' list was the importance he attached to it. He declared that his thirteen principles were the key determinant of Jewish identity. A Jew who was committed to those principles would be considered a member of the Jewish people and would receive a share in the world to come, no matter what other sins they had committed. A Jew who denied even one of these principles was a heretic and would have no share in the world to come. No Jewish thinker prior to Maimonides had given dogma so central a place in Judaism.[36]

Why was Maimonides' list so important to him? As already noted, the environments in which Jews lived during the medieval period may have motivated Jewish thinkers to show more interest in the dogmatic aspects of their religion than the earlier rabbis had. Even so, Maimonides' views on the importance of this element of Judaism were unique in their extremism and therefore are not sufficiently explained by this consideration. Scholars have tended to attribute Maimonides' emphasis on dogma to his interest in Greek and Islamic philosophy. As we have seen, Maimonides was the leading figure in medieval Jewish philosophy, and that approach to Judaism got much of its inspiration from ancient Greek philosophy as filtered through Islamic interpreters. One of the views that Maimonides adopted from them was that the only part of the individual that survived in the afterlife was the intellect. The intellect was immortal because ideas were not physical; that meant they were not subject to decay as our bodies were; that in turn meant that the intellect, being the part of us that contained our ideas, would survive in the afterlife, whereas our bodies would not. Therefore the more one cultivated one's intellect with correct ideas about the world, from science to metaphysics, the richer one's experience of the afterlife would be. Maimonides may have therefore composed his list of thirteen principles in order to give Jews the minimal list of intellectual beliefs that they had to adhere to in order to experience the afterlife, and he attached great importance to them for that reason.[37]

Maimonides' thirteen principles were influential in the same way that everything else he wrote was. They were summarized in a widely popular fourteenth-century hymn, Yigdal, which was eventually included in the Friday night prayer service. A summary of the principles also appears in the traditional weekday morning prayer service.[38]

Clearly then, the medieval period was a time when Jews showed greater interest in theological matters than had been the case in the early rabbinic period. We can also extend the same judgment to the early modern period, as illustrated by the treatment of Spinoza by the Jewish community in Amsterdam in the seventeenth century. Spinoza's excommunication was by no means as significant an event for Jews as the Karaite schism or the Maimonidean controversy had been. At the time of his excommunication, Spinoza was not yet famous and had not published any of his views, so the decision to push him out of the Jewish community was largely a local affair. But the treatment he received shows that matters of belief could be of great concern to the rabbis under the right circumstances. The precise reasons for Spinoza's excommunication have been a matter of debate, but there is evidence that he had been espousing heretical views to his fellow Jews for some time prior to being summoned before the rabbis, and those views included a devastating critique of the most sacrosanct Jewish beliefs. That, together with a number of other factors involving the make-up and character of the Amsterdam Jewish community at the time, prompted the rabbis to act as they did.[39]

However, we should not exaggerate the interest that medieval and early modern Jews had in theological matters. In these periods, law still remained the centre of life throughout the Jewish world, and while many Jews took an interest in philosophy and Kabbalah, the Talmud and the corpus of literature that grew out of it were still the most studied texts in medieval and early modern Judaism.

As for Maimonides' thirteen principles, their impact was limited. Jewish intellectuals mostly ignored them for a full three centuries after his death; they began seriously discussing them only in fifteenth-century Spain when Spanish Jews were being pressured to convert to Christianity and began examining what distinguished their religion from that of their non-Jewish neighbours. Most important, no prominent medieval Jewish thinker after Maimonides accorded the place to dogma that he had. Medieval rabbis did not subscribe to the notion that principles of belief were the key determinant of Jewish identity or necessary for survival in the afterlife. Observance of Jewish law remained the centre of Jewish life.[40]

Maimonides' principles also met with a good deal of opposition. Some Jewish thinkers were willing to support the notion that Judaism had fundamental dogmas, but they disagreed with the content of Maimonides' list and proposed lists of their own. In addition, in the centuries after Maimonides' lifetime, every one of his principles was challenged either explicitly or implicitly, and that was the case even before the nineteenth century when large parts of the Jewish community became modernized.[41]

Moreover, Maimonides composed the thirteen principles when he was relatively young, and some scholars have found evidence that even his own commitment to them waned in his later years. In his massive compendium of Jewish law, the *Mishneh Torah*, in which he revisited the question of what beliefs Jews should hold, he discussed only some of his thirteen principles, and they were not presented as a unit as they were in his earlier work. The same was true for his great philosophical work, *The Guide of the Perplexed*. In that work as well, only some of his principles were mentioned.[42]

Scholars have also argued that in his later works, Maimonides supported positions that actually undermined a good number of his original thirteen principles. As we have already discussed, there are even scholars who believe that by the time Maimonides wrote *The Guide of the Perplexed* late in his life, he was an Aristotelian heretic in disguise, and thus, according to these interpreters, Maimonides in his later years no longer believed in most of the thirteen principles he had set forth in his early writings.

At the tail end of the early modern period, the tendency of Jews to de-emphasize dogmas would be greatly strengthened by Mendelssohn's bold claim that dogmas were entirely absent in Judaism. However, there was interest in defining Jewish beliefs in some quarters of the Jew-ish intellectual world as Jews made the transition to modernity and had to define for themselves and for their Christian neighbours what it was precisely that they believed. We have already mentioned Saul Ascher, who, shortly after Mendelssohn's lifetime, argued that Judaism had an "essence" that included a number of dogmas. We have also noted that the Reform movement in Judaism that began to flourish in the nine-teenth century issued platforms that included a number of beliefs that the movement upheld. Nonetheless, in none of these instances was the claim being made that being a Jew required assent to a series of beliefs. Only in recent times has that claim been made, and it has come from figures in the right-wing sector of the Orthodox Jewish community in the US and Israel, who have stated that Maimonides' thirteen principles are the litmus test for whether a Jew is a true believer or a heretic. Yet this use of Maimonides' principles has little precedent.[43]

Where does all this leave us with regard to the concerns of this study? I think it is fair to say that while medieval and early modern Jews displayed a heightened interest in dogma and theological matters compared to early Rabbinic Judaism, their interest in this dimension of religion still paled in comparison to that of Christian thinkers, and for this reason Jews allowed for greater freedom when it came to ideas and their expression. That freedom certainly was not unlimited. The Karaite schism and the lengthy controversy over Maimonides' writings are proof of that. Furthermore, the rabbis certainly did not have tolerant views towards Christianity and Islam, even when they tried to find a positive place for them in God's plan. But what we do not have in medi-eval Judaism is the kind of consistent and intense focus on theological matters that we encounter in Christianity. Moreover, the debates about such matters were not as central to Judaism as they were for Christians, and as a result, the restrictions on the free expression of ideas in Juda-ism were not as severe as they were in Christianity. Thus, we have no real equivalent to the Arian Controversy in pre-modern Judaism. That controversy lasted about as long as the controversy over Maimonides' writings did, but it was of much greater consequence for the direction of Christianity than the Maimonidean controversy was for the direction of Judaism.

Jewish Law

So far, we have established that Rabbinic Judaism allowed for a relatively significant degree of free thought and expression in the realm of theology because the rabbis focused more on systematizing deeds, rather than beliefs. But even when it came to deeds, the rabbis displayed a marked tolerance for diversity of opinion. Although the rabbis were bent on creating a system of law that would standardize religious practice for all Jews, they also believed that the process leading to that end would require intense and lively debate. The prevailing attitude among the rabbis was that a proper understanding of God's directives could be achieved only by hashing out disagreements over the interpretation of every detail of the laws contained in his Written and Oral Torah.[44]

THE EARLY RABBINIC PERIOD

The importance the rabbis accorded to this process is evident in the very structure of the earliest texts they produced. The first major work of rabbinic law was the Mishnah, a six-volume compendium redacted around the year 200 by R. Judah the Patriarch. As a work of law, the Mishnah was quite strange. It was a meticulously organized collection of the disagreements about all matters of Jewish law up to R. Judah's period, but in the vast majority of these disagreements, no resolution was offered. The Mishnah was therefore a *work* of law but not a *code* of law, at least not in any obvious sense.[45]

The next major work of early rabbinic literature was the Gemara, which according to most scholars reached its final stage of redaction somewhere between 650 and 750, and it was not a law code either. It contained rabbinic discussions about the Mishnah that had taken place from the third to the sixth centuries, and its goal was to interpret the Mishnah and clarify its positions. Only on rare occasions did it rule in favour of one opinion or another. Thus, when the Talmud was created by bringing together the Mishnah and the Gemara into an enormous multi-volume work, there was still no clear code of law in Rabbinic Judaism, only a myriad of disputes about the law spanning five hundred years. Clearly, the early rabbis valued debate over legal issues.

The Talmud also contained a number of passages that *celebrated* its peculiarly argumentative character. An often cited source of this kind is

found in a passage in the Mishnah in which the rabbis ask why it is cus-
tomary to record the minority opinion in rabbinic disputes. The question
is predicated on the fact that the Mishnah often presents the majority
opinion of the rabbis on a given matter of law while also recording the
opinions of individual rabbis who disagree with them. Hence the question: why is there a need to present dissenting views, given that the law
is in accordance with those of the majority? The answer provided by the
Mishnah is that one never knows when a rabbinic court in the future
will revisit the same issue and overturn the original ruling in favour
of the rejected opinion, and so the latter opinion must be preserved.[46]
Diversity of opinion is clearly celebrated here.

A positive attitude towards debate comes through in another Talmudic passage worth citing in which the rabbis express sympathy for those
among their disciples who may experience confusion over the variety
of rabbinic opinions on any given matter of God's law. The passage tells
us that an individual studying the deliberations of the rabbis is liable
to throw up their hands in frustration and ask, "How in these circumstances is it possible to study Torah?" The passage attempts to appease
those who feel this way by declaring that all the opinions of the rabbis
were, in fact, directly imparted by God to Moses on Mount Sinai: "One
God gave them, one leader uttered them from the mouth of the Lord
of all creation."[47] That is, the debates *themselves* were communicated in
God's original revelation of the Oral Torah, and therefore the disciples
of the rabbis should not get upset about the argumentative nature of
rabbinic discourse; in fact, they should revel in it. The bewildering variety of rabbinic opinions on God's laws come from God himself, and
so understanding these opinions is as important as determining which
opinion is correct.

The notion that the rabbinic debates about God's laws were divine
in origin may seem odd, but as we saw in an earlier chapter, a number of medieval rabbis adopted this view based on remarks made by
Nahmanides. According to this perspective, when God gave Moses the
Torah, God taught Moses all the interpretations on every aspect of Jewish law that could possibly arise in the future, and those interpretations
were then passed on to the sages of subsequent generations as the Oral
Torah. It was then the obligation of the sages to determine which opinion they supported on a given issue when the need arose.[48]

As one might expect, not all rabbis were happy about the diversity
of opinion in their discourses on God's law. That is, the rabbis had a
diversity of opinion about their diversity of opinion! A more negative
view of rabbinic debate comes through in a Talmudic passage informing us that up to the time of the establishment of the schools of Hillel

and Shammai, two leading rabbis in the first century, disagreements on matters of Jewish law were few in number. Disagreements began to proliferate only after that time due to a deterioration in the quality of students in the two great schools.[49] In this source, then, diversity of opinion regarding God's laws is not the ideal. Had the students in the schools of Hillel and Shammai maintained higher standards in their study of the laws, disagreements would have remained rare. This negative perspective on debate was a minority view, but it still has to be acknowledged.[50]

Note also that the rabbis had to place limits on acceptable discourse within their ranks. A rabbi who insisted on making a ruling contrary to the major bodies of rabbinic authority could be punished, and rabbinic sources discuss this scenario and how it is to be handled.[51] But, of course, every legal system has to include such rules; otherwise, there would be chaos.

One more thing to note is that the positive view of debate among the rabbis did not mean that they were necessarily polite to each other when engaging in such discourse. In fact, they could be quite harsh. The culture of debate in the Babylonian rabbinic academies that redacted the Talmud at times featured outbursts of anger, abusive language, and insults. Nonetheless, the same culture, in principle, greatly valued debate as key to understanding God's laws.[52]

THE MEDIEVAL PERIOD

In the medieval period, a comprehensive law system emerged and became the centre of Jewish life, but debates among the rabbis did not disappear. New questions kept arising about the laws – as they do in every law system – and therefore disagreements between the rabbis about the laws persisted as well.

Medieval rabbis also enjoyed debating matters of law that were already settled. There was always room for new insights into how laws, long-established in Jewish practice, had been determined in Talmudic discussions centuries earlier. Every element in these discussions could be analysed in order to better understand how a particular ruling had been adjudicated. That was the case even when a Talmudic discussion had no final resolution. The medieval rabbis considered it meritorious to study these earlier debates for no other reason than to understand the differences of opinion among their rabbinic predecessors. The belief underlying this activity was that studying Jewish law was not just for the purpose of deciding how Jews should obey God's will; it was also because the "study of Torah" was a religious obligation in its own right, even when it had no immediate practical benefit.

A whole literature grew out of this exercise. It was referred to as the literature of the *hidushim* – often translated as *novellae*, though in more common language, it can be rendered as "insights." This literature is still studied today, mainly in Orthodox yeshivas.

In the medieval period, the rabbis also addressed, more directly than Talmudic literature, the question of why their discussions of law were filled with debates, and here too, their attitude towards this feature of their discourse was usually positive. We have just referred to one view on this issue that was inspired by Nahmanides, and one cannot have a more positive view on the matter than this one: according to this perspective, the viewpoints informing rabbinic debates were imparted by God himself to Moses on Mount Sinai.

We saw in an earlier chapter that Maimonides had another theory about why rabbinic discussions of God's laws were filled with debates, and that theory also presumed that this feature of Rabbinic Judaism was a positive one. According to Maimonides, such debates were necessary because the Oral Torah given by God to Moses consisted of a limited body of laws that supplemented those in the Written Torah, as well as rules of interpretation for expanding those laws. Most of the prescriptions of Jewish law were therefore the creation of the rabbis, who, over the generations, had engaged in debates about how to apply the laws of Moses and the rules of interpretation in new situations. Maimonides believed that there would have been no debates of this kind if all human beings had perfect intellects; the rabbis would have consistently arrived at the same interpretations of God's law. But given that intellectual talent varies among human beings, differences of opinion on the application of God's laws were inevitable.[53] Maimonides' views on debate were not quite as positive as those who followed Nahmanides. For the latter, the diverse rabbinic opinions regarding God's laws originated with God himself; for Maimonides, they were the result of human fallibility. Nonetheless, in Maimonides' thinking, such diversity was natural and expected.

The negative evaluation of rabbinic debate also had its supporters in the medieval period. Some rabbis upheld the view that debates about God's laws proliferated because the quality of the students in the schools of Hillel and Shammai had deteriorated.[54] Even so, the more positive understanding of rabbinic debates on matters of Jewish law seemed to be preponderant. Medieval thinkers tended to support viewpoints on this issue that were a variation on those of Maimonides or the disciples of Nahmanides.

As in Talmudic times, the positive view of debate did not mean that the rabbis were always polite in their disagreements. A rabbi's rhetoric could be quite harsh when he disagreed with a colleague. But again, the view seems to have been that debate was key to understanding God's laws.

What matters most for our concerns is whether rabbinic attitudes towards debate that we have been describing here had any analogue in pre-modern Christianity. It would appear that they did not. In pre-modern Christianity, the most significant debates were over theological matters, not legal ones, since theology was more central to Christianity than law. But what is more important is that for Christians the sole purpose of engaging in debate was to resolve the issue at hand. So once a debate was settled, the opinion of the losing side had no status. In fact, those supporting the minority viewpoint were liable to be labelled heretics unless they accepted the position of the majority. This was true, for instance, when Arius lost the dispute with Athanasius in the fourth century about the relationship between God and Jesus.[55] The same attitude towards debate was evident among Protestants. If a dispute could not be resolved, the two sides went their separate ways and formed different denominations, and each side usually considered the viewpoint of the other side to be heresy. This approach to religious truth changed only at the beginning of the twentieth century with the rise of ecumenism in Europe and the US. Only then was there recognition among Christians that there could be differing views among them and that this diversity had to be respected.[56]

As we have seen, pre-modern rabbis approached the issue of debate quite differently. They usually viewed this activity as valuable in its own right; the process of adjudicating God's word was nearly as important as the final decisions about how his word should be understood. That is why the Talmud consisted of an enormous number of debates about Jewish law that took place over five centuries yet left most of those debates unresolved.

Perhaps the only equivalent to rabbinic attitudes towards debate in pre-modern Christianity was the perspective that scholasticism had towards this activity. The great scholastic thinkers, such as Thomas Aquinas, believed that theological disagreements could be resolved only by presenting rational arguments on both sides of a given question, and they therefore invested great energy demonstrating how the different viewpoints had merit before determining which one was correct. The scholastics thus resembled the rabbis in the way they recorded the arguments of each side of the dispute and were interested in the process as much as in the final answer. However, scholasticism was only one school in medieval Christianity, and its views on debate did not have nearly the impact on Christianity that rabbinic views on this issue had on Judaism.

Conclusions

We have seen that in the medieval and early modern periods, the rabbis allowed their followers more freedom regarding what they could think and say than Christian authorities allowed their own followers. This distinction was most evident regarding matters of theology. Theology was central in Christianity, and therefore what one believed was key to membership in Christian communities. As a consequence, Catholic and Protestant Churches in the medieval and early modern periods were intent on regulating what people thought and said about religious matters. The rabbis, by contrast, had less interest in theology because their main focus was on developing and systematizing the commandments in the Hebrew Bible, and they were therefore more interested in regulating deeds than beliefs. In the late medieval period, there was increased interest among rabbis in systematic theology, and some rabbis, including Maimonides, attempted to delineate the fundamental dogmas that all Jews had to uphold. However, the level of interest in this exercise among Jews never approached that of Christians.

Yet the rabbis also granted a remarkable degree of freedom of expression, even in the area of religion, which they were intent on regulating. For the rabbis, the content of God's laws could be determined only through debate over how to properly interpret the norms of the Written and Oral Torah, and therefore the process of discerning what God's laws were was nearly as important as the laws that emerged from that process. The attitude that eventually developed in the medieval period among Judaism's most prominent rabbinic authorities was that God wanted it this way. He had given the Torah over to human beings to interpret, and therefore they were obliged to work out their differences over the meaning of its contents so that those differences could be reconciled and guidance could be provided to Jews on how to properly observe the divine commandments. Some rabbis even insisted that when God revealed the Torah to Moses, it came with the differing viewpoints about its interpretation along with the arguments that supported them. It is against this background that we can understand why the foundational text of Rabbinic Judaism, the Talmud, was a massive work consisting mainly of debates about God's laws that remained mostly unresolved. Again, process was as important as outcome.

Christians also engaged in lively debates about matters of religion, with the focus primarily on theology, but with the exception of scholasticism, the process was not nearly as important as it was in Rabbinic Judaism, and those who were on the losing side of these debates usually had to fall in line with the majority. Otherwise, they risked being labelled as heretics.

The rabbis cannot take all the credit for these developments, some of which came about because of historical circumstances. The rabbinic penchant for discussion and debate about matters of Jewish law can be explained this way. As we have already discovered in our treatment of human autonomy, the experience of exile inspired Jews to develop a rather high degree of independence in their relationship with God. If Judaism was going to survive, the rabbis would have to take their religion into their own hands and shape it so that it could deal with the reality of exile. The same sense of independence helps explain why the rabbis adopted a high degree of tolerance for each other's opinions on the meaning of God's laws. If the rabbis could argue with God, as they sometimes did, they could certainly argue with other rabbis.

It is important to recognize that the views that Christians and Jews developed on freedom of thought and expression in the medieval and early modern periods were as relevant for lay Christians and Jews as they were for intellectuals. After all, the limits that were placed on the expression of ideas in both Christian and Jewish communities affected ordinary people no less than they did the intellectual elite.

It must be emphasized that despite everything that has been said here, the freedoms the rabbis granted Jews regarding what they could think and say were not as comprehensive as those that modern Western democracies would eventually adopt. Even though Jews allowed a greater degree of freedom of thought and expression than Christians did prior to the modern period, once that period arrived, Christians quickly took the lead on this issue. Countries such as France and England gradually established comprehensive rights protecting free thought and expression so that individuals could express practically any opinion they wanted to on religious or political matters, no matter how offensive these opinions were to their fellow citizens. Before the modern period, the rabbis never went this far. In the medieval and early modern periods, the rabbis may not have regulated the views of their followers to the degree that Christian authorities did, but the rabbis still placed limits on them, limits that would be considered unacceptable by modern Western standards. Furthermore, the rabbis certainly did not accord equal status to other religions, nor did they have respect for the views of Jews who did not subscribe to the fundamental premises of the rabbinic world view, such as the Karaites. With regard to Jewish law, the rabbis were willing to entertain a diversity of opinion on most issues they discussed, but individuals or groups could not question the validity of the 613 commandments.

Similar observations can be made about democracy in its modern form. This type of government was the product of European society. Medieval and early modern Jewish communities governed themselves, and their governments were often chosen through democratic procedures, but they certainly were not democracies of the kind that eventually evolved in Europe.

Credit also has to be given to the European intellectuals of the Enlightenment and those carrying on its legacy in the nineteenth century for developing the theories that justified natural rights and democracy. While the rabbis ruminated on matters that were certainly relevant to these issues, they produced no literature that could compare in its sophistication on matters of theory to that of thinkers such as John Locke and John Stuart Mill.[57]

Still, it is significant that rabbinic Jewish culture prior to the nineteenth century allowed for a greater degree of freedom of thought and expression than Christian European culture did. It meant that when Jews joined European society in that century, they were, in key respects, better prepared than their non-Jewish neighbours for the momentous change that occurred when European countries finally gave their citizens the right of freedom of thought and expression in its mature modern form.

That may explain why Jews became important participants in the political and intellectual life of Europe after their emancipation with such remarkable speed. By the mid-nineteenth century, they were engaged in civil society and running for political office. They also flocked to the universities and began making great strides in a host of disciplines. Most of these Jews were no longer living the life of Rabbinic Judaism, but as I have argued, there is good reason to believe that some of its values remained with them, especially values that were of great utility to them as they adjusted to their new environment, such as the one we are now discussing.

One other factor may have helped prepare Jews for the notion of freedom of thought and expression in its modern form. In the medieval and early modern periods, Jews lived as a minority within a culture that was, in principle, hostile to their religion and way of life, and Jews were able to survive despite that hostility in part because of a fierce belief that they, not their non-Jewish neighbours, were the guardians of God's truth. We have to appreciate the courage that it took for Jews to think this way for almost 2,000 years. Inherent in Jewish culture throughout this lengthy stretch of time was an attitude of defiance towards the majority population among which they lived. Jews assumed that no matter how beleaguered they were, no matter how weak they appeared, it was they who were God's chosen.[58]

It was because of this strong sense of identity that attempts to convert Jews to Christianity largely failed in the medieval and early modern periods. There were periodic campaigns by the medieval Church to convince Jews to become Christians, campaigns usually spearheaded by monastic orders. We have records of public religious debates that the Church staged between Christians – usually monks – and rabbis in the hope of converting Jews to Christianity. It was also the practice in a number of times and places for Church authorities to force Jewish communities to listen to sermons from a priest or a monk about why they had to abandon their religion and become Christians. Yet, these efforts were largely futile. There were certainly instances of conversion, but over the centuries the vast majority of Jews remained Jews.

We need to keep in mind this dimension of the Jewish experience in the medieval and early modern periods when we try to understand why Jews adjusted so well to the political and intellectual life of modern European society. By the time Jews were invited to join that society, they came with almost 2,000 years of experience in being oppositional, in stubbornly adhering to beliefs that were objectionable to the populations among whom they lived and who were capable of doing them great harm. Jews were therefore unusually well-prepared for living in a society that rewarded those who thought independently.

Here too, the rabbis deserve much of the credit. The form of Judaism they constructed for their followers was clearly compelling enough to inspire the feistiness they would require when confronting their non-Jewish environment. Otherwise, one wonders whether Judaism would have survived.

Yet ironically, the independence of mind that the rabbis cultivated in their followers may have led to their undoing. In encouraging Jews over a period of centuries to think for themselves, the rabbis unwittingly encouraged Jews to question the premises of the way of life they had lived for so long. The result was that when Jews joined European society and were no longer under rabbinic authority, most of them either chose liberal forms of Judaism that rejected the premises of the premodern rabbinic tradition, or they became entirely secular. Even so, the rabbinic legacy was not lost as a result of this, just transformed. Most modern Jews did not realize that the independence of mind that led them to their new way of life was very much rooted in the old one.[59]

Chapter Seven

Valuing Life in This World I: 100–1000 CE

The next value we have to examine to understand why Jews became so successful in the modern period concerns the general question of how to relate to life in this world. To achieve success, both Christians and Jews in Europe not only had to believe that human beings possessed autonomy in relation to God and in relation to each other, they also had to channel these forms of autonomy into this-worldly goals, and that meant they had to view life in this world as good in itself. Yet we will see that prior to the modern period, this value, like the previous two we have discussed, was more strongly represented in Rabbinic Judaism than in Christianity.

The difference between the two religions on the value of the present world has been recognized for some time by both Christians and Jews. Christian thinkers began speaking of this difference long before the modern period, and they used it to criticize Judaism. They argued that Christianity was superior to Judaism because Christianity focused on lofty, spiritual matters, whereas Judaism was mired in the lowly concerns of the physical world. As the modern period got under way, Jews also began speaking about the difference between Judaism and Christianity regarding attitudes to this world. In their opinion, it was Judaism that was the superior religion because Judaism, in being more engaged with the mundane realm, was more ethically advanced than Christianity. Judaism's this-worldly focus meant that it had greater concern for the concrete needs of humanity than Christianity did.[1]

In this chapter, we will discover that there is much truth in the notion that Judaism has taken greater interest in the present world than Christianity has, but as we have seen with other generalizations of this kind, spokesmen for each side have greatly underestimated the complexities of Judaism and Christianity on this issue. So we will need to reassess how Jews and Christians approached this matter.[2]

The amount of material relevant to the topic being taken up here is extensive because it touches on almost every aspect of Christianity and Judaism, and therefore our discussion of it will be spread out over two chapters. This chapter will be devoted to Christian and Jewish views about life in this world up to the year 1000, which, on the Jewish side, roughly coincides with the end of the hegemony of Babylonian rabbinic culture, and, on the Christian side, coincides with the end of the early medieval period. In the next chapter, we will tackle Christian and Jewish views on this issue from 1000 up to the modern period.

There is one final introductory point I should make about terminology that will apply in this chapter and the next. In previous chapters, I have not had to be precise when differentiating between the early medieval period (500–1000) and the late medieval period (1000–1500) in Christian Europe. In this chapter and the next, however, I will be more careful in this regard because I will be focusing more intensively on each of these periods due to the nature of the material being analysed.

I.   Christian Perspectives

Early Christianity

The attitude of the New Testament to mundane existence is perhaps best characterized as ambivalent. A central feature – if not *the* central feature – of Jesus's mission, according to the New Testament, was the announcement that the Kingdom of God was unfolding. That is, the messianic process predicted centuries earlier by the Israelite prophets in Scripture was finally under way. History would come to an end and a new, idyllic world would come into existence.[3] Thus, from its very beginning, Christianity fixed its gaze on the future world, and that focus tended to diminish the value of the present world. However, it was not clear how much the value of this world was diminished in the New Testament because it was vague about how far along the world was in the messianic process, and it is for this reason that the attitude of the New Testament to the present world can be described as ambivalent.

Some passages in the New Testament, including the entire Book of Revelation, seemed to indicate that the messianic process was in its advanced stages and that the end of the present world was imminent. This way of thinking therefore presumed that the world in its current form did not have much worth because it would soon be superseded.

This perspective got much of its inspiration from apocalyptic literature, which was popular among Jews in the time of Jesus. Most of the authors of this literature were anonymous figures who were attempting to make sense of the troubles the Jews had been experiencing for some time. The Jews had been under foreign domination on and off for centuries and were quite distressed about it. The Romans, in particular, were heavy-handed overlords. The apocalyptic authors attempted to explain the situation by suggesting that the Jews were suffering because evil forces in the cosmos – usually identified with Satan – had taken control of the world, and, according to some of these authors, the Romans were agents of these forces. The same authors held out hope for the Jews by predicting that God would soon do battle with the forces of evil and defeat them, a victory that would result in the liberation of the Jews from foreign rule and the arrival of the messianic era. Thus, when the authors of the New Testament spoke of an imminent end to this world and the coming of the messianic period, they seemed to have taken at least part of their inspiration from apocalyptic literature. What is most important for our immediate purposes is that these ideas assumed a negative view of the present world. The world was under the sway of evil powers and had to be destroyed to make way for a far better one.[4]

Yet, some passages in the New Testament expressed a different view of the present world. The messianic process had begun, but the timing of its final completion was uncertain, and so the end of the present world was not necessarily imminent. That also meant that in the meantime, the present world still had value.

This way of thinking took hold in Christian communities scattered around the Mediterranean in the first century CE as they waited patiently for Jesus to return and complete the messianic process. As time went on, they began to realize that the final redemption might not occur as soon as they had hoped, and they wondered how they should live as Christians, given that the present world seemed to be staying in place for the time being. Paul's letters in the New Testament were composed in large part to address this question. Christian communities turned to Paul for guidance on this matter, and Paul's responses to their inquiries in his letters laid the groundwork for Christianity for centuries to come.[5] Thus, according to this perspective, the present world had more value than it had according to the apocalyptic view, which expected its imminent end.

Against this background, it is no surprise that the New Testament has inconsistent views about the attachments people have to the physical and material pleasures of life. Some passages encourage the minimization of such attachments. A well-known statement of this kind appears in Mark 8:34–35, in which Jesus says: "If any want to become my followers, let them deny themselves and take up their cross and follow me. For those who want to save their life will lose it, and those who lose their life for my sake, and for the sake of the gospel, will save it."

Some passages in the New Testament focus on more specific attachments in this world that should be resisted. The accumulation of wealth is a common target. In Mark 19:21–24, a rich young man asks Jesus what he should do to earn salvation, and Jesus replies, "Go sell your possessions and give the money to the poor." When the man walks away dejected, Jesus says to his disciples, "It is easier for a camel to pass through the eye of a needle than for someone rich to enter the kingdom of Heaven." In Matthew 6:24, we are told that one cannot serve God and money at the same time. In some passages, Jesus tells his followers that they should not only reject wealth, they should not even worry about their day-to-day material needs. In Matthew 6:25–26, he instructs them that when it comes to such basic needs as food, drink, and clothing, one should depend only on God in the same way the birds and the lilies do. Jesus's apostles also de-emphasized the material aspects of life by sharing their wealth and property in common (Acts 2:43–45; 4:22–26).[6]

However, Paul had a somewhat more positive view of material goods. In his writings, he declares that poverty is bad and that labour has value as a means to avoid it. He also states that one should not give so much of one's money to charity that one becomes poor oneself. So while Paul did not encourage the accumulation of material wealth, he apparently felt that it was important to maintain a minimum standard of living so as to avoid dependence on others.[7]

Of course, when we think of the pleasures of this world that preoccupy us, one of the first things that comes to mind is sex – and how a religion, or any thought system, deals with this issue is extremely important in determining its attitude towards life in this world in general. Sexuality, after all, concerns not just the sexual act but also marriage, children, and family life, which are commonly regarded as fundamental to mundane human existence.

The New Testament addresses these matters, but its views on them are as inconsistent as they are about other pleasures of this world. In Matthew 19:4–5, Jesus tells his disciples that marriage is ordained by God. However, later on in the same passage he expresses approval of those "who have made themselves eunuchs for the sake of the kingdom of heaven" (Matthew 19:12), a statement that seems to support celibacy. Jesus also appears to encourage celibacy in Luke 20:36, when he declares that those who remain unmarried are "equal to angels ... and sons of the resurrection." And, of course, Jesus himself did not marry.

Paul too expresses ambivalence about sex. He states explicitly that the virgin life is best, and Paul himself, like Jesus, did not marry. But

Paul says in the same passage that if people cannot exercise self-control in this area of life, they should marry, because "it is better to marry than to be aflame with passion" (1 Corinthians 7:8–9).[8]

After the New Testament achieved its final form, the Church Fathers offered views on wealth and sex that were based on those found in Scripture and were therefore mixed. Regarding wealth, the Church Fathers followed the New Testament in criticizing the amassing of material possessions, but the depth of their opposition varied. Some condemned materialism outright as Jesus had done in some passages of the New Testament, but others introduced a new perspective on the matter by arguing that even though wealth for its own sake was bad, it could be used to earn merit in God's eyes because one could give it away to charity. This way of thinking inspired some of the Church Fathers to conclude that ultimately the rich and the poor needed each other. The poor needed the rich for charity in order to survive, while the rich needed the poor because the poor provided them with the opportunity to earn reward from God through the giving of charity.[9]

On the issue of marriage and sex, the Church Fathers also followed the New Testament in having a range of views. Clement (150–215) spoke in favour of marriage and sex, while Tertullian (160–220) and Jerome (347–420) followed Paul in arguing that while marriage and sex were not forbidden, virginity was better.[10]

The most influential figure on this topic was Augustine, and his views on marriage and sex were mostly negative. As already noted, for Augustine the sexual impulse was the primary expression of Original Sin, and Augustine himself embraced celibacy at age thirty when he converted to Christianity. However, Augustine was not uncompromisingly harsh in his views on sexuality. He did not recommend celibacy for everyone. He saw marriage as potentially good because it produced children, encouraged fidelity between spouses, and allowed union between two individuals and their respective families. Still, Augustine had deep reservations about sexuality. He felt that even within marriage, sex could be a problem because of its overwhelming and distracting nature, and so he recommended that married couples engage in sex in moderation.[11]

While the Church Fathers were debating how much Christians should engage in the pleasures of this world, some Christians were making a clear commitment to a life of "denying" the present world, which is what Jesus had urged his disciples to do in the Gospel of Mark. In the fourth century, the first monasteries were established in the Christian world. In these institutions, men and women committed themselves to a life defined by "asceticism," a mode of living that involves consistently abstaining from the basic pleasures of the physical world. In this instance, that abstention focused mainly on material wealth and sexual activity. The monastics took vows to live in poverty and to abstain entirely from sex. Thus, while the New Testament and the Church Fathers expressed ambivalence towards the present world, the attitude of the monastic communities towards it leaned in a more negative direction.[12]

Ironically, one factor that inspired the development of monasticism was the material success of Christianity. When Christianity became the official religion of the Roman Empire in the fourth century, it became embroiled in political power, which meant that its focus shifted to worldly concerns. Moreover, though large numbers of inhabitants of the Roman Empire became Christians, many of them were not necessarily sincere about Christianity and merely saw it as fashionable.

Some Christians were deeply troubled by these developments and came to believe that the original message of Jesus and Paul was being lost. Some disaffected Christians therefore retreated from society to live in total isolation or to establish monastic communities so that they could live the pure religious life that they believed God wanted from Christians. Some went so far as to retreat to the desert where they could escape human society entirely.[13]

We can perhaps best sum up early Christian attitudes towards the present world by referring to Augustine's famous work, *The City of God*, written in 426, which captures the ambivalence of early Christianity towards the mundane realm. According to Augustine, Christians lived in the City of Man, but the City of God was a hidden city consisting of those whom God had selected for salvation. Eventually, the City of God would replace the City of Man when Jesus returned. In Augustine's thinking, the City of Man was of limited value and would be superseded, but it still had a positive purpose. Christians would have to make the best of an imperfect world until Jesus's return. Yet early Christianity also saw the beginnings of the monastic movement, which was more negative about the present world than Augustine and other Church Fathers were. In this movement, the best way of life was to minimize one's attachments to the world as much as was humanly possible in order to focus on one's spiritual relationship with God.

The Early Medieval Period

In many respects, the overall pattern of thinking about matters of this world that have been discussed up to this point would continue into the Middle Ages, though with some new twists.[14] On marriage and sexuality, the medieval Church remained ambivalent. The Church accepted the fact that most people married and that sex and the bearing of children were part of married life. However, the dangers of sexual lust were a constant concern, even for married couples, and the perils of this dimension of life were a common theme in Sunday sermons, Church decrees, and theological treatises. The Church therefore counselled that the purpose of sex was procreation, not pleasure, and that if one could remain celibate and not marry at all, that was best.[15]

But what about God's commandment to Adam and Eve to be "fruitful and multiply" (Gen. 1:28)? Medieval Christian thinkers tended to interpret this commandment in a figurative manner. God may have initially intended that the commandment be observed in a literal sense so that human beings would fill the earth, but the earth was now sufficiently populated, and therefore the commandment no longer referred to having children; it now had to be understood as a mandate for Christians to spread God's truth throughout the world.[16]

A major influence on how Christians viewed the pleasures of this world in the early medieval period was the remarkable growth and influence of monasticism. From the fourth century onwards, monasteries proliferated throughout Europe, so that by the year 1000, these institutions numbered in the thousands.[17] Moreover, some of the leading Church officials during the medieval period viewed monasticism as the most genuine form of Christianity, if not the *only* genuine form of Christianity. This high estimation of the monastic life was expressed by Pope Gregory the Great (c. 540–604), who did a great deal to shape medieval Christianity.[18]

Lay Christians were also impressed by monasticism in the early centuries of the medieval period. Not all communities in Europe in this period were served by priests, and when they were, the priests were not always well-trained or even well-behaved. As a result, ordinary Christians often looked up to the monastics as models of Christian piety. In fact, in the early medieval period, Christians commonly believed that the monastics were the ones most likely to be admitted to heaven in the afterlife. The chances of others achieving that goal were slim.[19]

What all this meant was that ascetic values that were central to monasticism had a more central place in early medieval Christianity than in prior centuries. Even though most Christians were not actually living that life, it coloured their perspective on the world.

What has been said thus far about medieval Christian attitudes towards the present world was not consistently implemented in practice. It is often the case that the ideal is one thing, the reality another, and here that gap was often striking. Throughout the Middle Ages – and here one can include the early *and* late medieval periods – Christian clergy up and down the Church hierarchy were known to indulge in material and physical pleasures in ways that were entirely inconsistent with the Church's teachings. The problem plagued even the highest offices in the Church. Some of the popes themselves were guilty of such transgressions, and a few of them led notoriously degenerate lives. The monastic communities suffered from similar problems: the vows of poverty and chastity were not always fulfilled.

At times, the fault for such failures did not lie with the clergy or the monastics themselves. Regional rulers and noblemen sometimes took charge of local churches and monasteries for their own material gain. They plundered them, channelled the taxes given to them into their own coffers, and installed their own officials to govern them. The result was that the churches and monasteries became corrupt. In other instances, the source of the problem was the churchmen themselves. The offices of the Church, especially the higher ones, conferred significant political power on those who held them, and their occupants were sometimes happy to exploit their positions to enrich themselves or indulge in pleasurable pursuits inconsistent with Christian ideals. The monasteries had additional problems. They often grew wealthy because lay people donated land and goods to them, with the result that monastic discipline declined and indulgence in material and physical pleasures increased.

These problems tended to occur in cycles. Throughout the Middle Ages, there were periods in which the Church's institutions became corrupted, but these would be followed by periods in which reforms were implemented to clean things up. The reforms would be effective for a century or two, but then a decline would set in once again.[20]

To sum up this section, the attitude in early medieval Christianity towards the present world continued to be ambivalent as it was in previous centuries, but the negative perspective was strengthened because of the growth and influence of monasticism. The challenge was implementing that negative perspective in practice, and neither the clergy nor the monastics were consistent in doing so. Still, by the end of the first millennium, Christianity, at least in theory, had significant reservations about the value of the mundane realm.

II.   Jewish Perspectives

As mentioned at the beginning of this chapter, it has long been recognized that the Jews were more positively disposed towards life in the present world than Christians were. The difference between the two religions on this issue goes back to the first two to three centuries CE when both Rabbinic Judaism and Christianity were in their early stages of development. In this period, Judaism and Christianity were not yet completely separated, and they faced similar challenges, but their respective answers to these challenges resulted in divergent views regarding the value of the present world, and that divergence would persist after they became separate religions.

We have already delineated the challenges both groups faced in these centuries. The land of Israel had been ruled for some time by the Romans, and the Jews had rebelled twice to achieve independence, but both rebellions had been crushed, leaving the land devastated and its population decimated. This situation prompted Jews and Christians to ask the same questions: How did the Roman domination accord with God's word as laid out in the Hebrew Bible? And what guidance could Scripture offer about how to react to this situation?

We discussed earlier in this chapter the theology that Christians formulated in response to these questions and how it affected their views on the present world. Christians settled into a way of thinking in which they remained devoted to their belief that Jesus was the messiah, but they also acknowledged that the world was not fully messianic just yet, and it was for this reason that Christians developed an ambivalence about the present world. They had one foot in the present world and another in the future world.

How did the rabbis deal with the questions that were prompted by this turbulent period of Roman rule? Some adopted a messianic theology, as the Christians did. A number of them seemed to have supported yet another revolt against Rome in 132, with a few believing that Shimon Bar Kokhba, its leader, was the messiah. Most rabbis, however, did not go in this direction; the majority adopted a theology that was less dramatic than that of Christianity but no less innovative.

That theology was spelled out in earlier chapters of this book, but we must now recast it in light of the issues of concern to us here. The view of the rabbis was that history was not coming to an end, and so they were willing to accept Roman domination as long as Jews could continue to live in accordance with God's commandments. The difficulty here was that Rome had destroyed the Temple in Jerusalem that had been the ritual centre of Judaism. Nonetheless, the rabbis, like the Christians, remained devoted to their religion and were bent on continuing to live life in accordance with the divine commandments that could still be observed after the loss of the Temple. They believed that if Jews lived by those commandments, God would relieve them of their suffering by sending his messiah, who would establish Jewish sovereignty in the land of Israel once again and rebuild the Temple.

The key point here is that the rabbis gave much less emphasis to the messianic theme than Christians did. For them, the messianic era remained in the future, and in the meantime, Jews had to live their lives in obedience to God's commandments as they had before, even if they could not observe those involving the Temple. Thus, the rabbis were not as ambivalent about the present world as Christians were. Life in this world would remain the focus as it had been prior to the Roman domination.

Rabbinic Judaism did not entirely ignore the messianic idea. But for the rabbis, the messiah had not yet appeared and there was no telling when he would, and the redemption was going to be achieved not through dramatic human gestures, physical or spiritual, but through the patient observance of God's commandments. The rabbis, then, were far more interested in defining the commandments so that they could be fulfilled in daily life than in thinking about the messiah and the future world. That is why there is very little treatment of the messianic period in rabbinic sources. The Talmud fills over twenty volumes, and yet discussions of the messianic era, which are scattered throughout these volumes, would take up only a few of pages.

The failure of the Bar Kokhba revolt helps explain why the rabbis did not focus on this issue. Once the rebellion was put down, most rabbis seem to have come to the conclusion that active messianism could be highly destructive and should be avoided. Living in peace under Roman rule was preferable to pushing a messianic agenda.[21]

Thus, the rabbinic attitude towards the messianic idea had a paradoxical element in it. The rabbis hoped and prayed for the coming of the messiah, but they also believed that Jews should not spend too much time thinking about it. The main concern for the rabbis was to regularize mundane life after two failed rebellions against Rome by living in accordance with God's laws, not to encourage messianism that might foment another rebellion.

This way of thinking is epitomized in a marvellous, pithy statement attributed to R. Yohanan ben Zakai, a first-century rabbi. He says, "If you are holding a sapling in your hand and someone tells you, 'Come quickly, the messiah is here!,' first finish planting the tree and then go to greet the messiah."[22] The message here is clear: mundane concerns take priority over messianic expectations.

The differences described here between early Christianity and early Rabbinic Judaism regarding the messianic period were connected to other divisions between the two religions. The Christian focus on an other-worldly messianic reality was part of a more general tendency to spiritualize the religious life. That tendency was not simply the result of an attempt to grapple with Roman domination; it was also born out of a desire to make God's truth available and easily accessible to all people, not just to those born as Jews. Paul argued that in the new semi-messianic reality, being a member of God's chosen did not require having Jewish lineage anymore, nor did it require the observance of a burdensome series of divine commandments. One's relationship with God was predicated on one's spiritual commitments and these commitments alone. If one had faith in God and his saviour Jesus, then one belonged to his chosen people. In this way, Paul was able to invite non-Jews to adopt the true religion without great difficulty.

The rabbis did not have Paul's universalist aspirations, and so their religion did not emphasize the spiritual dimension of Judaism in the way that Paul's did. The notion of chosenness remained physical in nature as it had been in the Hebrew Bible. One had to be born a Jew, or properly convert to Judaism, in order to belong to God's chosen people. Moreover, Jews had to continue observing the biblical commandments. That did not mean that the rabbis had no spiritual impulses at all, as their Christian opponents often claimed. It is just that rabbinic spirituality was based more on the experience of performing divinely mandated deeds than on inward experience.[23]

The Body, the Soul, and the Afterlife

Up to this point, we have explained the differences between early Rabbinic Judaism and Christianity regarding the present world by speaking about broad issues involving the two religions at the communal level – that is, by looking at how they each conceived of themselves as God's chosen people and where they believed they were located on the historical timeline leading up to their redemption in the messianic era. But the differences between the two religions on matters of this world were further accentuated by their divergent views about the individual – in particular, the relationship of the body to the soul and the fate of the soul after death.

We will begin with Christianity. By the fifth century, most Christians had adopted Plato's views on the body and the soul. In Plato's thinking, body and soul were separate entities that in this life were temporarily conjoined. The soul was the superior partner in this pairing. It was the essence of the individual, and it was also the source of their goodness because its desires were spiritual in nature. The soul's relationship with the body was therefore an uneasy one. The soul longed for the divine realm because it originated there and would return to it after death. The body, by contrast, was the source of evil in human beings in that it was responsible for their physical desires. The body's purpose was to provide a test for the soul to see whether it would cultivate a life devoted to spiritual concerns and minimize attention to the physical desires of the body during its temporary sojourn on earth. If the soul succeeded in doing so, it would be rewarded in the afterlife, where it would be free of physical wants and would persist in a state of spiritual bliss in close proximity to God. If the soul did not succeed in doing so, it was destined for punishment in hell. Augustine's influence was crucial here. While Christianity had adopted Greek ideas regarding the body and the soul before him, it was he who made these ideas into fundamental Christian doctrines.[24]

The rabbis saw things differently, and for those not familiar with Judaism, their views may seem strange. For the rabbis, the distinction between body and soul was not as sharp as it was for Christians; the two were believed to be commingled. Moreover, the body was more central to rabbinic thinking than it was to Christianity. As Daniel Boyarin puts it, whereas in Christianity the human being was viewed as a soul housed in a body, for the rabbis the human being was viewed as a body animated by a soul.[25]

Also, for the rabbis, evil did not originate in the body: the body was neither good nor evil. As we have already seen, a common view among the rabbis was that human beings acted in either a good or evil manner because of two inclinations within the soul that competed for dominance: the good inclination (*yetser ha-tov*) and the evil inclination (*yetser ha-ra*).[26] Thus, the body served as a neutral battleground for these two inclinations. People could be swayed to follow one inclination or the other depending on which of the two forces they were willing to accept guidance from at any given moment. Moreover, if they managed to keep the evil inclination at bay throughout their time on earth, their soul would be rewarded in the afterlife. If they did not, the soul would receive punishment in the afterlife.[27]

These observations help explain why the rabbis tended to have a more positive view of the present world than Christians did. Because the body was not associated with evil as it was in Christianity, physical and material desires were not necessarily evil either. They could be good *or* evil depending on which of the two inclinations in the soul was motivating them. If the good inclination channelled such desires towards worthy goals, those desires were good as well.

A charming rabbinic story illustrates the positive attitude the rabbis tended to adopt towards the body. We are told that Hillel, a great first-century Jewish sage, informed his students one day that he was going off to perform a "mitzvah," a divine commandment. When the students asked him what commandment he was about to fulfil, he replied that he was planning to take a bath in a bath-house. Understandably, the students wanted an explanation; bath-houses were not generally thought of as places of holy activity. Hillel responded by making note of the way in which the statues of the Roman emperors were cared for. These statues were cleaned and polished on a regular basis by people specially hired for the job, and those people were paid very well and were honoured for their work. Hillel then pointed out that he himself was created in the image and likeness of God as all human beings were according to the first chapter of Genesis, and God was a far greater king than any emperor. And so, the rabbi concluded, should not his body, which was modelled after God, be treated with at least the same dignity as statues modelled after rulers who were mere mortals? A bath was therefore an activity of sacred significance.[28]

One might be perplexed that Hillel apparently takes the notion that humans are created in the image of God quite literally here. He assumes that his body resembles God in some fashion, just as the statues of emperors resemble the human beings they portray. But we cannot dwell on this issue here. The important point is that we have an example here of a major rabbinic figure who believed that the human body was a holy creation and that it was a divine commandment to take care of it, even when it came to simple cleanliness. One would be hard-pressed to find an equivalent statement in early Christianity, or in medieval Christianity, for that matter. In Christian culture, the body was not something to be revered. It was usually viewed as the source of temptation and sin.

In light of these observations, it is not surprising that Rabbinic Judaism took much less interest in the afterlife than Christianity did. The afterlife was certainly a matter of concern for the rabbis. In fact, the rabbis inform us that one of the major issues that divided the Pharisees from the Sadducees was that the Pharisees believed in the afterlife and the Sadducees did not, and the rabbis were clearly on the side of the Pharisees here, as they were on other matters. But the rabbis were far less concerned about the afterlife than Christians were. Rabbinic literature contains very little discussion of this issue. Once again, the Talmud is largely preoccupied with God's commandments and how they are to be observed in this life.[29]

There is thus a parallel here to rabbinic attitudes towards the messiah. As with the concept of the messiah, the rabbis believed that the afterlife was certainly important and that one's goal should be to achieve reward in it, but they also felt that the afterlife should not preoccupy them or their constituents. One's focus should be on obedience to God, which meant observing his commandments in the present life.

The rabbinic emphasis on life in this world can be illustrated by a number of observations. First, it is clear that the rabbis did not see any rush in getting to the afterlife, a point that comes through very clearly in rabbinic law. According to the rabbis, when an individual's life was in danger, all the divine commandments were immediately suspended to save them, even if it meant that the person would live just a few more seconds. The underlying view here seems to have been that life in this world was so precious that one was mandated to prolong it even for a minuscule amount of time.[30]

The rabbinic emphasis on life in this world is also evident in a rather strange characterization of the afterlife that appears in several rabbinic sources. According to these sources, the greatest reward in the afterlife that one could achieve for one's good deeds in this life was to be admitted to a heavenly rabbinic academy where all the great rabbis studied Torah as they did on earth, with God himself presiding over the study sessions. The great irony inherent in this conception is that in this academy one would be studying the Talmud, a text that is devoted to mundane affairs. That is, the rabbis in heaven would be spending all their time studying such matters as what the laws should be when someone's ox gores their neighbour's ox, or how to ensure that one's pots and pans were fit for preparing kosher food – even though such earthly matters would presumably be of little relevance for the disembodied spirits studying in the heavenly academy.

This conception is less strange, however, in light of what we have said about rabbinic views of the present world. So enamoured were the rabbis of mundane matters that some of them envisioned themselves studying the laws pertaining to such matters even in the afterlife. For these rabbis, there was no greater bliss than studying the Torah's laws about earthly activities, even when one was no longer on earth to fulfill them.[31]

The rabbinic focus on matters of this world had an impact on how the rabbis conceived of the messianic period. It has already been noted that the rabbis deliberately downplayed the messianic idea, and therefore their literature contains relatively little material about this issue as well. But here again, what they *did* say about it is telling. The emphasis in their treatments of it was on the resurrection of the dead that would supposedly take place when the messiah arrived. The importance of this issue for the rabbis is reflected in the fact that in the *amidah*, the most central prayer in Rabbinic Judaism that is recited in all three daily prayer services, the rabbis included a blessing in its introductory section that praises God for resurrecting the dead in messianic times. Why this emphasis? In light of what has been said in this chapter, it makes perfect sense. The rabbinic interest in the resurrection underscores the extent to which the rabbis focused on the value of life in this world. The ideal existence for human beings in messianic times, as the rabbis conceived it, was not a disembodied one, but a fully embodied one on earth.[32]

To sum up our discussion thus far, early Rabbinic Judaism and Christianity in the first millennium developed different perspectives on the mundane realm, with the rabbis tending to have a more positive view of this realm than their Christian counterparts did. The differences here were rooted in fundamental disagreements about how to make sense of events in the first centuries CE. These events inspired Jews and Christians to come up with divergent views on the identity of God's chosen people, what was expected of them, and what stage of history they were in, and these views in turn spawned differing attitudes towards mundane existence. The difference in attitudes on this issue was accentuated by disagreements over the nature of the individual – in particular, the relationship of body to the soul and what happened to the soul in the afterlife.

Marriage, Sexuality, Procreation, and Family

The division between Rabbinic Judaism and Christianity regarding the theological matters discussed up to this point had important ramifications for a number of more concrete issues that we must now take up, beginning with marriage, sexuality, procreation, and family. We have seen that Christian views on marriage and sexuality in the Roman and early medieval periods were highly ambivalent because of Augustine's influence and the reverence that Christians had for the monastic life. Rabbinic views on such matters were generally more favourable, for several reasons. First and most obvious, since the rabbis had a more positive view of the mundane realm in general than Christians did, it makes sense that the rabbis also had more positive views of marriage and sexuality, given that these aspects of life were as mundane as any.

There were also more specific reasons why the rabbis had more favourable views of marriage and sexuality than Christians did. Perhaps the most important was that, according to the rabbis, procreation was a divine commandment. This imperative was based on God's instruction to Adam and Eve to "be fruitful and multiply." While Christians had spiritualized this commandment to mean that human beings were commanded to spread God's truth, the rabbis read this same verse quite literally, as a divine commandment that had to be obeyed not just by Adam and Eve but by all of their progeny.

Interestingly, the rabbis also believed that the commandment was directed specifically towards men, not women – though it goes without saying that women had to be involved as well.[33] The rabbis also had harsh things to say about men who neglected the duty to procreate, which underscores how important it was in rabbinic thinking. According to one source, a man who throughout his life had wilfully passed up the opportunity to have children would be barred from heaven.[34] In another passage, such a person is deemed a murderer, presumably because he has effectively denied life to his unborn children.[35]

Because the rabbis assumed that procreation would take place within the confines of marriage, marriage was not optional as it was in early and medieval Christianity. The commandment to procreate was, in effect, also a commandment to get married. But for many rabbis, marriage was a good thing not simply because it provided the opportunity to obey God's commandment to have children, but also because it was important for living a fulfilled life. According to one rabbinic passage, if one is widowed or divorced, one should remarry, even if one already has children. This piece of advice is premised on God's statement in the Bible prior to the creation of Eve that "it is not good for man to be alone" (Gen. 2:18).[36] Eve was meant to provide Adam with companionship, and companionship was thus an important component in all subsequent marital relationships as well. The same rabbinic passage contains other statements that equate marriage with companionship even more clearly. Thus, one rabbi tells us that "any man who lives without a wife, lives without happiness, without blessing, and without good." Another rabbi states that such an individual lives "without help, without wisdom, without Torah, without a wall, without a dwelling."[37]

The early rabbis also composed a series of seven blessings to be recited at weddings that extolled marriage as an institution bringing happiness and joy to husband and wife, and these blessings continue to be recited at traditional Jewish weddings to this very day.[38] What is significant about this custom is its public nature. In the period we are considering in this chapter, ordinary Jews might not have been familiar with the intricate rabbinic discussions that would eventually make up the Talmud, but we can assume that most of them attended weddings, and therefore, by instituting these blessings in wedding ceremonies, the rabbis clearly wanted Jews to view marriage as a happy and joyful institution.

Other passages in rabbinic literature express a positive view of marriage by implying that a man is somehow "incomplete" until he is married. Thus, in one Talmudic source, R. Elazar tells us that "any man without a wife is not a man."[39] This statement is not about marriage providing an opportunity for a man to prove his masculinity; rather, its message is that only through marriage does a man become fully human. R. Elazar draws this idea out of a verse in the fourth chapter of Genesis that informs us that when God created human beings, he created them "male and female" and "called them Adam" (Gen. 5:2). That God refers to his male and female creations as "Adam" seems odd because it implies the creation of a single being, not two. R. Elazar seems to make sense of the verse by playing on the fact that "Adam" is not just a proper name for the first man but also a noun that means "person" or "human being." What the verse is therefore teaching us, according to R. Elazar, is that only when both male and female were created did they become "complete" as humans.[40]

Yair Lorberbaum goes further, arguing that this passage, and a number of similar ones in rabbinic literature, imply that marriage is a cosmic event. It is not just that man becomes complete by marrying a woman – God becomes complete as well! That is because in the first chapter of Genesis, we are told that Adam was created in the "image" and "likeness" of God, and so if "Adam" here refers to a man and woman who have become conjoined as a complete being in marriage, then marriage, in effect, makes God himself complete as well. That may sound like a very peculiar notion, but we have already seen that the rabbis at times expressed radical ideas about God, and the passages being discussed here provide more instances of that tendency. The notion that marriage "completes" God may also explain why some of the rabbis saw procreation as a divine commandment; they believed that having children effectively increased God's presence in the world by filling it with people who would unite with each other in matrimony and would repeatedly "complete" the divine image.[41]

Against this background, we can make sense of another strange conception found in a number of rabbinic passages, which is that God is a matchmaker. In one passage, for example, the rabbis tell us that God determines whom a person will marry from the time they are conceived in the womb.[42] According to another source, matchmaking is, in fact, all that God does since he finished creating the world in six days.[43] These sources again reflect just how important marriage was for the rabbis.

From the rabbinic sources we have cited thus far about marriage, it is quite clear that a good number of early rabbis viewed marriage in more positive terms than Christian thinkers did. But what about sexuality? While marriage and sexuality often go together, positive views of the former do not necessarily imply positive views of the latter.

In early Rabbinic Judaism, positive views on marriage were matched by similarly positive views on sexuality, and here as well, there were specific reasons why the rabbis had more favourable views on this aspect of life than Christians did, reasons that went beyond the fact that the rabbis had more positive views about mundane life in general. Most important, early rabbinic thinking lacked the unpleasant associations that Christians had with sexuality, and so the rabbis could more easily affirm it as a necessary and important part of life than Christians could.

The positive view that the early rabbis had towards sexuality can be illustrated by the fact that, according to them, married men and women were mandated by divine law to fulfil each other's sexual needs quite apart from the goal of procreation. Sexual satisfaction was thus considered to be a legitimate part of marriage for both men and women.[44]

Early rabbinic sources often equated the sexual impulse with the "evil inclination" (*yetser ha-ra*) in all human beings, but as noted in an earlier chapter, some of these sources cast a positive light on the evil inclination by explaining that it was not evil if it was used for good purposes, and one such source brought that point across while making the connection between the evil impulse and sexuality. It stated that "were it not for the evil inclination, no man would build a house, nor marry a woman, nor would he have children." According to this passage, sexual desire can certainly lead to sin, but without it, no man would get married or have a family, and these are assumed to be very good things. Here, then, sexuality is viewed quite positively.[45]

The interest of the early rabbis in marriage and procreation went beyond just creating a family. A great deal of rabbinic ritual focused on the home that resulted from that enterprise, and this is also a key issue for our concerns because rabbinic attitudes towards the home also reflect the degree to which the rabbis focused on mundane matters.

Central in this regard were the Sabbath and religious festivals. The rabbis viewed it as a commandment to eat three meals on this hallowed day – Friday night, Saturday morning, and Saturday afternoon – and one had to eat all three whether or not one was hungry.[46] The notion that one is commanded to eat meals as a way of celebrating the holiest day of the week is in itself an indication of the rabbinic interest in mundane life, but this imperative had mundane ramifications well beyond the act of food consumption. It required families to come together to dine on a regular basis – the Sabbath, after all, came once every week – and this ensured that home life would be central for Jews.[47] There were also holidays throughout the rabbinic calendar year in which mandated meals figured just as prominently as they did on the Sabbath.

Yet, what has been said up until now about early rabbinic views on marriage and sexuality has to be qualified. The views of the rabbis on such matters were not always positive. With respect to marriage, we find sources in early rabbinic literature about married life that are decidedly less romantic than those cited earlier. Some rabbinic passages imply that marriage is primarily for the purpose of saving men from the sins that result from unregulated sexual lust. As we are told in one Talmudic passage, "if a man is twenty years old and is still unmarried, all of his days are spent in sin." A subsequent opinion revises the statement to say that "all of his days are spent in *thought* about sin" (my emphasis).[48] One also finds a number of stories in rabbinic literature in which some rabbis spent substantial amounts of time away from their wives in order to study Torah. Daniel Boyarin refers to such individuals as "married monks."[49]

On the specific issue of sexuality, we find sources in early rabbinic literature that are less sanguine about this aspect of life than those cited earlier. In some passages in which the sexual impulse is equated with the evil inclination, there is no attempt to explain why that impulse is actually good. In one Talmudic source, the wife of R. Eliezer, a towering rabbinic figure in second-century Palestine, reports that when her husband engages in sexual relations with her, "he unveils an inch and veils it again, and he appears as if he is driven by a demon."[50] Apparently, R. Eliezer believed that sexual pleasure was a bad thing and it therefore had to be minimized. We may also note again that some rabbis chose to leave their wives for extended periods to study Torah, and these rabbis, in doing so, were clearly not prioritizing their wives' sexual needs despite the imperative to do so. Finally, we should point out that while sexuality was at times celebrated in rabbinic literature, it was only sexuality as expressed within the confines of heterosexual marriage. Sex of any other kind and in any other context was prohibited.[51]

Clearly then, some of the early rabbis entertained unfavourable views on marriage and sexuality. In fact, these views appear to have been quite close to, or even overlapped with, those found in Christianity in the Roman and early medieval periods. Notions about marriage being mainly for procreation or that the sexual impulse was somehow demonic were certainly reminiscent of those espoused by Christian thinkers whom we looked at earlier. So if Rabbinic Judaism was not fully ascetic, it had what Steven Fraade refers to as "ascetic tensions."[52]

Yet despite these observations, rabbinic views on marriage and sexuality were still more positive than those of their Christian counterparts in fundamental respects. The rabbis, almost without exception, believed that marrying and having children were commanded by God, and that belief, in turn, presumed that engaging in sexual relations was divinely mandated as well. Even rabbis who had reservations about marriage and sexuality held these positions. Moreover, many of the early rabbis clearly celebrated marriage and sexuality. In Christianity, we find no parallel to these views in the Roman and early medieval periods. No prominent Christian thinker in these periods believed that marriage, procreation, and sexual activity were divinely mandated, nor did they make statements celebrating these elements of life in the way that some of the rabbis did. There were certainly no major Christian thinkers who suggested that marriage completed the Godhead. So while there is some overlap between views on marriage and sexuality in early Rabbinic Judaism and Christianity, Christians were willing to entertain negative views on these matters that are not found in early Rabbinic Judaism, and, conversely, the early rabbis were willing to entertain positive views on this subject not found in Christianity.

A core issue that set Rabbinic Judaism on a different path from Christianity regarding marriage and sexuality was procreation. Once the rabbis saw this activity as a divine imperative, positive views on marriage and sexuality followed. So an important question is why the rabbis took this position. Why did they turn God's imperative to Adam and Eve to procreate into a divine commandment that all Jews had to observe? Scholars have proposed several answers to this question, but to my mind, the obvious one is that this move was inspired by the failure of two rebellions against the Romans and the devastation these events caused. Hundreds of thousands of Jews were reported to have died, and the rabbis seem to have clearly understood that reconstructing Judaism and reviving the Jewish people required their followers to have children.[53] Procreation thus became a commandment.

The connection I am making here between the difficult circumstances of the Jews in this period and the imperative to procreate has been entertained by others, but it has also been disputed. I see it as perfectly plausible. This theory not only accounts for procreation becoming a commandment but also explains the rabbinic interest in marriage and family life in general. The rabbis believed that Jews had to reproduce in order to get past the catastrophes that had befallen the Jews in the first two centuries CE so that their communities could thrive again.[54]

Other Material and Physical Pleasures

WEALTH

The differences between Rabbinic Judaism and Christianity in the first millennium regarding the present world extended to their attitudes towards other material and physical pleasures, such as the accumulation and enjoyment of material goods. In early Rabbinic Judaism, perspectives on this dimension of life were more positive than those in Christianity in the same period.

According to the early rabbis, taking care of one's material needs was a legitimate part of life. This idea was reflected in the standard texts of the weekday prayer services the rabbis composed, which all adult male Jews were required to recite. These prayer services contained petitionary prayers for material blessing and are recited to this day by traditional Jews. Material well-being was thus viewed by the rabbis as a respectable goal to which everyone could aspire.

The early rabbis also believed that men had special obligations regarding this aspect of life. In several Talmudic passages, we are told that it was a divine duty for men to acquire a trade in order to make a living.[55] That prescription makes sense in light of a number of other duties that men had, according to the rabbis. It was incumbent on men to provide food and clothing to their wives; that requirement was part of the standard rabbinic marriage contract. Men also had to support their children.[56] Thus, for men, taking care of material needs was not just acceptable; it was imperative.

In early and medieval Christianity, work was valued as well. The Church Fathers spoke highly of work because they believed that it domesticated the natural world. The monastic communities also had high regard for work because, according to them, it enhanced the spiritual life.[57] However, as we saw earlier in this chapter, there was also an ambivalence towards wealth in early and medieval Christianity that had its roots in the New Testament. Thus, even though work was praised in early and medieval Christianity, the accumulation of goods was not necessarily seen as positive. In fact, the monastic communities glorified poverty. For these communities, work was only supposed to take care of one's most minimal needs and nothing more. The monastic life was supposed to be one of material deprivation. And we must keep in mind that the monastic attitude here was highly important for Christian society as a whole because by the early medieval period, the monastic life was widely respected in Christian Europe.

We find no parallel to these views in early Rabbinic Judaism. The early rabbis did not have the ambivalence towards wealth that their Christian counterparts did. Moreover, they viewed poverty quite negatively. According to one Talmudic passage, "poverty is worse than fifty plagues."[58] In another rabbinic passage, we are informed that "there is nothing in the world more grievous than poverty – the most terrible of sufferings."[59]

Most telling is how the early rabbis viewed their own wealth. Alyssa Gray has shown that these rabbis tended to portray themselves as being wealthy on the presumption that wealth was an important prerequisite for their role as leaders in Jewish society. The rabbis believed that by acquiring wealth, they would have the prestige to earn the respect of ordinary Jews and of the non-Jewish government officials under whose rule they lived.[60]

But were the rabbis actually wealthy? The way they portrayed themselves may have been more an ideal than a reality.[61] Still, it is highly significant that the rabbis depicted themselves in this manner because it implied that they openly embraced the notion that religious leadership required wealth in a way that early and medieval Christian authorities did not.[62]

There certainly were limits on how much the rabbis focused on material things and how much they wanted their followers to focus on them, and this is evident in the fact that the rabbis expected all Jews to observe the divine commandments, a way of life that required them to spend good portions of their time engaged in ritual activity, such as prayer. The Sabbath was an especially time-consuming commitment. It took up an entire day of each week, and work and the acquiring of goods on this day were expressly forbidden.

The rabbis also expected their followers to set aside as much time as they could to fulfil the commandment to study sacred texts. The question was how much time that activity should take up, and a number of suggestions were made. For instance, R. Gamliel, a third-century rabbi, believed that one should divide one's time between study and work.[63] R. Shimon bar Yohai, a second-century rabbi, contended that Jews should spend all their time engaged in study and not worry about work, on the belief that God would miraculously provide for their material needs.[64] But according to both views, the pursuit of wealth clearly had limits. The obligation to study Torah on a regular basis ensured that this was the case.[65]

Still, the early rabbis, on the whole, were not as ambivalent about wealth as Christians were. They certainly did not establish monastic communities in which the life of poverty was considered a virtue.

A critical factor explaining the differences between Rabbinic Judaism and Christianity regarding attitudes towards material wealth is the divergence between Jewish and Christian Scriptures on this issue. In the Hebrew Bible, wealth is seen as a divine blessing. In fact, the entire covenantal relationship between God and the Israelites in the Hebrew Bible is predicated on this notion. According to the terms of the covenant, if the Israelites obey God's commandments, they will be rewarded with material prosperity, and if they do not, they will be punished with poverty and exile. The rabbis continued to believe in this covenant, and they highlighted its importance by requiring Jews to recite the *Shema* prayer twice a day. This prayer consists of three paragraphs from the Torah, the second of which emphasizes the relationship between reward and punishment in the material realm, on the one hand, and obedience to God, on the other.[66] In Christianity, however, the belief was that this material understanding of the covenant had been superseded because of Jesus's arrival. In the New Testament, Jesus heralded the unfolding of the Kingdom of God so that the promise of material reward in this world was no longer of concern. Instead the focus was on the promise of spiritual reward in the future messianic world. The biblical background here therefore helps explain why Jews and Christians developed different approaches to wealth.

OTHER PLEASURES

The interest of the rabbis in the mundane realm also expressed itself in an appreciation for pleasures in life other than wealth – chief among them, food. As noted earlier, the Sabbath was structured around three meals that one was mandated to consume. Meals were also central to Jewish holidays throughout the calendar year. We can add here that all major life-cycle events, such as circumcisions and weddings, required special meals to mark the occasion. These observations help explain why the focus on food has remained a common feature of modern Jewish culture.

Moreover, meals served an important religious function in early Rabbinic Judaism even on weekdays. The rabbis viewed the dinner table as a symbolic replacement for the altar in the Temple in Jerusalem that no longer existed; thus, in rabbinic thinking, the dinner table was crucial for keeping Jews connected to God at a time when the Temple no longer existed.[67]

Here too there were limits to the positive attitude that the rabbis had to mundane needs. According to Rabbinic Judaism, Jews certainly were not permitted to eat everything they wanted to. Rabbinic law contained a myriad of intricate prescriptions regulating food consumption that were based on the dietary laws of the Torah. The rabbis also instituted several fast days during the year to commemorate the destruction of the Temple. They also declared fast days in times of drought and other natural disasters.[68] In addition, some rabbis fasted periodically to atone for their sins.[69]

But the focus on food and eating in Rabbinic Judaism is still striking in contrast to Christianity in the Roman and early medieval periods.

Christianity certainly had its own major food ritual: the Eucharist, which involved symbolically consuming Jesus's body and blood by eating bread and drinking a quantity of wine. But meals and food did not have the place in Christian ritual practice that they did in Rabbinic Judaism. Moreover, as meals went, the Eucharist was rather sparse.

One area of early rabbinic law that is especially significant for highlighting the discrepancy between early Rabbinic Judaism and Roman and early medieval Christianity is the one dealing with blessings. According to the rabbis, one had to recite a blessing over every pleasure one experienced in life, and the rabbis composed a wide variety of concise blessings for that purpose. In one Talmudic source, we are told that a person must utter one hundred such blessings every day.[70] These blessings included those that were to be said when witnessing natural events, such as lightning or falling stars; when seeing nature's beauty, such as mountains, seas, rainbows, beautiful animals, or even beautiful people; or when experiencing the gratification of a major new purchase, such as new clothing or a new house. There was even a blessing that one said after going to the bathroom. It expressed wonder at God's wisdom in creating the bodily organs and physical functions that kept us alive.[71]

Some scholars have argued that there was a theology underlying the rabbinic imperative to say blessings, based on a biblical law that specified that one was not allowed to use objects that belonged to the Temple in Jerusalem for personal use. All such objects essentially belonged to God, and therefore using the objects in the Temple in this manner was a serious violation.[72] It seems that the rabbis extended this rule to the world in general. The world was God's Temple as well, and so one was not allowed to derive pleasure from anything in the world unless one received authorization from God. The uttering of blessings was meant to provide just that. All blessings began with a standard formula acknowledging God's sovereignty over the world, and that gesture, in effect, secured the required permission to enjoy his world.[73]

Here again, we have no parallels in Christianity during the period of early Rabbinic Judaism. The notion that all pleasurable experiences should elicit a blessing went against the grain of Christian theology, which at the time was heavily influenced by Augustine and his negative views about such experiences. In fact, one can be sure that Augustine would have reacted with utter consternation to the notion that one should recite a blessing after seeing an exceptionally good-looking person, buying new clothing, or going to the bathroom.

Conclusions

As with all the other major topics we have discussed so far, neither Rabbinic Judaism nor Christianity in the first millennium expressed views on the present world that were monolithic. Each religion offered a variety of perspectives on the mundane realm and the major activities often associated with it, such as marriage, sexuality, family life, and the accumulation of wealth. Nonetheless, on a spectrum of views about mundane existence ranging from positive to negative, rabbinic views were skewed towards the positive end of the spectrum, while Christian views were skewed towards the negative end. The differences between the two religions here can be traced to the theological realm. They were rooted in divergent approaches to God's plan for history and the nature of the individual.

Our discussion is not yet complete. We have looked at how Jewish and Christian views on the present world evolved up to the year 1000, and we still have to look at how those views evolved in the second Christian millennium. But before we do that, I would like to finish this chapter with some general observations about how the early rabbis approached the mundane realm.

My sense is that the early rabbis, in constructing a religion that viewed the present world as positively as they did, did something rather unusual. Religious communities often respond to suffering by encouraging a retreat from the mundane world and focusing on other-worldly matters. Christianity in the Roman and early medieval periods is an excellent example of this tendency. In the face of Roman persecution and the execution of their founder, Christians constructed a religion with an other-worldly emphasis by focusing on the importance of the inward spiritual life, the afterlife, and the completion of the messianic process that had already begun. This other-worldly emphasis was particularly pronounced in the monastic communities that became so important in Christianity during the phase of its history that has been discussed in this chapter.

Other religions have advocated a retreat from the world not because of suffering they have experienced as a community but as a response to the ordinary suffering that so often suffuses the lives of human beings. Buddhism provides an example of a religion of this kind. Here the emphasis is on escaping this world as a response to the travails of disease, aging, and death that all people must confront. Moreover, here, as in Christianity, the monastic life is regarded as the preferred way of living.

The rabbis were remarkable in doing precisely the opposite of what these religions did. Their answer to the catastrophe that befell the Jewish community in the Roman period was to embrace life even more intensely than before. They constructed a religion consisting of a system of laws that regulated daily life so that Jews would connect to God in their mundane lives at every moment. The world of physical reality was their focus – not inward spirituality, not the afterlife, not the messianic era. I say this without forgetting the ascetic and other-worldly tensions that were present in early Rabbinic Judaism, for even with these tensions taken into account, it is still true that the religion the rabbis shaped was extraordinary in its positive engagement with mundane affairs. No rabbi, no matter how ascetic or detached from the world, could avoid observing the divine commandments, which included the requirement to get married, have children, support a family, eat three full meals on the Sabbath, and utter blessings over every pleasure experienced in God's world.[74]

To what extent the rabbis were truly unusual here would require a far more extensive investigation than I can provide. Still, I believe that what I am saying here has merit. Rabbinic religion did something out of the ordinary by embracing mundane existence in the face of catastrophe.

I can say with more certainty that regardless of whether rabbinic religion was unusual, it is understandable why the rabbinic response to catastrophe was so appealing to Jews. It was in fact quite a daring response. It was defiant regarding the ill fortune the Jews had experienced in urging them not to give up on finding God in this world despite the hardships they had experienced. Moreover, it represented a refusal to give in to any suggestion that the original covenant with God was no longer in effect. The Jews remained God's chosen people; it is just that they were being punished for their sins, and so they had to find a way back to him by observing the biblical commandments that they could still obey without the Temple.[75]

Should the rabbis alone take credit for the value they placed on the present world? One could argue that this emphasis was already present in the Hebrew Bible and that the rabbinic approach to the mundane world was simply a continuation of biblical thinking. There is certainly much truth in this assertion. The stories about the Patriarchs in the Book of Genesis, which have been taught to Jewish children since well before the rabbinic period and up to the modern era, focus on mundane issues. Much of their content is about family dynamics, including marital tensions and sibling rivalries. Furthermore, as already noted, the promises that God makes to the Patriarchs, which underpin the entire biblical narrative, are about rewards that are very much this-worldly in nature. God informs them that their descendants will grow into a large nation, inherit the land of Canaan, and prosper if they obey his will. Those same promises are reiterated generations later, when, according to the biblical narrative, the Israelites become a nation. Conversely, there is very little reference in the Hebrew Bible to other-worldly rewards. It rarely mentions the afterlife, and while the messianic period is often referred to in the books of the Prophets, here again, the emphasis is on the mundane realm. The idyllic world that the coming of the messiah will initiate is one in which the Israelites will return to their land and live materially prosperous lives.[76] So it has to be acknowledged that the Hebrew Bible had some influence on the rabbinic attitude towards the present world.

However, the rabbis should still take much of the credit here in constructing a form of religion focused on mundane matters. By the time the rabbinic period got under way, a large body of religious literature had been composed by Jews, including works that never made it into the Bible but were nonetheless influential, and much of this non-canonical literature was far more interested in the afterlife and the messianic period than the Hebrew Bible was. That meant that in the first centuries CE, as the Hebrew Bible came into its final form, Jews had a choice about how much to allow the non-canonical literature to influence their interpretation of the Bible. Some groups chose to take that literature quite seriously, with the result that they absorbed its other-worldly emphasis. Christians were one such group. Early Christianity was heavily influenced by the apocalyptic texts that were included in the non-canonical literature, and these texts, as we have noted, were concerned with the end of times and the events leading up to it. The rabbis also absorbed ideas from these texts, but apparently they were far less interested in their other-worldly themes than other contemporary Jewish groups. These themes were not developed extensively by the rabbis. Thus, while the focus of the rabbis on matters of this world was continuous with the Hebrew Bible, the rabbis made a conscious choice to make that focus central to their world view. They could have gone in the direction of Christianity and several other religious groups within Judaism and focused on other-worldly matters as found in the apocalyptic texts, but they clearly decided not to.

What emerges here is that the rabbis, in dwelling as much as they did on the concerns of this world, were motivated by a vision that they constructed quite deliberately. They believed that the best hope for the Jewish people to overcome their dire circumstances was to engage in the world as it was, not to retreat from it. As we will see in the next chapter, that vision helped Jews survive not just up to the year 1000 but in the late medieval and early modern periods as well, and once the modern period arrived, the same vision prepared them to achieve immense success when they were invited to become part of Western society.

Chapter Eight

Valuing Life in This World II: 1000–1800 CE

This chapter picks up where the last one left off by examining how the theme of valuing the present world developed in Christian and Jewish cultures in Europe during the late medieval and early modern periods. We will see that in this time frame, the gap between the two cultures regarding this issue significantly narrowed, with Christian culture unwittingly taking on features of Jewish culture and Jewish culture unwittingly taking on features of Christian culture.

Whether that gap ever closed entirely is a question we will have to examine. But whether it did or not, the confluence between the two cultures would have important ramifications for Jews in the modern period. By the time that period arrived, Christians had developed a far more positive attitude towards the mundane world than in prior centuries, and that attitude helped spur them to excel as never before in the economic, intellectual, and artistic spheres. Jews, for their part, had cultivated a positive relationship with the mundane world far longer than Christians had, and as a result, when Jews were invited to become part of non-Jewish European society, they were unusually well-prepared to participate in Europe's drive for excellence.

I. Christian Perspectives

The Late Medieval Period

We have already laid the groundwork for understanding Christian views of the mundane world in the later centuries of the medieval period. In the previous chapter, we saw that Christianity was fundamentally ambivalent about the present world. On the one hand, the present world was only of provisional importance because the Kingdom of God was unfolding and would be fully established when Jesus returned, but on the other hand, the present world still had to be dealt with as it was, as long as it remained in existence. This ambivalence resulted in mixed views on concrete issues in the mundane realm, such as marriage, sexuality, and the acquisition of wealth.

This approach to the mundane world would persist to the end of the Middle Ages, but there were some new and important developments regarding this issue after the year 1000. In some ways, Christians developed a greater interest in the mundane realm than in earlier centuries, while in other ways they developed greater reservations about it.

There was certainly a growing interest in the physical world in general among Europe's intellectuals. As noted in an earlier chapter, the twelfth century saw the rise of scholasticism, a school of Christian philosophy inspired by Aristotle that explored the truths of Christianity using a highly structured rational and empirical method, and this enterprise included the study of science on the premise that understanding God's creation was necessary in order to understand God himself. The assumption here was that the mundane world was very much worthy of our attention.[1]

The positive view of the present world in scholastic thought came through clearly in the writings of the movement's greatest representative: Thomas Aquinas. Aquinas not only explored the natural world as part of his quest for a better understanding of the divine, but he also emphasized that the natural world was good in itself because it was God's creation. If evil existed in the world, it was only because there were times when the good was mysteriously absent. Evil had no actual existence of its own.[2]

There were other developments in late medieval Europe that helped to create a more favourable attitude towards the present world than in earlier centuries, not just among Christian intellectuals but among ordinary Christians as well. Views on wealth became more positive in this period. Europe's economy steadily expanded, bringing unprecedented prosperity, particularly from the twelfth century onwards when cities throughout Europe were becoming sizeable and began functioning as centres of trade and commerce. Many Europeans clearly enjoyed this prosperity. More and more of them participated in the burgeoning economy as the medieval period progressed.[3]

The Church itself benefited from these developments. The revenues it received from landholdings, taxes, and gifts made it far richer than it had been in the past, and its leaders were happy to use that wealth to gain greater influence in Europe's political affairs. Here as well, Aquinas's views are worth noting. Aquinas seemed to be in line with the economic spirit of the age when he stated that material possessions were not necessarily bad. The pursuit of wealth was a problem only when it became excessive.[4]

In the same period, there were signs that European views on the very earthly issue of marriage and sexuality were becoming more positive across the intellectual and social spectrum. Despite the shadow of Augustine over the Church's views on such matters, the Church recognized marriage as a sacrament in the fourth Lateran Council of 1215, an action that elevated the status of marital life from a religious standpoint.[5] Around this time, we also see the emergence of more nuanced views among Christian thinkers on sexual pleasure that mitigated some of the harshness of Augustine's perspective. Aquinas, for instance, saw sexuality as a feature of God's natural world, and therefore, sexual pleasure had a place in it as well, as long as it was experienced in a marital context and with the proper intention.[6] A similarly positive view of sexual pleasure seems to come through in a regulation in Church canon law, according to which married spouses were each required to honour their partner's requests for sex. This regulation was referred to as the "marital debt," and it was based on a source in Paul.[7]

Positive views on romantic love and sexual desire were also expressed in the poetry, tales, and songs of the period. Troubadours and minstrels regaled audiences throughout Europe with stories about such matters. The theme of "courtly love" was also popular in poetry and literature. Stories of courtly love usually involved a knight falling in love with a noblewoman who was above his station and married, so that he was unable to consummate his feelings for her. He would nonetheless pine for her, and much of the story would focus on his unfulfilled passion for the woman he so desired but could not have.

Artistic expressions regarding love and sex, however, were not always so chaste or refined. The common folk often demonstrated its interest in these aspects of life in poetry, tales, and songs that were quite vulgar. We also know that what was depicted in these popular art forms had a basis in real life. We have plenty of evidence that considerable numbers of Europeans engaged in sexual behaviour that transgressed the Church's norms on such matters.[8]

Another important development in the late medieval Church that was evidence of its greater interest in mundane matters was that the Church began to organize its rules into a law-system which became known as "canon law," a corpus we referred to earlier. The goal here was to standardize these rules throughout Europe.[9]

Harold J. Berman has argued in two highly acclaimed studies that the development of medieval canon law was revolutionary in a number of respects. First, the Church lawyers who created canon law were the first

Europeans to conceive of law as a distinct discipline with its own theories and methods. Second, the canon lawyers were the first Europeans to see law as having applicability outside local jurisdictions. Up to this point, the laws that regulated everyday life in Europe consisted of a large and complex patchwork of local customs and regulations. Canon law, by contrast, was meant to govern the religious lives of Christians across the European continent. Third, the work of the canonists inspired medieval monarchs to create their own law systems to regulate secular affairs in their realms, a development that made European life far more organized and economically efficient. These law systems would lead to the evolution of modern secular law systems in the West, and they would also spawn the fundamental idea of the rule of law as a central principle in Western democracies. Berman's argument, in short, is that the medieval Catholic Church deserves much of the credit for initiating the whole idea of law as a central feature of Western society and for establishing the framework within which the secular law systems of the West would develop.[10] .

These observations are significant for our interests here because the creation of canon law by the medieval Church reflected a concern for the present world, and that is because law is, in essence, *always* about the present world, even law that is concerned with religious practice. Law that regulates religious activity provides rules for human deeds in the physical world no less than secular law does. The goal of religious law may ultimately be to transcend the present world, but the present world is still its focus. To put it in Christian terms, canon law was a concession to the fact that the final unfolding of the Kingdom of God had not yet occurred, that it might not happen for some time, and that the present world therefore had value. The Church assumed that the mundane realm was going to be around long enough to justify the great expenditure of energy that was needed to organize a large body of laws concerned with that realm.

Yet while the evidence adduced thus far suggests that in some respects, Christians in the late medieval period were cultivating positive views about the mundane realm, other factors were pushing them in precisely the opposite direction. The negative perspective on life in this world that was embedded in the Christianity of earlier times remained a potent factor in Christian life and thought.

On economic matters, Christian thinkers continued to have significant qualms about the accumulation of wealth. For instance, the Church, while benefiting greatly from Europe's growing wealth, had difficulty accepting the emerging banking system that was needed to support the new economy because this system depended on lending money with interest, an activity forbidden under canon law.[11] And while Aquinas had more positive views about economic matters than his predecessors did, his thinking was still permeated with reservations about material wealth that one finds in earlier Christian writers. For Aquinas, the acquisition of material goods could not be good in itself; it had to have some utility from the perspective of Christian morality, the sustenance of society being the most obvious. Aquinas also supported the prohibition against lending money with interest.[12]

On sexual matters, negative views were also still common in late medieval Christianity. It was not unusual for Christian thinkers in this period to express outright revulsion towards sexuality. Augustine's views on the connection between sexuality and Original Sin remained influential.[13]

Moreover, Christian thinkers still tended to see the ideal life as best represented by the monastic communities that dotted the European landscape and whose members were sworn to a life of celibacy and poverty. It is telling that Aquinas, despite his relatively moderate views on wealth acquisition and sexual pleasure, was himself a monk. So were many other prominent Christian intellectuals of this period.

Reservations about matters of this world were also expressed by ordinary Christians, for even though Europe as a whole was becoming increasingly wealthy, not everyone was prepared to indulge in that wealth. Many Christians who benefited from the growing economy felt a sense of profound unease about their newfound material comfort. In the period under discussion here, Christians were becoming more pious, and one way in which they expressed that piety was by embracing the notion of poverty as a Christian ideal. This ideal was connected to the belief that the best Christian life was one that was lived in imitation of Jesus, who during his life wandered the countryside without a home and lived in poverty as he preached God's message.[14]

The popularity of this ideal was evident in the success of several new monastic orders that were committed to a more extreme form of poverty than the older monastic orders were. The Cistercian Order, for instance, was founded in the eleventh century by monks who felt that the monasteries had become too comfortable and that monks were not taking the vow of poverty seriously enough. The Cistercians therefore established monasteries in which many of the material comforts of the monastic life, few as they were, were diminished even further.

The Franciscan and Dominican Orders that were established in the thirteenth century took matters even further. These "friars," as they were known, devoted themselves to the monastic ideal of poverty in radical fashion. For them, even having a monastery, or a home of any kind, was too much material comfort. They followed Jesus's example quite literally by wandering the countryside as homeless evangelists in threadbare clothes preaching to the common folk and spreading the word of God. They sustained themselves by begging for charity. That is why these monastic groups became known as the "mendicant orders."[15]

These new monastic orders were highly successful. They grew very quickly and soon competed quite well with the older ones. They established hundreds of monasteries throughout Europe. Moreover, lay people were moved by their example, and some formed organized groups affiliated with these orders that were committed to a semi-monastic lifestyle.[16]

Against this background, it is perhaps no surprise that lay people also began to express increasing concern about the Church's wealth and the corruption it engendered. The Church was not much of a role model for the notion of poverty that lay people and the new monastic orders had embraced. This concern would grow over time and would eventually help inspire the Protestant Reformation.

In sum, in later centuries of the medieval period, Christianity maintained the same ambivalence towards the mundane realm that we saw in earlier centuries, but both sides of that ambivalence were manifested in new ways, as Christianity and European society as a whole became more complex. Moreover, this ambivalence was manifested at all levels of European society, from lay people to the intellectual elite.

Perhaps a word is in order here about the Renaissance, which coincided with the final two centuries of the medieval period. As noted in an earlier chapter, some of the great intellectuals in Renaissance Italy developed an exalted view of human beings as creatures with a spark of divinity who had been put on this earth to improve it. For this reason, Humanist thinkers explored the classical literature of Greece and Rome to learn how to educate and cultivate individuals to become virtuous members of society. Therefore, the views of these thinkers appear to represent a shift towards a greater emphasis on this-worldly matters that one sees in the medieval period as a whole.

However, I also noted that the influence of the elite thinkers of Renaissance Italy on ordinary Europeans was limited. The Protestant Reformation, which began as the Renaissance waned, had far more of an effect on the common folk than the Renaissance did, and we will see in the next section, it imparted its own complex spin to European views on the value of the mundane realm.[17]

The Early Modern Period

The tensions between this-worldliness and other-worldliness in medieval Christianity seem to have been further accentuated in the Protestant Reformation. This movement in some respects represented an attempt to heighten the emphasis on other-worldly matters. As we saw in an earlier chapter, a feature of Luther's revolution was a return to a pure Augustinian perspective on sin, grace, and salvation, a perspective that presumed an attitude to life in this world that was quite negative.[18]

Furthermore, the harsh views that Luther and Calvin adopted from Augustine regarding the present world were no longer just for elite intellectuals. These views were eventually encapsulated in confessions and catechisms that all Protestants had to recite. Thus, doctrines, such as Original Sin and Predestination that had once been of interest mostly to Christian theologians, were now on the lips of large numbers of lay Christians.[19]

Yet in some respects, the Reformation also represented an attempt to shift the focus of life *towards* matters of this world. Luther and Calvin, despite their intense focus on other-worldly matters, both expressed an appreciation for the natural world as God's creation. Calvin, in particular, was enamoured of the natural world. In many passages in his writings, he expressed his awe for the world of nature and its role as a vehicle for appreciating God's wisdom and majesty.[20]

Perhaps the most important element in Protestantism that signalled an interest in life in this world was Luther's rejection of celibacy. Prior to his rebellion against the Church, Luther lived as a monk, and one of his most revolutionary actions in his campaign against the Church was his decision to get married. This decision was not just a personal one. He now opposed the life of celibacy on principle, and he urged his fellow monastics, male and female, to follow his example. And they did – in droves. Luther's own home served as an informal matchmaking centre for monks and nuns to find suitable mates. Thus, as the Reformation spread throughout Europe, one of its hallmarks was the emptying of the monasteries and convents.

The rejection of celibacy also applied to clergy who served in parishes. Priests practised celibacy inconsistently throughout most of the medieval period, but the Church made it the rule in the thirteenth century. From then on, all priests had to be celibate. Luther's revolution effectively reversed that decision. The priests were now enjoined to marry.[21]

These developments were of enormous significance, not just religiously but socially. As mentioned earlier, the issue of sexuality involved much more than just the sexual act itself. The role model for the new form of Christianity was now no longer the priest or monk living a life of detachment from the world; it was the minister with a wife and children living among lay people. The new way meant that the Christian life became more focused on the nuclear family than ever before. Getting married and having children were now seen as features of life completely consistent with the virtues of faith and piety.[22] It also meant that Christians would have to put more emphasis on this world in general. As anyone knows who has been married and raised a family, these commitments require one to be involved in matters of this world on a constant basis. There is nothing that gets one's head out of the clouds more quickly than having to attend to a child's needs![23]

There were limits, however, to the positive attitude towards marriage. That Luther and his successors embraced marriage did not mean they had a favourable view of sexuality. Luther, after all, was a devoted follower of Augustine, and he adopted Augustine's notion that sexual lust was the most powerful expression of Original Sin. It is just that Luther believed that this impulse was too great to overcome, and so it was better to engage in sex within the sanctified bounds of marriage than to try to quash the sexual urge altogether.[24]

The impact of Protestantism on attitudes towards the acquisition of material goods and the accumulation of wealth has been one of the most discussed issues in academia over the past century because of a famous theory proposed by Max Weber (1864–1920), a highly influential German intellectual who was one of the fathers of the field of sociology. In his book, *The Protestant Ethic and the Spirit of Capitalism*, Weber argued that the growth of capitalism in modern Europe was due to the influence of Protestantism, particularly in its Calvinist form.[25] Some scholars continue to support this intriguing theory, but most reject it or parts of it for a number of reasons.[26] So for the purposes of this discussion, Weber's thesis will be set aside.

However, there are other reasons not to set aside the possibility that Protestantism had an impact on economic matters. Some scholars have argued that Protestantism had a significant influence on the way Europeans approached the general issue of work and labour, and these arguments have merit.[27] Both Luther and Calvin stressed the notion that every individual had a "calling" or "vocation" ordained by God that determined the line of work they would adopt. This idea had roots in earlier Christian thinkers, but Luther put unprecedented emphasis on it. For both Luther and Calvin, fulfilling one's calling was nothing less than a sacred duty that was central to the life of faith. Both thinkers also believed that there were no differences between various professional occupations in God's eyes, as some previous Christian thinkers had suggested. As long as one was fulfilling one's calling, God would be pleased with one's choice of career. So, while it is unclear whether Protestantism promoted capitalism as Weber argued, it seems that Protestantism promoted the value of work more than Catholicism had, and this is highly significant for our concerns. It suggests that, once again, Protestantism inspired Europeans to view daily life in the present world as possessing more value than they had accorded it previously.

On balance, it would seem that while the Reformation accentuated the tensions between other-worldly and this-worldly concerns, the latter came out on top in critical respects because of the impact that Protestantism had on fundamental societal matters. Marriage, family, and work were valued more than ever before. Other-worldly concerns certainly remained important in Protestantism, as was evident in its emphasis on faith and its continued adherence to Augustinian views on Original Sin and sexuality. One must also keep in mind that not all Europeans became Protestants. Catholicism still reigned supreme in large parts of Europe, and its views on the mundane realm remained largely in line with those of the medieval period. Nonetheless, Protestantism introduced Europeans to a form of Christianity in which this-worldly matters had a greater place in life than ever before.

The Enlightenment

In the centuries following the Reformation, the positive valuation of the present world evident in Protestantism gained more strength. The Scientific Revolution in the seventeenth century was key in this regard. Europe's intellectuals were increasingly fascinated by the natural world and were determined to understand it better and to utilize it for human benefit. Another development around the same time, to which we alluded earlier, is that Europeans were beginning to speak about the notion that the law systems governing their society did not have to be entirely dependent on religion. The thinkers who began to think of law in this way were still Christians, and their views on law still betrayed religious influences, but there was growing interest in the notion of "natural law," the belief that human reason on its own could determine what the laws of society should be.[28]

During the Enlightenment, the positive valuation of the present world was strengthened even further. In fact, the Enlightenment represents something of a turning point in this regard. Some European intellectuals began to emphasize the value of the mundane realm in conscious opposition to its devaluation in Christianity.

This move was part of an overall offensive against Christianity in its institutional forms. Enlightenment intellectuals decried those aspects of Christianity that they saw as irrational and primitive, including its undue emphasis on other-worldly matters. Their view was that life in this world was good in itself, quite apart from the life that awaited human beings in the next world.[29]

A number of factors encouraged this new perspective. Revolutionary advances in science in the seventeenth century were starting to bring practical benefits to Europeans and to make life more pleasant. As the daily struggle for survival and well-being became less challenging, Europeans began to adopt a more optimistic view of mundane existence. This new perspective was strengthened by the rejection of Original Sin. As we have mentioned more than once, the dismissal of this doctrine was a hallmark of the Enlightenment. Intellectuals began to believe that people were born neither sinful nor virtuous and that they had a choice as to which they would be, and this way of thinking was key in inspiring Europeans to think of life in this world as good in itself.[30]

The new approach to the present world also inspired European intellectuals to believe that the enjoyment of such mundane pleasures as wealth and sex were not necessarily the evils they had been made out to be in the past. The more positive view of wealth was perhaps best reflected in the adoption of capitalism as the preferred economic system throughout Europe. Private enterprise and profit-making for the purpose of acquiring wealth were now embraced as never before.

It was Adam Smith (1723–90) who provided the most cogent and influential justification for capitalism. In *The Wealth of Nations*, Smith admitted that capitalism was predicated on the selfish desire that people had for luxury and status, but he saw that desire as serving a number of worthy purposes. First, capitalism would encourage people to adopt a life of hard work and discipline, traits that would ultimately make them better as individuals from a moral standpoint. Second, capitalism would morally improve society as a whole because in order to fulfil their selfish material needs, people would have an incentive to be good citizens and reduce conflicts with their neighbours. Third, capitalism would make people in society more equal, for as the lower and middle classes gained greater wealth, they would demand more say in government and would be given it. With this greater equality would also come greater freedom for everyone – yet another societal good. Finally, the world as a whole would be improved by capitalism because commerce was more profitable than war, and once the nations realized this, they would be reluctant to engage in armed conflict.

Smith famously referred to the "invisible hand" that he believed would guide people who took up capitalism. He believed that if society let people be motivated to generate wealth out of pure self-interest without government regulation, they not only would live better lives from a material standpoint, but they also would bring many other benefits to their society and the world in general. The invisible hand Smith referred to were the providential forces in the world that would cause all this to happen. Thus, for Smith, capitalism, far from being just a concession to all that was bad in human nature, could serve the highest of human purposes.[31]

The intellectual circles in the Enlightenment that began to take a more positive view of the present world than did their predecessors, also adopted a more positive view of sexuality. The new approach to this aspect of life was in part due to the widespread rejection of Original Sin among Enlightenment thinkers. As we have seen, there had been, since Augustine, a strong association between Original Sin and sexuality, and so when Enlightenment thinkers dismissed the notion of Original Sin, they also tended to dismiss the negative view of sexuality that came with it.

Many of these thinkers now viewed sex as a good thing, for they identified it with nature, which they saw as a guide for human conduct. Some even spoke of sexual pleasure as being highly important for human well-being and happiness. Some of the more radical Enlightenment figures went yet a step further, arguing for total freedom of sexual expression. Enlightenment thinkers of a more traditional bent did not go quite this far and held more conservative views. For them, sexual pleasure was a good thing, but only as long as it was indulged in within the confines of marriage and for the sake of procreation. Still, Enlightenment views on sexuality were on the whole more positive than those of earlier centuries. Furthermore, the new and more favourable attitudes towards sexuality were not confined to the elite; popular literature in the Enlightenment also reflected an increasingly positive view of sexuality.[32]

The growing focus in the Enlightenment on this-worldly matters was also reflected in the creation of secular law systems, which were now more detached than ever from the Church's jurisdiction. The belief began to take hold that the secular realm had value in its own right and it should not be regulated by religious authorities. This idea, which became known as the separation of church and state, would be fundamental to the development of the modern West.[33]

Yet, even though positive attitudes towards the present world were now more strongly represented in European culture than ever before, opposing attitudes were by no means vanquished. Alongside those in the Enlightenment who had favourable views of the mundane realm and its pleasures, there were some who continued to have far more reserved views about such matters. As noted in an earlier chapter, Enlightenment intellectuals were not all radicals as scholars once believed. Many of them continued to be devoted to traditional forms of Christianity and its mixed view of the present world. The same was true for large sectors of the European population. Many of the common folk in Europe remained untouched by the Enlightenment. In fact, some new forms of Christianity arose at this time that espoused an even deeper religiosity than the mainstream Churches did, such as Pietism in Germany, Jansenism in France, and Methodism in Britain.[34]

Conclusions

In earlier chapters, we learned that the two values we discussed – freedom in the metaphysical sense and freedom of thought and expression – were present to some degree in European Christian culture in the medieval and early modern periods, but they became far more pronounced during the Enlightenment and would eventually become central in European society. The same pattern is evident with regard to the notion that life in the mundane world was good in its own right. This value was present in medieval and early modern European culture, but it began to receive much more attention with the dawn of the Enlightenment, and it would eventually emerge as a basic principle in modern Western culture. According to this new way of thinking, life in this world was to be embraced. It was no longer just a corridor leading to a better life in the world to come.

This new attitude manifested itself in more favourable attitudes than in previous centuries towards a range of particular issues, such as the accumulation of wealth and sexual expression. It was now acceptable to view these aspects of life as facets of the human experience that enriched it, not as distractions that impeded the attainment of worthier spiritual goals. The new way of thinking was also expressed in the development of secular law systems that focused solely on mundane matters.

As with our analysis of the previous two values, we should not read too much of our contemporary viewpoint into the Enlightenment. During the Enlightenment, the positive approach to life in this world was not taken up by all Christians in Europe. Many of them remained devoted to traditional Christianity in which the present world continued to be viewed with ambivalence. Nonetheless, from the Enlightenment onwards, the general notion that life in this world was to be appreciated and even celebrated, now had widespread support, and that notion would soon filter down into popular culture and gain the upper hand among large sectors of European society. Eventually, this approach would also give rise to the phenomenon of secularism, which was the most extreme expression of the notion that the focus of life should be on the present world. After all, for the staunchest of secularists, there was no world to focus on other than the present one.

Most important, the positive attitude towards the present life that the Enlightenment nurtured was one reason why the West would achieve dominance in the world. This attitude towards the mundane realm spurred Westerners to look at the world as a place to explore and conquer, both literally and figuratively, and that is precisely what they did. Those ambitions, of course, predated the Enlightenment. Europeans had begun exploring the natural world and conquering large portions of the globe well before the eighteenth century, but such ambitions were given added impetus in the Enlightenment. It was in this period that Europeans began to engage the present world with unprecedented curiosity, interest, and energy.

II.   Jewish Perspectives

Late Medieval Rabbinic Judaism

Let us now return to Judaism to see how its views on the present world evolved in the late medieval and early modern periods and how these views compared with those of Christianity. We will begin with rabbinic views on marriage, sexuality, procreation, and family.

MARRIAGE, SEXUALITY, PROCREATION, AND FAMILY

Late medieval rabbinic views on these issues were in many respects continuous with rabbinic views of earlier centuries. As in early Rabbinic Judaism, late medieval rabbinic law specified that all Jews had to marry and have children and that men and women had to fulfil each other's sexual needs.[35] Medieval rabbis also endorsed the early rabbinic view that marriage was meant not just for procreation but for companionship as well.[36]

Some rabbis in the late medieval period focused on the importance of sexual pleasure even more than their predecessors. According to these rabbis, both husband and wife were supposed to enjoy sexual activity because it was deemed to be good for their own health and for producing healthy children. As we will see later on in this chapter, mystical motives may have also played a role in fostering this view. An excellent example of this tendency can be found in a passage from a work by R. Judah ben Samuel (1150–1217), a prominent German rabbi, who provided husbands with the following advice about how they should conduct themselves when engaging in sex with their wives: "Your wife should dress and adorn herself like a 'fruitful vine' (Ps. 128:3) so that your lust will become inflamed like a fire and you will shoot semen like an arrow … You should delay your orgasm until [your] wife has her orgasm first and then [she will conceive] sons."[37] There may be no better passage to dispel the stereotype that medieval rabbis were austere and severe characters.

However, some rabbis in the late medieval period displayed ascetic tendencies regarding marriage and sexuality. Some of the rabbis were far more reserved in their views about sexual pleasure than R. Judah ben Samuel. According to these rabbis, men had to engage in sex with their wives to fulfil the commandments to procreate and satisfy their wives' sexual needs, but their own pleasure should not be the focus.[38] A text from the thirteenth century had even more severe advice. It counselled married men to leave their homes during the week and live in houses away from their families so that they could devote their attention to studying sacred texts and avoid struggling with the sexual distractions that were inherent in married life.[39]

This range of views on marriage and sexuality reminds us of a similar range of views on these issues that developed in Christianity in the same period. Yet it is still safe to say that the views of the rabbis on marriage and sexuality were, on the whole, more positive than those of their Christians contemporaries, just as they had been in previous centuries. Late medieval rabbis never espoused an asceticism on sexual matters quite as extreme as that found among their Christian contemporaries. Marriage, sex, and child-bearing continued to be imperative for all Jews, including the rabbis themselves. So we have no parallel in late medieval Rabbinic Judaism to the option of monastic celibacy that was so common among Christians at this time and that was regarded by them as the highest expression of religious piety. It is telling that the rabbinic text that encouraged men to spend most of the week away from their wives to study sacred texts also instructed them to return home for the Sabbath in order to engage in sexual relations with their wives, since the requirements of procreation and providing for their wives' sexual needs were non-negotiable.[40] Furthermore, as several commentators have noted, late medieval rabbis, on the whole, were still more open than Christian thinkers were to the notion that pleasure was a legitimate component of the sexual experience.[41]

The distinction between the two groups of authorities on this issue is highlighted by the issue of contraception. Medieval Christian authorities generally forbade this practice on the premise that the purpose of sex was procreation. Some rabbis in the late medieval period, however, began to permit contraceptive practices on the presumption that sex was part of a normal and healthy relationship between husbands and wives and was not just for procreation.[42]

The discrepancy between Judaism and Christianity in the late medieval period with respect to married life was also highlighted by the fact that ritual practices involving the family continued to be central to Judaism in a way that had no analogue in Christianity. As in early Rabbinic Judaism, the week revolved around the Sabbath, and its celebration was built around family meals. The same was the case for Jewish festivals and major life-cycle events. Therefore, it was not just the approach to marriage that marked late medieval Rabbinic Judaism as different from Christianity, it was the approach of the rabbis to the institution of the family as a whole.

The distinctions we have drawn so far between late medieval Rabbinic Judaism and Christianity on marriage and sexuality are based primarily on the views of the intellectual elites in both communities, and there is good reason to question whether these distinctions were as great on the popular level. We saw earlier that ordinary Christians were prone to express themselves on matters of love and sexuality in ways of which their religious leaders did not approve. Moreover, these expressions reflected the fact that ordinary Christians were not as chaste about sexual norms in their personal lives as the Church's teachings expected them to be. Ordinary Jews were no different. Like their non-Jewish neighbours, Jews composed sensual poetry, tales, and songs about love and sexuality, and here as well, the sexual content of these popular art forms was matched by sexual activity in real life. There is ample evidence that Jews in the late medieval centuries could be lax about sexual mores in the same way that their Christian neighbours were.[43]

Nonetheless, we should not presume that the views of late medieval rabbis or Christian thinkers on marriage and sexuality had no significance in their respective societies. Lay people in the two religious communities who committed transgressions regarding these aspects of life were often troubled that they were engaging in such activities. We know this because many of the sources that tell us about these transgressions were composed by Jewish and Christian religious authorities who had been consulted by the perpetrators of such actions seeking repentance for their misdeeds, and we have many sources of this kind from both communities. Moreover, we can presume that many ordinary Jews and

Christians at the time heeded the sexual strictures of their respective religions; it is just that we do not hear as much about such conformity in the sources from this period because these sources were far more likely to report scandalous behaviour than behaviour that accorded with expectations. The argument can thus be made that the views of Jewish and Christian religious authorities on marriage and sexuality mattered to significant numbers of lay people in their respective communities, and therefore the distinctions we have drawn between the two groups of authorities on such matters were likely to be found among the common folk as well.

WEALTH

Regarding the accumulation of wealth, the rabbis in the late medieval period also followed their rabbinic predecessors in many respects. These rabbis adopted the Talmudic view mentioned in the previous chapter that men must acquire a trade in order to make a living and support their families. Some rabbis even argued that this imperative was one of the 613 commandments.[44]

But the rabbis of the late medieval period also followed their predecessors by emphasizing that the accumulation of wealth should not be excessive.[45] They instituted "sumptuary laws" in most European Jewish communities that were intended to limit the ostentatious display of wealth. These laws affected such matters as how expensively Jews were allowed to dress and how much money they were permitted to spend on family weddings.[46] The rabbis also continued to emphasize that the accumulation of wealth should not be one's only goal. According to late medieval rabbinic law, men had to set aside time to study sacred texts, even though this activity would impinge on their ability to acquire wealth.[47]

Thus, as with matters of sexuality and marriage, the rabbis entertained a significant range of views regarding wealth, much as their Christian contemporaries did. Yet here too, it is safe to say that the rabbis, on the whole, continued to espouse a more positive view of wealth than Christians did, as had been the case in prior centuries. Monasticism once again highlights the distinction. None of the late medieval rabbis saw making a living as optional or glorified a life devoted to poverty, a position that contrasted sharply with the support that Christians expressed for the monastic way of life.[48]

The contrast between late medieval rabbis and Christian thinkers on the accumulation of wealth and material well-being is wonderfully illustrated by the way the rabbis responded to a number of formidable obstacles in Jewish law that stood in the way of these activities.

Explaining this matter will require a substantial digression, but it will be well worth the effort. We will not only see the extent to which the rabbis valued mundane well-being; we will also see, once again, the extent to which the rabbis could be bold and innovative when it came to interpreting God's commandments.

As a tiny minority in medieval Europe, Jews had no choice but to do business with their Christian neighbours for their livelihood. Early rabbinic law, however, contained a series of restrictions on doing business with non-Jews who were idolaters, whom the rabbis defined as anyone who worshipped false gods. Thus, for example, a Jew was not permitted to conduct business with an idolater within a period of three days prior to one of their religious festivals out of fear that the idolater might give thanks to his false gods during the festival, and Jews were forbidden to promote the worship of gods other than the one true God even in this indirect manner.[49] The problem was that Christianity was presumed by later medieval rabbis to be idolatry because it was premised on the worship of Jesus, who, in Jewish thinking, was a false god, and so if the regulation just referred to had been applied to medieval European Jews doing business with Christians, Jews would have had to avoid doing business with their Christian neighbours for a good portion of the year. Medieval Christians not only celebrated major religious holidays such as Christmas and Easter, they also celebrated numerous other minor religious festivals throughout the year, such as specific days set aside for the veneration of individual saints. And then, of course, there was Sunday, which could be considered a holy day in its own right and happened every week. If Jews could not do business with Christians three days prior to these occasions, then Jewish business dealings with Christians would have been severely curtailed, and the result would have been economic ruin for Jews everywhere in Europe.

Another rabbinic rule that was potentially even more ruinous for Jewish economic life specified that Jews should avoid business relationships with idolaters entirely because if litigation were to arise between them, the idolater might be required to take an oath in court in the name of their false god, and it was forbidden for a Jew to prompt the mention of false gods, even if the person doing the mentioning was a non-Jew.[50] Had medieval European Jews been compelled to obey this particular rule, they would not have been permitted to do business with Christians at all because of the possibility that litigation might result in a non-Jew taking an oath invoking the name of Jesus. Thus, here again, restrictions on doing business with Christians would have resulted in economic ruin for Jews.

A more specific problem for Jews in medieval Europe was that many of them were moneylenders who made a living by providing loans to Christians and charging interest on the loans. Yet there was a Talmudic source suggesting that Jews were forbidden to lend money with interest to Jews and non-Jews alike.[51]

These were just some of the problems Jews faced when doing business with Christians, but the examples we have adduced here are sufficient to illustrate the nature and depth of the overall challenge. No European Jew in the medieval period could obey all the regulations in rabbinic law pertaining to conducting business with idolaters and hope to feed himself and his family. Most of the troubling rules had not been a problem when they were first set forth by the rabbis in Palestine in the first two centuries CE. In that place and time, Jews did not necessarily have to do business with non-Jews in order to survive economically, nor did they have to become moneylenders. The situation in medieval Europe was radically different: Jews were now wholly dependent for their livelihood on non-Jews, who were considered idolaters, and, in addition, money-lending was one of the few professions open to them.

The way in which the late medieval rabbis overcame these problems is a fascinating chapter in Jewish intellectual history.[52] The rabbis displayed great ingenuity and creativity to ensure that Jews could continue to transact business with Christians and avoid destitution. A full discussion of this matter is beyond the scope of this chapter, but we can give some idea of how the rabbis dealt with the difficulties that have been mentioned here. For instance, one rabbi got around the prohibition against lending money with interest simply by arguing that this rule was meant to apply only in situations in which it did not cause undue economic hardship; if it did so, the prohibition could be set aside.[53] Some rabbis were able to circumvent the various rules restricting business with idolaters by availing themselves of a Talmudic statement by R. Yohanan, who declared that non-Jews living outside the land of Israel were not true idolaters; they were idolaters only as a matter of "ancestral custom." The implication here seemed to be that these non-Jews practised idolatry because of long-standing tradition and without really believing in it. From this, some medieval rabbis concluded that business dealings with Christians were permitted.[54]

These examples were piecemeal attempts on the part of late medieval rabbis to allow Jews to conduct business with Christians in the sense that the rabbis targeted individual regulations that precluded such activity. In the fourteenth century, we have the first attempt by a prominent rabbi to deal with the problem holistically by entirely rethinking how Jews should view Christians. That rabbi was a French figure, R.

Menahem ha-Meiri (1249–1310), usually referred to simply as Meiri. According to Meiri, all the laws of the early rabbis that discriminated against non-Jews applied only to idolaters in ancient times because their societies were inherently immoral and violent. Those laws did *not* apply to non-Jewish nations that had created civilized societies based on what Meiri considered to be fundamental principles of religion. Meiri's great innovation was in defining idolaters not so much by what they believed but by how they acted. If non-Jews created an ordered, moral society with the rule of law and institutions that enforced that law, they were not idolaters, no matter what beliefs they held. Christians had created a society of this kind and therefore did not qualify as idolaters, which meant that all the problematic legislation about doing business with non-Jews did not apply to them either.[55]

There is plenty of room here for cynicism. One could say that the attempts of the medieval rabbis to allow Jews to transact business with non-Jews were motivated by purely pragmatic concerns. Moreover, in many instances, the rabbis were simply finding ways to approve of economic activities that Jews had already been engaging in for some time, long before the religious difficulties with those activities were brought to anyone's attention. One could therefore accuse the rabbis of circumventing God's laws rather than implementing them, of being more concerned about the material comfort of Jews than about their adherence to the divine will.

I would argue, however, that this is entirely the wrong way to interpret what the rabbis were doing here. As pointed out in an earlier chapter, in Rabbinic Judaism the rabbi's duty was not just to apply Jewish law as he understood it but to make it livable as well. The rabbi saw himself as an authority charged by God with the obligation to find the correct balance between the ideal and the practical, to implement the divine commandments while dealing creatively with the challenges that inevitably arise when laws are concretized in real life. So in finding innovative ways to allow Jews to conduct business with Christians, the rabbis did not see themselves as circumventing God's will; to their mind, they were fulfilling it. For the rabbis, it was inconceivable that God's laws would require his chosen people to live in complete destitution – even if they were being punished by having to live in exile – and so the rabbis interpreted God's laws in order to avoid that consequence.[56]

What is most important for our concerns is that this discussion tells us a great deal about the attitude of late medieval rabbis towards the accumulation of wealth and material well-being and how that attitude contrasted with that of their Christian neighbours. Clearly, the rabbis valued these aspects of life – so much so that they were willing to go to great lengths to reinterpret laws about the prohibition against idolatry, one of the most serious matters in Jewish law, in order to ensure that Jews could transact business and earn a decent living. It is hard to imagine Christians at this time doing the same thing, had they been in similar circumstances. For Christians, poverty was not necessarily bad; in fact, for some it was a great virtue.

FOOD

A word is in order about the differences between late medieval Rabbinic Judaism and Christianity regarding one other physical pleasure: eating. Here as well, the differences in earlier centuries between Rabbinic Judaism and Christianity persisted. Late medieval rabbis followed the earlier rabbis in making festive meals a prominent part of Jewish ritual life – particularly on the Sabbath, festivals, and during major life-cycle celebrations. In medieval Christianity, there was no precise equivalent. Some rabbis in the late medieval period encouraged ascetic practices regarding food that were similar to those in Christianity. Thus, in medieval Germany and northern France, some Jews had the custom of engaging in periodic fasting in order to atone for their sins.[57] Still, the enjoyment of food continued to have a place in Jewish religious life in the late medieval period that we do not see in Christianity.

LAW IN GENERAL

Perhaps the most important difference between late medieval Rabbinic Judaism and Christianity regarding the mundane realm had to do with the place of law in general in the two religions. In the late medieval period, Rabbinic Judaism continued to be a religion centred on law, and by this period that law had been developed and systematized so that it encompassed every aspect of life. Thus, it was the rabbinic legal enterprise itself, perhaps more than any other factor, that was responsible for the this-worldly character of late medieval Rabbinic Judaism. As already noted, law is always concerned with actions in the mundane realm, even when it is religious law, and that feature of law was particularly evident in rabbinic law given that its regulations addressed almost every type of human action.

In the late medieval period, the Church began developing its own law system in the form of canon law. However, canon law never became central to medieval Christianity in the way that rabbinic law did for Jews. Law was at the core of Rabbinic Judaism. It was its foundation. It encompassed all Jewish activity, not just in the religious realm but in the civil realm as well. In fact, in Rabbinic Judaism there was no easy way to separate the two. In Christianity, by contrast, canon law was certainly an important concern for the Church, but it was not the Church's central focus, and its regulations encompassed mostly religious matters, not civil ones. Thus, we see once again that while the late medieval Church had an interest in the mundane realm, that interest was not as intense as in Rabbinic Judaism.[58]

To summarize our discussion so far, we see in the late medieval period a contrast between Christianity and Rabbinic Judaism regarding attitudes towards the mundane realm that is similar to the contrast between the views of the two religions on this matter in earlier centuries. This contrast should not be exaggerated. Both the Church and the rabbis continued to entertain a range of views on the present world, and those views overlapped in some respects. But the Church's views on the present world continued to lean more towards the negative end of the spectrum, while those of the rabbis continued to lean more towards the positive end.

Medieval Philosophy and Kabbalah

Rabbinic Judaism is not the only lens through which to evaluate how Jews in the late medieval period viewed life in this world. As central as Jewish law was in late medieval Judaism, other factors emerged in Judaism in this period that influenced how Jews viewed the mundane realm. As we already know, the medieval period saw the rise of philosophical schools and schools of Kabbalah in Jewish communities in Europe, and some of these schools had a more ascetic bent than Rabbinic Judaism did. Philosophy and Kabbalah therefore introduced Jews to aspects of religion that were closer to Christianity regarding the mundane realm.

MEDIEVAL PHILOSOPHY

We are already somewhat familiar with medieval Jewish philosophy from previous chapters. Philosophical thinking arose in the tenth century among Jews in Islamic lands, who were inspired by the works of the great ancient Greek philosophers – most notably those of Plato and Aristotle in Arabic translation – to produce highly rational and comprehensive thought-systems of the sort that were absent in Rabbinic Judaism. By far the greatest of the medieval Jewish philosophers was Maimonides, who lived in the twelfth century.

Most significant for our purposes is that medieval Jewish philosophy introduced Jews to the same Greek views on the body and soul that centuries earlier had played such an important role in pushing Christianity in an other-worldly direction. As we have already seen, Christians absorbed the Greek notions that the essence of the human being was the soul, that the soul was by nature good because it came from the divine realm and remained focused on it, that the body was corrupt because of its physical desires, and that the goal of life was to be detached as much as possible from those desires so as to prepare the soul to return to the spiritual realm. The result was that Christianity developed negative views of the body and the mundane realm in general. Because medieval Jewish philosophy was based on Greek philosophy, it too developed negative views on these matters. For instance, Maimonides in his major philosophical work, *The Guide of the Perplexed*, had rather harsh things to say about the body and the mundane realm.[59]

But the other-worldly emphasis of medieval Jewish philosophy was not enough to inspire Jews who adopted this way of thinking to entirely reject Rabbinic Judaism and its mundane bent. Maimonides was a rabbi who observed the same laws that governed the lives of all Jews in the medieval period, laws that required them to be constantly engaged in matters of this world. In fact, Maimonides is widely regarded as the medieval period's greatest authority on Jewish law. He composed a fourteen-volume work that codified all of Jewish law, and it became the most important work of its kind up to his lifetime. Also, in his personal life, Maimonides married and had children, as other Jews did. He also had a profession: he was a physician. So there was a limit on how ascetic Maimonides could be in his thinking. Earlier, we raised the possibility that Maimonides was actually a radical Aristotelian philosopher in disguise who in his heart of hearts did not believe in many of the fundamental principles of Judaism, but even if that was true, he seems not to have displayed any of that radicalism in the way he lived.

Moreover, Maimonides' views on asceticism were inconsistent. True, he had negative things to say about physical desires, particularly in his major philosophical work, *The Guide of the Perplexed*, but in other writings, he extolled the virtue of moderation in satisfying these desires by following Aristotle's famous theory of the "golden mean." According to this theory, the best way to live life in this world was to consistently choose the middle path between extremes, and that included how one responded to one's instinctive impulses. That is, one should indulge in such impulses neither too much nor too little. This approach was therefore in tension with the more ascetic one found in his major philosophical treatise because it gave the satisfaction of physical desires a legitimate place in life.[60]

Maimonides and the school of Jewish Aristotelian philosophy that he spawned were also a major reason that medieval Jews took up the study of science, which was very much focused on the mundane realm. As we have seen, in the medieval period, the study of philosophy among Christians and Jews required the study of science as well.

Finally, we should add that the influence of medieval Jewish philosophy was limited in scope geographically. In Europe, it was popular among Jews in Spain throughout the late medieval period. It also made significant inroads in southern France and Italy. Among Jews in central and eastern Europe, it was less influential. So even if medieval Jewish philosophy had other-worldly tendencies, its influence was not felt by all Jews.

KABBALAH

The schools of Kabbalah also had attitudes towards the mundane realm that in some respects were closer to Christianity than to Rabbinic Judaism. Like the philosophers, Kabbalists followed in the footsteps of the ancient Greek philosophers – particularly Neoplatonists – in associating the physical world with evil. This way of thinking led them at times to adopt ascetic practices. Some of these practices were extreme. The Kabbalists in Palestine in the sixteenth century who belonged to the school of R. Isaac Luria were famous for such practices. They engaged in severe repentance rituals involving mortification of the flesh that were similar to those found in Christianity. These rituals included long periods of fasting and self-flagellation.[61] And these Kabbalists were not the first to practise such rituals. German Pietists in the twelfth and thirteenth centuries preceded the followers of Luria in engaging in these sorts of practices.[62] The interest of the Kabbalists in other-worldly matters was also evident in their discussions of the afterlife and the messiah, which were much lengthier and more detailed than those found in the standard texts of Rabbinic Judaism.[63] Here as well, the Kabbalists seemed to have more in common with Christianity than with Rabbinic Judaism.

Yet here too, Kabbalists placed limits on such other-worldly tendencies. Most of them did not deny the value of the present world, and in some ways, they embraced it as much as other Jews, if not more so. The Kabbalists held that the physical world was impregnated with the divine because it had been created through the unfolding of God's ten *sefirot*, or attributes, into the world below. They also strictly observed rabbinic law, which meant they were constantly engaged with the mundane through observance of the divine commandments. Thus, they, like all Jews, married and had children. As we have already discussed, the observance of the commandments in all their detail was central in Kabbalah because they were viewed as the means to repair God's broken being. The Kabbalists believed that the *sefirot* had been out of harmony with each other since the creation of the world and that they could be brought back into harmony only if Jews meticulously observed the commandments. So, like the medieval Jewish philosophers, Kabbalists had other-worldly tendencies, but these tendencies could not dominate their lives entirely because they lived by the strictures of Rabbinic Judaism, like the rest of the Jewish community.[64]

An aspect of Kabbalah that has received a good deal of attention from modern scholars and that highlights its positive attitude towards matters of this world is its approach towards sexuality.[65] Most scholars have argued that Kabbalah accentuated the erotic dimension of Judaism. In Kabbalah, the ten *sefirot* were divided by gender; some were male and others were female. This way of thinking resulted in the peculiar notion that God had both male and female attributes. By now, we are used to Kabbalists having radical ideas about God, and the notion that God is both male and female can be added to them. But it gets even stranger. The Kabbalists viewed human sexuality as vital to the process of repairing the *sefirot* because engaging in sex united the male *sefirot* with the female *sefirot*, thus helping repair God's broken being. That is, sex was necessary for "fixing" God. It is hard to imagine a view of sexuality more positive than this one. It turned sex into an event of cosmic significance.[66]

What emerges from this section of our discussion is that in some respects, medieval Jewish philosophy and Kabbalah reduced the gap between Judaism and Christianity regarding attitudes towards the mundane world. These branches of Judaism added an other-worldly dimension to Jewish thought and practice that was in tension with Rabbinic Judaism and more consistent with Christianity. However, the ascetic elements in medieval Jewish philosophy and Kabbalah never became as extreme as those in the European Christian world, nor did those elements become institutionalized in the way that they did in that world. Medieval Jewish philosophers and Kabbalists valued God's commandments, and these imperatives required constant engagement with the mundane realm. Both groups gave elaborate explanations about why this earthly regimen was necessary for achieving the other-worldly goals they sought, but neither group could escape that regimen. They certainly could not adopt the more extreme asceticism found in monastic Christianity.

The Early Modern Period

In the early modern period, the differences between European Jews and Christians regarding the value of this world narrowed even more because of changes taking place among Christians. We have seen how, in this era, Europeans gradually developed more positive views regarding the mundane realm on a number of fronts, and these changes, brought Europeans unwittingly closer to Rabbinic Judaism as well.

This was certainly true with respect to marriage and family. Luther's reforms rendered Protestantism far more similar to Rabbinic Judaism on these issues than Catholicism had been. Protestantism, like Rabbinic Judaism, saw marriage and family as natural and necessary for human beings.

On economic matters, the argument can be made that Protestant views were even closer to those of Rabbinic Judaism. In rejecting monasticism, Protestantism also rejected the ideal of poverty that had been popular in Catholicism. It also emphasized the value of work and labour as a calling that all people had to heed in order to properly serve God. Rabbinic Judaism was not much different from Protestantism on these matters. It had never embraced poverty as an ideal, and it too believed that by working and making a living, one fulfilled God's will.

The gap between European Jews and Christians regarding the value of the present world narrowed even further during the Enlightenment, and again, this was because of changes on the Christian side of the ledger. As we have seen, the Enlightenment saw dramatic developments in European thinking regarding the mundane realm. Life in this world was now seen as more than a way station en route to a better existence in the afterlife or the messianic era; it had merit in its own right. The pleasures of the mundane realm were also viewed as meritorious; the acquisition of wealth and sexual expression served worthy purposes. Thus, the way in which European intellectuals related to the present world was remarkably similar to that of Rabbinic Judaism. Enlightenment intellectuals certainly would not have seen it this way. They disparaged the rabbis and the religion they represented no less than previous European thinkers had. Yet, in fact, European views on the mundane realm now had a distinctly rabbinic character.

In some respects, Enlightenment thinkers espoused ideas that embraced the mundane realm even more than the rabbis did. Adam Smith's views on the acquisition of wealth are a case in point. For Smith, this activity was a virtue. It was not merely an acceptable feature of life; it made individuals better, as well as the society to which they belonged. There is no equivalent to Smith's philosophy in Rabbinic Judaism. The rabbis continued to hold the view that generating wealth was perfectly respectable, but they did not turn it into a great virtue the way Smith did. Moreover, the study of sacred texts was still the primary value for the rabbis, and men were encouraged to accept less prosperity in order to engage in this activity.

One could argue that developments on the Jewish side in the early modern period also narrowed the gap between Jews and Christians regarding the value of the present world. For while European intellectuals were discovering the value of the mundane realm that brought Europeans unwittingly closer to Judaism, Jews were conversely engaging in spiritualizing trends that brought them unwittingly closer to Christianity. In the second half of the seventeenth century, large parts of the Jewish world were engulfed by a messianic movement that lasted for a number of years. The story of this movement is absolutely fascinating, but for our purposes, we need only the bare facts. The movement revolved around the figure of Shabbetai Tsevi (1626–76), a Turkish Jew, whom many Jews believed to be the long-awaited messiah, and it was fuelled in part by Kabbalah, which had much to say about messianism. The Sabbatean movement, as scholars call it, was the most important messianic movement in Judaism since Christianity. It largely ended after Shabbetai was arrested by the Turkish authorities and was forced to convert to Islam. Yet while it existed, it showed that Judaism had its own other-worldly elements and that under the right condition, they could become dominant.[67]

An emphasis on other-worldly matters was also present in some sectors of Jewish society in Poland-Lithuania in the eighteenth century, which was home to the largest Jewish community in the world at the time. This emphasis was popular among the opponents of Hasidism. Hasidism emerged in Poland-Lithuania towards the end of the eighteenth century, and this movement, in many respects, emphasized the this-worldly character of Judaism. Hasidic preachers stressed the notion that God's presence pervaded the mundane realm and that he was therefore accessible to all Jews, not just through obedience to his commandments but also by connecting with his presence in their daily activities. Hasidic preachers thus encouraged Jews to engage life with a joyful disposition. However, a good portion of the Jews in Poland-Lithuania opposed Hasidism, and these "Mitnagdim," as they were called – which literally means "opponents" – often had a far more negative view of the mundane realm. The leader of this sector of eastern European Jewry, R. Elijah of Vilna (1720–97), was famous for his severe and ascetic lifestyle, and many of his disciples had similar tendencies. Furthermore, even Hasidism did not always have positive views of life in this world. It too had ascetic tendencies.[68] Thus, as we get towards the end of the early modern period, the value of life in this world was a contentious issue in the world's largest Jewish community, an observation that again underscores how early modern Judaism was close to Christianity regarding this issue.

Conclusions

What emerges from this chapter is that in the late medieval and early modern periods, the gap between Rabbinic Judaism and Christianity regarding attitudes towards the present world gradually became narrower compared to that of previous centuries, though perhaps it is more accurate to say that the ranges of attitudes towards the present world in the two religions increasingly overlapped. Neither religion ever had a monolithic view of the present world. Each had a variety of perspectives on the matter, with those of Jews skewed towards the this-worldly end of the spectrum and those of Christians skewed towards the other-worldly end. But in the time period under consideration here, the two sets of perspectives gradually became more congruent with each other.

On the Jewish side, philosophy and Kabbalah in the late medieval and early modern periods introduced Jews to forms of Judaism in which other-worldly matters were given greater emphasis than in Rabbinic Judaism. Kabbalah was especially important in this regard because it proved to be quite popular, and it also helped spawn a major messianic movement in the seventeenth century that epitomized its other-worldly emphasis. But most of the movement in this period in narrowing the gap between Judaism and Christianity regarding attitudes towards the mundane realm came from the Christian side. Christian thinkers developed a much greater interest in the mundane realm due to a sequence of three intellectual upheavals: the Protestant Reformation, the Scientific Revolution, and the Enlightenment. Thus, by the beginning of the nineteenth century, Christians and Jews had developed similar views on the value of the present world.

The question is whether at this point in history the gap between the two cultures on this issue completely disappeared. That is difficult to determine, but my sense is that it did not. Rabbinic Judaism and Christianity evolved parallel to each other from the first century onwards, but over the next 1,500 years or so of their evolution, Rabbinic Judaism attached far greater importance to the mundane realm than Christianity did. So even though Christians began coming around to a more favourable view of mundane existence in the early modern period, it is significant that this development occurred about a full millennium and a half later than it did in Rabbinic Judaism. By that time, the positive valuation of the present world permeated every aspect of Judaism because, from its very beginnings, rabbinic religion was centred on a system of law that was concerned primarily with daily activity. Therefore, even though there were spiritualizing tendencies in early modern Judaism, they would never entirely unseat the this-worldly orientation of Rabbinic Judaism and its centrality in Jewish life. It had become too fundamental to the Jewish world view. Most Jews in most places between the first century and the nineteenth were focused on how God's laws applied to their daily lives. On the Christian side, we see the converse. Christians increasingly appreciated the value of the mundane realm from the Reformation onwards, but Christianity in all its forms remained a religion focused on other-worldly matters. What continued to unite all Christians was the belief going back to the beginning of Christianity that the Kingdom of God heralded by Jesus was in process. Thus, in Christianity, it was the other-worldly orientation that had too much longevity to unseat. So it seems that even though the gap between Jews and Christians regarding the value of the present world had narrowed significantly by the nineteenth century, this value would remain more fundamental to rabbinic culture than to European culture.

I should add that the differences between Judaism and Christianity that are being addressed here were significant not just for the intellectual elites in both communities but for lay Jews and Christians as well. We are speaking here about issues that were central to the basic world view of both religions and that would thus have had an impact beyond the elites in the two communities.

Most important is that our observations in this chapter add to our understanding of why Jews were so well-suited to succeed in European culture in the modern period. One reason why modern Europeans achieved success in the economic, intellectual, and artistic realms was that they had developed a much greater interest in the mundane realm than ever before. Therefore, Jews, who were even more predisposed to this way of thinking, were in an excellent position to experience the success that came along with this way of thinking. All they needed was an invitation to become part of European society so that they could take advantage of what it had to offer, and that invitation came in most European countries by the end of the nineteenth century.

These conclusions are not at all inconsistent with the fact that most modern Jews who have succeeded in the economic, scientific, and artistic realms have been secular Jews, and that many of these Jews were rebelling *against* Rabbinic Judaism. As I have repeatedly argued in this study, it is quite common for proponents of a new cultural era to vilify the previous cultural era while unwittingly preserving some of its values. That is especially true when we are talking about a value of the kind being discussed here, one that was deeply ingrained in the culture of the previous era and thus was not easy to purge, but at the same time was highly useful to the new era.

The economic realm is perhaps the most obvious area in which modern Jews benefited from the positive attitude of Rabbinic Judaism towards the mundane realm. Jews entering the modern European world were primed to participate in the capitalist economic system that Europeans had adopted because Jews brought with them rabbinic views on wealth that allowed them to embrace the material dimension of life with a freer conscience than their Christian neighbours could.[69]

I would also argue that Rabbinic Judaism did not just make Jews receptive to capitalism, but it also made them good at it. Rabbinic law demanded that Jews live lives that were highly structured and routinized and required constant attention to minute actions in the realms of ethics and ritual. Yet the rewards of such a life were believed to be immense. Rabbinic Judaism held that if Jews observed God's laws in all their detail, they would be rewarded in this life and the next. Moreover, God would redeem the Jewish people and the world as a whole. One can easily see how this approach to life could be valuable for success in a modern capitalist society when transferred to the secular realm. It is a commonplace assumption in modern Western culture that economic success requires precisely the habits of mind that the rabbinic approach to life instilled in Jews: a determination to achieve long-term goals through patience, discipline, and attention to detail.[70]

Some of these observations can also be applied to other spheres. In the intellectual realm, modern Jews amassed an extraordinary record of achievement in the sciences, and this too, I believe, is attributable at least in part to the positive views that Rabbinic Judaism had regarding the mundane realm. After all, the study of science is based on the assumption that the world of nature is worthy of our attention and investigation, and the value that Rabbinic Judaism placed on the mundane realm resonated with this assumption. A religion that for centuries had attached profound religious significance to conducting detailed discussions about such earthly matters as the anatomy of animals to determine which defects rendered them non-kosher, or the movements of the sun and moon to decide the times of prayer, or the nature of the female menstrual cycle to make rulings on when married couples could engage in sexual activity – such a religion also prepared its adherents to be receptive to the study of those same earthly matters from a scientific standpoint.

The interest that modern Jews have had in science may also be attributable to the traditions of medieval and early modern Jewish philosophy in which the study of science figured prominently. However, far more Jews in the medieval and early modern periods were familiar with Rabbinic Judaism than with philosophy, and so my sense is that

Rabbinic Judaism, with its this-worldly focus, was more responsible for generating an interest in science among modern Jews than philosophy was.

And here too, the argument can be made that Rabbinic Judaism primed Jews not only to enter a new sphere in the European world but also to be good at it. If Jews did well in the economic realm because the rabbinic way of life had inculcated in them a determination to pursue long-term goals over an extended period of time with patience, discipline, and attention to detail, then the same can be said with respect to Jewish success in the sciences. Mastery of these disciplines required the same traits.

Of course, in the modern period, Rabbinic Judaism could also be a hindrance to the study of science because in this period science increasingly promoted views inimical to the rabbinic world view, and in fact for that reason, significant numbers of Jews over the past two centuries have approached science with great caution. But this response has been confined primarily to ultra-Orthodox Jews. Most other Jews have embraced science, and they have excelled at it in a way that no other group has in the Western world. And even ultra-Orthodox Jews have not rejected the sciences entirely. They have tended to accept the parts of science that do not conflict with their world view, which includes much of its application in various spheres of technology.[71]

The notion that Rabbinic Judaism prepared Jews for the study of science in the manner described here gains more credibility in light of observations made by Harold J. Berman. Berman, as we noted earlier, argues that the creation of medieval canon law by the Catholic Church was revolutionary because canon law laid the foundations for the law systems that would govern Western society in the following centuries. But Berman also argues that the creation of canon law influenced the development of Western science. He provides a number of arguments for this connection, and one of them makes the same association between the study of law and the study of science that I am making here with respect to Jews. According to Berman, the study of canon law prepared the West for the development of science because, in focusing on the minutiae of religious laws and their implementation in European society, the canonists prepared Europeans for the study of science, which was concerned with laws of nature and their implementation in the physical world. I am making precisely the same claim with respect to the rabbis. The rabbinic focus on law over the centuries prepared Jews for the study of science in the modern period in the same way that the Christian focus on canon law did for modern Europeans.[72]

One last series of observations is in order. As we have mentioned on a number of occasions, Rabbinic Judaism has often been vilified because its critics have been determined to cast its teachings in the most negative light possible, and the same goes for the features of Rabbinic Judaism we have discussed in this chapter. Christians have attacked Rabbinic Judaism throughout the centuries as a religion mired in the mundane world and therefore devoid of spirituality.

But the Christian critique has turned out to be both one-sided and short-sighted. Rabbinic Judaism was never as lacking in spirituality as Christians made it out to be. The rabbis took great interest in spiritual matters but believed that the realms of the spiritual and the mundane were more intertwined than Christians did. One's relationship with God came *through* the mundane world, not *despite* it. Moreover – and more germane to our concerns – the focus of Rabbinic Judaism on the mundane realm eventually conferred great advantages on Jews. It prepared them for the modern Western world when they were invited to become part of it.

Similar observations can be made about another feature of Rabbinic Judaism that has been discussed in this chapter and has been critiqued by Christians. Christians accused the rabbis of dwelling on the dead letter of biblical law, of focusing too much on observing the divine commandments in all their detail, while again ignoring the inward, spiritual dimension of religion.

Here again, the critique of Rabbinic Judaism was both one-sided and short-sighted. The rabbis simply had a different conception than Christians did regarding how one established a relationship with God. For the rabbis, one achieved access to God by observing his law in all its minutiae because this way of life allowed God's presence to be brought into one's life at practically every moment. And here as well, this way of thinking paid big dividends for modern Jews in the long run. It was ideally suited for the modern Western world, which valued discipline, patience, and attention to detail while providing great opportunity for those who possessed these qualities. The dead letter, as it turned out, was not really dead after all.

Chapter Nine

Education I: 100–1500 CE

We now come to the last of the four values that, according to my hypothesis, account for the success of Jews in the modern period. As I said in my introductory chapter, the most common explanation that people give for the disproportionate achievements of Jews over the past two centuries is that Jews have always placed great emphasis on education. In my experience, when Jews themselves are asked why they have done so well in the modern period, this explanation is usually the first one they mention; in fact, it is often the *only* one they mention.

This claim is based on the belief that Jews have prized education throughout their history. The assumption is that for centuries, Jews attached the highest importance to the amassing of religious knowledge and the cultivation of critical skills for analysing sacred texts, and they therefore invested enormous energy in the education of their young. The passion Jews had for education then paid great dividends when they joined modern Western society because a good education was required for entry into the most prestigious and best-paid professions in the new world they had entered. Those making this argument usually recognize that when pre-modern Jewish communities emphasized education, it was education focused mostly on religious matters that had no connection with the secular professions in which Jews would excel in the modern world. But the belief is that it was easy for Jews to transfer their drive for intellectual achievement from the religious to the secular realm.

Some scholars have gone along with this argument in one way or another, and we will confirm some aspects of it in the coming pages.[1] However, we will also see that matters are more complicated than the supporters of this argument have assumed. First, the view that education was always a Jewish ideal is not true; that ideal was specifically the product of rabbinic culture. Judaism had existed for centuries before the rabbis made education a central Jewish value. Second, and more important, we will see that when early Rabbinic Judaism made education central to Judaism, it did not necessarily result in the development of a robust system of schooling that provided equal opportunity for all Jews to develop their intellectual talents, nor was this the case for Rabbinic Judaism in the medieval and early modern periods.

A full account of the role of education in the success of modern Jews must also ask whether Jews were more devoted to education than Europeans were when the modern period began. One should not automatically assume that the answer to this question is yes. By the time the modern period arrived, Europeans understood quite well how important education was for them and their ambitions. The three values that have been analysed in this book thus far could carry Europe only so far. The first two encouraged Europeans to see themselves as sufficiently autonomous in relation to the cosmos and each other in order to undertake bold and innovative initiatives in the economic, intellectual, and artistic spheres. The third inspired Europeans to see the mundane world as sufficiently worthwhile to warrant such initiatives. But in order for Europe to become dominant in these spheres, another critical value was needed. Europeans had to build high-quality schools and universities to cultivate the talents of their citizens so that they could put the first three values into practice, and that is precisely what they did. So if Jews in the modern period did have an advantage over their non-Jewish neighbours regarding education, we will have to demonstrate that this was indeed true, and in what respects it was true.[2]

As with the last topic we analysed, the amount of material that needs to be covered here is too great for one chapter, and so this discussion will be divided into two parts. The present chapter will discuss Christianity and Judaism on education up to the year 1500, which marks the end of the medieval period. The following chapter will deal with the years 1500–1950, which cover the early modern period and most of the modern period.

I.   Christian Perspectives

The Early Medieval Period

It was around the beginning of the medieval period that European Christians began developing an interest in education. This interest started in the monasteries and it would remain centred in these institutions for several centuries.

The first monastic communities appeared in the fourth century in the eastern regions of the Mediterranean, and these communities often had schools that trained monks in Christian doctrines and guided them on how they should live their lives in devotion to God. The curriculum of these institutions was greatly strengthened in the sixth century by an Italian, Benedict of Nursia (c. 480–543 or 547), the most influential figure in Christian monasticism in its early phase and perhaps of all time. He composed the "Rule of St. Benedict," a comprehensive body of instructions for the monastic life that was widely accepted in monasteries throughout Europe in subsequent centuries. These instructions included directives about education. Benedict instituted a curriculum that ensured that monks would have the skills needed to perform the activities that were central to their daily routine, including the chanting of prayers and the study of sacred literature, such as the Bible and the works of the Church Fathers. The curriculum thus focused on teaching Latin, the language in which this literature was written. It also included the study of basic arithmetic, which was needed for several purposes, such as understanding the parts of Scripture that required some skill with numbers, and comprehending the intricacies of the religious calendar. The curriculum also included the study of music because of the centrality of chanting prayers in the daily monastic routine.[3]

By today's standards, this curriculum would seem rather sparse, but Europe was in a state of chaos in the early centuries of the medieval period, and the monasteries were the only places where education was taking place in a structured and disciplined way. The monasteries were also the only places in Europe that preserved not just Christian learning but pagan learning as well. The works of ancient Greek and Roman writers were often studied by the monastics alongside Christian texts.[4] The early medieval monasteries therefore have to be credited with keeping the light of learning alive in Europe.

The quality of learning in the monasteries varied with their overall fortunes, which fluctuated over time. As noted in an earlier chapter, throughout the Middle Ages, the monasteries had good and bad periods. There were centuries in which these institutions flourished, but there were also centuries in which they experienced decline because of a combination of forces both inside and outside the monastic communities.[5]

We have far less information about education outside the monasteries in early medieval Europe, but scholars keep unearthing evidence indicating that Europeans in this period were not as uneducated as they were once thought to be. In several regions, government bureaucracies were established that depended on written documents, and this meant that those who worked in government had to be literate. In some regions, the aristocracies were also able to read and write. Such skills were harder to find outside these groups, especially as one went down the social and economic hierarchy. However, in some places it was the custom for the common folk to conduct business transactions and land acquisitions with written documents, and so some portion of this population had to have been literate as well. It is not clear, however, how extensive this literacy was, or what form of schooling was responsible for it.[6]

The Late Medieval Period

In the later centuries of the medieval period (1000–1500), there were major developments in higher education. In the eleventh century, we begin to see the rise of schools affiliated with cathedrals, which opened up education to a larger audience than the monasteries had. The monasteries also provided opportunities for lay individuals to become educated, even those who were not planning to become monks, though such opportunities were limited.[7]

The cathedral schools were founded primarily to train individuals who wanted careers in the Church, but the skills taught by these schools also prepared people to work in government. The core curriculum in these institutions consisted of the "liberal arts," a phrase that had a different meaning in the medieval period than it does today. At that time, it referred to seven subjects that were prerequisites for the study of theology. The first three subjects were called the "trivium": grammar, logic, and rhetoric. Those who mastered these disciplines went on to the other four subjects, known as the "quadrivium": arithmetic, geometry, astronomy, and music.[8] Those who mastered these subjects were finally ready to engage in the study of theology.

The cathedral schools soon spawned a new type of educational institution: the university. It originated in the twelfth century after enrolments in the cathedral schools grew too large for the cathedrals to accommodate. This situation prompted students and teachers to organize separate institutions modelled on craftsmen's guilds, which were essentially labour unions that governed themselves and had their own regulations. The universities followed the cathedral schools in offering instruction in the liberal arts as preparation for a degree in theology, and again, the main purpose of this education was to train students for work in the Church or in government. However, the universities also offered professional degrees in medicine and law.[9]

The Church exercised control over the universities, which meant that there were limits on freedom of thought and expression in these institutions. Even so, a fair amount of free discourse was still permitted. The universities were home to scholasticism, a school of philosophy that encouraged argument and debate about all areas of knowledge studied at the time, and it was scholasticism that produced some of the most original minds in the medieval period, such as Thomas Aquinas and William of Ockham.[10]

Not long ago, it was believed that when the medieval period ended, education for the young was not much better than it was at the beginning of this period; however, scholars in recent decades have demonstrated that this assessment is inaccurate. The last two centuries of the medieval period (1300–1500) witnessed remarkable growth in educational opportunities for European children.[11] In this period, the number of elementary and grammar schools grew in various regions in Europe. This development was driven by the blossoming of trade and commerce, which demanded a workforce with basic skills in reading, writing, and math. It was also inspired by the increasing complexity of government bureaucracies across Europe, which required a workforce with similar skills.[12]

In some parts of Europe, these elementary and grammar schools were under the auspices of the Church. That was the case in England, Spain, and parts of Germany. However, in France, northern Italy, and northern Germany, schools were beginning to break free of the Church's oversight. In some places, that freedom was expressed in the teaching of literacy in vernacular languages rather than in Latin and in providing students with other skills to prepare them to become merchants. As a result, literacy rates in the vernacular languages greatly increased across Europe in the late medieval period. This development was also significant because it foreshadowed the growth of secular education in later centuries.[13]

A good deal more could be said about education in medieval Christian Europe, but I would like to hold off more discussion of this matter for the time being and turn now to Jewish perspectives on education in the medieval period. Exploring the Jewish side of the equation will provide ample opportunity to impart more information about education among medieval Christians because I will be making extensive comparisons between Christian and Jewish views on this issue during this period.

I. Jewish Perspectives

Early Rabbinic Judaism

Our discussion of education in Judaism will begin with an earlier phase of history than our discussion of education in Christianity did because there were important developments in Jewish views on education well before the medieval period. The first references to the importance of education in Judaism are contained in the Bible. In a number of passages in the Torah, the Israelites are instructed by God to teach their children the commandments he has given them.[14] In these passages, the imperative to educate the young clearly had a practical aim; children needed to learn God's laws in order to grow into adults who would adhere to them.[15] Education was not yet viewed as a value in its own right.

That would change with the rabbis. It was they who, in the first several centuries CE, conceived of the commandment to educate children in the grand terms that most Jews think of when they refer to the ideal of education in Jewish culture. For the rabbis, education fell under the larger rubric of the commandment to "study Torah." The rabbis believed that the study of Torah was an activity mandated by God himself as part of the covenant, and this commandment did not concern just the young; it was supposed to be a lifelong pursuit. Jews of all ages had to be occupied with it as much as possible. Moreover, when the rabbis referred to the study of "Torah" without the definite article – that is, "Torah" rather than "*the* Torah' – what they were thinking of included more than just the Five Books of Moses. It also included the rest of the Bible, as well as the enormous body of material that made up the Oral Torah. These had to be studied as well.

A full understanding of the rabbinic imperative to study Torah has to take into account the social context in which that activity took place. In the first two to three centuries CE, when the rabbis were beginning to emerge as a distinct group, they formed learning communities each of which consisted of a master rabbi and his disciples. There were as yet no written texts; the master rabbi's lessons were imparted orally and were memorized by his students. Moreover, the relationship the master rabbi had with his disciples went beyond his teachings. He was considered to be the very embodiment of Torah, which meant that his disciples, in addition to absorbing and memorizing his words, also saw him as a role model for how they should live their lives.[16]

The Mishnah, the first major work of rabbinic literature, revolutionized the learning that took place in these rabbinic communities by compiling their discussions into a single work. Rabbinic learning now became centralized as it began to focus on this one authoritative text.[17]

The rabbinic learning communities were exclusionary to the extent that they were entirely male, but membership in them was not based on ancestry. All male Jews were eligible to join one, so long as they accepted the premises of Rabbinic Judaism and were willing to be under the tutelage of a master rabbi.[18]

Why did the rabbis place so much emphasis on study? The practical goal of study already spelled out in the Torah was certainly a factor. For the rabbis, the meticulous observance of God's laws was the basis of his covenant with the Jewish people, which meant that Jews had to know what those laws demanded in order to practise them properly, which in turn meant that those laws had to be studied. Adding urgency to the matter was that there was much about God's laws that was unclear. The Written Torah was fixed, but the Oral Torah was not, and so there were disagreements among the rabbis over what the Oral Torah had to say about almost every one of the laws in the Written Torah. These disagreements had to be settled in order to clarify God's laws, and the rabbis believed that study was necessary for that purpose. Also, in the background here was the destruction of the Second Temple. The rabbis believed that this catastrophe occurred because of the sins of the Jewish people and that the only way they could repair their relationship with God was by properly observing the laws that were still applicable in the post-Temple era. This consideration added even greater urgency to studying God's laws because Jews could not afford to get things wrong about what God wanted from them; their redemption depended on it.

Another reason that the imperative to study Torah was so important had nothing to do with observing the commandments: the rabbis regarded this activity as a spiritual experience in its own right. It allowed Jews to connect directly with God and draw close to him, and that experience was particularly valuable now that Jews no longer had the Temple, the edifice in which God's presence had resided and that had served as a connecting point between him and the Jewish people.[19] Thus, some rabbinic sources suggested that attaching oneself to a teacher of Torah brought one into the presence of God, just as Moses had been brought into the presence of God when he received the Torah on Mount Sinai.[20] The spiritual dimension of Torah study was also expressed in the notion that such study was of value even when it dealt with laws that could not be practised. Thus, one was rewarded for studying the laws of sacrifices and other Temple rituals no less than for studying laws about the Sabbath, even though the laws regarding Temple ritual had been suspended after its destruction.[21]

We have also seen in an earlier chapter how the spiritual experience of studying Torah was exemplified in rabbinic notions of the afterlife. In a number of rabbinic passages, the ultimate heavenly reward for those who had left this world was to sit in the great rabbinic academy in heaven for all eternity and study Torah with the rabbis of the past. No idea, perhaps, illustrates better than this one the spiritual value that the rabbis attached to Torah study. In heaven, one could no longer

observe the commandments, but studying them was the greatest pleasure one could experience as a reward for one's righteousness while
on earth.[22]

We also noted in an earlier discussion that in some of the rabbinic
sources that speak about the heavenly rabbinic academy, God himself
presides over the study sessions. Did this mean that, according to the
rabbis, God himself studied Torah? Apparently, it did. In fact, a number
of rabbinic sources make that point quite explicitly. In one Talmudic
source, we are told that God spends one quarter of his day every day
engaged in this activity.[23] Thus, Torah study was so important for the
rabbis that they believed even God himself engaged in it.

In light of everything that has been said here, it makes sense that
in the Mishnah, we find a statement that the commandment to study
Torah was equivalent to all the other commandments combined.[24] For
the rabbis, Torah study was that important.

Did the passion for study in early Rabbinic Judaism include studying wisdom that came from outside Judaism? There are indications that
some Palestinian rabbis did engage in the pursuit of non-Jewish learning, which was available to them through the Roman culture in which
they found themselves embedded in the first few centuries CE. Several
rabbinic sources indicate that some rabbis were interested in Greek philosophy and literature, a body of learning that the Romans had preserved.[25] There are also indications that some rabbis were enamoured of
the sciences and pseudo-sciences of their time.[26] However, there is also
an opposing tendency in the rabbinic sources. Some of them speak out
against the study of foreign wisdom – Greek wisdom in particular.[27] But
even the rabbinic sources that do speak in favour of such wisdom are
few in number; we find no more than a handful of them in the massive
corpus of rabbinic literature. It is safe to say that for the rabbis, the value
of study was almost always equated with religious learning internal to
Judaism.

The importance of studying Torah in early rabbinic culture is evident
not just in the exalted terms the rabbis used to describe this activity, but
also in their views about how much time they believed Jews should
devote to it. So committed were the rabbis to Torah study that questions were raised about how one was supposed to observe God's commandments if one was constantly studying them. Some rabbis seemed
to believe that the study of Torah had priority over practising the commandments. Thus, one passage relates that R. Shimon bar Yohai would
not desist from study in order to recite the *Shema* prayer as mandated
by rabbinic law. Other rabbis, however, gave the practice of the commandments priority.[28]

Perhaps an even more significant dilemma for the rabbis concerned the relationship between Torah study and work. Most people do not have the luxury to study all day because they have to work for a living, and the rabbis and their followers were no exception in this regard. Thus, here too the rabbinic obsession with Torah study raised questions about how one should make the best use of one's time. Most rabbis seemed to understand that people had to engage in gainful employment to support themselves and their families and that Torah study had to be done in one's spare time.[29] However, as we noted in an earlier chapter, R. Shimon bar Yohai was unwilling to compromise. He believed that Jews should study Torah all day and that if they did, God would reward them by miraculously providing for their material needs. Their work, according to this rabbi, would be performed by others – presumably non-Jews. It seems that in R. Shimon's thinking, Jews just had to have faith in God's capacity to implement such an arrangement for it to become a reality.[30]

However, the rabbis were usually not so obsessed with Torah study that they advocated a life of deprivation of the kind we see among Christian monastics, who swore themselves to celibacy and poverty and retreated from communal life altogether. Torah study did not override the duty to get married, engage in sexual relations, and have children; nor was poverty worth the price of studying Torah, at least not as a rule.[31] Even extreme devotees to Torah study like R. Shimon bar Yohai did not go the way of the monastics. He married and had children, and when he declared that Jews could devote all their time to Torah study, he did not imagine that they would live a life of poverty; he believed that God would take care of their material needs. Still, the debates the rabbis had about the balance between Torah study and work indicate that they were deeply passionate about learning.

CHILDHOOD EDUCATION

Thus far, we have spoken about Torah study as an ideal for all Jews. What about the more specific question of educating the young? What did the rabbis have to say about this particular concern?

Not surprisingly, the rabbis were strong advocates of education. The rabbis recognized that if Jews were going to be deeply learned in Torah, they had to start at an early age. Moreover, the continuity of the rabbinic class itself was dependent on educating children so that some of them would grow up to become rabbis. Once again, the destruction of the Second Temple loomed large here. The education of the young was a particularly urgent matter for the rabbis after this catastrophe because education was key to rebuilding a vital Jewish community, one devoted to the rabbinic brand of Judaism.[32]

The rabbis inform us in the Mishnah that the responsibility for educating boys belonged specifically to their fathers.[33] When it came to the education of girls, matters were not as clear; in the Mishnah, opinions were divided on whether fathers had an obligation to teach Torah to their daughters.[34]

The rabbis recognized that most fathers were incapable of educating their children on their own, and so they established schools for this purpose. According to rabbinic sources, there were schools in every district in Roman Palestine by the end of the first century, and children were required to attend these schools from the age of six or seven onwards. Fathers could discharge their duty to educate their children by sending them to these schools.[35]

But the establishment of schools did not necessarily replace the home as a place for education. It is also likely that the home served as a place for education about other Jewish matters. In Roman Palestine, education also took place in the synagogue, not just for children but for adults as well. On the Sabbath, a portion of the Torah and a selection from the books of the Prophets were read in the synagogue publicly, a ritual that helped familiarize Jews with the Hebrew Bible. The rabbis also delivered sermons in the synagogue on the Sabbath, a custom that exposed those in attendance to a variety of biblical and rabbinic sources.[36] The level of education among Jewish children in the rabbinic period impressed at least one prominent observer. Jerome, the famous fourth-century Church Father, made note of the knowledge that Jewish children had of their religious traditions in two statements. In one of these, Jerome says as follows: "In childhood, they acquire the complete vocabulary of their language, and learn to recite all the generations from Adam to Zerubbabel with such accuracy and facility as if they were simply giving their names."[37] In another comment, Jerome praises the Jews for memorizing the Torah and the books of the Prophets.[38]

RECENT REVISIONIST SCHOLARSHIP

Modern academic scholars have recently cast doubt on many of the claims that the early rabbis made regarding education. They have also criticized previous academic scholars for painting too idyllic a picture of education in the rabbinic period.[39] Most current academic scholars of early Rabbinic Judaism now believe that the rabbis never established a network of schools for Jewish children in Roman Palestine in the first century CE, and a number of arguments support this assessment. Most important, rabbinic claims about establishing a network of schools first appear in rabbinic texts edited centuries after that system would have existed, and so such claims cannot be considered reliable. We also have no evidence of such a network of schools from non-Jewish sources composed at the time. Jewish children may have been educated by other means: parents may have taught their children at home, or they may have hired tutors for them. There are references in rabbinic literature to professional teachers who taught children, and these references may be alluding to these tutors. That may explain why Jerome encountered Jewish children who were so learned. However, what is doubtful is the rabbinic claim that in Roman Palestine the rabbis created an entire system of schools that gave all children the opportunity to be educated. Jewish education in this time and place was, in all likelihood, far more sporadic and uneven.[40]

Comments in rabbinic sources about the schoolteachers of their time also make one wonder how committed the rabbis actually were to educating the young. Isaiah Gafni has shown that while some sources in rabbinic literature praise schoolteachers, most sources, in fact, speak about them with derision. Apparently, many rabbis did not have much regard for the teaching profession; for them, it was a job for those who were not learned enough to join their elite circles.[41] None of this is to say that the rabbis were uninterested in educating children. The evidence adduced earlier in our discussion indicates that they were. But the rabbis may not have treated childhood education as the core value that modern Jews assume it was for them.

If Jewish children were not as educated in the rabbinic period as many have believed, there is also reason to believe that neither were Jewish adults. We have evidence that across the Jewish population in Roman Palestine during the first centuries CE, literacy rates were actually quite low. Jewish adults in this period may have absorbed rabbinic teachings orally in places like the synagogue, but most of them probably could not read rabbinic texts.[42] Thus, once again, we have to modify the common perception that Jews were always highly educated.

EDUCATION IN EARLY RABBINIC JUDAISM

What emerges from our discussion thus far is that in early Rabbinic Judaism, education was valued, but not necessarily valued as highly as modern Jewish scholars and popular writers, and Jewish lay people often imagine. The rabbis certainly believed that education was important, but one cannot assume that this belief translated into the establishment of schools or rabbinic efforts to reach out to common Jews so that all of them would become versed in rabbinic learning. It is more likely that Jews in both Roman Palestine and Babylonia became familiar with rabbinic learning sporadically and in settings other than schools, such as the home or the synagogue, or through private tutoring, and that large portions of the Jewish population in both regions remained unlearned or weakly learned when it came to rabbinic teachings.

Yet even if the rabbis were not as active in educating the masses as many have believed, they still revered learning and the cultivation of the intellect. The imperative to study Torah was fundamental to their world view, and that is evident from looking at any rabbinic text. Every page of rabbinic literature is filled with discourses and debates about the Written and Oral Torah. Rabbinic literature is essentially Torah study in textual form. Thus, we must still appreciate the enormous contribution the rabbis made in transforming Judaism into a highly intellectual religion. The emphasis the rabbis placed on the cultivation of the mind would also have an immense impact on Judaism for centuries to come. It would become one of its defining feature for the rest of its history.

Most important for our purposes here is that the obsession with learning and cultivating the intellect had no precise parallel in Christian Europe in the early medieval period. The Church required its followers to establish a relationship with God in a number of ways. They had to accept a series of fundamental beliefs that had been defined by the Church's creeds; they had to cultivate proper inner dispositions and traits of character that would lead them to a life of piety, which meant nurturing seven standard virtues and avoiding seven standard vices; they had to take part in a series of sacraments administered by the Church; and they had to obey the biblical commandments as interpreted by the Church.[43] But there were no imperatives to forge a relationship with God through learning or the cultivation of the intellect.

The closest we come in early medieval Europe to the rabbinic passion for studying Torah is the learning that took place in the monasteries. Yet the monastics did not accord study as exalted a place in their religious life as the rabbis did in theirs. The rabbis viewed studying Torah as the most important of the commandments – or perhaps, more accurately, as first among equals. All of God's commandments had to be obeyed, but a special place was given to Torah study; one was supposed to engage in it in every spare moment. For the monastics, study was only one of several activities that brought one close to God, and it usually was not the most important one. When one looks at the regimens of the various monastic orders throughout the medieval period, one finds that most orders spent the majority of their time chanting prayers.[44]

The Late Medieval Period

Let us now look at the period of 1000–1500. By the year 1000, Jews in both Christian and Muslim lands recognized the rabbis as their authorities on matters of religion, and as Rabbinic Judaism came to dominate the Jewish world, the intellectual component of Judaism that was so important to the rabbis became increasingly central to Jewish culture as a whole.[45] The rabbis continued to preach the notion that Torah study was a divine commandment for all men, and a particularly important one, and late medieval rabbinic works of Jewish law underscored its centrality; entire sections of these works were devoted to laying out the rules and regulations for Torah study. These works usually acknowledged that men had to work in order to make a living, and they therefore conceded that they could not study Torah all day; however, the rabbis instituted regulations specifying that time still had to be set aside on a regular basis for Torah study.[46]

It is difficult to determine the extent to which ordinary Jews were aware of these prescriptions, but they must have had some cognizance of them. The importance of studying Torah was underscored repeatedly in the daily morning prayer service that had been constructed and instituted by the rabbis in earlier centuries. The opening section of the prayer service contained two blessings in which one took upon oneself the duty to study Torah. No other commandment was singled out in this manner. The introductory section of the morning prayer service also contained the statement from the Mishnah noted earlier that Torah study was equivalent to all the other commandments combined. Jews thus began every day extolling the virtue of studying Torah.[47]

Later in the morning prayer service, one was required to recite the *Shema*, a prayer the rabbis regarded as one of the major focal points of morning worship. It consisted of three paragraphs from the Torah, and in the first two sections of this prayer, reference was made to the requirement to converse about God's words on a constant basis, an imperative the rabbis equated with Torah study. The *Shema* was then recited once more in the evening, further reminding Jews of the centrality of studying Torah.

In addition, Jews in late medieval Europe must have appreciated the importance of Torah study as a rabbinic ideal because of the role the rabbis themselves had begun to play in European Jewish communities. European rulers usually allowed Jews in their respective jurisdictions to govern themselves by Jewish law, and therefore rabbis were needed to give basic guidance about the law and to make rulings on new cases that constantly arose. And because Jewish law was concerned with both religious and civil matters, a rabbi's expertise was needed for rulings on virtually every aspect of life.[48]

By the early thirteenth century, most sizeable Jewish communities in Europe had at least one rabbi who served as an authority on Jewish law, and by the fourteenth century, the office of rabbi had become professionalized; communities usually had a rabbi who was hired and paid by them. In addition, these rabbis also preached in the synagogues on the Sabbath and served as teachers in the community. Many of the sermons given by medieval rabbis have been preserved, and they clearly gave lay people a sense of what Torah study was; they were chock full of biblical and rabbinic sources.[49]

Some communities also had highly learned rabbis who opened yeshivas, which were rabbinic institutions for advanced Talmudic studies, and students would come from other communities to study in them. The same rabbi might serve as a communal rabbi and head up a yeshiva, but often these positions were occupied by different individuals.[50] All of this meant that Jews in most medieval communities in Europe were reminded of the value of studying Torah not just because of what they recited in their daily prayers, but also because of the presence of the rabbis who embodied that value and served as public figures on account of it.

That medieval Jews had high regard for the intellectual component of Rabbinic Judaism is also evident from medieval marriage customs. Young men who were accomplished Torah scholars had higher value on the marriage market than other young men. A yeshiva student who was on his way to becoming an accomplished rabbi might therefore marry well above his class.[51]

The reverence for learning among Jews in late medieval Europe was also reflected in the fact that the stature of Jewish communities was tied to the intellectual achievements of their rabbis. A rabbi who was particularly learned, whether he was a communal rabbi or one who headed a yeshiva, gave the community in which he resided prestige in the eyes of Jews elsewhere. Such rabbis might therefore provide guidance on Jewish law not only for their own communities but also for surrounding communities when particularly complex or weighty questions arose that the rabbis in those communities could not handle.[52]

A rabbi who was exceptionally accomplished gave his community even greater status. His name and that of his community would be known throughout much of the Jewish world. A "pre-eminent rabbi of the generation" (*gedol ha-dor*), as such a rabbi was called, would receive written questions about Jewish law from Jewish communities that local rabbis could not answer. A rabbi of such distinction might field thousands of questions of this sort over the course of his lifetime.[53]

The common folk in medieval Jewish communities did not always treat their rabbis with reverence. The power of the rabbis was often limited by the wealthier sectors of the communities they served. As noted earlier, almost every Jewish community in late medieval Europe was governed by a council that consisted of local Jews elected by members of the community. That council was usually made up of the wealthiest Jews because they were the ones who financed the community's institutions and operations.[54] Thus, more often than not, ultimate power resided not with the rabbi but with the council that had hired him and paid his salary.[55]

The rabbi's weakness often became evident when he disagreed with the council's actions. Such disagreements were almost inevitable because, as one might expect, the council members often used their political power to protect their monetary interests, and they sometimes did so even when it meant violating Jewish law. The rabbi might protest, but he was often cowed into silence because his objections put him at risk for losing his job.[56]

But not all rabbis were powerless. If a rabbi had sufficient prestige, the lay council might be reluctant to go against him because the stature of their community depended on him, and they did not want him to leave for a position in another community.[57] Thus, the interests of the wealthy did not always trump Torah learning. The latter value could hold its own when it was embodied in a particularly distinguished individual.

CHILDHOOD EDUCATION

How did Jews in late medieval Europe educate their young? In the past several decades, our knowledge of Jewish educational practices in late medieval France, Germany, and Spain has grown significantly, and so I will concentrate on these regions.

Jewish communities in Germany and northern France shared a common culture, and therefore, in medieval Jewish literature, these regions are referred to collectively as "Ashkenaz."[58] For some time, modern scholars assumed that there had to have been an organized school system in Ashkenaz in the twelfth and thirteenth centuries. A defining feature of Ashkenazi culture in these centuries was its yeshivas, which were unmatched in Talmudic learning in the Jewish world. Therefore, the belief was that Ashkenazi communities must have established a network of publicly supported elementary schools to prepare young boys for higher Jewish learning.[59]

But here again, modern Jewish scholars have painted too idyllic a picture of how Jews approached education in pre-modern times. Recent research has shown that, just as with Jewish communities in the rabbinic period, Ashkenazi communities in the twelfth and thirteenth centuries did not establish publicly funded schools. In late medieval Jewish sources, we find no references to an organized system of education in Ashkenaz. Jews educated their children by other means. The great rabbis of the rabbinic academies tended to educate their children at home. As for the rest of the Jewish population, parents had to hire private tutors for their children. Sometimes groups of parents banded together for that purpose by hiring a tutor to teach their children collectively. Educational opportunities therefore depended on the availability of tutors in a given town, what parents could afford, and how much interest they had in educating their children. The result was that levels of education in Ashkenaz varied considerably even within the same Jewish community. Compounding this problem was that the status of teachers was no better in late medieval Ashkenaz than it was in the rabbinic period. Their pay was poor and their status was low, and thus the quality of instruction they provided was inconsistent. So we should not assume that all Jews in Ashkenazi culture were well-educated.[60]

None of this takes away from the fact that Ashkenaz was home to the greatest yeshivas in the Jewish world at the time. However, those who attended these yeshivas had been chosen early on in their education for advanced Talmudic study because of their exceptional talent, and they represented a small fraction of the population. Most Jews did not have the opportunity to develop their intellectual abilities beyond the elementary level.

Jewish communities thrived in Spain in the twelfth and thirteenth centuries, and these communities were better organized than those in Ashkenaz with respect to providing education for their children. Most Jewish communities in Spanish cities had elementary schools that were financially supported either by communal funds or by rich donors. However, education levels among Spanish Jews were actually lower than those of Jewish communities to the north, and they produced far fewer individuals who engaged in advanced Talmudic studies. It would seem, then, that while the Jews of Spain were diligent about educating their young people, their culture was not geared to intellectual accomplishment in the way that Ashkenazi culture was.[61] In sum, in medieval Jewish Europe the obligation to study Torah that was so central to Rabbinic Judaism was probably not fulfilled nearly as much as the rabbis wanted it to be, nor were educational levels among medieval European Jews nearly as high as modern Jews have often assumed.

CHRISTIANITY VS. JUDAISM

The critical question for us is how this situation compared to that of Christian society in late medieval Europe. The first thing to note is that the same modern Jewish academic scholars, who assumed that medieval European Jews were highly educated, also assumed that these Jews were far better educated than their Christian neighbours were, and there may be some truth to this assertion. We have testimony to that effect from a Christian source. A student of Peter Abelard, a French figure of the twelfth century who was one of the greatest Christian theologians of the medieval period, reports as follows about the educational levels of Jews he encountered:

> If the Christians educate their sons, they do so not for God, but for gain, in order that one brother, if he be a clerk, may help his father and his mother and his other brothers. They say that a clerk will have no heir and whatever he has will be ours and the other brothers'.... But the Jews, out of zeal for God and love of the law, put as many sons as they have to letters, that each may understand God's law.
>
> A Jew, however, poor, even if he had ten sons would put them all to letters, not for gain as Christians do, but for the understanding of God's law, and not only his sons but his daughters.[62]

So even if levels of education among medieval Jews were not as high as many modern Jews assume, they may still have been higher than those of their Christian peers.

Yet caution is in order here: the source just cited is unique. We have no others like it, and so it is hard to say to what extent the claims it makes are true. Moreover, the author praises the manner in which Jews educate their children in order to critique his fellow Christians, and one therefore wonders whether that praise has been exaggerated to make a point.

In addition, as noted earlier in this chapter, recent scholarship on the history of education in the West has demonstrated that the levels of education in late medieval Europe were greater than once thought, and new studies keep coming out that strengthen that assessment. Thus, if European Jews in the late medieval period were *less* educated than previously assumed, and Europeans Christians in this period were *more* educated than previously assumed, it is therefore difficult to determine whether there really was a gap in educational levels between the Jewish and non-Jewish communities in late medieval Europe, and if so, how great that gap was.

We also have to recognize that such comparisons are problematic because of large variations in educational levels between regions in both Jewish and non-Jewish communities in medieval Europe. Neither Jews nor Christians had stable, well-organized school systems run by a central government, and as a result, schooling was highly inconsistent *within* both groups.

Another relevant question here that complicates matters is how to define "education." What does it mean to say that Jews or non-Jews in the Middle Ages were educated? Which skills did they have to possess to deserve this designation? Discussions about this issue usually involve literacy, but this term itself is problematic. There are heated debates among modern scholars over what constitutes "literacy." For instance, does it mean to read, or to write, or both? And how proficient does one have to be in one or both these skills to be called literate? Modern scholars have widely different answers to these questions, and these answers affect how they assess educational levels in medieval Europe.[63] Thus, for many reasons, it is not easy to determine whether Jews in the late medieval period did better at educating their young people than Christians did, and if so, to what extent.

Nonetheless, one thing that I believe *can* be said with some degree of certainty is that in this period, learning and intellectual achievement were more *valued* in Jewish culture than in Christian culture. That is, even if it is not entirely clear whether Jews were better educated than Christians, we can be sure that Jews, on the whole, had greater reverence than Christians did for those who *were* educated.

The reason we can say this is that many of the differences between Jewish and Christian culture on this issue that we discerned in the early medieval period persisted into the late medieval period, even though Judaism and Christianity were now far more developed and consolidated than in the earlier centuries. As we have noted, late medieval rabbis continued to believe, as the earlier rabbis did, that the most important of God's commandments was to study Torah, and they even put rules in place requiring that Jews set aside time for it on a regular basis. Whether Jews obeyed those rules is again an open question, but the rules were there and figured prominently in medieval rabbinic literature. On the Christian side, there was still no precise parallel to the rabbinic emphasis on the intellectual dimension of religion, even as an ideal. According to the Church, Christian piety continued to consist of upholding the Church's creeds, living an ethical life defined by cultivating the seven virtues and avoiding the seven vices, participating in the officially sanctioned sacraments administered by the Church of which there were now seven, and obeying the biblical commandments as interpreted by the Church.[64] But there was still no imperative specifying that learning or the development of the intellect were central to the religious life.

The monasteries of the late medieval period were centres of learning, just as they had been in the early medieval period, but the discrepancy between the monks and the rabbis regarding the place of learning in religious life endured. The monks in the late medieval period certainly valued learning, as they had in earlier centuries. However, most monastic communities, like the Church in general, still had no equivalent to the rabbinic notion that studying God's word was a divine commandment, and certainly nothing resembling the rabbinic idea that study was supposed to occupy every minute of one's spare time. In the monasteries, engagement of the intellect for religious purposes was almost always secondary to more ritually oriented activities that filled the daily monastic routine. All of this meant that the monks had no motivation to encourage lay people with whom they had contact, to make study an important part of their lives.

There were exceptions. Some monks in the late medieval period became the era's leading intellectuals. The Dominican Order was unusual in making the cultivation of the intellect central to its mission. The Dominicans believed that people were led to faith primarily through reason, and so they engaged in intense study and the cultivation of rational skills so that they could wander the countryside and convince ordinary Christians through rational argumentation to become more devout.[65] As a result, the Dominicans resembled the rabbis more than any other monastic order in emphasizing the intellectual dimension of religious experience and the need for lay individuals to participate in it. However, the Dominicans were unique in this regard. Other monastic orders did not give the intellectual dimension of religion the attention the Dominicans did.

What about the priests who served Christian communities throughout Europe? Was there any analogue between these figures and the rabbis? Not when it came to intellectual matters. The priests had several functions, but by far the most important was to administer the sacraments. The priests were also expected to provide basic instruction to their constituents about fundamental elements of the Christian life – such as the Apostle's Creed, prayer, the sacraments, the Christian calendar, and ethics – and in order to fulfil these functions, the priests were supposed to have a modicum of education.[66] However, the priests were not expected to be role models of intellectual achievement. Moreover, many of them were not even knowledgeable enough to perform the minimal functions assigned to them, either because of poor training or because they had been placed in parishes by corrupt rulers who were intent on using them to siphon off tithes for their own purposes.[67] On the whole, then, the priests were nowhere near as learned in Christianity as the rabbis were in Judaism.[68]

A new class of religious figures appeared in the late medieval period that is very important for our discussion. It is in these centuries that we see the rise of the universities, and the scholars who led these institutions were much more similar to the rabbis in their devotion to intellectual matters than most monks and priests were. Many of these scholars, not surprisingly, were also Dominicans.

Like the rabbis, university scholars were passionately devoted to the accumulation of knowledge and the cultivation of the mind. The focus of university learning was somewhat different from that of the rabbis. In the universities, one sought to experience God by studying every aspect of existence from the created universe to the realm of the divine, and these interests, of course, involved a large number of disciplines. The universities also provided students with opportunities to study law and medicine.[69] The university curriculum was therefore much broader than the rabbinic one, which focused primarily on religious law. However, the point is that the universities introduced Europeans to figures who had an enthusiastic view of learning that was similar to that of the rabbis.

However, the emphasis on the intellectual dimension of religion among university faculty was still not quite equal to that of rabbis. Scholars in the universities, like the monks and the priests, did not espouse anything equivalent to the rabbinic notion that study was a divine commandment incumbent on all believers and that it should occupy every spare moment of one's time. The university scholars engaged in study as much as the rabbis did, but these scholars did not view this way of life as one that was incumbent on all Christians as a matter of divine imperative.

Furthermore, even if the faculty in the universities resembled the rabbis in their intense devotion to learning and intellectual achievement, they represented only one paradigm for Christian religiosity in late medieval Europe, and by no means the most popular one: monastic Christianity had far more adherents. While there were dozens of universities in Europe in the late medieval period, there were thousands of monasteries. On the Jewish side, the situation was entirely different. Here the rabbis had little competition. The religious leadership was almost exclusively in their hands, and so the life of learning and intellectual achievement the rabbis embodied was by far the most popular paradigm for Jewish religiosity.[70]

In sum, we have good reason to believe that the intellectual dimension of religion was valued more in late medieval Judaism than in late medieval Christianity. Yet, our focus here has been primarily on religious elites – rabbis on the Jewish side, and monks, priests, and university intellectuals on the Christian side. What about the common people? How did ordinary Jews and Christians compare in their attitudes towards intellectual achievement?

This question is very difficult to answer because sources on this issue are lacking. But on the basis of what we have said thus far, there is reason to believe that the differences we have seen between the elite groups in the two religious communities filtered down to some extent to the common people.

We have already discussed why ordinary Jews in late medieval Europe most likely had respect for learning and intellectual achievement even if they themselves were not educated. These Jews were reminded of the commandment to study Torah in their regular prayer services at several junctures of the day; they depended on the learning of rabbis for guidance on all things Jewish; and they measured the prestige of their communities by the intellectual accomplishments of these rabbis.

In Christian society, the situation was entirely different. Again, there was no divine commandment to study either for religious authorities or for the common folk. The figures who most closely resembled the rabbis and who could serve as role models in Christian society for intellectual achievement were university scholars. However, it is likely that ordinary Christians had less contact with these scholars than with priests or monks, given that in late medieval Europe there were many more priests and monks than university scholars. More important, ordinary Christians would likely have had less contact with university scholars than ordinary Jews had with rabbis. Besides the fact that there were relatively few universities, the population of Christian Europe was mostly rural in the late medieval period,[71] and so most Europeans would never have seen a university or encountered its faculty members, given that the universities were usually located in towns and cities. However, Jews lived in relatively close quarters in towns and cities, many of which had rabbis, and so contact between ordinary Jews and rabbis would have been reasonably common.

There were, of course, tens of thousands of students who came through the universities in the late medieval period and then returned to their home cities or towns, or went to other locations upon graduation, and it is likely that the common folk came into contact with them more often than with university faculty. Thus, university graduates would have familiarized ordinary Europeans with the intellectual life that the universities offered.

Yet the university students circulating in medieval Europe were a small part of the overall population.[72] More important, most Europeans studied in universities not because they wanted to spend their lives cultivating the intellect but for more practical reasons: a university degree in any field helped secure a well-paying job as a bureaucrat in the Church or in government, while a degree in law or medicine gave one credentials to practise in those professions. Some would have attended university out of a pure passion for learning, and they were the ones who often went on to join the faculty of these institutions after getting their degrees. But for most students, the university was a place for career advancement.[73] Therefore, most university graduates would not have necessarily been role models to other Europeans for a life devoted specifically to the intellect.

The group analogous to university students in the Jewish community were Jews who attended yeshivas, and it is instructive to compare the two groups. The goal of the yeshiva was to produce Torah scholars. Certainly, many of the students who graduated from the yeshivas went on to have careers as community rabbis, and so here as well, professional motives may have led students to attend yeshivas. We should also be reminded that a bright young Torah scholar of modest means might be able to advance his position in Jewish society by marrying a woman from a wealthy family, a factor that certainly increased the practical value of rabbinic training. However, when yeshiva students went on to become communal rabbis, they were still Torah scholars, and they got hired in Jewish communities as Torah scholars. Again, their purpose was to serve as intellectual masters of Jewish tradition, particularly Jewish law, in order to provide guidance on it. Moreover, even after yeshiva graduates were hired as rabbis, they presumably had to continue setting aside time for Torah study in order to maintain their qualifications as learned individuals on all things Jewish. A significant number of these rabbis also established yeshivas for nothing other than Torah study. The intellectual life of the yeshiva therefore carried over into the professional life of its graduates in a way that was less pronounced among the graduates of the universities. Thus, Jews were more likely than Christians to have in their midst religious role models who focused on intellectual achievement.

Furthermore, even if ordinary Christians had regular contact with university scholars, it is not clear that they would have admired that way of life. The Dominican Order placed more emphasis on the intellectual experience of religion than any other monastic order and fanned out across the countryside to preach its intellectual brand of Christianity, but this order was not terribly successful in convincing ordinary Christians to follow its ways. Lay Christians in the late medieval period were looking for a more emotional connection to religion than the Dominicans offered, which meant that the Dominicans' emphasis on the intellect had little appeal for them. Monastic orders that focused less on the intellect and more on piety were more popular.[74] In fact, as we have noted, ordinary Christians sometimes formed semi-monastic orders in emulation of these monastics.

A relatively clear picture therefore emerges here. There are a number of reasons to believe that in the late medieval period, common Jews had greater respect for the intellectual dimension of religious life than common Christians did, even if neither population was exceptionally learned.

CURIOSITY

Our observations regarding the differences between Jewish and Christian culture in medieval Europe are reinforced by exploring their respective attitudes towards human curiosity. In recent years, scholars have written a great deal about the history of curiosity in Europe. That may seem like a peculiar topic to examine, but the research that has been done on this issue has greatly illuminated our understanding of how Europeans before the modern period approached the world around them, and it has obvious implications for education.

Nowadays in the West, it is taken for granted that curiosity is a highly positive human trait. In fact, it is considered vital to our happiness and well-being. Curiosity energizes us, inspires us, and makes us creative in all aspects of our lives. Parents and educators therefore encourage curiosity in their children from the youngest age. The assumption is that children who develop a healthy sense of curiosity about the world around them will retain that trait as adults and go on to lead more fulfilled lives.

But it was not always this way. The leading figures in early Christianity saw curiosity not as a virtue but as a vice, and that way of thinking would persist throughout the medieval and early modern periods. Curiosity here was defined as either the desire to know things that were useless, or the desire to know things that were beyond human capacity. The latter form of curiosity was particularly offensive because it was connected to human pride, which was considered to be the worst of the vices. For this reason, curiosity was to be discouraged.[75]

This negative attitude towards curiosity was based on early Christian interpretations of the Garden of Eden story. The Church Fathers believed that curiosity was in part responsible for the fall of Adam and Eve. Adam and Eve disobeyed God because they were curious about the fruit of the Tree Knowledge of Good and Evil that they were forbidden to eat.[76]

Most significantly, Augustine incorporated this critique of curiosity into his views on Original Sin. We have already seen that in Augustine's thinking, the fall of Adam and Eve had been brought about by concupiscence, the tendency of human beings to focus on their own selfish needs rather than on service to God. We have also noted that according to Augustine, concupiscence expressed itself primarily in sexual lust.[77] Yet, according to Augustine, curiosity had contributed to the expulsion from Eden as well; Adam and Eve ate the forbidden fruit in part because curiosity inspired them to pursue knowledge that was beyond their capacity. Augustine also felt that curiosity was an expression of concupiscence because, like sexual lust, it led human beings away from God by focusing them on their own selfish interests. Curiosity, in Augustine's terminology, was "the lust of the eyes."[78] Other great medieval Christian thinkers followed Augustine's lead here. For instance, Thomas Aquinas condemned curiosity as well.[79]

The views of Augustine and Aquinas on curiosity may seem odd, given that they were the two most important intellectuals in medieval Christianity and that their writings reflect intense curiosity about a wide range of subjects. It seems particularly odd that Aquinas would have antipathy towards curiosity given that he was the leading figure in the school of scholasticism that emphasized the development of the intellect and believed that a rational understanding of God and his world was critical for the religious life. It would seem that Aquinas's entire way of thinking rested on a respect for curiosity. But neither Augustine nor Aquinas would have seen their intellectual endeavours as a problem because for them, curiosity was a vice only when it involved the pursuit of knowledge that was either useless or beyond one's capacity, and, presumably, they felt that their own intellectual pursuits had neither quality.

After the Reformation, the negative attitude towards curiosity transcended the Catholic-Protestant divide. Protestant thinkers in the sixteenth and seventeenth centuries often criticized curiosity as a vice. Only in the eighteenth century did attitudes towards curiosity begin to shift, and even then, scientists in this period often complained about having to explain why their endeavours were of any value. To explore the world just because it was interesting was considered by most people at the time to be a vain and useless way to spend one's time.[80]

There is no parallel to any of this in Rabbinic Judaism. The rabbis did not develop an antipathy towards curiosity in the way that Christian thinkers did, in part, it seems, because the rabbis did not share the Christian obsession with the Garden of Eden story. The differences between the rabbis and Christian thinkers regarding this story have been noted in this study in an earlier chapter, and here it is relevant again with respect to the issue of curiosity.[81]

The rabbis did express reservations similar to those of Christian thinkers about individuals studying subjects that were beyond their capacity. In a well-known passage in the Mishnah, the early rabbis warned their disciples not to teach certain esoteric subjects in public. What they had in mind here primarily were secret teachings studied in some rabbinic circles that dealt with two topics: the manner in which God created the world, and the nature of the heavenly realm in which God resided. Apparently, premature engagement with such esoteric matters was thought to be dangerous for all but the greatest of rabbis; for the uninitiated, it could lead to heresy, insanity, or even death. Ordinary minds simply could not handle areas of knowledge like these. The same passage in the Mishnah appears to warn the rabbis not to attempt to probe matters beyond the worlds of space and time that no one, not even they, can comprehend.[82] The warnings expressed in this source were highly influential among later medieval Jewish philosophers and Kabbalists, who interpreted these warnings in light of their own schools of thought. Some Jewish philosophers believed that the warnings were attempts to discourage people from pursuing the study of natural science and metaphysics before they were ready. For Kabbalists, the warnings concerned the premature study of their esoteric teachings regarding the ten *sefirot*, teachings that explained God's inner life and the operations of the universe he created.[83] Therefore, there was a continuous strand in Jewish thinking from the rabbinic period through the Middle Ages, according to which curiosity could be harmful, and the concern was focused on areas similar to those that Christians were concerned about.

However, there was an important difference between Judaism and Christianity on this issue. Once again, for Christians, curiosity was a fundamental vice connected to the fall of human beings in the Garden of Eden, and it remained a character flaw inherent in all human beings ever since. Jewish thinkers did not subscribe to these premises. For the rabbis, philosophers, and Kabbalists, curiosity had no associations of this kind. Some people were curious about esoteric matters that were beyond their capabilities, and they needed to be warned about their limits, lest they come to harm. But curiosity was not seen as a universal blemish on the human character.

Conclusions

What emerges from our discussion of the late medieval period is fairly consistent with our prior discussion of earlier centuries. In this period, European Jews were neither as devoted to education nor as far ahead of their Christian neighbours on this issue as modern Jews have often imagined. Nonetheless, Jews had greater reverence for learning and the cultivation of the intellect than Christians did. The rabbis emphasized in their writings that Torah study was mandated for all men, and even if in reality that ideal was not fulfilled nearly as often as the rabbis wanted it to be, by the later centuries of the medieval period, ordinary Jews certainly knew of the ideal since it was highlighted in their daily prayers and embodied in the figure of the communal rabbi. Medieval Christianity did not give the same place to intellectual achievement as Jews did. The medieval Church never conceived of study as an obligation for all Christians. Moreover, the notion that curiosity was a vice tied to the fall of Adam and Eve meant that one had to approach the pursuit of knowledge with great caution. This is not to say that medieval Christians had no interest in intellectual matters. The monasteries and the universities are evidence that they certainly did, and the learning that took place in these institutions could be highly sophisticated. It is just that the intellectual dimension of religion was accentuated more in medieval Judaism than in medieval Christianity.

Chapter Ten

Education II: 1500–1950 CE

In this chapter, we continue our discussion of education by examining Christian and Jewish perspectives on this issue in the early modern and modern periods. Our treatment of the other three values that are central to this study did not focus much on the modern period because our goal has been to show that Jews developed these values more than Christians did prior to the modern period. However, the value we are dealing with here is different because crucial developments took place in education among Jews and non-Jews in the Western world during the modern period itself, and these developments must therefore be included in our discussion.

I. Christian Perspectives

The Early Modern Period

The Reformation brought heightened interest in education to Christian Europe. A key element in Luther's revolution was a renewed emphasis on consulting the Bible directly for religious guidance. The Catholic Church viewed the Bible as the chief source of its doctrines and practices, but it also insisted that the Bible could be properly understood only with the help of interpretations officially sanctioned by Church authorities. Luther fervently rejected this approach. The concept of the "priesthood of all believers" meant that everyone should cultivate a relationship of faith with God without human intermediaries, and from this imperative, it followed that all people should read the Bible for themselves. For this reason, Luther encouraged literacy among lay Christians in a way that Catholicism had not.[1]

However, Luther soon became concerned about the dangers of allowing ordinary individuals to read the Bible without proper guidance, and as a result, he changed his mind on this issue; Bible reading now had to be done with the expert supervision of pastors and within the confines of the lessons taught by catechism. Nonetheless, Luther's emphasis on reading the Bible encouraged Protestants to become educated not just about this one text but about other areas of knowledge as well. As a consequence, by the end of the early modern period, levels of education in Protestant countries tended to be higher than in Catholic ones.[2]

The Catholic Church did not stand by passively in the face of these developments. The Catholic reaction to the Reformation, known as the "Counter-Reformation," saw the establishment of the Jesuit monastic order, which would have a significant impact on Catholic education. The Jesuits were an elite group directly responsible to the pope; their mission was to counter the effects of the Reformation and to convert non-Christians throughout the world to Christianity. To accomplish these goals, the Jesuits provided their members with rigorous intellectual training. The founder of the Jesuit Order, Ignatius Loyola (1491–1556), had once been a professional soldier, and he brought a military-style discipline to this training.[3] The result was a high standard of learning not just for members of the Jesuit Order but for Catholics in general. Jesuits became teachers at Catholic institutions throughout Europe and upgraded the quality of their schools. They also established their own educational institutions that were of high quality as well, and many of them are still in existence today.[4]

Another major development regarding education in this period had to do with the fact that nation-states had begun to emerge, with the ruler of each state determining which form of Christianity was to be the state's official religion. This meant that education was now under the jurisdiction not just of religious authorities but also of the sovereigns. In each state, Church officials worked together with the sovereigns to set educational standards, implement taxation to support the schools, and allocate resources to those schools. These changes were significant because now that political rulers were involved in education, the religious authorities saw their control over education weakened. Thus, Europe took an important step towards the development of secular education that would become widespread in later centuries.[5]

The Enlightenment

Throughout the early modern period, educational opportunities in Europe greatly expanded, with each country establishing a wide variety of educational institutions from the elementary to the university level. In the same country, one could find schools that were communally funded alongside those that were privately funded; those that were religious in orientation alongside those that were more vocational in focus; and those that catered to boys alongside those that catered to girls – and these were only some of the types of educational institutions that existed in this period. Moreover, rich Europeans often became educated without attending schools because they could afford private tutors. In addition, with the printing press operational throughout the early modern period, a far greater quantity of written material was available to Europeans than during the medieval period, which only increased the educational level of Europeans.[6] Literacy rates therefore climbed throughout Europe. For instance, it is estimated that by 1800, in most of northwestern Europe, more than half the males could sign their names, and even more could read a simple text.[7]

But access to education in Europe was by no means universal, and when it was available, its quality was highly uneven. This was in part because no European country had established an organized, government-run school system for all its citizens; the variety of schools just described were mostly independent of one another. Not surprisingly, it was the lower classes that were the most disadvantaged by this situation. Literacy rates were far lower in this sector of the population than among the middle and upper classes, and even when individuals in the latter classes were literate, their levels of education were minimal.[8] Thus, even when the Enlightenment got underway in the eighteenth century and brought forth new and exciting ideas in several areas of learning, the production and discussion of these ideas were confined mainly to an elite class of intellectuals.

However, some Enlightenment thinkers entertained views that would eventually inspire Europeans to believe that everyone should receive a formal education and that it should be of good quality. These thinkers argued that all human beings were born with the same intellectual capacities and that the only difference between them was how those capacities were cultivated. John Locke famously referred to the human mind at birth as a *tabula rasa*, a "blank slate," upon which new ideas could be imprinted. We take this viewpoint for granted nowadays, but at the time, it was revolutionary in pointing the way towards the belief that all people should become educated in order to lead better lives and to contribute to society.[9]

It was in the nineteenth century that these notions were put into actual practice. In the early part of this century, European countries began to greatly broaden people's access to formal education by building school systems with taxpayer money.[10] There were a number of drivers for publicly funded education. Some who supported it were idealists. Liberals in this era believed that humankind was steadily progressing towards perfection, and they regarded education as key to moving that process forward. Conservatives had more nationalistic interests. They saw education as a means to cultivate and solidify national identity among the masses in their respective countries. Still others supported public education for pragmatic reasons. People in the middle and upper classes saw it as a way to ensure stability in society; education would give people the skills to succeed in the new industrial economy so that they would obey the law and resist being involved in crime, which was growing in the crowded cities that had been created by industrialization. Education would also encourage the lower classes to reject political radicalism, which had attracted individuals from this sector of the population and had periodically inspired violent insurrection. But many in the lower classes also supported the idea of public education for pragmatic reasons. They saw education as a means to achieve upward mobility.[11]

The process of implementing public education varied considerably from one Western country to another. To simplify matters, I will briefly trace the development of public education in the US. That is a good country to look at here because it set trends for public education in the Western world as a whole.

The major figures who shaped the American republic in its early years of existence very much appreciated the value of making education available to everyone. Benjamin Franklin and Thomas Jefferson were Enlightenment thinkers heavily influenced by John Locke, and they were particularly outspoken about education. They saw it as a way to instil in Americans the ideals of freedom, liberty, and democracy upon which their new country had been founded. However, their views remained in the realm of theory and did not result in the reform of the spotty school system in this period or in the establishment of new educational institutions.[12]

Throughout the nineteenth century, a system of public education slowly began to take shape in the US. A number of arguments were made in support of such a system, some of them similar to those that had been made by Europeans. One was that the success of the American republic required that citizens think intelligently about the issues important to the nation in order to participate in its civic life, and public education was therefore needed to prepare them for this responsibility. Another argument was that the US was composed of diverse ethnic and religious groups, and public education was therefore necessary for them to coalesce into a unified nation. Finally, there was the pragmatic motive. Public education was needed to prepare individuals for employment in various professions and to create a healthy economy.[13]

The first major step in the founding of a public system of education in the US was the establishment of tax-supported elementary schools. According to the Tenth Amendment to the US Constitution, education was under the auspices of the individual states, and so it was up to each state to establish schools that were publicly funded. By 1870, all the states had done so. As a result, the US soon had one of the highest literacy rates in the world.[14]

The years between the end of the Civil War in 1865 and 1920 saw another series of important developments in American public education. One was a campaign to make a minimal level of education compulsory for all Americans. That initiative was highly successful. One by one, the American states passed legislation to that effect, and by 1918 all of them required children to complete elementary school.[15]

Another important development was the strengthening of high school education. Before the twentieth century, high schools in the US were private institutions, and they were attended by elite sectors of the population in preparation for college. But the idea gradually took hold that high school had to be made accessible to everyone, and the states therefore moved to ensure that high schools were publicly funded as well. As result, by the mid-twentieth century, high school graduation rates in the US were far ahead of those in Europe. In fact, the American policy of encouraging young adults to be educated past the age of fourteen set the US apart from Europe for most of the twentieth century.[16]

The rapid growth and improvement in education at the high school level was accompanied by similar trends at the college and university levels. Colleges had been established in America in colonial times, modelled after Oxford and Cambridge in England. Like their British counterparts, these institutions catered primarily to the wealthy. Their curriculum consisted of the seven liberal arts that had been taught in European universities since medieval times. Some colleges were also founded for the specific purpose of training ministers. These included Harvard and Yale.[17]

In the first decades of the twentieth century, American colleges grew in number, and the curriculums they offered became increasingly diverse as well. Some of the colleges were established by private donors, but public money also became available for that purpose.[18] Colleges and universities experienced a growth spurt after the Second World War, in part because of the large numbers of soldiers returning from military service who now needed an education and job training. From this point onwards, America led the world in higher education, and to a large extent that remains the case today.[19]

The US was by no means the only country in the West that made immense progress in education. Throughout the twentieth century, European countries increased the number of educational institutions at all levels, improved the curriculums offered in them, and expanded their accessibility. In recent decades, the quality of US education has declined in comparison to that of other Western countries at the elementary and secondary school levels, though American universities continue to be ranked among the best in the world.[20]

Conclusions

Once again, the Enlightenment appears to have been a turning point in European culture, this time with respect to education. In this period, the notion took root that every individual should have the opportunity to receive a formal education in order to become a contributing member of society to the best of their abilities. However, it would be well into the nineteenth century before that notion was implemented in practice, and even then, the rate of implementation varied considerably from country to country. Nonetheless, over the past two centuries, the West has built the best educational institutions in the world, and there is no question that these institutions have been a major factor in the success it has achieved in so many fields and disciplines. Western achievements in the economic, intellectual, and artistic spheres would not have been possible had schools and universities not provided access to the most advanced knowledge and the best training in these areas.

II.   Jewish Perspectives

The Early Modern Period

By the beginning of the early modern period, the Jewish population in Europe had shifted dramatically eastward. During the centuries of the late medieval period, Jews had been expelled from most of western and central Europe, and many of them had moved to Poland-Lithuania where regional rulers welcomed them because they believed that Jews had talents and skills for developing their economies. Jews, in fact, lived up to those expectations, and they soon became integral to economic life in this part of Europe.

In many respects, Jewish communities in Poland-Lithuania inherited the culture of medieval Ashkenaz in which Torah study was a central value, but eventually these communities developed an intellectual culture that exceeded that of their medieval predecessors. They built an unprecedented number of yeshivas, which became a source of great pride for Jews in this part of Europe, and their rabbis were among the most distinguished in the Jewish world at the time. Moreover, the culture of Torah study had an impact on the lay Jewish population. Significant numbers of ordinary Jews in Poland-Lithuania were lifelong students of rabbinic literature, even though they had no rabbinic titles and no official rabbinic positions in their communities.[21]

However, Jewish education for most Jews in eastern Europe in the early modern period was not much better than it had been in prior centuries. The gap between the intellectual elite and everyone else remained and may have even widened. Education had now become more of a communal responsibility than it had been in the medieval period, but this did not mean that the quality of education improved. Teachers continued to be paid poorly and to have low social standing, and the quality of instruction they provided was therefore wanting as well. Most important, the educational framework in medieval Ashkenaz persisted, and that framework allowed only a select group of young men to become accomplished Torah scholars. By the time boys reached their early teens, most were no longer in school and were being taught a trade. Only a small number of them, those deemed most gifted, went on to a yeshiva for higher learning. As a consequence, advancement to yeshivas tended to be limited to certain groups: boys from families of distinguished Torah scholars that provided children with the inspiration and home instruction to succeed in their studies, and boys from wealthy families that could pay for private education. Girls from all backgrounds had no opportunity to pursue education beyond the elementary level, though they often continued to receive informal education at home.[22]

In the early modern period, there were far fewer Jews in western and central Europe than in eastern Europe because of the expulsions mentioned earlier, but in the seventeenth century, western and central Europe saw growth in their Jewish communities once again as a more tolerant atmosphere began to take hold in these regions. This growth accelerated in the eighteenth century when the Enlightenment was in full swing.

Most important for our concerns is that significant developments were taking place in the central European part of the Jewish world with respect to education. Prominent Jewish figures were inspired by the relatively tolerant atmosphere there to engage in new and innovative thinking about this issue.

The impetus for such thinking came in part from outside the Jewish community. European intellectuals and political figures in central Europe who supported the Enlightenment began to believe that Jews, who had been mostly segregated from Europeans up to this point, could become valuable members of European society if given the chance. In their view, Jews just had to be "rehabilitated" by being taught the "superior" ways of European culture, which meant providing them with a European education. The first significant attempt to put this theory into practice was initiated by Joseph II (1741–90), the Habsburg emperor. In 1782, he issued an Edict of Toleration that, in the spirit of the Enlightenment, sought to create a more tolerant society, and it had provisions to integrate the Jews of Lower Austria into Austrian society. One of those provisions addressed education: Jews were now required either to attend European schools or to establish their own schools with a modern curriculum. The same edict also opened up the universities to Jews.[23]

The inspiration for making changes in Jewish education in central Europe came from within the Jewish community as well. Some Jewish intellectuals in this region joined their non-Jewish colleagues in hoping that Jews would become integrated into European society, and they too believed that reforms in Jewish education would accomplish this goal.

The interest taken by Jewish intellectuals in this matter in part reflected broader changes taking place in the Jewish communities of western and central Europe. Jews in these regions were beginning to question in unprecedented fashion the authority of the rabbis and the Judaism they represented. Jews were increasingly coming into contact with non-Jewish culture, and some were very attracted to it, and one consequence of these developments was that Jews were affected by the same forces of Enlightenment that had caused Christian Europeans to challenge religious dogmas. As a result, increasing numbers of Jews expressed a desire to leave their segregated Jewish communities and become part of European society. Thus, the Jewish intellectuals who pushed for the integration of Jews into European society were expressing views that reflected sentiments percolating in the Jewish community as a whole.[24]

There was one specific group of Jewish intellectuals that acted decisively to foster the integration of Jews into European society through education: the founders of the Haskalah. This movement, which began in Germany, is often referred to as "the Jewish Enlightenment." The goal of the Haskalah was to acculturate Jews to European society, and for that purpose, its leaders established schools for Jewish children in the late eighteenth century in major German cities to familiarize them with European culture. These schools combined a traditional Jewish curriculum with studies focused on science, European literature, and languages. The schools were specifically designed for poor Jewish children because their founders believed that this was the sector of the Jewish community most in need of enlightened education.[25]

It would take some time for initiatives of the kind undertaken by Joseph II and the proponents of the Haskalah to have an impact on Jews. At the end of the eighteenth century, the number of young Jews getting an education in secular studies was still quite small. Only in the nineteenth century would these numbers grow, and they would grow exponentially.

CHRISTIANITY VS. JUDAISM

Once again, the critical question is how the situation regarding education among Jews in early modern Europe compared to that of the surrounding non-Jewish culture. In addressing this question, we run into the same problems we faced earlier in our exploration of the medieval period. Comparisons of this kind are very difficult to make because the character of early modern Jewish culture varied considerably from region to region, as did that of European culture, and those variations affected the way education was handled. Moreover, how one makes such comparisons depends on the definitions of such terms like "education" and "literacy."

As was the case in our treatment of the late medieval period, we can say more about Jewish and European attitudes towards learning and the cultivation of the intellect, and it would seem that in the period we are now considering, the gap between the views of the two groups on this issue narrowed, largely because of developments on the non-Jewish side of the ledger. As we saw earlier in this chapter, the Protestant Reformation had an impact on European intellectual culture and education because a key element of Luther's revolution was his insistence that all believers should develop a direct relationship with God unmediated by Church authorities, and that in turn meant that believers had to be able to read the Bible. Literacy therefore became an important concern, and this led to a greater interest among Europeans in education in general. Europeans also made significant advances in intellectual culture outside the religious realm. There were now many more educational institutions and opportunities in Europe than there had been in the medieval era. In addition, the printing press, invented at the end of the medieval era, was making books far more available than they had been in prior centuries.[26]

However, my sense is that the differences between Jewish and Christian culture regarding attitudes to learning and intellectual achievement persisted in the early modern period, with Jews continuing to place greater emphasis on this dimension of life than Christians did. I say this despite the important developments in both cultures that I have spoken about here because traditional religion from earlier centuries still had great influence in both cultures. Most European Jews at this time lived in Poland-Lithuania where traditional Rabbinic Judaism still held sway, which meant that Jews there maintained a sense of reverence for the intellectual dimension of religion that had characterized Rabbinic Judaism for centuries. In western and central Europe, rabbinic authority was increasingly being challenged by Jews sympathetic to the Haskalah. However, the number of Jews in these parts of Europe was relatively small. Moreover, the inroads that the Haskalah made there were modest, with most Jews still maintaining a traditional rabbinic way of life. It is also important to keep in mind that the Haskalah, at least in its initial phase in Germany, did not reject Rabbinic Judaism. The schools it established provided an education in rabbinic texts while supplementing it with an education in secular subjects. On the Christian side, the Reformation did not go quite as far as Rabbinic Judaism in its emphasis on the intellectual dimension of religion. Literacy and direct engagement with the Bible did not become religious imperatives in the way that Torah study did among Jews. The Enlightenment certainly spawned much greater interest in learning and intellectual matters, but one has to keep in mind that most Europeans even during the Enlightenment remained devoted to traditional Christianity, a religion that accorded a place for the intellect less exalted than one finds in Rabbinic Judaism.

We must also highlight once again the difference between the two cultures with respect to curiosity. Despite the stunning advances in science in early modern Europe and the simultaneous growth of interest in education, there was still a prominent strand of thinking in European culture that saw curiosity as a manifestation of pride which was considered the worst of the vices and was rooted in Original Sin. Europeans in the early modern period recognized that curiosity could be good if the seeker was a moral person and the knowledge sought was for the good of human society. But curiosity was regarded as bad when it concerned worldly matters. Investigations of such matters were at best useless and frivolous and at worst led one to heresy or atheism. Many Europeans viewed the advances of the Scientific Revolution through this negative lens. The tide began to turn in favour of curiosity only in the eighteenth century, and even then it took some time before Europeans fully embraced curiosity as a positive human trait.[27]

In Jewish communities in the early modern period, curiosity was not viewed any more negatively than it had been in previous centuries. The rabbis continued to warn that the study of creation and the heavenly realm should be approached with great caution, and in this period this concern was focused primarily on Kabbalah, which had become the dominant source of Jewish theology. But curiosity was not regarded as a vice, nor was it seen as having brought about the fall of humanity in the Garden of Eden. Indeed, curiosity was to be embraced as long as it did not inspire the study of esoteric matters before one was truly ready.

The Modern Period

Our discussion in this chapter and the last reveals a remarkably consistent pattern in the way European Jews approached education from the second century CE up to the modern era. In the rabbinic, medieval, and early modern periods, European Jews greatly valued learning and the cultivation of the intellect more than Christians did. However, their feelings about education seem not to have had the same intensity. Jews may have revered the rabbis for their knowledge and sharp minds, but those sentiments did not translate into a willingness to invest in educational systems that would give all Jewish children an equal opportunity to develop these qualities. That opportunity was reserved for the select few.

As we move into the early nineteenth century, much about Jewish education in eastern Europe remained the same as it had been in prior centuries, and this would continue to be the case up until the mid-twentieth century when the Holocaust effectively put an end to Jewish culture in this part of the world. Eastern European Jewry maintained a vibrant rabbinic culture, and its yeshivas were among the most vibrant centres for Torah study that the Jewish world had ever seen. However, when it came to educating the young, eastern European Jews carried on the customs of earlier centuries. Education was of poor quality, teachers were badly paid and of low status, and only a small number of male students entered the yeshivas.[28]

It was a different story for the Jews of western and central Europe. The new direction in Jewish education that had been taken by some Jews in this part of the Jewish world at the end of the eighteenth century began to gain momentum in the nineteenth. Jews here became increasingly interested in secular education.

This trend was rooted in fundamental changes in the political status of Jews in western and central Europe in the nineteenth century.

Throughout this century, countries in these regions of Europe, one by one, granted Jews citizenship and full rights, and when Europeans welcomed Jews into their society, they did so with the expectation that Jews would become fully integrated from a cultural standpoint. Europeans also believed that education was critical for achieving that goal, much as earlier Enlightenment thinkers did. Thus, European governments made efforts to ensure that Jews would receive a modern secular education. In some places, it was the government that modernized school systems for Jews; in other places, Jews voluntarily modernized the curriculums of their own schools. Similar reforms were undertaken even in eastern Europe where the emancipation of Jews lagged behind that of other regions in Europe. Jews in eastern Europe were now under Russian rule, and the Russian government established state-sponsored schools for Jews in the 1830s and 1840s that included secular studies.[29]

In the first half of the nineteenth century, these initiatives were not terribly successful. Many Jews were leery of sending their children to modern schools, whether they were state-sponsored or run by fellow Jews, for they feared that the intent of the schools was to lead their children away from Judaism. Indeed, such fears were not unfounded. European schools in this period were often run by Christian clergy, who would have likely been happy to fulfil the worst fears of Jews on this issue. Moreover, Europeans in general were not positively disposed towards Judaism just because they believed in tolerance for Jews; the old prejudices remained. Even the most enlightened European intellectuals and government figures hoped that Jews would eventually leave behind their "primitive" religion and become Christians, and they saw education as a vehicle for accomplishing that goal.[30]

However, in the second half of the nineteenth century, Jews began to see the virtue of giving their children a modern education, and they increasingly gave preference to non-Jewish institutions of learning for that purpose. By the end of the nineteenth century, the rise in the numbers of Jews attending European schools and universities was dramatic, particularly in central Europe. In fact, Jewish enrolments in these institutions were now well out of proportion to their numbers in the population. For instance, in Austria in 1910, Jews made up 5 per cent of the population, but they accounted for 15 per cent of students in the gymnasia and *Realschulen* (the first two tiers of a three-tiered secondary school system), 33 per cent of students in the gymnasia in Vienna, and 18 per cent of university students. In 1880, Jews made up a stunning 50 per cent of the student body in the medical school of Vienna University, one of Europe's most prestigious institutions for training doctors. There were similar disproportions of Jews in schools and universities in Russia. The highest disproportions of this kind were to be found in German schools.[31]

In the US, there was a similar pattern. American Jews were granted citizenship and rights soon after the republic was founded, but up to the middle of the nineteenth century, Jews in the US generally did not send their children to non-Jewish schools, preferring to send them to their own. Yet by the end of the nineteenth century, Jews were taking advantage of the public school system and the universities in large numbers that here as well were disproportionate to their percentage of the population. In fact, American Jews developed something of a love affair with educational institutions in the US, expressing fervent enthusiasm for the opportunities they provided. Jews were also willing to sacrifice a great deal in order to get their children educated. Jews were unique among immigrants to America in the early twentieth century for sending their children to school rather than into the workforce, even if it meant that the parents had to work more hours and live in greater poverty than other immigrants did.[32]

The numbers of Jews in educational institutions in Europe and the US eventually stirred a backlash, and quotas on Jews attending these institutions were established in some countries, including the US. These measures diminished the high rate of Jewish enrolment in these institutions, but after the Second World War, the situation gradually improved as Western countries began to combat discrimination against minorities in general. Today, Jews remain disproportionately represented in educational institutions in the West, as I noted in my introductory chapter.[33]

What explains the passion for education among modernized Jews? They had certainly valued education prior to the modern period, but as we have seen repeatedly, they did not pay nearly as much attention to education as modern Jews often imagine. Only in the modern period has education become a near obsession among Jews.

The obvious answer is that modernized Jews were simply being sensible and pragmatic. They understood that one could succeed in Western culture through merit and that the type of merit this culture most valued could be acquired only through a good education. However, there were plenty of other minority and immigrant groups in the modern West that wanted to succeed, particularly in the US, but they did not focus on education the way Jews did. What then made Jews different? Why were they unusually passionate about education?

The answer to this question, I believe, is provided by the central argument of this book: Jews were different on the issue of education because rabbinic culture for centuries had ingrained in them a number of values, one of them being a deep reverence for learning and intellectual achievement, and so by the time the modern period arrived, the centuries-long obsession that Jews had with the intellectual dimension of life had become almost instinctive. So it is no surprise that Jews continued to uphold that value when they became modernized. Not only was it embedded in their mindset, it also happened to be a value that was of great utility for succeeding in the non-Jewish world of which they were now part.

Modern Jews took two important steps to translate the esteem accorded to intellectual achievement in Rabbinic Judaism into a value that served their purposes. First, they transformed the passion for intellectual achievement in Rabbinic Judaism into a secular ideal. The focus was no longer on religious learning but on learning in the secular sphere. Second, they gave their children far more opportunities than rabbinic culture did to excel intellectually. A comprehensive education was no longer just for the select few who were gifted, but for everyone.

These transformations in Jewish attitudes towards education were not necessarily conscious. For most Jews, they probably were not. Yet as I have argued repeatedly, important cultural transformations can take place unconsciously, and the matter we are discussing here, I believe, provides an excellent example of this phenomenon.

Jews cannot take all the credit here. An important factor that helped Jews pursue education in the modern West was its availability. Western countries funded public schools that everyone could attend and universities were open to all. As we have noted, in the early twentieth century, quota systems were eventually established by some universities in some countries to limit the number of Jews admitted to these institutions, and yet Jews remained determined to take advantage of educational opportunities in the West at all levels in a way that no other subgroup in the West was.

There is an irony in all this. Rabbinic Judaism had made intellectual achievement a core value in Jewish culture since the first century CE, but it was only in the modern period when Jews finally left behind the life of Rabbinic Judaism that they cultivated that value on a broad scale.[34]

Conclusions

We can now summarize what we have learned in the last two chapters. It seems that prior to modernity, Jewish culture did not differ from Christian culture in Europe regarding education nearly as much as modern Jews have often assumed. Jews invested far less in education, and Christians far more in it, than has commonly been believed. The key difference between the two cultures had to do with a related issue: their divergent attitudes towards learning and the cultivation of the intellect. Jewish culture tended to value these traits more than Christian culture did.

The difference in attitudes towards the intellectual dimension of life would eventually result in differences regarding education, but this would happen quite late. When the modern period arrived, Western Jews developed a strong desire to send their children to public schools, and then to universities to get advanced degrees. While there were certainly pragmatic motives here, the rabbinic obsession with intellectual achievement undoubtedly provided impetus to Jews to look to education as the key to success, even if they were not necessarily conscious of the rabbinic origins of that impetus. And succeed they did. Education helped Jews enter high-paying professions, become leading thinkers in a range of intellectual disciplines, and rack up achievements in the arts.

I am not the first one to suggest a connection between the centuries-old rabbinic emphasis on intellectual accomplishment and the overrepresentation of Jews in modern Western institutions of higher learning. Nor am I the first to suggest that the focus on education among Western Jews paid huge dividends in bringing them immense success. As I noted in the introduction to the previous chapter, other scholars and popular commentators have made the same points. To my knowledge, however, no one has made the important distinction between Jewish attitudes towards intellectual accomplishment and Jewish attitudes towards education. The two are not necessarily the same, and as we have seen throughout the past two chapters, they were not connected in Jewish culture for the better part of two millennia prior to modernity. Jews could have great admiration for the knowledge and intellectual abilities of their rabbis, but that did not mean that they were willing to invest resources in providing all Jewish children with a high-quality education.

Still, the reverence that Jews had for learning and the cultivation of the intellect across so many centuries was highly significant. It meant that when Jews entered the modern period and became part of the European world around them, ingrained in them was a value that was crucial for success in their new environment. Even more important, they transformed that value into a passion for educating their young. Cultivating the intellect was no longer just for the select few; rather, it was something that Jews should undertake on a mass scale, and thus Jews became deeply devoted to providing the best education for their children. If education had not been a central concern in Jewish culture up to that point, it certainly was now.

Some may wonder whether this chapter has undermined the central argument of this book. If Jews were not all that interested in education in the medieval and early modern periods, how could they have absorbed the four rabbinic values that, I claim, prepared them for modernity? Did that not require a certain amount of education in the teachings of the rabbis? As I have repeatedly argued, those values were so fundamental to Rabbinic Judaism that even without a high-level education, Jews would have been familiar with them, even if only on a subliminal level. They were the unwritten premises on which much of Rabbinic Judaism was based, and it was this form of Judaism that had governed their lives for so many centuries.

PART THREE

Final Matters

Chapter Eleven

Conclusions

In the opening chapter, I described the tantalizing mystery that prompted me to write this book: how have Jews achieved success in the modern world that has been wildly disproportionate to their numbers? Over the past two centuries, Jews in the West have amassed a record of accomplishments in the economic, intellectual, and artistic realms unlike that of any other minority or subgroup, and no clear or obvious reason explains why. Deepening the mystery is how quickly this success came about. Jews began excelling in the nineteenth century within a mere generation of gaining citizenship and equal rights in Western countries, and two generations later they were already overrepresented in some of the West's most prestigious fields and disciplines. Deepening the mystery even further is the historical background against which this success occurred. Before the modern period, Jews had lived as a marginalized and often persecuted minority for the better part of two millennia, and even though the situation for Jews in the West improved considerably when the modern period arrived, marginalization and persecution remained a problem. In fact, it was in this period that Jews experienced the worst catastrophe in their history: the Holocaust. Jews therefore had to overcome remarkably difficult historical conditions to experience the success they did in the modern period. How then did Jews do it? What accounts for their disproportionate achievements over the past two centuries? No minority in the modern era, or perhaps in any other, has been able to accomplish so much, so quickly, and under such challenging circumstances.

Numerous solutions to this mystery have been proposed. The soundest of these from an academic standpoint have attempted to account for the success of Jews in one or another endeavour by arguing that modern Jews were in the right place at the right time with the right skills. Jewish economic historians have been particularly enamoured of this approach. I emphasized early on in this study that this approach has merit and that scholars who have adopted it have done a great deal to illuminate our understanding of modern Jewish achievement. The difficulty with this approach is that it is piecemeal. It fails to see the larger picture. Modern Jews have had extraordinary success in too many fields, locations, and times for it to be attributed solely to specific historical circumstances in each instance. There must therefore be some unifying factor in addition to these explanations that accounts for the broad and variegated success that Jews have experienced.

The cultural hypothesis, which I have adopted in this book, provides this type of explanation and must therefore be seen as a critical ingredient, if not *the* critical ingredient, in accounting for the success of modern Jews. It surmises that modern Jews achieved success because of cultural traits that had been ingrained in them for centuries by their religion. However, this hypothesis has shortcomings of its own. Some of these shortcomings have to do with the limitations of the individuals who have supported the cultural hypothesis. They have tended to be popular writers whose arguments have not been detailed or informed enough to be convincing. Their arguments have also been plagued by inaccuracies and exaggerations.

Other problems with the cultural hypothesis have to do with more serious issues involving the hypothesis itself. Scholars, especially in recent years, have tended to reject the cultural hypothesis, and for sound reasons. The difficulty most often cited as its fatal flaw is that the cultural traits deemed responsible for the success of modern Jews are religious in origin, but many of the most successful modern Jews have been secular. A second difficulty is that the cultural hypothesis fails to explain why the greatest achievements of modern Jews have been heavily concentrated among Western Jews, not Jews from Muslim lands. A third difficulty that, to my knowledge, has not been noticed by others, but is just as serious as the other two, is that the cultural traits often identified as responsible for modern Jewish achievement are shared by modern Western culture as a whole. Thus, the cultural hypothesis may explain how Jews succeeded in Western culture but not how they succeeded in such disproportionate fashion.

Despite these challenges, I embarked on this project with the belief that the cultural hypothesis still held the greatest promise for explaining the success of modern Jews and that its difficulties could be overcome. The preceding chapters have been dedicated to this task, and it is now time to sum up my findings and formulate a series of conclusions that, I hope, will be persuasive and compelling.

The Four Values in Western Culture

My explanation for the success of Jews in the modern period began with the premise that Jews could not have achieved what they did in the Western world had the West itself not experienced similar success as well, and therefore I expended considerable effort explaining the success of the West. I argued, as others have, that the West's dominance in the economic, intellectual, and artistic realms in the modern period can be attributed at least in part to the development of certain values in Western culture that began reaching a critical stage of maturity just as the modern period began. I focused on four of those values: human autonomy in relation to God and the cosmos, freedom of thought and expression, an emphasis on life in this world, and education. These values as a group were not the only reasons for the success of the West. Other factors undoubtedly played a role, such as geography and demography, factors about which recent authors have written extensively. Nonetheless, I focused exclusively on those four values because I felt they were most relevant for explaining the success of Jews.

My analysis of the evolution of these values in Western culture was not as comprehensive as my treatment of their development in Jewish culture. Still, that analysis provided the necessary context for evaluating the success of modern Jews.

Two general observations that are important for this study emerge from my discussion of the development of the four values in Western culture. First, all four values evolved in the West rather slowly. This point has to be emphasized because it has been common for historians of the West to project their own modern perspective onto the past eras in which they specialize. The result has been that past eras have often been depicted as periods of dramatic breakthrough regarding the four values, when in fact that was not the case.

This tendency is still evident in some quarters. Scholars of the Renaissance at one time spoke with great enthusiasm about the contributions this era made to the development of the modern world. It was here, according to these scholars, that we find the roots of the modern notions of individualism and secularism. Some textbooks on European history still depict the Renaissance in this manner. Recent scholarship, however, has shown that such judgments have been exaggerated. The Renaissance was certainly an extraordinary period, but it was less modern than it has often been made out to be. It was an era that in a number of respects was actually quite religious and conservative.

The same can be said about other major periods. Scholars of the Reformation era, for instance, have often identified this period as the source of the modern concept of the individual, much as Renaissance scholars had claimed regarding the era they studied. But once again, more recent scholarship has shown that this claim lacks support. Luther's notion of the "priesthood of all believers" did not mean that everyone had a right to decide for themselves how to relate to God, and therefore he was not really espousing individualism in its modern form.

If there *was* a period that did indeed mark a turning point in the development of the four values, it was perhaps the Enlightenment. That was the era when all these values went through significant transformations. However, if the Enlightenment was a turning point for the four values, it was not necessarily as sharp a turning point as some have imagined. Each value continued evolving over the two centuries that followed the Enlightenment until it achieved its fully modern form. Moreover, not all Westerners were willing to adopt the modern versions of these values. Many adhered to older versions of them or rejected them altogether, and this remains the case today, especially in the US, which has a large population of conservative Christians. Thus, the Enlightenment did not represent as clean a break with the past as many scholars, until recently, have depicted it to be.

Another important point that becomes clear from my investigation of the evolution of the four values in Western culture is that their evolution was not inevitable. This point needs to be emphasized because academics have often portrayed the development of Western ideas over the centuries as a process of continuous progress towards modernity. In truth, the development of the four values was neither continuous nor inevitable. The process was often "two steps forward, one step back," or, in some instances, "one step forward, two steps back," and it was not inevitable that the process would lead to modernity.

Again, the preceding chapters provided examples of this point. For instance, with regard to our first value – human autonomy in the metaphysical sense – the Protestant Reformation in some respects represented a step *away* from the form this value would later take in modernity. The medieval Church had allowed elements of Pelagianism to seep into its thinking on human autonomy before God, and that element left room for human initiative in the salvation process, but Luther and others in the Protestant revolution wanted to return to a purely Augustinian understanding of Original Sin and Predestination, which essentially precluded this sort of autonomy. Only in later centuries did the idea of human autonomy in the metaphysical sense re-emerge, with renewed vigour.

I highlight these observations as they pertain to the four values of concern to us in order to ensure an accurate understanding of their evolution in Western culture, for only with such an understanding in place can we comprehend how Jews flourished so impressively when the modern period dawned. If there is a common link in these observations, it is that they all point to the importance of exercising caution against the temptation of reading too much of our own modern values back into history.

There is one more point to be emphasized regarding my treatment of the four values in Western culture: it should not be regarded as an attack on Christianity. Certainly, the development of these values, in many respects, represented an attempt to overcome Christian thinking. Yet in a good number of instances, it was Christianity that inspired their development. Thus, for example, if Luther's notion of the priesthood of all believers was not yet the beginning of the modern notion that the individual had autonomy in relation to the cosmos, it certainly made that notion possible in later centuries. This view of autonomy was encouraged by the pursuit of philosophy and science in medieval and early modern Christianity. Those disciplines regarded reason as a divine gift that human beings were required to use to gain insight into the world around them.

Similarly, the invention of the concept of natural rights, including freedom of thought and expression, owed something to Christianity. Like the notion of the autonomous individual in the metaphysical sense, this idea grew out of the notion of the priesthood of all believers. The belief that human beings should form a direct relationship with God without the assistance of Church intermediaries evolved into the view that the individual had a right to determine what their relationship with God should be to begin with, even if it displeased the Church.

The value of education had Christian roots as well. In the medieval period, Christian institutions were largely responsible for preserving ancient learning, not just that of Christianity but also that of Greece and Rome, and these institutions also developed new types of learning. Initially, the monasteries were important in this regard, but they were eventually superseded by the universities, which began as institutions affiliated with the Church. In sum, Christianity is to be commended for its contributions to the modernization of the West.

The Four Values in Jewish Culture

It is against all this background that we can best understand the success of Jews in the modern period. In the pre-modern Western world, Jews developed the same four values that Christians did, but in Jewish culture, these values were developed earlier, they achieved a more robust form, and they were therefore more deeply ingrained in Jewish culture than in Christian culture when the modern period began. As a result, Jews were, in critical respects, better equipped to take on the challenges of modernity than Christians were, and that is why Jews began to amass achievements in so many areas, with such speed, and despite their history of marginalization and persecution.

The irony in this argument is that it has required us to spend far less time on the modern period than on the eighteen or so centuries prior to that period, even though it is the success of Jews in the modern period that we have been attempting to explain. The claim here is that Jews were unusually well-prepared for success in modernity because of the trajectory of their culture from Late Antiquity onwards, and therefore, we have had to focus our attention mostly on pre-modern Jewish and Christian culture.

One of my assumptions in comparing pre-modern Jewish and Christian cultures with respect to the four values was that the longer a people possesses a particular value, the more deeply embedded it becomes in its collective psychology. That is, the robustness of a value in a culture is determined not only by the emphasis given to it by that culture, but also by its longevity within that culture. Not everyone may agree with this assumption. The argument can be made that if two cultures possess a value and place the same emphasis on it for at least a generation, then that value will be ingrained equally in the two cultures in subsequent generations, regardless of its prior history. But I do not take this view. I believe that the length of time here matters, that the longer a culture upholds a value, the more it seeps into the thinking of its constituents, becomes instinctive to them, and influences their thinking and behaviour. Thus, my argument that modern Jews possessed the four values in more robust form than non-Jewish Westerners did is based in part on the greater longevity of these values in Jewish culture than in Christian culture. In some instances, the discrepancy was substantial. Some aspects of the four values developed in Jewish culture centuries before they developed in Christian culture.

It is important to emphasize that my arguments focused not just on the views of intellectual elites in Jewish and non-Jewish societies in the West but also on those of ordinary people in these societies. In order to explain the success of Jews in the modern West, all sectors of the Jewish population had to be taken into account, not just the intellectual sector, because much of the success that Jews achieved in the modern period was experienced by ordinary Jews. Such success was not just about Jews winning Nobel Prizes; it was also about Jews having high

average income levels or attending Ivy League schools in disproportionate numbers – markers that concerned ordinary Jews, not just those
who were unusually distinguished.

It was, of course, more difficult to determine what the common folk
in Jewish and non-Jewish society were thinking on any given issue
than it was to make such determinations about the intellectual elites in
the two societies. Jewish and Christian intellectual elites left us with far
more written material about their thought-worlds than ordinary people did, and we cannot assume that the latter were consistently aware
of, let alone agreed with, the views of the intellectual elites. However,
I tried to make reasonable judgments about what ordinary Jews and
Christians in the pre-modern West were thinking on the issues of concern to this study. Those judgments led me to argue throughout this
book that, from the beginning of the medieval period up to the modern period, what Jewish and Christian intellectual elites were thinking regarding the four values had to have influenced ordinary people
in their respective communities. The four values were tied to features
that were so fundamental to Jewish and Christian culture throughout
the centuries that ordinary people in both cultures would have likely
absorbed, in some measure, the views of their intellectuals on these
values.

When I speak of the advantage that ordinary Jews had over Christians regarding the four values, I include women. These values were so
fundamental to rabbinic culture that Jewish women would have also
absorbed the four values in unusually robust form in the medieval and
early modern periods just as men did. Of course, Jewish women did
not have the opportunity that men had to shape these values in pre-
modern Jewish culture or to make use of them in the modern period.
Prior to the modern period, women could not become rabbis, the figures most responsible for cultivating the four values.[1] And once the
modern period got under way and Jews began to succeed on account of
these values, opportunities for Jewish women to participate in that success were highly restricted, at least until relatively recently. Far fewer
modern Jewish women than men became leading figures in the economic, intellectual, and artistic realms until the advent of feminism in
the 1960s.[2]

However, this discrepancy between Jewish men and women both
prior to and after the advent of the modern period was not necessarily any worse that it was between men and women in the Western
world. I would also argue that Jewish women throughout the medieval
and early modern periods still played a crucial role in bringing about
the success of modern Jews by maintaining the four values in Jewish

culture. After all, it was they who were most responsible for raising Jewish children, male and female, and one can assume that they passed on to their children the four values alongside other rabbinic norms.[3] The communication of these values may not have been conscious, but there is good reason to believe that such communication took place. The four values were, again, fundamental to Jewish culture, and I have argued on more than one occasion that, like many cultural norms, they were often passed on without conscious intent.

Jewish women from the early rabbinic period onwards would have been especially important with regard to the cultivation of the third value: the emphasis placed on life in this world. I noted in my discussion of this value that the Jewish home was an important locus for its inculcation, and from the early rabbinic period up to the modern era, the home again was mostly under the jurisdiction of women. It was in the home that Jewish children were raised, an activity central to the this-worldly agenda of Rabbinic Judaism. The home was also critical for weekly Sabbath observance, which reinforced the importance of the present world by requiring Jewish families to gather for three mandatory meals once a week.

One may be tempted to argue that, prior to the modern period, the critical difference between Jewish men and women had to do with the last value I considered in this study: education. Here men clearly had opportunities denied to women, and if one accepts the old adage that "knowledge is power," this discrepancy had important negative consequences for women as the modern period began. Yet my chapter on education indicates that matters were not so simple. It is true that in the medieval and early modern periods, men could become rabbis while women could not, and that rabbis had considerable power in the shaping of Jewish culture. But I also demonstrated in that chapter that the vast majority of Jewish men from the rabbinic period onwards did not become rabbis, nor were they well-educated. So the discrepancy between Jewish men and women on this issue in pre-modern times was not as great as one might assume.[4]

However, these observations about Jewish women only graze the surface of a complex issue that cannot be adequately analysed here. The role that women have played in the success of modern Jews requires separate study.

Can any judgments be made about the relative importance of one or another of the four values in paving the way for Jewish success? Were some of these values more influential than others in helping Jews achieve what they did in the modern West?

It is difficult to answer these questions given the complex manner in which the four values evolved in Jewish and Christian culture over the centuries. However, there is one striking point that emerged from my analysis of these values that is relevant to this question. The value that is most commonly identified in modern popular culture as the reason for the success of Jews in the modern period is education. According to many people – and this includes not just Jews but a substantial number of non-Jews as well – education is usually the first thing that comes to mind as an explanation for the achievements of Jews in the modern era. The assumption is that Jews have excelled in the modern West because of their long-standing dedication to the education of their young.

Yet my chapter on education has shown that this view is highly problematic. Education, in fact, may have been the least important of the four values I have examined in this book to explain Jewish success. My analysis of this value demonstrated that over the centuries, Jews were not nearly as interested in educating their young as many have been led to believe. The more important value for Jewish success was a high regard for the cultivation of the intellect, a value that was related to education but did not necessarily translate into the belief that all Jews should be educated and educated well.

Eventually, education did become important for Jews, and one can assume that this interest was inspired in part by the reverence that Jews had always had for the cultivation of the intellect. But that interest appeared quite late. Only in the latter half of the nineteenth century did European and American Jews begin to focus on education to a disproportionate degree, and that was because they recognized that it was the best way to achieve success in Western society. Thus, the notion that everyone should be educated and educated well from a young age onwards is a relatively recent development in Jewish culture.

A major benefit of my comparison of Jewish and Christian cultures regarding the four values is that it allowed for a rigorous examination of the differences between the two cultures. These differences have been discussed for some time in the modern period but have never been subjected to a thorough academic inquiry. We noted in chapter 1 that rabbis, Jewish intellectuals, and popular Jewish writers throughout the modern period have spoken about the contrasts between Jewish and Christian culture regarding one or another of the four values, but they have not examined them sufficiently to see whether they were indeed valid. What has emerged from this study is that these differences hold up rather well in the face of close scrutiny. Jewish and Christian cultures did in fact differ in many of the ways that have been commonly pointed out.

There were, however, important discoveries that require us to qualify those differences. First of all, the differences were not nearly as stark as popular views have often made them out to be. Jewish and Christian cultures displayed a wide variety of opinions on each of the four values, and so when the two groups of opinions regarding a particular value were placed on a single spectrum, there was much overlap between them in the middle of the spectrum. It was only on the extreme ends of the spectrum that the differences were evident. Second, the differences between Jewish and Christian cultures regarding a particular value were dynamic; that is, they changed over time. For instance, even though, in our examination of the third value, Judaism tended to be more focused on matters of this world than Christianity was, the gap between the two religions changed significantly over time, so that by the time the early modern period was under way, the distinctions between them became increasingly narrow. Finally, there was one difference between the two cultures that has been much discussed in popular discourse but turned out to be inaccurate, and that again had to do with education. It is not clear that there was a distinction between Jewish and Christian cultures on this issue. We did discover, however, that the two cultures differed significantly on the related issue of their attitudes towards the cultivation of the intellect.

Caveats and Qualifications

It is important that I add a number of caveats and qualifications to the conclusions I have drawn here so that the nuances of my arguments are not lost. Specifically, I would like my readers to understand not just what I *am* saying in this book, but also what I am *not* saying. The following is a list of points to that effect:

1) I am not claiming that the contrasts I have drawn throughout this study between Jewish and Christian culture are absolute; they are only relative. It is not that Jewish culture developed the four values, while Christian culture did not. Both cultures cultivated the four values; it is just that Jews developed stronger versions of these values prior to the modern period.

2) I am not arguing that Jewish culture was modern before the modern period. Some Jewish scholars have treated one or another of the four values in Jewish culture in the same problematic manner that Western scholars have treated them in Christian culture. That is, Jewish scholars have sometimes made pre-modern Judaism sound more modern than it really was. I have done my best to resist that tendency. I have certainly given credit to the innovations of pre-modern Jewish culture regarding the four values, innovations that

put Jews ahead of their non-Jewish neighbours in the anticipation of modernity, but I have also done so cautiously in order to avoid giving the impression that Jews in pre-modern times were more advanced than was actually the case. In other words, I have tried to show that in key respects, pre-modern Jewish culture *anticipated* modernity more than pre-modern Christian culture did, not that it *was* modern.

3) I am not claiming that in the West, Jews were better prepared for modernity than Christians in all respects. Such a claim would be absurd. By the beginning of the nineteenth century, Western Christians were ahead of Jews in several areas – in some instances, far ahead:

a) Christians had developed an entire body of sophisticated scientific learning. Jews were certainly interested in science before the modern period, and some studied it avidly, but they were not innovators in this area of learning in the way that Christians were.

b) Christians had developed capitalism, as well as a body of economic theory that justified it. Jews in some parts of Europe participated in the capitalist system as it started to develop in the early modern period, and they were quite successful at it, but here again, Jews were not innovators either in the practice of capitalism or in the development of its theory.

c) Christians had established societies based on democracy and natural rights, and here too their innovations were accompanied by a well-developed body of theory. In fact, their writings on these matters were among the most important contributions that Western culture made to the world. Jews also had democratic institutions in their communities from the medieval period onwards. One could also argue that they had some idea of natural rights. However, by the beginning of the modern period, their thinking on such matters was not nearly as developed as it was in the Christian West.

d) Christians had developed a rich tradition of art and music. There were certainly Jewish artists and musicians prior to the modern period, but they made few meaningful original contributions in their respective fields compared to their Christian counterparts.

Nonetheless, I argue that once Jews were admitted to Western society, they were in a position to catch up quickly and move ahead of their non-Jewish neighbours in many of these areas, because again, the four values had a longer history and took on a more pronounced form in Jewish culture than they did in Christian culture. That is why Jews were highly receptive to modern science, capitalism, politics, and the arts and were able to advance in them with remarkable speed.

4) I do not want to give the impression that before modernity, Jewish culture in the West evolved in complete isolation from Christian culture. We have noted a number of instances in which European Jews absorbed ideas from Christianity along the way, perhaps without knowing it. For example, Jews in medieval Ashkenaz may have absorbed ascetic practices from medieval Christians. Therefore, Jewish culture in Europe, to some extent, evolved in tandem with Christian culture in the medieval and early modern periods, and thus the manner in which Jews understood the four values was likely affected by their Christian environment as well. Still, these observations do not undermine my hypothesis, which is predicated on the assumption that in key respects, Jews and Christians followed different cultural trajectories. Pre-modern Jewish culture in Europe had enough independence from its surroundings to be considered separate from Christian culture – though there was considerable variation as to how much that was the case, depending on time and place. The two cultures, in fact, *wanted* their independence. For the most part, Christians and Jews viewed each other negatively and were happy to live in their separate spheres.

5) I have done my best throughout this study not to engage in what academics refer to as "essentializing. Perhaps more accurately, I have done my best not to engage in it any more than I have had to. In the context of the present study, essentializing refers to the notion that one can evaluate a given culture by identifying its "essential" attributes – that is, traits that clearly define the character of that culture, are unchangeable, and are timeless. This approach to culture was once common among academics and is still common in popular discourse, but academics have come to abhor it on the belief that no culture can be defined so simplistically. It is often difficult if not impossible to find attributes in any culture that define what it is in all places and times. Moreover, academics have often pointed out that those who attempt to identify essential attributes in a particular culture usually have an underlying agenda, which is to valorize their own culture and demean someone else's. That is, authors often tend to identify the best features of their own culture as its essential characteristics, while identifying the worst features of another culture as *its* essential characteristics.

The problem of essentializing has plagued discussions among modern Jewish thinkers when they compare Judaism and Christianity on one or another of the four values. As I have noted, rabbis and Jewish intellectuals throughout the modern period have often spoken about differences between the two religions regarding these values in order to demonstrate the moral superiority of Judaism over Christianity, and they have done so by essentializing – that is, by making glib generalizations about both religions.

I have made every effort to avoid this problem. First, in order to ensure that I did not indulge in misleading generalizations about the two religions, I have taken care throughout this study to treat the differences between them in a far more nuanced and accurate way than my predecessors have. With each topic I discussed, I demonstrated that Judaism and Christianity had a range of views and that neither religion should be caricatured as upholding a typical position.

Most important, the comparisons I have made between Judaism and Christianity does not mask an agenda. I hope it is clear by now that my book in no way represents an attempt to argue that Judaism is superior to Christianity. My entire focus has been on explaining a historical phenomenon: the disproportionate success of Jews in the modern period. Moreover, my study is predicated on the presumption that Jews could not have achieved the success they did, had the Christian culture of the West not been successful and had Christians not invited Jews to participate in that culture. The Christian West and the culture it developed provided the ideal environment for Jews to excel.

While I avoided the worst type of essentializing, I acknowledge that I have still made judgments in this study that essentialize to some degree, and I make no apology for that. While on most of the matters I discussed in this study, Jewish and Christian culture each had a variety of opinions, I demonstrated that the two ranges of views were never entirely congruent, even though they may have overlapped to some extent. Again, the views of each culture on a given topic, when placed on a single spectrum, tended to occupy different parts of the spectrum. It was therefore possible to make meaningful generalizations about the differences between the two cultures and to see each of them as having its own approach to the issues being considered.

One last general thought is in order about essentializing. Not only was essentializing in some degree required for this project, to my mind, it is required for *any* project that deals with culture.

If one resists all essentialist claims about culture, if no generalizations are ever acceptable, then one robs cultures of their unique character. Every culture becomes nothing but a morass of ideas and practices that constantly shift over time and have no coherence, and that is a perspective I cannot accept. It deprives us of much of the richness of the human experience, which includes a myriad of cultures, each with its own distinct personality. We can certainly debate how the character of a particular culture should be depicted, and that is no simple matter. But we must not in principle rule out the possibility that cultures have their own idiosyncratic features. I believe they do.

The Slezkine Hypothesis Refashioned

A fascinating implication of everything I have said here is that as Europe became modernized, it unwittingly became more Jewish! The process of Jewish modernization is usually depicted as one in which Jews, as a small minority living among Christian Europeans, transformed their culture in order to fit into the culture of the majority. What has not been sufficiently appreciated is that, in some measure, the reverse was also true: when Christian European culture became modern, that culture, in key respects, also became less Christian and more Jewish in character. Christian Europe adopted a world view based on ideas and patterns of thought that in some ways were more in line with Jewish culture than with its own Christian culture. That is why Jews succeeded as they did in Europe: Christian Europeans had created an environment in which Jews could thrive. Jews, who had recently been invited to become part of non-Jewish society, found themselves entering a world that was built on ideas that were already deeply entrenched in their own collective mindset.

These claims may sound strange – even absurd to those versed in Jewish and European history – but some clarification will, I think, make them less so. I am not saying that Christian European culture became more Jewish in all respects, only in some – that is, those involving the four values. Nor am I suggesting that Christian European culture became more Jewish intentionally: the process was completely inadvertent. In fact, most Christians would have been outraged by the very suggestion that their culture had become more Jewish; they saw Judaism as backward, primitive, and unenlightened compared to Christianity. Nor am I even suggesting that Christian European culture became more Jewish because Christians were influenced by Jews or Judaism subconsciously. Christians had a very poor and often distorted understanding of Judaism, and so they could not have possibly absorbed Jewish cultural traits in this manner.[5] My claim is only that as Europeans gradually adopted a modern outlook, they happened to develop ways of thinking that distanced them from their Christian roots and, unbeknownst to them, moved them closer to a Jewish orientation.

There is a resemblance here between the argument I am proposing and that of Yuri Slezkine in his book, *The Jewish Century*, which I discussed in my opening chapter. Slezkine's claim was that the twentieth century was the "Jewish century" because it was in that century that the Western world unwittingly adopted a lifestyle that Jews had been living for centuries. Jews were "Mercurians," a class of people commonly found in human history who live as perpetual nomads and wanderers providing goods and services to the more settled "Appollonians." Mercurians are marked by adaptability, wit, and ingenuity, because these qualities are needed for their restless way of life. However, when capitalism became the dominant economic system in the West in the modern period, Westerners, who up to that time had been Appollonians, had to become Mercurians, because success in capitalism depended on adopting Mercurian traits. That is why Jews have done so well in the modern period. The Jewish way of life has long been well-suited to the new capitalist age.

My theory resembles that of Slezkine in that I too am arguing that in the modern period, Western non-Jews unwittingly adopted key aspects of the Jewish way of life. The major difference is that Slezkine's theory focuses entirely on the socio-economic aspects of Jewish life, whereas my theory is concerned with its religious aspects.

I believe that my theory is more convincing than Slezkine's for a number of reasons. In my initial presentation of Slezkine's theory, I noted several of its flaws. Slezkine does not adequately explain why Jews succeeded in such disproportionate fashion when they became part of non-Jewish society in the Western world. He also does not adequately explain why Jews have done so much better in the modern period than other minorities and subgroups.[6] The arguments I have presented in this book do not suffer from such difficulties. I have been able to explain the disproportionate nature of Jewish success in the modern period by showing that while Jews and non-Jews in the West shared much in common with respect to the four values, Jews cultivated these values in a manner that prepared them better for success in modernity than non-Jews did. The question about why other groups have not experienced the success that Jews have, is not a problem either, according to my theory, because one of its premises is that there *are* no groups similar to Jews. My theory is predicated on the assertion that Jews had a unique cultural trajectory that unfolded over many centuries and that finds no exact parallel in any other ethnic or national community.

Perhaps the most important reason why my argument is stronger than Slezkine's is that Slezkine focuses solely on the socio-economic dimension of Jewish life that evolved over the centuries prior to modernity, and it ignores the dimension of Jewish life that was, by far, more important for Jews in pre-modern times: religion. Religious culture defined Jewish life before modernity far more than any other factor, and so if one is going to formulate a theory to explain why modern Jews achieved immense success in Western culture in so many fields, in so many places, and over such an extended period of time, it is more likely to involve the religious features of the Jewish experience than the socio-economic features in which Slezkine is interested.

Rabbinic Judaism

Perhaps the most important finding of this study is that much of the credit for Jewish success in the modern West goes to Rabbinic Judaism. We have seen how the rabbis in the first seven or eight centuries CE reconstructed Judaism as a religion in which the four values were embedded in order to survive the destruction of the Second Temple and the Jewish commonwealth, and this form of Judaism became the Judaism that practically all Jews adhered to in the medieval and early modern periods. The rabbis never spoke about these values explicitly, nor could they have imagined how the religion they constructed would do so much for Jews in subsequent centuries. But the four values were critical to the rabbinic agenda, and they ended up playing a key role both in helping Jews survive centuries of persecution and in paving the way for their success in the modern period. So Rabbinic Judaism has to be regarded as one of the most remarkable manifestations of religion in history. It was the religion of the rabbis that gave a small minority the tools to deal with hundreds of years of adversity and emerge as the most successful group in the modern era.

The role of Rabbinic Judaism in the success of Jews in the modern era has often been ignored by the writers who have addressed this issue. Most do not even mention it, including those who support the cultural hypothesis. They simply refer to "Judaism," making no differentiation between the various forms Judaism has taken over the centuries.

Worse than this oversight are the negative attitudes towards Rabbinic Judaism that have been commonly expressed by Jews and non-Jews in a variety of contexts in the modern period. We delineated these attitudes at the beginning of this book. Leading the way here were scholars of

Christianity, particularly early Christianity, in the nineteenth century and the better part of the twentieth, who were highly critical of Rabbinic Judaism because it had grown out of the Judaism of the Pharisees who opposed Jesus, and it was therefore seen as the obstacle to Jews discovering the truth of Christianity. These scholars had different opinions on precisely what was wrong with Rabbinic Judaism, with some arguing that the rabbis were too harsh and severe regarding religious matters, and others claiming that the rabbis were too flexible on such matters to the point of being manipulative. Over the past half century, Christian scholars have revised their views of Rabbinic Judaism and have purged themselves of many of their prejudices towards it. The difficulty is that many of these prejudices have morphed into criticisms of Judaism in general and, in this form, survive in popular Christian discourse. Furthermore, even Christian scholars who now speak positively of Rabbinic Judaism seem unaware of just how extraordinary a phenomenon it is.

And it is not just Christians who have had prejudices against Rabbinic Judaism; Jews themselves have succumbed to these prejudices as well. Many Jews have adopted the view that Rabbinic Judaism is harsh and severe, on the assumption that before the modern period, the Judaism of the rabbis was akin to the Judaism of today's ultra-Orthodox Jews, even though that was not true.

This study has shown that when one has a proper understanding of Rabbinic Judaism, the negative views that have been expressed about it by Christians and Jews prove to be highly distorted. For those who think that Rabbinic Judaism is harsher than Christianity, this study has shown that, in many respects, the precise opposite was true. Regarding metaphysical autonomy, the first of the four values, the rabbis were on the whole less severe than their Christian counterparts. The most influential theologian in medieval Christianity, Augustine, espoused the doctrines of Original Sin and Predestination that greatly hampered or entirely negated human freedom in relation to God and the cosmos, and the two most influential theologians in Protestantism, Martin Luther and John Calvin, largely adopted these doctrines as well. Rabbinic Judaism was never so restrictive in its views on metaphysical autonomy. In rabbinic thinking, we find no equivalent to Original Sin and Predestination – at least, not in their Augustinian form. Moreover, the rabbis entertained ideas about metaphysical autonomy that were so permissive that they at times shocked Christians – most notably, the notion that one could argue with God.

A similar judgment can be made about our second value: freedom of thought and expression. Here too Rabbinic Judaism tended to be less severe than Christianity. Christians were perpetually concerned with dogma, and therefore their leaders invested great energy over the centuries in creating uniformity on matters of belief and enforcing it among their constituents, actions that restricted what Christians were allowed to think and say. The rabbis had far less concern for dogma and they therefore had far less interest in regulating what people thought and said. Also, on legal matters, which *were* the primary concern of the rabbis, we find that the rabbis to a large extent celebrated diversity of opinion; they encouraged debate on all matters having to do with God's laws and their implementation.

Attitudes towards the mundane realm, our third value, provide yet another example of how Rabbinic Judaism was less harsh than Christianity. The rabbis tended more than Christians to see the present world as the primary locus for relating to the divine. God's commandments, after all, focused on actions in this world, which meant that one's connection to God was forged in the activities of daily life. Therefore, the rabbis tended to see life in this world as a greater source of joy than Christians did.

What about the other critique of Rabbinic Judaism? Was Rabbinic Judaism perhaps too flexible? Were the rabbis so willing to exercise their freedom when interpreting God's word that they manipulated their readings of the Bible in order to bypass God's will and suit the practical needs of their constituents? This book has shown that such a critique also reflects a poor understanding of the rabbis. As Rabbinic Judaism matured in the medieval period, the rabbis came to believe that they indeed had the freedom to interpret God's word in light of practical concerns, but this belief was predicated on the notion that God had granted them that freedom. God had given them his Written and Oral Torah with the understanding that they would shape its meaning as they applied it to everyday life and that this process would involve taking pragmatic considerations into account. Thus, the rabbis, in interpreting God's word as they did, were not intent on bypassing God's will; as far as they were concerned, they were *implementing* it. What underlay this approach was an exalted view of human beings, one that was, on the whole, more exalted than is usually found in Christianity. For the rabbis, human beings were partners with God in determining the meaning of his revelation.

In addition, the Christian critique of the rabbis as overly flexible interpreters of God's words fails to take into account that they clearly set limits on how far they could go in this regard. The rabbis did not accept any and all interpretations of Scripture. In determining the meaning of the Written and Oral Torah, they grappled with the challenge of finding a proper balance between what they perceived to be God's will and practical considerations, and sometimes the former trumped the latter.

The picture of the rabbis that emerges from this study is striking. The rabbis were feisty, daring, and courageous leaders who revolutionized Judaism so that it could survive. In the first few centuries CE, they were determined not to be defeated by the tragic events that occurred under Roman domination, and in later centuries they were similarly determined not to succumb to the physical and spiritual pressures exerted on them by their Christian and Muslim overlords. They dealt with these challenges by insisting that they had the autonomy to creatively mould Judaism to the needs of their time, by fashioning a lively intellectual culture in which debate and disagreement were honoured, by convincing Jews that the best way forward was to embrace life in this world rather than escape from it, and by championing the intellectual dimension of religion in order to keep Judaism vibrant. Underpinning all these initiatives was the defiant belief of the rabbis that if Jews followed their program, God would eventually send his messiah and redeem them from exile. The power of the Roman, Christian, and Islamic empires was not going to vanquish them.

Most important for this book is that these very same qualities of Rabbinic Judaism allowed Jews to experience remarkable success when they finally became part of Western culture in the modern period. Rabbinic feistiness, daring, and courage were precisely what Jews needed to overcome the prejudices against them that had long defined their relationship with Christian Europe and that persisted after their emancipation, and these qualities were also what Jews needed in order to rise to the top of Western society in almost every field and discipline they touched. To put it succinctly, in fashioning a Judaism that allowed Jews to *survive* centuries of subjugation, the rabbis also fashioned a Judaism that allowed Jews to *thrive* in the modern period.

I am not the first to speak about the dynamism of the rabbis. But I do not believe that their accomplishments have been fully appreciated even by Jews who are versed in their literature.

I recognize that the claims I am making regarding Rabbinic Judaism will likely be controversial for some of my colleagues in Jewish Studies. Rabbinic Judaism is often regarded as the antithesis of everything in Judaism that is modern. The assumption is that it was this form of Judaism that Jews over the past two centuries were trying to overcome in order to become part of the modern world. I believe that the discussion I have provided in this book requires a rethinking of these premises but not a total rejection of them. Indeed, Rabbinic Judaism was in some respects an obstacle to the modernization of Jews, but I also believe that in other crucial respects, it was an aid to it. That Rabbinic Judaism played this dual role is not strange for those who are familiar with the evolution of cultures. Cultural revolutions often have a paradoxical relationship with the past. They overturn many elements of the bygone era even while co-opting others.

Other Factors

Lest anyone think that my praise of the rabbis is excessive, I would now like to identify a number of factors that contributed to the success of Jews that were not at all the product of rabbinic initiative. As I have already noted, historical circumstances certainly helped modern Jews succeed in a variety of endeavours, as Jewish historians have argued.[7] But even the success of the rabbis themselves was due in part to historical circumstances over which they had little control. In fact, Rabbinic Judaism came into existence *because* of such circumstances. The rabbis became leaders in the Jewish community in the first centuries CE in the wake of the destruction of the Second Temple and the Jewish commonwealth at the hands of the Romans. These events gave the rabbis the opportunity to lead the Jewish people that they might not have had otherwise.

Moreover, historical circumstances did not just create a vacuum of leadership that the rabbis were happy to fill; they compelled the rabbis to come up with a creative agenda that would allow Jews to survive over the long term. In other words, the rabbinic agenda was in part the product of sheer necessity. The rabbis had to fashion a Judaism that would outlast the catastrophes that had befallen Jews or risk the demise of Judaism altogether.

I have also argued that the same historical circumstances fostered the development of the four values that have been at the core of this study. The first value – human autonomy in the metaphysical sense – may have been shaped by the need of the rabbis to feel empowered when historical events seemed to indicate that God had become distant from them and the Jewish people.

The development of the second value – freedom of thought and expression – seems to have been encouraged by historical circumstances in the medieval period. The capacity for Jews in pre-modern times to think more freely about religious matters than Christians did was made possible in part by the peculiar situation of Jews in Christian Europe. From the beginning of the medieval period onwards, the Church willingly relinquished its coercive power over the Jews in religious matters. The Church believed that Jews should be allowed to live as Jews because they were a testimony to God's truth that had been revealed to them in the Hebrew Bible. Not that the Church was entirely tolerant of Jews; its policy was that Jews should live in lowly conditions and be treated with disdain because they had rejected Christianity. But in the meantime, according to the Church, Jews should not be coerced into becoming Christians. Moreover, the Church believed that it was only a matter of time before Jews came around to the truth. When Jesus returned to usher in the final stages of the messianic era, Jews would finally become Christians.

Yet, if the Church did not exercise coercive power over the Jews regarding religious matters, it was not as if the religious leadership in the Jewish community could fill the void. The rabbis lacked the power to punish Jews who deviated from their path. They certainly could threaten excommunication to force Jews to conform to their will, a punishment that consisted primarily of social ostracism, but that weapon was of limited effectiveness. In some communities, the rabbis were allowed to use excommunication only with the approval of the lay communal leadership.[8] Furthermore, excommunication was effective only to the extent that Jews were willing to enforce it not just locally but in other Jewish communities in the region to which the person being punished might flee, and a decree of excommunication did not always reach far beyond the community or region where it had been issued. Finally, excommunication, while being a serious punishment, was not nearly as frightening as arrest, torture, or execution – forms of punishment that the Church had at its disposal.[9]

As a consequence, Jews did not have to fear expressing their views on religious matters in the same way that Christians did. The controversy over Maimonides' writings is a case in point. Some of the rabbis who opposed the study of Maimonides' philosophy and the Greek philosophy upon which it was based excommunicated those who insisted on indulging in this literature. But rabbis who were part of the latter group strongly supported the study of Maimonidean and Greek philosophy, and they issued their own orders of excommunication against the first group of rabbis. Thus, in the end, none of the punishments had much effect. Each side continued doing precisely what it had been doing prior to the controversy. Unlike the situation in Christian Europe, there was no all-powerful arbiter equivalent to the Church that could settle the disagreement.

Scholars have identified other factors to help explain the success of modern Jews that I have not treated in this book but should be taken seriously. For instance, an argument has often been made that Jews achieved economic success in the West because they took advantage of their "social capital." That is, Jews did well economically because they were extremely supportive of one another from a material standpoint. For example, they offered charity to Jews in need, founded Jewish organizations that offered low-interest loans to other Jews, and employed fellow Jews in their businesses and professional practices. According to this theory, these practices gathered steam throughout the modern period until large numbers of Jews occupied the upper rungs of the economic ladder.[10]

This theory falls well short of a full explanation for Jewish economic success. No amount of social capital would have helped Jews if they had not also been good at what they did. In fact, they had to be exceptionally good, because whatever their professions were, they were not going to achieve success by relying solely on their fellow Jews for help. Their success was dependent on interactions with non-Jews who were their employers, peers, clients, and customers, and with antisemitism continuing to be common among non-Jews, Jews had to make the case that the goods and services they offered were of superior quality for non-Jews to overcome their antipathy to Jews and purchase them. And here, again, is where the influence of Rabbinic Judaism was key; Jews became good at what they did because of its legacy. Nonetheless, there is no question that social capital helped Jews to some extent in their quest for economic success.

Challenges: Mizrahi Jews, Secular Jews, Modernizing Jewish Movements

I had to address the difficulties with the cultural hypothesis that I mentioned earlier. I chose not to deal with the problem posed by Mizrahi Jews, and for good reasons. For most of the modern period, Mizrahi Jews lived in Muslim countries, the culture of which was very different from that of the West and that in many respects was not modern. Therefore, an evaluation of what "success" has meant for Mizrahi Jews over the past two centuries would have to be done according to standards appropriate for their host societies, not modern Western ones. I was reluctant to take up this task because our knowledge of Mizrahi Jews over the past two hundred years is more elementary than it is for Jews of Western origin.

Yet leaving Mizrahi Jews out of this study has not necessarily hampered my investigation because the vast majority of Jews in the modern period lived in the West. Thus, by focusing on the success of Western Jews in the modern period, I have in effect focused on the success of most Jews in this period.

Incidentally, the discrepancy in population numbers here may explain why modern Western Jews have so many more achievements to their credit than Mizrahi Jews do; there were simply many more of the former than the latter. But again, that still leaves open the question of whether Mizrahi Jews achieved success according to the standards of the Muslim societies in which they resided for most of the modern period, and a full investigation of that matter will have to be taken up by a specialist in Mizrahi Jewry, which I am certainly not.

The most formidable obstacle to my explanation for the success of Jews in the modern period and to any explanation of this phenomenon involving the cultural hypothesis was that many of the most accomplished modern Jews were secular. These Jews had left the life of Rabbinic Judaism behind, and therefore it seemed unlikely that Rabbinic Judaism or its four values could be responsible for their achievements.

I devoted an entire chapter to explain why this presumption was not necessarily correct and that it was quite plausible that secular Jews continued to be influenced by Rabbinic Judaism and its four values. I began with the general observation we are already familiar with – that ethnic groups, nations, and even whole civilizations undergoing major cultural transformations always retain elements of the culture that is being superseded, even if their intent is to rid themselves of the past culture entirely and start the new era with a clean slate. The culture of the new era will be marked, at the very least, by vestiges of the older culture when it comes to thought patterns, speech, and behaviour. Change is always accompanied by some degree of continuity.

Modern secular Jews would have been no different from other groups in this regard, and therefore, they would have retained some elements of pre-modern rabbinic culture even as they did their best to move past it. The chances of this happening would have been greatly increased by the fact that Jews, including secular Jews, continued to live lives that were mostly segregated from non-Jews, even though the legal barriers between Jews and non-Jews had been removed. Of course, this situation changed in the 1960s when Jews in the US began assimilating into non-Jewish society more than ever before. Jews started to intermarry with non-Jews in large numbers and to relinquish their Jewish commitments as they were welcomed into non-Jewish society to an unprecedented degree. But even then, secular Jews who joined non-Jewish society may still have carried with them vestiges of Jewish culture without being aware of it, including the rabbinic values we have been speaking about. The assimilation of groups into a majority culture does not happen suddenly; it is gradual, and Jews are only in the second generation of a process of assimilation that began in the 1960s.

Most important, the four values at the core of this book were likely to have been included among the features of rabbinic culture that secular Jews retained, for at least two reasons. First, these values were fundamental to Rabbinic Judaism, and so if any rabbinic values were carried over into the modern period, they would have been among them. Second, the four values could be easily adapted to the needs of secular Jews once they had been stripped of their religious meaning. In secularized form, these values meshed perfectly with the ones that were driving the Western world to become dominant in so many spheres.

I now take up one more challenge to my arguments that I have not yet broached in this book. Jewish scholars who specialize in Jewish history or Jewish thought in the eighteenth and nineteenth centuries are likely to greet the claims I am making with scepticism. They will point out that in these centuries, what led Jews to adopt the four values at the core of this study were not the rabbis, but a number of other groups. Most important among these were Jewish intellectuals in various movements that attempted to modernize Judaism. There was the Haskalah, the Jewish Enlightenment mentioned earlier in this book, which arose in central Europe in the eighteenth century and spread to western and eastern Europe in the nineteenth century. There was also the Reform movement, which developed in central Europe in the nineteenth century. And there were various movements that arose among Jews that were secular in orientation, such as the Bund, a Jewish socialist party; Yiddishism, which focused on various aspects of Jewish culture rooted in the Yiddish language; and Zionism, which was largely a secular political movement. An argument could be made that it was these movements that brought Jews into the modern world along with the four values, not Rabbinic Judaism.

We should also mention other Jewish groups that eroded the authority of the rabbis in the early modern period and are seen by scholars as factors in preparing Jews for modernity. One such group was the *conversos*. The *conversos* were Jews who had converted to Christianity in Spain and Portugal in the fifteenth and sixteenth centuries in order to avoid expulsion from those countries. In the seventeenth century, many of these converts left their native countries, settled in other places in Europe, and began returning to Judaism. Amsterdam, for instance, was one such destination. For a generation or two, these Jews had at most a tenuous link to their Jewish heritage. They had little knowledge of Rabbinic Judaism, and some therefore resisted the authority of the rabbis after their return to the Jewish community, thereby paving the way for modern forms of Judaism.

Rabbinic authority in western and central Europe in the early modern period may also have been weakened by the Sabbatean movement, which we mentioned in an earlier chapter. This messianic movement, which was centred on the figure of Shabbetai Tsevi engulfed large numbers of Jewish communities throughout Europe and the Islamic world, and when that movement failed, it spawned radical groups that deliberately transgressed some of the divine commandments. Clearly, these Jews also represented a challenge to rabbinic authority and in doing so prepared Jews for modernity.[11]

I have a number of responses to this line of argument. First, the movements and groups listed here were certainly important in the modernization of Jews. That I will not deny. But the question I am asking in this study is not about how Jews were modernized, nor even why they became successful in the modern Western world, but why they became *inordinately* successful in that world, and as I stated in chapter 1, these questions are not the same. Over the past two centuries, Jews did not just become modern, or just successful; they became far more successful than their non-Jewish counterparts, and this phenomenon is not readily explained by the modernizing movements in Judaism such as the Haskalah and Reform Judaism, the presence of *conversos*, or the aftereffects of Sabbateanism. One would have to show how these factors gave Jews a significant advantage over their Christian counterparts, and I am not aware of any arguments to that effect. Yet the inordinate success of modern Jews *can* be explained by some of the core values of Rabbinic Judaism, as I have argued throughout this book.

Second, while many of the aforementioned movements and groups were intent on rejecting Rabbinic Judaism, there were elements of them that did not. The Haskalah was not initially interested in overturning the rabbinic way of life. Instead, it wanted to supplement this way of life with secular education and training so that Jews could become productive members of European society. Moses Mendelssohn, who inspired the Haskalah, was himself an observant Jew who had great reverence for rabbinic tradition. It was only later on that more radical versions of the Haskalah arose in central and eastern Europe. The Reform movement, as already noted, did not represent a wholesale rejection of Rabbinic Judaism. While it was intent on refashioning Judaism by emphasizing monotheism and ethics, its leaders still made use of rabbinic sources when it suited their purposes.[12] Sabbateanism may have spawned radical groups, but it also fed into a movement that was highly traditional in character: Hasidism.[13]

Third, we have to keep in mind that the modernizing movements and groups being discussed here had limited influence. Not all Jews

were affected by them. Eastern Europe had by far the largest population of Jews in the eighteenth and nineteenth centuries, and its culture remained largely rabbinic in character due to the slow pace of
emancipation in these parts of Europe. The modernizing movements
therefore did not reach large numbers of European Jews. Moreover,
the vast majority of Jews who immigrated to the US at the end of
the nineteenth century and the beginning of the twentieth were from
eastern Europe, and even when they dropped religious observance,
they did not tend to identify with modernizing movements such as
the Haskalah and the Reform movement.[14] The number of *conversos*
and Sabbateans was even more limited in size than that of the modernizing movements. These movements and groups therefore cannot
explain the widespread nature of Jewish success over the past two
centuries. Far more Jews succeeded in the economic, intellectual, and
artistic realms than those Jews who identified with one or another of
these movements or groups. Yet almost all Jews in the eighteenth and
nineteenth centuries and a good part of the twentieth century were
connected to Rabbinic Judaism in one way or another. Either they
themselves were living in accordance with rabbinic tradition, or they
had parents or grandparents who had lived that way – and as I have
argued, it is highly likely that even Jews who were one or two generations removed from Rabbinic Judaism still inherited from it patterns
of thought, speech, and behaviour. The influence of Rabbinic Judaism
is therefore a far better candidate for explaining the disproportionate success of modern Jews than the various movements and groups
being discussed here. And once again, the fact that many modern Jews
openly rebelled against Rabbinic Judaism does not negate what I am
claiming here. It is quite common for representatives of a new cultural
era to vilify the culture of the previous era even while absorbing some
of its values, especially when those values serve an important function in the new era.

The Veblen Hypothesis Refashioned

My discussion of secular Jews in chapter 2 allowed me to add another
dimension to my explanation of Jewish success. In the early twentieth
century, Thorstein Veblen theorized that Jews became highly accomplished scientists in the modern period because many of them had left
Jewish culture behind without becoming fully part of Western culture.
They therefore found themselves in a void between the two cultures,
and in that space, they were able to think freely and creatively in ways
they could not have, had they been ensconced in and beholden to either

one of the two cultures. Veblen's hypothesis illuminated my discussion of secular Jews because it could be expanded to explain why some of the most successful Jews in the modern period were secular. It was not just secular Jewish scientists who occupied a space between Jewish and non-Jewish Western culture, but secular Jews in other professions as well. Secular Jews may have left Rabbinic Judaism behind, but most of them retained their Jewish identity and did not fully assimilate into the Western world. Thus, secular Jews in general occupied a space between Jewish and non-Jewish culture that Veblen believed bred unusual creativity.

I expanded Veblen's theory even further: the success of religiously affiliated Jews in the modern period could be explained in a similar manner. These Jews did not abandon Jewish culture in the way that secular Jews did; they carried much of Rabbinic Judaism with them quite consciously into their new life in the modern world. But with the notable exception of ultra-Orthodox Jews, religiously affiliated Jews were not beholden to Rabbinic Judaism in its pre-modern form; instead, they reshaped it to suit their modern environment – sometimes drastically, as in the case of Reform Judaism. Therefore, these Jews too occupied a space between pre-modern Jewish culture and modern Western culture similar to that occupied by secular Jews, and they benefited from being in that space in the same way secular Jews did.

I also modified Veblen's theory with the claim that the space Jews occupied between the two cultures was not the void Veblen imagined. Quite the opposite. It was a space in which Jews brought together the best of both cultures, and that is why they were so successful. This space was an unusually fertile one for Jews because it provided opportunities for them to bring together two culturally rich worlds.

These observations added a sociological dimension to my theory of Jewish success. My theory was focused almost entirely on the realm of ideas. It was concerned with values – four, in particular – that explained why Jews achieved disproportionate success in the modern world. My modified version of the Veblen hypothesis added another layer to that theory because it suggested that the anomalous social position of Jews in modern Western society contributed to their success by enhancing their capacity to take advantage of the four values. The space that Jews occupied between pre-modern Jewish society and modern non-Jewish society gave them room to combine these values with the best features of non-Jewish Western culture and create a hybrid culture that was remarkably dynamic.

Weber vs. Marx

My theory about the success of Jews in the modern period raises questions beyond the Jewish sphere that concern the manner in which cultures change. A question that has been debated by modern intellectuals is whether cultural change occurs mainly because of revolutions in economic conditions or because of revolutions in the realm of ideas. Karl Marx was the great champion of the first approach. His theory of dialectical materialism presumed that cultures advance from one stage to the next because of changes in economic conditions. Max Weber took the second approach. In an earlier chapter, I alluded to Weber's famous work, *The Protestant Ethic and the Spirit of Capitalism*, in which he argued that the growth of capitalism in Europe resulted from the transmutation of ideas and habits ingrained in Europeans by Protestantism.[15] I also noted that while most scholars today do not support Weber's theory for various reasons, Weber's approach can be applied to explain the development of a work ethic in European culture that inspired Europeans to view daily life in the present world as possessing greater value than it had before.[16]

Clearly, this study sides with Weber in its approach to the success of Jews in the modern period. Essentially, I have argued that ideas really do matter. Rabbinic values that had been fundamental to Jewish life for many hundreds of years prepared Jews for success in the modern period, not just in the economic realm but also in the intellectual and artistic realms.

As I discussed in my introductory chapter, most modern Jewish historians account for the success of modern Jews by taking an approach that is closer to that of Marx: economic circumstances – or perhaps more broadly, material circumstances – explain why Jews have done so well in the modern period. Yet as I said earlier, one does not have to necessarily choose one approach to the exclusion of the other. I have acknowledged the fine work of Jewish historians of the modern period that has illuminated why Jews have done so well in the modern West.[17] It is just that the explanations offered by these historians for the success of modern Jews are implausible unless one inserts the cultural factor as the motivating element that ties together the success that Jews experienced across a wide range of locations and professions over the past two centuries.

A Circumstantial Case

The arguments I have presented in this book are the best I can do to explain the success of Jews in the modern period. For some, it may not be enough, and I can understand why they may feel that way. I admitted towards the end of chapter 2 on secular Jews that my arguments about the success of Jews in the modern period – secular or religiously affiliated – were speculative because they were based on insights about subconscious processes that are difficult to analyse. When Jews became part of the modern Western world, they did not have a conscious plan about how they were going to use the four values to succeed in it, and so we have no explicit testimonies to prove that my theory is correct.

I must reiterate, however, what I said in the continuation of the same discussion, which is that *any* theory about Jewish success has to be speculative to some extent because it is a phenomenon that is so elusive and diffuse. It spans two centuries and encompasses a wide variety of Jewish subcultures across the modern Western world, and so anyone proposing an explanation for the success of modern Jews has to explore subliminal processes that affected them across the many historical contexts in which they lived.

I also pointed out that not all speculations are equal; some are better than others, and their relative merit can be determined by the arguments that support them. For this reason, I believe that my theory for the success of modern Jews, if not objectively verifiable, is nonetheless the best that has been offered. It explains this phenomenon more convincingly than competing theories do.

Another way to phrase this is that any theory about the success of modern Jews can only be "circumstantial." One cannot provide direct evidence about why Jews became so successful because again, Jews, as a people, did not consciously plan their success, and there are thus no documents that attest to such a plan. As a consequence, circumstantial evidence is the best evidence that one can provide here. But circumstantial evidence is still evidence. When assembled in sufficient quantity, it can add up to a convincing case, and I believe that this is what I have done here. I have adduced enough evidence of this kind to make my theory about the success of modern Jews as persuasive as I believe any theory about this issue can be. I hope that the jury – that is, you, my readers – will concur.

Lessons for Jews, Lessons for Everyone

This epilogue is devoted to exploring the lessons that can be learned from this book. What lessons can Jews learn from their success in the past in order to perpetuate their success in the future? What lessons can non-Jews learn from the success of Jews so that they can experience similar success if they so wish?

Lessons for Jews

What lessons can Jews learn from this book? Perhaps the most important one is that the success of modern Jews has come about by finding the right balance between two factors that have been in tension with each other throughout the modern period: maintaining Jewish identity and being open to Western culture. Therefore, Jews will be able to sustain the kind of success they have experienced in the past two centuries if they preserve the balance between these two tendencies. It is not clear, however, that they will be able to do so.

In order to understand why, a bit of information about world Jewry is needed. Of the 15 million Jews in the world, almost half live in Israel, and the rest are located in Western countries, with the vast majority of these Jews residing in the US.[1] Thus, for all intents and purposes, the future of Jews and Judaism is in the hands of Israeli and American Jews.

The two communities are quite different from each other, and so to determine whether Jews can sustain their past success, we must look at these communities separately. We will begin with the Jewish community in Israel. Here, many of the factors that have led to the success of modern Jews are still in place. The vast majority of Israeli Jews maintain some form of Jewish identity. Fully half of Israeli Jews are secular, while the other half are religiously observant to varying degrees. Those in the latter category range from *masorti*, or traditional (i.e., semi-religious), to ultra-Orthodox. Nonetheless, just about all Israeli Jews identify as Jews. Moreover, they marry other Jews and socialize with other Jews.[2]

Therefore, Israeli society provides the same type of environment for the preservation of the four rabbinic values that led to the success of modern Jews up to now. And here again, secular Jews are included in that assessment on the assumption that they too have retained the four values, albeit in secular form. In fact, in our chapter on secular Jews, we noted two studies done by sociologists demonstrating that secular Israeli Jews have retained the modes of discourse and speech patterns characteristic of Rabbinic Judaism without being aware of it, and this suggested that secular Israeli Jews may have also unwittingly retained basic rabbinic values as well.[3]

Alongside their commitment to Jewish identity, the vast majority of Israelis are open to Western culture, particularly in its American form. In fact, they are awash in it. Israelis watch American TV and movies and listen to American popular music. Most are comfortable with English. Israelis are also open to more sophisticated expressions of Western culture in the intellectual and artistic realms. Israeli universities are fully Western with regard to the content of the learning they offer. Israelis also take great interest in the Western arts in their various forms, including classical music, theatre, and dance. Israeli Jews therefore have a relationship with the Western world that, as we have seen, has been central to the success of modern Jews up to now.

The capacity of Israelis to maintain Jewish identity while interacting with the Western world helps explain Israel's remarkable accomplishments in the short period that it has been in existence. As noted in the introductory chapter, Israel has done very well in the economic, intellectual, and artistic spheres. Its thriving hi-tech industry is perhaps the best example of its achievements.[4]

There are, however, clouds on the horizon. The biggest is Israel's political situation. The Israeli–Palestinian conflict continues to fester and shows no signs of abating anytime soon. At the time of this writing, Israel has better relations with the Arab and Muslim countries than it has ever had, but some of Iran's leaders still speak openly about destroying Israel. Moreover, even in Arab and Muslim countries that have peace treaties with Israel or have developed warmer relations with Israel, anti-Israel and anti-Jewish sentiments are widespread, and a change of leadership could quickly result in renewed hostilities towards the Jewish state. These problems have been an enormous drain on Israel's material and human resources. Thus, while Israel appears to be quite strong and stable, anyone familiar with Israel and its environment knows that its situation remains precarious.

Another cloud on the horizon is that the ultra-Orthodox community in Israel is by far the fastest-growing sector of its population. This community currently makes up only 9 per cent of the Jewish population in Israel, but it has a very high birth rate – 7.1 births per ultra-Orthodox woman compared to 3.1 for women in the general Israeli population – and this community will therefore become an ever larger and more powerful portion of Israeli society in the coming years.[5] This does not bode well for Israel to continue the success it has experienced up to now. While ultra-Orthodox Jews certainly live according to the four values that have made modern Jews successful, they live largely segregated lives, and they therefore avoid contact with modern Western culture. In consequence, there is an absence here of a critical factor that has brought Jews success in the past two centuries.

In recent years, some of the barriers between ultra-Orthodox Israelis and the outside world have begun to erode. For instance, some of these Jews have begun to enter the hi-tech industry and have done very well in it.[6] But as things stand, the ultra-Orthodox community remains sufficiently closed off from the modern world, that it is hard to imagine its constituents becoming agents of the type of success that Jews have achieved thus far in the modern period.

These observations should not be construed as a criticism of ultra-Orthodox Jews. They have every right to live the lives they have chosen. They are also a far more interesting and multifaceted community than outsiders have given them credit for. Ultra-Orthodox communities also have virtues that others can learn from. Still, when it comes to the question of whether Israeli Jews can continue to succeed as modern Jews have in the past two centuries, the growth of the ultra-Orthodox community in Israel raises serious doubts about that possibility.

Another issue to mention here is that Israel is a country with a high degree of economic inequality. A 2015 report from the Organisation for Economic Co-operation and Development found that the gap between rich and poor in both the US and Israel was much higher than in the rest of the developed world.[7] This problem should be seen as a threat to Israeli Jews maintaining the past success that modern Jews have experienced. Israeli Jews will not be able to extend that record of success if their society does not provide opportunities for more of its constituents to live well from a material standpoint.

As for the American Jewish community, the factors that have led to the success of modern Jews are not as firmly in place as they are in Israel, for a number of reasons. Most important, the rate of intermarriage between American Jews and non-Jews has skyrocketed over the past several decades, mostly because of intermarriage between non-Orthodox Jews and non-Jews, who constitute the vast majority of the Jewish population in the US. For instance, in a 2013 survey, half of all Jews who identified with Reform Judaism, the largest of the Jewish denominations in the US, were married to a non-Jewish spouse.[8] Intermarried Jews do not necessarily lose their Jewish identity once they marry non-Jews. However, a substantial percentage of the children of these Jews do not identify as Jews. As a result, the number of non-Orthodox Jews in the US is steadily shrinking.[9] That trend is being accelerated by low birth rates among these Jews – even those who marry other Jews. The current birth rate among non-Orthodox Jews in the US is 1.7, a figure that represents negative population growth.[10]

In addition, many non-Orthodox Jews in the US, regardless of whom they marry, have become detached from Judaism and highly Westernized. At no time in history have Jews felt as comfortable in a non-Jewish country as they do in America today. This is not just because of changing attitudes among American Jews towards non-Jews, but it is also because of changing attitudes among American non-Jews towards Jews. Over the past half century, Americans have welcomed Jews into their society in ways that are unprecedented. As late as the 1950s, it was taboo for American non-Jews to marry or even socialize with Jews, but that is no longer the case in large portions of American society. I make these claims fully aware that antisemitism has made a comeback in recent years in the US. Despite this phenomenon, non-Jews in America have been more welcoming to Jews in recent decades than they have been in any other place or period in Jewish history. These are wonderful developments. However, the downside is that in the current circumstances, any vestiges of Rabbinic Judaism that non-Orthodox American Jews still carry with them, consciously or subconsciously, are likely to dissipate in the coming years.

The situation with ultra-Orthodox Jews in the US is similar to the one in Israel. American ultra-Orthodox Jews at present constitute a small portion of the American Jewish population, only 6 per cent, but their birth rates are much higher than those of non-Orthodox Jews, and so if Jewish birth rates remain the same, ultra-Orthodox Jews will constitute an increasing portion of the American Jewish community.[11] Moreover, American ultra-Orthodox Jews exhibit resistance to modern Western culture, though not to the extent that their Israeli counterparts do.

Modern Orthodox Jews in the US attempt to combine traditional Rabbinic Judaism with an openness to Western culture. However, they are only 3 per cent of the American Jewish population, and their birth rates are also lower than those of ultra-Orthodox Jews. Furthermore, this sector of the American Jewish community is losing a lot of its young people to the ultra-Orthodox community. Therefore, Modern Orthodox Jews are not much of a factor in the population trends I am discussing here.[12]

What all these observations about American Jews add up to is that the number of individuals in the US who have a strong Jewish identity but are also open to modern Western culture is diminishing, and if this trend continues, there will be fewer and fewer American Jews who possess the critical characteristics that have so far allowed Jews to achieve success in the modern period. That, of course, calls into question whether the success of American Jews is sustainable.

Very good minds in the American Jewish community have been working hard for some time to revitalize Jewish life in America, and if they are able to do so, American Jews may be able to extend their record of achievement. For instance, one avenue that is being explored is to increase the number of non-Orthodox children who are educated in private Jewish schools on the premise that religiously educated Jews will be more inclined to have a strong Jewish identity. This initiative, if successful, would help give young Jews the tools to succeed as Jews have in the past. A good Jewish education would familiarize young Jews from non-Orthodox backgrounds with the rabbinic tradition, which, as we have seen, has played such a vital role in the success of Jews up to this point.

But the challenges are substantial here. The American Jewish community has not yet found a way to offer private Jewish education that is both high in quality and affordable for people on modest incomes – and not all Jews are wealthy. Moreover, it is not easy to teach Rabbinic Judaism in a way that makes it easily digestible for young Americans who have become thoroughly Westernized. Rabbinic texts are notoriously difficult and can come across as completely foreign to those with a Western mindset. I am personally familiar with the problem, having taught a college-level course in Rabbinic Judaism for a number of years at an American university. And even if young Jews find a way to relate to rabbinic texts, mastering them takes years of study. So there is no guarantee that teaching these texts to young Jews will revitalize American Judaism or ensure that American Jews will be as successful as they have been in the past. In short, American Jews are rapidly losing their connection with their rabbinic heritage, and it is going to be very difficult to revive it.

To summarize, the Israeli and American Jewish communities are quite different from each other, as are their challenges, but the challenges that each of them is facing are quite daunting and raise serious questions about whether modern Jews will be able to sustain the success they have experienced up to now. However, it is difficult to make firm predictions here. The prospects of modern Jews sustaining their record of success depend a great deal on whether the current birth rates in the Israeli and American Jewish communities continue, and whether the current intermarriage rates in the American Jewish community continue as well, and as any demographer will tell you, current trends of behaviour regarding such matters in any population are often unreliable predictors of future trends. The future of Israel's success will also depend on where its geopolitical situation is headed, and here too, it is difficult to make reliable predictions. So while pessimism is warranted about the prospects for Jews maintaining their record of success in the modern period, the future is quite uncertain.

Lessons for Everyone

Let us now look at what lessons this study can offer *all* people about success, not just Jews. The most fundamental lesson of this kind is that one can succeed in the contemporary Western world by adopting a number of key values that underlie modern Western culture – four, in particular: human autonomy, freedom of thought and expression, valuing life in this world, and education. Jews have done remarkably well in the modern Western world because their religious culture inculcated in them unusually strong versions of these values, and so it stands to reason that others can achieve similar success by cultivating these values as well.

I have also explored a number of other secondary values in Jewish culture that were connected, in one way or another, to the primary four and were important in helping Jews achieve success, and non-Jews can learn from these values as well. For instance, in my discussion of the third value, appreciating life in this world, I spoke about the rabbinic focus on family life. Rabbinic Judaism believed that God's presence was experienced in the mundane realm, and therefore the rabbis looked at everyday pleasures as religiously significant, including those associated with the family. Modern Jews clearly benefited from the tradition of strong family life in Jewish culture for obvious reasons, and therefore, if non-Jews want to emulate the success of Jews, they should seek ways to support the family as well.

The same can be said about other values that, I argued, were connected to the Jewish emphasis on life in this world, such as patience, discipline, and long-term planning. These values were inculcated by a system of Jewish law that the rabbis implemented for centuries and served modern Jews well, and they are also instructive for non-Jews in the modern world, again for reasons that do not require explanation.

Also instructive for anyone – Jew or non-Jews – looking to succeed in the modern world is the entire saga of Jewish history that has been discussed throughout this book. It shows how perseverance in the face of adversity can pay off in the long term. The fact that Jews were able to survive almost two millennia of exile and subjugation and then thrive in the modern period is about as powerful a testimony to the strength of the human spirit as any that one will ever find. The same can be said about Jews in the twentieth century, who were determined to resume their record of achievement after the devastation of the Holocaust. Not only did Jews manage to continue their push for success after this catastrophe, it was only three years later that Jews created their own sovereign state after so many centuries without one.

Of course, what I have said thus far about the lessons that non-Jews can learn from the success of Jews is not terribly innovative. One does not need to read this book to know that one can achieve success in the modern world by cultivating the four values that have been at the centre of this study, as well the values secondary to them that have just been mentioned. Also, while Jews provide a salient example of the value of perseverance in the face of adversity, it is not as if Jews are unique in this regard. But what this book has highlighted is just how important these values are. Jews achieved success in such disproportionate fashion in the past two centuries because they have exemplified these values in a particularly bold manner.

There are also lessons that both Jews and non-Jews can glean from this book that are not so obvious. One is that religion can be a force for the good. Over the past several decades, this notion has not been taken as a given among Western thinkers and writers. A number of Western intellectuals have gone as far as saying that religion is malevolent and best got rid of. This book has demonstrated that much of what is considered valuable in both modern Jewish and Western culture in fact has roots in religion. The four values that resulted in immense achievements in both cultures evolved from religious values.

This is not to say that the aforementioned authors are entirely wrong in their assessment of religion. Religion has indeed been a source of great suffering, and it continues to be in large parts of the world. My argument is only that this assessment is one-sided.

I also acknowledge that the values explored in this study often inspired the achievements they did in the modern world only after they had been secularized. However, this does not diminish the valuable role that religion played in the development of these values. Religion still deserves much of the credit here. Moreover, the four values did not have to be secularized to be of great benefit in the modern world,

and Jews provide an excellent example of that. As we have seen, it was
not just secular Jews who were successful, but also religiously affiliated
Jews who managed to combine the religious and the secular in dynamic
fashion.

These observations lead us to another valuable lesson that comes out
of this book and may not be so obvious: the religious and the secular
may coexist and they may even be brought together in ways that are
beneficial in the modern world. Jews provide an unusually good example of how this is possible, but I believe that adherents to other religions
can follow their lead. All the major religions of the world are sufficiently
rich and complex to find ways to combine the religious and the secular
in a vibrant manner.

MINORITIES

This study may offer helpful insights for more specific groups and cultures outside the Jewish community, and I will begin with minorities in
the Western world. As noted in the previous chapter, one reason why
modern Jews achieved the success they did is that they were determined
to participate in the majority culture around them and to derive the
best from it while maintaining their own culture. They created a space
between the two cultures in which there could be a dynamic interplay
between them.

I wonder whether there are lessons here for other minorities that have
had difficulty succeeding in the Western world. Might these minorities
find success by striking the right balance between participating in the
majority culture and maintaining their own identity, as Jews did?

It is hard to say. There are certainly reasons to doubt this possibility.
First of all, every minority has its own unique history and challenges,
and the path that Jews took to achieve success may not work for others.
This path would be especially difficult to duplicate given its long and
complex history. Second, the argument can be made that in the end, the
Jewish quest for finding a balance between participating in the majority culture and maintaining a separate identity did not work even for
them. In Europe, Jews made immense contributions to Western society
once they were invited to become part of it, but they discovered that
antisemitism was a sickness in Western culture that was not going to go
away so easily. Their success, far from leading to the retreat of antisemitism, only inflamed it further, and the result was the murder of 6 million
Jews in the Second World War. And if one argues that this catastrophe
marked the end of the problem, that the West had finally learned its lesson about the consequences of antisemitism, events in recent times raise
questions about that assessment. The return of antisemitism in the past

few years in Europe and America makes one wonder whether the West will ever rid itself of this sickness.

Nonetheless, I believe it is still worth asking whether other minorities in the West may learn something from the Jewish experience that could help them with their own challenges. For even though that experience has been marked by tragedy, it has also been marked by extraordinary accomplishments that no tragedy can negate and that should be of interest to minorities who are trying to make their own way in the Western world. At the very least, the Jewish model may help minorities shape the questions that need to be asked. In particular, what kind of balance should be struck between cooperating with the majority culture – even when it is oppressive – and maintaining one's distance from it in order to preserve one's own identity?

AMERICAN CULTURE

There are lessons in this book that I believe are particularly valuable for contemporary American culture, and I will focus here on lessons involving education. As we have seen, one reason for the success of modern Jews is that they inherited from Rabbinic Judaism an admiration for learning. According to the rabbis, one was commanded to study in order to understand God's laws, but in their eyes, the activity of study did much more than that. It was a spiritual experience in its own right, and as such, it was considered highly pleasurable – so pleasurable, in fact, that according to some rabbinic sources, the ultimate reward in the afterlife was to be able to engage in study for all eternity. Not all Jews throughout the centuries occupied themselves with study, nor did they educate their children nearly as much as people often imagine, but they certainly absorbed the rabbinic reverence for intellectual achievement, and that sentiment played a critical role in preparing Jews for success in the modern world.

Americans could learn from this aspect of Jewish culture. They increasingly see education as nothing more than a means to a job. Academics like myself are being pressured more and more to construct curriculums and teach courses that will lead to employment. I, of course, understand how valuable it is to have a decent job, and I am by no means denying the importance of that goal. However, the ideal of education for its own sake is gradually being lost, and that, to my mind, is a terrible development. The rabbis were right to view learning as one of life's greatest pleasures, and it is something that can be appreciated even without the religious framework of Rabbinic Judaism to support it. Americans therefore have much to lose by viewing learning as serving only practical ends. They will end up leading far less fulfilled lives.

The argument can also be made that not only will the erosion of the ideal of learning for its own stake take away from the pleasure of life in general, ironically it may take away from the practical goals that Americans increasingly believe are the entire reason why people should be educated. My sense is that professional success is more likely to occur when people remain lifelong students and when curiosity and a desire to learn permeate their lives. Individuals who approach the world as a fascinating place to be explored on a constant basis bring that way of thinking into the workplace, and as a result, they become better at what they do. They are energized for their work because it becomes one more opportunity for them to learn about the world. Thus, the irony of Americans pressuring educators to train students for the workplace and nothing more is that students will end up performing more poorly in the workplace.

In light of these considerations, I wonder if Jews did well in the modern world in part because they brought into the workplace a sense of curiosity and an excitement about learning that had been central to their religious culture. This speculation would be difficult to prove, but it is worth considering.

I recognize that most people are not blessed with professions that allow them to constantly learn new things. But I would maintain that whatever one does professionally will be enhanced if one has a love of learning and a fundamentally curious disposition. Moreover, work is just one part of life. There is the rest of life to live, and the desire to learn and curiosity about the world can bring great enjoyment to the hours of the week that are not devoted to one's job.

In order for Americans to appreciate learning for its own sake, they need to demand that their educational institutions inculcate that ideal. Yet Americans also need something more. They also need to cultivate role models for their youth who embody learning for its own sake. The role models in American society have to include intellectuals. Much of the success that modern Jews have experienced has been due to the fact that for centuries Jews did just that; they chose intellectuals as their heroes. The rabbis in medieval and early modern Europe were revered by Jews for their knowledge and their powerful minds. And here again, modern Jews translated that value into a secular ideal. Contemporary American culture, in contrast, is wanting in this regard. The heroes that young Americans emulate are distinguished by superficial qualities: physical beauty, bravado, and wealth, and that is unlikely to change any time soon. Most Americans are willing to pay far more money to see a great basketball player dunk a ball into a hoop than to listen to a great scholar lecture on morality or the meaning of existence. American youth would be better served if their role models also included great intellectuals.

My arguments here also have ramifications for the curriculums in American schools, particularly middle school and high school. When I speak about the reverence that Jews had for intellectual achievement prior to the modern period, I am speaking about intellectual achievement that was focused mostly on the mastery of Jewish law. Rabbis over the centuries were respected for their knowledge of the law's contents as well as for their ability to use reason to interpret it.

Modern Western educators can learn something here. Why not make the study of law a core component of the American educational system in the way that Jews did? What would be studied here would be secular American law, not religious law, but students would benefit from studying this body of law in the same way that Jewish students over the centuries benefited from studying Jewish law. A serious engagement with American law would help American students gain concrete knowledge of the central political and social issues affecting their society, while also developing in them the capacity to formulate arguments about those issues. American young people would then be much better prepared than they currently are to engage in debates about such issues, and as they grow into adulthood, they would be much better prepared to participate in civil society and respond to the challenges facing their country. Currently, some high schools in the US offer courses on American law. What I am suggesting is much more ambitious: make the study of law a core subject in American schools from middle school onwards.

Interestingly, South Koreans have recently begun to include the study of the Talmud in their high school curriculums on the premise that Jews have been successful because Talmud study helped them develop powerful thinking skills. This novel project has received a fair amount of attention in the Israeli press and from Jews elsewhere.[13] While I greatly commend Koreans for understanding the significance of studying Talmud for the success of Jewish culture, I think their experiment is somewhat misguided. Much of what is contained in the Talmud is of little relevance to Korean society. Koreans would be much better served by doing what I propose Americans should do; Koreans should have their students study their *own* legal system. That way, their young people will not only develop good thinking skills, they will also gain knowledge of the law system by which they live their lives.

I recognize, of course, that American schools are facing far more basic challenges that will have to be confronted before implementing the suggestion I have just made. However, Americans should still aspire to making the study of law a core subject in their schools. This subject should be on a par with English literature and history. To my mind, the study of law is that important.

A Final Thought

These then are the lessons that I believe can be gleaned from this book. They are by no means exhaustive. My readers may find in it lessons of their own, and I invite them to add to those I have offered.

I want to conclude this book with a personal wish, but I must preface it with some general observations about success. In my introductory chapter, I emphasized that the type of success I would be concerned with did not include success in the moral realm; my focus was going to be on success in the economic, intellectual, and artistic realms. However, I also argued that while the subject matter of this book would not be morality, it did have moral implications because those who do not achieve success in any of the realms just mentioned often have great difficulty achieving happiness in life in general, and that is certainly a moral concern. Deprivation in the economic sphere is especially harmful to human happiness.[14]

This last point can be expanded upon by noting that there is wide recognition that economic deprivation is indeed a moral concern. This premise is, in fact, fundamental to the domestic and international policies of most Western countries. The presumption is that economic success is extremely important for human well-being, and so we have to do our best to provide those who are materially deprived with the resources they need to improve their situation. There is much debate, particularly in the US, about who should offer such assistance and what it should consist of. Yet, there is consensus that economic deprivation is indeed a moral issue.

Similar arguments can be made about the harm inflicted by deprivation in the other two areas of success focused on in this book: the intellectual and artistic realms. Deprivation in these areas may be less damaging than economic deprivation, but it is deprivation nonetheless in that it robs people of the full richness of life's experiences. Much in life is missing if one is unable to develop one's intellect through education or to enjoy the pleasure of artistic creation, be it one's own or that of others. The claim can also be made that deprivation in the intellectual realm can lead to economic deprivation since one's educational level has ramifications for one's career opportunities. Thus, deprivation in the intellectual and artistic spheres is a moral issue as well.

Yet, too many people in our world do not experience anything close to the kind of success we have been discussing. Hundreds of millions of people in our world live lives mired in poverty, have no access to education, and have little opportunity to express themselves artistically. Even Western countries have poverty rates that are too high, given how much wealth they have. In the US, for instance, the poverty rate has hovered around 10 per cent in recent years. I noted in my introductory chapter that even Jews, despite their immense success, have rates of poverty that are not negligible.[15]

So I leave my readers with a personal wish, a wish that the kind of success this book discusses will be made available to far more people in our world than it currently is. Everyone should have the opportunity to achieve success in the three spheres that have been the focus of our discussion. Everyone should experience the security of economic well-being, the excitement that comes with intellectual growth, and the emotional enrichment that accompanies engagement with the arts. These experiences are too basic to the welfare of human beings to be the property of select groups. No one – Jew or non-Jew, Westerner or non-Westerner – should be deprived of them. And if this wish seems too grandiose, too unrealistic to be fulfilled – let us keep in mind the words of Rabbi Tarfon, a prominent rabbi of the second century, who, in reflecting on the obligations of the religious life, said as follows:

> It is not incumbent upon you to bring the task to completion,
> but you are also not at liberty to be relieved of it altogether.
>
> (M *Avot* 2:16)

Notes

Introduction: The Mystery of Jewish Success

1 See the website of the Museum of the Jewish People at Beit Hatfutsot, https://nobel.bh.org.il/en.

2 Sergio Della Pergola, "World Jewish Population, 2017," *American Jewish Year Book 2017*, ed. Arnold Dashefsky and Ira M. Sheskin, vol. 117 of *American Jewish Year Book* (Cham, Switzerland: Springer International, 2018), 297–377.

3 Steven L. Pease has tirelessly documented Jewish achievement over the past two centuries in two books. The first is *The Golden Age of Jewish Achievement: The Compendium of a Culture, a People, and Their Stunning Performance* (Sonoma: Deucalion, 2009). This book is an enormous anthology of facts and statistics about Jewish success in the modern period, along with an analysis of explanations for this phenomenon. The second is, *The Debate over Jewish Achievement: Exploring the Nature and Nurture of Human Accomplishment* (Sonoma: Deucalion, 2015). This book traces the history of the theories that have been proposed to explain Jewish success. It also provides a convenient summary of the major statistics that Pease compiled in the first book (9–16). Some of the statistics I cite below are from Pease's two books. However, the tripartite scheme I adopt here for analysing the accomplishments of Jews in the modern world is my own.

4 Gabe Friedman, "Forbes' Billionaires List Features Old and New Jewish Faces," *Jewish Telegraphic Agency*, 2 March 2015, https://www.jta.org /2015/03/02/culture/forbes-billionaires-list-features-new-and-old -jewish-faces.

5 In an article published in 2003, Lisa A. Keister showed that, according to data compiled in the 1980s, Jews ranked first in annual income among various religious groups in the US. See Keister, "Religion and Wealth:

The Role of Religious Affiliation and Participation in Early Adult Asset Accumulation," *Social Forces* 82, no. 1 (September 2003): 175–205, https://doi.org/10.1353/sof.2003.0094. See also Keister's discussion of Jews in her subsequent study on the relationship between religion and income, *Faith and Money: How Religion Contributes to Wealth and Poverty* (Cambridge: Cambridge University Press, 2011), 169–81, https://doi.org/10.1017/CBO9781139028547. The Pew Research Center has also compiled statistics in recent years on the average annual income of religious groups in the US. A Pew survey in 2009 ranked Jews second in annual income among religious groups, just behind Hindus. See "Income Distribution within U.S. Religious Groups," Pew Research Center, 30 January 2009, https://www.pewresearch.org/religion/2009/01/30/income-distribution-within-us-religious-groups. Another survey in 2014 ranked Jews first in this regard. See, David Masci, "How Income Varies among U.S. Religious Groups," Pew Research Center, 11 October 2016, https://www.pewresearch.org/fact-tank/2016/10/11/how-income-varies-among-u-s-religious-groups.

6 Jacob Berkman, "At Least 139 of the Forbes 400 Are Jewish," *Jewish Telegraphic Agency*, 5 October 2009, https://www.jta.org/2009/10/05/united-states/at-least-139-of-the-forbes-400-are-jewish.

7 Jonathan Hornstein, *Jewish Poverty in the United States: A Survey of Recent Research* (Owing Mills: Harry and Jeanette Weinberg Foundation, 2019), 3–4, https://hjweinbergfoundation.org/wp-content/uploads/dlm_uploads/2019/03/jewish-poverty-in-the-united-states.pdf; Jane Eisner, "Why We Do Not Talk about Jewish Poverty – and Why We Should," *The Forward*, 19 March 2019, https://forward.com/culture/421071/why-we-dont-talk-about-jewish-poverty-and-why-we-should.

8 See, "Jewish Recipients of the Pulitzer Prize for General Non-Fiction," accessed 4 January 2023, http://www.jinfo.org/Pulitzer_Non-Fiction.html; and "Jewish Recipients of the Pulitzer Prize for Fiction," accessed 4 January 2023, http://www.jinfo.org/Pulitzer_Fiction.html.

9 Pease, *The Golden Age*, 50; Pease, *The Debate*, 13.

10 Pease, 56–7; Pease, 13.

11 Ulrich Charpa, "Jews and Science," in *The Modern World, 1815–2000*, ed. Mitchel B. Hart and Tony Michels, vol. 8 of *The Cambridge History of Judaism* (Cambridge: Cambridge University Press, 2018), 988–1016, https://doi.org/10.1017/9781139019828.037.

12 I cite statistics here only up to 2008 because the most up-to-date numbers I could find on the achievements of Jews in the performing arts were those provided by Pease, whose research went no further than that year.

13 Pease, *The Golden Age*, 118; Pease, *The Debate*, 13.

14 Pease, *The Golden Age*, 125–6; Pease, *The Debate*, 17.

15 Pease, *The Golden Age*, 156–7; Pease, *The Debate*, 13.

16 Pease, *The Golden Age*, 121–2; Pease, *The Debate*, 15.

17 Pease, *The Golden Age*, 88–90; Pease, *The Debate*, 15.

18 The modest contribution of Jews to medieval science is noted by Gad Freudenthal, "Introduction: The History of Science in Medieval Jewish Cultures: Toward a Definition of the Agenda," in *Science in Medieval Jewish Cultures*, ed. Gad Freudenthal (Cambridge: Cambridge University Press, 2011), 4–5, https://doi.org/10.1017/CBO9780511976575.002. As for the arts, there were no famous European Jewish painters in the medieval and early modern periods – at least none with the stature of such famous modern Jewish figures as Camille Pissarro and Marc Chagall. The same could be said about other branches of the arts.

19 Jonathan D. Sarna, *American Judaism: A History*, 2nd ed. (New Haven: Yale University Press, 2019), 31.

20 Pease, *The Debate*, 21.

21 Mark Twain, "Concerning the Jews," *Harper's Magazine* 99 (September 1899), 535.

22 Noah J. Efron, *A Chosen Calling: Jews in Science in the Twentieth Century* (Baltimore: Johns Hopkins University Press, 2014), 1–12, https://doi.org/10.1353/book.29450.

23 Robert Chazan, in a recent book, argues that Jewish historians have exaggerated the impact of expulsions on Jewish communities in medieval Europe. He claims that Jews often migrated voluntarily in order to achieve better conditions for themselves. See Robert Chazan, *Refugees or Migrants: Premodern Jewish Population Movement* (New Haven: Yale University Press, 2018), https://doi.org/10.12987/yale/9780300218572.001.0001. It is too early to tell whether Chazan's thesis will be accepted by other historians. Jonathan D. Sarna offers a somewhat critical appraisal of the thesis in a brief review in *Choice: Current Reviews for Academic Libraries* 56, no. 9 (May 2019): 1167. I want to thank the anonymous reviewer who brought this book to my attention.

24 Even in ancient Israel, Jews had not had an easy time. Jewish history goes back at least 3,000 years, and in the first thousand years, when Jews lived in their own homeland, they were frequently attacked by and subjugated to larger empires – the Assyrians, Babylonians, Persians, Greeks, and Romans. Their commonwealth was entirely destroyed twice, once in the sixth century BCE by the Babylonians, and again in the first century CE at the hands of the Romans. It was after the second destruction that Jews effectively went into exile and began to live in Europe and in lands later conquered by Islam.

25 This point was first made by Baron in his article, "Ghetto and Emancipation," *The Menorah Journal* 14, no. 6 (June 1928): 515–26.

26 As Robert Liberles has demonstrated, even Baron himself did not intend that his anti-lachrymose view of Jewish history should minimize the extent of Jewish persecution throughout the centuries. He simply wanted to ensure that Jewish historians give attention to the richness of pre-modern Jewish culture that he felt it deserved. See Robert Liberles, *Salo Wittmayer Baron: Architect of Jewish History* (New York: NYU Press, 1995), 345.

27 Pease, *The Golden Age*, 45, 55, 405.

28 The story of Israel's rise as an economic and technological power is analysed in Dan Senor and Saul Singer, *Startup Nation: The Story of Israel's Economic Miracle* (New York: Twelve, 2011).

29 Thomas Sowell, *Race and Culture: A World View* (New York: Basic Books, 1994); Sowell, *Migrations and Cultures: A World View* (New York, Basic Books, 1996); Sowell, *Conquest and Cultures: An International History* (New York: Basic Books, 1998); Lawrence E. Harrison, *Jews, Confucians, and Protestants: Cultural Capital and the End of Multiculturalism* (Lanham, MD: Rowman and Littlefield, 2012); Amy Chua and Jed Rubenfeld, *The Triple Package: How Three Unlikely Traits Explain the Rise and Fall of Cultural Groups in America* (London: Penguin Books, 2014).

30 See Harrison, *Jews, Confucians, and Protestants*; and Chua and Rubenfeld, *The Triple Package*.

31 Jennifer Lee and Min Zhou, *The Asian American Achievement Paradox* (New York: Russell Sage Foundation, 2015). Lee and Zhou reject the notion argued by Harrison, and Chua and Rubenfeld, that the success of Asian Americans has been due to cultural factors.

32 My focus here is on the modern period. However, it is appropriate to note that some groups achieved success, as I have defined it, just before the modern period. The immense accomplishments of the Dutch in the seventeenth century have been studied by Simon Schama in *The Embarrassment of Riches: An Interpretation of Dutch Culture in the Golden Age* (New York: Alfred A. Knopf, 1987). The accomplishments of the Scots in the eighteenth and early nineteenth centuries have been discussed by Arthur Herman in *How the Scots Invented the World* (New York: Random House, 2001). A comparison between the success of modern Jews in the West and that of these earlier cultures would be most instructive.

33 For a Jewish perspective of this kind, see, for instance, Shawn Lazar, "Jewish Genius and the Existence of God," Grace Evangelical Society, 1 March 2016, https://faithalone.org/journal-articles/jewish-genius-and-the-existence-of-god. For a Christian perspective, see, for instance, Jim Gerrish, "Why the Jews Succeed," Church and Israel Forum, accessed 4 January 2023, https://www.churchisraelforum.com/jews-succeed.

34 The most notorious representative of this viewpoint is the *Protocols of the Elders of Zion*, a document composed by the Russian secret police and

published in Russia in 1903. It purported to be a record of discussions from meetings among Jews who were planning to take over the world.

35 My discussion of genetic explanations for Jewish success is much indebted to Pease, *The Debate*, ch. 2; and Pinker, "Groups and Genes: The Lessons of the Ashkenazim," *The New Republic*, 26 June 2006, 25–8, https://newrepublic.com/article/77727/groups-and-genes.

36 For a recent attempt to support the genetic hypothesis for Jewish success, see Richard Lynn, *The Chosen People: A Study of Jewish Intelligence and Achievement* (Whitefish: Washington Summit, 2011). Lynn entertains a number of other theories for Jewish success as well.

37 Lynn, *The Chosen People*, 329–31. A variation on this hypothesis that attracted a great deal of attention was presented by Gregory Cochran, Jason Hardy, and Henry Harpending in an article, "Natural History of Ashkenazi Intelligence," *Journal of Biosocial Sciences* 38, no. 5 (September 2006): 659–93, https://doi.org/10.1017/S0021932005027069.

38 Ernest Van den Haag, *The Jewish Mystique* (New York: Stein and Day, 1969); Lynn, *The Chosen People*, 325–9.

39 Pease, *The Debate*, 26–33; Robert Plomin, "Is Intelligence Hereditary?" *Scientific American Mind* 27, no. 3 (1 May 2016), 73.

40 Pease, *The Debate*, 32–3, 37–42. There is also the problem of the "Flynn effect," which refers to a gradual increase in IQ scores from the 1930s to the present day in many parts of the world. There is much debate about the meaning of this phenomenon. See Pease, 32–3.

41 Plomin notes that genetics explains only about half the differences between individuals when it comes to intelligence.

42 Hasia Diner, *Roads Taken: The Great Jewish Migrations to the New World and the Peddlers Who Forged the Way* (New Haven: Yale University Press, 2015), https://doi.org/10.12987/9780300210194.

43 Adam D. Mendelsohn, *The Rag Race: How Jews Sewed Their Way to Success in America and the British Empire* (New York: NYU Press, 2015), https://doi.org/10.18574/nyu/9781479860258.001.0001. Eli Lederhendler provides another example of the historical approach to explain the economic success of Jews in the US in *Jewish Immigrants and American Capitalism, 1880–1920: From Caste to Class* (Cambridge: Cambridge University Press, 2009). Lederhendler traces the process by which eastern European Jewish immigrants to the US at the turn of the twentieth century became economically successful by fashioning a social identity in response to their new circumstances. According to Lederhendler, that identity was entirely their own creation and bore no relation to the life they left behind in Europe.

44 Thorstein Veblen, "The Intellectual Pre-Eminence of Jews in Modern Europe," *Political Science Quarterly* 34, no. 1 (March 1919): 33–43.

45 Efron, *A Chosen Calling*.

46 Lederhendler also allows room for human initiative in his treatment of Jewish economic success in America.

47 Diner casts a wide net by looking at Jewish peddling in a number of Western countries, but her main focus is on the US. Mendelsohn compares Jewish participation in the garment industry in nineteenth-century America with Jewish participation in the same industry in England in the same century, and he demonstrates that US Jews did much better than their British counterparts. Mendelsohn therefore concludes that what led to Jewish success in the garment industry in America was historical circumstance, not culture. Otherwise, Jews in Britain's garment industry would have been just as successful as those in US. Mendelsohn thus attempts a comparative approach to Jewish economic success in the modern period. However, Mendelsohn analyses the economic success of Jews in only two countries and in one industry, a focus that is still too narrow to draw any firm conclusions about their economic success in the modern period in general.

48 Jonathan I. Israel, *European Jewry in the Age of Mercantilism, 1550–1750* (Oxford: Oxford University Press, 1991), https://doi.org/10.1093/acprof:oso /9780198219286.001.0001; Israel, *Diasporas within a Diaspora: Jews, Crypto-Jews, and the World of Maritime Empires, 1540–1740*, vol. 30 of *Brill's Series in Jewish Studies*, ed. David S. Katz (Leiden: E.J. Brill, 2002), https://doi .org/10.1163/9789004500969.

49 Gershon David Hundert, "The Role of Jews in Commerce in Early Modern Poland-Lithuania," *Journal of European Economic History* 16, no. 2 (1987): 245–75; Hundert, *Jews in a Polish Private Town: The Case of Opatòw in the Eighteenth Century* (Baltimore: Johns Hopkins University Press, 1992), https://doi.org/10.1353/book.71395; Hundert, *Jews in Poland-Lithuania in the Eighteenth Century: A Genealogy of Modernity* (Berkeley: University of California Press, 2004), ch. 2, https://doi.org/10.1525/9780520940321 -008; Moshe J. Rosman, *The Lords' Jews: Magnate-Jewish Relations in the Polish-Lithuanian Commonwealth in the Eighteenth Century* (Cambridge, MA: Harvard University Press, 1990); Adam Teller, *Money, Power, and Influence in Eighteenth-Century Lithuania: The Jews on the Radziwiłł Estates* (Stanford: Stanford University Press, 2016), https://doi.org/10.1515 /9780804799874.

50 Avraham Barkai, "German Jews at the Start of Industrialization – Structural Change and Mobility, 1835–1860," in *Revolution and Evolution: 1848 in German-Jewish History*, ed. Werner E. Mosse, Arnold Pauker, Reinhard Rürup, and Robert Weltsch (Tübingen: JCB Mohr, 1981), 123–45; Jerry Z. Muller, *Capitalism and the Jews* (Princeton: Princeton University Press, 2010), 94–103, https://doi.org/10.1515/9781400834365; Jonathan

Karp, "Jews and Commerce," in Hart and Michels, *The Modern Period, 1815–2000*, 8:420–1, 8:425, https://doi.org/10.1017/9781139019828.016.

51 Karp's essay, "Jews and Commerce," gives a wonderful whirlwind tour of Jewish economic activity in the modern period.

52 Norman Lebrecht, *Genius and Anxiety: How Jews Changed the World, 1847–1947* (New York: Scribner, 2019), xii, xiv, 26–7.

53 One also has to question whether anxiety is as productive as Lebrecht claims. Anxiety can often cripple an individual's ability to achieve, not enhance it.

54 Yuri Slezkine, *The Jewish Century* (Princeton: Princeton University Press, 2004), https://doi.org/10.1515/9781400828555.

55 Slezkine, *The Jewish Century*, 40–1.

56 Werner Sombart, *Die Juden und das Wirtschaftsleben* (Leipzig: Duncker & Humblot, 1911).

57 Derek J. Penslar, *Shylock's Children: Economics and Jewish Identity in Modern Europe* (Berkeley: University of California Press, 2001), 163–73.

58 Muller, *Capitalism and the Jews*, 83–6.

59 Efron, *A Chosen Calling*, 1–3.

60 Some of the writers who support this approach are identified in my next footnote.

61 These writers have presented their views in various books, journals, newspapers, and websites. Book-length attempts to argue in favour of the cultural hypothesis include Pease's two books, as well as Steven Silbiger, *The Jewish Phenomenon: Seven Keys to the Enduring Wealth of a People*, 2nd ed. (Lanham, MD: M. Evans, 2009). In this category is also Thomas Cahill's very popular book, *The Gift of the Jews: How a Tribe of Desert Nomads Changed the Way Everyone Thinks and Feels* (New York: Anchor Books, 1999). However, Cahill's book, despite the title, deals only with the period of the Hebrew Bible before Judaism appeared in its classical form. As for the internet, a simple search with the keywords "Jews" and "success," or "Jews" and "achievement," will yield scores of sources in which popular writers argue in favour of the cultural hypothesis. Norman Lebrecht also hints at the cultural hypothesis in a number of places in his book, *Genius and Anxiety*. In some of his biographical sketches of major modern Jewish figures, he notes how their thinking was beholden to biblical or rabbinic principles and ideas. See, for instance, his discussion of the Jewish sources of Freud's views, pp. 172–5. Lebrecht, however, in focusing on the biographies of prominent Jews, does not provide a systematic exposition of the cultural hypothesis.

62 Paul Johnson, *A History of the Jews* (New York: Harper Perennial, 1988), 44.

63 Johnson, *A History of the Jews*, 591.

64 See note 3 above.

65 Raphael Patai, *The Jewish Mind* (Detroit: Wayne State University Press, 1996).

66 Stella Botticini and Zvi Eckstein, *The Chosen Few: How Education Shaped Jewish History, 70–1492* (Princeton: Princeton University Press, 2012).

67 See Shaul Stampfer, review of Eckstein and Botticini, *The Chosen Few* in *Jewish History* 29, nos. 3–4 (December 2015): 373–9, https://doi.org/10.1007/s10835-015-9247-0. See also Barry Chazan, Robert Chazan, and Benjamin M. Jacobs, *Cultures and Contexts of Jewish Education* (New York: Palgrave Macmillan, 2017), 29n13.

68 The "r" in Rabbinic Judaism is often lower-case. However, I have chosen to make it upper-case in this book in order to underscore the importance and independent character of this form of Judaism.

69 I base this figure on the statistics of Sergio Della Pergola, "Some Fundamentals of Jewish Demographic History," *Papers in Jewish Demography 1977*, ed. S. Della Pergola and J. Even (Jerusalem: Hebrew University, 2001), 21.

70 This is perhaps more true in the economic and scientific realms than in other areas.

71 My observations here explain why I have deliberately avoided referring to "Ashkenazi" and "Sephardi" Jews. Jews in the West are the focus of this book because it is in the West that most modern Jews have lived and experienced success in such disproportionate fashion. The terms "Ashkenazi" and "Sephardi" would complicate matters. Most Western Jews are, in fact, Ashkenazi; that is, they are Jews who can trace their origins to communities in medieval Germany and northern France. However, the West also contains sizeable numbers of Sephardi Jews, who are of Spanish origin, and Mizrahi Jews, who hail from Muslim countries, and it is difficult to differentiate the various types of Western Jews with respect to the issue of success because we do not have the data to make such distinctions. As I have already pointed out, when American Jews are surveyed regarding income and education levels, the surveys do not tend to distinguish among Ashkenazi, Sephardi, and Mizrahi Jews. They are all lumped together as "Jews." The term "Ashkenazi," therefore, is not helpful here, and it is much better that we speak of "Western Jews" instead. The term "Sephardi" is problematic for other reasons. Spanish Jews were expelled from Spain in 1492 and established communities in Christian Europe and Islamic lands, and their histories in these two cultures were quite different. We know that Sephardi Jews did quite well in Western countries and that this success carried over to some extent into the modern period as well. However, we are less sure about the success of Sephardi Jews in Islamic lands given how little we know about the success of Jews in Islamic lands in general. Thus, the term "Sephardi" is not

helpful either. Moreover, the term "Sephardi" has often been mistakenly used for all Jews in Islamic lands, an identification that only confuses the picture even more, and this therefore provides yet another reason to avoid the term.

72 My thinking here is substantially the same as that of Moshe J. Rosman in, *How Jewish Is Jewish History?* (Portland, OR: Oxford, 2007), 148–9.

73 Rosman, *How Jewish Is Jewish History?*, 20–35.

74 One could refine the definition a bit further by saying that Jews include those who have not only identified themselves as such throughout the centuries but who have been identified as such by the majority of others in the same period who identify themselves as Jews. That is, it is perhaps not enough to say that one is a Jew; one must also be viewed as a Jew by the majority of others in one's era who say they are Jews. This definition would preclude such groups as Messianic Jews in our own period, who claim to be Jews but are not regarded as Jews by the vast majority of other people who call themselves Jews.

75 Some scholars claim that the modern period ended in the 1980s and that we now live in the period of postmodernity. However, I will not be engaging with this demarcation in this study. First, many scholars claim that the modern period never ended and that we are still living in it. Second, even those who believe that we are currently in the period of postmodernity have not been able to agree on what its characteristics are. I cannot enter into these debates in this book, nor do I need to. Even if the argument can be made that we are living in a postmodern age, that reality is not relevant to my analysis of Jewish success. The reasons for the success of Jews from the beginning of the modern period up to the 1980s are, to my mind, the same for the success of Jews since the 1980s.

1. Western Culture, Jewish Culture, and Four Key Values

1 These values are referred to frequently in two excellent books that describe the evolution of modern intellectual culture: Richard Tarnas, *The Passion of the Western Mind: Understanding the Ideas That Have Shaped Our World View* (New York: Ballantine Books, 1991), chs. 5–6; and Jacques Barzun, *From Dawn to Decadence: 1500 to the Present: 500 Years of Western Cultural Life* (New York: HarperCollins, 2001).

2 This is the main emphasis of Philip T. Hoffman's, *Why Did Europe Conquer the World?* (Princeton: Princeton University Press, 2015), https://doi.org /10.1515/9781400865840. Hoffman also ties the military advantages of the West to political, economic, and geographical factors.

3 This approach is taken in Jared Diamond's study, *Guns, Germs, and Steel: The Fate of Human Societies* (New York: W.W. Norton, 1999). Diamond

argues that geography, demography, and ecological circumstances
were the key to the West's success. These factors allowed Europeans to
develop strong agricultural societies, a form of community that gave them
enormous advantages over their rivals. Ian Morris highlights geographic
circumstances in his explanation of Western dominance in his book *Why
the West Rules – For Now: The Patterns of History and What They Reveal About
the Future* (New York: Farrar, Straus and Giroux, 2010).

4 David S. Landes, in *The Wealth and Poverty of Nations: Why Some Are So
Rich and Some So Poor* (New York: W.W. Norton, 1999), argues that the
cultural traits that have allowed the West to dominate the world include
an emphasis on work, thrift, honesty, patience, and tenacity, as well as
a commitment to democracy and an openness to new ideas. However,
Landes does not clearly differentiate these cultural factors from material
factors. In Niall Ferguson's *Civilization: The West and the Rest* (London:
Penguin Group, 2011), the cultural traits responsible for Western
dominance are competition, science, property rights, modern medicine,
consumerism, and a strong work ethic. Rodney Stark, in *How the West
Won: The Neglected Story of the Triumph of Modernity* (Wilmington: ISI Books,
2014), argues that it was primarily the West's intellectual culture that made
it successful by emphasizing the ideas of human freedom, the pursuit of
knowledge, and the rationality of God and the universe. Stark gives much
credit to Christianity, which, he believes, was the primary source of these
ideas. Charles Murray, in *Human Accomplishment: The Pursuit of Excellence
in the Arts and Sciences, 800 B.C. to 1950* (New York: HarperCollins, 2003),
argues that the West's accomplishments are attributable to its emphasis
on human individualism and autonomy, which were harnessed for the
purpose of achieving excellence in the pursuit of truth, beauty, and the
good.

5 From among the authors cited in my previous note, the approaches of
Murray and Stark most resemble mine; however, I have sharp differences
with Murray and Stark that will come out in this book. They tend to
exaggerate the superiority of the West over other cultures. Moreover,
as I will point out later, Murray's treatment of Jewish culture is entirely
inaccurate.

6 Ricardo Duchesne provides a detailed history of this approach in his book,
The Uniqueness of Western Civilization, vol. 28 of *Studies in Critical Social
Studies*, edited by David Fasenfest (Leiden: E.J. Brill, 2012), https://doi
.org/10.1163/ej.9789004192485.i-527.

7 Duchesne's book is largely dedicated to that goal.

8 This matter is discussed throughout the study of Walter Jacob, *Christianity
through Jewish Eyes: The Quest for Common Ground* (Cincinnati: Hebrew
Union College Press, 1974).

9 Two books published in the middle of the twentieth century that were widely read by Jews at the time epitomized this interest: Trude Weiss-Rosmarin, *Judaism and Christianity: The Differences* (New York: Jewish Book Club, 1943); and Abba Hillel Silver, *Where Judaism Differed: An Inquiry into the Distinctiveness of Judaism* (New York: Macmillan, 1965).

10 This approach is decried by Eugene J. Fisher, a Christian scholar and theologian, in his article, "Typical Jewish Misunderstandings of Christianity," *Shofar* 28, no. 3 (Spring 2010): 57–69.

11 The notion that there are 613 commandments is stated in a number of places in early rabbinic literature. The best known is BT *Makkot* 23b. Medieval Jewish thinkers attempted to provide a list of these commandments. The most famous was that of Maimonides, who devoted an entire book to this project.

12 The reign of Solomon is described in I Kings 1–11.

13 Shaye J.D. Cohen, *From the Maccabees to the Mishnah*, 3rd ed. (Louisville: Westminster John Knox Press, 2014), 25–6.

14 Martin S. Jaffee, *Early Judaism: Religious Worlds of the First Judaic Millennium*, 2nd ed. (Bethesda: University Press of Maryland, 2006), 78–81, 161–2.

15 Robert Goldenberg, "The Destruction of the Jerusalem Temple: Its Meaning and Its Consequences," in *The Late Roman-Rabbinic Period*, ed. Steven T. Katz, vol. 4 of *The Cambridge History of Judaism* (Cambridge: Cambridge University Press, 2006), 199, https://doi.org/10.1017/CHOL9780521772488.009. A number of passages attempt to identify the sins responsible for the destruction of the Temple. For example, a passage in BT *Yoma* 9a claims that "groundless hatred" between Jews was its cause.

16 See, for instance, Deut. 4:25–31.

17 See, for instance, Is. 2:1–14.

18 Goldenberg, "The Destruction of the Jerusalem Temple," 199–201.

19 BT *Berakhot* 26b.

20 Jaffee, *Early Judaism*, ch. 5. Synagogues existed even before the destruction of the Second Temple, but it was the rabbis who gave them a central place in the religious life of the Jewish community by making prayer a substitute for sacrifice.

21 Jaffee, 92–4, 104–13, 117–21; Lawrence H. Schiffman, "Messianism and Apocalypticism in Rabbinic Texts," in Katz, *The Late Roman-Rabbinic Period*, 4:1053–72, https://doi.org/10.1017/CHOL9780521772488.042.

22 David Biale, *Not in the Heavens: The Tradition of Jewish Secular Thought* (Princeton: Princeton University Press, 2011), https://doi.org/10.1515/9781400836642.

23 In Matthew 23:7, Jesus refers to the Pharisees as those who like to be called "rabbi." It is unlikely that Jesus was referring to a formal designation here.

As noted, the term "rabbi" literally means "my master," and at this point in the history of Judaism, it was used as a title of honour in the way that modern Americans use the title "sir." However, one can see how, in light of Jesus's statement, the equation between the Pharisees and the rabbis was an easy one to make for Christians in subsequent centuries.

24 See, for instance, 2 Corinthians 3:6.

25 My analysis in the preceding paragraphs of the negative portrayal of Rabbinic Judaism among Western academics is based on E.P. Sanders, *Paul and Palestinian Judaism* (Philadelphia: Fortress Press, 1977), esp. 1–59, and Charlotte Klein, *Anti-Judaism in Christian Theology*, trans. Edward Quinn (Philadelphia: Fortress Press, 1978), esp. chs. 1–3. Neither Sanders nor Klein breaks down the prejudices against the rabbis into the opposing camps that have been described here, but if one reads their descriptions of these prejudices carefully, one finds both perspectives.

26 These thinkers wanted Jews to go into agriculture and crafts on the belief that these occupations constituted "real" work, as opposed to money-lending, banking, and commerce – the professions in which Jews were involved. See Derek J. Penslar, *Shylock's Children: Economics and Jewish Identity in Modern Europe* (Berkeley: University of California Press, 2001), 62–3, 84–5.

27 I am always struck by how few of my Jewish students have any real knowledge of Rabbinic Judaism. They have certainly heard of rabbis, but they often know little about Rabbinic Judaism as a historical phenomenon.

28 Pioneers of this reading of Paul were Sanders, *Paul and Palestinian Judaism*; James D.G. Dunn, *The New Perspectives on Paul*, 2nd ed. (Grand Rapids, MI: Wm. B. Eerdmans, 2008); and Paula Fredriksen, *Paul: The Pagans' Apostle* (New Haven: Yale University Press, 2018), https://doi.org/10.12987/9780300231366. I would like to thank Paul Duff, my colleague at GW and an accomplished scholar of the New Testament, for educating me about the Jewish dimension of Paul's thought.

29 In recent decades, for instance, some Jewish academics have made the case that Rabbinic Judaism anticipated the main features of postmodernism, an argument that presumes that the rabbis were sophisticated intellectuals and well ahead of their time. Discussions of this matter can be found in Susan A. Handelman, *The Slayers of Moses: The Emergence of Rabbinic Interpretation in Modern Literary Theory* (Albany: SUNY Press, 1983); Daniel Boyarin, *Intertextuality and the Reading of Midrash* (Bloomington: Indiana University Press, 1991); and David Stern, *Midrash and Theory: Ancient Jewish Exegesis and Contemporary Literary Studies* (Evanston, IL: Northwestern University Press, 1998).

30 Nora L. Rubel, *Doubting the Devout: The Ultra-Orthodox in the Jewish American Imagination* (New York: Columbia University Press, 2009), 148,

https://doi.org/10.7312/rube14186-006. Ruben notes that "Mainstream Jews have – until recently – maintained the impression that the ultraorthodox are the 'real' Jews."

2. Secular Jews (and Other Jews)

1 A survey by the Pew Research Center in 2013 found that 62 per cent of American Jews identified themselves as Jews mainly on the basis of ancestry or culture, not religion. See Drew Desilver, "Jewish Essentials: For Most American Jews, Ancestry and Culture Matter More than Religion," Pew Research Center, 1 October 2013, http://www.pewresearch.org/fact -tank/2013/10/01/jewish-essentials-for-most-american-jews-ancestry -and-culture-matter-more-than-religion. According to a Pew survey of Israeli Jews in 2016, 40 per cent of Jews identified themselves as *hiloni*, which is usually translated as "secular." See, "Israel's Religiously Divided Society," Pew Research Center, 8 March 2016, https://www.pewresearch .org/religion/2016/03/08/israels-religiously-divided-society.

2 I will be referring to these debates in the course of this study, particularly those involving the Renaissance and the Enlightenment.

3 This point has been painfully evident in international debates over human rights since the Universal Declaration of Human Rights (UDHR) was issued by the United Nations in 1948. Non-Western cultures, particularly those of Asia and the Islamic world, have objected consistently to what they perceive as the Western biases of the UDHR, as well as to subsequent attempts by the West to define human rights, and one of the major points of contention has involved the question of the individual and the individual's place in society. Representatives of Asian countries have pointed out that when Westerners speak of human rights, they often place great emphasis on the value of the individual and assume that all other cultures do as well, but, the Asian representatives argue, this is not necessarily the case. In Asian countries, the collective has more importance than the individual. See R. Scott Appleby, *The Ambivalence of the Sacred* (Lanham, MD: Rowman and Littlefield, 2000), 247–64, esp. 248–9.

4 Brad S. Gregory discusses this issue in *The Unintended Reformation: How a Religious Revolution Secularized Society* (Cambridge, MA: Belknap Press, 2012), ch. 2 – though Gregory's presentation has a polemical edge to it in that he criticizes modern individualism and other ideas that can be traced back to the Reformation as ultimately detrimental to Western culture.

5 The debate began in 1966 with the publication of Blumenberg's book, *The Legitimacy of the Modern Age*, trans. Robert M. Wallace (Cambridge, MA: MIT Press, 1985), which attacked Löwith's views in the *Meaning in History: The Theological Implications of the Philosophy of History* (Chicago: University

of Chicago Press, 1949). The debate was carried on in subsequent publications by the two scholars. An excellent review of the debate can be found in Robert M. Wallace, "Progress, Secularization, and Modernity: The Löwith-Blumenberg Debate," *The New German Critique* 22 (Winter 1981): 63–79, https://doi.org/10.2307/487864.

6   Charles Taylor's most important work on the secularization question is his widely read book, *A Secular Age* (Cambridge, MA: Harvard University Press, 2007), https://doi.org/10.4159/9780674044289. There, Taylor argues for continuity between modernity and pre-modern Christianity by claiming that the roots of secularization can be found in the Protestant Reformation. Marcel Gauchet presents an even stronger case for the Christian origins of secularization in his book, *The Disenchantment of the World: A Political History of Religion*, trans. Oscar Burge (Princeton: Princeton University Press, 1999), https://doi.org/10.1515/9780691238364. Recent treatments of this issue can also be found in Michael Allen Gillespie, *The Theological Origins of Modernity* (Chicago: University of Chicago Press, 2009), https://doi.org/10.7208/9780226293516; Gregory, *The Unintended Reformation*; and Alec Ryrie, *Protestants: The Faith That Made the Modern World* (New York: Viking, 2017). All three authors are on the side of the debate that argues for continuity between Christianity and modernity. Gregory, however, attributes secularization to Protestant Christianity in order to critique this form of Christianity. Scholarly analyses of the debate can be found in Stijn Latré, Walter Van Herck, and Guido Vanheeswijck, eds., *Radical Secularization? An Inquiry into the Religious Roots of Secular Culture* (London: Bloomsbury Press, 2016).

7   Jonathan Frankel, "Assimilation and the Jews in Nineteenth-Century Europe: Toward a New Historiography?," in *Assimilation and Community: The Jews in Nineteenth-Century Europe*, ed. Jonathan Frankel and Steven J. Zipperstein (Cambridge: Cambridge University Press, 1992), 21–3; Pierre Birnbaum and Ira Katznelson, "Emancipation and the Liberal Offer," in *Paths of Emancipation: Jews, States, and Citizenship*, ed. Pierre Birnbaum and Ira Katznelson (Princeton: Princeton University Press, 1995), 17–19, https://doi.org/10.1515/9781400863976.1.

For a good portion of the twentieth century, Jewish historians believed that in the nineteenth century, the Jews of western and central Europe were focused on revolutionary change while the Jews of eastern Europe and Russia were focused on continuity with the past. This paradigm originated with the great Jewish historian, Simon M. Dubnov (1860–1941). However, since the 1960s, Jewish historians have come to recognize that the differences here were not as stark as Dubnov and his disciples believed. Jewish communities both east and west were, in fact, trying to strike a balance between change and continuity, and the differences between them had to do with where the emphasis should lie. Frankel's essay provides a detailed account of how the historiography on this issue evolved.

It should also be pointed out that while the modernization of Jewish culture was similar to the modernization of Western culture, the two were not identical. For instance, Jews struggled with the tension between change and continuity more than their non-Jewish neighbours did. Jews feared that modernizing influences, combined with the breaking down of barriers between Jews and non-Jews, would spell the end of the Jewish people. The concern was that Jews would assimilate into the non-Jewish world around them in large numbers and leave their former world behind. Resolving the tension between change and continuity was therefore a matter of survival for European Jews in a way that it was not for Europeans in general.

8 Todd Endelman, who has written extensively on this group, estimates that throughout the modern period it numbered in the hundreds of thousands. However, that means that at any one time – say, over the course of any decade in the modern period – this group was a fraction of this number, and given that Jews numbered in the millions at any one time in the modern period, the relative number of Jews converting to Christianity was relatively small. See Todd M. Endelman, "Assimilation and Assimilationism," in *The Modern Period, 1815–2000*, ed. Mitchell B. Hart and Tony Michels, vol. 8 of *The Cambridge History of Judaism* (Cambridge: Cambridge University Press, 2018), 333, https://doi.org/10.1017/9781139019828.012.

9 As noted earlier, however, while ultra-Orthodox Jews claimed to be the only Jews living a life truly continuous with the Jewish past, that was not necessarily true. Ultra-Orthodox Judaism was a product of modernity as much as the more liberal denominations were. It, along with other forms of Jewish Orthodoxy, were created in response to the rise of Reform Judaism in the early nineteenth century.

10 Zvi Gitelman, ed., *Religion or Ethnicity? Jewish Identities in Evolution* (New Brunswick: Rutgers University Press, 2009); David Biale, *Not in the Heavens: The Tradition of Secular Jewish Thought* (Princeton: Princeton University Press, 2011), https://doi.org/10.1515/9781400836642; David M. Gordis and Zachary I. Heller, eds., *Jewish Secularity: The Search for Roots and the Challenges of Relevant Meaning* (Lanham, MD: University Press of America, 2012); Ari Joskowicz and Ethan B. Katz, eds., *Secularism in Question: Jews and Judaism in Modern Times* (Philadelphia: University of Pennsylvania Press, 2015), https://doi.org/10.9783/9780812291513. Mention should also be made of an essay by Naomi Seidman, "Religion/Secularity," in *The Routledge Handbook of Contemporary Jewish Cultures*, ed.

Laurence Roth and Nadia Valman (London: Routledge, 2017), 151–61, https://doi.org/10.4324/9780203497470. Seidman's piece is brief but highly informative about the issues relevant to my discussion here.

11 Biale's book is cited in my previous note. My only quarrel with Biale is that in tracing the roots of Jewish secularism to pre-modern Jewish sources, he gives little attention to Rabbinic Judaism. He mentions in his introductory chapter that Rabbinic Judaism contained the seeds of modern Jewish secularism (7–8), but throughout the rest of his book, his focus is mostly on other forms of pre-modern Judaism that foreshadowed it, including the Bible, medieval Jewish philosophy, Kabbalah, and biblical exegesis. As I will argue below, I believe that Rabbinic Judaism also had a role to play in shaping modern Jewish secularism.

I have noted that Jewish secularism assumed a wide variety of expressions, but a full treatment of these expressions is well beyond the scope of this chapter. My analysis will therefore discuss this topic in broad strokes.

12 Biale, *Not in the Heavens*, ch. 1; see also 82–4; Ari Joskowicz and Ethan B. Katz, "Rethinking Jews and Secularism," in Joskowicz and Katz, *Secularism in Question*, 7–8, 14–15, https://doi.org/10.9783/9780812291513 -002. Scholars of the German Haskalah – the Haskalah was the Jewish Enlightenment – have also come to recognize that this movement attempted to preserve key features of Judaism even as it reshaped them to be in harmony with the European Enlightenment. See David Sorkin, *The Religious Enlightenment: Protestants, Jews, and Catholics from London to Vienna* (Princeton: Princeton University Press, 2008), https:// doi.org/10.1515/9780691188188. Shmuel Feiner paints a complex picture of the Haskalah in *The Jewish Enlightenment*, trans. Chaya Naor (Philadelphia: University of Pennsylvania Press, 2003), https://doi .org/10.9783/9780812200942. However, one of the strands that runs through his analysis is that the Haskalah thinkers battled radical Jewish secularity as much as they battled the traditional Judaism of the rabbis.

13 Biale, *Not in the Heavens*, 81–91, 95–6; Anita Shapira, "The Religious Motifs of the Labor Movement," in *Zionism and Religion*, ed. Shmuel Almog, Jehuda Reinharz, and Anita Shapira (Hanover, NH: University of New England Press, 1998), 251–72; Shlomo Avineri, "Zionism and Jewish Religious Tradition: The Dialectics of Redemption and Secularization," in Almog, Reinharz, and Shapira, *Zionism and Religion*, 5–6; Ehud Luz, *Wrestling with an Angel: Power, Morality, and Jewish Identity*, trans. Michael Swirsky (New Haven: Yale University Press, 2003), 104–8, https://doi .org/10.12987/9780300129298.

14 Biale's book, for instance, is focused almost solely on secular Jews who belonged to the intellectual elite.

15 Maud Mandel nicely summarizes the literature that deals with this phenomenon in "Assimilation and Cultural Exchange in Modern Jewish History," in *Rethinking European Jewish History*, ed. Jeremy Cohen and Moshe Rosman (Portland, OR: Littman Library of Jewish Civilization, 2009), 72–85. See also Frankel, "Assimilation and the Jews," 22.

16 See sources cited in the previous note.

17 Todd M. Endelman, "Jewish Self-Identification and West European Categories of Belonging: From the Enlightenment to World War II," in Gitelman, *Religion or Ethnicity?*, 116. It should be understood that the generalizations being made here mask regional variations. Thus, for instance, rates of Jewish conversion to Christianity, intermarriage, and assimilation were greater in Berlin the late 1700s and early 1800s than in other major Jewish centres in Europe at the time.

18 Jonathan D. Sarna, "The Rise, Fall, and Rebirth of Secular Judaism," *Contemplate: The International Journal of Cultural Thought* 4 (2007): 3–13. Sarna points out that in the 1800s, prior to the great migration, there were substantial numbers of American Jews who were secular in orientation and that these Jews retained a sense of Jewishness despite a lack of interest in Judaism. However, the allure and incidence of intermarriage for these Jews posed a significant challenge for the Jewish community. Between 1776 and 1840, 28.7 per cent of marriages involving American Jews were interfaith marriages, mostly because in this era, the population of Jews was relatively small and spread out in the US, and in these circumstances, it was likely that Jews would find non-Jewish partners. This was not the case for Jews of the immigrant wave post-1881. Intermarriage rates for American Jews between 1900 and 1950 were relatively low, ranging from 2 per cent in the early decades of this time span to just under 7 per cent at its conclusion. Many of these Jews lived in New York in Jewish neighbourhoods where they socialized with each other, and therefore for these Jews, in-marriage was the norm. The figures cited here are discussed by Sarna in his survey, *American Judaism: A History*, 2nd ed. (New Haven: Yale University Press, 2019), 45, 222.

19 For instance, Shmuel Feiner has argued that Jewish secularization in Europe began in the eighteenth century among ordinary German Jews who wanted to throw off the yoke of the rabbinic way of life. See Shmuel Feiner, *The Origins of Jewish Secularization in Eighteenth-Century Europe*, trans. Chaya Naor (Philadelphia: University of Pennsylvania Press, 2010), https://doi.org/10.9783/9780812201895. A similar position is taken by Endelman, "Jewish Self-Identification," 118, and Seidman, "Religion/Secularity," 153–5, 159, regarding the process of secularization among European Jews in general.

20 Steven Beller, for instance, argues that in the nineteenth century, the Jews of Vienna excelled intellectually because they preserved the emphasis that the rabbinic tradition had placed on education. See Steven Beller, *Vienna and the Jews 1867–1938: A Cultural History* (Cambridge: Cambridge University Press, 1989), pt. 2, esp. ch. 7; and Beller, "How Modern Were Vienna's Jews? Preconditions of 'Vienna 1900' in the Worldview of Viennese Jewry, 1860–1890," *Austrian Studies* 16 (2008): 19–31. Jerry Z. Muller in his study of Jews and capitalism makes a similar but even broader argument by suggesting that Western Jews in general did well economically when they became part of Western society because they inherited from Rabbinic Judaism the values of education, discipline, and worldliness that prepared them well for modern capitalism. See Jerry Z. Muller, *Capitalism and the Jews* (Princeton: Princeton University Press, 2010), 82–91, https://doi.org/10.1515/9781400834365. Yet, the insights of Beller and Muller about the connection between modern secular Jews and Rabbinic Judaism are general and impressionistic because this issue is not their main concern. In the second part of this study, I will take up these insights and explore them in a more in-depth manner.

   Biale's study is hard to classify with respect to the issue being discussed here. It is predicated on the notion that the secularism of the Jewish intellectual elite was rooted in pre-modern Jewish sources, and as I have noted above, he acknowledges at the beginning of his study that the roots of this secularism can be found in early Rabbinic Judaism. However, as I have also pointed out, Biale's study ends up focusing on sources that are not at the core of the rabbinic tradition. He is far more interested in medieval Jewish philosophy, Kabbalah, and medieval biblical commentaries. See chapter 2, under "The Modernization and Secularization of Jewish Culture," p. 67.

21 S.Y. Agnon, an Israeli writer, won the Nobel Prize in Literature in 1966, and Robert Auman, another Israeli, won the Nobel Prize in Economics in 2005.

22 A notable exception is Julia Wolfe, an Orthodox Jew who won a Pulitzer Prize in the field of music in 2015.

23 Ultra-Orthodox Jews have not been quite as closed off from the outside world to the extent that stereotypes would have one believe. Moreover, in recent years, ultra-Orthodox Jews have discovered that they need to interact with the outside world more than in the past.

24 This way of life is proving to be unsustainable, and thus many are entering the workforce. In Israel, many ultra-Orthodox Jews who have done so have taken up careers in hi-tech, and they have been quite successful at it. See the CNN report by Oren Lieberman, "Israel's Tech Whiz-Kids-In -Training? Ultra-Orthodox Jews," 8 July 2015, https://www.cnn.com

/2015/07/08/world/israel-Ultra-orthodox-jews-high-tech/index.html.
Still, ultra-Orthodox have engaged with the modern world only in limited
ways.

25 See my introductory chapter, note 5.

26 According to a report on Jewish Americans by the Pew Research Center
in 2013, Orthodox Jews constitute 10 per cent of the Jewish population in
the US, with 6 per cent of the population identifying as ultra-Orthodox
and 3 per cent identifying as Modern Orthodox. See "A Portrait of
Jewish Americans," Pew Research Center, 1 October 2013, ch. 3, https://
www.pewresearch.org/religion/2013/10/01/chapter-3-jewish-identity.
According to another report done by the Pew Research Center on Israeli
demography in 2016, 8 per cent of Israel's population identifies as ultra-
Orthodox, while 10 per cent of the population identifies as just Orthodox.
See, "Israel's Religiously Divided Society," Pew Research Center, 8 March
2016, https://www.pewresearch.org/religion/2016/03/08/israels
-religiously-divided-society.

27 However, in recent years, the ranks of unaffiliated Jews have grown
substantially, and so there may soon come a time when most American
Jews no longer identify with one of the three major denominations. See
"A Portrait of Jewish Americans," Pew Research Centre.

28 I have had to simplify matters for the sake of this discussion. For a brief
but highly insightful discussion of how Reform Judaism has related to
the Jewish past, see Michael A. Meyer, *Response to Modernity: A History
of the Reform Movement in Judaism* (New York: Oxford University Press,
1988), 3–9.

29 See chapter 1, under "The Four Values and the Success of Jews," pp. 45–6.

30 See my introductory chapter, under "The Historical Hypothesis," p. 15.

31 Menahem Blondheim and Shoshana Blum-Kulka, "Literacy, Orality,
Television: Mediation and Authenticity in Jewish Conversational Arguing,
1–2000 C.E.," *The Communication Review* 4, no. 4 (2001): 511–40, https://
doi.org/10.1080/10714420109359483.

32 Shoshana Blum-Kulka, Menahem Blondheim, and Gonen Hacohen,
"Traditions of Dispute: From Negotiations of Talmudic Texts to the
Arena of Political Discourse in the Media," *Journal of Pragmatics* 34,
nos. 10–11 (October–November 2002): 1569–94, https://doi.org
/10.1016/S0378-2166(02)00076-0. See also Blum-Kulka's book, *Dinner
Talk: Cultural Patterns of Sociability and Socialization in Family Discourse*
(Mahwah: Lawrence Erlbaum Associates, 1997), 273–4, 277–8, https://
doi.org/10.4324/9780203053225.

33 Deborah Schiffrin, "Jewish Argument as Sociability," *Language and Society*
13, no. 3 (September 1984): 311–35, esp. 332, https://doi.org/10.1017
/S0047404500010526. Shaul Stampfer, a modern historian who has written

a great deal about Orthodox Jews in the nineteenth and early twentieth centuries, also believes, on the basis of the studies cited here, that the style of modern Jewish discourse is rooted in Talmudic literature. See his, *Families, Rabbis, and Education: Traditional Jewish Society in Nineteenth-Century Eastern Europe* (Portland, OR: Littman Library of Jewish Civilization, 2010), 247–51.

Part Two – The Cultural Hypothesis Revisited: The Core Argument

1 See chapter 1, under "The Four Values and the Success of the Jews," pp. 45–6.
2 See chapter 1, under "The Success of the West: Four Critical Values," pp. 39–40.
3 See chapter 1, under "Rabbinic Judaism and the Four Values," p. 53.

3. Human Autonomy I: Sin, Grace, and Salvation

1 See chapter 1, under "The Success of the West: Four Key Values," p. 41.
2 Among the many surveys of the history of Christian theology, particularly helpful for the topic being examined in this chapter is Roger E. Olson, *The Story of Christian Theology: Twenty Centuries of Tradition and Reform* (Downers Grove: InterVarsity Press, 1999). Olson focuses a great deal on the tension suffusing the history of Christian thought between those who espoused "monergism," a theology in which events in this world are controlled by God, and God alone – and "synergism," a theology in which humans have some degree of control over these events. That tension is the central concern of this chapter.
3 An enormous amount has been written on this issue. Introductory expositions are contained in the following sources and will be cited throughout my presentation: Olson, *The Story of Christian Theology*, ch. 17; Henry Chadwick, *Augustine: A Very Short Introduction* (New York: Oxford University Press, 2001), chs. 3 and 10, https://doi.org/10.1093 /actrade/9780192854520.001.0001; Tatha Wiley, *Original Sin: Origins, Developments, Contemporary Meanings* (Mahwah: Paulist Press, 2002), ch. 3; Alister E. McGrath, *Christian Theology: An Introduction*, 4th ed. (Victoria, Australia: Blackwell, 2007), 364–9; Gregg R. Allison, *Historical Theology: An Introduction to Christian Doctrine* (Grand Rapids: Zondervan, 2011), chs. 16 and 21; Peter Sanlon, "Original Sin in Patristic Theology," in *Adam, the Fall, and Original Sin: Theological, Biblical, and Scientific Perspectives*, ed. Hans Madueme and Michael R.E. Reeves (Grand Rapids: Baker Academic, 2015), 85–108; James Boyce, *Born Bad: Original Sin and the Making of the Western World* (Berkeley: Counterpoint, 2015), chs. 1–2; Matthew Levering, *Predestination: Biblical and Theological Paths* (New York: Oxford University Press, 2011), 44–54, https://doi.org/10.1093/ac

prof:oso/9780199604524.001.0001. Other more specialized treatments of Augustine's views on sin, grace, and salvation will be cited as needed.

4   Wiley, *Original Sin*, 64.

5   Augustine's views on these matters appear in a number of works devoted to his polemic against Pelagius that will be described shortly: *On the Spirit and the Letter* (412), *On Nature and Grace* (415), *On the Grace of Christ and on Original Sin* (418), *On Grace and Free Will* (427), and *On Predestination of the Saints* (429). Augustine also discussed his disagreements with Pelagius in other works, such as *The Enchiridion: On Faith, Hope, and Love* (421) and *The City of God* (430). The harshness of Augustine's thinking on Original Sin was evident in his views on baptism. According to Augustine, you were born with an inherently corrupt nature, and you were therefore guilty in God's eyes and worthy of punishment the minute you emerged from the womb. Baptism took away that guilt, but you were still left with the tendency to sin because of your corrupt nature, and that inclination guaranteed that you would do evil and merit divine punishment. A point that followed from this position was that, according to Augustine, babies who died before they were baptized were destined for hell. Everyone was born with the guilt of Original Sin, and without baptism to wipe away that guilt, punishment in hell inevitably followed.

6   T. Kermit Scott, *Augustine: His Thought in Context* (Mahwah: Paulist Press, 1995), 153, 227; Olson, *The Story of Christian Theology*, 273–4; Chadwick, *Augustine*, ch. 10; Jesse Couenhoven, "Augustine's Rejection of the Free-Will Defence: An Overview of the Late Augustine's Theodicy," *Religious Studies* 43, no. 3 (September 2007): 279–98, https://doi.org/10.1017/S0034412507009018; Eric L. Jenkins, *Free to Say No? Free Will and Augustine's Evolving Doctrines of Grace and Election* (Cambridge: James Clarke, 2013), esp. 106–12.

7   Chadwick, *Augustine*, 125. This statement appears in Augustine's *The Retractions*, trans. Mary Inez Bogan, R.S.M. (Washington, D.C.: Catholic University of America), 1999, 120, though Bogan's translation of the same statement differs from Chadwick's, which is cited here, and reads as follows: "In the solution of this question, I indeed labored in defense of the free choice of the human will, but the grace of God conquered."

8   Olson, *The Story of Christian Theology*, 278–85; Boyce, *Born Bad*, 23; Allison, *Historical Theology*, 349–50.

9   Olson, 285; Allison, *Historical Theology*, 350.

10   Olson, 289; Bernard Hamilton, *Religion in the Medieval West*, 2nd ed. (London: Hodder Arnold, 2003), 91–3, 107–9; Clifford R. Backman, *The Worlds of Medieval Europe*, 3rd ed. (New York: Oxford University Press, 2015), 484–5.

11   Gregory the Great, who served as pope from 590 to 604 and was one of the most important figures in shaping medieval Christianity, supported

Augustine's position in some passages in his writings, and the Semi-Pelagian view in other passages. See Olson, 285–9; and Justo L. Gonzalez, *The Story of Christianity*, 2nd ed. (New York: HarperOne, 2010), 1:288.

12 Charles Trinkaus, *In Our Image and Likeness: Humanity and Divinity in Italian Humanist Thought* (Notre Dame: University of Notre Dame Press, 1995); William Caferro, *Contesting the Renaissance* (West Sussex: Wiley-Blackwell, 2011), ch. 7, https://doi.org/10.1002/9781444324501.ch7.

13 See Trinkaus's discussion of Petrarch, 30–41.

14 John Jeffries Martin discusses this and other developments in religion during the Renaissance from the standpoint of social history in "Religion," in *Palgrave Advances in Renaissance Historiography*, ed. Jonathan Woolfson (New York: Palgrave Macmillan, 2005), 193–209.

15 Luther's views on Original Sin and Predestination are scattered throughout his writings. For his position on Original Sin, see, for instance, *Lectures on Romans*, in *Luther's Works*, vol. 25, trans. Walter G. Tillmanns and Jacob A.O. Preus (St. Louis: Concordia, 1972), esp. 299–307; and *The Bondage of the Will*, trans. J.I. Packer and O.R. Johnston (Grand Rapids: Baker Academic, 2012), 273–8. For Luther's views on Predestination, see *The Bondage of the Will*, 168. For basic treatments of Luther's views on these matters, see Olson, *The Story of Christian Theology*, ch. 24; Wiley, *Original Sin*, 88–90; Gonzalez, *The Story of Christianity*, 2:272–4; Allison, *Historical Theology*, 353–4, 461–2; and Robert Kolb, "The Lutheran Doctrine of Original Sin," in Madueme and Reeves, *Adam, the Fall, and Original Sin*, 109–16.

16 Olson, 408–13; McGrath, *Christian Theology*, 381–2; Levering, *Predestination*, 103–10; Allison, *Historical Theology*, 354–7, 463–6; Boyce, *Born Bad*, ch. 9.

17 Olson, 459–60; McGrath, 381–2; Allison, *Historical Theology*, 466–7. Key in this regard was the Synod of Dort in Holland held in 1618–19. At this gathering, leaders of the Reformed Church spelled out five points regarding sin, grace, and salvation that all Reformed Christians had to uphold; these points essentially summarized Calvin's views on Original Sin and Predestination. The five points were subsequently adopted by all major branches of the Reformed Church throughout Europe.

18 Olson, 435–44, esp. 437, 441, and 443. The emphasis on Original Sin and Predestination in Protestantism was not necessarily in accord with what Luther or Calvin would have wanted. That was especially the case with Predestination. There is evidence that neither Luther nor Calvin thought of this doctrine as central to Christianity in the way that those shaping the confessions did. Both Luther and Calvin believed that Predestination was a divine mystery that human beings could not fathom, and so people should go about their business without being overly focused on it; there were more immediate concerns to worry about. However, the framers of

the confessions were now in charge, and, according to them, the doctrines of Original Sin and Predestination were both essential to Christian faith. See McGrath, 382–3; and Allison, *Historical Theology*, 466–7.

It is worth adding here that not everything in Luther's and Calvin's attitudes towards the human condition was gloom and doom. Luther was capable of saying positive things about human beings and their capabilities. Calvin was even more sanguine on such matters. While he believed, as Luther did, in Original Sin and Predestination, he also spoke frequently in favour of positive engagement with life in this world. The world was, after all, God's creation, and it therefore had much goodness in it. Calvin also acknowledged that even if Luther was right in assuming that all human actions were motivated to some extent by selfish desires, human beings were still capable of producing things with those desires that were worthy of praise, including science and literature. These accomplishments would not bring salvation, but they were still positive contributions to God's world. Nonetheless, both Luther and Calvin supported a view of human beings implying that they had little autonomy in their relationship with God when it came to the issue of salvation, and that view was highly influential in the major branches of Protestantism in the sixteenth and seventeenth centuries. See C. Scott Dixon, *Contesting the Reformation* (West Sussex: Wiley Blackwell, 2012), 191–2.

19 Dixon, *Contesting the Reformation*, 188–91; Carlos Eire, "Calvinism and the Reform of the Reformation," in *The Oxford Illustrated History of the Reformation*, ed. Peter Marshall (Oxford: Oxford University Press, 2015), 109–14. Much has been written on the inner life of American Puritanism. See, for instance, Andrew Delbanco, *The Puritan Ordeal* (Cambridge, MA: Harvard University Press, 1989), https://doi.org/10.4159/9780674034174.

20 Dixon, *Contesting the Reformation*, 184–5.

21 Eire, "Calvinism and the Reform," 108.

22 The first representatives of this viewpoint belonged to a branch of the Reformation commonly referred to as the "Radical Reformation." Many of the Radical Reformers were branded as heretics and many of them died for their beliefs. See Olson, *The Story of Christian Theology*, ch. 26, esp. 421–2, 425–46; and McGrath, *Christian Theology*, 48. But the Semi-Pelagian position eventually attracted the attention of more mainstream Protestants. One such individual was the sixteenth-century Dutch thinker, Jakob Arminius (1560–1609), who began in the Calvinist tradition but ultimately turned away from it. Arminius's followers, known as the Remonstrants, were eventually accused of heresy in the Netherlands where the Reformed Church reigned supreme. See Olson, ch. 28; McGrath, 383–4; Allison, *Historical Theology*, 357, 467–8.

23 Olson, 510–16; Wiley, *Original Sin*, 91–9; McGrath, 352–8; Allison, 469–72.

24 Olson, 444–9; McGrath, 49–50, 52–3; Allison, 466. The Catholic Church's reaction to the positions of Luther and Calvin on Original Sin and Predestination was foreshadowed by the great Dutch humanist, Erasmus, an older contemporary of Luther who engaged in direct dialogue with the founder of Protestantism over these very issues. Erasmus was essentially a Semi-Pelagian. He supported the doctrine of Original Sin but emphatically rejected Predestination on the presumption that all human beings had to have some element of free will in their relationship with God. As we have seen, that way of thinking had been presumed in the official teachings of the Catholic Church throughout the medieval period but had not been explicitly articulated. Erasmus's disagreement with Luther on this issue effectively ended their friendship.

25 See Wiley, *Original Sin*, 109.

26 Dorinda Outram, *The Enlightenment*, 3rd ed. (Cambridge: Cambridge University Press, 2013), 114–15, https://doi.org/10.1017/CBO9781139226318. It is important to recognize that the thinkers of the Enlightenment did not necessarily abandon religion. Until recently, it was a common view among scholars that the rejection of Christianity was a primary characteristic of the Enlightenment. However, more recent scholarship has shown that this assessment is not accurate. Some Enlightenment thinkers certainly left Christianity, particularly in France and in England, but most did not. They regarded themselves as Christians but were interested in fashioning a rational Christianity – a "religion of reason," as they called it. I will say more about this issue in later chapters in this study.

27 Dorinda Outram, *The Enlightenment*, 114–15.

28 Prominent European Jewish intellectuals who took this position include nineteenth-century figures such as Ludwig Steinheim, as well twentieth-century figures such as Leo Baeck and Max Brod. For Steinheim, see Walter Jacob, *Christianity through Jewish Eyes: The Quest for Common Ground* (Cincinnati: Hebrew Union College Press, 1974), 64; for Brod, see Jacob, *Christianity through Jewish Eyes*, 113, 115; and for Baeck, see Fritz A. Rothschild, ed., *Jewish Perspectives on Christianity* (New York: Crossroad, 1990), 66, 102. Prominent US thinkers in the nineteenth century include Emil G. Hirsch, and in the twentieth century, Abba Hillel Silver and Samuel S. Cohon. For Hirsch, see Naomi W. Cohen, *What the Rabbis Said: The Public Discourse of Nineteenth-Century American Rabbis* (New York: NYU Press, 2008), 30, https://doi.org/10.18574/nyu/9780814772942.003.0005. For Abba Hillel Silver, see his book, *Where Judaism Differed: An Inquiry into the Distinctiveness of Judaism* (New York: Macmillan, 1965), 166, 244–51. For Samuel S. Cohon, see his article, "Original Sin," *Hebrew Union College Annual* 21 (1948): 275–330. For the views of popular writers, a search on the internet for the terms "Judaism" and "Original Sin" yields dozens of

sites in which such writers proclaim that Judaism has no doctrine of this sort.

29 This question has been addressed by a number of scholars. See Ephraim E. Urbach, *The Sages: Their Concepts and Beliefs*, trans. Israel Abrahams (Cambridge, MA: Harvard University Press, 1987), 421–36; Alan Cooper, "A Medieval Jewish Version of Original Sin: Ephraim of Luntshits on Leviticus 12," *Harvard Theological Review* 97, no. 4 (October 2004): 445–59, https://doi.org/10.1017/S0017816004000781; Steven T. Katz, "Man, Sin, and Redemption in Rabbinic Judaism," in *The Late Roman-Rabbinic Period*, ed. Steven T. Katz, vol. 4 of *The Cambridge History of Judaism* (Cambridge: Cambridge University Press, 2006), 934–5, https://doi.org/10.1017/CHOL9780521772488.038; Michael Graves, "Classic Rabbinic Literature," in *T and T Clark Companion to the Doctrine of Sin*, ed. Keith L. Johnson and David Lauber (London: Bloomsbury T and T Clark, 2016), 138–41. I would like to thank Michael Graves for sharing his excellent article with me prior to its publication.

30 BT *Shabbat* 146a.

31 Joel Kaminsky analyses a number of early rabbinic sources that develop this theme in "Paradise Regained: Rabbinic Reflections on Israel at Sinai," in *Jews, Christians, and the Theology of the Hebrew Scriptures*, ed. Alice Ogden Bellis and Joel S. Kaminsky (Atlanta: Society of Biblical Literature, 2000), 15–43.

32 E.g., BT *Sanhedrin* 102a. This theme is also discussed in Kaminsky's analysis.

33 BT *Berakhot* 61a; Urbach, *The Sages*, 471–83; Katz, "Man, Sin, and Redemption," 935–7; Graves, "Classic Rabbinic Literature," 134–6.

34 *Genesis Rabbah* 58:2–3; BT *Sanhedrin* 97b, 98a.

35 BT *Hulin* 7b. See also BT *Yoma* 38b; *Ecclesiastes Rabbah* 10:11.

36 Urbach, *The Sages*, 265; Katz, "Man, Sin, and Redemption," 928; Graves, "Classic Rabbinic Literature," 132–4.

37 M *Avot* 3:15. The translation here is that of Graves, "Classic Rabbinic Literature," 132, and it is the most common one. Urbach suggests an alternative reading. According to him, R. Akiva's statement does not mean that everything is "foreseen" by God but only that everything is "seen" by God. That is, God "sees" all our actions no matter how private. R. Akiva's statement is therefore about human responsibility, not the paradox between divine foreknowledge and human free will. R. Akiva's point is that human beings are accountable for their actions for two reasons: God sees everything that we do, public and private, and we have the freedom to choose what we do. See Urbach, *The Sages*, 256–8. I prefer the translation I have given here because the majority of later Jewish thinkers understood R. Akiva's statement in this way. I also find Urbach's reading problematic

because it is not entirely clear why, according to his rendering, the freedom to choose has to be asserted alongside the idea that God sees everything we do. The assertion make more sense if it is in juxtaposition to God's foreknowledge of future events, which would seem to preclude such freedom.

38 See chapter 3, under "The Medieval Period," p. 90.

39 See Aquinas's *Summa Theologiae* I, q. 23 a. 5, in which he connects Predestination to divine will but rules out a connection to divine foreknowledge.

40 We might also add that Christian theologians in the Augustinian tradition would have vehemently disagreed with R. Akiva's notion that a person could win God's favour if only the majority of their deeds were righteous. According to the Christian theologians who supported the doctrine of Predestination, the sins that such a person committed would have made them undeserving of divine reward. Moreover, the assumption would have been that even a person's good deeds were tainted by sinful motivations. These observations underscore that R. Akiva's view of God is less harsh than that of Augustine and his followers.

41 BT *Berakhot* 33b, *Megilah* 25a, *Nidah* 16b.

42 BT *Berakhot* 7a, *Menahot* 29b. David C. Kraemer discusses these sources and others similar to them in *Responses to Suffering in Classical Rabbinic Literature* (New York: Oxford University Press, 1994), 193–200. Kraemer claims that the notion of God's ways being mysterious with respect to reward and punishment are to be found primarily in the Babylonian Talmud, not the Jerusalem Talmud.

43 BT *Ta'anit* 11a; JT *Pe'ah* 1:1, *Sanhedrin* 10:1; *Genesis Rabbah* 33:1; Urbach, *The Sages*, 436–7; Katz, p. 934. This idea is nicely illustrated in *Eccelsiastes Rabbah* 7:8:1 which deals with R. Elisha ben Abuyah who became a heretic because he witnessed injustice in the world. R. Akiva is quoted as saying that Elisha's mistake was in not understanding that the injustices in this world are rectified by God in the world to come. These and other sources that present reward in the afterlife as a solution to the problem of evil in this world are analyzed by Kraemer, 71–73, 91–94.

44 Here again, one need only go to the web and search for "Judaism" and "free will," and one will find dozens of websites supporting this view.

45 BT *Kidushin* 30b. Graves cites a number of other sources to this effect. See Graves, "Classic Rabbinic Literature," 136.

46 *Mekhilta de-R. Ishmael* on Ex. 16:10; *Leviticus Rabbah* 27:4; BT *Shabbat* 55a, *Rosh Hashanah* 16b-17a; Katz, "Man, Sin, and Redemption," 934–5.

47 Urbach, *The Sages*, 475; Katz, "Man, Sin, and Redemption," 936; Graves, "Classic Rabbinic Literature," 134–5.

48 *Genesis Rabbah* 9:9.

49 Urbach, *The Sages*, 462–71; Katz, "Man, Sin, and Redemption," 938–40; Graves, "Classic Rabbinic Literature," 143–5.

50 See, for instance, BT *Berakhot* 12b, *Hagigah* 5a. However, that may not be the case with the most serious of sins. In BT *Yoma* 86a, the rabbis tell us that the sin of *hillul ha-shem* – desecrating of God's name by engaging in unethical conduct in public – can only be repented for by one's death.

51 The theme of protest against God in biblical and rabbinic literature is analysed by Anson Laytner, *Arguing with God: A Jewish Tradition* (Northvale: Jason Aronson, 1977); and Dov Weiss, *Pious Irreverence: Confronting God in Rabbinic Judaism* (Philadelphia: University of Pennsylvania Press, 2016), https://doi.org/10.9783/9780812293050.

52 Ex. 3:21, 11:2, 12:35.

53 BT *Berakhot* 32a.

54 Cited in Laytner, *Arguing with God*, ch. 7, with some adjustments to the translation. Ellipses added.

55 Weiss, *Pious Irreverence*, ch. 1.

56 This has been noted by a number of scholars. See Weiss, 2. Weiss also notes, however, that modern Christian theologians have begun co-opting the protest motif into their thinking, and they have done so at the inspiration of this theme in Judaism.

57 Gen. 18:16–33; Ex. 32:7–14; Laytner, *Arguing with God*, ch. 1; Weiss, 4–6.

58 See, for instance, Mt. 26:47–54.

59 Weiss suggests similar reasons for the discrepancy between Jews and Christians regarding the protest motif. See Weiss, *Pious Irreverence*, 184–6.

60 BT *Shabbat* 104a, *Sukkah* 25b; Graves, "Classic Rabbinic Literature," 137–8.

61 BT *Bava Batra* 164a–165b, *Sanhedrin* 101a, *Arakhin* 17a.

62 BT *Sukkah* 52b; *Leviticus Rabbah* 10:1; Katz, "Man, Sin, and Redemption," 931; Graves, "Classic Rabbinic Literature," 136–8.

63 This theme is prominent in the Jewish prayerbook, especially on Rosh Hashanah and Yom Kippur, when Jews engage in repentance. On these holidays, the traditional liturgy is filled with prayers expressing hope that God's mercy will prevail over his anger so that he can judge his people in a generous state of mind. See, for instance, the famous prayer recited on Rosh Hashanah and Yom Kippur, *U-Netaneh Tokef*. The regular weekday morning service also makes allusion to this notion. See, for instance, *Ahavah Rabbah*, which is recited just prior to the *Shema* prayer in the morning service.

64 *Genesis Rabbah* 12:15.

65 Haym Soloveitchik, "Three Themes in *Sefer Hasidim*," *AJS Review* 1 (April 1976): 311–58, https://doi.org/10.1017/S0364009400000155; Ivan G. Marcus, *Piety and Society: The Jewish Pietists of Medieval Germany*, vol. 10 of *Études sur le judaïsme médiéval*, ed. Georges Vajda. (Leiden: E.J. Brill, 1981), https://doi.org/10.1163/9789004497818.

66 Talya Fishman, "The Penitential System of Hasidei Ashkenaz and the Problem of Cultural Boundaries," *Journal of Jewish Thought and Philosophy* 8, no. 2 (January 1999): 201–29, https://doi.org/10.1163/147728599794761608.

67 Cooper, "A Medieval Jewish Version of Original Sin."

68 Deborah Schechterman, "The Doctrine of Original Sin and Maimonidean Interpretation in Jewish Philosophy of the Thirteenth and Fourteenth Centuries" [in Hebrew], *Da'at* 20 (Winter 1988): 65–90.

69 Shaul Magid, *From Metaphysics to Midrash: Myth, History, and the Interpretation of Scripture in Lurianic Kabbala* (Bloomington: Indiana University Press, 2008); see esp. ch. 1. A Kabbalist who perhaps comes the closest to espousing a view on sin that is reminiscent of Augustine is R. Isaiah Horowitz (1560–1630). In his major work, *The Two Tables of the Covenant* (*Sheney Luhot ha-Berit*) (Warsaw: n.p., 1930), he speaks about the overwhelming power of the evil inclination. See Jacob Elbaum, *Repentance and Self-Flagellation in the Writings of the Sages of Germany and Poland, 1348–1648* [in Hebrew] (Jerusalem: Magnes Press, 1993), 181–94; and Cooper, "A Medieval Jewish Version," 447–8.

70 The Kabbalists believed that their thought-system was divine in origin. The basic doctrines of Kabbalah had been given by God to Moses on Mount Sinai and had been passed down orally from generation to generation. The Kabbalists therefore believed that there were essentially *three* Torahs that Moses received: the Written Torah, the Oral Torah that was the basis of Rabbinic Judaism, and another Oral Torah that conveyed the truths of Kabbalah – that is, truths about God and the universe. These views on the origin of Kabbalah also explain its name, which means "tradition." Kabbalah was believed by its adherents to be a body of wisdom known through an unbroken chain of oral transmission going all the way back to the revelation at Mount Sinai.

71 Gershom Scholem, *Major Trends in Jewish Mysticism* (Jerusalem: Schocken, 1941), 283–4.

72 E.g., *Lamentations Rabbah* 1:6:33. This motif is examined by Michael Fishbane in *Biblical Myth and Rabbinic Mythmaking* (New York: Oxford University Press, 2003), 173–91, https://doi.org/10.1093/0198267339.003.0009. Moshe Idel examines the same motif both in rabbinic and Kabbalistic literature in *Kabbalah: New Perspectives* (New Haven: Yale University Press, 1988), chs. 7 and 8.

73 Augustine makes this very argument in his debate against Pelagius, pointing out that if Pelagius was correct and human beings could achieve salvation entirely on their own, then Jesus died in vain. See Olson, *The Story of Christian Theology*, 274.

74 Stephen K. Moroney, *God of Love and God of Judgment* (Eugene: Wipf and Stock, 2009), 73–4. The key figure who developed this outlook was the

German Protestant theologian, Adolf von Harnack (1851–1930). See Olson, 551–2.

75 Wiley, *Original Sin*, 113.

76 Kant believed that Judaism failed to provide guidance on moral issues because in Judaism, human behaviour was dictated by divine commandments, and for Kant, actions could be moral only if they were completely autonomous. Moreover, in Judaism, the divine commandments were only for Jews, and this too precluded the commandments from having moral force. Moral prescriptions had to be universal for them to be truly moral. See Emil L. Fackenheim, "Kant and Judaism," *Commentary* 36, no. 6 (July 1963): 460–7, https://doi.org/10.2307/1453762.

77 That was certainly true of the Jewish community in Poland-Lithuania in the early modern period, the largest Jewish community in this era. See Gershon David Hundert, *Jews in Poland-Lithuania: A Genealogy of Modernity* (Berkeley: University of California Press, 2004), ch. 9, https://doi.org/10.1525/9780520940321-015.

4. Human Autonomy II: Religious Authority

1 Mat. 16:18.

2 Edward LeRoy Long Jr., *Patterns of Polity: Varieties of Church Government* (Cleveland: Pilgrim Press, 2001), 14–26; Justo L. Gonzalez, *The Story of Christianity*, 2nd ed. (New York: HarperOne, 2010), 1:79–81; Gregg R. Allison, *Historical Theology: An Introduction to Christian Doctrine* (Grand Rapids: Zondervan, 2011), 588–601.

3 Gonzalez, *The Story of Christianity*, 2:52–3; Allison, *Historical Theology*, 601–2.

4 Long, *Patterns of Polity*, 64–77; 603–4.

5 Long, chs. 7–9; Allison, 604.

6 Allison, 604–5.

7 Moreover, Luther usually gets more credit for being the harbinger of the modern notion of the individual than he deserves. His contemporary, Huldrych Zwingli, who led the Reformation in Switzerland, was as innovative as Luther on this point, if not more so. I wish to thank my colleague, Jon Wood, for these observations and for having taught me a great deal about Luther, the Reformation, and Protestantism.

8 Dixon, *Contesting the Reformation*, 187–8.

9 Andrew Delbanco, *The Puritan Ordeal* (Cambridge, MA: Harvard University Press, 1989), https://doi.org/10.4159/9780674034174; Dixon, *Contesting the Reformation*, 188–91.

10 Dorinda Outram, *The Enlightenment*, 3rd ed. (Cambridge: Cambridge University Press, 2013), 118–19, https://doi.org/10.1017/CBO9781139226318.

It is not clear that religion was really the central issue in the conflicts that tore Europe apart during this period. William T. Cavanaugh has argued that there were other issues that caused the violence, and they had nothing to do with religion. See his study, *The Myth of Religious Violence: Secular Ideology and the Roots of Modern Conflict* (New York: Oxford University Press, 2009), https://doi.org/10.1093/acprof:oso/9780195385045.001.0001. Still, even if Cavanaugh is right, what is important for our concerns is that religion was perceived to be the cause of these wars, and as a result of that perception, Europeans made significant changes in their societies concerning the relationship between religion and state.

11 Hanina Ben-Menahem, "Talmudic Law: A Jurisprudential Perspective," in *The Late Roman-Rabbinic Period*, ed. Steven T. Katz, vol. 4 of *The Cambridge History of Judaism* (Cambridge: Cambridge University Press, 2006), 886–98, https://doi.org/10.1017/CHOL9780521772488.036; Elizabeth Shanks Alexander, "The Orality of Rabbinic Writing," in *The Cambridge Companion to the Talmud and Rabbinic Literature*, ed. Charlotte Elisheva Fonrobert and Martin S. Jaffee (Cambridge: Cambridge University Press, 2007), 38–48, https://doi.org/10.1017/CCOL0521843901.003. Azzan Yadin has done important scholarship on the question of whether the rabbis saw themselves as passive recipients of the Oral Torah or creators of it. His theory is that the school of R. Akiva supported the former viewpoint whereas that of R. Ishmael supported the latter viewpoint. See Azzan Yadin, *Scripture as Logos: Rabbi Ishmael and the Origins of Midrash* (Philadelphia: University of Pennsylvania Press, 2004), https://doi.org/10.9783/9780812204124; Yadin, *Scripture and Tradition: Rabbi Akiva and the Triumph of Midrash* (Philadelphia: University of Pennsylvania Press, 2014), https://doi.org/10.9783/9780812290431. Menachem Fisch, in *Rational Rabbis: Science and Talmudic Culture* (Bloomington: Indiana University Press, 1997), deals with similar issues in attempting to show that the early rabbis were divided between "traditionalists," who believed that Jewish law was based only on accumulated traditions, and "anti-traditionalists," who held that traditions could be constantly interpreted and revised.

12 Ex. 21:24, Lev. 24:20, Deut. 19:21.

13 BT *Bava Kama* 84a.

14 Baruch A. Levine, *The JPS Torah Commentary: Leviticus* (New York: Jewish Publication Society of America, 1989), 270; Jacob Milgrom, "Lex Talionis and the Rabbis," *Bible Review* 12, no. 2 (April 1996), 16, 48.

15 M *Sanhedrin* 8:1–5; BT *Sanhedrin* 71a.

16 BT *Sanhedrin* 71a.

17 The case of the rebellious son and its ramifications have been analysed by many scholars. See, for instance, Moshe Halbertal, *Commentary Revolutions*

in the Making: Values as Interpretative Considerations in Midrashei Halakhah
[in Hebrew] (Jerusalem: Magnes Press, 1999), ch. 2; and Christine Hayes,
What's Divine about Divine Law: Early Perspectives (Princeton: Princeton
University Press, 2015), 314–17, https://doi.org/10.1515/9781400866410.
Halbertal also analyses several other instances in which he believes the
rabbis consciously used moral considerations to modify or disable a
biblical law.

18 BT *Sanhedrin* 71a.
19 Yitzhak D. Gilat, "A Rabbinical Court May Decree the Abrogation of the
    Law of the Torah" [in Hebrew], *Annual of Bar-Ilan University* 7–8 (1970):
    117–32; Menachem Elon, "Takkanot," in *The Principles of Jewish Law*,
    ed. Menachem Elon (Jerusalem: Keter, 1972), 73–83; Elon, *Jewish Law:
    History, Sources, Principles*, trans. Bernard Auerbach and Melvin J. Sykes
    (Philadelphia: Jewish Publication Society of America, 1994), vol. 2,
    chs. 13–16.
20 BT *Shabbat* 14b, *Yevamot* 89b, *Ketubot* 82b.
21 Aaron D. Panken, *The Rhetoric of Change: Self-Conscious Legal Change in
    Rabbinic Literature* (Lanham, MD: University Press of America, 2005),
    171–4.
22 Ex. 23:10–11, Lev. 25:1–7, 25:20–22.
23 This law is best understood in light of the seven-day week in the Bible. Just
    as the Israelites were commanded by God to work six days and rest on the
    seventh, so too were they commanded to cultivate their fields for six years
    and take the seventh year off. Refraining from the cultivation of land in
    the seventh year seems to have been a way of acknowledging that nothing,
    not even one's own land, belonged entirely to human beings; everything
    in this world ultimately belonged to God. See Meir Tamari, *With All Your
    Possessions: Jewish Ethics and Economic Life* (Northvale: Jason Aronson Press,
    1987), 36–9.
24 Deut. 15:1–10.
25 Panken, *The Rhetoric of Change*, 194.
26 M *Gittin* 4:3; Panken, *The Rhetoric of Change*, 192–7.
27 According to the Gemara, Hillel did not actually overturn a biblical law
    here. Hillel lived in an era in which, for technical reasons, the law of
    debt cancellation was no longer required according to biblical law, but it
    continued to be observed because the rabbis decreed that it should remain
    in effect as a matter of custom. Therefore, when Hillel implemented his
    amendment, he was actually overturning a rabbinic decree, not a biblical
    one. See BT *Gittin* 36a-b; Hayes, *What's Divine about Divine Law*, 294–9.
        However, the rabbis in the Talmud could not soften the radicalism of
    their predecessors entirely, for in light of the explanation just given, they
    then had to justify the fact that the earlier rabbis extended the law of

debt cancellation in the first place. Imposing this extension was a serious matter because it meant that lenders were not able to collect money from borrowers that would have normally belonged to them after the seventh year according to biblical law. The extension of debt cancellation was thus tantamount to justifying theft on the part of the borrower, and theft was a serious violation of biblical law.

The Talmudic rabbis provide a couple of reasons to explain why the extension of the law was justified. One is that in imposing the extension, the rabbis were not ordering people to violate biblical law actively but only passively (*shev ve-al ta'aseh*, meaning "sit and do nothing"). That is, the effect of the extension was that the money remained with the borrower after the seventh year and did not go back to the lender, and this passive violation was deemed acceptable. Thus, according to this reasoning, biblical law was still being violated here, but it was not because of Hillel's ruling; it was because the earlier rabbis had extended the law of debt cancellation prior to that ruling. The consolation was that this ruling had the advantage of violating the law only passively, not actively.

The Gemara provides another justification for the extension of the law of debt cancellation that is based on the principle of *hefker bet din hekfer*. This phrase, literally translated, means that "a rabbinic court may declare [property] ownerless." This principle, which is similar to that of "eminent domain" in US law, allows a rabbinic court to confiscate property or money from an individual when needed. The rabbis based this principle on a biblical source. In the book of Ezra, Ezra the Scribe orders Jews living in Judah and Jerusalem to assemble in Jerusalem for a convocation, and he threatens to confiscate the property of those who fail to obey his decree. The rabbis assume that the same right to confiscate property that Ezra apparently exercised here can be exercised by a rabbinic court as well. See Ez. 8:9–10; BT *Mo'ed Katan* 16a, *Yevamot* 89b.

This second explanation for the rabbinic extension of debt cancellation goes further in softening the radicalism of the rabbis than the first explanation did because here the extension is based on a principle derived from the Bible. Therefore, in this instance, the rabbis do not seem to see themselves as violating God's law. Rather, they are showing preference for one biblically derived principle – *hefker bet din hefker* – over another, the prohibition against theft that the extension of debt cancellation is in danger of violating. My interpretation of the Talmudic sources being discussed here is closer to that of Panken than that of Hayes (see notes 26 and 27 above), but it includes some of my own insights.

28 Medieval rabbinic authorities had to explain how the implementation of a *takkanah* did not violate the biblical prohibition against adding to the laws

of the Torah (Deut. 4:2, 13:1). For strategies to deal with this problem, see Elon, *The Principles of Jewish Law*, 75.

29 See Elon, *The Principles of Jewish Law*; and Gilat, "A Rabbinical Court May Decree."

30 Ex. 34:7; BT *Gittin* 60b; *Temurah* 14b.

31 The Oral Torah in Hebrew literally means "Torah by the mouth." In the verse, the phrase "in accordance with" literally means "according to the mouth of" (*al pi*), and is therefore taken as allusion to the Oral Torah.

One can speculate why the rabbis believed there was a need for such a rule. It may be that they wanted to protect their authority as the guardians of the traditions contained in the Oral Torah, and they therefore believed that it should not be committed to writing since that would put it in the public domain. This point is made in a midrashic passage in *Tanhuma, Ki Tissa* 44 that expresses a fear that writing down the Oral Torah will result in it being taken away from the Jews the way the Written Torah has been. This passage clearly has Christianity in mind, which laid claim to the Written Torah as part of its own Scripture. See Martin S. Jaffee, *Early Judaism: Religious Worlds of the First Judaic Millennium*, 2nd ed. (Bethesda: University Press of Maryland, 2006), 237–40. The suggestion has also been made that the rabbis were concerned that writing down the traditions of the Oral Torah would make it appear as if the Oral Torah had the same level of authority as the Written Torah, and they wanted to avoid making such an impression. See Shaye J.D. Cohen, *From the Maccabees to the Mishnah*, 3rd ed. (Louisville: Westminster John Knox Press, 2014), 196.

32 This reasoning is implied in a passage in BT *Gittin* 60a.

33 BT *Bava Metsi'a* 59b.

34 Recent academic commentators have shown that this passage is a good deal more complicated than it would seem at first glance. A close reading raises questions about whether the rabbis have, in fact, "defeated" God here. However, the way I have presented the passage here is the way it has been read by Jews up until recently, and that is what is most significant for our concerns. Most Jews throughout the centuries read this passage to mean that the rabbis did indeed overrule God. The following is a partial list of studies on this passage: Itzhak Englard, "Majority Decision vs. Individual Truth: The Interpretations of the 'Oven of Achnai' Aggadah," *Tradition* 15, nos. 1–2 (Spring–Summer 1975): 137–52; Daniel J.H. Greenwood, "Akhnai: Legal Responsibility in the World of the Silent God," *Utah Law Review* 1997, no. 2 (1997): 309–58; Jeffrey L. Rubenstein, *Talmudic Stories: Narrative Art, Composition, and Culture* (Baltimore: Johns Hopkins University Press, 1999), ch. 2; David Luban, "The Coiled Serpent of Argument: Reason, Authority, and Law in a Talmudic Tale," *Chicago-Kent Law Review* 79, no. 3 (2004): 1253–88.

35 Deut. 17:8–13.
36 BT *Shabbat* 23a. According to the opinion of R. Nehemiah, the source is Deut. 32:7: "Ask your father, he will inform you, / Your elder, they will tell you."
37 As I noted in note 11 above in this chapter, Fisch attempts to show that the early rabbis were divided between traditionalists and anti-traditionalists, and R. Eliezer belonged to the latter group.
38 Panken, *The Rhetoric of Change*, 127, makes this point.
39 The description of the two viewpoints that follow is based on Moshe Halbertal, *People of the Book: Canon, Meaning, and Authority* (Cambridge, MA: Harvard University Press, 1997), ch. 2, https://doi.org/10.4159 /9780674038141-004. Halbertal discusses a third viewpoint, but it was far less influential than the two discussed here.
40 *Sifra*, Introduction (*Baraita de-R. Yishma'el*).
41 Maimonides makes these points in the introduction to his *Commentary on the Mishnah* and in his introduction to the *Mishneh Torah*. See Halbertal, *People of the Book*, 59–63.
42 Nahmanides, *Hasagot le-Sefer ha-Mitsvot shel ha-Rambam* (*Glosses to Maimonides'* Book of the Commandments), gloss to principle #1; R. Yom Tov Ishbili, *Hiddushei Ritba* (*Novellae of R. Yom Tov Ishbili*), 21 vols. (Jersualem: Mosad ha-Rav Kuk, n.d.) on BT *Eruvin* 13b; R. Nissim Gerondi, *Dersashot ha-Ran* (*Sermons of R. Nissim Gerondi*), ed. Aryeh L. Feldman (Jerusalem: Makhon Shalem, 1977), sermons 5 and 7; and Halbertal, 63–7.
43 Elon, *Jewish Law*, vol. 2, chs. 18, 20. The amendments of the later rabbis did not have quite the same authority that those of their predecessors had. A rabbinic amendment issued in medieval Europe might have authority among European Jews but not among Jews living in Islamic lands. See Elon, "Takkanot," 85–6; Elon, *Jewish Law*, vol. 2, ch. 18.
44 See Menachem Elon, "Takkanot ha-Kahal," in Elon, *The Principles of Jewish Law*, 654–62; Elon, "Public Authority and Administrative Law," in Elon, *The Principles of Jewish Law*, 645–54; Elon, "Power and Authority: Halachic Stance of the Traditional Community and Its Contemporary Implications," in *Kinship and Consent: The Jewish Political Tradition and Its Contemporary Uses*, ed. Daniel J. Elazar (Lanham, MD: University Press of America, 1983), 183–217; Elon, *Jewish Law*, vol. 2, ch. 19.
    Elon, "Power and Authority," 191, provides several examples of such *takkanot*: 1. In one community, witnesses were allowed to testify in cases involving their personal lives in some way when the cases concerned communal matters, such as taxation and charitable trusts. According to Jewish law, personal connections to a case would have normally disqualified such individuals from serving as witnesses, but the reasoning

was that if this rule were enforced regarding communal matters, virtually no one could serve as witnesses since these cases touched on the lives of almost everyone in the community. 2. In several communities from the twelfth century onwards, governing communal bodies were allowed to conduct legal transactions without a *kinyan*, a formal act that was normally required by Jewish law to complete such transactions. The reasoning here was that a *kinyan* unnecessarily hampered governing bodies from conducting their business. 3. There was widespread acceptance of the principle that governing communal bodies could mete out punishment to criminals beyond that which was specified by Jewish law for the sake of the public good.

In some of these instances, the authority given to the governing communal bodies was rooted in the notion that they had the same status as a rabbinic court (*bet din*). That was the case with the second and third examples just cited. Rabbinic courts were allowed to conduct legal transactions without a *kinyan* and could impose punishments beyond what Jewish law normally required.

45 Jay R. Berkovitz, "Rabbinic Culture and the Historical Development of Halakhah," in *The Early Modern World, 1500–1815*, ed. Jonathan Karp and Adam Sutcliffe, vol. 7 of *The Cambridge History of Judaism* (Cambridge: Cambridge University Press, 2018), 351–6, https://doi. org/10.1017/9781139017169.015.

46 On papal authority, see Joseph H. Lynch and Phillip C. Adamo, *The Medieval Church: A Brief History*, 2nd ed. (London: Routledge, 2014), ch. 12, https://doi.org/10.4324/9781315735221. James A. Brundage discusses the limitations of canon lawyers in interpreting canon law due to the immutability of the divine will in *Medieval Canon Law* (London: Longman, 1995), 168, 173. Some recent scholars of canon law have questioned these limitations on the premise that canon law must evolve in order to deal with ever-changing human circumstances. See Joseph J. Koury, "*Ius Divinum* as a Canonical Problem: On the Interaction of Divine and Ecclesiastical Laws," *The Jurist* 53 (1993), 131. A most interesting discussion of this matter is provided by Judith Hahn, who dedicates an entire article to the question of whether the story about the oven of Akhnai in the Talmud has lessons to teach canon lawyers about how to negotiate the relationship between human and divine will in the legislation and interpretation of canon law. See Hahn, "'Not in Heaven:' What the Talmudic Tale on the Oven of Akhnai May Contribute to the Recent Debates on the Development of Catholic Canon Law," *Oxford Journal of Law and Religion* 6, no. 2 (June 2017): 372–98, https://doi.org/10.1093/ojlr/ rwx001. The contrast I draw here between Catholic and rabbinic views on religious authority vis-à-vis the divine will is similar to that drawn by Hahn.

47 This issue is examined by Itzhak Brand, "The 'Oven of Akhnai' and Polemics" [in Hebrew], *Tarbiz* 75 (2006): 437–67. See esp. 439–42. See also Kenneth R. Stow, "The Burning of the Talmud in 1553, in Light of Sixteenth-Century Catholic Attitudes toward the Talmud," in *Essential Papers on Judaism and Christianity in Conflict: From Late Antiquity to the Reformation*, ed. Jeremy Cohen (New York: NYU Press, 1991), 409–10.

48 See chapter 1, under "Views of Rabbinic Judaism," pp. 54–5.

49 See chapter 1, under "Views of Rabbinic Judaism," p. 55.

5. Human Autonomy III: Reason and Philosophy

1 For instance, Augustine affirmed free will, but he defined it in his own idiomatic way. Human beings had free will, according to Augustine, when their actions followed from their desires, and even if those desires were placed in them by God so that they were not able to act otherwise, Augustine still regarded them as acting freely. We moderns would tend to disagree. We would say that for human beings to be free, our actions not only have to follow from our desires, but that we have to have some degree of control over the desires that lead to those actions. Yet, that is precisely what Augustine denied. For Augustine, our desires were by nature evil, and therefore we were unable to do good even if we exerted our best effort. Thus, even though Augustine affirmed free will in his later years, he rejected it in the form that we normally think of when we speak about free will. My reading here is indebted to T. Kermit Scott, *Augustine: His Thought in Context* (Mahwah: Paulist Press, 1995), 181.

2 A helpful overview of the relationship between philosophy and theology throughout the history of Christianity is provided by Alister E. McGrath, *Christian Theology: An Introduction*, 4th ed. (Victoria, Australia: Blackwell, 2007), ch. 8.

3 See Charles Murray's *Human Accomplishment: The Pursuit of Excellence in the Arts and Sciences, 800 B.C. to 1950* (New York: HarperCollins, 2003), esp. ch. 19. Murray argues that the West, throughout its history, accentuated human rational capabilities more than all other major cultures and that medieval Christian philosophy was emblematic of that tendency. However, Murray makes no mention of the restrictions that were placed on the exercise of reason by Christians in both the medieval and early modern periods. The same tendency to exaggerate the rationalism of Western culture can be found in Rodney Stark, in *How the West Won: The Neglected Story of the Triumph of Modernity* (Wilmington: ISI Books, 2014), esp. ch. 8.

4 Roger E. Olson, *The Story of Christian Theology: Twenty Centuries of Tradition and Reform* (Downers Grove: InterVarsity Press, 1999), chs. 3 and 5; Justo L.

Gonzalez, *The Story of Christianity*, 2nd ed. (New York: HarperOne, 2010), 1:63–8.

5 Olson, *The Story of Christian Theology*, 257, 263–5; Gonzalez, *The Story of Christianity*, 1:244–6.

6 Olson, chs. 21–3; Gonzalez, 1: 369–80.

7 They had been preserved in Muslim culture in Arabic translation, and Christians in this era were intersecting with that culture more than ever before since they were now getting the upper hand in their wars with the Islamic Empire and conquering large sectors of its territory. The Christians became familiar with Aristotle through this contact.

8 Olson, 313, 333–6, 338–42; Gonzalez, 1:374–9.

9 Olson, 356.

10 Olson, 356. Hans Thijssen, "Condemnation of 1277," in *The Stanford Encyclopedia of Philosophy*, ed. Edward N. Zalta, Winter 2016 ed. (Stanford: Stanford University, 1997–), article 30 January 2003, last modified 24 September 2013, https://plato.stanford.edu/archives/win2016/entries/condemnation.

11 See chapter 3, under "The Renaissance," p. 92. William Caferro summarizes the academic work that has been done on this issue in *Contesting the Renaissance* (West Sussex: Wiley-Blackwell, 2011), 193–204, https://doi.org/10.1002/9781444324501.ch7.

12 Caferro, *Contesting the Renaissance*, 193–204.

13 Craig Martin, "Pietro Pomponazzi," in Zalta, *The Stanford Encyclopedia of Philosophy*, Winter 2017 ed., article published 7 November 2017, https://plato.stanford.edu/archives/win2017/entries/pomponazzi.

14 Dilwyn Knox, "Giordano Bruno," in Zalta, *The Stanford Encyclopedia of Philosophy*, Summer 2019 ed., article published 30 May 2018, last modified 28 May 2019, https://plato.stanford.edu/archives/sum2019/entries/bruno.

15 George Klosko, *History of Political Theory: An Introduction*, 2nd ed. (Oxford: Oxford University Press, 2013), 2:37–8.

16 Olson, *The Story of Christian Theology*, 315; Alisha Rankin, "Natural Philosophy," in *The Oxford Handbook of the Protestant Reformations*, ed. Ulinka Rublack (Oxford: Oxford University Press, 2017), 729, https://doi.org/10.1093/oxfordhb/9780199646920.013.22.

17 Paul Althaus, *The Theology of Martin Luther*, trans. Robert C. Schultz (Philadelphia: Fortress Press, 1966), 64–71; Randall C. Zachman, *John Calvin as Teacher, Pastor, and Theologian: The Shape of His Writings and Thought* (Grand Rapids, MI: Baker Academic Press, 2006), 231–42; C. Scott Dixon, *Contesting the Reformation* (West Sussex: Wiley Blackwell, 2012), 191–2. Some scholars have claimed that the Reformation aided in the development of science by desacralizing or disenchanting the world.

This theory is based on the notion that Protestantism de-emphasized or eliminated Catholic rituals and sacraments that were believed to attract divine grace and, by doing so, it emphasized God's transcendence rather than his immanence in creation. However, recently scholars have argued that this was not the case and that the disenchantment of the world occurred much later in the Enlightenment. See Dixon, *Contesting the Reformation*, 194–6.

18 John Henry, *The Scientific Revolution and the Origins of Modern Science*, 3rd ed. (New York: Palgrave Macmillan, 2008), chs. 3 and 4.

19 This group of philosophers included René Descartes (1596–1650), Baruch Spinoza (1632–77), and George Berkeley (1685–1753).

20 This group included Thomas Hobbes (1588–1679) and John Locke (1632–1704). It was Immanuel Kant (1724–1804) who created a synthesis between these two approaches.

21 Stewart Duncan, "Thomas Hobbes," in Zalta, *The Stanford Encyclopedia of Philosophy*, Spring 2017 ed., article published 11 March 2009, last modified 27 January 2017, https://plato.stanford.edu/archives/spr2019/entries/hobbes.

22 Jonathan Israel argues that Spinoza was the key figure who shaped the radical branch of the Enlightenment in France in the eighteenth century. This theory has been criticized. There are doubts about whether Spinoza's influence was as great as Israel believes. Still, we can certainly look to Spinoza as a foreshadowing of things to come in European thought. See Jonathan I. Israel, *Radical Enlightenment: Philosophy and the Making of Modernity 1650–1750* (Oxford: Oxford University Press, 2002), https://doi.org/10.1093/acprof:oso/9780198206088.001.0001; and Israel, *Enlightenment Contested: Philosophy, Modernity, and the Emancipation of Man 1670–1752* (Oxford: Oxford University Press, 2006), https://doi.org/10.1093/acprof:oso/9780199279227.001.0001. For criticisms of Israel's views, see Dorinda Outram, *The Enlightenment*, 3rd ed. (Cambridge: Cambridge University Press, 2013), 144–6, https://doi.org/10.1017/CBO9781139226318, and Dan Edelstein, *The Enlightenment: A Genealogy* (Chicago: University of Chicago Press, 2010), 8–9, https://doi.org/10.7208/9780226184500-003.

23 Henry, *The Scientific Revolution*, ch. 6. Protestantism may have played a role in inspiring the Scientific Revolution. Scholars have noted that scientific advances occurred disproportionately in Protestant countries in the late seventeenth and early eighteenth centuries, and some have surmised that the reason for this was the Protestant emphasis on the direct reading of Scripture. A core principle of the Protestant Reformation was the rejection of the Catholic notion that the Bible could be read and interpreted only by Church authorities. Protestants insisted that all people should read the Bible and interpret it themselves. Protestants were aware that people

might come up with different interpretations of God's word, which could result in chaos, but concerns about that possibility were allayed by the belief that the correct reading could be determined by simply looking at the text. The unforeseen consequence here was that Protestants began to look at nature in the same way that they looked at the Bible. Nature was God's "other book," which could also be "read" in order to understand the divine mind. This way of thinking encouraged Protestants to pursue science in a way that Catholics did not. For a discussion about the merits and criticisms of this theory, see Dixon, *Contesting the Reformation*, 192–4; Henry, 95–6; Rankin, "Natural Philosophy," 729–31.

24 Outram, *The Enlightenment*, 106–9.

25 Outram, 113; Edelstein, *The Enlightenment*, 33–4.

26 Stephen J. Pope, "Natural Law and Christian Ethics," in *The Cambridge Companion to Christian Ethics*, ed. Robin Gill, 2nd ed. (Cambridge: Cambridge University Press, 2012), 66–77, https://doi.org/10.1017/CCOL9781107000070.007.

27 Outram, *The Enlightenment*, 109–13, 123–4, 125–6.

28 Outram, 124–5.

29 Outram, 123.

30 He also felt that even though Christianity was false, it was important for social stability, and he therefore did not believe it should be got rid of entirely. The masses needed it. See Outram, 114–17.

31 Gonzalez, *The Story of Christianity*, 2:349–55.

32 McGrath, *Christian Theology*, 67–9; Outram, *The Enlightenment*, 115–17, 122. Kant's presence loomed large in this endeavour. His book, *Religion Within the Limits of Reason Alone*, translated by J.W. Semple (Edinburgh: Thomas Clark, 1838), originally published in German in 1793, was a pioneering work for adherents of a religion of reason.

33 Olson, *The Story of Christian Theology*, chs. 29 and 30.

34 Olson, chs. 29 and 30; Gonzalez, *The Story of Christianity*, vol. 2, ch. 24, 288–90; Outram, *The Enlightenment*, 117–18, 127–8.

35 Moses Maimonides, *The Guide of the Perplexed*, trans. Shlomo Pines (Chicago: University of Chicago Press, 1963), 5–20.

36 The two approaches to Maimonides are discussed by Aviezer Ravitzky, "The Secrets of the *Guide of the Perplexed*: From the Thirteenth to the Twentieth Centuries," in *Studies in Maimonides*, ed. Isadore Twersky (Cambridge, MA: Harvard University Press, 1990), 159–207. See also Howard Kreisel, "Moses Maimonides," in *History of Jewish Philosophy*, ed. Daniel H. Frank and Oliver Leaman, 250–2 (London: Routledge, 1997), https://doi.org/10.4324/9780203983102.

37 The philosophy of Aristotle described here was not pure Aristotle. In the medieval period, what was called "Aristotle" was really an amalgam of

Aristotle's philosophy and that of Plato. Still, medieval thinkers in all three Abrahamic faiths referred to this philosophy as that of Aristotle, and so I will too.

38 The modern scholar who has been most responsible for championing this approach is Leo Strauss (1899–1973), a specialist in political theory who was famous for his original works in his field among both Jewish and non-Jewish scholars. Strauss's reading of Maimonides can be found in such works as "The Literary Character of the *Guide of the Perplexed*," in *Persecution and the Art of Writing* (Glencoe, IL: Free Press, 1952), 38–94; and *Philosophy and Law*, trans. Fred Baumann (Philadelphia: Jewish Publication Society of America, 1987).

39 See my study, *The Book of Job in Medieval Jewish Philosophy* (New York: Oxford University Press, 2004), ch. 3, https://doi.org/10.1093/acpro f:oso/9780195171532.003.0003, in which I argue for a radical reading of Maimonides' interpretation of Job and the views of providence that underlie that interpretation.

40 These figures include Samuel ibn Tibbon (1150–1230), Isaac Albalag (second half of the thirteenth century), Joseph ibn Kaspi (1280–1345), and Moses Narboni (second half of the fourteenth century). Relatively little has been written about these figures. On Samuel ibn Tibbon and Joseph ibn Kaspi as radical thinkers, see Idit Dobbs-Weinstein, "The Maimonidean Controversy," in Frank and Leaman, *History of Jewish Philosophy*, 340–5.

41 These figures included R. Moses Isserles (Rema), R. Judah Loew ben Betstal'el (Maharal), and R. Yom Tov Lipmann Heller. See David B. Ruderman, *Jewish Thought and Scientific Discovery in Early Modern Europe* (New Haven: Yale University Press, 1995), ch. 2, https://doi .org/10.12987/9780300145953-004; Hava Tirosh-Samuelson, "Jewish Philosophy on the Eve of Modernity," in Frank and Leaman, *History of Jewish Philosophy*, 499–576. See also Jay R. Berkowitz, "Rabbinic Culture and the Historical Development of Halakhah," in *The Early Modern World, 1500–1815*, ed. Jonathan Karp and Adam Sutcliffe, vol. 7 of *The Cambridge History of Judaism* (Cambridge: Cambridge University Press, 2018), 352, https://doi.org/10.1017/9781139017169.015.

42 This claim was made despite the fact that Kabbalah had been influenced from its very inception by philosophy. The system of emanation of the *sefirot* that was at the centre of Kabbalah was clearly modelled in part on Neoplatonic philosophy.

43 Michael L. Morgan, "Moses Mendelssohn," in Frank and Leaman, *History of Jewish Philosophy*, 660–81.

44 Mordecai Finley, "Nineteenth-Century German Reform Philosophy," in Frank and Leaman, *History of Jewish Philosophy*, 682–705.

45 Seymour Feldman, "Spinoza," in Frank and Leaman, *History of Jewish Philosophy*, 612–35. For discussions of the influence of Maimonides and Gersonides on Spinoza's thinking, see most recently Steven Nadler, "Virtue, Reason, and Moral Luck: Maimonides, Gersonides, Spinoza," in *Spinoza and Medieval Jewish Philosophy*, ed. Steven Nadler (Cambridge: Cambridge University Press, 2014), 152–76, https://doi.org/10.1017/CBO9781139795395.009; and Alexander Green, "A Portrait of Spinoza as a Maimonidean Reconsidered," *Shofar* 34, no. 1 (Fall 2015): 81–106, https://doi.org/10.1353/sho.2015.0052.

46 Kenneth Seeskin, "Jewish Neo-Kantianism: Hermann Cohen," in Frank and Leaman, *History of Jewish Philosophy*, 786–98. Daniel B. Schwartz examines the reception of Spinoza among Jews in the three centuries after his death in *The First Modern Jew: Spinoza and the History of an Image* (Princeton: Princeton University Press, 2012), https://doi.org/10.1515/9781400842261. It should be noted, however, that while Hermann Cohen adopted an impersonal conception of God, he was in many ways opposed to Spinoza's views because of their pantheism.

47 The best-known collection of this sort is *Malmad ha-Talmidim* by the French figure, Jacob Anatoli (c. 1194–1256). It is not clear how many of Anatoli's written sermons were actually delivered, and if they were, whether the written versions were identical with the oral ones. Still, he certainly viewed his sermons as appropriate for public consumption, and they contained copious amounts of philosophical material. See Marc Saperstein, *Jewish Preaching, 1200–1800: An Anthology* (New Haven: Yale University Press, 1989), 15–16, 56–7. Saperstein also analyses the philosophical content of rabbinic sermons in late medieval Spain in, "Sermons as Evidence for the Popularization of Philosophy in Fifteenth-Century Spain," in *Your Voice is Like a Ram's Horn: Themes and Texts in Traditional Jewish Preaching* (Cincinnati: Hebrew Union College Press, 1997), 75–88.

48 See Seymour Feldman, introduction to *The Wars of the Lord: Book One: Immortality of the Soul*, by Levi ben Gershom (Gersonides), trans. Seymour Feldman (Philadelphia: Jewish Publication Society of America, 1984), 11–17. Gersonides's commentaries on the Torah and the Book of Job were particularly popular. They were both printed early and often.

49 The controversy in medieval Judaism over the study of philosophy is discussed by Joseph Sarachek, *Faith and Reason: The Conflict over the Rationalism of Maimonides* (Williamsport: Bayard Press, 1935); Daniel Jeremy Silver, *Maimonidean Criticism and Maimonidean Controversy 1180–1240* (Leiden: E.J. Brill, 1965); Dobbs-Weinstein, "The Maimonidean Controversy," 331–49; and Gregg Stern, *Philosophy and Rabbinic Culture: Jewish Interpretation and Controversy in Medieval Languedoc* (Abingdon, UK: Routledge, 2009), https://doi.org/10.4324/9780203884195.

50 Hayim Hillel Ben-Sasson implies that two of the three major phases of
the controversy – the first, in the 1230s, and the second, in the first decade
of 1300s – affected all strata of the Jewish community. According to
Ben-Sasson, both these phases reflected socio-economic divisions within
the Jewish community, with the lower classes opposing the study of
philosophy and the upper classes supporting it. See Hayim Hillel Ben-
Sasson, *Chapters in the History of Jews in the Middle Ages* [in Hebrew] (Tel
Aviv: Am Oved, 1969), 224–6, 230.

51 Historians in the nineteenth and early twentieth centuries claimed
that the doctrines condemned in 1277 were espoused by radical
Aristotelians, who were called "Latin Averroists" on the presumption
that they were influenced by the thinking of Averroes, a Muslim
Aristotelian philosopher whose writings were available in Latin.
However, subsequent research has shown that these Christian
thinkers were *not* Averroists, nor was their thinking that radical. For
a good summary of the historiography on this issue, see Thijssen,
"Condemnation of 1277," sections 4 and 5.

52 Sometimes medieval rabbis implemented more violent punishments,
including capital punishment, but only on rare occasions. See Aaron
M. Schreiber, *Jewish Law and Decision-Making: A Study through Time*
(Philadelphia: Temple University Press, 1979), 402–5; and Kenneth R. Stow,
Alienated Minority: The Jews of Medieval Latin Europe (Cambridge, MA:
Harvard University Press, 1992), 176.

53 This matter is touched on by Georges Vajda, *Isaac Albalag : Averroïste juif,
tradacteur et annotateur d'Al-Ghazâlî* (Paris: J. Vrin, 1960), 256–8.

54 See my introductory chapter, pp. 6–7.

55 See chapter 2, under "Jewish Secularism," p. 62.

6. Freedom of Thought and Expression

1 Paul speaks about salvation in a number of places in his writings. See, for
instance, Rom. 3:21–31; Gal. 2:15–21, 3:6–9, 4:21–30.

2 Until recently, scholars of the New Testament interpreted Paul to be
saying that faith had completely displaced the law in the wake of Jesus's
death and resurrection. Christians, whether born as Jews or gentiles, did
not need to observe the commandments in the Torah in order to achieve
salvation; faith was sufficient. Certainly there are passages in Paul that
support this interpretation. However, many scholars now argue that
Paul did not dismiss the law as completely as earlier scholars claimed.
There are many inconsistencies in Paul's writings, and some passages
suggest that the law still had relevance, particularly for Jews who had
become Christians. See, Bart D. Ehrman, *The New Testament: A Historical*

Introduction to the Early Christian Writings, 2nd ed. (New York: Oxford University Press, 2000), 308–11, 321–9.

But even if one accepts this latter interpretation, there is no question that Paul emphasized the importance of faith, and his statements about it had a great impact on the direction that Christianity took. Moreover, Christian interpreters in later centuries took the view that, for Paul, faith did, in fact, replace the law, and this one-sided reading of Paul is important for our concerns in this chapter because it resulted in Christianity being highly focused on matters of belief for the rest of its history.

3 The Apostles' Creed was further refined and expanded over subsequent centuries, achieving its final form in the eighth century. In the ninth century, it was given official status by the Church, and it is still used today by many Christian denominations in the West. See Roger E. Olson, *The Story of Christian Theology: Twenty Centuries of Tradition and Reform* (Downers Grove: InterVarsity Press, 1999), 128–31; Alister E. McGrath, *Christian Theology: An Introduction*, 4th ed. (Victoria, Australia: Blackwell, 2007), 14–15; Justo L. Gonzalez, *The Story of Christianity*, 2nd ed. (New York: HarperOne, 2010), 1:77–9.

4 There were, however, dissenters. For instance, a group known as the Monophysites believed that Jesus was entirely divine, and they went on to found the Syrian, Armenian, Coptic, and Ethiopic Churches. See Olson, *The Story of Christian Theology*, chs. 9–16; McGrath, *Christian Theology*, 283–9; Gonzalez, *The Story of Christianity*, vol. 1, chs. 17–19; and Gregg R. Allison, *Historical Theology: An Introduction to Christian Doctrine* (Grand Rapids: Zondervan, 2011), 368–77.

5 Clifford R. Backman, *The Worlds of Medieval Europe*, 3rd ed. (New York: Oxford University Press, 2015), 43, 46–8.

6 See, for instance, Rom. 13:8–14, Gal. 5:16–26, I Cor. 6:9–12. I have also noted in note 2 above that according to recent research, Paul did not entirely dismiss the value of observing "the law," as Christians interpreters have usually claimed.

7 Backman, *The Worlds of Medieval Europe*, 373–9. The Cathars, who were centred in France, were dualists who believed that God and Satan were both eternal and powerful deities. The Waldensians, who were in central Europe and southern France, called on all Christians to live a life of poverty and to read the Bible in the vernacular. It is not entirely clear what precipitated the violence against heretical groups in this period, but what we do know is that at this time, as mentioned earlier, intolerance towards heretics in Europe was part of a much wider phenomenon. There was also intolerance against other outsiders – such as Jews, gays, and lepers (467–9, 580–2).

8 See chapter 5, under "Christian Perspectives" within "The Medieval Period," p. 156. See also David C. Lindberg, "Science and the Medieval

Church," in *Medieval Science*, ed. David C. Lindberg and Michael H. Shank, vol. 2 of *The Cambridge History of Science*, ed. David C. Lindberg and Ronald L. Numbers (Cambridge: Cambridge University Press, 2013), 276–8, https://doi.org/10.1017/CHO9780511974007.012. Lindberg downplays the opposition of the Church to science in the thirteenth and fourteenth centuries with the claim that its various condemnations either were ignored or were eventually rescinded. This may be true; however, my guess is that the Church's condemnations were effective in precluding the most radical thinking, given that the Church had great power and had demonstrated its willingness to use it to suppress heresy. I will have more to say about this issue later on in this chapter.

9 The Catholic Church did not always instigate the violence against Protestants. The violence was often directed by local rulers, but at times it was also perpetrated by mobs that were under no one's direction in particular. Nonetheless, the root of the violence was the Catholic Church's intolerance of dissent.

10 See chapter 3, under "The Reformation," p. 93.

11 Olson, *The Story of Christian Theology*, 417; Gonzalez, *The Story of Christianity*, 2:83–4. Perhaps the best example of tit-for-tat violence between Catholics and Protestants in the early modern period is provided by England. In the sixteenth and seventeenth centuries, the two groups took turns persecuting each other depending on who was in power.

12 See chapter 4, under "The Reformation," p. 122.

13 Studies that support this approach include the following: John Hedley Brooke, *Science and Religion: Some Historical Perspectives* (Cambridge: Cambridge University Press, 1991), https://doi.org/10.1017/CBO9781107589018; David C. Lindberg and Ronald L. Numbers, eds., *When Christianity and Science Meet* (Chicago: University of Chicago Press, 2003), https://doi.org/10.7208/9780226482156; and John Henry, *The Scientific Revolution and the Origins of Modern Science*, 3rd ed. (New York: Palgrave Macmillan, 2008), ch. 6. My analysis in the rest of this section reflects the works of these scholars.

14 See Charles Murray, *Human Accomplishment: The Pursuit of Excellence in the Arts and Sciences, 800 B.C. to 1950* (New York: HarperCollins, 2003) and Rodney Stark, *How the West Won: The Neglected Story of the Triumph of Modernity* (Wilmington: ISI Books, 2014).

15 Similar observations can be made about other restrictions put in place by the Condemnation of 1277. For instance, some of the ideas banned here concerned speculations about the intellect. This topic had religious significance because the intellect was the means by which truth was determined and because it was considered by medieval Christian philosophers to be the faculty through which prophecy was received. Yet this topic also included matters that we would now classify under one or

another field in the sciences, such as neuroscience and psychology. Thus, here as well, the Church's offensive against ideas that were religious in nature was also an offensive against an area of knowledge that was scientific in orientation.

According to some scholars, the Condemnation of 1277 not only failed to impede the development of science but also resulted in its progress. Aristotelian science had been adhered to by Christian philosophers in dogmatic fashion, but because the Church criticized that science, it paved the way for alternative ways of thinking. See Hans Thijssen, "Condemnation of 1277," in *The Stanford Encyclopedia of Philosophy*, ed. Edward N. Zalta, Winter 2016 ed. (Stanford: Stanford University, 1997–), article published 30 January 2003, last modified 24 September 2013, https://plato.stanford.edu/archives/win2016/entries/condemnation. I find myself sceptical about this claim. Proponents of this view would have to show that the alternative ways of thinking opened up by the Church's condemnation did indeed represent progress, and I am doubtful that this can be demonstrated.

16 As noted in chapter 5, note 10, religion was not necessarily the sole cause of the violence here, but it was perceived to be, and that perception motivated Europeans to make changes in the way they related to religion.

17 Dorinda Outram, *The Enlightenment*, 3rd ed. (Cambridge: Cambridge University Press, 2013), 118–22, https://doi.org/10.1017/CBO9781139226318.

18 A.C. Grayling, *Toward the Light of Liberty: The Struggles for Freedom and Rights That Made the Modern Western World* (New York: Walker, 2007), 72–9; Alan Ryan, *On Politics: A History of Political Thought: From Herodotus to the Present* (New York: Liveright, 2012), 2:491–4.

19 John Milton, the great poet, was a key figure here. He addressed the right to free speech in 1644 in his famous work, *Areopagitica*. Milton's specific target was the practice of censorship by the British Parliament. Publications in England had to be licensed by the Parliament, and the Parliament could deny a licence if a publication had objectionable material in it. Milton himself was a victim of this practice, which is what prompted him to write his treatise. Milton's defence of free speech was both eloquent and passionate, and it was highly influential. It inspired a debate in subsequent years that eventually achieved the desired result. Parliament no longer had power over what could be published. See, Grayling, *Toward the Light of Liberty*, 63–70.

20 Grayling, 141–6; Ryan, *On Politics*, vol. 2, ch. 16.

21 In England, for instance, freedom of worship for British Catholics was finally granted in 1791, more than a century after the same right had been given to non-Anglican Protestants in England. Other discriminatory practices against Catholics, such as restrictions on holding public office,

were gradually removed by a number of acts of Parliament throughout
the nineteenth century. Jews won similar concessions, particularly with
the passage of the Jews Relief Act in 1858. See Ian Machin, "British
Catholics," in *The Emancipation of Catholics, Jews, and Protestants: Minorities
and the Nation-State in Nineteenth-Century Europe*, ed. Rainer Liedtke and
Stephan Wendehorst (Manchester: Manchester University Press, 2011),
15; and David Cesarini, "British Jews," *The Emancipation*, ed. Liedtke and
Wendehorst, 43–4.

22 The well-known case of John Wilkes in England in the 1760s provides a
good illustration. Wilkes was jailed simply because his radical political
views offended those in power, and it took some effort for him to win his
freedom. Problems of this sort persisted in the West, but gradually the
idea took hold among those in power in their respective countries that the
public was not going to stand for the jailing of political opponents. See
Joris van Eijnatten, "In Praise of Moderate Enlightenment: A Taxonomy of
Early Modern Arguments in Favor of Freedom of Expression," in *Freedom
of Speech: The History of An Idea*, ed. Elizabeth Powers (Lanham, MD:
Rowman and Littlefield, 2011), 38–9.

23 The right of all adults to vote took longer than most Westerners realize.
When the English civil wars of the seventeenth century ended, only men
who had property qualifications were given the right to vote. That right
was gradually expanded in England in the next two and a half centuries.
By 1918, men over the age of twenty-one without property could vote. A
parallel but slower process enfranchised women. It was not until 1928 that
women in England were given voting rights. A similar process occurred in
the US. Voting rights were gradually extended from landowning males to
all males, and then to women, with the last of these rights secured in 1919.
France went through a more tumultuous process. During the nineteenth
century, France lost its democracy completely when Napoleon took the
reins of government, but recovered it when Napoleon was deposed. But
here again, full voting rights for the adult population that did not own
land would have to wait until the twentieth century. And women did not
have the right to vote in France until 1945!

It is hard to nail down precise dates when male suffrage was granted
without property or wealth qualifications in the US, England, and
France. A number of scholars discuss this issue, but, to my mind,
the best treatment of it can be found in David Alexander Bateman,
*Disenfranchising Democracy: Constructing the Electorate in the United States,
the United Kingdom, and France* (Cambridge: Cambridge University Press,
2018), https://doi.org/10.1017/9781108556323. I want to thank David
Bateman for a wonderfully helpful correspondence that we had about
these issues.

24 This position was central to Mendelssohn's most important work on Judaism, *Jerusalem: Or on Religious Power and Judaism*, trans. Allan Arkush (Waltham, MA: Brandeis University Press, 1983).

25 Solomon Schechter, *Studies in Judaism: First Series* (Philadelphia: Jewish Publication Society of America, 1896), ch. 6.

26 Leo Baeck, "Does Traditional Judaism Possess Dogmas?," in *Studies in Jewish Thought: An Anthology of German Jewish Scholarship*, ed. Alfred Jospe (Detroit: Wayne State University Press, 1981), 41–53.

27 See, for instance, the statement by Rabbi Emil G. Hirsch (1851–1923), an American Reform rabbi, cited in Naomi W. Cohen, *What the Rabbis Said: The Public Discourse of Nineteenth-Century Rabbis* (New York: NYU Press, 2008), 30, https://doi.org/10.18574/nyu/9780814772942.003.0005. See also Abba Hillel Silver, *Where Judaism Differed: An Inquiry into the Distinctiveness of Judaism* (New York: Macmillan, 1965), 115–20.

28 See, for instance, Deut. 11:13–21, which became the second paragraph of the celebrated *Shema* prayer.

29 Marc B. Shapiro, *The Limits of Orthodox Theology: Maimonides' Thirteen Principles Reappraised* (Portland, OR: Littman Library of Jewish Civilization, 2004), 29–32.

30 M *Sanhedrin* 10:1.

31 Menachem Kellner, *Must a Jew Believe Anything?* (Portland, OR: Littman Library of Jewish Civilization, 1999), 36; Shapiro, *The Limits of Orthodox Theology*, 29–30. There are even harsher texts suggesting that one throw sectarians into a pit and abandon it, which would effectively result in their death. See T *Bava Metsi'a* 2:13.

32 See chapter 5, under "Jewish Philosophy vs. Christian Philosophy," pp. 172–3.

33 Menachem Kellner, *Dogma in Medieval Jewish Thought: From Maimonides to Abravanel* (Portland, OR: Littman Library of Jewish Civilization, 2004).

34 Yoseif Yaron, Joe Pessah, Avraham Qanaï, and Yosef El-Gamil, *An Introduction to Karaite Judaism: History, Theology, Practice, and Culture* (Albany: Qirqisani Center, 2003).

35 Maimonides, *Commentary on the Mishnah*, introduction to *Sanhedrin* 10; Kellner, *Must a Jew Believe Anything?* 53.

36 Kellner, 53–6.

37 Kellner, 74–5; Shapiro, *The Limits of Orthodox Theology*, 13.

38 Kellner, p. 53; Shapiro, 17–19.

39 Steven Nadler, *Spinoza: A Life* (Cambridge: Cambridge University Press, 1999; Cambridge Core, 2013), ch. 6, https://doi.org/10.1017/CBO9780511815713.007. Nadler's views on Spinoza's excommunication are neatly summarized in his article, "Why Spinoza was Excommunicated," *Humanities* 34, no. 5 (September–October 2013), https://www.neh.gov/article/why-spinoza-was-excommunicated.

40 Kellner, *Must a Jew Believe Anything?*, 67, 70; Shapiro, *The Limits of Orthodox Theology*, 4, 20–4, 32–7.

41 Shapiro's book, *The Limits of Orthodox Theology*, is dedicated to demonstrating this point.

42 Shapiro, 6–8.

43 Shapiro, 14–15.

44 Much has been written on the remarkably pluralistic attitude of the rabbis that underlay their deliberations about Jewish law. See, for instance, Moshe Halbertal, *People of the Book: Canon, Meaning, and Authority* (Cambridge, MA: Harvard University Press, 1997), ch. 2, https://doi .org/10.4159/9780674038141-004; Avi Sagi, *The Open Canon: On the Meaning of Halakhic Discourse* (New York: Continuum, 2007); Richard Hidary, *Dispute for the Sake of Heaven: Legal Pluralism in the Talmud* (Providence, RI: Brown Judaic Studies, 2010); and Christine Hayes, *What's Divine about Divine Law? Early Perspectives* (Princeton: Princeton University Press, 2015), especially ch. 5, https://doi.org/10.1515/9781400866410-011.

45 Some scholars have argued that there is evidence that the Mishnah *was* a law code because most of the disagreements recorded in it include an opinion not attributed to a specific rabbi. This anonymous opinion is presumed to be that of the majority of rabbis and is therefore the one that the redactor of the Mishnah favoured. However, the fact that the disputes in the Mishnah are not resolved explicitly still makes it an odd work of law. Usually law codes strive for greater clarity in presenting their rulings than is the case here. For a discussion of this issue and the overall character of the Mishnah, see David Kraemer, "The Mishnah," in *The Late Roman-Rabbinic Period*, ed. Steven T. Katz, vol. 4 of *The Cambridge History of Judaism* (Cambridge: Cambridge University Press, 2006), 299–315, esp. 311–13, https://doi.org/10.1017/CHOL9780521772488.014.

46 M *Eduyot* 1:5–6. However, in the same passage, R. Judah suggests that the minority opinion is recorded so that if, in future disputes, there is a sage who supports that opinion, the Mishnah can be cited to prove that his opinion is incorrect. In other words, R. Judah's opinion is precisely the opposite of the anonymous opinion alongside which it is cited. The irony here is that R. Judah's opinion is itself a minority opinion and would therefore be negated by the very rule that R. Judah himself lays down. See Kraemer, "The Mishnah," 305–6, who discusses this passage and the irony of R. Judah's position.

47 BT *Hagigah* 3b.

48 See chapter 4, under "The Late Medieval and Early Modern Periods," p. 141.

49 See, for instance, BT *Sanhedrin* 88b.

50 A number of scholars argue that the positive attitude towards disputation is more evident in the Babylonian Talmud than in the Jerusalem Talmud. Hidary's book, for instance, develops that position. Hidary also asks a critical question here: to what extent did tolerance in early Rabbinic Judaism for different opinions on legal matters also result in tolerance for different legal practices? One can allow for a diversity of opinion on a particular issue, but that does not mean that one will also have tolerance for the practices based on those opinions. One may insist that in the realm of practice, there must be uniformity. Hidary argues that the rabbis of the Babylonian Talmud did indeed extend their tolerance for different opinions to the practices resulting from those opinions, though that tolerance had certain limits.

51 BT *Sanhedrin* 87a.

52 Jeffrey L. Rubenstein, *The Culture of the Babylonian Talmud* (Baltimore: Johns Hopkins University Press, 2005), 54–66, 147–51, https://doi.org/10.1353/book.20647.

53 See chapter 4, under "The Late Medieval and Early Modern Periods," pp. 140–1.

54 The viewpoint was supported by Abraham ibn Da'ud (1110–80), but he was not a prominent figure in the way that Maimonides and Nahmanides were. See Halbertal, *People of the Book*, 54–71.

55 Arius, however, did have the support of some of the Roman emperors in the next century, before his viewpoint was discarded.

56 Ecumenism has roots in the seventeenth and eighteenth centuries, but it does not become a movement until the beginning of the twentieth century. For a succinct history of ecumenism, see Daniel Kasomo, Nicholas Ombachi, Joseph Musyoka, and Naila Napoo, "Historical Survey of the Concept of Ecumenical Movement, Its Model, and Contemporary Problems," *International Journal of Applied Sociology* 2, no. 5 (2012): 47–51, https://doi.org/10.5923/j.ijas.20120205.01.

57 I should also point out that the modern notion of freedom of thought and expression was viewed by Westerners as a "right," and that conception was foreign to rabbinic thinking prior to the nineteenth century. The idea of "rights" implied that human beings had protections they were born with. Rabbinic Judaism had no such notion. The rabbis tended to think more in terms of duties than rights. People had obligations to serve God, not rights that protected them.

Some Jewish thinkers have argued, however, that the distinction here is misleading and ultimately false because rights imply duties and vice versa. That is, when a thinker supports the right of an individual to free speech, they are not just saying that such speech is protected by law; they are also saying that the individual's fellow citizens have the duty to enforce that law. The same can be said in reverse, that duties imply rights. Thus, the duty that citizens have to protect free speech implies the right of free speech for the particular individual who chooses to speak his mind on a given issue.

58 My remarks here are focused on Jews in Europe, but they are also applicable to Jews living in Islamic lands.

59 Charles Murray, in his study, *Human Accomplishment*, claims that modern Jews were highly successful in the West because they learned individualism from the surrounding non-Jewish culture. According to Murray, individualism was the legacy of Christianity. While Murray admits that Jews were well-educated, he claims that Jews could not have developed a sense of individualism from their own culture because that culture emphasized duty to family and community more than the cultivation of the individual. See Murray, *Human Accomplishment*, 404. In light of everything I have said in this chapter and the preceding three chapters dealing with autonomy, Murray's claims are difficult to sustain. Murray's views are also undermined by the fact that as the modern period progressed, Jews were, in fact, far more successful than their Western neighbours in many of the areas that Murray focuses on in his arguments about the success of the West.

7. Valuing Life in This World I: 100–1000 CE

1 Prominent modern Jewish intellectuals who have taken this view include Abraham Geiger, Kauffmann Kohler, Max Brod, and Abba Hillel Silver. For Abraham Geiger, see Walter Jacob, *Christianity through Jewish Eyes: The Quest for Common Ground* (Cincinnati: Hebrew Union College Press, 1974), 47. For Kaufmann Kohler, see Naomi W. Cohen, *What the Rabbis Said: The Public Discourse of Nineteenth-Century American Rabbis* (New York: NYU Press, 2008), 185–6, https://doi.org/10.18574/nyu/9780814772942.003.0013; for Max Brod, see Jacob, 113–20. For Abba Hillel Silver, see *Where Judaism Differed: An Inquiry into the Distinctiveness of Judaism* (New York: Macmillan, 1965), ch. 11.

2 Eugene J. Fisher, a Christian scholar and theologian, is particularly unhappy about the way in which this common comparison caricatures Christianity. See his article, "Typical Jewish Misunderstandings of Christianity," *Shofar* 28, no. 3 (Spring 2010): 57–69.

3 There are dozens of passages about the Kingdom of God in the New Testament. See, for instance, Mk. 1:15, 6:10, 9:1, 13:32–5, 14:25; Lk. 21: 34–6; 1 Cor. 10:11; and 2 Cor. 5:17.

4 Bart D. Ehrman, *The New Testament: A Historical Introduction to the Early Christian Writings*, 2nd ed. (New York: Oxford University Press, 2000), 225–8, 241–50.

5 This tension is evident, for instance, in 1 Cor. 3:6. See Ehrman's discussion, *The New Testament*, ch. 20.

6 Alan S. Kahan, *Mind vs. Money: The War between Intellectuals and Capitalism* (New Brunswick: Transaction, 2010), 42–4.

7 Cosimo Perrotta, *Consumption as an Investment I: The Fear of Goods from Hesiod to Adam Smith*, trans. Joan McMullin (London: Routledge, 2004), 47, https://doi.org/10.4324/9780203694572.

8 Merry E. Wiesner-Hanks, *Christianity and Sexuality in the Early Modern World: Regulating Desire, Reforming Practice*, 2nd ed. (London: Routledge, 2010), 26–7, https://doi.org/10.4324/9781315787350.

9 Perrotta, *Consumption as an Investment I*, 47–8; Kahan, *Mind vs. Money*, 44. Underlying this more lenient attitude towards wealth was the idea that all wealth actually belonged to God and that human beings were only its stewards. Therefore, ideally, everyone should share wealth in common as Jesus's apostles had, but if people were not willing to – and most people were not – the next best thing was for them to share their wealth with the poor.

10 Wiesner-Hanks, *Christianity and Sexuality*, 32–3.

11 James Boyce, *Born Bad: Original Sin and the Making of the Western World* (Berkeley: Counterpoint, 2015), 18–19. The matter was quite personal for Augustine. In his *Confessions*, Augustine speaks a great deal about his own struggles with sexual lust.

12 Justo L. Gonzalez, *The Story of Christianity*, 2nd ed. (New York: HarperOne, 2010), vol. 1, ch. 15; Clifford R. Backman, *The Worlds of Medieval Europe*, 3rd ed. (New York: Oxford University Press, 2015), 89–102.

13 Backman, *The Worlds of Medieval Europe*, 89–102.

14 My remarks here will be concerned mainly with Christianity prior to the year 1000, but I will be dealing with matters that are also applicable to Christianity past that point in time.

15 Wiesner-Hanks, *Christianity and Sexuality*, 39–47; Ruth Mazo Karras, *Sexuality in Medieval Europe: Doing unto Others* (New York: Routledge, 2005), 59–60, 67.

16 Jeremy Cohen, *"Be Fertile and Increase, Fill the Earth and Master It": The Ancient and Medieval Career of a Biblical Text* (Ithaca: Cornell University Press, 1989), ch. 5, esp. 225–6.

17 Backman, *The Worlds of Medieval Europe*, ch. 4.

18 Roger E. Olson, *The Story of Christian Theology: Twenty Centuries of Tradition and Reform* (Downers Grove: InterVarsity Press, 1999), 287–9. Gregory himself had been a monk before he became the pope, and he saw in the monastic communities the essence of the Christian life. He believed that if Christians wanted to live as Jesus intended them to, they had to be "crucified with him," and that meant denying oneself bodily pleasures

in order to cultivate one's spirituality. For Gregory, the ideal life was therefore a monastic one. Others who did not live that life should at least do their best to imitate the monastic regimen by minimizing indulgence in earthly pleasures, particularly sex. The association between asceticism and Jesus's suffering was significant. Denying oneself pleasure had great value because it allowed one to have communion with Jesus, who suffered on the cross. This theme would crop up in medieval Christianity and would become especially popular in the later centuries of the Middle Ages. In doing so, it would provide a powerful argument for resisting the pleasures of this world.

19 Bernard Hamilton, *Religious Life in the Medieval West*, 2nd ed. (London: Hodder Arnold, 2003), 43–4; Backman, *The Worlds of Medieval Europe*, 100.

20 For a discussion of the corruption in the early medieval Church and attempts at reform, see Gonzalez, *The Story of Christianity*, 1:327–38, 1:357–68, 1:393–431; and Backman, 208–10, 310–15, 533–42.

21 This position is evident in the negative depiction of the figure of Bar Kokhba in rabbinic texts. Early rabbinic opinion was divided over whether he was a messianic impostor or a failed military hero, but in both depictions he was criticized for his arrogance and self-aggrandizement. See Richard G. Marks, *The Image of Bar Kokhba in Traditional Jewish Literature: False Messiah and National Hero* (University Park: Pennsylvania State University Press, 1994), ch. 1, https://doi.org/10.1515/9780271075495-005. Differences of rabbinic opinion on Bar Kokhba are found in a number of sources, most notably JT *Ta'anit 4:8, and Lamentations Rabbah* 2:4.

22 *Avot de-Rabi Natan*, version B, 31. The fact that this statement is attributed to R. Yohanan ben Zakai does not mean that he said it or that it dates from the first century. Scholars tend to believe that this source has its origin in the fifth or sixth century. I would like to thank Jeffrey Rubenstein for this insight.

23 Daniel Boyarin, *Carnal Israel: Reading Sex in Talmudic Culture* (Berkeley: University of California Press, 1995), 1–2, 233–4.

24 Boyarin, *Carnal Israel*, 31–2.

25 Boyarin, 33–4.

26 See chapter 3, under "Original Sin," p. 100.

27 Ephraim E. Urbach, *The Sages: Their Concepts and Beliefs*, trans. Israel Abrahams (Cambridge, MA: Harvard University Press, 1987), 433–5, 472; Reuven Kimelman, "The Rabbinic Theology of the Physical: Blessings, Body and Soul, Resurrection, and Covenant and Election," in *The Late Roman-Rabbinic Period*, ed. Steven T. Katz, vol. 4 of *The Cambridge History of Judaism* (Cambridge: Cambridge University Press, 2006), 952–6, https://doi.org/10.1017/CHOL9780521772488.039.

28 *Leviticus Rabbah* 34:3.

29 M *Avot* 1:3; *Avot de-Rabi Natan*, ch. 5; Simcha Paull Raphael, *Jewish Views of the Afterlife*, 2nd ed. (Lanham, MD: Rowman and Littlefield, 2009), 120–1; Alan L. Mittleman, *A Short History of Jewish Ethics: Conduct and Character in the Context of Covenant* (Malden: Wiley-Blackwell, 2012), 66–7, https://doi .org/10.1002/9781444346619.ch2.

30 BT *Yoma* 84b–85b.

31 BT *Pesahim* 53b; *Bava Metsi'a* 85a, 86a. The notion of a heavenly yeshiva appears only in a handful of early rabbinic sources, and therefore there is no proof that it was widely accepted among the early rabbis. Nevertheless, this motif seems to have had some weight in rabbinic circles, for even though the rabbis said very little about the afterlife in their literature, the idea of the heavenly yeshiva appears in several sources. Moreover, the rabbis who mentioned it saw no reason to justify it; they spoke about it as if it was common knowledge.

32 Kimelman, "The Rabbinic Theology of the Physical," 956–65.

33 M *Yevamot* 6:6.

34 BT *Pesahim* 113a.

35 BT *Yevamot* 63ba.

36 BT *Yevamot* 61b.

37 BT *Yevamot* 62b. Michael Satlow argues in *Jewish Marriage in Antiquity* (Princeton: Princeton University Press, 2001), 5, https://doi.org/10.1515 /9780691187495, that the emphasis in this passage is on marriage as a means for a man to create a household. Yet while the statement certainly mentions that an unmarried man lives without a "wall" or a "dwelling," the passage also says he lives without "help," "Torah," and "wisdom," which are abstract and have nothing to do with a household. I therefore prefer to read the statement to be imparting a more general message about a number of different aspects of life, domestic and religious.

38 BT *Ketubot* 8a.

39 BT *Yevamot* 63a.

40 The passage is focused on men and could therefore be criticized as having a sexist message, but that is a concern we cannot take up here.

41 Yair Lorberbaum, *In God's Image: Myth, Theology, and Law in Classical Judaism* (Cambridge: Cambridge University Press, 2015), ch. 8, https://doi.org /10.1017/CBO9781107477940.010.

42 BT *Sotah* 2a, *Sanhedrin* 22a; *Leviticus Rabbah* 29:8.

43 *Leviticus Rabbah* 8:1.

44 The obligation for men to fulfil their wives' sexual needs can be found in M *Ketubot* 5:6. The obligation is based on Ex. 21:10, which deals with a man who has married his female slave. Reference is made here to the man owing his wife "conjugal rights" (*onah*), and those rights are interpreted

by the rabbis as a reference to sexual pleasure. The obligation of women to fulfil their husbands' sexual needs is implied in M *Ketubot* 5:7, where it is stated that the refusal by a woman to have sex with her husband was grounds for divorce. According to later interpreters, this rule applied if the refusal was without legitimate cause and was steadfast.

45 *Genesis Rabbah* 9:7; see chapter 3, under "Pelagian Elements in Early Rabbinic Judaism," p. 104.

46 BT *Shabbat* 117b.

47 Moreover, because rabbinic law prohibited cooking food on the Sabbath itself, preparation for the three Sabbath meals had to begin well in advance so that part of the week was taken up with the effort of getting ready for the rich home experience the Sabbath provided.

48 BT *Yevamot* 62b.

49 Boyarin, *Carnal Israel*, ch. 5. In a number of these sources, the Torah is depicted as the "other woman" who seduces men away from their wives. These sources hardly reflect a view of marriage in which companionship is celebrated.

50 BT *Nedarim* 20a.

51 Boyarin, *Carnal Israel*, 46–57, discusses the tensions in early Rabbinic Judaism regarding sexuality that are outlined here. Some medieval rabbis permitted the institution of concubinage, which allowed a man to have a kind of semi-marriage to a woman other than this wife, as one finds in the Bible. However, most rabbis forbade the custom. See *Shulhan Arukh, Even ha-'Ezer*, 26:1.

52 Steven D. Fraade, "Ascetical Aspects of Ancient Judaism," in *Jewish Spirituality: From the Bible through the Middle Ages*, ed. Arthur Green (New York: Crossroad, 1986), 253–88. See also Eliezer Diamond, *Holy Men and Hunger Artists: Fasting and Asceticism in Rabbinic Culture* (New York: Oxford University Press, 2003), https://doi.org/10.1093/acprof:oso /9780195137507.001.0001; Joshua Schwartz, "Material Culture in the Land of Israel: Monks and Rabbis on Clothing and Dress in the Byzantine Period," in *Saints and Role Models in Judaism and Christianity*, ed. Joshua Schwartz and Marcel Poorthuis, vol. 7 of *Jewish and Christian Perspectives Series*, ed. Doron Bar, Leo Mock, Eric Ottenheijm, Eyal Regev, and Lieve Teugels (Leiden: E.J. Brill, 2004), 121–38, https://doi .org/10.1163/9789047401605_009; and Michal Bar-Asher Siegal, "Shared Worlds: Rabbinic and Monastic Literature," *Harvard Theological Review* 105, no. 4 (2012): 423–56, esp. 427–8, https://doi.org/10.1017 /S001781601200020X. Diamond provides a good summary of academic treatments of asceticism in the rabbinic and medieval periods in "Asceticism," *Reader's Guide to Judaism*, ed. Michael Terry (Abingdon, UK: Routledge, 2013), 45–6, https://doi.org/10.4324/9781315062488.

53 Mireille Hadas-Lebel, *Jerusalem Against Rome*, trans. Robyn Fréchet (Leuven: Peeters, 2006), 398–9.

54 The connection between the rabbinic idea that there is a commandment to procreate and the historical circumstances of the rabbis is argued by David Daube, *The Duty of Procreation* (Edinburgh: Edinburgh University Press, 1977), 36–67; and Robert Gordis, "'Be Fruitful and Multiply': Biography of a Mitzvah," *Midstream* 28, no. 7 (August–September 1982): 21–9. Jeremy Cohen, who has studied this issue far more comprehensively than anyone else, has mixed views about Daube's and Gordis's position. Cohen is open to the possibility that there is a connection between the rabbinic notion of an imperative to procreate and the historical context. According to Cohen, such a theory is "plausible" (126, 159–60). But Cohen rejects some of the particulars in Daube's and Gordis's formulations of that theory. Cohen does not support Daube's view that the rabbis were influenced by a decree promulgated by the Roman emperor Augustus, according to which Roman citizens who had children were rewarded, and those who did not were punished. Cohen also rejects Gordis's argument that the rabbinic idea of a duty to procreate was taken more seriously by the rabbis in the medieval period than by the rabbis in late antiquity (159–60). Satlow goes further than Cohen in rejecting any connection whatsoever between the rabbinic notion of a biblical commandment to procreate and the historical circumstances in which that commandment was formulated because there is no explicit mention of any concern in rabbinic sources regarding the decimation of the Jewish population in the first and second centuries CE (18).

I support Cohen's view that there is indeed such a connection, but I would go further and say that it is highly probable rather than merely plausible. I find it hard to believe that the devastation that Jews experienced due to the two failed rebellions against Rome did not have an influence on the rabbis here. Moreover, as I have argued, the notion that there was an imperative to procreate was not an isolated idea in rabbinic thinking. The rabbis emphasized the importance of the home and the family in other ways, and the home could exist only through procreation. We therefore have to see the views of the rabbis on procreation as part of a larger thrust to revive the Jewish community in a time of catastrophe. As for Satlow's argument that the rabbis never explicitly mention any concern about the decline in Jewish population, I do not see this observation as an effective rebuttal to the argument that historical circumstance played a role in inspiring the rabbis to see procreation as a commandment. The rabbis were writing for an audience that would not have needed an explicit reminder about the catastrophes that had befallen the Jewish people in the first two centuries CE.

55 BT *Kidushin* 30b; JT *Pe'ah* 1:1. There were rabbinic sources that spoke positively about poverty. See BT *Hagigah* 9b; *Avot de-Rabi Natan*, version A 11. Such sources, however, are rare. Note also that the statement praising poverty in *Avot de-Rabi Natan* is contained in a chapter in which numerous other statements takes the opposite view.

56 The obligation of men to provide their wives with food and clothing is found in BT *Ketubot* 47b, 56a, and is based on Ex. 21:9–10. The obligation of men to support their children up to the age of six is found in BT *Ketubot* 65b and is considered a rabbinic, not a biblical enactment. Later medieval rabbinic authorities would extend the obligation to the age of puberty.

57 Catharina Lis and Hugo Soly, *Worthy Efforts: Attitudes to Work and Workers in Pre-Industrial Europe*, vol. 10 of *Studies in Global Social History*, ed. Marcel van der Linden (Leiden: E.J. Brill, 2012), 104–7, 114–16, https://doi.org/10.1163/9789004232778_005.

58 BT *Bava Batra* 116a.

59 *Exodus Rabbah* on 31:12.

60 Alyssa M. Gray, "Wealth and Rabbinic Self-Fashioning in Late Antiquity," in *Wealth and Poverty in Jewish Tradition*, ed. Leonard J. Greenspoon (West Lafayette: Purdue University Press, 2015), 53–81. Gray shows that the rabbis certainly understood the potential of wealth to corrupt, but they nonetheless felt that their own leadership depended on it. They also emphasized that their own wealth had not been acquired through nefarious means. Gray also shows that there were differences in attitudes towards wealth between the early rabbis in Palestine and those in Babylonia. For instance, Babylonian rabbis tended to be more hostile towards lay people who were wealthy than the Palestinian rabbis were.

61 Gray, "Wealth and Rabbinic Self-Fashioning."

62 However, we do read in M *Avot* 6:4 as follows: "Such is the way [of a life] of Torah: you shall eat bread with salt, and rationed water shall you drink; you shall sleep on the ground, your life will be one of privation, and in Torah shall you labour. If you do this, 'Happy shall you be and it shall be good for you' (Ps. 128:2): 'Happy shall you be' in this world, 'and it shall be good for you' in the world to come." As is often the case, rabbinic literature often contains dissenting views on just about every issue it treats.

63 M *Avot* 2:2.

64 BT *Berakhot* 35b.

65 Incidentally, one should not misunderstand R. Shimon to be saying that poverty was virtuous. He was in no way advocating that Jews lead a destitute life. His view was only that if Jews engaged in Torah study on a constant basis, God would somehow provide for their material needs.

66 Deut. 11:13–21.

67 BT *Hagigah* 27a. It does not take much reflection to understand why the rabbis looked to the dinner table as a reminder of the Temple. Meals took place one or more times every day, and therefore attaching the commemoration of the Temple to meals meant that the Temple would be remembered on a constant basis. Moreover, meals were often social affairs with family and friends, and therefore, by connecting meals to the Temple, the Temple would not only be remembered, it would be remembered in a social setting. Finally, meals were an ideal time to contemplate one's connection to God in the absence of the Temple because they provided an opportunity to reflect on God's role as the sustainer of life in providing food. This issue is discussed by Baruch M. Bokser, *The Origins of the Seder: The Passover Rite and Early Rabbinic Judaism* (Berkeley: University of California Press, 1984), 10, https://doi .org/10.1525/9780520317376-003; and Jacob Neusner, *From Politics to Piety: The Emergence of Pharisaic Judaism*, 2nd ed. (Eugene: Wipf and Stock, 2003), ch. 5.

68 M *Ta'anit* 1–3.

69 BT *Ta'anit* 11b–12b.

70 BT *Menahot* 43b.

71 Kimelman, 948–49.

72 E.g. Lev. 5:15.

73 Kimelman, "The Rabbinic Theology of the Physical," 947.

74 In a number of rabbinic passages, one of the early sages, Shimon ben Azzai, was criticized for not being married. See T *Yevamot* 8:4; BT *Yevamot* 63b.

75 There is something surprisingly contemporary about the rabbinic reaction to suffering and the path taken to overcome it. It is common wisdom in our culture that one of the best ways to deal with suffering is to get back into life and its ordinary experiences. If, for instance, one has lost a loved one, what any psychologist or any number of self-help books will recommend is that after allowing oneself a period of mourning, the healthy thing is to return to the routine of everyday life. In essence, the rabbis understood this, if not consciously, then at least instinctively. They seemed to know on some level that the best way to rebuild a vibrant Jewish community was to focus on the mundane, which for them, meant keeping God's commandments. Marriage, family, the basic sensual and aesthetic pleasures of life – these things would help Jews get past the destruction of their Temple and the loss of their homeland. Thus, the response of the early rabbis to the turbulence of their time, in addition to being bold from a theological standpoint, was simply good psychology, and in that respect it was ahead of its time.

76 See, for example, Is. 11:1–9, Ez. 36:29–30; Am. 9:13–15.

8. Valuing Life in This World II: 1000–1800 CE

1 See chapter 5, under "Christian Perspectives" within "The Medieval Period," p. 155.
2 Thomas Aquinas, *Summa Theologiae* (New York: Bezinger Brothers, 1947), I, q. 49 a. 1.
3 Clifford R. Backman, *The Worlds of Medieval Europe*, 3rd ed. (New York: Oxford University Press, 2015), 450–5.
4 Aquinas, *Summa Theologiae* I–II, q. 2 a. 1; II–II, q. 77 a. 1; Cosimo Perrotta, *Consumption as an Investment I: The Fear of Goods from Hesiod to Adam Smith*, trans. Joan McMullin (London: Routledge, 2004), 57, 70–3, https://doi .org/10.4324/9780203694572; Alan S. Kahan, *Mind vs. Money: The War between Intellectuals and Capitalism* (New Brunswick: Transaction, 2010), 47–8.
5 Ruth Mazo Karras, *Sexuality in Medieval Europe: Doing unto Others* (New York: Routledge, 2005), 68.
6 John Giles Milhaven, "Thomas Aquinas on Sexual Pleasure," *Journal of Religious Ethics* 5, no. 2 (Fall 1977): 157–81.
7 James A. Brundage, *Law, Sex, and Christian Society in Medieval Europe* (Chicago: University of Chicago Press, 1990), 240–1, https://doi.org /10.7208/9780226077895-011.
8 Anna Clark, *Desire: A History of European Sexuality* (New York: Routledge, 2008), ch. 4, https://doi.org/10.4324/9780203723678.
9 Backman, *The Worlds of Medieval Europe*, 326–30.
10 Harold J. Berman, *Law and Revolution: The Formation of the Western Legal Tradition* (Cambridge, MA: Harvard University Press, 1983); Berman, *Law and Revolution II: The Impact of the Protestant Reformations on the Western Legal Tradition* (Cambridge, MA: Belknap Press, 2006), https://doi.org /10.4159/9780674020863.
11 Backman, *The Worlds of Medieval Europe*, 366.
12 Aquinas, *Summa Theologiae* I–II, q. 2 a. 1; Kahan, *Mind vs. Money*, 47–8.
13 Gratian, author of the *Decretum* and founder of medieval canon law, is a good example of a prominent Christian figure who had strongly negative views of sexual activity. It was an aspect of life that he believed should be avoided altogether. See James A. Brundage, "Sex and Canon Law," in *Handbook of Medieval Sexuality*, ed. Vern L. Bullough and James A. Brundage (New York: Garland, 1996), 39–40.
14 Backman, *The Worlds of Medieval Europe*, 487–9.
15 Backman, 312,15, 485–7, 489–93; C.H. Lawrence, *Medieval Monasticism: Forms of Religious Life in Western Europe in the Middle Ages*, 4th ed. (London: Routledge, 2015), chs. 8–10, 13, https://doi.org/10.4324/9781315715667.
16 Backman, 488; Lawrence, *Medieval Monasticism*, 162–5, 238–40.

17 See chapter 3, under "The Renaissance," p. 92. William Caferro, *Contesting the Renaissance* (West Sussex: Wiley-Blackwell, 2011), 187, 194–7, 205, https://doi.org/10.1002/9781444324501.ch7.

18 See chapter 3, under "The Reformation," p. 93.

19 See chapter 3, under "The Reformation," p. 93.

20 See chapter 5, under "The Reformation," p. 158.

21 Justo L. Gonzalez, *The Story of Christianity*, 2nd ed. (New York: HarperOne, 2010), 2:42–3; Merry E. Wiesner-Hanks, *Christianity and Sexuality in the Early Modern World: Regulating Desire, Reforming Practice*, 2nd ed. (London: Routledge, 2010), 73–82, https://doi.org/10.4324/9781315787350. Charles Taylor has highlighted the importance of the affirmation of ordinary life as one of the key factors in the development of the modern notion of the self, and he locates the beginnings of this emphasis in the Reformation. See his *Sources of the Self: The Making of The Modern Identity* (Cambridge, MA: Harvard University Press, 1989), 211–32.

22 John Witte Jr., "Sex and Marriage in the Protestant Tradition, 1500–1900," in *The Oxford Handbook of Theology, Sexuality, and Gender*, ed. Adrian Thatcher (Oxford: Oxford University Press, 2015), 304–22, https://doi.org/10.1093/oxfordhb/9780199664153.013.012; Kathleen E. Crowther, "Sexuality and Difference," in *The Oxford Handbook of the Protestant Reformations*, ed. Ulinka Rublack (Oxford: Oxford University Press, 2017), 668–73, https://doi.org/10.1093/oxfordhb/9780199646920.013.19.

23 Wiesner-Hanks, *Christianity and Sexuality*, 88–91; C. Scott Dixon, *Contesting the Reformation* (West Sussex: Wiley Blackwell, 2012), 135; James Boyce, *Born Bad: Original Sin and the Making of the Western World* (Berkeley: Counterpoint, 2015), 61.

24 Wiesner-Hanks, 76–8; Crowther, "Sexuality and Difference," 671–2. Luther struggled with the sexual impulse in much the same way Augustine had. Luther spent a great deal of energy as a monk trying to keep his lustful thoughts at bay, only to fail time and time again. This failure led him to despair, which sparked his insight that God saves us through faith alone. Human beings were simply too sinful to be granted salvation on the basis of their deeds. But in contrast to Augustine, who found celibacy to be the best way to combat sexual lust, Luther felt that embracing marriage was the only way to deal with the problem.

25 Max Weber, *The Protestant Ethic and the Spirit of Capitalism*, trans. Talcott Parsons (London: Routledge, 2001), https://doi.org/10.4324/9780203995808.

26 Dixon, *Contesting the Reformation*, 184–7; Donald Frey, "The Protestant Ethic Thesis," EH.net, website for the Economic History Association, https://eh.net/encyclopedia/the-protestant-ethic-thesis.

27 This argument is made by two prominent scholars, Catharina Lis and Hugo Soly, in *Worthy Efforts: Attitudes to Work and Workers in Pre-Industrial*

Europe, vol. 10 of *Studies in Global Social History*, ed. Marcel van der
Linden (Leiden: E.J. Brill, 2012), 148–55, esp. 154, https://doi.org/10.1163
/9789004232778_005. A great deal has been written in recent years on
attitudes to work and labour in European history, but the study by Lis and
Soly is perhaps the most definitive work on the subject to date.

28 These developments are analysed by Berman in *Law and Revolution II*.

29 Samuel Fleischacker highlights the appreciation of the mundane world
as one of the hallmarks of the Enlightenment. See his study, *What Is
Enlightenment?* (Abingdon, UK: Routledge, 2013), 3, https://doi.org/10.4324
/9780203070468.

30 See chapter 3, under "The Enlightenment," p. 162.

31 Much of what Smith argued turned out to be incorrect. Capitalism was not
the panacea he hoped for. But what is important for our purposes is how
Smith's thinking reflected an interest in wealth and material prosperity
that characterized the age he lived in.

32 Clark, *Desire*, ch. 7.

33 Berman, *Law and Revolution II*.

34 See chapter 5, under "The Enlightenment," p. 164.

35 For the obligation to marry and procreate, see Maimonides, *Mishneh Torah*,
Laws of Marriage 15:2; R. Jacob ben Asher, *Arba'ah Turim*; and R. Joseph
Karo, *Shulhan Arukh, Even ha-'Ezer* 1. The obligation of men to fulfil their
wives' sexual needs is found in *Mishneh Torah, Laws of Marriage*, 14:1;
Arba'ah Turim; and *Shulhan Arukh, Even ha-'Ezer* 76. This imperative in
early and medieval rabbinic literature is analysed by David M. Feldman,
Marital Relations, Birth Control, and Abortion in Jewish Law (New York:
Schocken Books, 1974), ch. 4.

36 *Tur, Even ha-'Ezer* 1:1; Feldman, *Marital Relations*, 28–9.

37 R. Judah ben Samuel, *Book of the Pious*, no. 1084, cited and translated
in David Biale, *Eros and the Jews: From Biblical Israel to Contemporary
America* (Berkeley: University of California Press, 1997), 78, https://doi
.org/10.1525/9780520920064-005.

38 Such was the advice of R. Abraham ben David of Posquières (c. 1120–98), a
renowned French rabbi who wrote *Ba'aley ha-Nefesh*, one of the first Jewish
marriage manuals. See Biale, *Eros and the Jews*, 95–7.

39 Biale, 81–2. The text that suggested this regimen was titled *Laws of the Torah*
(*Hukkey Torah*) and was produced by the Tosafists, a major rabbinic school
that thrived in thirteenth-century Germany and France.

40 Biale, 81–82.

41 The contrast being drawn here between medieval Christian and Jewish
views on marriage and sexuality conforms to the assessment of Kenneth
R. Stow, *Alienated Minority: The Jews of Medieval Latin Europe* (Cambridge,
MA: Harvard University Press, 1992), 205–9. A similar contrast is made by

Feldman throughout his study. However, Feldman tends to exaggerate the differences between the two religions, with the apparent intent of casting Judaism in a more favourable light than Christianity regarding sexual matters. This tendency is not surprising given that Feldman's book was published in 1968 when it was fashionable for Jewish writers to make comparisons between Judaism and Christianity in order to show Judaism's superiority. Karras also addresses the contrast being drawn here between medieval Christian and Jewish views on marriage and sexuality, for even though Karras's book is devoted primarily to sexuality in medieval Christianity, she also deals with medieval Jewish and Muslim views on sexuality and draws helpful comparisons among the three religions on this issue. See Karras, *Sexuality in Medieval Europe*, 25.

42 Much of Feldman's book is devoted to this issue. See esp. 103–5. See also Stow, *Alienated Minority*, 205–6, and Karras, 72–3, 74.

43 Biale, *Eros and the Jews*, 73, 87–9.

44 Yehudah Levi, *Torah Study: A Survey of Classic Sources on Timely Issues* (Jerusalem: Feldheim, 1990), 7, citing R. Mordekhai ben Hillel (1240–98) a German rabbi and commentator on the Talmud, and R. Shimon ben Tsemah Duran (1361–1444), a figure who lived in Spain and North Africa.

45 See, for instance, Rashi on Deut. 32:6.

46 Meir Tamari, *With All Your Possessions: Jewish Ethics and Economic Life* (Northvale: Jason Aronson, 1998), 57–8.

47 Maimonides, *Mishneh Torah, Laws of Torah Study* 3:7; Levi, *Torah Study*, 23–31.

48 Stow, *Alienated Minority*, ch. 10.

49 M *Avodah Zarah* 1:1.

50 BT *Sanhedrin* 63b based on Ex. 23:13.

51 The original biblical prohibition was against lending money on interest to "your brother" (Ex. 22:24, Lev. 25:35–7, Deut. 23:20). The rabbis therefore ruled in the Mishnah that lending money on interest to non-Jews was permitted (M *Bava Metsi'a* 5:6). However, in BT *Bava Metsi'a* 70b-71a, it is reported that R. Huna extended the biblical prohibition to non-Jews in order to discourage social intercourse with them. There is another tradition reported here regarding R. Huna's views on the matter that disputes this claim.

52 This issue is analysed in Jacob Katz's classic study, *Exclusiveness and Tolerance: Studies in Jewish–Gentile Relations in Medieval and Modern Times* (New York: Behrman House, 1961).

53 Katz, *Exclusiveness and Tolerance*, 30. This is the opinion of R. Isaac ben Samuel of Dampierre (death c. 1189), a French rabbi who belonged to the school of the Tosafists. See *Tosafot*, BT *Bava Metsi'a* 70b.

54 Katz, 32–3. The statement of R. Yohanan is found in BT *Hullin* 13b.

55 Katz devotes all of chapter 10 to a discussion of Meiri. Meiri in no way
felt that Christianity was on a par with Judaism; that would have been too
much to ask of a medieval rabbi. He continued to regard Christianity as
a flawed and inferior religion. Nonetheless, his position was remarkably
daring and enlightened for a medieval rabbi in that it exhibited a degree of
appreciation and respect for Christians and the society they had created.
  From the seventeenth century onwards, other rabbis developed
similar theories independently of Meiri, whose writings by that time
were mostly lost. See Katz, *Exclusiveness and Tolerance*, 164–6; and
Jay R. Berkovitz, "Rabbinic Culture and the Historical Development
of Halakhah," in *The Early Modern World, 1500–1815*, ed. Jonathan
Karp and Adam Sutcliffe, vol. 8 of *The Cambridge History of Judaism*
(Cambridge: Cambridge University Press, 2018), 371–5, https://doi.
org/10.1017/9781139017169.015.

56 See chapter 4, under "Conclusions," pp. 148–9.

57 An argument can be made that these practices were directly inspired by
the Christian environment in which Jews in these locations lived. See
Elisheva Baumgarten, *Practicing Piety in Medieval Ashkenaz: Men, Women,
and Everyday Religious Observance* (Philadelphia: University of Pennsylvania
Press, 2014), ch. 2, https://doi.org/10.9783/9780812290127.51. However,
that does not make such practices any less rabbinic. The rabbis willingly
chose to co-opt those customs into their way of life.

58 There was a certain irony in the Church's creation of canon law.
Christianity from Paul onwards had decried Judaism's focus on law.
With the coming of Jesus, the old law had been superseded, and human
beings now should relate to God primarily by committing themselves
to Jesus as saviour. Yet the medieval Church came to the conclusion
that law had a place in Christianity after all, and it therefore set about
organizing and systematizing its laws in a manner similar to the way in
which Jews had been doing for centuries. And even though the Church
did not accord law nearly so central a place in Christianity as the rabbis
accorded it in Judaism, the fact that the Church took as much interest in
law as it did is remarkable in light of the Church's scathing criticisms
of Judaism as a religion much too preoccupied with this dimension of
religious experience.

59 Maimonides, *Guide of the Perplexed*, trans. Shlomo Pines (Chicago:
University of Chicago Press, 1963), II:36, II:40; III:8, and III:33; Alan L.
Mittleman, *A Short History of Jewish Ethics: Conduct and Character in the
Context of Covenant* (Malden: Wiley-Blackwell, 2012), 116–17, https://
doi.org/10.1002/9781444346619.ch3. Another Jewish intellectual figure
who lived in the Muslim world, espoused ascetic views, and had a big
influence on European Jews once his works were translated, was Bahya

ibn Pakuda (1050–1120). His work, *Duties of the Heart*, was widely read by Jews in medieval Europe.

60 Maimonides, *Mishneh Torah, Laws of Character Traits*, chs. 1–2; Mittleman, *A Short History of Jewish Ethics*, 108–12. A lucid and informative discussion of the inconsistences in Maimonides' views here can be found in Howard Kreisel, *Maimonides' Political Thought: Studies in Ethics, Law, and the Human Ideal* (Albany: SUNY Press, 1999), ch. 5.

61 Lawrence Fine, *Physician of the Soul, Healer of the Cosmos: Isaac Luria and His Kabbalistic Fellowship* (Stanford: Stanford University Press, 2003), 171–86, https://doi.org/10.1515/9781503618619-009.

62 Baumgarten, *Practicing Piety in Medieval Ashkenaz*, ch. 2.

63 Simcha Paull Raphael, *Jewish Views of the Afterlife*, 2nd ed. (Lanham, MD: Rowman and Littlefield, 2009), ch. 8; Moshe Idel, *Messianic Mystics* (New Haven: Yale University Press, 1998), esp. chs. 2–6, https://doi.org /10.12987/9780300145533.

64 See chapter 3, under "Sin, Grace, and Salvation in Medieval and Early Modern Judaism," pp. 112–14.

65 My discussion of this issue is much indebted to Hava Tirosh-Samuelson, "Gender in Jewish Mysticism," in *Jewish Mysticism and Kabbalah: New Insights and Scholarship*, ed. Frederick E. Greenspahn (New York: NYU Press, 2011), 191–230, https://doi.org/10.18574/nyu/9780814732885.003.0013.

66 The foremost scholar in support of this perspective is Moshe Idel. See his *Kabbalah and Eros* (New Haven: Yale University Press, 2005). An analysis of his views and those of others who support the notion that Kabbalah has a mostly positive perspective on sexuality can be found in Tirosh-Samuelson, "Gender in Jewish Mysticism," 205–11. Opinions on this issue, however, are not unanimous. Elliot Wolfson has argued that there was still an ascetic dimension in the Kabbalistic approach to sex because the focus of the Kabbalists was not on the sexual act itself but on the intentions of those engaging in it. One had to engage in sex with the mind focused on uniting the *sefirot* in order for the sexual act to have the effect on God that it was supposed to have. Thus, the physical pleasure of the sexual act itself was not really valued, and that meant, in turn, that the Kabbalistic approach to sexuality was, in effect, ascetic in orientation. See, Elliot R. Wolfson, *Language, Eros, Being: Kabbalistic Hermeneutics and Poetic Imagination* (New York: Fordham University Press, 2005), https://doi .org/10.1515/9780823237852; and Tirosh-Samuelson, "Gender in Jewish Mysticism," 202–5. Still, those who believe that Kabbalah had a positive view of sexuality seem to be more numerous than those who deny that view.

67 The classic study of this movement remains Gershom Scholem, *Sabbatai Zevi: The Mystical Messiah* (Princeton: Princeton University Press, 1973).

Information regarding more recent scholarship on this movement can be found in Matt Goldish, "Sabbatai Zevi and the Sabbatean Movement," in *The Early Modern World, 1500–1815*, ed. Jonathan Karp and Adam Sutcliffe, vol. 7 of *The Cambridge History of Judaism* (Cambridge: Cambridge University Press, 2018), 491–521, https://doi.org/10.1017/9781139017169.020.

68 The world view of the Mitnagdim has received relatively little attention from scholars, but Allan Nadler provides a thorough analysis of the thought of R. Phinehas of Polotsk, who is representative of this group and its ascetic views, in *The Faith of the Mithnagdim: Rabbinic Responses to Hasidic Rapture* (Baltimore: Johns Hopkins University Press, 1997). Immanuel Etkes examines the figure of R. Elijah of Vilna in *The Gaon of Vilna: The Man and His Image*, trans. Jeffrey Green (Berkeley: University of California Press, 2002). Gershon David Hundert discusses mystic ascetics in eighteenth-century Poland-Lithuania prior to the division between Hasidim and Mitnagdim in *Jews in Poland-Lithuania: A Genealogy of Modernity* (Berkeley: University of California Press, 2004), 131–7, https://doi.org/10.1525/9780520940321-013. Ascetic tendencies in Hasidism are discussed in David Biale et al., *Hasidism a New History* (Princeton: Princeton University Press, 2018), 174–9, https://doi.org/10.1515/9781400889198.

69 Jerry Muller makes this same argument. See Muller, *Capitalism and the Jews* (Princeton: Princeton University Press, 2010), 82–6, https://doi.org/10.1515/9781400834365. There is a widespread belief that in the modern period, Jews have been far more attracted to socialism than to capitalism. Muller has shown convincingly, however, that the association between Jews and socialism is overblown. See Muller, *Capitalism and the Jews*, ch. 2, esp. 106–32.

70 Others have made similar claims. See Jacob Katz, *Tradition and Crisis: Jewish Society at the End of the Middle Ages* (New York: Schocken Books, 1972), 72; and Victor Karady, *The Jews of Europe in the Modern Era: A Social-Historical Outline*, trans. Tim Wilkinson (Budapest: Central European University Press, 2004), 49–52, 57–9, 62–4; and Muller, 87–8. However, all these authors speak about the contributions made by Judaism in general to the economic success of Jews in Europe. None of them hone in on Rabbinic Judaism *per se* as the aspect of Judaism most responsible for that success.

71 Steven Gimbel attempts to prove in his book, *Einstein's Jewish Science: Physics at the Intersection of Politics and Religion* (Baltimore: Johns Hopkins University Press, 2012), that there was a connection between Albert Einstein's accomplishments in physics and his Jewish background. According to Gimbel, some of Einstein's most important innovations in physics were inspired by the legacy of rabbinic thinking that he and

other modern secular Jews unwittingly inherited. Gimbel's arguments are similar to mine and are intriguing, but it is beyond the scope of this discussion to take them up. Gimbel's work deals with issues highly specific to Einstein's work, while my interest here is in the scientific accomplishments of modern Jews in general.

72 Berman, *Law and Revolution*, 151–64. One can also extend this argument to just about any domain in which Jews excelled – perhaps even to the arts in which modern Jews have experienced disproportionate success as well. As noted at the beginning of this book, Jews have done extremely well in such areas as classical and popular music, fiction-writing, and film-making, and these accomplishments may also be connected to the mindset that Rabbinic Judaism instilled in Jews over centuries regarding the mundane realm. The arts by definition are focused on this realm. They are a commentary on how we as human beings experience the world, and they use physical media for that purpose. Certainly, the arts often attempt to transcend the mundane realm. Some of the greatest classical music ever written, for instance, was composed for religious purposes. But the media of the arts are always physical, and they appeal to our physical senses. Therefore, here too the success of Jews may be rooted in the emphasis that Rabbinic Judaism placed on the present world.

9. Education I: 100–1500 CE

1 Marsha L. Rozenblit, *The Jews of Vienna 1867–1914: Assimilation and Identity* (Albany: SUNY Press, 1983), 99–126; Steven Beller, *Vienna and the Jews, 1867–1938: A Cultural History* (Cambridge: Cambridge University Press, 1989), 43–70; Victor Karady, *The Jews of Europe in the Modern Era: A Socio-Historical Outline* (Budapest: Central European University Press, 2004), 88–113; Jerry Z. Muller, *Capitalism and the Jews* (Princeton: Princeton University Press, 2010), 87–9, https://doi.org/10.1515/9781400834365.

2 Little academic work has been done on the history of Jewish education, as noted by Robert Chazan in "The Historiography of Premodern Jewish Education," *Journal of Jewish Education* 71, no. 1 (January 2005): 23–32; and Barry Chazan, Robert Chazan, and Benjamin M. Jacobs, *Cultures and Contexts of Jewish Education* (New York: Palgrave Macmillan, 2017), ch. 1. One of the few studies addressing the history of education in Judaism in recent years is Maristella Botticini and Zvi Eckstein, *The Chosen Few: How Education Shaped Jewish History, 70–1492* (Princeton: Princeton University Press, 2012). However, as I mentioned in an earlier chapter, this study has been criticized for several reasons by a number of reviewers, including Shaul Stampfer. See my introductory chapter, under "The Cultural Hypothesis," p. 26.

3 Gerald L. Gutek, *A History of the Western Educational Experience*, 2nd ed.
   (Prospect Heights, IL: Waveland Press, 1995), 79–87; Justo L. Gonzalez,
   The Story of Christianity, 2nd ed. (New York: HarperOne, 2010), 1:277–81;
   Clifford R. Backman, *The Worlds of Medieval Europe*, 3rd ed. (New York:
   Oxford University Press, 2015), 102–10.
4 Backman, *The Worlds of Medieval Europe*, 109–10.
5 See chapter 7, under "The Early Medieval Period," pp. 218–9.
6 Rosamond McKitterick, "Conclusions," in *The Uses of Literacy in
   Early Medieval Europe*, ed. Rosamond McKitterick (Cambridge:
   Cambridge University Press 1990), 328–31, https://doi.org/10.1017/
   CBO9780511584008.
7 Gutek, *A History of the Western Educational Experience*, 84–5.
8 Gutek, 87–9; Joseph A. Lynch and Phillip C. Adamo, *The Medieval Church:
   A Brief History*, 2nd ed. (London: Routledge, 2014), 270–3, https://doi
   .org/10.4324/9781315735221; Backman, *The Worlds of Medieval Europe*,
   338–40. The phrase "liberal arts" was first used in ancient Greek and
   Roman culture to refer to the fundamental skills that were believed to be
   needed by a free citizen to participate productively in civic life. Non-free
   citizens were excluded from civic life and were instead given technical or
   vocational training. Hence the word "liberal," which is related to the same
   Latin term that gives us the word "liberty." In the medieval period, the
   liberal arts curriculum of the cathedral schools taught many of the same
   skills that were part of the liberal arts curriculum in classical antiquity,
   but those skills were now seen as necessary for the study of theology. See
   Gutek, *A History of the Western Educational Experience*, 51, 87.
9 Gutek, 96–106; Lynch and Adamo, *The Medieval Church*, 275–9; Backman,
   340–5.
10 See chapter 5, under "The Medieval Period," p. 155.
11 See David Sheffler's brief but highly informative historiographical essay
   on this issue: "Late Medieval Education: Continuity and Change," *History
   Compass* 8, no. 9 (September 2010): 1067–82, https://doi.org/10.1111/j.1478
   -0542.2010.00726.x.
12 Sheffler, "Late Medieval Education," 1068.
13 Sheffler, 1068, 1074–5.
14 Deut. 4:9; 6:7, 20–5; 11:19.
15 Marc Hirshman, "Torah in Rabbinic Thought: The Theology of Learning,"
   in *The Late Roman-Rabbinic Period*, ed. Steven T. Katz, vol. 4 of *The
   Cambridge History of Judaism* (Cambridge: Cambridge University Press,
   2006), 901–2, https://doi.org/10.1017/CHOL9780521772488.037.
16 Martin S. Jaffee, *Early Judaism: Religious Worlds of the First Judaic Millennium*,
   2nd ed. (Bethesda: University Press of Maryland, 2006), 231–3, 237–40.

17 Jaffee, *Early Judaism*, 233–4.
18 BT *Makkot* 10a, *Nedarim* 81a; Jaffee, 240.
19 M *Avot* 3:2, 6:1; BT *Berakhot* 6a.
20 Steve D. Fraade, "The Early Rabbinic Sage," in *The Sage and the Ancient Near East*, ed. John G. Gammie and Leo G. Perdue (Winona Lake: Eisenbrauns, 1990), 434–5.
21 One could argue that laws involving Temple ritual did have practical relevance because the rabbis anticipated the rebuilding of the Temple and the reconstitution of its rituals, and therefore Jews had to be prepared for the resumption of those rituals. However, a number of rabbinic sources suggest that studying the laws of sacrifices was itself a substitute for the Temple sacrifices. Some even suggest that such study was superior to the sacrifices. These latter sources therefore underscore the importance of Torah study as an end in itself. See BT *Menahot* 110a, *Makkot* 10a.
22 See chapter 7, under "The Body, the Soul, and the Afterlife," p. 225.
23 BT *Avodah Zarah* 3b.
24 M *Pe'ah* 1:1.
25 BT *Sotah* 49b; JT *Avodah Zarah* 2:2; *Shabbat* 6:1.
26 BT *Sukkah* 28; Hirshman, "Torah in Rabbinic Thought," 910–11.
27 BT *Bava Kama* 82b-83a, *Menahot* 99b; Sacha Stern, *Jewish Identity in Early Rabbinic Writings*, vol. 23 of *Arbeiten zur Geschichte des antiken Judentums und des Urchristentums/Ancient Judaism & Early Christianity*, ed. Martin Hegel, Peter Schäfer, Pieter W. van der Horst, Martin Goodman, and Daniel R. Schwartz (Leiden: E.J. Brill, 1994), 176–81, https://doi.org/10.1163/9789004332768.
28 JT *Berakhot* 1:3. A debate between two prominent rabbis recorded in the Talmud illustrates the tension here. One rabbi claimed that study was more important than observance of the commandments, while the other argued the reverse, that observance of the commandments was more important than study. The matter was ultimately decided in favour of the first opinion, and the reason given was that study led to the observance of the commandments. That response, however, is rather confusing. We are being told that study is of greater value than the practice of the commandments, but that is only because study leads to the practice of the commandments! So which of the two activities is really more important here? It is not clear. See *Sifrey Deuteronomy* 4; BT *Kiddushin* 40b; Hirshman, "Torah in Rabbinic Thought," 909. This issue is analyed by Ephraim E. Urbach, *The Sages: Their Concepts and Beliefs*, trans. Israel Abrahams (Cambridge, MA: Harvard University Press, 1987), 603–20.
29 This is the opinion of Rabban Gamliel ben Judah, as reported in M *Avot* 2:2; and R. Ishmael, as reported in BT *Berakhot* 35b.

30 See chapter 7, under "Other Material and Physical Pleasures," p. 233; *Sifrey Deuteronomy* 42; BT *Berakhot* 35b. Other sources pertaining to the tension between Torah study and work are adduced by Urbach in his discussion of this issue. See Urbach, *The Sages*, 593–603.

31 See chapter 7, under "Other Material and Physical Pleasures," pp. 230–1, 233–4.

32 Shmuel Safrai, "Education and the Study of Torah," in *The Jewish People in the First Century: Historical Geography, Political History, Social, Cultural, and Religious Life and Institutions*, ed. Shmuel Safrai and Menachem Stern (Philadelphia: Fortress Press, 1976), 2:945–58, https://doi.org/10.1163/9789004275096_010; Hirshman, "Torah in Rabbinic Thought," 908.

33 M *Kidushin* 11:1.

34 M *Sotah* 3:4.

35 BT *Bava Batra* 21a; *Sanhedrin* 17b. The importance the rabbis attached to childhood education is evident in a number of pronouncements in their literature that express reverence for schoolchildren. One Talmudic passage records a statement by one rabbi that the very existence of the world is dependent on schoolchildren: "the world endures only for the sake of the breath of schoolchildren" (BT *Shabbat* 119a). In the same passage, another rabbi declares that "schoolchildren may not be made to neglect their studies even for the sake of building the Temple" (BT *Shabbat* 119a). This latter statement is quite striking in that it reflects the determination of the rabbis to move beyond the Temple era, with the learning of schoolchildren being emblematic of that resolve.

36 T *Sotah* 7:9; Safrai, "Education and the Study of Torah," 966–8; Chazan et al., *Cultures and Contexts of Jewish Education*, 16–17.

37 S. Krauss, "The Jews in the Works of the Church Fathers," *Jewish Quarterly Review*, old series 6, no. 2 (January 1894): 231–2, quoted in Hirshman, "Torah in Rabbinic Thought," 907–8.

38 Krauss, "The Jews in the Works of the Church Fathers," 231–2.

39 Such criticisms have been directed at scholars such as Shmuel Safrai, whose essay on Jewish education in first-century Roman Palestine has been cited in some of my previous notes.

40 Catherine Hezser, *Jewish Literacy in Roman Palestine* (Tubingen: Mohr Siebeck, 2001), 40–90; Hirshman, "Torah in Rabbinic Thought," 908; Chazan et al., *Cultures and Contexts of Jewish Education*, 17.

41 Isaiah Gafni, "The Education of Children in the Period of the Talmud – Tradition and Reality" [in Hebrew], in *Education and History: Political and Cultural Contexts*, ed. Rivkah Feldhay and Immanuel Etkes [in Hebrew] (Jerusalem: Zalman Shazar, 1999), 6–68.

42 See Heszer, *Jewish Literacy in Roman Palestine*.

43 Bernard Hamilton, *Religion in the Medieval West*, 2nd ed. (London: Arnold, 2003), chs. 5–11.

44 Other activities included meditation, and, for some orders, manual labour. The major exception here was the Dominican Order, which was established in the late medieval period. For the Dominicans, learning and the cultivation of the intellect were central to their mission. We will discuss the Dominican Order later in this chapter. Other monastic orders in the medieval period were known for their interest in intellectual matters; these orders included Irish monasteries in the early centuries of the medieval period, monasteries in the Frankish kingdom under Charlemagne's reign in the ninth century, and the Cluniac monasteries in the later centuries of the medieval period. But none of them made intellectual matters the focus of their mission in the way the Dominicans did. See C.H. Lawrence, *Medieval Monasticism: Forms of Religious Life in Western Europe in the Middle Ages*, 4th ed. (London: Routledge, 2015), 41, 71–2, 104–6, https://doi.org/10.4324/9781315715667.

45 Simon Schwarzfuchs, *A Concise History of the Rabbinate* (Oxford: Blackwell, 1993), ch. 1.

46 Maimonides, *Mishneh Torah, Laws of Studying Torah*; R. Jacob ben Asher, *Arba'ah Turim, Yoreh De'ah*, sections 445–6; *Sefer ha-Hinukh*, commandment 419.

47 In various passages in rabbinic literature, other commandments are singled out as being equivalent to the rest of the commandments, including Sabbath observance, the giving of charity, and circumcision. However, only Torah study is mentioned in this regard in the opening section of the morning liturgy.

48 Kenneth R. Stow, *Alienated Minority: The Jews of Medieval Latin Europe* (Cambridge, MA: Harvard University Press, 1992), 164–77; Schwarzfuchs, *A Concise History of the Rabbinate*, ch. 2; Marc Saperstein, *Jewish Preaching, 1200–1800: An Anthology* (New Haven: Yale University Press, 1989). European rulers obviously did not allow Jewish communities independence on all matters. The rulers maintained control on issues that were important for their interests, and they did so by appointing either a Jew or a non-Jew to serve as an intermediary between them and the Jewish communities. See Stow, *Alienated Minority*, 159–66.

49 Stow, 164–77; Schwarzfuchs, ch. 2.

50 Schwarzfuchs, 17.

51 Elisheva Baumgarten, "The Family," in *The Middle Ages: The Christian World*, ed. Robert Chazan, vol. 6 of *The Cambridge History of Judaism* (Cambridge: Cambridge University Press, 2018), 447, 455–6, https://doi.org/10.1017/9781139048880.018.

52 Schwarzfuchs, *A Concise History of the Rabbinate*, 17, 22.

53 Stow, *Alienated Minority*, 173–5, 176–7; Schwarzfuchs, 22, 55–6.

54 See chapter 4, under "Communal Amendments," pp. 142–3.

55 Stow, *Alienated Minority*, 166–8; Schwarzfuchs, *A Concise History of the Rabbinate*, 19–22.

56 Schwarzfuchs, 19–22.

57 Stow, *Alienated Minority*, 173–5, 176–7; Schwarzfuchs, 22, 55–6.

58 This term has a long history. It appears in the Bible and rabbinic literature, but only in the medieval period did it begin referring to the regions of Germany and northern France.

59 Ephraim Kanarfogel, *Jewish Education and Society in the High Middle Ages* (Detroit: Wayne State University Press, 1992), 16–18.

60 Kanarfogel, *Jewish Education and Society*, 18–30; Kanarfogel, "Schools and Education," in Robert Chazan, *The Middle Ages: The Christian World*, 6:403–12, https://doi.org/10.1017/9781139048880.016.

61 Karnarfogel, *Jewish Education and Society*, 62–65; Karnarfogel, "Schools and Education," 394–400.

62 A. Landgraf, ed., *Commentarius Cantabrigienis in Epistolas Pauli e Schola Petri Petri Abeldardi* (Notre Dame, 1937), 2:434, translated in B. Smalley, *The Study of the Bible in the Middle Ages* (Oxford: Blackwell, 1952), 78.

63 R.A. Houston, *Literacy in Early Modern Europe: Its Growth, Uses, and Impact, 1500–1800*, 2nd ed. (London: Routledge, 2002), 125–39, https://doi.org /10.4324/9781315839233.

64 See this chapter, under "Early Rabbinic Judaism," pp. 281–2.

65 Backman, *The Worlds of Medieval Europe*, 485–7; Lawrence, *Medieval Monasticism*, 233–44.

66 Hamilton, *Religion in the Medieval West*, 34–5, 39–40.

67 Hamilton, 34–5, 39–40; Backman, *The Worlds of Medieval Europe*, 167–8. These problems festered until the tenth century, when the Church finally made reforms that greatly improved matters. The priests were now more educated and disciplined. Still, the problems did not entirely go away, and by the thirteenth century, they had returned. The Church was now wealthier and more powerful than ever before, and the priests again were accused of corruption. This time, however, the Christian public, which was more devout than in previous centuries, was beginning to lose its patience not just with the priests but with the entire Church hierarchy that was mired in corruption, and this unhappiness would set the stage for the Reformation. See Backman, 487–98, 539.

There was certainly corruption in medieval Jewish communities as well. However, the rabbis tended not to be the problem but rather the individuals who governed these communities. As already noted, the town councils were often populated with wealthy Jews, who passed legislation and set policies designed to protect their monetary interests. The rabbis sometimes protested such corruption, but more often they were forced to remain silent because they were employees of the town councils whose members financed their salaries. See Schwarzfuchs, *A Concise History of the Rabbinate*, 57. I am not suggesting here that the rabbis were inherently more virtuous than the Christian clergy. Rather, the rabbis may have avoided corruption because they did not control large amounts of wealth in the way that the Church did. Corruption tends to arise when riches are up for grabs, and the rabbis, for better or for worse, were spared that temptation, while the Christian clergy were not.

68 In fact, the priests were, in some sense, a mirror image of the rabbis. The job of the communal rabbis was very much centred on intellectual matters. They were hired to be experts in Jewish law and to issue rulings on it. However, they had no official sacramental functions as the priests did. The rabbis certainly officiated at weddings, circumcisions, funerals, and other important religious events, and they were preferred for guiding these ceremonies on account of their knowledge of the laws governing them. But rabbinic law did not technically require a rabbi to perform such functions. Any Jew could.

69 See this chapter, under "Christian Perspectives" within "The Late Medieval Period," pp. 274–5. Backman, *The Worlds of Medieval Europe*, 317–18.

70 The rabbis had competition from medieval Jewish philosophers and Kabbalists, who often felt that the learning they did was of greater value than that focused on traditional rabbinic texts. However, many of the philosophers and Kabbalists were themselves rabbis. More important, their brands of Judaism also put great emphasis on study and the intellectual mastery of their respective disciplines.

71 Backman, 455.

72 Backman, 317, notes that university students may have numbered in the tens of thousands in the late medieval period, or perhaps even in the hundreds of thousands. However, the population of Europe during this period was in the tens of millions ("Medieval Sourcebook: Tables on Population in Medieval Europe," in *Internet Medieval Sourcebook*, ed. Paul Halsall [Bronx: Fordham University Center for Medieval Studies, 1996], https://sourcebooks.fordham.edu/source/pop-in-eur.asp), and therefore even if Backman's figures are correct, the number of university students would have been small relative to Europe's overall population.

73 Walter Rüegg, "Themes," in *Universities in the Middle Ages*, ed. Hilde de Ridder-Symoens, vol. 1 of *A History of the University in Europe*, ed. Walter Rüegg (Cambridge: Cambridge University Press, 1992), 9–14, 20–3, https://doi.org/10.1017/CBO9780511599507.003. Rüegg explains that a university degree did not necessarily guarantee a good job. Ancestry and wealth were important as well. However, a university degree certainly helped.

74 Backman, *The Worlds of Medieval Europe*, 487.
75 Peter Harrison, "Curiosity, Forbidden Knowledge, and the Reformation of Natural Philosophy in Early Modern England," *Isis* 92, no. 2 (June 2001): 265–90, https://doi.org/10.1086/385182; Sari Kivistö, *The Vices of Learning: Morality and Knowledge at Early Modern Universities*, vol. 48 of *Education and Society in the Middle Ages and Renaissance*, ed. William J. Courtenay, Jürgen Miethke, Frank Rexroth, and Jacques Verger (Leiden: E.J. Brill, 2014), https://doi.org/10.1163/9789004276451.
76 Harrison, "Curiosity, Forbidden Knowledge," 266; Kivistö, *The Vices of Learning*, 202.
77 See chapter 3, under "The Medieval Period," pp. 88–9.
78 Harrison, "Curiosity, Forbidden Knowledge," 267; Kivistö, *The Vices of Learning*, 202.
79 Harrison, 270; Kivistö, 202.
80 Harrison's article examines attitudes towards curiosity in early modern England, while Kivistö's book explores those in early modern Germany. See also the remarks of Dorinda Outram about this issue as it pertains to the Enlightenment in *The Enlightenment*, 3rd ed. (Cambridge: Cambridge University Press, 2013), 103. https://doi.org/10.1017/CBO9781139226318.
81 See chapter 3, under "Original Sin," pp. 99–100.
82 M *Hagigah* 2:1; Ithamar Gruenwald, *Apocalyptic and Merkavah Mysticism*, 2nd rev. ed., vol. 90 of *Ancient Judaism and Early Christianity* (Leiden: E.J. Brill, 2014), https://doi.org/10.1163/9789004279209.
83 See chapter 3, under "Sin, Grace, and Salvation in Medieval and Early Modern Judaism," pp. 112–3. Aviezer Ravitzky, "The Secrets of the *Guide of the Perplexed*: From the Thirteenth to the Twentieth Centuries," in *Studies in Maimonides*, ed. Isadore Twersky (Cambridge, MA: Harvard University Press, 1990), 159–207; Moshe Idel, "On the History of the Interdiction against the Study of Kabbalah before the Age of Forty," *AJS Review* 5, no. 1 (April 1980): 1–20 [Hebrew section], https://doi.org/10.1017/S0364009400011880.

10. Education II: 1500–1950 CE

1 Gerald L. Gutek, *A History of the Western Educational Experience*, 2nd ed. (Prospect Heights, IL: Waveland Press, 1995), 143–8; R.A. Houston, *Literacy in Early Modern Europe: Its Growth, Uses and Impact, 1500–1800*, 2nd ed. (London: Routledge, 2002), 37–8, https://doi.org/10.4324/9781315839233.
2 Houston, *Literacy in Early Modern Europe*, 37–8.
3 Gutek, *A History of the Western Educational Experience*, 149–50.
4 Gutek, 150–2; Houston, *Literacy in Early Modern Europe*, 38–9.
5 Gutek, 156.

6 This variety of educational institutions is thoroughly described in Houston, *Literacy in Early Modern Europe*, ch. 2.

7 Houston, 166.

8 Houston, 16, 24, 54–6.

9 Gutek, *A History of the Western Educational Experience*, 163–4, 168, 170.

10 Gutek, ch. 11.

11 Gutek, 202–6.

12 Gutek, 175–83.

13 Gutek, 454–6.

14 Gutek, 460–1.

15 Michael S. Katz, *A History of Compulsory Education Laws* (Bloomington: Phi Delta Kappa Educational Society, 1974), 17.

16 Gutek, *A History of the Western Educational Experience*, 492–4; Claudia Goldin, "America's Graduation from High School: The Evolution and Spread of Secondary Schooling in the Twentieth century," *Journal of Economic History* 58, no. 2 (June 1998): 345–74, https://doi.org/10.1017/S0022050700020544. The quality of education in the US was also enhanced by the research of scholars who made progress in understanding how education could be made most effective. The greatest of these scholars was John Dewey (1859–1952), who taught at the University of Chicago and then at Columbia University. See Gutek, *A History of the Western Educational Experience*, 482–6.

17 Gutek, 467–9.

18 Gutek, 470–2.

19 Gutek, 497–9.

20 Gutek, 513–20; Robert J. Gordon, "The Great Stagnation of American Education," *New York Times*, 7 September 2013, https://archive.nytimes.com/opinionator.blogs.nytimes.com/2013/09/07/the-great-stagnation-of-american-education/.

21 Israel Bartal, "The Establishment of Eastern European Jewry," in *The Early Modern World, 1500–1815*, ed. Jonathan Karp and Adam Sutcliffe, vol. 7 of *The Cambridge History of Judaism* (Cambridge: Cambridge University Press, 2018), 243, 244, 247, https://doi.org/10.1017/9781139017169.010; Marc Saperstein, "Education and Homiletics," in Karp and Sutcliffe, *The Early Modern World, 1500–1815*, 7:416–17, https://doi.org/10.1017/9781139017169.017.

22 Elisheva Carlebach, "The Early Modern Jewish Community and Its Institutions," in Karp and Sutcliffe, *The Early Modern World, 1500–1815*, 7:188; Bartal, "The Establishment of Eastern European Jewry," 243, 246–7; Saperstein, "Education and Homiletics," 7:415–17.

23 Saperstein, 7:419; Gary B. Cohen, "Education and the Politics of Jewish Integration," in *The Modern Period, 1815–2000*, ed. Mitchell B. Hart and

Tony Michels, vol. 8 of *The Cambridge History of Judaism* (Cambridge: Cambridge University Press, 2018), 479, https://doi.org/10.1017/9781139019828.018.

24 Edward Breuer, "Enlightenment and Haskalah," in Karp and Sutcliffe, *The Early Modern World, 1500–1815,* 7:658.

25 Saperstein, "Education and Homiletics," 419; Breuer, "Enlightenment and Haskalah," 7:655–65.

26 See this chapter, under "Christian Perspectives" within "The Early Modern Period," pp. 297–8.

27 Peter Harrison, "Curiosity, Forbidden Knowledge, and the Reformation of Natural Philosophy in Early Modern England," *Isis* 92, no. 2 (June 2001), 270–5, 279–82, 287–9, https://doi.org/10.1086/385182; Sari Kivistö, *The Vices of Learning: Morality and Knowledge at Early Modern Universities,* vol. 48 of *Education and Society in the Middle Ages and Renaissance,* ed. William J. Courtenay, Jürgen Miethke, Frank Rexroth, and Jacques Verger (Leiden: E.J. Brill, 2014), 203–17, 226–30, https://doi.org/10.1163/9789004276451.

28 Shaul Stampfer, *Families, Rabbis, and Education: Traditional Jewish Society in Nineteenth-Century Eastern Europe* (Portland, OR: Littman Library of Jewish Civilization, 2010), ch. 7.

29 Cohen, "Education and the Politics of Jewish Integration," 480–3.

30 Cohen, 480–3.

31 Cohen, 484–8.

32 Jerry Z. Muller, *Capitalism and the Jews* (Princeton: Princeton University Press, 2010), 92–3, https://doi.org/10.1515/9781400834365; Barry Chazan, Robert Chazan, and Benjamin M. Jacobs, *Cultures and Contexts of Jewish Education* (New York: Palgrave Macmillan, 2017), 87–92; Cohen, "Education and the Politics of Jewish Integration," 484, 488–9.

33 Cohen, 489–95. See my introductory chapter, p. 4.

34 Shaul Stampfer presents an argument that is similar to the one offered here. According to Stampfer, modernized Jews developed a passion for education in the following manner: eastern European Jews developed the myth that learning was a means to advancement because any young man could become a great Torah scholar and marry a rich girl. Wealthy Jews in eastern Europe often sought to marry off their daughters to the most accomplished yeshiva students, and therefore Jewish boys, even poor ones, could hope to achieve economic security by devoting themselves to their studies. The reality, as we have already seen, was quite different. Most Jewish boys had no chance to fulfil the hope of a rich marriage, given the poor state of education, and that is why Stampfer refers to such expectation as a "myth." But it was a powerful myth nonetheless, and thus, when the Jews of eastern Europe emigrated in large numbers to western Europe and the US, they carried it with them, even when they

became secularized. They continued to believe that learning brought one economic advancement, but they came to understand that instead of achieving advancement by using education to marry into wealth, one achieved it by using education to enter high-paying professions. See Stampfer, *Families, Rabbis, and Education*, 166. The scheme I am suggesting here is simpler. I believe that when Jews in Europe and the US abandoned traditional Judaism, they secularized the basic values of rabbinic culture, and these values included the ideal of learning and the cultivation of the intellect. That ideal in secularized form then provided Jews with the desire to educate their children in Western schools, an aspiration that was made possible by public education.

11. Conclusions

1 Even in the modern period, women could not become rabbis until relatively recently. The Reform movement ordained its first female rabbi in 1972, the Conservative movement followed suit in 1985, and the Orthodox movement still does not ordain women.

2 This is evident by perusing the names of modern Jews who have won major international awards, such as Nobel Prizes. References to these lists can be found in my introductory chapter.

3 Elisheva Baumgarten, "The Family," in *The Middle Ages: The Christian World*, ed. Robert Chazan, vol. 6 of *The Cambridge History of Judaism* (Cambridge: Cambridge University Press, 2018), 456–8, https://doi.org/10.1017/9781139048880.018.

4 It is also noteworthy that young Jewish women in nineteenth-century eastern Europe were exposed to knowledge that young men were not. For instance, young women received informal education in their homes that allowed them to read Yiddish literature, learn foreign languages, and engage in non-Jewish learning, areas of study not included in the traditional yeshiva curriculum designed for young men. See Shaul Stampfer, *Families, Rabbis, and Education: Traditional Jewish Society in Nineteenth-Century Eastern Europe* (Portland, OR: Littman Library of Jewish Civilization, 2010), ch. 8. This observation is important, given that the largest Jewish community in the world at this time was that of eastern Europe. Moreover, it was this community that supplied the vast majority of immigrants to the US in the late nineteenth and early twentieth centuries.

5 See, however, Maud Mandel, "Assimilation and Cultural Exchange in Modern Jewish History," in *Rethinking European Jewish History*, ed. Jeremy Cohen and Moshe Rosman (Portland, OR: Littman Library of Jewish Civilization, 2009), 72–92, esp. 85–92. Mandel suggests that Jews may have

indeed had some influence on the modernization of Europe, though not necessarily with respect to the four values that have been my focus in this book.

6 See my introductory chapter, under "The Slezkine Hypothesis," pp. 20–1.

7 See my introductory chapter, under "The Historical Hypothesis," pp. 14–9.

8 Kenneth R. Stow, *Alienated Minority: The Jews of Medieval Latin Europe* (Cambridge, MA: Harvard University Press, 1992), 168–9, 171.

9 Though as noted in an earlier discussion, Jews sometimes did impose capital punishment, when it came to the most serious of crimes. See chapter 5, note 53.

10 Jerry Z. Muller, *Capitalism and the Jews* (Princeton: Princeton University Press, 2010), 91–2, https://doi.org/10.1515/9781400834365.

11 See chapter 8, under "Jewish Perspectives" within "The Early Modern Period," p. 265. The role of the *conversos* and the Sabbateans in challenging rabbinic authority is discussed by David B. Ruderman, *Early Modern Jewry* (Princeton: Princeton University Press, 2010), chs. 2 and 4, https://doi.org/10.1515/9781400834693, and in his updated summary of the findings in this book in "Looking Backward and Forward: Rethinking Jewish Modernity in Light of Early Modernity," in *The Early Modern World, 1500–1815*, ed. Jonathan Karp and Adam Sutcliffe, vol. 7 of *The Cambridge History of Judaism* (Cambridge: Cambridge University Press, 2018), 1089–110, https://doi.org/10.1017/9781139017169.043; Jay R. Berkovitz, "Rabbinic Culture and the Historical Development of Halakhah," in Karp and Sutcliffe, *The Early Modern World, 1500–1815*, 7:350–2, https://doi.org/10.1017/9781139017169.015; Matt Goldish, "Sabbatai Zevi and the Sabbatean Movement," in Karp and Sutcliffe, *The Early Modern World, 1500–1815*, 7:518–19, https://doi.org/10.1017/9781139017169.020.

12 See chapter 2, under "Reform and Conservative Jews," pp. 75–6.

13 Gershon David Hundert, *Jews in Poland-Lithuania: A Genealogy of Modernity* (Berkeley: University of California Press, 2004), 153–9, https://doi.org/10.1525/9780520940321-013.

14 Jonathan D. Sarna, *American Judaism: A History*, 2nd ed. (New Haven: Yale University Press, 2019), 159–75.

15 Daniel Pals, *Nine Theories of Religion* (New York: Oxford University Press, 2015), 175–7.

16 See chapter 8, under "The Early Modern Period," pp. 247–8.

17 As Pals notes, even Weber himself was not always consistent about the motivations for cultural change. There are instances in which he sees economic conditions as the sources of change, much as Marx did. See Pals, *Nine Theories of Religion*, 177–8.

Epilogue: Lessons for Jews, Lessons for Everyone

1 These are rough figures. An estimate of how many US Jews there are depends on whom you count as Jews, and there has been much debate about this question. See "A Portrait of Jewish Americans," Pew Research Center, 1 October 2013, https://www.pewresearch.org/religion/2013/10/01/jewish-american-beliefs-attitudes-culture-survey; Emily Guskin, "How Many Jews Live in the U.S.? That Depends on How You Define 'Jewish,'" *Washington Post*, 23 February 2018, https://www.washingtonpost.com/news/post-nation/wp/2018/02/23/measuring-the-size-of-the-u-s-jewish-population-comes-down-to-identity/.

2 See, "Israel's Religiously Divided Society," Pew Research Center, 8 March 2016, https://www.pewresearch.org/religion/2016/03/08/israels-religiously-divided-society.

3 See chapter 2, under "Conclusions," pp. 78–9.

4 See my introductory chapter, p. 10.

5 "Israel's Religiously Divided Society," Pew Research Center; Gilad Malach and Lee Cahaner, "2018 Statistical Report on Ultra-Orthodox Society in Israel," Israel Democracy Institute, 19 December 2018, https://en.idi.org.il/articles/25385.

6 See chapter 2, note 24.

7 Alanna Petroff, "U.S. and Israel Have Worst Inequality in the Developed World," *CNN Business*, 21 May 2015, https://money.cnn.com/2015/05/21/news/economy/worst-inequality-countries-oecd. One has to be aware, however, that the poverty figures among Israeli Jews are inflated by the fact that in the ultra-Orthodox community, a large percentage of men do not work and are supported by their community in order to engage in full-time Torah study. Moreover, the same men are fathers in families with large numbers of children. The poverty rate for ultra-Orthodox Jews in Israel, according to 2017 figures, was 43.1%. See, Alon Einhorn, "21.2% of the Israeli Population Lives below the Poverty-Line," *Jerusalem Post*, 31 December 2018, https://www.jpost.com/Israel-News/212-percent-of-Israeli-population-lives-below-the-poverty-line-new-report-575883.

8 "A Portrait of Jewish Americans," Pew Research Center.

9 Children from intermarriages between Jews and non-Jews are increasingly identifying as Jews. A survey by the Pew Research Center conducted in 2013 showed that children of such marriages who are older than 65 identify as Jews at a rate of 25 per cent, while those who are under 30 identify as Jews at a rate of 59 per cent. See Alan Cooperman and Gregory A. Smith, "What Happens When Jews Intermarry," Pew

Research Center, 12 November 2013, https://www.pewresearch.org/fact
-tank/2013/11/12/what-happens-when-jews-intermarry. However, even
according to the latter figure, 41 per cent of children from marriages
between Jews and non-Jews do not identify as Jews.

10 "A Portrait of Jewish Americans," Pew Research Center.

11 Ari Feldman and Laura E. Adkins, "Orthodox to Dominate American
Jewry in Coming Decades as Population Booms," *The Forward*, 12 June
2018, https://forward.com/news/402663/orthodox-will-dominate
-american-jewry-in-coming-decades-as-population; "A Portrait of
American Orthodox Jews," Pew Research Center, 26 August 2015,
https://www.pewresearch.org/religion/2015/08/26/a-portrait-of
-american-orthodox-jews.

12 "A Portrait of Jewish Americans," Pew Research Center, 1 October 2013,
https://www.pewresearch.org/religion/2013/10/01/jewish-american
-beliefs-attitudes-culture-survey; Samuel Heilman, *Sliding to the Right: The
Contest for the Future of American Jewish Orthodoxy* (Berkeley: University of
California Press, 2006).

13 Ross Arbeis, "How the Talmud Became a Best-Seller in South Korea,"
The New Yorker, 23 June 2015), https://www.newyorker.com/books/page
-turner/how-the-talmud-became-a-best-seller-in-south-korea; Tim Alper,
"Talmud-Inspired Learning Craze Sweeps South Korea," *Jewish Telegraph
Agency*, 14 January 2019, https://www.jta.org/2019/01/14/global/talmud
-inspired-learning-craze-sweeps-south-korea.

14 See my introductory chapter, p. 5.

15 See my introductory chapter, p. 4.

Bibliography

Alexander, Elizabeth Shanks. "The Orality of Rabbinic Writing." In *The Cambridge Companion to the Talmud and Rabbinic Literature*, edited by Charlotte Elisheva Fonrobert and Martin S. Jaffee, 38–48. Cambridge: Cambridge University Press, 2007. https://doi.org/10.1017/CCOL0521843901.003.

Allison, Gregg R. *Historical Theology: An Introduction to Christian Doctrine*. Grand Rapids, MI: Zondervan, 2011.

Almog, Shmuel, Jehuda Reinharz, and Anita Shapira, eds. *Zionism and Religion*. Hanover, NH: University of New England Press, 1998.

Alper, Tim. "Talmud-Inspired Learning Craze Sweeps South Korea." *Jewish Telegraph Agency*, 14 January 2019. https://www.jta.org/2019/01/14/global/talmud-inspired-learning-craze-sweeps-south-korea.

Althaus, Paul. *The Theology of Martin Luther*. Translated by Robert C. Schultz. Philadelphia: Fortress Press, 1966.

Appleby, R. Scott. *The Ambivalence of the Sacred*. Lanham, MD: Rowman and Littlefield, 2000.

Aquinas, Thomas. *Summa Theologiae*. 5 vols. New York: Bezinger Brothers, 1947.

Arbeis, Ross. "How the Talmud Became a Best-Seller in South Korea." *The New Yorker*, 23 June 2015. https://www.newyorker.com/books/page-turner/how-the-talmud-became-a-best-seller-in-south-korea.

Avineri, Shlomo. "Zionism and Jewish Religious Tradition: The Dialectics of Redemption and Secularization." In Almog, Reinharz, and Shapira, *Zionism and Religion*, 1–9.

Avot de-Rabi Natan. Edited by Solomon Schechter. London, 1887.

Babylonian Talmud. Standard ed.

Backman, Clifford R. *The Worlds of Medieval Europe*, 3rd ed. New York: Oxford University Press, 2015.

Baeck, Leo. "Does Traditional Judaism Possess Dogmas?" In *Studies in Jewish Thought: An Anthology of German Jewish Scholarship*, edited by Alfred Jospe, 41–53. Detroit: Wayne State University Press, 1981.

Barkai, Avraham. "German Jews at the Start of Industrialization – Structural Change and Mobility, 1835–1860." In *Revolution and Evolution: 1848 in German-Jewish History*, edited by Werner E. Mosse, Arnold Pauker, Reinhard Rürup, and Robert Weltsch, 123–45. Tübingen: JCB Mohr, 1981.

Baron, Salo W. "Ghetto and Emancipation." *The Menorah Journal* 14, no. 6 (June 1928): 515–26.

Bartal, Israel. "The Establishment of Eastern European Jewry." In Karp and Sutcliffe, *The Early Modern World, 1500–1815*, 7:226–56. https://doi.org /10.1017/9781139017169.010.

Barzun, Jacques. *From Dawn to Decadence: 1500 to the Present: 500 Years of Western Cultural Life*. New York: HarperCollins, 2001.

Bateman, David A. *Disenfranchising Democracy: Constructing the Electorate in the United States, the United Kingdom, and France*. Cambridge: Cambridge University Press, 2018. https://doi.org/10.1017/9781108556323.

Baumgarten, Elisheva. "The Family." In Chazan, *The Middle Ages: The Christian World*, 6:440–62. https://doi.org/10.1017/9781139048880.018.

– *Practicing Piety in Medieval Ashkenaz: Men, Women, and Everyday Religious Observance*. Philadelphia: University of Pennsylvania Press, 2014. https:// doi.org/10.9783/9780812290127.

Beller, Steven. "How Modern Were Vienna's Jews? Preconditions of 'Vienna 1900' in the Worldview of Viennese Jewry, 1860–1890." *Austrian Studies* 16 (2008): 19–31.

– *Vienna and the Jews 1867–1938: A Cultural History*. Cambridge: Cambridge University Press, 1989.

Ben-Menahem, Hanina. "Talmudic Law: A Jurisprudential Perspective." In Katz, *The Late Roman–Rabbinic Period*, 4:877–98. https://doi.org/10.1017 /CHOL9780521772488.036.

Ben-Sasson, Hayim Hillel. *Chapters in the History of Jews in the Middle Ages* [in Hebrew]. Tel Aviv: Am Oved, 1969.

Berkman, Jacob. "At Least 139 of the Forbes 400 Are Jewish." *Jewish Telegraphic Agency*, 5 October 2009. https://www.jta.org/2009/10/05/united-states/at -least-139-of-the-forbes-400-are-jewish.

Berkovitz, Jay R. "Rabbinic Culture and the Historical Development of Halakhah." In Karp and Sutcliffe, *The Early Modern World, 1500–1815*, 7:349–77. https://doi.org/10.1017/9781139017169.015.

Berman, Harold J. *Law and Revolution: The Formation of the Western Legal Tradition*. Cambridge, MA: Harvard University Press, 1983.

– *Law and Revolution II: The Impact of the Protestant Reformations on the Western Legal Tradition*. Cambridge, MA: Belknap Press, 2006. https://doi.org/10.4159 /9780674020863.

Biale, David. *Eros and the Jews: From Biblical Israel to Contemporary America*. Berkeley: University of California Press, 1997. https://doi.org/10.1525/9780520920064.

– *Not in the Heavens: The Tradition of Jewish Secular Thought*. Princeton: Princeton University Press, 2011. https://doi.org/10.1515/9781400836642.

Biale, David, David Assaf, Benjamin Brown, Uriel Gellman, Samuel Heilman, Moshe Rosman, Gadi Sagiv, and Marcin Wodziński. *Hasidism: A New History*. Princeton: Princeton University Press, 2018. https://doi.org/10.1515/9781400889198.

Birnbaum, Pierre, and Ira Katznelson. "Emancipation and the Liberal Offer." In *Paths of Emancipation: Jews, States, and Citizenship*, edited by Pierre Birnbaum and Ira Katznelson, 3–36. Princeton: Princeton University Press, 1995. https://doi.org/10.1515/9781400863976.1.

Blondheim, Menahem, and Shoshana Blum-Kulka. "Literacy, Orality, Television: Mediation and Authenticity in Jewish Conversational Arguing, 1–2000 C.E." *The Communication Review* 4, no. 4 (2001): 511–40. https://doi.org/10.1080/10714420109359483.

Blumenberg, Hans. *The Legitimacy of the Modern Age*. Translated by Robert M. Wallace. Cambridge, MA: MIT Press, 1985.

Blum-Kulka, Shoshana. *Dinner Talk: Cultural Patterns of Sociability and Socialization in Family Discourse*. Mahwah: Lawrence Erlbaum Associates, 1997. https://doi.org/10.4324/9780203053225.

Blum-Kulka, Shoshana, Menahem Blondheim, and Gonen Hacohen. "Traditions of Dispute: From Negotiations of Talmudic Texts to the Arena of Political Discourse in the Media." *Journal of Pragmatics* 34, nos. 10–11 (October–November 2002): 1569–94. https://doi.org/10.1016/S0378-2166(02)00076-0.

Bokser, Baruch M. *The Origins of the Seder: The Passover Rite and Early Rabbinic Judaism*. Berkeley: University of California Press, 1984. https://doi.org/10.1525/9780520317376.

Botticini, Stella, and Zvi Eckstein. *The Chosen Few: How Education Shaped Jewish History, 70–1492*. Princeton: Princeton University Press, 2012.

Boyarin, Daniel. *Carnal Israel: Reading Sex in Talmudic Culture*. Berkeley: University of California Press, 1995.

– *Intertextuality and the Reading of Midrash*. Bloomington: Indiana University Press, 1991.

Boyce, James. *Born Bad: Original Sin and the Making of the Western World*. Berkeley: Counterpoint, 2015.

Brand, Itzhak. "The 'Oven of Akhnai' and Polemics" [in Hebrew]. *Tarbiz* 75 (2006): 437–67.

Breuer, Edward. "Enlightenment and Haskalah." In Karp and Sutcliffe, *The Early Modern World, 1500–1815*, 7:652–76. https://doi.org/10.1017/9781139017169.026.

Brooke, John Hedley. *Science and Religion: Some Historical Perspectives*. Cambridge: Cambridge University Press, 1991. https://doi.org/10.1017/CBO9781107589018.

Brundage, James A. *Law, Sex, and Christian Society in Medieval Europe*. Chicago: University of Chicago Press, 1990. https://doi.org/10.1525/9780520317376.
– *Medieval Canon Law*. London: Longman, 1995.
– "Sex and Canon Law." In *Handbook of Medieval Sexuality*, edited by Vern L. Bullough and James A. Brundage, 33–50. New York: Garland, 1996.
Caferro, William. *Contesting the Renaissance*. West Sussex: Wiley-Blackwell, 2011. https://doi.org/10.1002/9781444324501.
Cahill, Thomas. *The Gift of the Jews: How a Tribe of Desert Nomads Changed the Way Everyone Thinks and Feels*. New York: Anchor Books, 1999.
Carlebach, Elisheva. "The Early Modern Jewish Community and Its Institutions." In Karp and Sutcliffe, *The Early Modern World, 1500–1815*, 7:168–98. https://doi.org/10.1017/9781139017169.008.
Cavanaugh, William T. *The Myth of Religious Violence: Secular Ideology and the Roots of Modern Conflict*. New York: Oxford University Press, 2009. https://doi.org/10.1093/acprof:oso/9780195385045.001.0001.
Cesarini, David. "British Jews." In Liedtke and Wendehorst, *The Emancipation*, 33–55.
Chadwick, Henry. *Augustine: A Very Short Introduction*. New York: Oxford University Press, 2001. https://doi.org/10.1093/actrade/9780192854520.001.0001.
Charpa, Ulrich. "Jews and Science." In Hart and Michels, *The Modern World, 1815–2000*, 8:988–1016. https://doi.org/10.1017/9781139019828.037.
Chazan, Barry, Robert Chazan, and Benjamin M. Jacobs. *Cultures and Contexts of Jewish Education*. New York: Palgrave Macmillan, 2017.
Chazan, Robert. "The Historiography of Premodern Jewish Education." *Journal of Jewish Education* 71, no. 1 (January 2005): 23–32. https://doi.org/10.1080/00216240590924006.
–, ed. *The Middle Ages: The Christian World*. Vol. 6 of *The Cambridge History of Judaism*. Cambridge: Cambridge University Press, 2018. https://doi.org/10.1017/9781139048880.
– *Refugees or Migrants: Premodern Jewish Population Movement*. New Haven: Yale University Press, 2018. https://doi.org/10.12987/yale/9780300218572.001.0001.
Chua, Amy, and Jed Rubenfeld. *The Triple Package: How Three Unlikely Traits Explain the Rise and Fall of Cultural Groups in America*. London: Penguin Books, 2014.
Clark, Anna. *Desire: A History of European Sexuality*. New York: Routledge, 2008. https://doi.org/10.4324/9780203723678.
Cochran, Gregory, Jason Hardy, and Henry Harpending. "Natural History of Ashkenazi Intelligence." *Journal of Biosocial Sciences* 38, no. 5 (September 2006): 659–93. https://doi.org/10.1017/S0021932005027069.

Cohen, Gary B. "Education and the Politics of Jewish Integration." In Hart and Michels, *The Modern Period, 1815–2000*, 8:477–504. https://doi.org /10.1017/9781139019828.018.

Cohen, Jeremy. *"Be Fertile and Increase, Fill the Earth and Master It": The Ancient and Medieval Career of a Biblical Text*. Ithaca: Cornell University Press, 1989.

Cohen, Naomi W. *What the Rabbis Said: The Public Discourse of Nineteenth-Century American Rabbis*. New York: NYU Press, 2008. https://doi.org /10.18574/nyu/9780814772942.001.0001.

Cohen, Shaye J.D. *From the Maccabees to the Mishnah*, 3rd ed. Louisville: Westminster John Knox Press, 2014.

Cohon, Samuel S. "Original Sin." *Hebrew Union College Annual* 21 (1948): 275–330.

Cooper, Alan. "A Medieval Jewish Version of Original Sin: Ephraim of Luntshits on Leviticus 12." *Harvard Theological Review* 97, no. 4 (October 2004): 445–59. https://doi.org/10.1017/S0017816004000781.

Cooperman, Alan, and Gregory A. Smith. "What Happens When Jews Intermarry?" Pew Research Center, 12 November 2013. https://www .pewresearch.org/fact-tank/2013/11/12/what-happens-when-jews -intermarry.

Couenhoven, Jesse. "Augustine's Rejection of the Free-Will Defence: An Overview of the Late Augustine's Theodicy." *Religious Studies* 43, no. 3 (September 2007): 279–98. https://doi.org/10.1017/S0034412507009018.

Crowther, Kathleen E. "Sexuality and Difference." In Rublack, *The Oxford Handbook of the Protestant Reformations*, 667–87. https://doi.org/10.1093 /oxfordhb/9780199646920.013.19.

Daube, David. *The Duty of Procreation*. Edinburgh: Edinburgh University Press, 1977.

Delbanco, Andrew. *The Puritan Ordeal*. Cambridge, MA: Harvard University Press, 1989. https://doi.org/10.4159/9780674034174.

Della Pergola, Sergio. "Some Fundamentals of Jewish Demographic History." In *Papers in Jewish Demography 1977*, edited by Paul Glikson, Sergio Della Pergola, and Usiel Oskar Schmelz, 11–33. Jerusalem: Hebrew University, 2001.

– "World Jewish Population, 2017." In *American Jewish Year Book 2017*, edited by Arnold Dashefsky and Ira M. Sheskin, 297–377. Vol. 117 of *American Jewish Year Book*. Cham, Switzerland: Springer International, 2018. https:// doi.org/10.1007/978-3-319-70663-4_7.

Desilver, Drew. "Jewish Essentials: For Most American Jews, Ancestry and Culture Matter More Than Religion." Pew Research Center, 1 October 2013. https://www.pewresearch.org/fact-tank/2013/10/01/jewish-essentials -for-most-american-jews-ancestry-and-culture-matter-more-than-religion/.

Diamond, Eliezer. "Asceticism." In *Reader's Guide to Judaism*, edited by Michael Terry, 45–6. Abingdon, UK: Routledge, 2013. https://doi.org/10.4324/9781315062488.

– *Holy Men and Hunger Artists: Fasting and Asceticism in Rabbinic Culture*. New York: Oxford University Press, 2003. https://doi.org/10.1093/acprof:oso/9780195137507.001.0001.

Diamond, Jared. *Guns, Germs, and Steel: The Fate of Human Societies*. New York: W.W. Norton, 1999.

Diner, Hasia. *Roads Taken: The Great Jewish Migrations to the New World and the Peddlers Who Forged the Way*. New Haven: Yale University Press, 2015. https://doi.org/10.12987/9780300210194.

Dixon, C. Scott. *Contesting the Reformation*. West Sussex: Wiley Blackwell, 2012.

Dobbs-Weinstein, Idit. "The Maimonidean Controversy." In Frank and Leaman, *History of Jewish Philosophy*, 331–49.

Duchesne, Ricardo. *The Uniqueness of Western Civilization*. Vol. 28 of *Studies in Critical Social Sciences*, edited by David Fasenfest. Leiden: E.J. Brill, 2012. https://doi.org/10.1163/ej.9789004192485.i-527.

Duncan, Stewart. "Thomas Hobbes." In Zalta, *The Stanford Encyclopedia of Philosophy*, Spring 2017 ed. Article published 11 March 2009; last modified 27 January 2017. https://plato.stanford.edu/archives/spr2019/entries/hobbes.

Dunn, James D.G. *The New Perspectives on Paul*, 2nd ed. Grand Rapids, MI: Wm. B. Eerdmans, 2008.

Ecclesiastes Rabbah. In *Midrash Rabbah*, standard ed.

Edelstein, Dan. *The Enlightenment: A Genealogy*. Chicago: University of Chicago Press, 2010. https://doi.org/10.7208/9780226184500.

Efron, Noah J. *A Chosen Calling: Jews in Science in the Twentieth Century*. Baltimore: Johns Hopkins University Press, 2014. https://doi.org/10.1353/book.29450.

Ehrman, Bart D. *The New Testament: A Historical Introduction to the Early Christian Writings*, 2nd ed. New York: Oxford University Press, 2000.

Einhorn, Alon. "21.2% of the Israeli Population Lives below the Poverty-Line." *Jerusalem Post*, 31 December 2018. https://www.jpost.com/Israel-News/212-percent-of-Israeli-population-lives-below-the-poverty-line-new-report-575883.

Eire, Carlos. "Calvinism and the Reform of the Reformation." In *The Oxford Illustrated History of the Reformation*, edited by Peter Marshall, 109–14. Oxford: Oxford University Press, 2015.

Eisen, Robert. *The Book of Job in Medieval Jewish Philosophy*. New York: Oxford University Press, 2004. https://doi.org/10.1093/acprof:oso/9780195171532.001.0001.

Eisner, Jane. "Why We Do Not Talk about Jewish Poverty – and Why We Should." *The Forward*, 19 March 2019. https://forward.com/culture/421071/why-we-dont-talk-about-jewish-poverty-and-why-we-should.

Elbaum, Jacob. *Repentance and Self-Flagellation in the Writings of the Sages of Germany and Poland, 1348–1648* [in Hebrew]. Jerusalem: Magnes Press, 1993.

Elon, Menachem. *Jewish Law: History, Sources, Principles.* 4 vols. Translated by Bernard Auerbach and Melvin J. Sykes. Philadelphia: Jewish Publication Society of America, 1994.

– "Power and Authority: Halachic Stance of the Traditional Community and Its Contemporary Implications." In *Kinship and Consent: The Jewish Political Tradition and Its Contemporary Uses,* edited by Daniel J. Elazar, 183–217. Lanham, MD: University Press of America, 1983.

–, ed. *The Principles of Jewish Law.* Jerusalem: Keter, 1972.

– "Public Authority and Administrative Law." In Elon, *The Principles of Jewish Law,* 645–52.

– "Takkanot." In Elon, *The Principles of Jewish Law,* 73–83.

– "Takkanot ha-Kahal." In Elon, *The Principles of Jewish Law,* 654–62.

Endelman, Todd M. "Assimilation and Assimilationism." In Hart and Michels, *The Modern Period, 1815–2000,* 8:312–36. https://doi.org/10.1017 /9781139019828.012.

– "Jewish Self-Identification and West European Categories of Belonging: From the Enlightenment to World War II." In Gitelman, *Religion or Ethnicity?,* 104–30.

Englard, Itzhak. "Majority Decision vs. Individual Truth: The Interpretations of the 'Oven of Achnai' Aggadah." *Tradition* 15, nos. 1–2 (Spring–Summer 1975): 137–52.

Etkes, Immanuel. *The Gaon of Vilna: The Man and His Image.* Translated by Jeffrey Green. Berkeley: University of California Press, 2002.

Exodus Rabbah. In *Midrash Rabbah,* standard ed.

Fackenheim, Emil L. "Kant and Judaism." *Commentary* 36, no. 6 (July 1963): 460–7. https://doi.org/10.2307/1453762.

Feiner, Shmuel. *The Jewish Enlightenment.* Translated by Chaya Naor. Philadelphia: University of Pennsylvania Press, 2003. https://doi.org/10.9783 /9780812200942.

– *The Origins of Jewish Secularization in Eighteenth-Century Europe.* Translated by Chaya Naor. Philadelphia: University of Pennsylvania Press, 2010. https://doi.org/10.9783/9780812201895.

Feldman, Ari, and Laura E. Adkins. "Orthodox to Dominate American Jewry in Coming Decades as Population Booms." *The Forward,* 12 June 2018. https://forward.com/news/402663/orthodox-will-dominate-american -jewry-in-coming-decades-as-population.

Feldman, David M. *Marital Relations, Birth Control, and Abortion in Jewish Law.* New York: Schocken Books, 1974.

Feldman, Seymour. Introduction to *The Wars of the Lord: Book One: Immortality of the Soul,* by Levi ben Gershom (Gersonides), 1–61. Translated by Seymour Feldman. Philadelphia: Jewish Publication Society of America, 1984.

– "Spinoza." In Frank and Leaman, *History of Jewish Philosophy*, 612–35.

Ferguson, Niall. *Civilization : The West and the Rest*. London: Penguin Group, 2011.

Fine, Lawrence. *Physician of the Soul, Healer of the Cosmos: Isaac Luria and His Kabbalistic Fellowship*. Stanford: Stanford University Press, 2003. https://doi .org/10.1515/9781503618619.

Finley, Mordecai. "Nineteenth-Century German Reform Philosophy." In Frank and Leaman, *History of Jewish Philosophy*, 682–705.

Fisch, Menachem. *Rational Rabbis: Science and Talmudic Culture*. Bloomington: Indiana University Press, 1997.

Fishbane, Michael. *Biblical Myth and Rabbinic Mythmaking*. New York: Oxford University Press, 2003. https://doi.org/10.1093/0198267339.001.0001.

Fisher, Eugene J. "Typical Jewish Misunderstandings of Christianity." *Shofar* 28, no. 3 (Spring 2010): 57–69.

Fishman, Talya. "The Penitential System of Hasidei Ashkenaz and the Problem of Cultural Boundaries." *Journal of Jewish Thought and Philosophy* 8, no. 2 (January 1999): 201–29. https://doi.org/10.1163/147728599794761608.

Fleischacker, Samuel. *What Is Enlightenment?* Abingdon, UK: Routledge, 2013. https://doi.org/10.4324/9780203070468.

Fraade, Steven D. "Ascetical Aspects of Ancient Judaism." In *Jewish Spirituality: From the Bible through the Middle Ages*, edited by Arthur Green, 253–88. New York: Crossroad, 1986.

– "The Early Rabbinic Sage." In *The Sage and the Ancient Near East*, edited by John G. Gammie and Leo G. Perdue, 417–36. Winona Lake: Eisenbrauns, 1990.

Frank, Daniel H., and Oliver Leaman, eds. *History of Jewish Philosophy*. London: Routledge, 1997. https://doi.org/10.4324/9780203983102.

Frankel, Jonathan. "Assimilation and the Jews in Nineteenth-Century Europe: Towards a New Historiography?" In *Assimilation and Community: The Jews in Nineteenth-Century Europe*, edited by Jonathan Frankel and Steven J. Zipperstein, 1–38. Cambridge: Cambridge University Press, 1992.

Fredriksen, Paula. *Paul: The Pagans' Apostle*. New Haven: Yale University Press, 2018. https://doi.org/10.12987/9780300231366.

Freudenthal, Gad. "Introduction: The History of Science in Medieval Jewish Cultures: Toward a Definition of the Agenda." In *Science in Medieval Jewish Cultures*, edited by Gad Freudenthal, 1–13. Cambridge: Cambridge University Press, 2011. https://doi.org/10.1017/CBO9780511976575.002.

Frey, Donald. "The Protestant Ethic Thesis." EH.net, website for the Economic History Association. https://eh.net/encyclopedia/the-protestant-ethic -thesis.

Friedman, Gabe. "Forbes' Billionaires List Features Old and New Jewish Faces." Jewish Telegraphic Agency, 2 March 2015. https://www.jta.org

/2015/03/02/culture/forbes-billionaires-list-features-new-and-old-jewish
-faces.

Gafni, Isaiah. "The Education of Children in the Period of the Talmud –
Tradition and Reality" [in Hebrew]. In *Education and History: Political
and Cultural Contexts*, edited by Rivkah Feldhay and Immanuel Etkes
[in Hebrew], 63–78. Jerusalem: Zalman Shazar, 1999.

Gauchet, Marcel. *The Disenchantment of the World: A Political History of Religion*.
Translated Oscar Burge. Princeton: Princeton University Press, 1999.
https://doi.org/10.1515/9780691238364.

Genesis Rabbah. In *Midrash Rabbah*, standard ed.

Gerondi, R. Nissim. *Dersashot ha-Ran (Sermons of R. Nissim Gerondi)*. Edited by
Aryeh L. Feldman. Jerusalem: Makhon Shalem, 1977.

Gerrish, Jim. "Why the Jews Succeed." Church and Israel Forum. Accessed
4 January 2013. https://www.churchisraelforum.com/jews-succeed.

Gilat, Yitzhak D. "A Rabbinical Court May Decree the Abrogation of the Law
of the Torah" [in Hebrew]. *Annual of Bar-Ilan University* 7–8 (1970): 117–32.

Gillespie, Michael Allen. *The Theological Origins of Modernity*. Chicago:
University of Chicago Press, 2009. https://doi.org/10.7208/9780226293516.

Gimbel, Steven. *Einstein's Jewish Science: Physics at the Intersection of Politics and
Religion*. Baltimore: Johns Hopkins University Press, 2012.

Gitelman, Zvi, ed. *Religion or Ethnicity? Jewish Identities in Evolution*. New
Brunswick: Rutgers University Press, 2009.

Goldenberg, Robert. "The Destruction of the Jerusalem Temple: Its Meaning
and Its Consequences." In Katz, *The Late Roman-Rabbinic Period*, 4:191–205.
https://doi.org/10.1017/CHOL9780521772488.009.

Goldin, Claudia. "America's Graduation from High School: The Evolution
and Spread of Secondary Schooling in the Twentieth century." *Journal of
Economic History* 58, no. 2 (June 1998): 345–74. https://doi.org/10.1017
/S0022050700020544.

Goldish, Matt. "Sabbatai Zevi and the Sabbatean Movement." In Karp and
Sutcliffe, *The Early Modern World, 1500–1815*, 7:491–521. https://doi.org
/10.1017/9781139017169.020.

Gonzalez, Justo L. *The Story of Christianity*, 2nd ed. 2 vols. New York:
HarperOne, 2010.

Gordis, David M., and Zachary I. Heller, eds. *Jewish Secularity: The Search for
Roots and the Challenges of Relevant Meaning*. Lanham, MD: University Press
of America, 2012.

Gordis, Robert. "'Be Fruitful and Multiply': Biography of a Mitzvah."
Midstream 28, no. 7 (August–September 1982): 21–9.

Gordon, Robert J. "The Great Stagnation of American Education." *New York
Times*, 7 September 2013. https://archive.nytimes.com/opinionator.blogs
.nytimes.com/2013/09/07/the-great-stagnation-of-american-education/.

Graves, Michael. "Classic Rabbinic Literature." In *T and T Clark Companion to the Doctrine of Sin*, edited by Keith L. Johnson and David Lauber, 129–47. London: Bloomsbury T and T Clark, 2016.

Gray, Alyssa M. "Wealth and Rabbinic Self-Fashioning in Late Antiquity." In *Wealth and Poverty in Jewish Tradition*, edited by Leonard J. Greenspoon, 53–81. West Lafayette: Purdue University Press, 2015.

Grayling, A.C. *Toward the Light of Liberty: The Struggles for Freedom and Rights That Made the Modern Western World*. New York: Walker, 2007.

Green, Alexander. "A Portrait of Spinoza as a Maimonidean Reconsidered." *Shofar* 34, no. 1 (Fall 2015): 81–106. https://doi.org/10.1353/sho.2015.0052.

Greenwood, Daniel J.H. "Akhnai: Legal Responsibility in the World of the Silent God." *Utah Law Review* 1997, no. 2 (1997): 309–58.

Gregory, Brad S. *The Unintended Reformation: How a Religious Revolution Secularized Society*. Cambridge, MA: Belknap Press, 2012.

Gruenwald, Ithamar. *Apocalyptic and Merkavah Mysticism*, 2nd rev. ed. Vol. 90 of *Ancient Judaism and Early Christianity*. Leiden: E.J. Brill, 2014. https://doi.org/10.1163/9789004279209.

Guskin, Emily. "How Many Jews Live in the U.S.? That Depends on How You Define 'Jewish.'" *Washington Post*, 23 February 2018. https://www.washingtonpost.com/news/post-nation/wp/2018/02/23/measuring-the-size-of-the-u-s-jewish-population-comes-down-to-identity/.

Gutek, Gerald L. *A History of the Western Educational Experience*, 2nd ed. Prospect Heights, IL: Waveland Press, 1995.

Hadas-Lebel, Mireille. *Jerusalem Against Rome*. Trans. Robyn Fréchet. Leuven: Peeters, 2006.

Hahn, Judith. "'Not in Heaven': What the Talmudic Tale on the Oven of Akhnai May Contribute to the Recent Debates on the Development of Catholic Canon Law." *Oxford Journal of Law and Religion* 6, no. 2 (June 2017): 372–98. https://doi.org/10.1093/ojlr/rwx001.

Halbertal, Moshe. *Commentary Revolutions in the Making: Values as Interpretative Considerations in Midrashei Halakhah* [in Hebrew]. Jerusalem: Magnes Press, 1999.

– *People of the Book: Canon, Meaning, and Authority*. Cambridge, MA: Harvard University Press, 1997. https://doi.org/10.4159/9780674038141.

Hamilton, Bernard. *Religion in the Medieval West*, 2nd ed. London: Hodder Arnold, 2003.

Handelman, Susan A. *The Slayers of Moses: The Emergence of Rabbinic Interpretation in Modern Literary Theory*. Albany: SUNY Press, 1983.

Harrison, Lawrence E. *Jews, Confucians, and Protestants: Cultural Capital and the End of Multiculturalism*. Lanham, MD: Rowman and Littlefield, 2012.

Harrison, Peter. "Curiosity, Forbidden Knowledge, and the Reformation of Natural Philosophy in Early Modern England." *Isis* 92, no. 2 (June 2001): 265–90. https://doi.org/10.1086/385182.

Hart, Mitchell B., and Tony Michels, eds. *The Modern Period, 1815–2000*. Vol. 8 of *The Cambridge History of Judaism*. Cambridge: Cambridge University Press, 2018. https://doi.org/10.1017/9781139019828.

Hayes, Christine. *What's Divine about Divine Law? Early Perspectives*. Princeton: Princeton University Press, 2015. https://doi.org/10.1515/9781400866410.

Heilman, Samuel. *Sliding to the Right: The Contest for the Future of American Jewish Orthodoxy*. Berkeley: University of California Press, 2006.

Henry, John. *The Scientific Revolution and the Origins of Modern Science*, 3rd ed. New York: Palgrave Macmillan, 2008.

Herman, Arthur. *How the Scots Invented the World*. New York: Random House, 2001.

Hezser, Catherine. *Jewish Literacy in Roman Palestine*. Tubingen: Mohr Siebeck, 2001.

Hidary, Richard. *Dispute for the Sake of Heaven: Legal Pluralism in the Talmud*. Providence, RI: Brown Judaic Studies, 2010.

Hirshman, Marc. "Torah in Rabbinic Thought: The Theology of Learning." In Katz, *The Late Roman-Rabbinic Period*, 4:899–924. https://doi.org/10.1017/CHOL9780521772488.037.

Hoffman, Philip T. *Why Did Europe Conquer the World?* Princeton: Princeton University Press, 2015. https://doi.org/10.1515/9781400865840.

Hornstein, Jonathan. *Jewish Poverty in the United States: A Survey of Recent Research*. Owing Mills: Harry and Jeanette Weinberg Foundation, 2019. https://hjweinbergfoundation.org/wp-content/uploads/dlm_uploads/2019/03/jewish-poverty-in-the-united-states.pdf.

Horowitz, Isaiah. *The Two Tables of the Covenant (Sheney Luhot ha-Berit)*. Warsaw: n.p., 1930.

Houston, R.A. *Literacy in Early Modern Europe: Its Growth, Uses, and Impact, 1500–1800*, 2nd ed. London: Routledge, 2002. https://doi.org/10.4324/9781315839233.

Hundert, Gershon David. *Jews in a Polish Private Town: The Case of Opatòw in the Eighteenth Century*. Baltimore: Johns Hopkins University Press, 1992. https://doi.org/10.1353/book.71395.

– *Jews in Poland-Lithuania in the Eighteenth Century: A Genealogy of Modernity*. Berkeley: University of California Press, 2004. https://doi.org/10.1525/9780520940321.

– "The Role of Jews in Commerce in Early Modern Poland-Lithuania." *Journal of European Economic History* 16, no. 2 (1987): 245–75.

Idel, Moshe. *Kabbalah and Eros*. New Haven: Yale University Press, 2005.

– *Kabbalah: New Perspectives*. New Haven: Yale University Press, 1988.

– *Messianic Mystics*. New Haven: Yale University Press, 1998. https://doi.org/10.12987/9780300145533.

– "On the History of the Interdiction against the Study of Kabbalah before the Age of Forty." *AJS Review* 5, no. 1 (April 1980): 1–20 [Hebrew section]. https://doi.org/10.1017/S0364009400011880.

"Income Distribution within U.S. Religious Groups." Pew Research Center, 30 January 2009. https://www.pewresearch.org/religion/2009/01/30/income-distribution-within-us-religious-groups/.

Ishbili, R. Yom Tov. *Hiddushei Ritba (Novellae of R. Yom Tov Ishbili)*. 21 vols. Jersualem: Mosad ha-Rav Kuk, n.d.

Israel, Jonathan I. *Diasporas within a Diaspora: Jews, Crypto-Jews, and the World of Maritime Empires, 1540–1740*. Vol. 30 of *Brill's Series in Jewish Studies*, edited by David S. Katz. Leiden: E.J. Brill, 2002. https://doi.org/10.1163/9789004500969.

– *Enlightenment Contested: Philosophy, Modernity, and the Emancipation of Man, 1670–1752*. Oxford: Oxford University Press, 2006. https://doi.org/10.1093/acprof:oso/9780199279227.001.0001.

– *European Jewry in the Age of Mercantilism, 1550–1750*. Oxford: Oxford University Press, 1991. https://doi.org/10.1093/acprof:oso/9780198219286.001.0001.

– *Radical Enlightenment: Philosophy and the Making of Modernity 1650–1750*. Oxford: Oxford University Press, 2002. https://doi.org/10.1093/acprof:oso/9780198206088.001.0001.

"Israel's Religiously Divided Society." Pew Research Center, 8 March 2016. https://www.pewresearch.org/religion/2016/03/08/israels-religiously-divided-society/.

Jacob ben Asher. *Arba'ah Turim*, standard ed.

Jacob, Walter. *Christianity through Jewish Eyes: The Quest for Common Ground*. Cincinnati: Hebrew Union College Press, 1974.

Jaffee, Martin S. *Early Judaism: Religious Worlds of the First Judaic Millennium*, 2nd ed. Bethesda: University Press of Maryland, 2006.

Jenkins, Eric L. *Free to Say No? Free Will and Augustine's Evolving Doctrines of Grace and Election*. Cambridge: James Clarke, 2013.

Jerusalem Talmud. Standard ed.

"Jewish Recipients of the Pulitzer Prize for Fiction." Accessed 4 January 2023. http://www.jinfo.org/Pulitzer_Fiction.html.

"Jewish Recipients of the Pulitzer Prize for General Non-Fiction." Accessed 4 January 2023. http://www.jinfo.org/Pulitzer_Non-Fiction.html.

Johnson, Paul. *A History of the Jews*. New York: Harper Perennial, 1988.

Joskowicz, Ari, and Ethan B. Katz, "Rethinking Jews and Secularism." In Joskowicz and Katz, *Secularism in Question*, 1–24. https://doi.org/10.9783/9780812291513-002.

Joskowicz, Ari, and Ethan B. Katz, eds. *Secularism in Question: Jews and Judaism in Modern Times*. Philadelphia: University of Pennsylvania Press, 2015. https://doi.org/10.9783/9780812291513.

Kahan, Alan S. *Mind vs. Money: The War between Intellectuals and Capitalism.* New Brunswick: Transaction, 2010.

Kaminsky, Joel. "Paradise Regained: Rabbinic Reflections on Israel at Sinai." *Jews, Christians, and the Theology of the Hebrew Scriptures*, edited by Alice Ogden Bellis and Joel S. Kaminsky, 15–43. Atlanta: Society of Biblical Literature, 2000.

Kanarfogel, Ephraim. *Jewish Education and Society in the High Middle Ages.* Detroit: Wayne State University Press, 1992.

– "Schools and Education." In Chazan, *The Middle Ages: The Christian World*, 6:393–415. https://doi.org/10.1017/9781139048880.016.

Kant, Immanuel. *Religion Within the Limits of Reason Alone.* Trans. J.W. Semple. Edinburgh: Thomas Clark, 1838. Originally published as *Die Religion innerhalb der Grenzen der bloßen Vernunft* (Königsberg: Friedrich Nicolovius, 1793).

Karady, Victor. *The Jews of Europe in the Modern Era: A Social-Historical Outline.* Translated by Tim Wilkinson. Budapest: Central European University Press, 2004.

Karo, Joseph. *Shulhan Arukh*, standard ed.

Karp, Jonathan, and Adam Sutcliffe, eds. *The Early Modern World, 1500– 1815.* Vol. 7 of *The Cambridge History of Judaism.* Cambridge: Cambridge University Press, 2018. https://doi.org/10.1017/9781139017169.

Karp, Jonathan. "Jews and Commerce." In Hart and Michels, *The Modern Period, 1815–2000*, 8:414–49. https://doi.org/10.1017/9781139019828.016.

Karras, Ruth Mazo. *Sexuality in Medieval Europe: Doing unto Others.* New York: Routledge, 2005.

Kasomo, Daniel, Nicholas Ombachi, Joseph Musyoka, and Naila Napoo. "Historical Survey of the Concept of Ecumenical Movement, Its Model, and Contemporary Problems." *International Journal of Applied Sociology* 2, no. 5 (2012): 47–51. https://doi.org/10.5923/j.ijas.20120205.01.

Katz, Jacob. *Exclusiveness and Tolerance: Studies in Jewish–Gentile Relations in Medieval and Modern Times.* New York: Behrman House, 1961.

– *Tradition and Crisis: Jewish Society at the End of the Middle Ages.* New York: Schocken Books, 1972.

Katz, Michael S. *A History of Compulsory Education Laws.* Bloomington: Phi Delta Kappa Educational Society, 1974.

Katz, Steven T., ed. *The Late Roman-Rabbinic Period.* Vol. 4 of *The Cambridge History of Judaism.* Cambridge: Cambridge University Press, 2006. https://doi.org/10.1017/CHOL9780521772488.

– "Man, Sin, and Redemption in Rabbinic Judaism." In Katz, *The Late Roman-Rabbinic Period*, 4:925–45. https://doi.org/10.1017/CHOL9780521772488.038.

Keister, Lisa A. *Faith and Money: How Religion Contributes to Wealth and Poverty.* Cambridge: Cambridge University Press, 2011. https://doi.org/10.1017 /CBO9781139028547.

– "Religion and Wealth: The Role of Religious Affiliation and Participation in Early Adult Asset Accumulation." *Social Forces* 82, no. 1 (September 2003): 175–207. https://doi.org/10.1353/sof.2003.0094.

Kellner, Menachem. *Must a Jew Believe Anything?* Portland, OR: Littman Library of Jewish Civilization, 1999.

Kimelman, Reuven. "The Rabbinic Theology of the Physical: Blessings, Body and Soul, Resurrection, and Covenant and Election." In Katz, *The Late Roman-Rabbinic Period*, 4:946–76. https://doi.org/10.1017 /CHOL9780521772488.039.

Kivistö, Sari. *The Vices of Learning: Morality and Knowledge at Early Modern Universities.* Vol. 48 of *Education and Society in the Middle Ages and Renaissance,* edited by William J. Courtenay, Jürgen Miethke, Frank Rexroth, and Jacques Verger. Leiden: E.J. Brill, 2014. https://doi.org/10.1163/9789004276451.

Klein, Charlotte. *Anti-Judaism in Christian Theology.* Translated by Edward Quinn. Philadelphia: Fortress Press, 1978.

Klosko, George. *History of Political Theory: An Introduction,* 2nd ed. Oxford: Oxford University Press, 2013.

Knox, Dilwyn. "Giordano Bruno." In Zalta, *The Stanford Encyclopedia of Philosophy,* Summer 2019 ed. Article published 30 May 2018; last modified 28 May 2019. https://plato.stanford.edu/archives/sum2019/entries/bruno.

Kolb, Robert. "The Lutheran Doctrine of Original Sin." In Madueme and Reeves, *Adam, the Fall, and Original Sin,* 109–16.

Koury, Joseph J. "*Ius Divinum* as a Canonical Problem: On the Interaction of Divine and Ecclesiastical Laws." *The Jurist* 53 (1993): 104–31.

Kraemer, David C. "The Mishnah." In Katz, *The Late Roman-Rabbinic Period,* 4:299–315. https://doi.org/10.1017/CHOL9780521772488.014.

– *Responses to Suffering in Classical Rabbinic Literature.* New York: Oxford University Press, 1994.

Kreisel, Howard. *Maimonides' Political Thought: Studies in Ethics, Law, and the Human Ideal.* Albany: SUNY Press, 1999.

– "Moses Maimonides." In Frank and Leaman, *History of Jewish Philosophy,* 245–80.

Landes, David S. *The Wealth and Poverty of Nations: Why Some Are So Rich and Some So Poor.* New York: W.W. Norton, 1999.

Latré, Stijn, Walter Van Herck, and Guido Vanheeswijck, eds. *Radical Secularization? An Inquiry into the Religious Roots of Secular Culture.* London: Bloomsbury Press, 2016.

Lawrence, C.H. *Medieval Monasticism: Forms of Religious Life in Western Europe in the Middle Ages,* 4th ed. London: Routledge, 2015. https://doi.org /10.4324/9781315715667.

Laytner, Anson. *Arguing with God: A Jewish Tradition*. Northvale: Jason Aronson, 1977.

Lazar, Shawn. "Jewish Genius and the Existence of God." Grace Evangelical Society, 1 March 2016. https://faithalone.org/journal-articles/jewish-genius-and-the-existence-of-god/.

Lebrecht, Norman. *Genius and Anxiety: How Jews Changed the World, 1847–1947*. New York: Scribner, 2019.

Lederhendler, Eli. *Jewish Immigrants and American Capitalism, 1880–1920: From Caste to Class*. Cambridge: Cambridge University Press, 2009.

Lee, Jennifer, and Min Zhou. *The Asian American Achievement Paradox*. New York: Russell Sage Foundation, 2015.

Levering, Matthew. *Predestination: Biblical and Theological Paths*. New York: Oxford University Press, 2011. https://doi.org/10.1093/acprof:oso/9780199604524.001.0001.

Levi, Yehudah. *Torah Study: A Survey of Classic Sources on Timely Issues*. Jerusalem: Feldheim, 1990.

Levine, Baruch A. *The JPS Torah Commentary: Leviticus*. New York: Jewish Publication Society of America, 1989.

Leviticus Rabbah. In *Midrash Rabbah*, standard ed.

Liberles, Robert. *Salo Wittmayer Baron: Architect of Jewish History*. New York: NYU Press, 1995.

Lieberman, Oren. "Israel's Tech Whiz-Kids-In-Training? Ultra-Orthodox Jews" *CNN*, 8 July 2015. https://www.cnn.com/2015/07/08/world/israel-Ultra-orthodox-jews-high-tech/index.html.

Liedtke, Rainer, and Stephan Wendehorst, eds. *The Emancipation of Catholics, Jews and Protestants: Minorities and the Nation-State in Nineteenth-Century Europe*. Manchester: Manchester University Press, 2011.

Lindberg, David C. "Science and the Medieval Church." In *Medieval Science*, edited by David C. Lindberg and Michael H. Shank, 268–85. Vol. 2 of *The Cambridge History of Science*, edited by David C. Lindberg and Ronald L. Numbers. Cambridge: Cambridge University Press, 2013. https://doi.org/10.1017/CHO9780511974007.012.

Lindberg, David C., and Ronald L. Numbers, eds. *When Christianity and Science Meet*. Chicago: University of Chicago Press, 2003. https://doi.org/10.7208/9780226482156.

Lis, Catharina, and Hugo Soly. *Worthy Efforts: Attitudes to Work and Workers in Pre-Industrial Europe*. Vol. 10 of *Studies in Global Social History*, edited by Marcel van der Linden. Leiden: E.J. Brill, 2012. https://doi.org/10.1163/9789004232778.

Long, Edward LeRoy, Jr. *Patterns of Polity: Varieties of Church Government*. Cleveland: Pilgrim Press, 2001.

Lorberbaum, Yair. *In God's Image: Myth, Theology, and Law in Classical Judaism*. Cambridge: Cambridge University Press, 2015. https://doi.org/10.1017/CBO9781107477940.

Löwith, Karl. *Meaning in History: The Theological Implications of the Philosophy of History*. Chicago: University of Chicago Press, 1949.

Luban, David. "The Coiled Serpent of Argument: Reason, Authority, and Law in a Talmudic Tale." *Chicago-Kent Law Review* 79, no. 3 (2004): 1253–88.

Luther, Martin. *The Bondage of the Will*. Translated by J.I. Packer and O.R. Johnston. Grand Rapids, MI: Baker Academic, 2012.

– *Lectures on Romans*. In *Luther's Works*, vol. 25. Translated by Walter G. Tillmanns and Jacob A.O. Preus. St. Louis: Concordia, 1972.

Luz, Ehud. *Wrestling with an Angel: Power, Morality, and Jewish Identity*. Translated by Michael Swirsky. New Haven: Yale University Press, 2003. https://doi.org/10.12987/9780300129298.

Lynch, Joseph H., and Phillip C. Adamo. *The Medieval Church: A Brief History*, 2nd ed. London: Routledge, 2014. https://doi.org/10.4324/9781315735221.

Lynn, Richard. *The Chosen People: A Study of Jewish Intelligence and Achievement*. Whitefish: Washington Summit, 2011.

Machin, Ian. "British Catholics." In Liedtke and Wendehorst, *The Emancipation*, 11–32.

Madueme, Hans and Michael R.E. Reeves, eds. *Adam, the Fall, and Original Sin: Theological, Biblical, and Scientific Perspectives*. Grand Rapids, MI: Baker Academic, 2015.

Magid, Shaul. *From Metaphysics to Midrash: Myth, History, and the Interpretation of Scripture in Lurianic Kabbala*. Bloomington: Indiana University Press, 2008.

Maimonides. *Commentary on the Mishnah*. In *Babylonian Talmud*, standard ed.

– *The Guide of the Perplexed*. Translated by Shlomo Pines. Chicago: University of Chicago Press, 1963.

– *Mishneh Torah*. Standard ed.

Malach, Gilad, and Lee Cahaner. "2018 Statistical Report on Ultra-Orthodox Society in Israel." Israel Democracy Institute, 19 December 2018. https://en.idi.org.il/articles/25385.

Mandel, Maud. "Assimilation and Cultural Exchange in Modern Jewish History." In *Rethinking European Jewish History*, edited by Jeremy Cohen and Moshe Rosman, 72–92. Portland, OR: Littman Library of Jewish Civilization, 2009.

Marcus, Ivan G. *Piety and Society: The Jewish Pietists of Medieval Germany*. Vol. 10 of *Études sur le judaïsme médiéval*, edited by Georges Vajda. Leiden: E.J. Brill, 1981. https://doi.org/10.1163/9789004497818.

Marks, Richard G. *The Image of Bar Kokhba in Traditional Jewish Literature: False Messiah and National Hero*. University Park: Pennsylvania State University Press, 1994. https://doi.org/10.1515/9780271075495.

Martin, Craig. "Pietro Pomponazzi." In Zalta, *The Stanford Encyclopedia of Philosophy*, Winter 2017 ed. Article published 7 November 2017. https://plato.stanford.edu/archives/win2017/entries/pomponazzi.

Martin, John Jeffries. "Religion" In *Palgrave Advances in Renaissance Historiography*, edited by Jonathan Woolfson, 193–209. New York: Palgrave Macmillan, 2005.

Masci, David. "How Income Varies among U.S. Religious Groups." Pew Research Center, 11 October 2016. https://www.pewresearch.org/fact -tank/2016/10/11/how-income-varies-among-u-s-religious-groups.

McGrath, Alister E. *Christian Theology: An Introduction*, 4th ed. Victoria, Australia: Blackwell, 2007.

McKitterick, Rosamond. "Conclusions." In *The Uses of Literacy in Early Mediaeval Europe*, edited by Rosamond McKitterick, 319–33. Cambridge: Cambridge University Press 1990. https://doi.org/10.1017/CBO9780511584008.

"Medieval Sourcebook: Tables on Population in Medieval Europe." In *Internet Medieval Sourcebook*, edited by Paul Halsall. Bronx: Fordham University Center for Medieval Studies, 1996. https://sourcebooks.fordham.edu /source/pop-in-eur.asp. Originally published in Josiah C. Russell. "Population in Europe," in *The Middle Ages*, edited by Carlo M. Cipolla, 25–71, vol. 1 of *The Fontana Economic History of Europe* (Glasgow: Collins/ Fontana, 1972).

Mekhilta de-R. Ishmael. Edited by H.S. Horowitz and I.A. Rabin. Frankfurt am Main: J. Kauffmann, 1931.

Mendelsohn, Adam D. *The Rag Race: How Jews Sewed Their Way to Success in America and the British Empire*. New York: NYU Press, 2015. https://doi.org /10.18574/nyu/9781479860258.001.0001.

Mendelssohn, Moses. *Jerusalem: Or on Religious Power and Judaism*. Translated by Allan Arkush. Waltham, MA: Brandeis University Press, 1983.

Meyer, Michael A. *Response to Modernity: A History of the Reform Movement in Judaism*. New York: Oxford University Press, 1988.

Milgrom, Jacob. "Lex Talionis and the Rabbis." *Bible Review* 12, no. 2 (April 1996): 16–48.

Milhaven, John Giles. "Thomas Aquinas on Sexual Pleasure." *Journal of Religious Ethics* 5, no. 2 (Fall 1977): 157–81.

Mittleman, Alan L. *A Short History of Jewish Ethics: Conduct and Character in the Context of Covenant*. Malden: Wiley-Blackwell, 2012. https://doi.org /10.1002/9781444346619.

Morgan, Michael L. "Moses Mendelssohn." In Frank and Leaman, *History of Jewish Philosophy*, 660–81.

Moroney, Stephen K. *God of Love and God of Judgment*. Eugene: Wipf and Stock, 2009.

Morris, Ian. *Why the West Rules – For Now: The Patterns of History and What They Reveal about the Future*. New York: Farrar, Straus and Giroux, 2010.

Muller, Jerry Z. *Capitalism and the Jews*. Princeton: Princeton University Press, 2010. https://doi.org/10.1515/9781400834365.

Murray, Charles. *Human Accomplishment: The Pursuit of Excellence in the Arts and Sciences, 800 B.C. to 1950*. New York: HarperCollins, 2003.

Nadler, Allan. *The Faith of the Mithnagdim: Rabbinic Responses to Hasidic Rapture*. Baltimore: Johns Hopkins University Press, 1997.

Nadler, Steven. *Spinoza: A Life*. Cambridge: Cambridge University Press, 1999; Cambridge Core, 2013. https://doi.org/10.1017/CBO9780511815713.

– "Virtue, Reason, and Moral Luck: Maimonides, Gersonides, Spinoza." In *Spinoza and Medieval Jewish Philosophy*, edited by Steven Nadler, 152–76. Cambridge: Cambridge University Press, 2014. https://doi.org/10.1017/CBO9781139795395.009.

– "Why Spinoza Was Excommunicated." *Humanities* 34, no. 5 (September–October 2013), https://www.neh.gov/article/why-spinoza-was-excommunicated.

Nahmanides. *Hasagot le-Sefer ha-Mitsvot shel ha-Rambam (Glosses to Maimonides' Book of the Commandments)*. In Maimonides, *Mishneh Torah*, standard ed.

Neusner, Jacob. *From Politics to Piety: The Emergence of Pharisaic Judaism*, 2nd ed. Eugene: Wipf and Stock, 2003.

Olson, Roger E. *The Story of Christian Theology: Twenty Centuries of Tradition and Reform*. Downers Grove: InterVarsity Press, 1999.

Outram, Dorinda. *The Enlightenment*, 3rd ed. Cambridge: Cambridge University Press, 2013. https://doi.org/10.1017/CBO9781139226318.

Pals, Daniel. *Nine Theories of Religion*. New York: Oxford University Press, 2015.

Panken, Aaron D. *The Rhetoric of Change: Self-Conscious Legal Change in Rabbinic Literature*. Lanham, MD: University Press of America, 2005.

Patai, Raphael. *The Jewish Mind*. Detroit: Wayne State University Press, 1996.

Pease, Steven L. *The Debate over Jewish Achievement: Exploring the Nature and Nurture of Human Accomplishment*. Sonoma: Deucalion, 2015.

– *The Golden Age of Jewish Achievement: The Compendium of a Culture, a People and Their Stunning Performance*. Sonoma: Deucalion, 2009.

Penslar, Derek J. *Shylock's Children: Economics and Jewish Identity in Modern Europe*. Berkeley: University of California Press, 2001.

Perrotta, Cosimo. *Consumption as an Investment I: The Fear of Goods from Hesiod to Adam Smith*. Translated by Joan McMullin. London: Routledge, 2004. https://doi.org/10.4324/9780203694572.

Petroff, Alanna. "U.S. and Israel Have Worst Inequality in the Developed World." *CNN Business*, 21 May 2015. https://money.cnn.com/2015/05/21/news/economy/worst-inequality-countries-oecd.

Pinker, Steven. "Groups and Genes: The Lessons of the Ashkenazim." *The New Republic*, 26 June 2006, 25–8. https://newrepublic.com/article/77727/groups-and-genes.

Plomin, Robert. "Is Intelligence Hereditary?" *Scientific American Mind* 27, no. 3 (1 May 2016), 73.

Pope, Stephen J. "Natural Law and Christian Ethics." In *The Cambridge Companion to Christian Ethics*, 2nd ed., edited by Robin Gill, 67–86. Cambridge: Cambridge University Press, 2012. https://doi.org/10.1017/CCOL9781107000070.007.

"A Portrait of American Orthodox Jews." Pew Research Center, 26 August 2015. https://www.pewresearch.org/religion/2015/08/26/a-portrait-of-american-orthodox-jews.

"A Portrait of Jewish Americans." Pew Research Center, 1 October 2013. https://www.pewresearch.org/religion/2013/10/01/chapter-3-jewish-identity/.

Rankin, Alisha. "Natural Philosophy." In Rublack, *The Oxford Handbook of the Protestant Reformations*, 726–46. https://doi.org/10.1093/oxfordhb/9780199646920.013.22.

Raphael, Simcha Paull. *Jewish Views of the Afterlife*, 2nd ed. Lanham, MD: Rowman and Littlefield, 2009.

Ravitzky, Aviezer. "The Secrets of the *Guide of the Perplexed*: From the Thirteenth to the Twentieth Centuries." In *Studies in Maimonides*, edited by Isadore Twersky, 159–207. Cambridge, MA: Harvard University Press, 1990.

Rosman, Moshe J. *How Jewish Is Jewish History?* Portland, OR: Littman Library of Jewish Civilization, 2007.

– *The Lords' Jews: Magnate-Jewish Relations in the Polish-Lithuanian Commonwealth during the Eighteenth Century*. Cambridge, MA: Harvard University Press, 1990.

Rothschild, Fritz A., ed. *Jewish Perspectives on Christianity*. New York: Crossroad, 1990.

Rozenblit, Marsha L. *The Jews of Vienna, 1867–1914: Assimilation and Identity*. Albany: SUNY Press, 1983.

Rubel, Nora L. *Doubting the Devout: The Ultra-Orthodox in the Jewish American Imagination*. New York: Columbia University Press, 2009. https://doi.org/10.7312/rube14186.

Rubenstein, Jeffrey L. *The Culture of the Babylonian Talmud*. Baltimore: Johns Hopkins University Press, 2005. https://doi.org/10.1353/book.20647.

– *Talmudic Stories: Narrative Art, Composition, and Culture*. Baltimore: Johns Hopkins University Press, 1999.

Rublack, Ulinka, ed. *The Oxford Handbook of the Protestant Reformations*. Oxford: Oxford University Press, 2017. https://doi.org/10.1093/oxfordhb/9780199646920.001.0001.

Ruderman, David B. *Early Modern Jewry*. Princeton: Princeton University Press, 2010. https://doi.org/10.1515/9781400834693.

– *Jewish Thought and Scientific Discovery in Early Modern Europe*. New Haven: Yale University Press, 1995. https://doi.org/10.12987/9780300145953.

– "Looking Backward and Forward: Rethinking Jewish Modernity in Light of Early Modernity." In Karp and Sutcliffe, *The Early Modern World, 1500–1815*, 7:1089–110. https://doi.org/10.1017/9781139017169.043.

Rüegg, Walter. "Themes." In *Universities in the Middle Ages*, edited by Hilde de Ridder-Symoens, 3–34. Vol. 1 of *A History of the University in Europe*, edited by Walter Rüegg. Cambridge: Cambridge University Press, 1992. https://doi.org/10.1017/CBO9780511599507.003.

Ryan, Alan. *On Politics: A History of Political Thought: From Herodotus to the Present*. 2 vols. New York: Liveright, 2012.

Ryrie, Alec. *Protestants: The Faith That Made the Modern World*. New York: Viking, 2017.

Safrai, Shmuel. "Education and the Study of Torah." In *The Jewish People in the First Century: Historical Geography, Political History, Social, Cultural, and Religious Life and Institutions*, edited by Shmuel Safrai and Menachem Stern, vol. 2, 945–70. Philadelphia: Fortress Press, 1976. https://doi.org/10.1163/9789004275096_010.

Sagi, Avi. *The Open Canon: On the Meaning of Halakhic Discourse*. New York: Continuum, 2007.

Sanders, E.P. *Paul and Palestinian Judaism*. Philadelphia: Fortress Press, 1977.

Sanlon, Peter. "Original Sin in Patristic Theology." In Madueme and Reeves, *Adam, the Fall, and Original Sin*, 85–108.

Saperstein, Marc. "Education and Homiletics." In Karp and Sutcliffe, *The Early Modern World, 1500–1815*, 7:407–36. https://doi.org/10.1017/9781139017169.017.

– *Jewish Preaching, 1200–1800: An Anthology*. New Haven: Yale University Press, 1989.

– "Sermons as Evidence for the Popularization of Philosophy in Fifteenth-Century Spain." In *Your Voice is Like a Ram's Horn: Themes and Texts in Traditional Jewish Preaching*, 75–88. Cincinnati: Hebrew Union College Press, 1997.

Sarachek, Joseph. *Faith and Reason: The Conflict over the Rationalism of Maimonides*. Williamsport: Bayard Press, 1935.

Sarna, Jonathan D. *American Judaism: A History*, 2nd ed. New Haven: Yale University Press, 2019.

– Review of *Refugees or Migrants: Premodern Jewish Population Movement*, by Robert Chazan. *Choice: Current Reviews for Academic Libraries* 56, no. 9 (May 2019): 1167.

– "The Rise, Fall, and Rebirth of Secular Judaism." *Contemplate: The International Journal of Cultural Thought* 4 (2007): 3–13.

Satlow, Michael. *Jewish Marriage in Antiquity*. Princeton: Princeton University Press, 2001. https://doi.org/10.1515/9780691187495.

Schama, Simon. *The Embarrassment of Riches: An Interpretation of Dutch Culture in the Golden Age*. New York: Alfred A. Knopf, 1987.

Schechter, Solomon. *Studies in Judaism: First Series*. Philadelphia: Jewish Publication Society of America, 1896.

Schechterman, Deborah. "The Doctrine of Original Sin and Maimonidean Interpretation in Jewish Philosophy of the Thirteenth and Fourteenth Centuries" [in Hebrew]. Da'at 20 (Winter 1988): 65–90.

Schiffman, Lawrence H. "Messianism and Apocalypticism in Rabbinic Texts." In Katz, The Late Roman-Rabbinic Period, 4:1053–72. https://doi.org/10.1017/CHOL9780521772488.042.

Schiffrin, Deborah. "Jewish Argument as Sociability." Language and Society 13, no. 3 (September 1984): 311–35. https://doi.org/10.1017/S0047404500010526.

Scholem, Gershom. Major Trends in Jewish Mysticism. Jerusalem: Schocken, 1941.

– Sabbatai Zevi: The Mystical Messiah. Princeton: Princeton University Press, 1973.

Schreiber, Aaron M. Jewish Law and Decision-Making: A Study through Time. Philadelphia: Temple University Press, 1979.

Schwartz, Daniel B. The First Modern Jew: Spinoza and the History of an Image. Princeton: Princeton University Press, 2012. https://doi.org/10.1515/9781400842261.

Schwartz, Joshua. "Material Culture in the Land of Israel: Monks and Rabbis on Clothing and Dress in the Byzantine Period." In Saints and Role Models in Judaism and Christianity, edited by Joshua Schwartz and Marcel Poorthuis, 121–38. Vol. 7 of Jewish and Christian Perspectives Series, edited by Doron Bar, Leo Mock, Eric Ottenheijm, Eyal Regev, and Lieve Teugels. Leiden: E.J. Brill, 2004. https://doi.org/10.1163/9789047401605_009.

Schwarzfuchs, Simon. A Concise History of the Rabbinate. Oxford: Blackwell, 1993.

Scott, T. Kermit. Augustine: His Thought in Context. Mahwah: Paulist Press, 1995.

Seeskin, Kenneth. "Jewish Neo-Kantianism: Hermann Cohen." In Frank and Leaman, History of Jewish Philosophy, 786–98.

Sefer ha-Hinukh. Standard ed.

Seidman, Naomi. "Religion/Secularity." In The Routledge Handbook of Contemporary Jewish Cultures, edited by Laurence Roth and Nadia Valman, 151–61. London: Routledge, 2017. https://doi.org/10.4324/9780203497470.

Senor, Dan, and Saul Singer. Startup Nation: The Story of Israel's Economic Miracle. New York: Twelve, 2011.

Shapira, Anita. "The Religious Motifs of the Labor Movement." In Almog, Reinharz, and Shapira, Zionism and Religion, 251–72.

Shapiro, Marc B. The Limits of Orthodox Theology: Maimonides' Thirteen Principles Reappraised. Portland, OR: Littman Library of Jewish Civilization, 2004.

Sheffler, David. "Late Medieval Education: Continuity and Change." History Compass 8, no. 9 (September 2010): 1067–82. https://doi.org/10.1111/j.1478-0542.2010.00726.x.

Siegal, Michal Bar-Asher. "Shared Worlds: Rabbinic and Monastic Literature." *Harvard Theological Review* 105, no. 4 (October 2012): 423–56. https://doi .org/10.1017/S001781601200020X.

Sifrey Deuteronomy. In *Midrash Rabbah*, standard ed.

Silbiger, Steven. *The Jewish Phenomenon: Seven Keys to the Enduring Wealth of a People*, 2nd ed. Lanham, MD: M. Evans, 2009.

Silver, Abba Hillel. *Where Judaism Differed: An Inquiry into the Distinctiveness of Judaism*. New York: Macmillan, 1965.

Silver, Daniel Jeremy. *Maimonidean Criticism and Maimonidean Controversy 1180–1240*. Leiden: E.J. Brill, 1965.

Slezkine, Yuri. *The Jewish Century*. Princeton: Princeton University Press, 2004. https://doi.org/10.1515/9781400828555.

Smalley, Beryl. *The Study of the Bible in the Middle Ages*. Oxford: Blackwell, 1952.

Soloveitchik, Haym. "Three Themes in *Sefer Hasidim*." *AJS Review* 1 (April 1976): 311–58. https://doi.org/10.1017/S0364009400000155.

Sombart, Werner. *Die Juden und das Wirtschaftsleben*. Leipzig: Duncker & Humblot, 1911.

Sorkin, David. *The Religious Enlightenment: Protestants, Jews, and Catholics from London to Vienna*. Princeton: Princeton University Press, 2008. https://doi .org/10.1515/9780691188188.

Sowell, Thomas. *Conquest and Cultures: An International History*. New York: Basic Books, 1998.

– *Migrations and Cultures: A World View*. New York, Basic Books, 1996.

– *Race and Culture: A World View*. New York: Basic Books, 1994.

Stampfer, Shaul. *Families, Rabbis, and Education: Traditional Jewish Society in Nineteenth-Century Eastern Europe*. Portland, OR: Littman Library of Jewish Civilization, 2010.

– Review of *The Chosen Few: How Education Shaped Jewish History, 70–1492*, by Stella Botticini and Zvi Eckstein. *Jewish History* 29, nos. 3–4 (December 2015): 373–9. https://doi.org/10.1007/s10835-015-9247-0.

Stark, Rodney. *How the West Won: The Neglected Story of the Triumph of Modernity*. Wilmington: ISI Books, 2014.

Stern, David. *Midrash and Theory: Ancient Jewish Exegesis and Contemporary Literary Studies*. Evanston, IL: Northwestern University Press, 1998.

Stern, Gregg. *Philosophy and Rabbinic Culture: Jewish Interpretation and Controversy in Medieval Languedoc*. Abingdon, UK: Routledge, 2009. https://doi.org/10.4324/9780203884195.

Stern, Sacha. *Jewish Identity in Early Rabbinic Writings*. Vol. 23 of *Arbeiten zur Geschichte des antiken Judentums und des Urchristentums/Ancient Judaism & Early Christianity*, edited by Martin Hegel, Peter Schäfer, Pieter W. van der Horst, Martin Goodman, and Daniel R. Schwartz. Leiden: E.J. Brill, 1994. https://doi.org/10.1163/9789004332768.

Stow, Kenneth R. *Alienated Minority: The Jews of Medieval Latin Europe*. Cambridge, MA: Harvard University Press, 1992.

– "The Burning of the Talmud in 1553, in Light of Sixteenth-Century Catholic Attitudes toward the Talmud." In *Essential Papers on Judaism and Christianity in Conflict: From Late Antiquity to the Reformation*, edited by Jeremy Cohen, 401–30. New York: NYU Press, 1991.

Strauss, Leo. *Persecution and the Art of Writing*. Glencoe, IL: Free Press, 1952.

– *Philosophy and Law*. Translated by Fred Baumann. Philadelphia: Jewish Publication Society of America, 1987.

Tamari, Meir. *With All Your Possessions: Jewish Ethics and Economic Life*. Northvale: Jason Aronson Press, 1987.

Tarnas, Richard. *The Passion of the Western Mind: Understanding the Ideas That Have Shaped Our World View*. New York: Ballantine Books, 1991.

Taylor, Charles. *A Secular Age*. Cambridge, MA: Harvard University Press, 2007. https://doi.org/10.4159/9780674044289.

– *Sources of the Self: The Making of the Modern Identity*. Cambridge, MA: Harvard University Press, 1989.

Teller, Adam. *Money, Power, and Influence in Eighteenth-Century Lithuania: The Jews on the Radiziwiłł Estates*. Stanford: Stanford University Press, 2016. https://doi.org/10.1515/9780804799874.

Thijssen, Hans. "Condemnation of 1277." In Zalta, *The Stanford Encyclopedia of Philosophy*, Winter 2016 ed. Article published 30 January 2003; last modified 24 September 2013. https://plato.stanford.edu/archives/win2016/entries/condemnation.

Tirosh-Samuelson, Hava. "Gender in Jewish Mysticism." In *Jewish Mysticism and Kabbalah: New Insights and Scholarship*, edited by Frederick E. Greenspahn, 191–230. New York: NYU Press, 2011. https://doi.org/10.18574/nyu/9780814732885.003.0013.

– "Jewish Philosophy on the Eve of Modernity." In Frank and Leaman, *History of Jewish Philosophy*, 499–576.

Trinkaus, Charles. *In Our Image and Likeness: Humanity and Divinity in Italian Humanist Thought*. Notre Dame: University of Notre Dame Press, 1995.

Twain, Mark. "Concerning the Jews." *Harper's Magazine* 99 (September 1899): 527–35.

Urbach, Ephraim E. *The Sages: Their Concepts and Beliefs*. Translated by Israel Abrahams. Cambridge, MA: Harvard University Press, 1987.

Vajda, Georges. *Isaac Albalag 6: Averroïste juif, traducteur et annotateur d'Al-Ghazâlî*. Paris: J. Vrin, 1960.

Van den Haag, Ernest. *The Jewish Mystique*. New York: Stein and Day, 1969.

Van Eijnatten, Joris. "In Praise of Moderate Enlightenment: A Taxonomy of Early Modern Arguments in Favor of Freedom of Expression." In *Freedom of*

Speech: The History of An Idea, edited by Elizabeth Powers, 19–44. Lanham, MD: Rowman and Littlefield, 2011.

Veblen, Thorstein. "The Intellectual Pre-Eminence of Jews in Modern Europe." *Political Science Quarterly* 34, no. 1 (March 1919): 33–43.

Wallace, Robert M. "Progress, Secularization, and Modernity: The Löwith-Blumenberg Debate." *The New German Critique* 22 (Winter 1981): 63–79. https://doi.org/10.2307/487864.

Weber, Max. *The Protestant Ethic and the Spirit of Capitalism.* Translated by Talcott Parsons. London: Routledge, 2001. https://doi.org/10.4324/9780203995808.

Weiss, Dov. *Pious Irreverence: Confronting God in Rabbinic Judaism.* Philadelphia: University of Pennsylvania Press, 2016. https://doi.org/10.9783/9780812293050.

Weiss-Rosmarin, Trude. *Judaism and Christianity: The Differences.* New York: Jewish Book Club, 1943.

Wiesner-Hanks, Merry E. *Christianity and Sexuality in the Early Modern World: Regulating Desire, Reforming Practice*, 2nd ed. London: Routledge, 2010. https://doi.org/10.4324/9781315787350.

Wiley, Tatha. *Original Sin: Origins, Developments, Contemporary Meanings.* Mahwah: Paulist Press, 2002.

Witte, John, Jr. "Sex and Marriage in the Protestant Tradition, 1500–1900." In *The Oxford Handbook of Theology, Sexuality, and Gender*, edited by Adrian Thatcher, 304–22. Oxford: Oxford University Press, 2015. https://doi.org/10.1093/oxfordhb/9780199664153.013.012.

Wolfson, Elliot R. *Language, Eros, Being: Kabbalistic Hermeneutics and Poetic Imagination.* New York: Fordham University Press, 2005. https://doi.org/10.1515/9780823237852.

Yadin, Azzan. *Scripture and Tradition: Rabbi Akiva and the Triumph of Midrash.* Philadelphia: University of Pennsylvania Press, 2014. https://doi.org/10.9783/9780812290431.

– *Scripture as Logos: Rabbi Ishmael and the Origins of Midrash.* Philadelphia: University of Pennsylvania Press, 2004. https://doi.org/10.9783/9780812204124.

Yaron, Yoseif, Joe Pessah, Avraham Qanaï, and Yosef El-Gamil. *An Introduction to Karaite Judaism: History, Theology, Practice, and Culture.* Albany: Qirqisani Center, 2003.

Zachman, Randall C. *John Calvin as Teacher, Pastor, and Theologian: The Shape of His Writings and Thought.* Grand Rapids, MI: Baker Academic Press, 2006.

Zalta, Edward N., ed. *The Stanford Encyclopedia of Philosophy.* Stanford: Stanford University, 1997–. https://plato.stanford.edu/archives/.

Index

Abelard, Peter, 287
Abraham, 107, 108
Academy Awards, 4
Adam and Eve: Augustine on, 89,
  294, 296; and curiosity, 294, 296;
  Kabbalah on, 112, 113, 114; Luther
  on, 158; Pelagius on, 90; and
  procreation, 218, 226, 227, 231;
  Rabbinic Judaism on, 98–9, 228
afterlife: Aristotle on, 167; Augustine
  on, 89, 93, 100; Christianity on 42,
  223, 224–5, 236; the Enlightenment
  on, 96, 163, 264; Hebrew Bible
  on, 238; Kabbalah on, 262;
  Maimonides on, 200–1; Plato on,
  223; Rabbinic Judaism on, 102–3,
  201, 224–5, 237, 277, 353, 384n46,
  411n31; Semi-Pelagians on, 91
Akiva, R., 101–2, 383n37, 384n40,
  384n43
Albalag, Isaac, 398n40
amendment: in American law, 132;
  in Jewish law, see *takkanah*
Anatoli, Jacob, 399n47
Anglican Church, 93
antisemitism, x, 69, 70, 72, 254, 336,
  348, 352
apocalyptic literature, 213–4, 238
Apostle's Creed, 183

apostolic succession, 121, 125
Aquinas, Thomas, 91, 155–6, 187,
  189, 207, 241, 244, 294
arguing with God. *See* God: arguing
  with
Arian Controversy, 184–5
Aristotle, 153, 155, 166–8, 174, 176,
  188, 241, 260, 261, 397n37
Arminius, Jacob, 381n22
arts, accomplishments of Jews in, 4,
  179, 325, 423n72
asceticism, 216–17, 237, 261, 262,
  409n18
Ascher, Saul, 194–5, 202
Ashkenazi Jews, 366n71
Asian Americans, 11
Augustine, 88–90, 90–1, 92, 93, 94,
  95, 97, 98–9, 101, 109, 123, 130, 155,
  216, 235, 244, 246, 248, 294, 331,
  379n5, 394n1
authority, religious, 120–50
autonomy, metaphysical, 39, 41, 65,
  84, 87–179, 180–1, 192, 317, 318,
  319, 331, 334. *See also* free will
Averroes, 189, 400n51

Baeck, Leo, 195
Bahya ibn Pakuda, 420n59
baptism, 379n5